# Database Concepts

# Database Concepts

**Third Edition**

## David M. Kroenke
*University of Washington*

## David J. Auer
*Western Washington University*

PEARSON

Prentice Hall

Upper Saddle River, New Jersey 07458

Library of Congress Cataloging-in-Publication Data

Kroenke, David.
    Database concepts / David M. Kroenke, David J. Auer. – 3rd ed.
        p. cm.
    ISBN-13: 978-0-13-198625-1
    ISBN-10: 0-13-198625-2
    1. Database management. 2. Relational databases. I. Auer, David J. II. Title.
    QA76.9.D3K736 2007
    005.74—dc22

                                                    2006100979

**AVP/Executive Editor:** Bob Horan
**VP/Editorial Director:** Jeff Shelstad
**Manager, Product Development:** Pamela Hersperger
**Project Manager:** Ana Jankowski
**Editorial Assistant:** Kelly Loftus
**Associate Director, Production Editorial:** Judy Leale
**Managing Editor:** Cynthia Zonneveld
**Production Editor:** Melissa Feimer
**Permissions Coordinator:** Charles Morris
**Associate Director, Manufacturing:** Vinnie Scelta
**Manufacturing Buyer:** Michelle Klein
**Design/Composition Manager:** Christy Mahon
**Composition Liaison:** Suzanne Duda
**Cover Design:** Bruce Kenselaar
**Cover Illustration/Photo:** Getty Images
**Composition/Full-Service Project Management:** GGS Book Services
**Printer/Binder:** Quebecor
**Typeface:** 10/12, Simoncinigaramond

Credits and acknowledgments borrowed from other sources and reproduced, with permission, in this textbook appear on appropriate page within.

Microsoft® and Windows® are registered trademarks of the Microsoft Corporation in the U.S.A. and other countries. Screen shots and icons reprinted with permission from the Microsoft Corporation. This book is not sponsored or endorsed by or affiliated with the Microsoft Corporation.

MySQL® , the MySQL Command Line Client™, the MySQL Query Brower™ and the MySQL Administrator™ and the MySQL 5.0 Reference Manual are copyright, trademarks, and/or registered trademarks of MySQL AB and MySQL Inc. in the U.S.A and other countries.  Screenshots and icons reprinted with permission of MySQL AB and MySQL Inc.  This book is not sponsored or endorsed by or affiliated with MySQL AB or MySQL Inc.

Pearson Education LTD.                      Pearson Education Australia PTY, Limited
Pearson Education Singapore, Pte. Ltd       Pearson Education North Asia Ltd
Pearson Education, Canada, Ltd              Pearson Educación de Mexico, S.A. de C.V.
Pearson Education–Japan                     Pearson Education Malaysia, Pte. Ltd.

10 9 8 7 6 5 4 3 2 1
ISBN-13: 978-0-13-198625-1
ISBN-10:    0-13-198625-2

# Brief Contents

# Contents

## ▶ PART 2   DATABASE DESIGN AND MANAGEMENT     189

### 4   Data Modeling and the Entity-Relationship Model     191

### 5   Database Design     231

6    Database Administration    **269**

7    Database Processing Applications and Business
      Intelligence    **325**

# Preface

Colin Johnson is a production supervisor for a small manufacturer in Seattle. Several years ago, Colin wanted to build a database to keep track of components in product packages. At the time, he was using a spreadsheet to perform this task, but he could not get the reports that he needed from the spreadsheet. Colin had heard about Microsoft Access, and he tried to use it to solve his problem. After several days of frustration, he bought several popular Access books and attempted to learn from them. Ultimately, he gave up and hired a consultant who built an application that more or less met Colin's needs. Over time, Colin wanted to change his application, but he did not dare to try.

Colin was a successful businessperson who was highly motivated to achieve his goals. A seasoned Windows user, he had been able to teach himself how to use Excel, PowerPoint, and a number of production-oriented application packages. He was flummoxed at his inability to use Access to solve his problem. "I'm sure I could do it, but I just don't have any more time to invest," he thought. This story is even more remarkable because it has occurred thousands of times over the last decade.

Microsoft Corporation, Oracle Corporation, and other database management system (DBMS) vendors are aware of such scenarios and have invested millions of dollars in creating better graphical user interfaces, hundreds of multipanel wizards, and many sample applications. Unfortunately, such efforts treat the symptom and not the cause. Most users have no clear idea of what wizards are doing on their behalf. As soon as these users require changes to database structure or to components, such as forms and queries, they drown in a sea of complexity for which they are unprepared. With little understanding of the underlying fundamentals, these users grab at any straw that appears to lead in the direction they want. The consequence is poorly designed databases and applications that fail to meet the users' requirements.

Why can people like Colin learn a word processor or a spreadsheet product, yet fail when trying to learn to use a DBMS product? First, the underlying database concepts are unnatural to most people. Whereas everyone knows what paragraphs and margins are, no one knows what a relation is. Second, it seems like using a DBMS product ought to be easier than it is. "All I want to do is keep track of something. Why is it so hard?" people ask. Without knowledge of the relational model, breaking a sales invoice into five separate tables before storing the data is mystifying to business users.

## ▶ THE NEED FOR ESSENTIAL CONCEPTS

With today's technology, it is impossible to utilize a DBMS successfully without first learning fundamental concepts. After years of developing databases with business users, we believe that the following database concepts are essential.

> Fundamentals of the relational model
> Structured Query Language (SQL)
> Data modeling
> Database design
> Database administration

And because of the increasing use of the Internet and the World Wide Web today, one more essential concept can be added:

> Web database processing

Users like Colin—and students who will accept jobs similar to his—do not need to learn these topics to the same depth as future information systems professionals. Consequently, this textbook presents only essential concepts—those that are necessary for users, like Colin, who want to create and use small databases. Many of the discussions in this book are rewritten and simplified explanations of topics that you will find fully discussed in David Kroenke's *Database Processing: Fundamentals, Design, and Implementation*.[1] However, in adapting the material for this text, we have endeavored to ensure that the discussions remain accurate and do not mislead. Nothing here will need to be unlearned if students take more advanced database courses.

## ► TEACHING CONCEPTS INDEPENDENT OF DBMS PRODUCTS

This book does not assume that any particular DBMS product will be used by students. The book does illustrate database concepts with Microsoft Access, SQL Server 2005 Express Edition, and MySQL 5.0 so that students can use these products as tools and actually try out the material, but all the concepts are presented in a DBMS-agnostic manner. When learned this way, students come to understand that the fundamentals pertain to any database, from the smallest Access database to the largest Oracle or DB2 database.

Moreover, this approach avoids a common pitfall. When concepts and products are taught at the same time, students frequently confound concepts with product features and functions. For example, consider referential integrity constraints. When taught from a conceptual standpoint, students learn that there are times when the values of a column in one table must always be present as values of a column in a second table. Students also will learn how this constraint arises in the context of relationship definition, and how either the DBMS or the application must enforce this constraint. If taught in the context of a DBMS—for example, in the context of Access—students will only learn that in some cases you check a check box, and in other cases you don't. The danger is that the underlying concept will be lost in the product feature.

All this is not to say that a DBMS should not be used in this class. On the contrary, students can best master these concepts by applying them using a commercial DBMS product. This edition of the book was written to include enough basic information about Access, SQL Server 2005 Express Edition, and MySQL 5.0 so that you can introduce these products in your class without the need for a second book or other materials. Access is covered in some depth because of its popularity as a personal database (and its inclusion in the Microsoft Office Professional suite of applications). This coverage of Access will allow students to complete all the database assignments in this book, and may be sufficient for some classes. However, if you want to cover a particular DBMS in depth or use a DBMS product not discussed in the book, you will have to supplement this book with another text or additional materials. Prentice Hall provides a number of books for Microsoft Access 2003 and other DBMS products, and many of them can be packaged with this text.

## ► THE ACCESS WORKBENCH

Previous editions of this text included an introduction to Microsoft Access in an appendix. Because Access is widely used in first database classes, this edition includes more information on using Access. Each chapter has an accompanying section of "The Access

---

[1]David M. Kroenke, *Database Processing: Fundamentals, Design, and Implementation*, 10th Edition (Upper Saddle River, NJ: Prentice-Hall, 2006).

Workbench," which illustrates the chapter's concepts and techniques using Access. "The Access Workbench" topics start with creating a database and a single table in Section One and end with Web database processing against an Access database in Section Seven. This material is not intended to be a comprehensive coverage of Access, but all the necessary basic Access topics are covered so that your students can effectively build and use Access databases.

## ▶ REVIEW QUESTIONS, EXERCISES, AND PROJECTS

Because it is so important for students to apply the concepts they learn, each chapter concludes with sets of review questions, exercises (including exercises tied to "The Access Workbench"), and three projects that run throughout the book. Students should be able to answer the review questions if they have read and understood the chapter material. The exercises require the students to apply the chapter concepts to a small problem or task.

The first of the projects, Garden Glory, concerns the development and use of a database for a partnership that provides gardening and yard maintenance services to individuals and organizations. The second project, James River Jewelry, addresses the need for a database to support a frequent-buyer program for a retail store, and the third project, the Queen Anne Curiosity Shop, concerns the sales and inventory needs of a retail business. These three projects appear in all of the book's chapters and in Appendix C on SQL views. In each instance, students are asked to apply concepts from the chapter to the project. Instructors will find more information on the use of these projects in the instructor's manual and can obtain databases and data from the password-protected instructor's portion of our Web site (**www.prenhall.com/kroenke**). Over the past 30-plus years, we have found the development of databases and database applications to be an enjoyable and rewarding activity. We believe that the number, size, and importance of databases will increase in the future, and that the field will achieve even greater prominence. It is our hope that the concepts, knowledge, and techniques presented in this book will help students participate successfully in database projects now and for many years to come.

## ▶ CHANGES FROM THE SECOND EDITION

Major changes include:

> Coverage of SQL views (Appendix C)
> Coverage of subtype/supertype entities (Chapters 4 and 5)
> Coverage of associative entities and association relationships (Chapter 5)
> Use of IE Crow's Foot E-R diagrams instead of UML E-R models for ease of use and consistency with *Database Processing*, 10th Edition (Chapter 4 and following)
> Rearrangement of the topics in Chapters 6 and 7—distributed database and object-relational databases are covered as part of database administration in Chapter 6
> Additional coverage of Web-based database processing including specific steps and code examples to create Web pages that display data stored in databases (Chapter 7)

> Coverage of concepts of business intelligence (Bl) systems (Chapter 7)
> The use of "The Access Workbench" sections in each chapter and Appendix C to provide coverage of Access fundamentals
> Introductions to the use of SQL Server 2005 Express Edition (Appendix A)and MySQL 5.0 (Appendix B)

In addition, three example database that run throughout various portions of the book—the Wedgewood Pacific Corporation and Heather Sweeney Designs in the chapters, and Wallingford Motors in "The Access Workbench"—are fully developed with example datasets. The use of these databases provides continuity of the concept examples throughout the various chapters and can be created in actual databases by the students to try out the topics discussed in each chapter.

And, although it is not a change, it should be mentioned that this edition has retained the more effective discussion of normalization added in the second edition, and uses a prescriptive procedure for normalizing relations. Whereas the first edition described normalization principles but left it to the student to apply those principles, Chapter 2 of the second edition presented a four-step process that students could use to normalize. This change not only made the normalization task easier, it also made normalization principles easier to understand. Therefore, this approach is the same in this edition. For those instructors wanting a bit more detail on normal forms, short definitions of 2NF and 3NF have been added to the discussion of normal forms in Chapter 5.

## ▶ BOOK OVERVIEW

This textbook consists of seven chapters and three appendices. Chapter 1 explains why databases are used, what their components are, and how they are developed. Students will learn the purpose of databases and their applications, and how databases differ from and improve on keeping lists in spreadsheets. Chapter 2 introduces the relational model and defines basic relational terminology. It also introduces the fundamental ideas that underlie normalization and describes the normalization process.

Chapter 3 presents fundamental SQL statements. Basic SQL statements for data definition are described, as are SQL SELECT and data modification statements. No attempt is made to present advanced SQL statements; only the essential statements are described. Appendix C adds coverage of SQL views. The next three chapters consider database design and management. Chapter 4 addresses data modeling using the entity-relationship (E-R) model. The need for data modeling is described, basic E-R terms and concepts are introduced, and a short case application (Heather Sweeney Designs) of E-R modeling is presented. Chapter 5 describes database design and explains the essentials of normalization. The data model from the case example in Chapter 4 is transformed into a relational design in Chapter 5.

Chapter 6 provides an overview of database administration. The case example database is built as a functioning database, and it serves as the example for a discussion of the need for database administration. The chapter surveys concurrency control, security, and backup and recovery techniques. Database administration is an important topic because it applies to all databases, even for personal, single-user databases. In some ways, this topic is more important for such databases because no professional database administrator is present to ensure that critical tasks are performed. Chapter 6 also provides a discussion of distributed databases and object-relational databases.

Finally, Chapter 7 introduces the use of Web-based database processing, including a discussion of Open Database Connectivity (ODBC), Active Data Objects (ADO), and Active Serve Pages (ASPs). The emergence and basic concepts of extensible markup language (XML) are discussed, and business intelligence (Bl) systems are introduced.

A short introduction to SQL Server 2005 Express Edition is provided in Appendix A, and a similar introduction for MySQL 5.0 is provided in Appendix B. Microsoft Access is covered in "The Access Workbench" included in each chapter and Appendix C.

## ► ACKNOWLEDGMENTS

The authors would like to thank the following reviewers for their insightful and helpful comments:

Ann Aksut, Central Piedmont Community College
Tina Ashford, Macon State College
Karin Bast, University of Wisconsin–La Crosse
Jean-Francois Blanchette, University of California–Los Angeles
Shoba Chengular-Smith, State University of New York at Albany
Sam Chung, Pacific Lutheran University
Mary Daul, Marian College
Jamie Doll, Foothill College
Deena Engel, New York University
Larry Fudella, Erie Community College
Thanh Giang, Leeward Community College
Don Goelman, Villanova University
Constanza Hagmann, Kansas State University
Edward P. Holden, Rochester Institute of Technology
Larry Holt, Rollins College
Peter Johnson, Humboldt State University
Ted Lemser, Oklahoma City Community College
Brian Mennecke, Iowa State University
Anne Nelson, High Point University
Terry Redman. Webster University
Kamaljeet Sanghera, George Mason University
Eileen Sikkema, University of Washington
Pat Smith, Temple College
Charles Stout, High Point University
Richard Tibbs, Radford University
Susan E. Yager, Southern Illinois University–Edwardsville

David Kroenke would like to thank:

In addition, I would like to thank my editor, Bob Horan, and my assistant editor, Ana Jankowski, for their continued support, insight, and assistance in the development of this project.

David Auer would like to thank:

David Kroenke for his generosity, insight, and support during this project. Our editor, Bob Horan, our assistant editor, Ana Jankowski, and our production editor Melissa Feimer for their professionalism, insight, support, and assistance in the development of this project. My wife Donna Auer for her love, encouragement, and patience while I was completing this project.

David Kroenke
Seattle, Washington
David Auer
Bellingham, Washington

# About the Authors

**David M. Kroenke** entered the computing profession as a summer intern at the Rand Corporation in 1967. Since then, his career has spanned education, industry, consulting, and publishing.

He has taught at Colorado State University, Seattle University, and the University of Washington, where he currently teaches. Over the years he has led dozens of teaching seminars for college professors. In 1991 the International Association of Information Systems named him Computer Educator of the Year.

In industry, Kroenke has worked for the U.S. Air Force and Boeing Computer Services, and he was a principal in the startup of three companies. He also was vice president of product marketing and development for the Microrim Corporation and was chief technologist for the database division of Wall Data, Inc. He is the father of the semantic object data model. Kroenke's consulting clients include the IBM Corporation, Microsoft, Computer Sciences Corporation, and numerous other companies and organizations.

His text *Database Processing* was first published in 1977 and is now in its tenth edition. He has published many other textbooks, including the classic *Business Computer Systems* (1981). More recently he authored *Using MIS* which is in its first edition. An avid sailor, Kroenke also wrote *Know Your Boat: The Guide to Everything That Makes Your Boat Work.* Kroenke lives in Seattle, Washington. He is married and has two children and two grandchildren.

**David J. Auer** is currently the Director of Information Systems and Technology Services at Western Washington University's College of Business and Economics (CBE), and a Lecturer in CBE's Department of Decision Sciences. He has taught for CBE since 1981, teaching courses in Quantitative Methods, Production and Operations Management, Statistics, Finance and Management Information Systems. In 1994, he was hired into his current position at CBE. Besides managing CBE's computer, network, and other technology resources, he also teaches Management Information Systems courses. He has taught the Principles of Management Information Systems and Business Database Development courses, and he was responsible for developing CBE's network infrastructure courses including Computer Hardware and Operating Systems, Telecommunications, and Network Administration. He has coauthored several MIS related text books.

Auer holds a B.A. in English Literature from the University of Washington, a B.A. in Mathematics and Economics from Western Washington University, an M.A. in Economics from Western Washington University, and an M.S. in Counseling Psychology from Western Washington University. He served as a commissioned officer in the U.S. Air Force, and has also worked as an organizational development specialist and therapist for an Employee Assistance Program (EAP). He and his wife Donna live in Bellingham, Washington, where he is currently a member of the local Planning Commission, and where he is involved with community growth and development issues. He has two children and three grandchildren.

# PART I

# Fundamentals

**P**art I introduces fundamental concepts and techniques of relational database management. Chapter 1 explains database technology, why databases are used, and describes the components of a database system. Chapter 2 introduces the relational model and defines key relational terms. It also presents basic relational design principles. Finally, Chapter 3 presents Structured Query Language, an international standard for creating and processing relational databases.

Once you have learned these fundamental database concepts, we will then focus on database modeling, design, implementation and management in Part II.

# CHAPTER 1

# Getting Started

> Identify the purpose and scope of this book
> Know the potential problems with lists
> Understand the reasons for using a database
> Understand how related tables avoid the problems of lists
> Know the components of a database system
> Learn the elements of a database
> Learn the purpose of the database management system (DBMS)
> Understand the functions of a database application

**K**nowledge of database technology increases in importance every day. Databases are used everywhere: They are key components of e-commerce and other Web-based applications. They lay at the heart of organization-wide operational and decision support applications. Databases also are used by thousands of work groups and millions of individuals. Estimates of the number of active databases in the world today exceed 10 million.

The purpose of this book is to teach you the essential database concepts, technology, and techniques that you will need to begin a career as a database developer. This book does not teach everything of importance in database technology, but it will give you sufficient background to be able to create your own personal databases and to participate as a member of a team in the development of larger, more complicated databases. You will also be able to ask the right questions to learn more on your own.

In this first chapter, we will investigate the reasons for using a database. We begin by describing the problems that can occur when using lists. Using a series of examples, we will illustrate how sets of related tables avoid those problems. Next, we will describe the components of a database system and explain the elements of a database, the purpose of the database management system (DBMS), and the functions of a database application.

## ▶ WHY USE A DATABASE?

A database is used to help people keep track of things. You might wonder why we need a special term (and course) for such technology when a simple list could serve the same purpose. Many people do keep track of things using lists, and sometimes such lists are valuable. In other cases, however, simple lists lead to data inconsistencies and other problems.

In this section, we will examine several different lists and show some of these problems. As you will see, we can solve the problems by splitting lists into tables of data. Such tables are the key components of a database. A majority of this text concerns the design of such tables and techniques for manipulating the data they contain.

### Problems with Lists

Figure 1-1 shows a simple list of student data, named the Student List[1], stored in a spreadsheet. The Student List is a very simple list, and for such a list, a spreadsheet works quite well. Even if the list is long, you can sort it alphabetically by name or email address to find any entry you want. You can change the data values, add data for a new student, or delete student data. With a list like the Student List in Figure 1-1, none of these actions is problematic, and a database is unnecessary. Keeping this list in a spreadsheet is just fine.

Suppose, however, we change the Student List by adding adviser data as shown in Figure 1-2. You can still sort the new Student with Adviser List any way you want to find an entry, but making changes to this list causes **modification problems**. Suppose, for example, you want to delete the data for the student Chip Marino. As shown in Figure 1-3, if

**FIGURE 1-1**

**The Student List in a Spreadsheet**

|   | A | B |
|---|---|---|
| 1 | **Name** | **Email** |
| 2 | Andrews, Matthew | MattA@ourcampus.edu |
| 3 | Brisbon, Lisa | LisaB@ourcampus.edu |
| 4 | Fischer, Douglas | DougF@ourcampus.edu |
| 5 | Hwang, Terry | TerryH@ourcampus.edu |
| 6 | Marino, Chip | ChipM@myserver.com |
| 7 | Lai, Tzu | TzuL@ourcampus.edu |
| 8 | Thompson, James | JamesT@myserver.com |

[1] In order to easily identify and reference the lists being discussed, we will capitalize the list names in this chapter. Similarly, we will capitalize the names of the databases associated with the lists.

**FIGURE 1-2**

The Student with
Adviser List

| | A | B | C | D |
|---|---|---|---|---|
| 1 | Name | Email | Adviser | AdviserEmail |
| 2 | Andrews, Matthew | MattA@ourcampus.edu | Baker | Baker@ourcampus.edu |
| 3 | Brisbon, Lisa | LisaB@ourcampus.edu | Valdez | Valdez@ourcampus.edu |
| 4 | Fischer, Douglas | DougF@ourcampus.edu | Baker | Baker@ourcampus.edu |
| 5 | Hwang, Terry | TerryH@ourcampus.edu | Taing | Taing@ourcampus.edu |
| 6 | Marino, Chip | ChipM@myserver.com | Tran | Tran@ourcampus.edu |
| 7 | Lai, Tzu | TzuL@ourcampus.edu | Valdez | Valdez@ourcampus.edu |
| 8 | Thompson, James | JamesT@myserver.com | Taing | Taing@ourcampus.edu |

**FIGURE 1-3**

Modification Problems in the Student with Adviser List

| | A | B | C | D |
|---|---|---|---|---|
| 1 | Name | Email | Adviser | AdviserEmail |
| 2 | Andrews, Matthew | MattA@ourcampus.edu | Baker | Baker@ourcampus.edu |
| 3 | Brisbon, Lisa | LisaB@ourcampus.edu | Valdez | Valdez@ourcampus.edu |
| 4 | Fischer, Douglas | DougF@ourcampus.edu | Baker | Baker@ourcampus.edu |
| 5 | Hwang, Terry | TerryH@ourcampus.edu | Taing | Taing@ourcampus.edu |
| 6 | Marino, Chip | ChipM@myserver.com | Tran | Tran@ourcampus.edu |
| 7 | Lai, Tzu | TzuL@ourcampus.edu | Valdez | Valdez@ourcampus.edu |
| 8 | Thompson, James | JamesT@myserver.com | Taing | Taing2@ourcampus.edu |
| 9 | ?? | ?? | Greene | Greene@ourcampus.edu |

Deleted row—
Too much lost

Changed row—
Inconsistent data

Inserted row—
Data missing

you delete the sixth row, you will not only remove Chip Marino's data, but you will also remove the fact that there is an adviser named Tran and that Professor Tran's email address is Tran@ourcampus.edu.

Similarly, updating a value in this list can have unintended consequences. If, for example, you change AdviserEmail in the eighth row, you will have inconsistent data. After the change, the fifth row indicates one email address for professor Taing, and the eighth row indicates a different email address for the same professor. Or is it the same professor? From this list, we cannot tell if there is one professor Taing with two inconsistent email addresses or whether there are two professors named Taing with different email addresses. By making this update, we add confusion and uncertainty to our list.

Finally, what do we do if we want to add data for a professor who has no advisees? For example, Professor Greene has no advisees, but we still want to record his or her email address. As shown in Figure 1-3, we must insert a row with incomplete values, or as they are called in the database field, **null values**. As you will learn in the next chapter, null values are always problematic and we want to avoid them whenever possible.

What happened in these two examples? We had a simple list with two columns, added two more columns to it, and thereby created several problems. But it isn't just that the list has four columns instead of two. The Student with Dorm List in Figure 1-4 has four columns, yet it suffers from none of the problems that the Student with Adviser List in Figure 1-3 does.

In the Student with Dorm List in Figure 1-4, we can delete the data for student Chip Marino and lose only data for that student. No unintended consequence occurs. Similarly, we can change the value of Dorm for student Tzu Lai without introducing any inconsistency. Finally, we can add data for student Garret Ingram and not have any null values.

An essential difference exists between the Student with Adviser List in Figure 1-3 and the Student with Dorm List in Figure 1-4. See if you can determine this difference before continuing. The essential difference is that the Student with Dorm List in Figure 1-4 is all about a *single thing:* All the data in that list concern *students.* In contrast,

**FIGURE 1-4**

**The Student with Dorm List**

the Student with Adviser List in Figure 1-3 is about *two things*: Some of the data concerns *students* and some of the data concerns *advisers*. In general, whenever a list has data about two or more different things, modification problems will result.

To reinforce this idea, examine the Student with Adviser and Department List in Figure 1-5. This list has data about three different things: students, advisers, and departments. As you can see in the figure, the problems with inserting, updating, and deleting data just get worse. A change in the value of Adviser, for example, might necessitate a change in only AdviserEmail, or it might require a change in AdviserEmail, Department, and Admin. As you can imagine, if this list is long—for example, if it has thousands of rows—and if several people process it, it will be a mess in a very short time.

## Using Relational Database Tables

The problems of using lists were first identified in the 1960s, and a number of different techniques were developed to solve them. Over time, a methodology called the **relational model** emerged as the leading solution, and today almost every commercial database is based on the relational model. We will examine the relational model in detail

**FIGURE 1-5**

**The Student with Adviser and Department List**

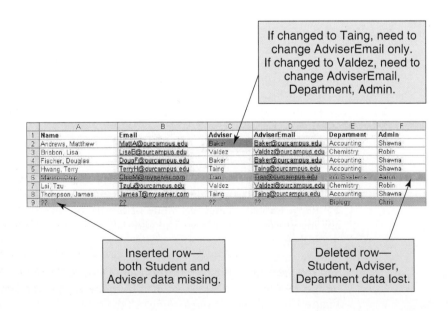

in Chapter 2. Here, however, we will introduce the basic ideas of the relational model by showing how it solves the modification problems of lists.

Remember your eighth-grade English teacher? He or she said that a paragraph should have a single theme. If you have a paragraph with more than one theme, you need to break it up into two or more paragraphs, each with a single theme.

That idea is the foundation of the design of relational databases. A **relational database** contains a collection of separate tables. A **table** holds data about one and only one theme in most circumstances. If a table has two or more themes, we break it up into two or more tables.

---

**B T W**

A table and a spreadsheet are very similar in that you can think of both as having rows, columns, and cells. The details that define a table as something different from a spreadsheet will be discussed in Chapter 2. For now, the main differences you will see are that tables have column names instead of identifying letters (*Name* instead of *A*) and that the rows are not necessarily numbered.

---

**A Relational Design for the Student with Adviser List** The Student with Adviser List in Figure 1-2 has two themes: *students* and *advisers*. If we put this data into a relational database, we place the student data in one table named STUDENT and the adviser data in a second table name ADVISER.

---

**B T W**

In this book, table names will be in all capital or upper-case letters (STUDENT, ADVISER). Column names will have initial capitals (Phone, Address), and where column names consist of more than one word, the initial letter of each word will be capitalized (StudentName, AdviserEmail).

---

We still want to show which students have which advisers, however, so we leave AdviserName in the ADVISER table. As shown in Figure 1-6, the values of AdviserName now let us link rows in the two tables to each other.

Now consider possible modifications to these tables. As you saw in the last section, three basic **modification actions** are possible: **insert**, **update**, and **delete**. To evaluate a design, we need to consider each of these three actions. As shown in Figure 1-7, we can insert, update and delete in these tables with no modification problems.

For example, we can insert the data for Professor Greene by just adding his or her data to the ADVISER table. No student references Professor Greene, but this is not a problem. Perhaps a student will have Greene as an adviser in the future. We can also update data values without unintended consequences. The email address for Professor Taing can be changed to Taing2@ourcampus.edu, and no inconsistent data will result because Taing's email address is stored just once in the ADVISER table. Finally, we can delete data without associated consequences. For example, if we delete the data for student Marino from the STUDENT table, we lose no adviser data.

## FIGURE 1-6

**The Adviser and Student Tables**

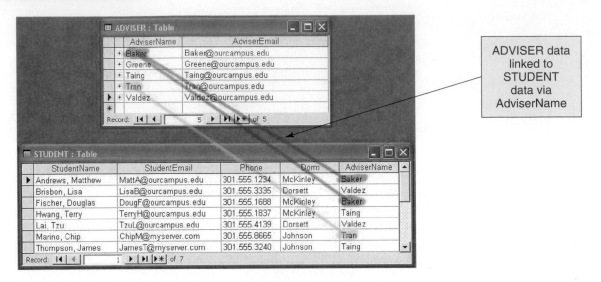

ADVISER data linked to STUDENT data via AdviserName

## FIGURE 1-7

**Modifying the Adviser and Student Tables**

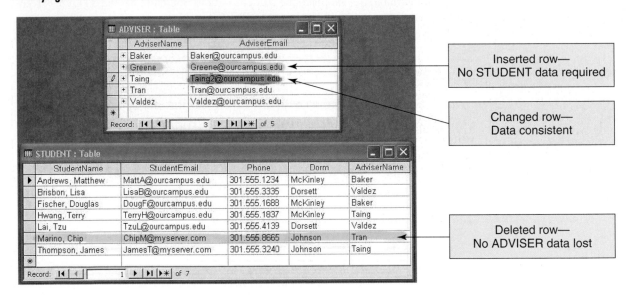

Inserted row—
No STUDENT data required

Changed row—
Data consistent

Deleted row—
No ADVISER data lost

### A Relational Design for the Student with Adviser and Department List

We can use a similar strategy to develop a relational database for the Student with Adviser and Department List as shown in Figure 1-5. This list has three themes: students, advisers, and departments. Accordingly, we create three tables, one for each of these three themes as shown in Figure 1-8.

As illustrated in Figure 1-8, we will use AdviserName and Department to link the tables. Also as shown in this figure, there are no modification problems with this set of tables. We can insert new data without creating null values, we can modify data without creating inconsistencies, and we can delete data without unintended consequences. Notice in particular that when we add a new row to DEPARTMENT, we can add rows

**FIGURE 1-8**

**The Department, Adviser, and Student Tables**

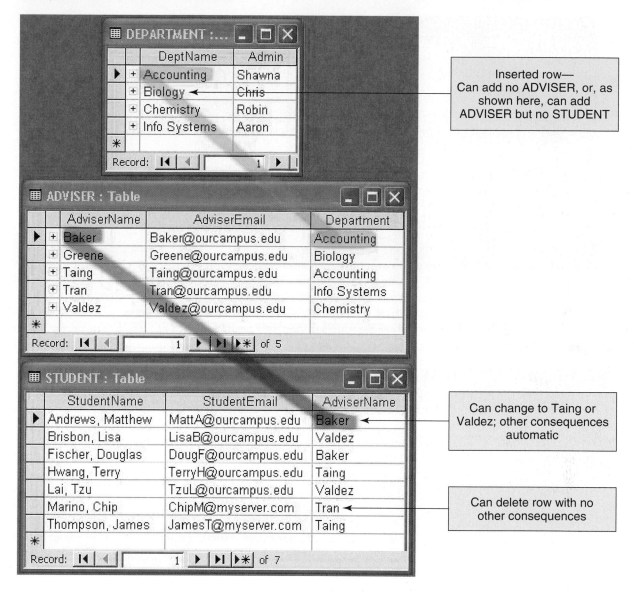

in ADVISER if we want, and we can add rows in STUDENT for each of the new rows in ADVISER, if we want. However, all of these actions are independent. None of them leaves the tables in an inconsistent state.

Similarly, when we modify the AdviserName of a row in STUDENT, we automatically pick up the correct email and department. If we change AdviserName in the first row of STUDENT to Taing, it will be connected to the row that has the correct AdviserEmail and Department values. If we want, we can use the value of Department in ADVISER to obtain the correct DEPARTMENT data, as well. Finally, notice that we can delete the row for student Marino without a problem.

As an aside, the design in Figure 1-8 has removed the problems that occur when modifying a list, but it has also introduced a new problem. Specifically, what happens if we delete the first row in ADVISER? Students Andrews and Fischer would have an invalid value of AdviserName because a Baker would no longer exist in the ADVISER table. To prevent this

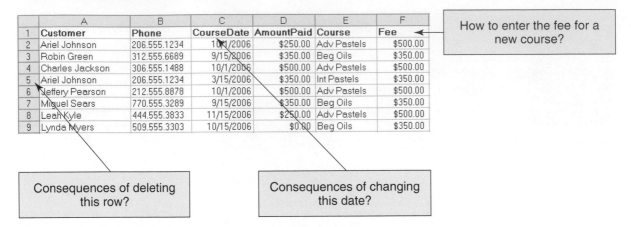

**FIGURE 1-9**

**The Art Course List with Problematic Changes**

| | A | B | C | D | E | F |
|---|---|---|---|---|---|---|
| 1 | Customer | Phone | CourseDate | AmountPaid | Course | Fee |
| 2 | Ariel Johnson | 206.555.1234 | 10/1/2006 | $250.00 | Adv Pastels | $500.00 |
| 3 | Robin Green | 312.555.6689 | 9/15/2006 | $350.00 | Beg Oils | $350.00 |
| 4 | Charles Jackson | 306.555.1488 | 10/1/2006 | $500.00 | Adv Pastels | $500.00 |
| 5 | Ariel Johnson | 206.555.1234 | 3/15/2006 | $350.00 | Int Pastels | $350.00 |
| 6 | Jeffery Pearson | 212.555.8878 | 10/1/2006 | $500.00 | Adv Pastels | $500.00 |
| 7 | Miguel Sears | 770.555.3289 | 9/15/2006 | $350.00 | Beg Oils | $350.00 |
| 8 | Leah Kyle | 444.555.3833 | 11/15/2006 | $250.00 | Adv Pastels | $500.00 |
| 9 | Lynda Myers | 509.555.3303 | 10/15/2006 | $0.00 | Beg Oils | $350.00 |

How to enter the fee for a new course?

Consequences of deleting this row?

Consequences of changing this date?

problem, we can design the database so that a deletion of a row is not allowed if other rows depend on it, or we can design it so that the dependent rows are deleted, as well. We're skipping way ahead here, however, and we will discuss such issues in later chapters.

**A Relational Design for Art Course Enrollments**    To fix these ideas in your mind, consider the Art Course List in Figure 1-9, which is used by an art school that offers art courses to the public. This list has modification problems. For example, suppose we change the value of CourseDate in the first row. This change might mean that the date for the course is changing, in which case the CourseDate values should be changed in other rows, as well. Alternatively, this change could mean that a new Advanced Pastels (Adv Pastels) course is being offered. Either is a possibility.

As with the previous examples, we can remove the problems and ambiguities by creating a separate table for each theme. However, in this case, the themes are more difficult to determine. Clearly, one of the themes is *customer,* and another one is *art course.* However, a third theme exists that is more difficult to bring to light. The customer has paid a certain amount toward a course. The amount paid is not a property of the customer because it varies depending on which course the customer is taking. For example, customer Ariel Johnson paid $250 for the Advanced Pastels (Adv Pastels) course and $350 for the Intermediate Pastels (Int Pastels) course. Similarly, the amount paid is not a property of the course, because it varies with which customer has taken the course. Therefore, the third theme of this list must concern the enrollment of a particular student in a particular class. Figure 1-10 shows a design of three tables that correspond to these three themes.

Notice that this design assigns an **ID column** named CustomerNumber that assigns a unique identifying number to each row of CUSTOMER; this is necessary because some customers might have the same name. Another ID column named CourseNumber has also been added to COURSE. This is necessary because some courses have the same name. Finally, notice that the rows of the ENROLLMENT table show the amount paid by a particular customer for a particular course while using the ID columns CustomerNumber and CourseNumber as linking columns to the other tables.

**A Relational Design for Parts and Prices**    Now consider a more complicated example. Figure 1-11 shows a spreadsheet that holds the Project Equipment List used by a housing contractor named Carbon River Construction to keep track of the parts that it buys for various construction projects.

Suppose your job is to maintain this list, and your boss tells you that customer Elizabeth Barnaby changed her phone number. How many changes would you need to

**FIGURE 1-10**

### The Art Course Tables with Changes

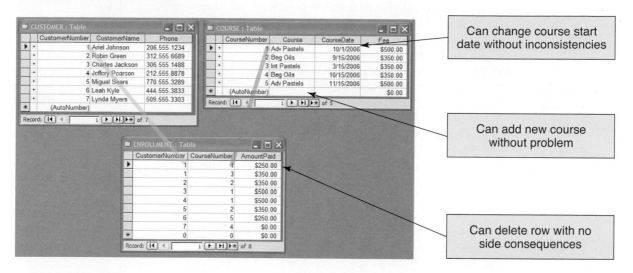

**FIGURE 1-11**

### The Project Equipment List as a Spreadsheet

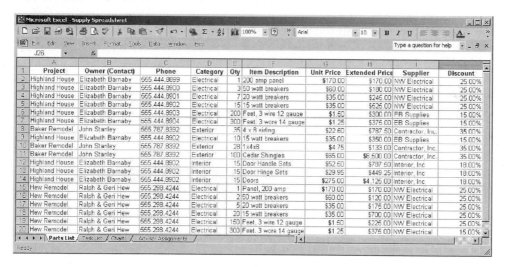

make to this spreadsheet? For the data in Figure 1-11, you would need to make this change 10 times. Now suppose the spreadsheet has 5,000 rows. How many changes might you need to make? The answer could be dozens, and you need to worry not only about the time this will take but also about the possibility of errors—you might miss her name in a row or two.

Consider a second problem with this list. In this business, each supplier agrees to a particular discount for all parts it supplies. For example, in Figure 1-11 the supplier NW Electrical has agreed to a 25 percent discount. With this list, every time you enter a new part quotation, you must enter the supplier of that part along with the correct discount. If dozens or hundreds of suppliers are used, there is always the chance that you will enter the wrong discount. Then the list would have more than one discount for one supplier—a situation that is incorrect and confusing.

For another problem, consider what happens when you enter data correctly but inconsistently. The first row has a part named 200-amp panel, whereas the fifteenth row has a part named Panel, 200-amp. Are these two parts the same item, or are they different? It turns out that they are the same item, but they were named differently.

A fourth problem concerns partial data. Suppose you know that a supplier offers a 20 percent discount, but Carbon River has not yet ordered from the supplier. Where do you record the 20 percent discount?

Just as we did for the previous examples, we can fix the Project Equipment List by breaking it up into separate tables. Because this list is more complicated, we will use more tables. Analyzing the Project Equipment List we find data about four themes: *projects*, *items*, *price quotations*, and *suppliers*. Accordingly, we create a database with four tables, and relate those four tables using linking values as before. Figure 1-12 shows our four tables and their relationships.

In Figure 1-12, note that the QUOTE table holds a unique quote identifier (QuoteID), a quantity, a price, and then three ID columns as linking values: ProjectID for PROJECT, ItemNumber for ITEM, and SupplierID for SUPPLIER.

Now, if Elizabeth Barnaby changes her phone number, we need to make that change only once—in the PROJECT table. Similarly, we need to record a supplier discount only once—in the SUPPLIER table.

## Processing the Relational Tables

By now, you may have a burning question: It may be fine to tear the lists up into pieces in order to eliminate processing problems, but what if the users want to view their data in the format of the original list? With the data separated into different tables, the users will have to jump from one table to another to find the information they want, and this jumping around will become tedious.

This is an important question and one that many people addressed in the 1970s and 1980s. Several approaches were invented for combining, querying, and processing sets

---

### FIGURE 1-12

**The Project Equipment List Tables**

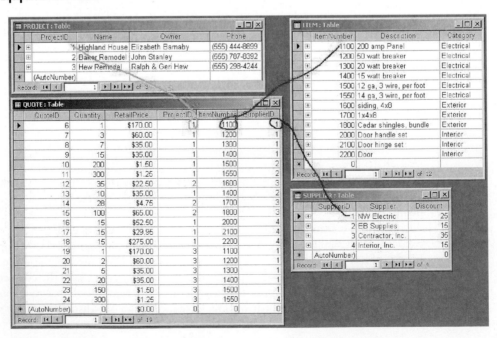

of tables. Over time, one of those approaches, a language called **Structured Query Language (SQL)** emerged as the leading technique for data definition and manipulation. Today, SQL is an international standard. Using SQL, you can reconstruct lists from their underlying tables; you can query for specific data conditions; you can perform computations on data in tables; and you can insert, update, and delete data.

**Processing Tables with SQL**  You will learn how to code SQL statements in Chapter 3. However, to give you an idea of the structure of such statements, the following SQL statement will join the three tables in Figure 1-10 to produce the original Art Course List. Don't worry about understanding all of the syntax of this statement now; just realize that it produces the result shown in Figure 1-13, which contains all the Art Course List data (although it is in a slightly different row order[2]).

```
SELECT   CUSTOMER.CustomerName, CUSTOMER.Phone,
         COURSE.CourseDate, ENROLLMENT.AmountPaid,
         COURSE.Course, COURSE.Fee
FROM     CUSTOMER, ENROLLMENT, COURSE
WHERE    CUSTOMER.CustomerNumber = ENROLLMENT.CustomerNumber
         AND COURSE.CourseNumber = ENROLLMENT.CourseNumber;
```

As you will learn in Chapter 3, it is also possible to select rows, to order them, and to make calculations on row data values. Figure 1-14 shows the result of a SQL statement that joins the Art Course tables together, computes the difference between the course Fee and the AmountPaid, and stores this result in a new column called AmountDue. The SQL statement then selects only rows for which AmountDue is greater than zero and presents the results sorted by CustomerName. Compare the data in Figure 1-13 with the results in Figure 1-14 to ensure that the results are correct.

---

**FIGURE 1-13**

**Results of SQL Query to Recreate the Art Course List**

| | CustomerName | Phone | CourseDate | AmountPaid | Course | Fee |
|---|---|---|---|---|---|---|
| ▶ | Ariel Johnson | 206.555.1234 | 10/1/2006 | $250.00 | Adv Pastels | $500.00 |
| | Ariel Johnson | 206.555.1234 | 3/15/2006 | $350.00 | Int Pastels | $350.00 |
| | Robin Green | 312.555.6689 | 9/15/2006 | $350.00 | Beg Oils | $350.00 |
| | Charles Jackson | 306.555.1488 | 10/1/2006 | $500.00 | Adv Pastels | $500.00 |
| | Jeffery Pearson | 212.555.8878 | 10/1/2006 | $500.00 | Adv Pastels | $500.00 |
| | Miguel Sears | 770.555.3289 | 9/15/2006 | $350.00 | Beg Oils | $350.00 |
| | Leah Kyle | 444.555.3833 | 11/15/2006 | $250.00 | Adv Pastels | $500.00 |
| | Lynda Myers | 509.555.3303 | 10/15/2006 | $0.00 | Beg Oils | $350.00 |

Record: 1 of 8

**Amount Due Query : Select Query**

| | CustomerName | Phone | Course | Fee | AmountPaid | AmountDue |
|---|---|---|---|---|---|---|
| ▶ | Ariel Johnson | 206.555.1234 | Adv Pastels | $500.00 | $250.00 | $250.00 |
| | Leah Kyle | 444.555.3833 | Adv Pastels | $500.00 | $250.00 | $250.00 |
| | Lynda Myers | 509.555.3303 | Beg Oils | $350.00 | $0.00 | $350.00 |

Record: 1 of 3

**FIGURE 1-14**

**Results of the SQL Query to Compute Amount Due**

---

[2]We will discuss how to sort data to control the row order in Chapter 3.

# ▶ WHAT IS A DATABASE SYSTEM?

As shown in Figure 1-15, a database system consists of the four components: users, the database application, the database management system (DBMS), and the database. Starting from the right of Figure 1-15, the **database** is a collection of related tables and other structures. The **database management system (DBMS)** is a computer program used to create, process, and administer the database. The DBMS receives requests encoded in SQL and translates those requests into actions on the database. The DBMS is a large, complicated program that is licensed from a software vendor—companies almost never write their own DBMS programs.

A **database application** is a set of one or more computer programs that serves as an intermediary between the user and the DBMS. Application programs read or modify database data by sending SQL statements to the DBMS. Application programs also present data to users in the format of forms and reports. Application programs can be acquired from software vendors, and they are also frequently written in-house. The knowledge you gain from this text will help you write database applications.

**Users** are the fourth component of a database system. Users employ the database application to keep track of things. They use forms to read, enter, and query data, and they produce reports.

Of these components, we'll consider the database, the DBMS, and database application in more detail.

## The Database

In the most general case, a database is defined as a self-describing collection of related records. For all relational databases (almost all databases today, and the only type considered in this book), this definition can be modified to indicate that a database is a self-describing collection of related tables.

The two key terms in this definition are **self-describing** and **related tables**. You already have a good idea of what we mean by *related tables*. One example of related tables consists of the ADVISER and STUDENT tables, which are related by the common column of AdviserName. We will build on this idea of relationships further in the next chapter.

*Self-describing* means that a description of the structure of the database is contained within the database itself. Because this is so, the contents of a database can always be determined just by looking inside the database itself. It is not necessary to look anywhere else. This situation is akin to that at a library, where you can tell what is in the library by examining the catalog that resides within the library.

Data about the structure of a database are called **metadata**. Examples of metadata are the names of tables, the names of columns and the tables to which they belong, properties of tables and columns, and so forth.

All DBMS products provide a set of tools for displaying the structure of their databases. For example, Figure 1-16 shows a diagram produced by Microsoft Access that displays the relationships between the Art Course database tables shown in Figure 1-10. Other tools describe the structure of the tables and other components.

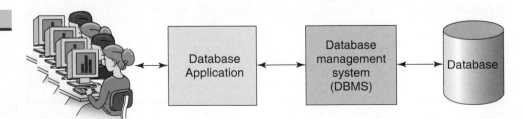

**FIGURE 1-15**

**Components of a Database System**

Users

**FIGURE 1-16**

Example Metadata–Relationship Diagram for the Art Course Tables in Figure 1-10

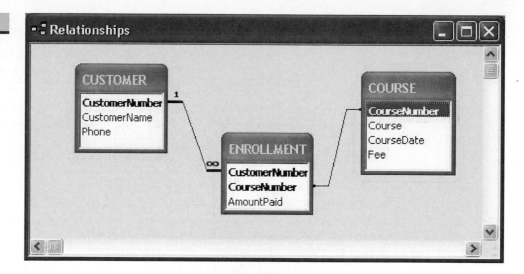

**FIGURE 1-17**

Database Contents

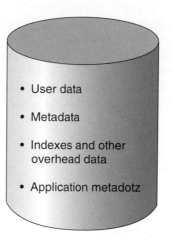

- User data

- Metadata

- Indexes and other overhead data

- Application metadotz

The contents of a database are illustrated in Figure 1-17. A database has user data and metadata as just described. A database also has indexes and other structures that exist to improve database performance, and we will discuss such structures in later chapters. Finally, some databases contain application metadata; these are data that describe application elements, such as forms and reports. For example, Microsoft Access carries application metadata as part of its databases.

## The DBMS

The purpose of the DBMS is to create, process, and administer the database. The DBMS is a large, complicated product that is almost always licensed from a software vendor. One DBMS product is Microsoft Access. Other commercial DBMS products are Oracle, from Oracle Corporation; DB2, from IBM Corporation; SQL Server, from Microsoft Corporation; and MySQL from MySQL AB. Dozens of other DBMS products exist, but these five have the lion's share of the market.

Figure 1-18 lists the functions of a DBMS. The DBMS is used to create the database itself and to create tables and other supporting structures inside that database. As an example of the latter, suppose that we have an EMPLOYEE table with 10,000 rows and that this table includes a column, DepartmentName, that records the name of the department in which an employee works. Furthermore, suppose that we frequently need to access employee data by DepartmentName. Because this is a large database, searching through the table to find, for example, all employees in the accounting department would take

**FIGURE 1-18**

**Functions of a DBMS**

- Create database
- Create tables
- Create supporting structures (e.g., indexes, etc.)
- Read database data
- Modify (insert, update, or delete) database data
- Maintain database structures
- Enforce rules
- Control concurrency
- Provide security
- Perform backup and recovery

a long time. To improve performance, we can create an index (akin to the index at the back of a book) for DepartmentName to show which employees are in which departments. Such an index is an example of a supporting structure that is created and maintained by the DBMS.

The next two functions of the DBMS are to read and modify database data. To do this, the DBMS receives SQL and other requests and transforms those requests into actions on the database files. Another DBMS function is to maintain all of the database structures. For example, from time to time it might be necessary to change the format of a table or other supporting structure. Developers use the DBMS to make such changes.

With most DBMS products, it is possible to declare rules about data values and have the DBMS enforce them. For example, in the Art Course database tables in Figure 1-10, what would happen if a user mistakenly entered a value of 9 for CustomerID in the ENROLLMENT table? No such customer exists, so such a value would cause numerous errors. To prevent this situation, it is possible to tell the DBMS that any value of CustomerID in the ENROLLMENT table must already be a value of CustomerID in the CUSTOMER table. If no such value exists, the insert or update request should be disallowed. Such rules, called **referential integrity constraints**, are enforced by the DBMS.

The last three functions of the DBMS listed in Figure 1-18 have to do with database administration. The DBMS controls **concurrency** by ensuring that one user's work does not inappropriately interfere with another user's work. This important (and complicated) function will be discussed in Chapter 6. Also, the DBMS contains a security system that is used to ensure that only authorized users perform authorized actions on the database. For example, users can be prevented from seeing certain data. Similarly, users' actions can be confined to making only certain types of data changes on specified data.

Finally, the DBMS provides facilities for backing up database data and recovering it from backups when necessary. The database, as a centralized repository of data, is a valuable organizational asset. Consider, for example, the value of a book database to a company like Amazon.com. Because the database is so important, steps need to be taken to ensure that no data will be lost in the event of errors, hardware or software problems, or natural catastrophes.

**Application Programs**   Figure 1-19 lists the functions of database applications. First, the application program creates and processes forms. Figure 1-20 shows a typical form for entering and processing customer data for the Art Course application.

Notice that this form hides the structure of the underlying tables from the user. Comparing the tables and data in Figure 1-10 to the form in Figure 1-20, we can see that data from the CUSTOMER table appears at the top of the form, while data from the

**FIGURE 1-19**

**Functions of
Application Programs**

- Create and process forms
- Process user queries
- Create and process reports
- Execute application logic
- Control application

**FIGURE 1-20**

**Example Data Entry Form**

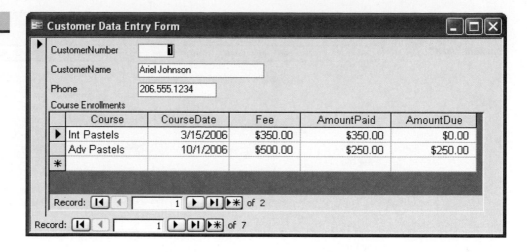

ENROLLMENT and the COURSE tables is combined and presented in a tabular section labeled Course Enrollments.

The goal of this form, like that for all data entry forms, is to present the data in a format that is most useful for the users, regardless of the underlying table structure. Behind the form, the application processes the database in accordance with the users' actions. The application generates a SQL statement to insert, update, or delete data for any of the three tables that underlie this form.

The second function of application programs is to process user queries. The application program first generates a query request and sends it to the DBMS. Results are then formatted and returned to the user. The forms in Figure 1-21 illustrate this process in a query of the Art Course database in Figure 1-10.

In Figure 1-21(a), the application obtains the name or part of a name of a course. Here, the user has entered the characters *pas*. When the user clicks OK, the application then constructs a SQL query statement to search the database for any course containing these characters. The result of this SQL query is shown in Figure 1-21(b). In this particular case, the application queried for the relevant course and then joined the ENROLLMENT and CUSTOMER data to the qualifying COURSE rows. Observe that the only rows shown are those with a course name that includes the characters *pas*.

**FIGURE 1-21**

**Example Query**

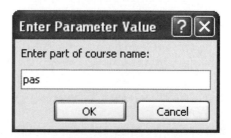

**(a) Query Parameter Form**

| CustomerName | Course | CourseDate | Fee | AmountPaid | Amount Due |
|---|---|---|---|---|---|
| Ariel Johnson | Int Pastels | 3/15/2006 | $350.00 | $350.00 | $0.00 |
| Ariel Johnson | Adv Pastels | 10/1/2006 | $500.00 | $250.00 | $250.00 |
| Charles Jackson | Adv Pastels | 10/1/2006 | $500.00 | $500.00 | $0.00 |
| Jeffery Pearson | Adv Pastels | 10/1/2006 | $500.00 | $500.00 | $0.00 |
| Leah Kyle | Adv Pastels | 11/15/2006 | $500.00 | $250.00 | $250.00 |

Record: 1 of 5

**(b) Query Results**

| FIGURE 1-22 | *Course Enrollment Report* |
| --- | --- |

**Example Report**

| Course | CourseDate by Month | CustomerName | Phone | CourseDate | Fee | AmountPaid | AmountDue |
| --- | --- | --- | --- | --- | --- | --- | --- |
| **Adv Pastels** | | | | | | | |
| | October 2006 | | | | | | |
| | | Ariel Johnson | 208.555. | 10/1/2006 | $500.00 | $250.00 | $250.00 |
| | | Charles Jackson | 308.555. | 10/1/2006 | $500.00 | $500.00 | $0.00 |
| | | Jeffery Pearson | 212.555. | 10/1/2006 | $500.00 | $500.00 | $0.00 |
| | November 2006 | | | | | | |
| | | Leah Kyle | 444.555. | 11/15/2006 | $500.00 | $250.00 | $250.00 |
| **Beg Oils** | | | | | | | |
| | September 2006 | | | | | | |
| | | Miguel Sears | 770.555. | 9/15/2006 | $350.00 | $350.00 | $0.00 |
| | | Robin Green | 312.555. | 9/15/2006 | $350.00 | $350.00 | $0.00 |
| | October 2006 | | | | | | |
| | | Lynda Myers | 509.555. | 10/15/2006 | $350.00 | $0.00 | $350.00 |
| **Int Pastels** | | | | | | | |
| | March 2006 | | | | | | |
| | | Ariel Johnson | 208.555. | 3/15/2006 | $350.00 | $350.00 | $0.00 |

The third function of an application is to create and process reports. This function is somewhat similar to the second because the application program first queries the DBMS for data (again using SQL). The application then formats the query results as a report. Figure 1-22 shows a report displaying all of the Art Course database enrollment data in order by course. Notice that the report, like the form in Figure 1-20, is structured according to the users' needs and not according to the underlying table structure.

In addition to generating forms, queries, and reports, the application program takes other actions to update the database in accordance with application-specific logic. For example, suppose a user using an order-entry application requests 10 units of a particular item. Suppose further that when the application program queries the database (via the DBMS), it finds that only eight items are in stock. What should happen? It depends on the logic of that particular application. Perhaps no items should be removed from inventory and the user should be notified, or perhaps the eight items should be removed and two more placed on back order. Perhaps some other action should be taken. Whatever the case, it is the job of the application program to execute the appropriate logic.

Finally, the last function for application programs listed in Figure 1-19 is to control the application. There are two ways in which this is done. First, the application needs to be written so that only logical options are presented to the user. For example, the application may generate a menu with user choices. If so, the application needs to ensure that only appropriate choices are available. Second, the application needs to control data activities with the DBMS. The application might direct the DBMS, for example, to make a certain set of data changes as a unit. The DBMS might be told either to make all of these changes or none of them. You will learn about such control topics in Chapter 7.

## Personal Versus Enterprise-Class Database Systems

Database technology can be used in a wide array of applications. On one end of the spectrum, a researcher might use database technology to track the results of experiments performed in a lab. Such a database might include only a few tables, and each table would have, at most, several hundred rows. The researcher would be the only user of this application. This is a typical use of a **personal database system**.

At the other end of the spectrum, some enormous databases support international organizations. Such databases have hundreds of tables with millions of rows of data and support thousands of concurrent users. These databases are in use 24 hours a day, seven days a week. Just making a backup of such a database is a difficult task. These databases are typical uses of **enterprise-class database systems**.

Figure 1-23 shows the four components of a personal database application. As you can see from this figure, Microsoft Access (and other personal DBMS products) takes on the role of both the database application and the DBMS. Microsoft designed Access this way to make it easier for people to build personal database systems. Using Access, one can switch back and forth from DBMS functions to application functions and never know the difference.

By designing Access this way, Microsoft has hidden many aspects of database processing. For example, behind the scenes, Access uses SQL just as all relational DBMS products do. One must look hard, however, to find it. Figure 1-24 shows the SQL that was used by Access for the query in Figure 1-21. As you examine this figure, you're probably thinking, "I'm just as glad they hid it—it looks complicated and hard." In fact, it looks harder than it is, but we will leave that topic for Chapter 3.

The problem with hiding database technology (and with using lots of wizards to accomplish database design tasks) is that you do not understand what is being done on your behalf. As soon as you need to perform some function that was not anticipated by the Access team, you are lost. Therefore, to be even an average database developer, you have to learn what is behind the scenes.

Furthermore, such products are useful only for personal database applications. When you want to develop larger database systems, you will have to learn all of the hidden technology. For example, Figure 1-25 shows an enterprise-class database system that has three different applications, and each application has many users. The storage of the database itself is spread over many different disks—perhaps even over different specialized computers known as database servers.

**FIGURE 1-23**

**Personal Database System**

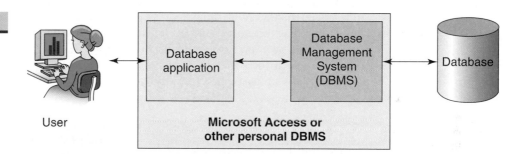

User

Microsoft Access or other personal DBMS

**FIGURE 1-24**

**SQL Generated by Access Query**

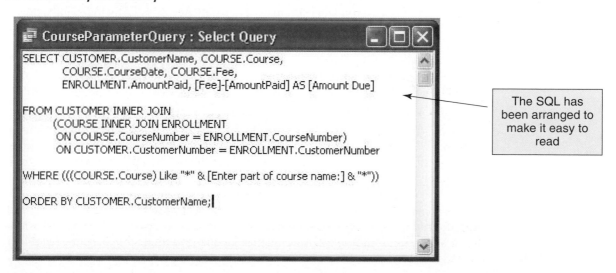

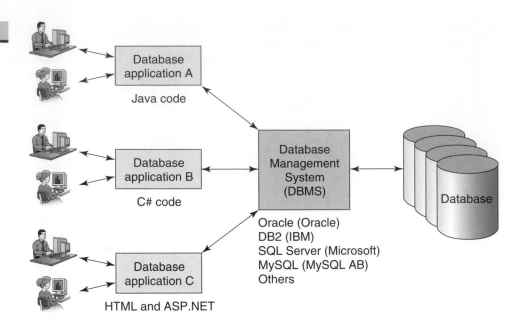

**FIGURE 1-25**

Enterprise-Class
Database System

Notice that in Figure 1-25 the applications are written in three different languages: Java, C#, and a blend of HTML and ASP.NET. These applications call upon an industrial-strength DBMS product to manage the database. No wizards or simple design tools are available to develop a system like this; instead, the developer writes program code using standard tools, such as those in integrated development environments. To write such code, you will need to know SQL and other data access standards.

While hiding technology and complexity is good in the beginning, business requirements will soon take you to the brink of your knowledge, and then you will need to know more. To be a part of a team that creates such a database application, you will need to know everything in this book. Over time, you will need to learn more.

# THE ACCESS WORKBENCH

## Section 1

### Getting Started with Microsoft Access

"The Access Workbench" is designed to reinforce the concepts you learn in each chapter. Additionally, you will learn many Microsoft Access skills by following along on your computer. In this section of "The Access Workbench," we'll review some database basics from Chapter 1 as we learn the basic steps necessary to build and use Access database applications.

As discussed in Chapter 1, Microsoft Access is a personal database that combines a DBMS with an application generator. The DBMS performs the standard DBMS functions of database creation, processing and administration, while the application generator adds the abilities to create and store forms, reports, queries, and other application-related functions. In this section, we will work with only one table in a database; in the next section, we will expand this to include two or more tables.

### Creating an Access Database

The first step is to create the Access database that will store the database tables and the application forms, reports, and queries. In this section, we will work with basic forms and reports, and we will leave queries for a later section.

Our Access database will be used by a car dealership named Wallingford Motors, which is located in the Wallingford district of Seattle, Washington. Wallingford Motors is the dealer for a new line of hybrid cars named Gaea.[3] Instead of using only a gasoline or diesel engine, hybrid cars are powered by a combination of energy sources, such as gasoline and electricity. Gaea produces the following four models:

1. **SUHi** — The Sport Utility Hybrid (Gaea's answer to the SUV)
2. **HiLuxury** — A luxury class four-door sedan hybrid
3. **HiStandard** — A basic four-door sedan hybrid
4. **HiElectra** — A variant of the HiStandard that uses a higher proportion of electrical power

There is an increasing interest in hybrid cars—and specifically in the Gaea product line. The sales staff at Wallingford Motors needs a way to track its customer contacts. Therefore, our database application will be a simple example of what is known as a **customer relationship management system (CRM)**. A CRM is used (among other uses) by a sales staff to track current, past, and potential customers as well as the sales staff's contacts with these customers. We will start out with a personal CRM used by one salesperson and expand it into a companywide CRM in later sections.[4]

We will name our Access application and its associated database **WMCRM**.

### Creating the Access Database WMCRM

1. **Start Microsoft Access**. The Microsoft Access window appears as shown in Figure AW-1-1.
   - **NOTE:** Microsoft Access 2003 is used in these sections, and the wording of the steps and appearance of the screenshots reflect its use. If you have a different version of Access, there will be some differences in the step details and in what you see on screen. However, the basic functionality is the same, and you can complete "The Access Workbench" operations in any version of Access.
   - **NOTE:** The first time you start Microsoft Access 2003, a dialog box will appear asking if you want to block unsafe expressions. Click the **Yes** button. At this point, another dialog box will appear, telling you that you must restart Access so that a new security level can take effect. Restart Access.
   - **NOTE:** You will also get a Microsoft Access 2003 Security Warning dialog box each time you open an *existing* database file. This is warning you about possible macro viruses. Since you don't have much choice if you want to use the database, click the **Open** button to open the file. Of course, you should only do this for database files that you are familiar with.
2. In the Getting Started task pane, click **Create a new file** . . . under Open. The New File task pane appears as shown in Figure AW-1-2.
3. In the New File task page, Click **Blank Database** . . . . The File New Database dialog box appears as shown in Figure AW-1-3.

---

[3]Gaea was the Greek goddess of the Earth (see **www.windows.ucar.edu/tour/link=/ mythology/gaea.html**). For information on hybrid cars, see **www.hybridcars.com/**.
[4]There are already many CRM applications in the marketplace. In fact, Microsoft has one: **Microsoft CRM** (see **www.microsoft.com/businesssolutions/crm/crm_productoverview.mspx**).

*(Continued)*

**FIGURE AW-1-1**

**The Microsoft Access 2003 Window**

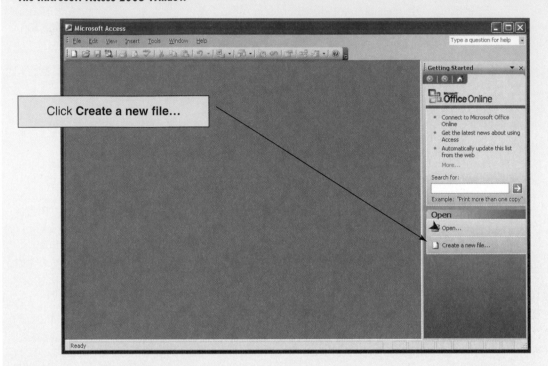

Click **Create a new file...**

**FIGURE AW-1-2**

**The New File Task Pane**

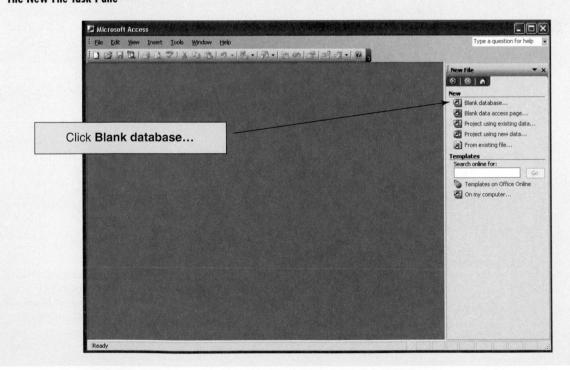

Click **Blank database...**

**FIGURE AW-1-3**

**The File New Database Dialog Box**

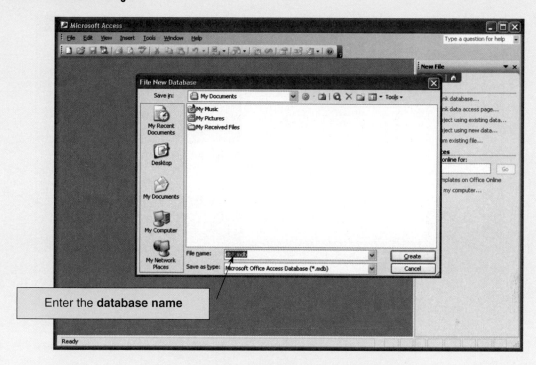

Enter the **database name**

4. Note that by default this file is being stored in My Documents on the workstation. If you need to change to another directory, do it now. In the File Name text box, type in the database name **WMCRM.mdb**, and then click the **Create** button. Note that the file extension *mdb* is the Microsoft Access file extension for Access databases. The WMCRM.mdb database is created, and the WMCRM : Database window is displayed as shown in Figure AW-1-4.

In Figure AW-1-4, notice that the WMCRM database is in the Access 2000 format. The file format used by Access has changed from version to version, and newer file formats incorporate features that make the databases unusable by older versions of Access. The default file format for Access 2003 is the Access 2000 format, which allows databases to be shared with other users running Access 2000 or Access XP. We will use the Access 2000 format to maintain backwards compatibility. Unless specifically noted, all the features of Access described in this book are available in all versions of Access starting with Access 2000.

This means that certain newer features in Access 2003 will not be available to us. However, if we need any of these features, we can select the Access 2002-2003 file format by using the **Tools | Options** command in the Access menu and then selecting the settings on the Advanced tab as shown in Figure AW-1-5.

### Creating Database Tables

For use by one salesperson, we only need two tables in the WMCRM database—CUSTOMER and CONTACT. We'll create the CUSTOMER table first.

The CUSTOMER table will contain the columns shown in the table in Figure AW-1-6. The table shows the column name and characteristics for each column. The column characteristics are type, key, required, and remarks.

*(Continued)*

## FIGURE AW-1-4

**The WMCRM : Database Window**

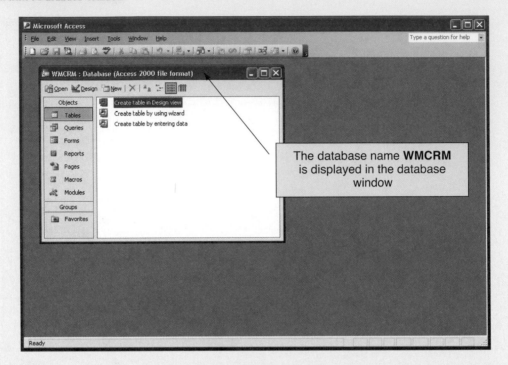

The database name **WMCRM** is displayed in the database window

## FIGURE AW-1-5

**The Advanced Options Settings**

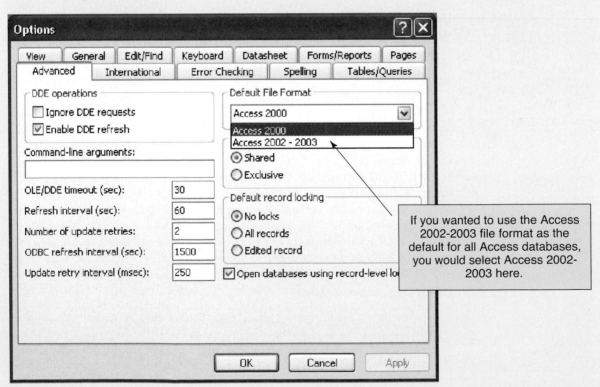

If you wanted to use the Access 2002-2003 file format as the default for all Access databases, you would select Access 2002-2003 here.

## FIGURE AW-1-6

**Database Column Characteristics for the CUSTOMER Table**

| Column Name | Type | Key | Required | Remarks |
|---|---|---|---|---|
| CustomerID | AutoNumber | Primary Key | Yes | Surrogate Key |
| LastName | Text (25) | No | Yes | |
| FirstName | Text (25) | No | Yes | |
| Address | Text (35) | No | No | |
| City | Text (35) | No | No | |
| State | Text (2) | No | No | |
| ZIP | Text (10) | No | No | |
| Phone | Text (12) | No | Yes | |
| Fax | Text (12) | No | No | |
| E-mail | Text (100) | No | No | |

## FIGURE AW-1-7

**Microsoft Access Data Types**

| Name | Type of Data | Size |
|---|---|---|
| Text | Characters and numbers | Maximum 255 characters |
| Memo | Large text | Maximum 65,535 characters |
| Number | Numeric data | Varies with Number type |
| Date/Time | Dates and times from the year 100 to the year 9999 | |
| Currency | Numbers with decimal places | 1 to 4 decimal places |
| AutoNumber | A unique sequential number | Incremental by 1 each time |
| Yes/No | Fields that can contain only two values | Yes/No, On/Off, True/False, etc. |
| Hyperlink | A hyperlink address | Maximum 2,048 characters in each of three parts of the hyperlink address |
| OLE Object | An object embedded in or linked to an Access table | Maximum 1 gigabyte |

**Type** refers to the kind of data that the column will store. Some possible Access data types are shown in Figure AW-1-7. For CUSTOMER, most data is being stored as **text** data (also commonly called **character** data), which means we can enter strings of letters, numbers, and symbols (a space is considered a symbol). The number behind the word *Text* indicates how many characters may be stored in the column. For example, customer last names may be up to 25 characters long. The only **number** or **numeric** data column in the CUSTOMER table is CustomerID, which is listed as AutoNumber. This indicates that ACCESS will automatically provide a sequential number for this column for every new customer that is added to the table.

**Key** refers to table identification functions assigned to the column. These will be described in detail in Chapter 2, "The Relational Model." At this point, you simply need to know that a **primary key** is a column value used to identify each row—and,

*(Continued)*

therefore, the values in this column must be unique. This is the reason for using an AutoNumber data type, which automatically assigns a unique number to each row in the table as it is created.

**Required** refers to whether or not the column must have a data value. If *Yes*, a value must be present in the column. If *No*, the column may be blank. Note that since CustomerID is a primary key used to identify each row, it *must* have a value.

**Remarks** contains comments about the column or how it is used. For CUSTOMER, the only comment is that CustomerID is a **surrogate key**. Surrogate keys are discussed in Chapter 2, "The Relational Model." At this point, you simply need to know that surrogate keys are usually computer-generated unique numbers used to identify rows in a table (i.e., a primary key). This is done by using the Access AutoNumber data type.

### Creating the CUSTOMER Table

1.  In the WRCRM : Database dialog box, note that Tables should already be selected in the Objects pane. If it isn't, click **Tables** to select it.
2.  Double-click **Create table in Design view** as shown in Figure AW-1-8. The Table1 : Table window appears as shown in Figure AW-1-9.
    *   **NOTE:** It seems like now would be a good time to name the new table CUS-TOMER. With Access, however, you don't name the table until you save it the first time, and you can't save the table until you have at least one column defined. So, we will define the columns, and then we will save and name the table. If you want, save the table after you've defined just one column. This will close the table, so you'll have to reopen it to define the remaining columns.

---

**FIGURE AW-1-8**

**Create Table in Design View**

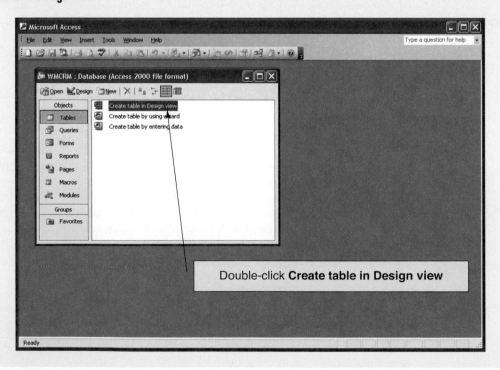

Double-click **Create table in Design view**

**FIGURE AW-1-9**

**The Table1 : Table Window**

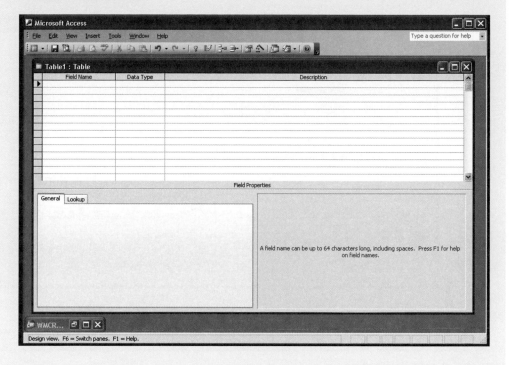

3. In the Field Name column text box of the first line, **type** the column name *CustomerID*, and then press the **Tab** key to move to the Data Type column (you can also click the Data Type column to select it).
   - **NOTE:** The terms *column* and *field* are considered synonyms in database work. The term *attribute* is also considered to be equivalent to these two words.
4. Select the **AutoNumber** Data Type for CustomerID from the **Data Type drop-down list** as shown in Figure AW-1-10.
5. An optional comment may be stored in the Description column. To do so, move to the Description column by pressing the **Tab** key or clicking in the Description text box. **Type** the text *Surrogate key for CUSTOMER*, then press the **Tab** key to move to the next row. The Table1: Table dialog box now appears as shown in Figure AW-1-11.
6. The other columns of the CUSTOMER table are created using the sequence described in steps 3 through 5.
7. In order to set the number of characters in text columns, edit the **Text Field Size** text box as shown in Figure AW-1-12. The default Field Size is 50, and the maximum value is 255.
8. In order to set a column to required, select **Yes** in the column Data Type **Required** property drop-down list as shown in AW-1-13. The default is *No* (not required), and *Yes* must be selected to make the column required.[5]

---

[5]MS Access has an additional Data Type property named Allow Zero Length. This property confounds the settings necessary to truly match the SQL constraint NOT NULL discussed in Chapter 3. However, the discussion of Allow Zero Length is beyond the scope of this book. See the MS Access Help system for more information.

*(Continued)*

**FIGURE AW-1-10**

**Selecting the Data Type**

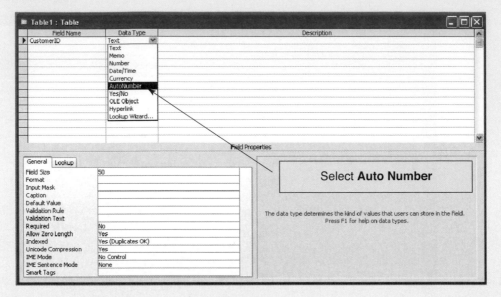

**FIGURE AW-1-11**

**The Completed CustomerID Column**

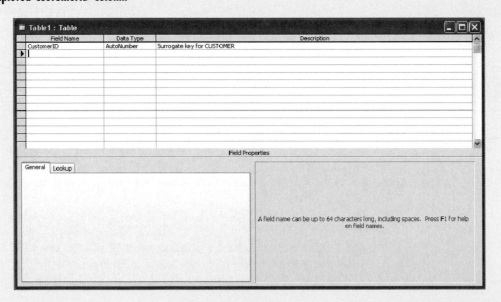

*Setting the CUSTOMER Table Primary Key*

1. Move the mouse cursor to the row selector column of the row containing the CustomerID properties as shown in Figure AW-1-14, and click to select the row.
2. Click the **Primary Key** button in the Table Design toolbar, as shown in Figure AW-1-15. CustomerID is selected as the primary key for the CUSTOMER table.

**FIGURE AW-1-12**

**Editing the Text Field Size**

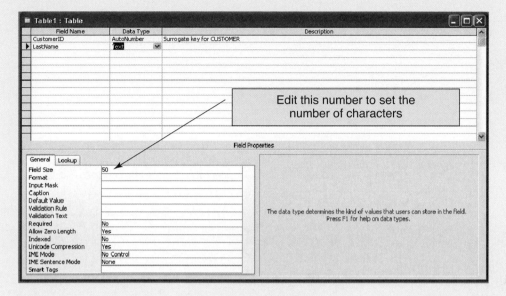

**FIGURE AW-1-13**

**Setting the Column Required Property Value**

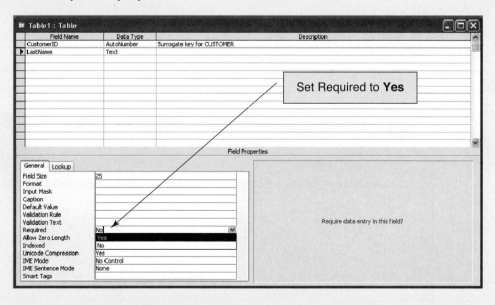

*Naming, Saving, and Closing the CUSTOMER Table*

1. To name and save the CUSTOMER table, click the **Save** button in the Table Design toolbar. The Save As dialog box appears as shown in Figure AW-1-16.
2. **Type** the table name *CUSTOMER* into the Save As dialog box **Table Name text box**, the click the **OK** button. The table is named and saved, and now appears with the table name CUSTOMER as shown in Figure AW-1-17.

*(Continued)*

## FIGURE AW-1-14

### Selecting the CustomerID Row

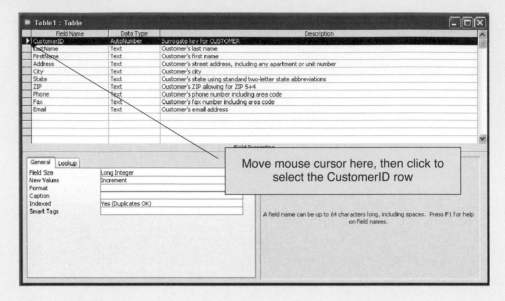

## FIGURE AW-1-15

### Setting the Primary Key

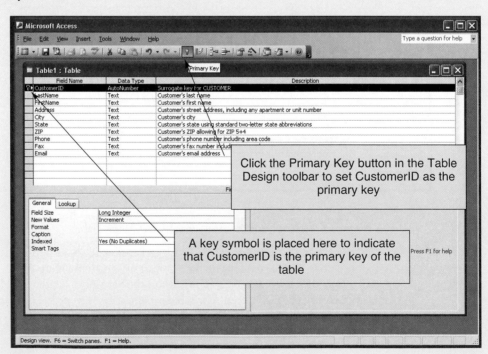

## FIGURE AW-1-16

**Naming and Saving the CUSTOMER Table**

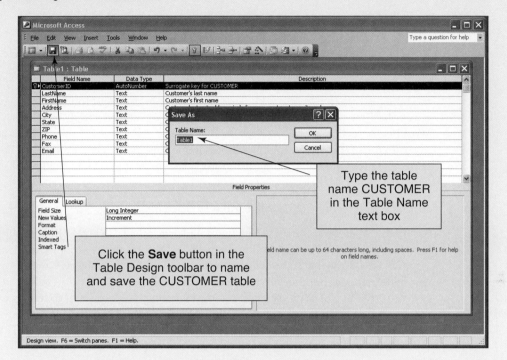

Type the table name CUSTOMER in the Table Name text box

Click the **Save** button in the Table Design toolbar to name and save the CUSTOMER table

## FIGURE AW-1-17

**The Completed CUSTOMER Table**

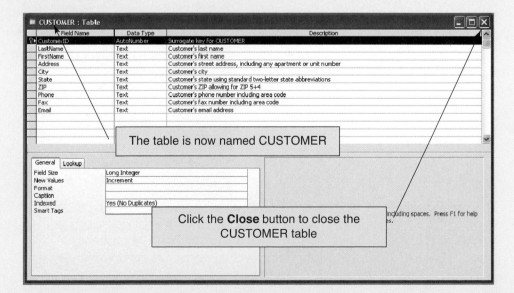

The table is now named CUSTOMER

Click the **Close** button to close the CUSTOMER table

*(Continued)*

3. To close the CUSTOMER table, click the **Close** button in the upper right corner of the CUSTOMER table window. The CUSTOMER table now appears as a table object in the WMCRM : Database window, as shown in Figure AW-1-18.

### Inserting Data into Tables—The Datasheet View

There are three commonly used methods for adding data to a table. First, we can use the table much like we would use a spreadsheet and enter the data cell by cell. When we do this, the table is in **Datasheet view**. Second, we can build a data entry form for the table, and then use it to add data. Third, we can use SQL to insert data. We will cover the first two of these in this section, and we will use SQL in a later Access Workbench section.

Of course, before we can use either method we need some data to put into the table. Data for some of Wallingford Motors customers is shown in Figure AW-1-19.

### Adding Data to the CUSTOMER Table in Datasheet View

1. In the WMCRM : Database window, double-click the **CUSTOMER** table object. The CUSTOMER : Table window appears in Datasheet view as shown in Figure AW-1-20. Note that some columns on the right side of the datasheet do not appear in the window, but they may be accessed by scrolling.
   * **NOTE:** Just as in a spreadsheet, the intersection of a row and column is called a *cell* in a datasheet.
2. Press the **Tab** key to move to the LastName cell in the new row of the CUSTOMER datasheet. For customer Ben Griffey, **type** *Griffey* into the LastName cell. Note

---

**FIGURE AW-1-18**

**The CUSTOMER Table Object**

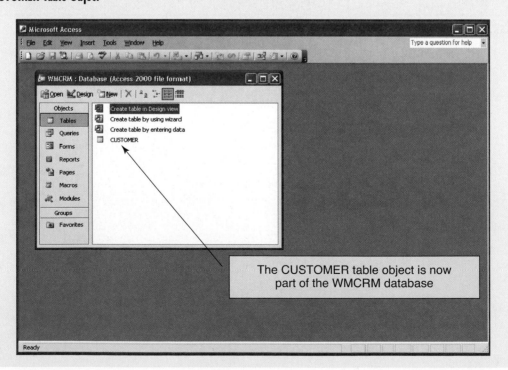

The CUSTOMER table object is now part of the WMCRM database

---

**FIGURE AW-1-19**

---

**CUSTOMER Data**

| LastName | FirstName | Address | City | State | ZIP |
|---|---|---|---|---|---|
| Griffey | Ben | 5678 25th NE | Seattle | WA | 98178 |
| Christman | Jessica | 3456 36th SW | Seattle | WA | 98189 |
| Christman | Rob | 4567 47th NW | Seattle | WA | 98167 |
| Hayes | Judy | 234 Highland Place | Edmonds | WA | 98210 |

| LastName | FistName | Phone | Fax | Email |
|---|---|---|---|---|
| Griffey | Ben | 206-456-2345 | | BGriffey@somewhere.com |
| Christman | Jessica | 206-467-3456 | | JChristman@somewhere.com |
| Christman | Rob | 206-478-4567 | 206-478-9998 | RChristman@somewhere.com |
| Hayes | Judy | 425-354-8765 | | JHayes@somewhere.com |

that as soon as you do this, the AutoNumber function puts the number *1* into the CustomerID cell, and a new row is added to the datasheet, as shown in Figure AW-1-21.

3. Using the **Tab** key to move from one column to another in the CUSTOMER datasheet, enter the rest of the data values for Ben Griffey. When you enter the

---

**FIGURE AW-1-20**

---

**The CUSTOMER Table in Datasheet View**

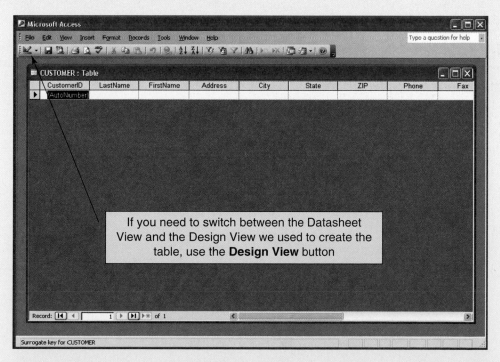

If you need to switch between the Datasheet View and the Design View we used to create the table, use the **Design View** button

*(Continued)*

---

**FIGURE AW-1-21**

**Entering Data Values for Ben Griffey**

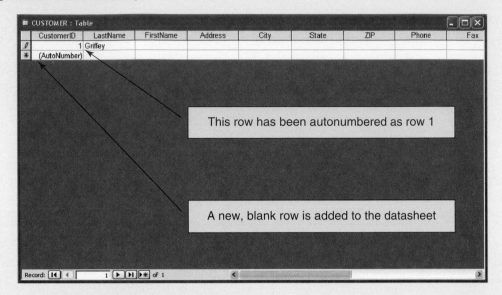

---

email address *BGriffey@somewhere.com*, the Access editor (just like in Microsoft Word) does not like the two capital letters at the start of the address and will change the second capital to lowercase—so be sure you edit this back to two capitals!

4. The final result is shown in Figure AW-1-22. Note that column width of the Email column was expanded using the mouse to move the right-hand border of the column—just like you do in an Excel spreadsheet.

---

**FIGURE AW-1-22**

**The Completed Row of Data Values**

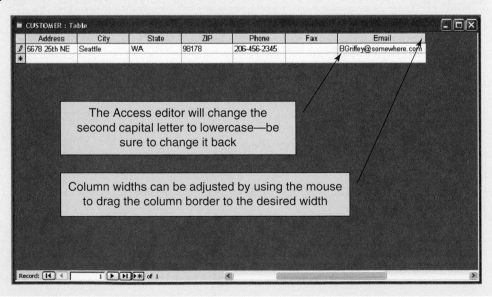

- **NOTE:** If you make a mistake and need to return to a cell, click the cell to select it—you will be in edit mode. Alternatively, you can use **Shift-Tab** to move to the right in the datasheet, and then press **F2** to edit the contents of the cell.
- **NOTE:** Remember that LastName, FirstName, and Phone *require* a data value. You will not be able to move to another row or close the table window until you have some value in each of these cells!

5. Use the **Tab** key to move to the next row of the CUSTOMER datasheet and enter the data for Jessica Christman.
6. Adjust the datasheet column widths so that the contents of the datasheet can be seen in one screen. The final result is shown in Figure AW-1-23.
7. Click the **Close** button in the upper right corner of the CUSTOMER datasheet window to close the CUSTOMER datasheet. A dialog box will appear asking if you want to save the changes you made to the column widths. Click the **Yes** button.

## Modifying Data in Tables—The Datasheet View

Once data is entered into a table, you can modify or change it by editing the data values in the datasheet view. To illustrate this, we will temporarily change Jessica Christman's phone number to 206-467-9876.

### Modifying Data in the CUSTOMER Table in Datasheet View

1. In the WMCRM : Database window, double-click the **CUSTOMER** table object. The CUSTOMER : Table window appears in datasheet view
2. Click the cell containing Jessica Christman's phone number to select it. Access automatically puts the cell into edit mode.
   - **NOTE:** If alternatively you use the **Tab** key (or **Shift-Tab** to move to the right in the datasheet) to select the cell, press the **F2** key to edit the contents of the cell.

---

### FIGURE AW-1-23

**The Completed CUSTOMER Datasheet**

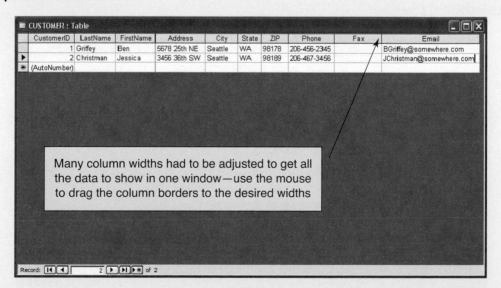

*(Continued)*

3. Edit the phone number to 206-467-9876.
   - **NOTE:** Remember that Phone has a 12-character field size. You will have to delete characters before you can enter new ones!
4. Press the **Enter** key, or otherwise move to another cell, or click the **Save** button to complete the edit. The CUSTOMER datasheet appears as shown in Figure AW-1-24.
5. Since we really don't want to change Jessica's phone number, edit the Phone value back to its original value of 206-467-3456. Complete the edit, then click the **Save** button in the Table Datasheet toolbar to save the changes.
6. Click the **Close** button in the upper right corner of the CUSTOMER datasheet window to close the CUSTOMER datasheet.

### Deleting Rows in Tables—The Datasheet View

Once data is entered into a table, you can delete the entire row in the datasheet view. To illustrate this, we will temporarily delete Jessica Christman's data.

#### Deleting a Row in the CUSTOMER Table in Datasheet View

1. In the WMCRM : Database window, double-click the **CUSTOMER** table object. The CUSTOMER : Table window appears in datasheet view.
2. Right-click the **row selector cell** on the right side of the CUSTOMER datasheet for the row containing Jessica Christman's data. This selects the entire row and displays a shortcut menu, as shown in Figure AW-1-25.
   - **NOTE:** The terms *row* and *record* are synonymous in database usage.
3. Click **Delete Record** in the shortcut menu. As shown in Figure AW-1-26, an Access dialog box appears warning you that you are about to permanently delete the record.
   - **NOTE:** As also shown in Figure AW-1-26, Access 2003 with default settings also performs the visual trick of actually removing the row! However, the row is

---

**FIGURE AW-1-24**

**The Modified CUSTOMER Datasheet**

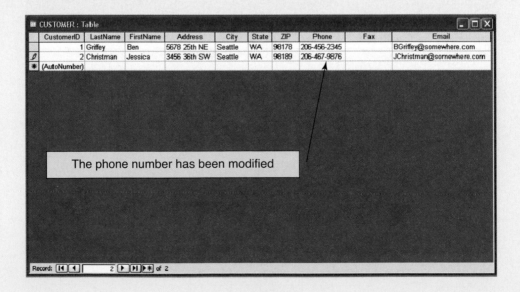

The phone number has been modified

**FIGURE AW-1-25**

### Deleting a Row in the CUSTOMER Datasheet

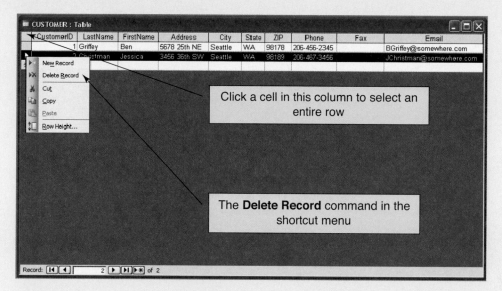

**FIGURE AW-1-26**

### The Access Dialog Box Warning About the Deletion

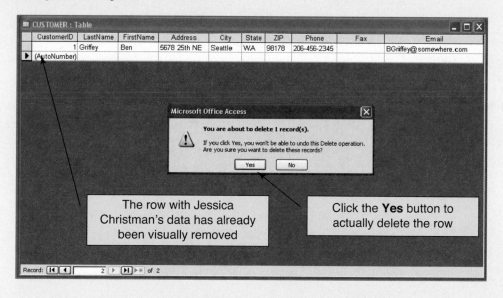

not permanently deleted until you click the **Yes** button in the Access dialog box. If you click the **No** button, the row will reappear.

4. Click the **Yes** button to complete the deletion of the row.

- **NOTE:** Alternatively, you can also delete the row by clicking the **row selector cell**, then pressing the **Delete** key. The same Access dialog box shown in Figure AW-1-26 will appear at this point.

*(Continued)*

**FIGURE AW-1-27**

**The New CustomerID Number**

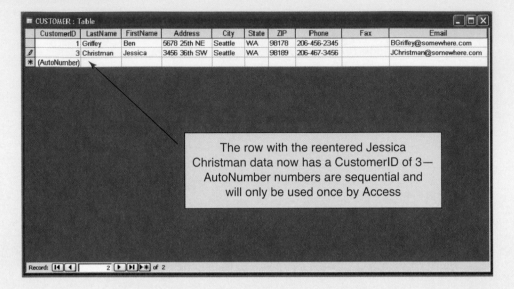

The row with the reentered Jessica Christman data now has a CustomerID of 3—AutoNumber numbers are sequential and will only be used once by Access

5. Since we do not want to really lose Jessica's data at this point, add a new row to the CUSTOMER datasheet containing Jessica's data. As shown in Figure AW-1-27, note that the CustomerID number for Jessica is now 3 instead of 2. In an autonumbered column, each number is only used once!

6. Click the **Close** button in the upper right corner of the CUSTOMER datasheet window to close the CUSTOMER datasheet.

## Inserting Data into Tables—Using a Form

Now, let's create and use an Access form to insert data into a table. Access has a form generator as part of its application generator functions. We could build a form manually in Form Design View, but we'll take the easy route and use an Access Form Wizard instead.

### Creating a Data Entry Form for the CUSTOMER Table

1. In the WMCRM : Database window, click **Forms** in the Objects pane to display the Forms pane as shown in Figure AW-1-28.

2. Double-click **Create form by using wizard** as shown in Figure AW-1-28. The Form Wizard appears as show in Figure AW-1-29.

3. The CUSTOMER table is already selected as the basis for the form, so we only have to select which columns we want on the form. We can choose columns one at a time by highlighting the column name and clicking the right-facing single chevron button. We can also choose all the columns at once by clicking the right-facing double chevron button. We will add all the columns, so click the **right-facing double chevron** button to add all of the columns, then click the **Next >** button.

   - **NOTE:** In a real-world situation, we may not want to display the CustomerID value. If so, we would unselect it by highlighting it and clicking the left-facing single chevron key.

## FIGURE AW-1-28

**The Forms Pane Objects**

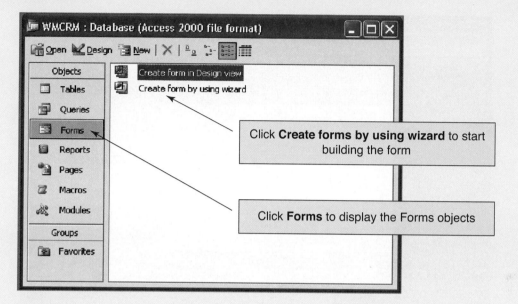

Click **Create forms by using wizard** to start building the form

Click **Forms** to display the Forms objects

## FIGURE AW-1-29

**The Forms Wizard**

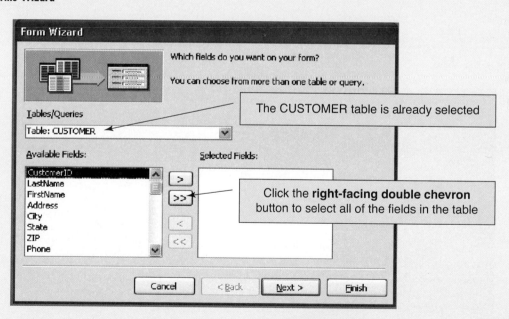

The CUSTOMER table is already selected

Click the **right-facing double chevron** button to select all of the fields in the table

4. We are now asked "What layout would you like for your form?" We will use the default Columnar layout, so click the **Next >** button.
5. We are now asked, "What style would you like? We will use the default Standard style, so click the **Next >** button.

*(Continued)*

## FIGURE AW-1-30

**The Completed WMCRM Customer Data Form**

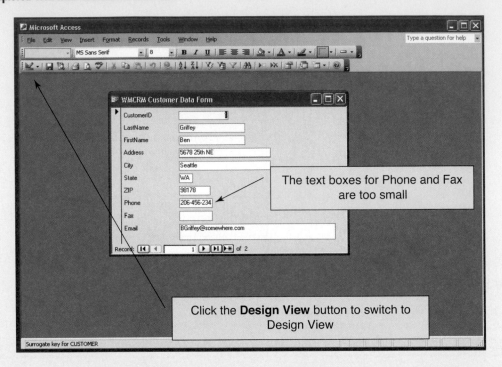

## FIGURE AW-1-31

**The Form in Design View**

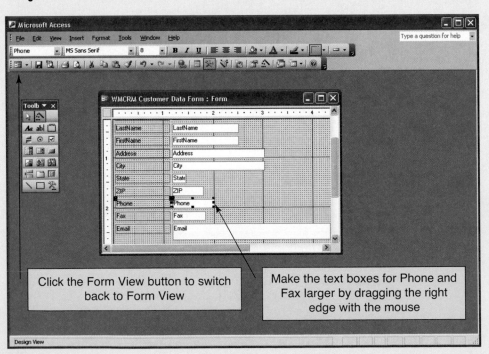

6. We are now asked "What title do you want for your form?" **Type** the form title *WMCRM Customer Data Form* in the text box, and then click the **Finish** button. The completed form appears, as shown in Figure AW-1-30.
7. Unfortunately, the Access wizard made the text boxes for Phone and Fax too small. We will fix this manually. Click the **Design View** button, shown in Figure AW-1-30, to switch the form into the design view.
8. Click on the **Phone field text box** to select it, and then use the mouse to drag the left border to the right to increase the size of the text box. The result is shown in Figure AW-1-31.
9. Repeat the actions in Step 8 to increase the size of the **Fax field text box**—make it match the new size of the Phone field text box.
10. Click the **Form View** button to return the form to its normal view. The result with the adjusted text boxes is shown in Figure AW-1-32.

### Inserting Data Into the CUSTOMER Table Using a Form

1. Click the **New Record** button shown in Figure AW-1-32. A blank form appears.
2. Click the **LastName** text box to select it. Enter the data for Rob Christman shown in Figure AW-1-19. You can either use the **Tab** key to move from text box to text box, or you can click on the text box you want to edit.

---

**FIGURE AW-1-32**

**The Corrected and Final Form in Form View**

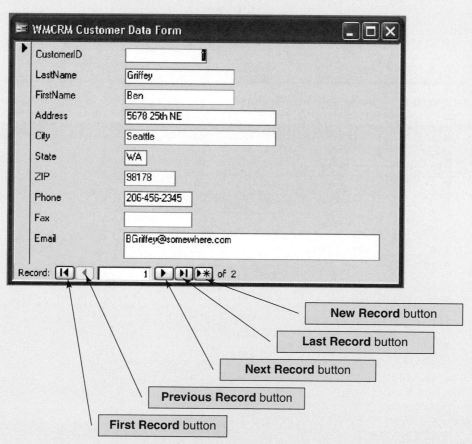

*(Continued)*

3. When you are done, use Steps 1 and 2 to enter the data for Judy Hayes. When you are done, your form will appear as shown in Figure AW-1-33.
4. Click the **Close** button in the upper right corner of the WMCRM Customer Data Form to close the form window. When you are asked "Do you want to save changes to the design of form 'WMCRM Customer Data Form'?" click the **Yes** button.

### Modifying Data and Deleting Records—Using a Form

Just as we can modify data and delete rows in a Datasheet view, we can edit data and delete records using a form. Editing data is simple—click on the appropriate field text box, and then edit the contents. Deleting a record is also simple—move to the record you want to delete by using the record navigation buttons (**First Record**, **Previous Record**, etc.), and then click the **Delete Record** button shown in Figure AW-1-33. We will not use these capabilities at this time.

### Creating Single Table Access Reports

One common function of an application is to generate printed reports. MS Access has a report generator as part of its application generator functions. Just as with forms, we could build a form manually, but we'll take the easy route and use an Access Report Wizard instead.

#### Creating a Report for the CUSTOMER Table

1. In the WMCRM : Database window, click **Reports** in the Objects pane to display the Reports pane as shown in Figure AW-1-34.
2. Double-click **Create report by using wizard** as shown in Figure AW-1-34. The Report Wizard appears as show in Figure AW-1-35.

---

### FIGURE AW-1-33

**The WMCRM Customer Data Form for Customer Judy Hayes**

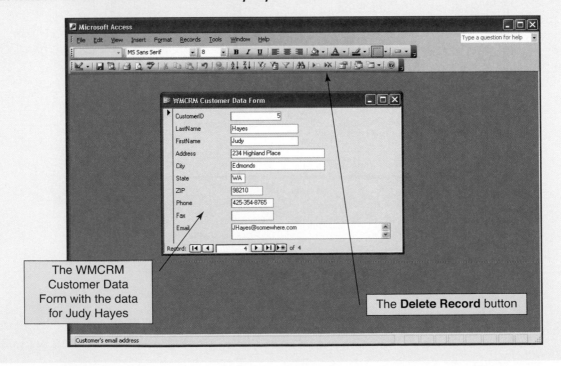

The WMCRM Customer Data Form with the data for Judy Hayes

The **Delete Record** button

**FIGURE AW-1-34**

**The Reports Pane Objects**

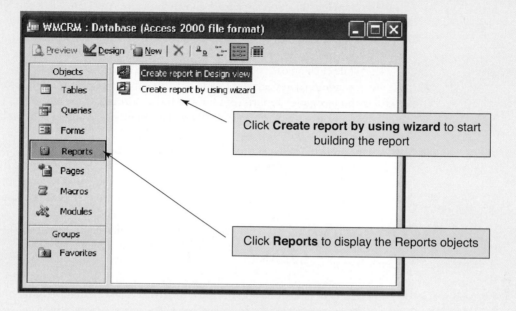

**FIGURE AW-1-35**

**The Report Wizard**

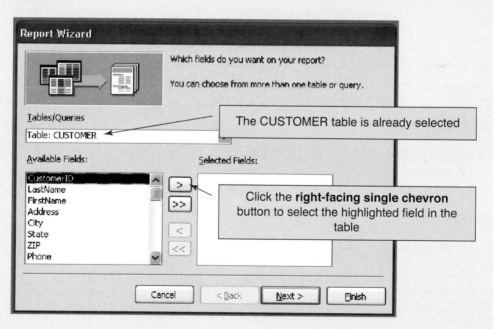

3.  The CUSTOMER table is already selected as the basis for the report, so we only have to select which columns we want on the form. Just as with the form wizard, we can choose columns one at a time by highlighting the column name and clicking the right-facing single chevron button. We can also choose all the columns at once by clicking the right-facing double chevron button. We will use only the following

*(Continued)*

columns: **LastName**, **FirstName**, **Phone**, **Fax**, and **Email**. Click each column name to select it, then click the **right-facing chevron** button to move each column to Selected Fields.

The complete selection appears as shown in Figure AW-1-36. Click the **Next >** button.

- **NOTE:** You can only select one column at a time—the usual technique of selecting more than one column name at a time by pressing and holding the **Ctrl** key while clicking each additional column name does NOT work.

4. We are now asked, "Do you want to add any grouping levels?" Grouping can be useful in more complex reports, but for a simple report listing the customers we don't need any groupings. Instead, we'll use the default nongrouped column listing, so click the **Next >** button.

5. We are now asked, "What sort order do you want for your records?" as shown in Figure AW-1-37. The most useful sorting order is by last name, with sorting by first name within identical last names. For both sorts we will want an *ascending* sort (from A to Z). Click the **sort field 1** drop-down list arrow and select **LastName**. Leave the sort order button on its current setting of Ascending.

6. Click the **sort field 2** drop-down list arrow and select **FirstName**, leave the sort order button on its current setting of Ascending, and then click the **Next >** button.

7. We are now asked, "How would you like to lay out your report?" We will use the default setting of tabular layout, but click the **Landscape orientation** radio button to change the report orientation to landscape. Then click the **Next >** button.

8. Now we are asked, "What style would you like?" We will use the default setting of **Corporate**. Then click the **Next >** button.

9. Finally, we are asked, "What title do you want for your report?" **Edit** the report title to read *Wallingford Motors Customer Report*. Leave the **Preview the report** radio

---

## FIGURE AW-1-36

**The Completed Column Selection**

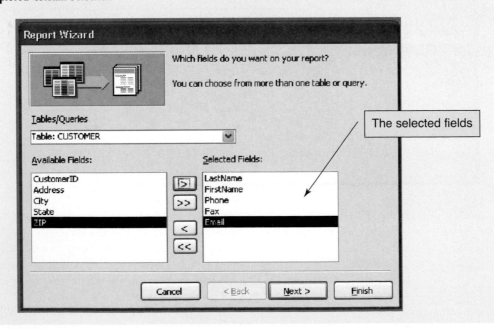

button selected. Click the **Finish** button. The completed report appears as shown in Figure AW-1-38

10. Click the **Close** button in the upper right corner of the Wallingford Motors Customer Report to close the report window.

---

**FIGURE AW-1-37**

**Choosing the Sort Order**

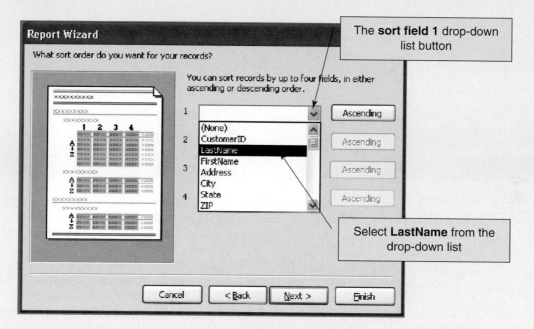

---

**FIGURE AW-1-38**

**The Finished Report**

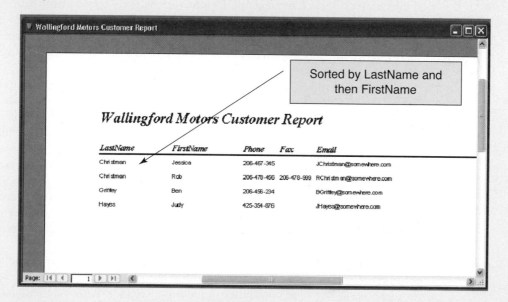

*(Continued)*

### Closing a Database and Exiting Access

That completes the work we'll do in this section of "The Access Workbench." We will finish by closing the database and Access.

#### Closing the WMCRM Database

1. To close the WMCRM : Database window, click the **Close** button in the upper right corner of the WMCRM : Database window.

#### Exiting Access

1. To exit Access, click the **Close** button in the upper right corner of the Microsoft Access window.

## SUMMARY

The importance of database processing increases every day because databases are used in information systems everywhere—and increasingly so. The purpose of this book is to teach you essential database concepts and to help you get started using and learning database technology.

The purpose of a database is to help people keep track of things. Lists can be used for this purpose, but if a list involves more than one theme, modification problems will occur when data are inserted, updated, or deleted.

Relational databases store data in the form of tables. Almost always, the tables are designed so that each table stores data about a single theme. Lists that involve multiple themes need to be broken up and stored in multiple tables, one for each theme. When this is done, a column needs to be added to link the two tables to each other so that the relationship from a row in one table to a row in a second table can be shown.

Structured Query Language (SQL) is an international language for processing relational tables. Using SQL, data in separated tables can be joined together, new tables can be queried, and data can be inserted, updated, and deleted. Using SQL, tables of data can be queried in many ways. Tables can also be joined together to form new tables. SQL can be used to insert, modify, and delete data as well.

The components of a database system are the database, the database management system (DBMS), one or more database applications, and users. A database is a self-describing collection of related records. A relational database is a self-describing collection of related tables. A database is self-describing because it contains a description of its contents within itself, which is known as metadata. Tables are related by storing linking values of a common column. The contents of a database are user data, metadata, supporting structures like indexes, and sometimes application metadata.

A database management system (DBMS) is a large, complicated program used to create, process, and administer the database. DBMS products are almost always licensed from software vendors. Specific functions of the DBMS are summarized in Figure 1-18.

The functions of database applications are to create and process forms, to process user queries, and to create and process reports. Application programs also execute specific application logic and control the application. Users provide data and data changes and read data in forms, queries, and reports.

DBMS products for personal database systems provide functionality for application development and database management. They hide considerable complexity, but at a cost: Requirements unanticipated by the DBMS features cannot be readily implemented. Enterprise-class database systems include multiple applications that might be written in multiple languages. These systems may support hundreds or thousands of users.

## REVIEW QUESTIONS

**1.1**  Why is the study of database technology important?

**1.2**  What is the purpose of this book?

**1.3**  Describe the purpose of a database.

**1.4**  What is a *modification problem?* What are the three possible modification problems?

**1.5**  Figure 1-26 shows a list that is used by a veterinary office. Describe three modification problems that are likely to occur when using this list.

**1.6**  Name the two themes in the list in Figure 1-26.

**1.7**  What is an *ID column?*

**1.8**  Break the list in Figure 1-26 into two tables, each with data for a single theme. Assume that owners have a unique phone number but that pets have no unique column. Create an ID column for pets like the one created for customers and courses for the Art Course database tables in Figure 1-10.

**1.9**  Show how the tables you created for question 1.8 solve the problems you described in question 1.5.

**1.10**  What does *SQL* stand for, and what purpose does it serve?

**1.11**  Another version of the list used by the veterinary office is shown in Figure 1-27. How many themes does this list have? What are they?

**1.12**  Break the list in Figure 1-27 into tables, each with a single theme. Create ID columns as you think necessary.

**1.13**  Show how the tables you created for question 1.12 solve the three problems of lists identified in this chapter.

**1.14**  Describe in your own words and illustrate with tables how relationships are represented in a relational database.

## FIGURE 1-26

**The Veterinary Office List—Version One**

|   | A | B | C | D | E | F | G |
|---|---|---|---|---|---|---|---|
| 1 | PetName | Type | Breed | DOB | Owner | OwnerPhone | OwnerEmail |
| 2 | Kino | Dog | Std. Poodle | 27-Feb-05 | Marsha Downs | 555-123-6788 | MD@somewhere.com |
| 3 | Teddy | Cat | Cashmier | 1-Feb-04 | Richard James | 555-444-0098 | RJ@somewhere.com |
| 4 | Filo | Dog | Std. Poodle | 17-Jul-06 | Marsha Downs | 555-123-6788 | MD@somewhere.com |
| 5 | AJ | Dog | Collie Mix | 5-May-05 | Liz Frier | 555-444-5596 | LF@somewhere.com |
| 6 | Cedro | Cat | Unknown | 6-Jun-01 | Richard James | 555-444-0098 | RJ@somewhere.com |
| 7 | Woolley | Cat | Unknown | ??? | Richard James | 555-444-0098 | RJ@somewhere.com |
| 8 | Buster | Dog | Border Collie | 11-Dec-00 | Miles Trent | 555-999-8861 | MT@somewhere.com |

**FIGURE 1-27**

**The Veterinary Office List—Version Two**

| | A | B | C | D | E | F | G | H | I | J |
|---|---|---|---|---|---|---|---|---|---|---|
| 1 | PetName | Type | Breed | DOB | Owner | OwnerPhone | OwnerEmail | Service | Date | Charge |
| 2 | Kino | Dog | Std. Poodle | 27-Feb-05 | Marsha Downs | 555-123-6788 | MD@somewhere.com | Ear Infection | 17-Aug-06 | $ 65.00 |
| 3 | Teddy | Cat | Cashmier | 1-Feb-04 | Richard James | 555-444-0098 | RJ@somewhere.com | Nail Clip | 5-Sep-06 | $ 27.50 |
| 4 | Filo | Dog | Std. Poodle | 17-Jul-06 | Marsha Downs | 555-123-6788 | MD@somewhere.com | | | |
| 5 | AJ | Dog | Collie Mix | 5-May-05 | Liz Frier | 555-444-5596 | LF@somewhere.com | One year shots | 5-May-06 | $ 42.50 |
| 6 | Cedro | Cat | Unknown | 6-Jun-01 | Richard James | 555-444-0098 | RJ@somewhere.com | Nail Clip | 5-Sep-06 | $ 27.50 |
| 7 | Woolley | Cat | Unknown | ??? | Richard James | 555-444-0098 | RJ@somewhere.com | Skin Infection | 3-Oct-06 | $ 35.00 |
| 8 | Buster | Dog | Border Collie | 11-Dec-00 | Miles Trent | 555-999-8861 | MT@somewhere.com | Laceration Repair | 5-Oct-06 | $ 127.00 |

**1.15** Name the four components of a database system.

**1.16** Define the term *database*.

**1.17** Why do you think it is important for a database to be self-describing?

**1.18** List the components of a database.

**1.19** Define the term *metadata*.

**1.20** Describe the use of an index.

**1.21** What are *application metadata?*

**1.22** What is the purpose of the DBMS?

**1.23** List specific functions of the DBMS.

**1.24** Define the term *referential integrity constraint*. Give an example of a referential integrity constraint for the tables you created for question 1.8.

**1.25** Explain the difference between a DBMS and a database.

**1.26** List the functions of a database application.

**1.27** Explain the differences between a personal database system and an enterprise-class database system.

**1.28** What is the advantage of hiding complexity from the user of a DBMS? What is the disadvantage?

**1.29** Summarize the differences in the database systems in Figures 1-23 and 1-25.

## EXERCISES

The following are a set of named spreadsheets with the indicated column headings. Use these spreadsheets to answer exercises 1.30 through 1.32.

**A.** Name of Spreadsheet: EQUIPMENT
Column Headings:
(Number, Description, AcquisitionDate, AcquisitionPrice)

**B.** Name of Spreadsheet: COMPANY
Column Headings:
(Name, IndustryCode, Gross Sales, OfficerName, OfficerTitle)

**C.** Name of Spreadsheet: COMPANY
Column Headings:
(Name, IndustryCode, Gross Sales, NameOfPresident)

**D.** Name of Spreadsheet: COMPUTER
Column Headings:
(SerialNumber, Make, Model, DiskType, DiskCapacity)

**E.** Name of Spreadsheet: PERSON
Column Headings:
(Name, DateOfHire, DeptName, DeptManager, ProjectID, NumHours, ProjectManager)

**1.30** For each of the spreadsheets provided, indicate the number of themes you think the spreadsheet includes and give an appropriate name for each theme. For some of them, the answer may depend on the assumptions you make. In these cases, state your assumptions.

**1.31** For the spreadsheets that have more than one theme, show at least one modification problem that will occur when inserting, updating, or deleting data.

**1.32** For the spreadsheets that have more than one theme, break up the columns into tables such that each table has a single theme. Add ID columns if necessary, and add a linking column (or columns) to maintain the relationship between the themes.

## ACCESS WORKBENCH EXERCISES

**AW.1.1** The Wedgewood Pacific Corporation (WPC) was founded in 1957 in Seattle, Washington, and has grown into an internationally recognized organization. The company is housed in two buildings. One building houses the Administration, Accounting, Finance, and Human Resources departments, while the second houses the Production, Marketing and Information Systems departments. The company database contains data about company employees, departments, company projects, company assets such as computer equipment, and other aspects of company operations.

**A.** Create an Access database named *WPC.mdb*.

**B.** Figure 1-28 shows the column characteristics for the WPC EMPLOYEE table. Using the column characteristics, create the EMPLOYEE table in the WPC.mdb database.

**C.** Figure 1-29 shows the data for the WPC EMPLOYEE table. Using Datasheet View, enter the data for the first three rows of data in the EMPLOYEE table shown in Figure 1-29 into your EMPLOYEE table.

### FIGURE 1-28

**Database Column Characteristics for the EMPLOYEE Table**

| Column Name | Type | Key | Required | Remarks |
|---|---|---|---|---|
| Employee Number | AutoNumber | Primary Key | Yes | Surrogate Key |
| FirstName | Text (25) | No | Yes | |
| LastName | Text (25) | No | Yes | |
| Department | Text (35) | No | Yes | |
| Phone | Text (12) | No | No | |
| Email | Text (100) | No | Yes | |

| FIGURE 1-29 | | | | | |
|---|---|---|---|---|---|
| **Wedgewood Pacific Corporation EMPLOYEE Data** | | | | | |
| Employee Number | First Name | LastName | Department | Phone | Email |
| [AutoNumber] | Mary | Jacobs | Administration | 360-285-8110 | MJacobs@WPC.com |
| [AutoNumber] | Rosalle | Jackson | Administration | 360-285-8120 | RJackson@WPC.com |
| [AutoNumber] | Richard | Bandalone | Legal | 360-285-8210 | RBandalone@WPC.com |
| [AutoNumber] | Tom | Caruthers | Accounting | 360-285-8310 | TCaruthers@WPC.com |
| [AutoNumber] | Heather | Jones | Accounting | 360-285-8320 | HJones@WPC.com |
| [AutoNumber] | Mary | Abemathy | Finance | 360-285-8410 | MAbernathy@WPC.com |
| [AutoNumber] | George | Smith | Human Resources | 360-285-8510 | GSmith@WPC.com |
| [AutoNumber] | Tom | Jackson | Production | 360-287-8610 | TJackson@WPC.com |
| [AutoNumber] | George | Jones | Production | 360-285-8620 | TJones@WPC.com |
| [AutoNumber] | Ken | Numoto | Marketing | 360-287-8710 | KNumoto@WPC.com |
| [AutoNumber] | James | Nestor | InfoSystems | | JNestor@WPC.com |
| [AutoNumber] | Rick | Brown | InfoSystems | 360-287-8820 | RBrown@WPC.com |

**D.** Create a data input form for the EMPLOYEE table named *WPC Employee Data Form*. Make any adjustments necessary to the form so that all data displays properly. Use this form to enter the rest of the data in the EMPLOYEE table shown in Figure 1-29 into your EMPLOYEE table.

**E.** Create a report named *Wedgewood Pacific Corporation Employee Report* that presents the data contained in your EMPLOYEE table sorted first by employee last name and second by employee first name. Make any adjustments necessary to the report so that all headings and data display properly. Print out a copy of this report.

## GARDEN GLORY PROJECT QUESTIONS

Garden Glory is a partnership that provides gardening and yard maintenance services to individuals and organizations. Garden Glory is owned by two partners, who employ two office administrators and a number of full- and part-time gardeners. Garden Glory will provide one-time garden services, but it specializes in ongoing service and maintenance. Many of its customers have multiple buildings, apartments, and rental houses that require gardening and lawn maintenance services.

**A.** Create a sample list of owners and properties. Your list will be similar in structure to that in Figure 1-26, but it will concern owners and properties rather than owners and pets. Your list should include, at the minimum, owner name, phone, and billing address, as well as property name, type, and address.

**B.** Describe modification problems that are likely to occur if Garden Glory attempts to maintain the list in a spreadsheet.

**C.** Split the list into tables such that each has only one theme. Create appropriate ID columns. Use a linking column to represent the relationship between a property and an owner. Demonstrate that the modification problems you identified in B have been eliminated.

**D.** Create a sample list of owners, properties, and services. Your list will be similar to that in Figure 1-27. Your list should include the data items from question A as well as the date, description, and amount charged for each service.

**E.** Illustrate modification problems that are likely to occur if Garden Glory attempts to maintain the list from question D in a spreadsheet.

**F.** Split the list from question D into tables such that each has only one theme. Create appropriate ID columns. Use linking columns to represent relationships. Demonstrate that the modification problems you identified in E have been eliminated.

## JAMES RIVER JEWELRY PROJECT QUESTIONS

James River Jewelry is a small jewelry shop that specializes in hard-to-find Asian jewelry. It has a small but loyal clientele, and it wants to further increase customer loyalty by creating a frequent buyer program. In this program, after every 10 purchases customers will receive a credit of 50 percent of the sum of their 10 most recent purchases.

**A.** Create a sample list of customers and purchases, and a second list of customers and credits. Your lists should include customer data you think would be important to James River along with typical purchase data. Credit data should include the date of the credit, the total amount of the 10 purchases used as the basis of the credit, and the credit amount.

**B.** Describe modification problems that are likely to occur if James River attempts to maintain the lists in a spreadsheet.

**C.** Split the lists into tables that each have only a single theme. Create appropriate ID columns. Use an ID to represent the relationship between a purchase and a customer, and another ID to represent the relationship between a credit and a customer.

**D.** Attempt to combine the two lists you created in question A into a single list. What problems occur as you try to do this? Look closely at Figure 1-27. An essential difference exists between a list of the three themes *customer*, *purchase*, and *credit* and a list of the three themes *PetName*, *Owner*, and *Service* in Figure 1-27. What do you think that difference is?

**E.** Change the tables from question C so that the Purchase list has not only the ID of Customer but also the ID of Credit. Compare this arrangement to the tables in your answer to question 1.10. What is the essential difference between these two designs?

## THE QUEEN ANNE CURIOSITY SHOP PROJECT QUESTIONS

The Queen Anne Curiosity Shop sells both antiques and current production household items that complement or are useful with the antiques. For example, the store sells antique dining room tables and new tablecloths. The antiques are purchased from both individuals and wholesalers, and the new items are purchased from distributors. The store's customers include individuals, owners of bed-and-breakfast operations, and local interior designers who work with both individuals and small businesses. The antiques are unique, although some multiple items, such as dining room chairs, may be available as a set (sets are never broken). The new items are not unique, and an item may be reordered if out of stock. New items are also available in various sizes and colors (for example, a particular style of tablecloth may be available in several sizes and in a variety of colors).

**A.** Create a sample list of purchased inventory items and vendors, and a second list of customers and sales. Your first list should include Inventory data such as a description, manufacturer and model (if available), item cost, and vendor identification and contact data you think should be recorded. Your second list should include customer data you think would be important to The Queen Anne Curiosity Shop along with typical sales data.

**B.** Describe problems that are likely to occur when inserting, updating, and deleting data in these spreadsheets.

**C.** Attempt to combine the two lists you created in question A into a single list. What problems occur as you try to do this?

**D.** Split the spreadsheets you created in question A into tables having only one theme each. Create appropriate ID columns.

**E.** Explain how the tables in your answer to question C will eliminate the problems you identified in question B.

**F.** What is the relationship between the tables you created from the first spreadsheet and the tables you created from the second spreadsheet? If your set of tables does not already contain this relationship, how will you add it into your set of tables?

# CHAPTER 2

# The Relational Model

> Learn the conceptual foundation of the relational model
> Understand how relations differ from nonrelational tables
> Learn basic relational terminology
> Learn the meaning and importance of keys, foreign keys, and related terminology
> Understand how foreign keys represent relationships
> Learn the purpose and use of surrogate keys
> Learn the meaning of functional dependencies
> Learn to apply a process for normalizing relations

**T**his chapter explains the relational model, the single most important standard in database processing today. This model, which was developed and published in 1970 by Edgar Frank Codd, commonly referred to as E. F. Codd,[1] then an employee at IBM, was founded on the theory of relational algebra. The model has since found widespread practical application, and today it is used for the design and implementation of almost every commercial database worldwide. This chapter describes the conceptual foundation of this model.

---

[1]E. F. Codd, "A Relational Model of Data for Large Shared Databanks," *Communications of the ACM* (June 1970): 377–387.

# ▶ RELATIONS

Chapter 1 stated that databases help people keep track of things, and that relational DBMS products store data in the form of tables. Here we need to clarify and refine these statements. First, the formal name for a "thing" that is being tracked is **entity**, which is defined as something of importance to the user that needs to be represented in the database. Further, it is not entirely correct to say the DBMS products store data in tables. DBMS products store data in the form of relations, which are a special type of table. Specifically, a **relation** is a two-dimensional table that has the following characteristics:

- Each row of the table holds data that pertain to some entity or a portion of some entity.
- Each column of the table contains data that represent an attribute of the entity. For example, in an EMPLOYEE relation, each row would contain data about a particular employee, and each column would contain data that represented an attribute of that employee, such as Name, Phone, or EmailAddress.
- The cells of the table must hold a single value, and thus no repeating elements are allowed in a cell.
- All of the entries in any column must be of the same kind. For example, if the third column in the first row of a table contains EmployeeNumber, then the third column in all other rows must contain EmployeeNumber as well.
- Each column must have a unique name, but the order of the columns in the table is unimportant.
- The order of the rows is unimportant.
- No two rows in the table may hold identical data values.

The characteristics of a relation are summarized in Figure 2-1.

## A Sample Relation and Two Nonrelations

Figure 2-2 shows a sample EMPLOYEE table. Consider this table in light of the characteristics discussed earlier. First, each row is about an EMPLOYEE entity, and each column represents an attribute of employees, so those two conditions are met. Each cell has only one value, and all entries in a column are of the same kind. Column names are unique, and we could change the order of either the columns or the rows and not lose any information. Finally, no two rows are identical. Because this table meets all requirements of the definition of a relation, we can classify it as a relation.

| **FIGURE 2-1**<br><br>Characteristics of<br>a Relation | • Rows contain data about an entity<br>• Columns contain data about attributes of the entity<br>• Cells of the table hold a single value<br>• All entries in a column are of the same kind<br>• Each column has a unique name<br>• The order of the columns is unimportant<br>• The order of the rows is unimportant<br>• No two rows may be identical |
| --- | --- |

**FIGURE 2-2**

Sample EMPLOYEE Table

| EmployeeNumber | FirstName | LastName | Department | Email | Phone |
| --- | --- | --- | --- | --- | --- |
| 100 | Jerry | Johnson | Accounting | JJ@somewhere.com | 236-9987 |
| 200 | Mary | Abernathy | Finance | MA@somewhere.com | 444-8898 |
| 300 | Liz | Smathers | Finance | LS@somewhere.com | 777-0098 |
| 400 | Tom | Caruthers | Accounting | TC@somewhere.com | 236-9987 |
| 500 | Tom | Jackson | Production | TJ@somewhere.com | 444-9980 |
| 600 | Eleanore | Caldera | Legal | EC@somewhere.com | 767-0900 |
| 700 | Richard | Bandalone | Legal | RB@somewhere.com | 767-0900 |

Now consider the tables shown in Figures 2-3 and 2-4. Neither of these tables is a relation. The EMPLOYEE table in Figure 2-3 is not a relation because the Phone column has cells with multiple entries. For example, Tom Caruthers has three values for phone, and Richard Bandalone has two values. Multiple entries per cell are not permitted in a relation.

The table in Figure 2-4 is not a relation for two reasons. First, the order of the rows is important. Since the row under Tom Caruthers contains his fax number, we may lose track of the correspondence between his name and his fax number if we rearrange the rows. The second reason this table is not a relation is that not all values in the Email column are of the same kind. Some of the values are e-mail addresses, and others are types of phone numbers.

Although each cell can have only one value, that value can vary in length. Figure 2-5 shows the table in Figure 2-2 with an additional variable-length Comment attribute. Even though a comment can be lengthy and varies in length from row to row, there is still only one comment per cell. Thus, the table in Figure 2-5 is a relation.

## A Note on Presenting Relation Structures

When we need to write out the relation structure of a relation that we are discussing, we will use the following format:

RELATION_NAME (Column01, Column02, . . . , LastColumn)

**FIGURE 2-3**

**Nonrelational Table—Multiple Entries per Cell**

| EmployeeNumber | FirstName | LastName | Department | Email | Phone |
|---|---|---|---|---|---|
| 100 | Jerry | Johnson | Accounting | JJ@somewhere.com | 236-0000 |
| 200 | Mary | Abernathy | Finance | MA@somewhere.com | 444-8898 |
| 300 | Liz | Smathers | Finance | LS@somewhere.com | 777-0098 |
| 400 | Tom | Caruthers | Accounting | TC@somewhere.com | 236-0000, 236-0991, 236-0991 |
| 500 | Tom | Jackson | Production | TJ@somewhere.com | 444-9980 |
| 600 | Eleanore | Caldera | Legal | EC@somewhere.com | 767-0900 |
| 700 | Richard | Bandalone | Legal | RB@somewhere.com | 767-0900, 767-0011 |

**FIGURE 2-4**

**Nonrelational Table—Order of Rows Matters and Kind of Column Entries Differs in Email Column**

| EmployeeNumber | FirstName | LastName | Department | Email | Phone |
|---|---|---|---|---|---|
| 100 | Jerry | Johnson | Accounting | JJ@somewhere.com | 236-9987 |
| 200 | Mary | Abernathy | Finance | MA@somewhere.com | 444-8898 |
| 300 | Liz | Smathers | Finance | LS@somewhere.com | 777-0098 |
| 400 | Tom | Caruthers | Accounting | TC@somewhere.com | 236-9987 |
| | | | | Fax: | 236-9987 |
| | | | | Home: | 555-7171 |
| 500 | Tom | Jackson | Production | TJ@somewhere.com | 444-9980 |
| 600 | Eleanore | Caldera | Legal | EC@somewhere.com | 767-0900 |
| | | | | Fax: | 236-9987 |
| | | | | Home: | 555-7171 |
| 700 | Richard | Bandalone | Legal | RB@somewhere.com | 767-0900 |

**FIGURE 2-5**

**Relation with Variable Length Column Values**

| EmployeeNumber | FirstName | LastName | Department | Email | Phone | Comment |
|---|---|---|---|---|---|---|
| 100 | Jerry | Johnson | Accounting | JJ@somewhere.com | 236-9987 | Joined the Accounting Department in March after completing his MBA at night. Will sit for CPA exam this fall. |
| 200 | Mary | Abernathy | Finance | MA@somewhere.com | 444-8898 | |
| 300 | Liz | Smathers | Finance | LS@somewhere.com | 777-0098 | |
| 400 | Tom | Caruthers | Accounting | TC@somewhere.com | 236-9987 | |
| 500 | Tom | Jackson | Production | TJ@somewhere.com | 444-9980 | |
| 600 | Eleanore | Caldera | Legal | EC@somewhere.com | 767-0900 | |
| 700 | Richard | Bandalone | Legal | RB@somewhere.com | 767-0900 | Is a full time consultant to legal on a retainer basis. |

The relation name will be written first, and it will be written in all capital (uppercase) letters, for example, *EMPLOYEE*. If the relation name is a combination of two or more words, we will join the words with an underscore, as in *EMPLOYEE_PROJECT_ASSIGNMENT*. Column names will be contained in parentheses, and will be written with an initial capital letter followed by lowercase letters, as in *Department*. If the column name is a combination of two or more words, the first letter of each word will be capitalized, as in *EmployeeNumber* and *LastName*. Thus, the EMPLOYEE relation shown in Figure 2-2 would be written as:

EMPLOYEE (EmployeeNumber, FirstName, LastName, Department, Email, Phone)

---

**B  T  W**

Relation structures, such as the one shown earlier, are part of a database schema. A database schema is the design upon which the database and its associated applications are built.

---

## A Note on Terminology

In the database world, people generally use the terms *table* and *relation* interchangeably. Accordingly, from now on, this book will do the same. Thus, any time we use the term *table*, we will mean a table that meets the characteristics required for a relation. Keep in mind, however, that strictly speaking, some tables are not relations.

Sometimes, especially in traditional data processing, people will use the term *file* instead of table. When they do so, they will use the term **record** for *row* and the term **field** for *column*. To further confound the issue, database theoreticians sometimes use yet another set of terms: Although they do call a table a *relation*, they call a *row* a **tuple** (rhymes with *couple*) and a *column* an **attribute**. These three sets of terminology are summarized in Figure 2-6.

To make things even more confusing, people often mix up these sets of terms. It is not unusual to hear someone refer to a relation that has rows and fields. As long as you know what is intended, this mixing of terms is not important.

There is one other source of confusion that should be discussed. According to Figure 2-1, a table that has duplicate rows is not a relation. However, in practice this condition is often ignored. Particularly when manipulating relations with a DBMS, we may end up with a table that has duplicate rows. To make that table a relation, we should eliminate the duplicates. On a large table, however, checking for duplication can be time-consuming. Therefore, the default behavior for DBMS products is not to check for duplicate rows. Hence, in practice, tables might exist with duplicate rows that are still called relations. You will see examples of this situation in the next chapter.

---

**FIGURE 2-6**

**Equivalent Sets of Terms**

| Table | Row | Column |
|---|---|---|
| File | Record | Field |
| Relation | Tuple | Attribute |

## ▶ TYPES OF KEYS

A **key** is one or more columns of a relation that is used to identify a row. A key can be **unique** or **nonunique**. For example, for the EMPLOYEE relation in Figure 2-2, EmployeeNumber is a *unique key* because a value of EmployeeNumber identifies a unique row. Thus, a query to display all employees having an EmployeeNumber of 200 will produce a single row. On the other hand, Department is a *nonunique key*. It is a key because it is used to identify a row, but it is nonunique because a value of Department potentially identifies more than one row. Thus, a query to display all rows having a Department value of Accounting will produce several rows.

From the data in Figure 2-2, it appears that EmployeeNumber, LastName, and Email are all unique identifiers. However, to decide whether or not this is true, database developers must do more than examine sample data. Rather, the developers must ask the users or other subject-matter experts whether a certain column is unique. The column LastName is an example where this is important. It might turn out that the sample data just happen to have unique values for LastName. The users, however, might say that LastName is not always unique.

### Composite Keys

A key that contains two or more attributes is called a **composite key**. For example, suppose that we're looking for a unique key for the EMPLOYEE relation, and that the users say that while LastName is not unique, the combination of LastName and Department is unique. Thus, for some reason, the users know that two people with the same last name will never work in the same department. Two Johnsons, for example, will never work in accounting. If that is the case, then the combination LastName, Department is a unique composite key.

Alternatively, the users may know that the combination (LastName, Department) is not unique, but that the combination (FirstName, LastName, Department) is unique. The latter combination, then, is a composite key with three attributes.

Composite keys, like one-column keys, can be unique or nonunique.

### Candidate and Primary Keys

**Candidate keys** are keys that uniquely identify each row in a relation. Candidate keys can be single-column keys or they can be composite keys. The **primary key** is the candidate key that is chosen as the key that will actually be used by the DBMS to uniquely identify each row in a relation. For example, suppose that we have the following EMPLOYEE relation:

EMPLOYEE (EmployeeNumber, FirstName, LastName, Department, Email, Phone)

The users tell us that EmployeeNumber is a unique key, that Email is a unique key, and that the composite key (FirstName, LastName, DepartmentName) is a unique key. Therefore, we have three candidate keys. When designing the database, we choose one of the candidate keys to be the primary key. In this case, for example, we will use EmployeeNumber as the primary key.

> **B T W**
>
> It may help you to understand why the unique keys that could be used as the main identifier for the relation are referred to as candidate keys if you think of them as the "candidates" in the running to be elected "primary key"—but remember that only one candidate will win the election.

The primary key is important not only because it can be used to identify unique rows, but also because it can be used to represent rows in relationships. Although we did not indicate it in Figure 1-10 in Chapter 1, CustomerNumber was the primary key of CUSTOMER. As such, we used CustomerNumber to represent the relationship between CUSTOMER and ENROLLMENT by placing CustomerNumber as a column in the ENROLLMENT table to create the link between the two tables. Additionally, many DBMS products use values of the primary key to organize storage for the relation. They also build indexes and other special structures for fast retrieval of rows using primary key values.

We will indicate primary keys by underlining them. Since EmployeeNumber is the primary key of EMPLOYEE, we will write the EMPLOYEE relation as:

EMPLOYEE (EmployeeNumber, FirstName, LastName, Department, Email, Phone)

Different DBMS programs each have their own way of creating and indicating a primary key. In Chapter 1's "The Access Workbench," we briefly discussed primary keys and explained how to set a primary key in Microsoft Access. Figure 2-7 shows the CUSTOMER table from the Art Course database in Figure 1-10 in the Access table Design view. In the Access table Design view, we can spot the primary key of the table by finding the key symbol next to the Field Names of the columns in the primary key. In this case, there is a key symbol next to CustomerNumber, which means that the developer has defined CustomerNumber as the primary key for this table.

Figure 2-8 shows the same CUSTOMER table in Microsoft SQL Server 2005 Express Edition[2] as seen in the Microsoft SQL Server Management Studio Express

**FIGURE 2-7**

**Defining the Primary Key in Microsoft Access**

---

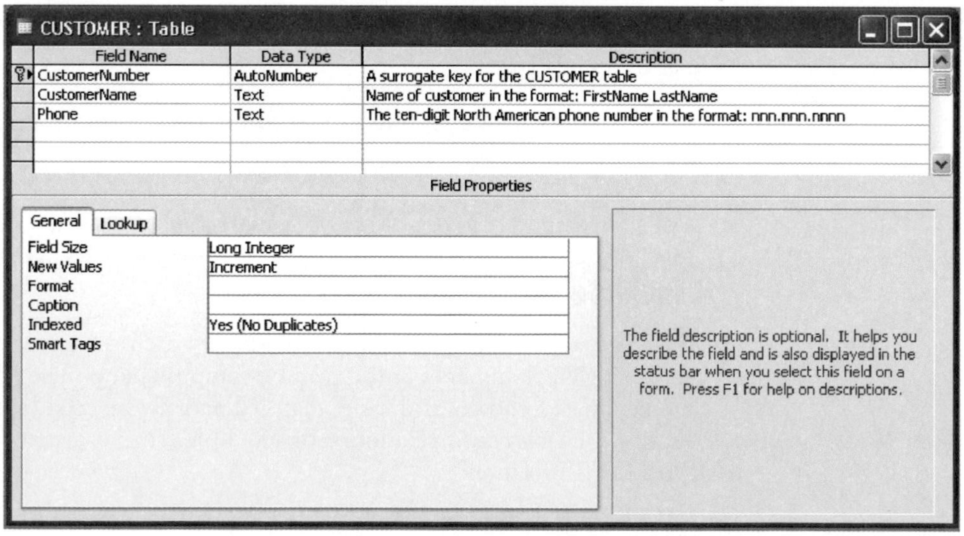

[2]Microsoft has released four versions of SQL Server 2005. SQL Server 2005 Express is the least powerful version, but it is intended for general use and can be downloaded for free from the Microsoft SQL Server home page at **www.microsoft.com/sql/default.mspx**. For more information see Appendix A—Getting Started with Microsoft SQL Server 2005 Express Edition.

**FIGURE 2-8**

Defining the Primary
Key in Microsoft SQL
Server 2005 Express
Edition

graphical utility program. This display is more complex, but again we can spot the primary key of the table by finding the key symbol next to ColumnNames of the columns in the primary key. Again, there is a key symbol next to CustomerNumber indicating that CustomerNumber is the primary key for this table.

> **B T W**
>
> In Figure 2-8, the table names are often listed with a dbo preceding the table name, as in dbo.CUSTOMER. The dbo stands for database owner, and this is a common occurrence in SQL Server.

Figure 2-9 shows the same CUSTOMER table in the MySQL[3] as seen in the MySQL Table Designer, which is accessed from the MySQL Query Browser graphical utility program. This display is more complex than MS Access, but we can spot the primary key of the table by finding the key symbol next to ColumnNames of the columns in the primary key. Again, there is a key symbol next to CustomerNumber indicating that CustomerNumber is the primary key for this table.

A common method of specifying primary keys is to use SQL, which we briefly introduced in Chapter 1. We will see how SQL is used to designate primary keys in the next chapter.

---

[3]Released in the fall of 2005, MySQL 5.0 is the latest version of the popular MySQL DBMS (later versions may be available as you read this). MySQL and the associated GUI utilities MySQL Query Browser and MySQL Administrator can be downloaded for free from the MySQL Web site at **www.mysql.com**. Like SQL Server 2005, MySQL is an enterprise-class DBMS and, as such, is much more complex than Microsoft Access. Also like SQL Server 2005, MySQL does not include application development tools, such as form and report generators. For more information see Appendix B—Getting Started with MySQL.

**FIGURE 2-9**

**Defining the Primary Key in MySQL**

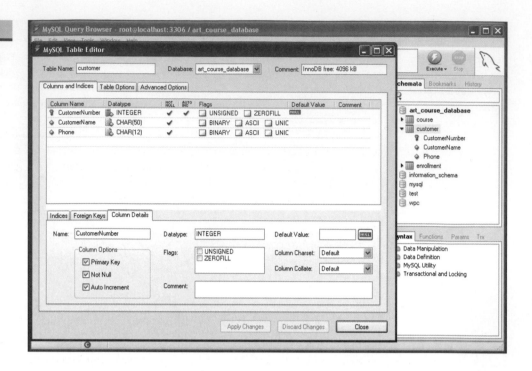

## Surrogate Keys

A **surrogate key** is a column with a unique, DBMS-assigned identifier that has been added to a table to be the primary key. The unique values of the surrogate key are assigned by the DBMS each time a row is created, and the values never change.

An ideal primary key is short, numeric, and never changes. Sometimes one column in a table will meet these requirements or come close to them. For example, EmployeeNumber in the EMPLOYEE relation should work very well as a primary key. But in other tables, the primary key does not come close to being ideal. For example, consider the relation PROPERTY:

PROPERTY (<u>Street</u>, <u>City</u>, <u>State</u>, <u>ZIP</u>, OwnerID)

The primary key of PROPERTY is (*Street, City, State, ZIP*), which is long and non-numeric (although it probably won't change). This is not an ideal primary key. In cases like this, the database designer will add a surrogate key, such as PropertyID:

PROPERTY (<u>PropertyID</u>, Street, City, State, ZIP, OwnerID)

Surrogate keys are short, numeric, and never change—they are ideal primary keys. Since the values of the surrogate primary key will have no meaning to users, they are often hidden on forms and reports.

Surrogate keys have already been used in the databases we have discussed. For example, in the Art Course database shown in Figure 1-10, we added the surrogate keys CustomerNumber to the CUSTOMER table and CourseNumber to the COURSE table.

Most DBMS products have a facility for automatically generating key values. In Figure 2-7, we can see how surrogate keys are defined with Microsoft Access. In Access, the Data Type is set to AutoNumber. With this specification, Access will assign a value of 1 to CustomerNumber for the first row of CUSTOMER, a value of 2 to CustomerNumber for the second row, and so forth.

Enterprise–class DBMS products, such as Microsoft's SQL Server, offer more capability. For example, with SQL Server, the developer can specify the starting value of the surrogate key as well as the amount to increment the key for each new row. Figure 2-8 shows how this is done for the definition of the surrogate key CustomerNumber for the CUSTOMER table. In the Column Properties window, which is below the Table-dbo.CUSTOMER column details window, there are a set of Identity specifications (**Is Identity**) that has been set to Yes to indicate to SQL Server that a surrogate key column exists. In SQL Server, the starting value of the surrogate key is called the **Identity Seed**. For CustomerNumber, it is set to 1. Furthermore, the amount that is added to each proceeding key value to create the next key value is called the **Identity Increment**. In this example, it is set to 1. These settings mean that when the user creates the first row of the CUSTOMER table, SQL Server will give the value 1 to CustomerNumber. When the second row of CUSTOMER is created, SQL Server will give the value 2 to CustomerNumber, and so forth.

MySQL uses the **AUTO_INCREMENT** function to automatically assign surrogate key numbers. In AUTO_INCREMENT, the starting value can be any value (the default is 1), but the increment will always be 1. Figure 2-9 shows that CustomerNumber is a surrogate key for CUSTOMER because AUTO_INCREMENT is being used to set the value of that column.

## Foreign Keys and Referential Integrity

As described in Chapter 1, we place values from one relation into a second relation to represent a relationship. The values we use are the primary key values (including composite primary key values when necessary) of the first relation. And when we do this, the attribute in the second relation that holds these values is referred to as a **foreign key**. For example, in the Art Course database shown in Figure 1-10, we represent the relationship between customers and the art courses they are taking by placing CustomerNumber, the primary key of CUSTOMER, into the ENROLLMENT relation. In this case, CustomerNumber in ENROLLMENT is referred to as a foreign key. This term is used because CustomerNumber is the primary key of a relation that is foreign to the table in which it resides.

Consider the following two relations, where besides the EMPLOYEE relation we now have a DEPARTMENT relation to hold data about departments.

EMPLOYEE (<u>EmployeeNumber</u>, FirstName, LastName, Department, Email, Phone)

and

DEPARTMENT (<u>DepartmentName</u>, BudgetCode, OfficeNumber, DepartmentPhone)

where EmployeeNumber and DepartmentName are the primary keys of EMPLOYEE and DEPARTMENT, respectively.

Now suppose that Department in EMPLOYEE contains the names of the departments in which employees work, and that DepartmentName in DEPARTMENT also contains these names. Then, Department in EMPLOYEE is said to be a foreign key to DEPARTMENT. In this book, we will denote foreign keys by displaying them in italics. Thus, we would write these two relation descriptions as follows.

EMPLOYEE (<u>EmployeeNumber</u>, FirstName, LastName, *Department*, Email, Phone)

and

DEPARTMENT (<u>DepartmentName</u>, BudgetCode, OfficeNumber, DepartmentPhone)

Note that it is not necessary for the primary key and the foreign key to have the same column name. The only requirement is that they have the same set of values.

In most cases, it is important to ensure that every value of a foreign key matches a value of the primary key. In the previous example, the value of Department in every row of EMPLOYEE should match a value of DepartmentName in DEPARTMENT. If this is the case (and it usually is), then we declare the following rule:

Department in EMPLOYEE must exist in DepartmentName in DEPARTMENT

Such a rule is called a **referential integrity constraint**. Whenever you see a foreign key, you should always look for an associated referential integrity constraint.

Consider the Art Course database shown in Figure 1-10. The structure of this database is:

CUSTOMER (<u>CustomerNumber</u>, CustomerName, Phone)

COURSE (<u>CourseNumber</u>, Course, CourseDate, Fee)

ENROLLMENT (*<u>CustomerNumber</u>*, *<u>CourseNumber</u>*, AmountPaid)

The ENROLLMENT table has a composite primary key of (CustomerNumber, CourseNumber), where CustomerNumber is a foreign key linking to CUSTOMER and CourseNumber is a foreign key linking to COURSE. Therefore, there are two referential integrity constraints required:

CustomerNumber in ENROLLMENT must exist in CustomerNumber in CUSTOMER

and

CourseNumber in ENROLLMENT must exist in CourseNumber in COURSE

Just as DBMS products have a means of specifying primary keys, they also have a way to set up foreign key referential integrity constraints. We will discuss the details of setting up referential integrity constraints in "the Access Workbench" section later in this chapter. Figure 2-10 shows the tables from the Art Course database in Figure 1-10 in the Access Relationships window and with the Edit Relationship dialog box showing the details of the relationship between CUSTOMER and ENROLLMENT. Notice that the Enforce Referential Integrity check box is checked, so the referential integrity constraint between CustomerNumber in ENROLLMENT (the foreign key) and CustomerNumber in CUSTOMER (the primary key) is being enforced.

**FIGURE 2-10**

**Enforcing Referential Integrity in Microsoft Access**

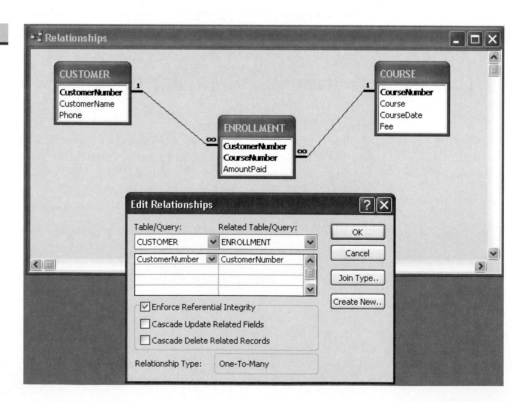

Figure 2-11 shows the same foreign key relationship between CUSTOMER and ENROLLMENT in the Microsoft SQL Server Management Studio Express program. Again, this display is more complex, but notice that the property Table Designer: Enforce Foreign Key Constraint is set to *Yes*. This means that the referential integrity constraint between CustomerNumber in ENROLLMENT (the foreign key) and CustomerNumber in CUSTOMER (the primary key) is being enforced.

Figure 2-12 shows foreign keys in MySQL. Here the Foreign Keys tab in the MySQL Table Designer GUI utility displays the properties of each foreign key.

Just as SQL can be used to specify primary keys, it can also be used to set referential integrity constraints. We will see how to use SQL to do this in the next chapter.

**FIGURE 2-11**

**Enforcing Referential Integrity in Microsoft SQL Server 2005 Express Edition**

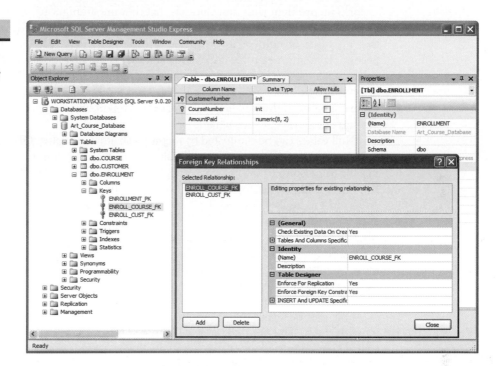

**FIGURE 2-12**

**Enforcing Referential Integrity in MySQL**

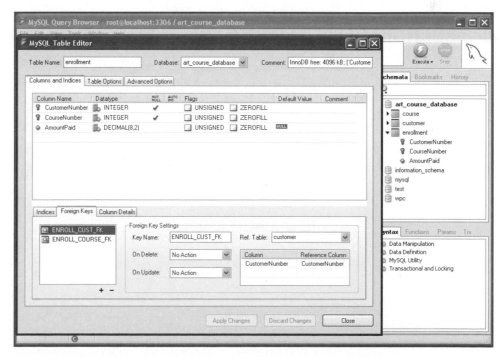

# THE PROBLEM OF NULL VALUES

Before we leave this discussion of relations and the relationships between them, we will discuss a subtle but important topic: null values. A **null value** is a missing value in a cell in a relation. Consider the following relation that is used to track finished goods for an apparel manufacturer.

ITEM (<u>ItemNum</u>, ItemName, Color, Quantity)

Sample data for this table are shown in Figure 2-13. Notice that in the last row of data, the row with ItemNumber 400 and ItemName Spring Hat, that there is no value for Color. The problem with null values is that they are ambiguous; we do not know how to interpret them because three possible meanings can be construed. First, it might mean that no value of color is appropriate; Spring Hats do not come in different colors. Second, it might mean that the value is known to be blank; that is, Spring Hats have a color, but the color has not yet been decided. Maybe the color is established by placing ribbons around the hats, but this is not done until an order arrives. Or third, the null value might mean that the hats' color is simply unknown; the hats do have a color, but no one has checked yet to see what it is.

Null values can be eliminated by requiring an attribute value. DBMS products have the means to specify whether or not a null value can occur in a column. We discussed how to do this for Microsoft Access in Chapter 1's "The Access Workbench." For SQL Server 2005 Express Edition, notice the column in the Table-dbo.CUSTOMER window labeled "Allow Nulls" in Figure 2-8. A check box without a check mark means that null values are not allowed in this column. For MySQL, note that in Figure 2-9 the Column Details tab in the MySQL Table Editor shows a check box indicating whether or not null values are allowed in the column. Regardless of the DBMS being used, if nulls are not allowed, then some value must be entered for each row in the table. If the attribute is a text value, users can be allowed to enter values such as "not appropriate," "undecided," or "unknown" when necessary. If the attribute is not text, then some other coding system can be developed.

For now, be aware that null values can occur and that they always carry an ambiguity with them. The next chapter will show another, possibly more serious problem of null values.

# FUNCTIONAL DEPENDENCIES AND NORMALIZATION

This section introduces some of the concepts used for relational database design; these concepts will be used in the next several chapters and then expanded in scope in Chapter 5. This book presents only the essentials. To learn more, you should consult other, more comprehensive references.[4]

| **FIGURE 2-13** |
| :--- |
| **Example ITEM Relation and Data** |

| ItemNum | ItemName | Color | Quantity |
| --- | --- | --- | --- |
| 100 | Small T-Shirt | Red | 15 |
| 150 | Small T-Shirt | Blue | 5 |
| 200 | Small T-Shirt | Green | 7 |
| 300 | Med T-Shirt | Red | 8 |
| 400 | Spring Hat | | 5 |

---

[4]See David M. Kroenke, *Database Processing: Fundamentals, Design, and Implementation*, 10th Edition (Upper Saddle River, NJ: Prentice Hall, 2006), and C. J. Date, *An Introduction to Database Systems*, 8th Edition (Boston, MA: Addison-Wesley, 2004).

## Functional Dependencies

To get started, let's take a short excursion into the world of algebra. Suppose you are buying boxes of cookies and someone tells you that each box costs $5. Knowing this fact, you can compute the cost of several boxes with the formula:

CookieCost = NumberOfBoxes × $5

A more general way to express the relationship between CookieCost and Number-OfBoxes is to say that CookieCost depends upon NumberOfBoxes. Such a statement tells the character of the relationship of CookieCost and NumberOfBoxes, even though it doesn't give the formula. More formally, we can say that CookieCost is **functionally dependent** on NumberOfBoxes. Such a statement can be written as follows:

NumberOfBoxes → CookieCost

This expression also can be read as NumberOfBoxes determines CookieCost. The variable on the left, NumberOfBoxes, is called the **determinant**.

Using another example, we can compute the extended price of a part order by multiplying the quantity of the item times its unit price, or:

ExtendedPrice = Quantity × UnitPrice

In this case, we would say that ExtendedPrice is functionally dependent on Quantity and UnitPrice, or:

(Quantity, UnitPrice) → ExtendedPrice

The composite (Quantity, UnitPrice) is the determinant of ExtendedPrice.

Now, let's expand these ideas. Suppose you know that a sack contains either red, blue, or yellow objects. Further suppose you know that the red objects weigh 5 pounds, the blue objects weigh 3 pounds, and the yellow objects weigh 7 pounds. If a friend looks into the sack, sees an object, and tells you the color of the object, you can tell the weight of the object. We can formalize this in the same way we did in the previous example.

ObjectColor → Weight

Thus, we can say that Weight is functionally dependent on ObjectColor and that ObjectColor determines Weight. The relationship here does not involve an equation, but this functional dependency is still true. Given a value for ObjectColor, you can determine the object's weight.

In addition, if we know that the red objects are balls, the blue objects are cubes, and the yellow objects are cubes, then:

ObjectColor → Shape

Thus, ObjectColor also determines Shape. We can put these two together and state:

ObjectColor → (Weight, Shape)

Thus, ObjectColor determines Weight and Shape.

Another way to represent these facts is to put them into a table as shown in Figure 2-14. Note that this table meets all of the conditions in our definition of a relation as listed in Figure 2-1, so we can refer to it as a relation. We will call it the OBJECT relation, and use ObjectColor as the primary key. We can write this relation as:

OBJECT (<u>ObjectColor</u>, Weight, Shape)

**FIGURE 2-14**

**Example OBJECT Relation and Data**

| Object Color | Weight | Shape |
|---|---|---|
| Red | 5 | Ball |
| Blue | 3 | Cube |
| Yellow | 7 | Cube |

Now, you may be thinking that we have just performed some trick or sleight of hand to arrive at a relation, but one can make the argument that the only reason for having relations is to store instances of functional dependencies. Consider a relation such as the CUSTOMER relation from the Art Course database in Figure 1-10:

CUSTOMER (<u>CustomerNumber</u>, CustomerName, Phone)

Here, we are simply storing facts that express the following functional dependency:

CustomerNumber → (CustomerName, Phone)

## Primary and Candidate Keys Revisited

With the concept of functional dependency, we can now define primary and candidate keys more formally. Specifically, a primary key of a relation can be defined as "one or more attributes that functionally determine all of the other attributes of the relation." The same definition holds for candidate keys, as well.

Recall the EMPLOYEE relation from Figure 2-2 (shown without primary or foreign keys indicated).

EMPLOYEE (EmployeeNumber, FirstName, LastName, Department, Email, Phone)

As we previously discussed, based on information from users, this relation has three candidate keys: EmployeeNumber, Email, and the composite (FirstName, LastName, Department). Because this is so, we can state the following:

EmployeeNumber → (FirstName, LastName, Department, Email, Phone)

Equivalently, if we are given a value for EmployeeNumber, we can determine FirstName, LastName, Department, Email, and Phone. Similarly, we can state that:

Email → (EmployeeNumber, FirstName, LastName, Department, Phone)

That is, if we are given a value for Email, we can determine EmployeeNumber, FirstName, LastName, Department, and Phone. Finally, we also can state that:

(FirstName, LastName, Department) → (EmployeeNumber, Email, Phone)

This means that if we are given values of FirstName, LastName, and Department, we can determine the EmployeeNumber, Email, and Phone.

These three functional dependencies express the reason the three candidate keys *are* candidate keys. When we choose a primary key from the candidate keys, we are choosing which functional dependency we want to define as the one that is most meaningful or important to us.

## Normalization

The concepts of functional dependencies and determinants can be used to help in the design of relations. Recalling the concept from Chapter 1 that a table or relation should only have one theme, we will define **normalization** as the process of breaking a table or relation with more than one theme into a set of tables such that each has only one theme. Normalization is a complex topic, and it consumes one or more chapters of more theoretically oriented database books. Here, we will reduce this topic to a few ideas that capture the essence of the process, and we will expand this discussion in Chapter 5. After that, if you are interested in the topic, you should consult the references mentioned earlier for more information.

The problem that normalization addresses is the following: A table can meet all of the characteristics listed in Figure 2-1 and still have the modification problems we identified for lists in Chapter 1. Specifically, consider the following ADVISER_LIST relation:

ADVISER_LIST (AdviserID, AdviserName, Department, Phone, Office, StudentNum, StudentName)

What is the primary key of this relation? Given the definitions of candidate key and primary key, it has to be an attribute that determines all of the other attributes. The only attribute that has this characteristic is StudentNum. Given a value of StudentNum, we can determine the values of all of the other attributes:

StudentNum → (AdviserID, AdviserName, Department, Phone, Office, StudentName)

We can then write this relation as follows:

ADVISER_LIST (AdviserID, AdviserName, Department, Phone, Office, <u>StudentNum</u>, StudentName)

However, this table has modification problems. Specifically, an adviser's data are repeated many times in the table, once for each advisee. This means that updates to adviser data might need to be made multiple times. If, for example, an adviser changes offices, that change will need to be completed in all the rows for the person's advisees. If an adviser has 20 advisees, that change will need to be entered 20 times.

Another modification problem can occur when we delete a student from this list. If we delete a student who happens to be the only advisee for an adviser, we will delete not only the student's data, but also the adviser's data. Thus, we will unintentionally lose facts about two entities while attempting to delete one.

If you look closely at this relation, you will see a functional dependency that involves the adviser's data. Specifically:

AdviserID → (AdviserName, Department, Phone, Office)

Now, we can state the problem with this relation more accurately—in terms of functional dependencies. Specifically, this relation is poorly formed because it has a functional dependency that does not involve the primary key. Stated differently, AdviserID is a determinant of a functional dependency, but it is not a candidate key and thus cannot be the primary key under any circumstances.

## Relational Design Principles

From this discussion, we can formulate the following design principles for what we will call a **well-formed relation**.

1. To be a well-formed relation, every determinant must be a candidate key.
2. Any relation that is not well formed should be broken into two or more relations that are well formed.

These two principles are the heart of normalization—the process of examining relations and modifying them to make them well formed. This process is called normalization because you can categorize the problems to which relations are susceptible into different types called normal forms.

There are many normal forms. Technically, our well-formed relations are those that are said to be in **Boyce-Codd normal form**. There are many defined normal forms. For example, any relation that has the characteristics listed in Figure 2-1 is called a relation in **first normal form (1NF)**. Besides first normal form and Boyce-Codd normal form, other normal forms exist, such as second, third, fourth, fifth, and domain/key normal form. We will further describe normal forms in Chapter 5.

However, if we simply follow the aforementioned design principles, we will avoid almost all of the problems associated with unnormalized tables. Some rare problems arise that these principles do not address (see questions 2.40 and 2.41 in the Exercises section), but if you follow these principles, you will be safe most of the time.

## The Normalization Process

We can apply the principles just described to formulate the following process for normalizing relations.

**1.** Identify all the candidate keys of the relation.
**2.** Identify all the functional dependencies in the relation.
**3.** Examine the determinants of the functional dependencies. If any determinant is not a candidate key, the relation is not well-formed. In this case:
   **a.** Place the columns of the functional dependency in a new relation of their own.
   **b.** Make the determinant of the functional dependency the primary key of the new relation.
   **c.** Leave a copy of the determinant as a foreign key in the original relation.
   **d.** Create a referential integrity constraint between the original relation and the new relation.
**4.** Repeat Step 3 as many times as necessary until every determinant of every relation is a candidate key.

To understand this process, consider the following relation:

PRESCRIPTION (PrescriptionNumber, Date, Drug, Dosage, CustomerName, CustomerPhone, CustomerEmail)

Sample data for the PRESCRIPTION relation are shown in Figure 2-15.

**Step 1**   According to the normalization process, we first identify all candidate keys. PrescriptionNumber clearly determines Date, Drug, and Dosage. If we assume that a prescription is for only one person, then it also determines CustomerName CustomerPhone, and CustomerEmail. By law, prescriptions must be for only one person, so PrescriptionNumber is a candidate key.

Does this relation have other candidate keys? None of Date, Drug, or Dosage determine PrescriptionNumber because many prescriptions can be written on a given date, many prescriptions can be written for a given drug, and many prescriptions can be written for a given dosage.

What about customer columns? If a customer had only one prescription, then we could say that some identifying customer column—for example, CustomerEmail—would determine the prescription data. However, people can have more than one prescription, so this assumption is invalid.

Given this analysis, then the only candidate key of PRESCRIPTION is PrescriptionNumber.

**Step 2**   According to Step 2 in the normalization process, we now identify all functional dependencies. PrescriptionNumber determines all of the other attributes as just described. If a drug had only one dosage, then we could state that:

Drug → Dosage

But this is not true, because some drugs have several dosages. Therefore, Drug is *not* a determinant. Furthermore, Dosage is not a determinant because the same dosage can be given for many different drugs.

However, examining the customer columns, we do find a functional dependency:

CustomerEmail → (CustomerName, CustomerPhone)

**FIGURE 2-15**

**Example PRESCRIPTION Relation and Data**

| PrescriptionNumber | Date | Drug | Dosage | CustomerName | CustomerPhone | CustomerEmail |
|---|---|---|---|---|---|---|
| P10001 | 10/17/2006 | DrugA | 10mg | Alvin Smith | 575.323.2233 | ASmith@somewhere.com |
| P10003 | 10/17/2006 | DrugB | 35mg | Jeff Rhodes | 575.334.4455 | JRhodes@somewhere.com |
| P10004 | 10/17/2006 | DrugA | 20mg | Sarah Smith | 575.323.2233 | SSmith@somewhere.com |
| P10007 | 10/18/2006 | DrugC | 20mg | Michael Frye | 575.345.6677 | MFrye@elsewhere.com |
| P10010 | 10/18/2006 | DrugC | 25mg | Jeff Rhodes | 575.334.4455 | JRhodes@somewhere.com |

(Again, to know if this is true for a particular application, we need to look beyond the sample data in Figure 2-15 and to ask the users. For example, it is possible that some customers share the same e-mail address; it is also possible that some customers do not have e-mail. For now, assume the users say that CustomerEmail is a determinant of the customer attributes.)

**Step 3**    Now, according to Step 3, we ask whether a determinant exists that is *not* a candidate key. In this example, CustomerEmail is a determinant and not a candidate key. Therefore, PRESCRIPTION has normalization problems and is not well formed. According to Step 3, we then split the functional dependency into a relation of its own:

CUSTOMER (CustomerName, CustomerPhone, <u>CustomerEmail</u>)

We make the determinant of the functional dependency, CustomerEmail, the primary key of the new relation.

We leave a copy of CustomerEmail in the original relation as a foreign key. Thus, PRESCRIPTION is now:

PRESCRIPTION (<u>PrescriptionNumber</u>, Date, Drug, Dosage, *<u>CustomerEmail</u>*)

Finally, we create the referential integrity constraint.

CustomerEmail in PRESCRIPTION must exist in CustomerEmail in CUSTOMER

At this point, if we move through the three steps, we find that neither of these relations has a determinant that is not a candidate key, and we can say the two relations are now well formed.

## Normalization Examples

We will now illustrate the use of the normalization process with four examples.

**Normalization Example 1**    The relation in Figure 2-16 shows a table of student residence data named STU_DORM. The first step in normalizing it is to identify all candidate keys. Because StudentNum determines each of the other columns, it is a candidate key. StudentName cannot be a candidate key because two students have the name Smith. None of the other columns can be an identifier either, so StudentNum is the only candidate key.

Next, in Step 2, we look for the functional dependencies in the relation. Besides those for StudentNum, a functional dependency appears to exist between DormName and DormCost. Again, we would need to check this out with the users. In this case, assume that the functional dependency

DormName → DormCost

is true, and assume that our interview with the users indicates that no other functional dependencies exist.

According to Step 3, we now ask if any determinants exist that are not candidate keys. In this example, DormName is a determinant, but it is not a candidate key. Therefore, this relation is not well formed and has normalization problems.

**FIGURE 2-16**

**Example STU_DORM Relation and Data**

| StudentNum | StudentName | DormName | DormCost |
|---|---|---|---|
| 100 | Smith | Stephens | $3,500.00 |
| 200 | Johnson | Alexander | $3,800.00 |
| 300 | Abernathy | Horan | $4,000.00 |
| 400 | Smith | Alexander | $3,800.00 |
| 500 | Wilcox | Stephens | $3,500.00 |
| 600 | Webber | Horan | $4,000.00 |
| 700 | Simon | Stephens | $3,500.00 |

To fix those problems, we place the columns of the functional dependency (DormName, DormCost) into a relation of their own and call that relation DORM. We make the determinant of the functional dependency the primary key. Thus, DormName is the primary key of DORM. We leave the determinant DormName as a foreign key in STU_DORM. Finally, we find the appropriate referential integrity constraint. The result is:

STU_DORM (<u>StudentNum</u>, StudentName, *<u>DormName</u>*)

DORM (<u>DormName</u>, DormCost)

With constraint:

DormName in STU_DORM must exist in DormName in DORM

The same data for these relations appear as shown in Figure 2-17.

**Normalization Example 2**   Now consider the EMPLOYEE table in Figure 2-18. First, we identify the candidate keys in EMPLOYEE. From the data, it appears that EmployeeNumber and Email each identify all of the other attributes. Hence, they are candidate keys (again, with the proviso that we cannot depend on sample data to show all cases; we must verify this assumption with the users).

Step 2 is to identify other functional dependencies. From the data, it appears that the only other functional dependency is:

Department → DeptPhone

Assuming that this is true, then according to Step 3, we have a determinant, Department, that is not a candidate key. Thus, EMPLOYEE has normalization problems.

To fix those problems, we place the columns in the functional dependency in a table of their own and make the determinant the primary key of the new table. We leave the determinant as a foreign key in the original table. The result is the two tables:

EMPLOYEE (<u>EmployeeNumber</u>, LastName, Email, *Department*)

and

DEPARTMENT (<u>Department</u>, DeptPhone)

With referential integrity constraint:

Department in EMPLOYEE must exist in Department in DEPARTMENT

---

**FIGURE 2-17**

**Normalized Student Residence Relations and Data**

| StudentNum | StudentName | DormName |
|---|---|---|
| 100 | Smith | Stephens |
| 200 | Johnson | Alexander |
| 300 | Abernathy | Horan |
| 400 | Smith | Alexander |
| 500 | Wilcox | Stephens |
| 600 | Webber | Horan |
| 700 | Simon | Stephens |

| DormName | DormCost |
|---|---|
| Stephens | $3,500.00 |
| Alexander | $3,800.00 |
| Horan | $4,000.00 |

---

**FIGURE 2-18**

**Example EMPLOYEE Relation and Data**

| EmployeeNumber | LastName | Email | Department | DeptPhone |
|---|---|---|---|---|
| 100 | Johnson | JJ@somewhere.com | Accounting | 236-9987 |
| 200 | Abernathy | MA@somewhere.com | Finance | 444-8898 |
| 300 | Smathers | LS@somewhere.com | Finance | 444-8898 |
| 400 | Caruthers | TC@somewhere.com | Accounting | 236-9987 |
| 500 | Jackson | TJ@somewhere.com | Production | 444-9980 |
| 600 | Caldera | EC@somewhere.com | Legal | 767-0900 |
| 700 | Bandalone | RB@somewhere.com | Legal | 767-0900 |

**FIGURE 2-19**

Normalized EMPLOYEE and DEPARTMENT Relations and Data

| EmployeeNumber | LastName | Email | Department |
|---|---|---|---|
| 100 | Johnson | JJ@somewhere.com | Accounting |
| 200 | Abernathy | MA@somewhere.com | Finance |
| 300 | Smathers | LS@somewhere.com | Finance |
| 400 | Caruthers | TC@somewhere.com | Accounting |
| 500 | Jackson | TJ@somewhere.com | Production |
| 600 | Caldera | EC@somewhere.com | Legal |
| 700 | Bandalone | RB@somewhere.com | Legal |

| Department | DeptPhone |
|---|---|
| Accounting | 236-9987 |
| Finance | 444-8898 |
| Production | 444-9980 |

**FIGURE 2-20**

Example MEETING Relation and Data

| Attorney | ClientNumber | ClientName | MeetingDate | Duration |
|---|---|---|---|---|
| Boxer | 1000 | ABC, Inc | 5/5/2006 | 2.00 |
| Boxer | 2000 | ZZZ Partners | 5/5/2006 | 5.50 |
| James | 1000 | ABC, Inc | 5/7/2006 | 3.00 |
| Boxer | 1000 | ABC, Inc | 5/9/2006 | 4.00 |
| Wu | 3000 | Malcomb Zoe | 5/11/2006 | 7.00 |

The result for the sample data is shown in Figure 2-19.

**Normalization Example 3**   Now consider the MEETING table in Figure 2-20. We begin by looking for candidate keys. No column by itself can be a candidate key. Attorney determines different sets of data, so it cannot be a determinant. The same is true for ClientNumber, ClientName, and MeetingDate. In the sample data, the only column that does not determine different sets of data is Duration, but this uniqueness is accidental. It is easy to imagine that two more meetings would have the same duration.

The next step is to look for combinations of columns that can be candidate keys. (Attorney, ClientNumber) is one combination, but the values (Boxer, 1000) determine two different sets of data. They cannot be a candidate key. The combination (Attorney, ClientName) fails for the same reason. The only combinations that can be candidate keys of this relation are (Attorney, ClientNumber, MeetingDate) and (Attorney, ClientName, MeetingDate).

Consider those possibilities further. The name of the relation is MEETING and we're asking whether (Attorney, ClientNumber, MeetingDate) or (Attorney, ClientName, MeetingDate) can be a candidate key. Do these combinations make sense as an identifier of a meeting? They do unless more than one meeting of the same attorney and client occurs on the same day. In that case, we need to add a new column, MeetingTime, to the relation and make this new column part of the candidate key. In this example, we will assume this is not the case and that (Attorney, ClientNumber, MeetingDate) and (Attorney, ClientName, MeetingDate) are the candidate keys.

The second step is to identify other functional dependencies. Here, two exist:

ClientNumber → ClientName

and

ClientName → ClientNumber

Each of these determinants is part of one of the candidate keys. For example, ClientNumber is part of (Attorney, ClientNumber, MeetingDate). However, being part of a candidate key is not enough. The determinant must be the same as the entire candidate key. Thus, the MEETING table is not well formed and has normalization problems.

When you are not certain whether or not normalization problems exist, consider the three modification operations discussed in Chapter 1: insert, update, and delete. Do problems exist with any of them? For example, in Figure 2-18, if you change ClientName in the first row to ABC, Limited, do inconsistencies arise in the data? The answer is yes because ClientNumber 1000 would have two different names in the table. This and any of the other problems that were identified in Chapter 1 when inserting, updating, or deleting data are a sure sign that the table has normalization problems.

To fix the normalization problems, we create a new table CLIENT with columns ClientNumber and ClientName. Both of these columns are determinants; thus, either can be the primary key of the new table. However, whichever one is selected as the primary key also should be made the foreign key in MEETING. Thus, two correct designs are possible. First, we can use:

MEETING (Attorney, *ClientNumber*, MeetingDate, Duration)

CLIENT (ClientNumber, ClientName)

ClientNumber in MEETING must exist in ClientNumber in CLIENT

Second, we can use:

MEETING (Attorney, *ClientName*, MeetingDate, Duration)

CLIENT (ClientNumber, ClientName)

ClientName in MEETING must exist in ClientName in CLIENT

Data for the first design are shown in Figure 2-21.

Notice in these two designs that either the attribute ClientNumber or ClientName is both a foreign key and also part of the primary key of MEETING. This illustrates that foreign keys can be part of a composite primary key.

One final comment about this design needs to be made: When two attributes, such as ClientNumber and ClientName, each determine one another, they are **synonyms**. They both must appear in a relation to establish their equivalent values. Given that equivalency, the two columns are interchangeable; one can take the place of the other in any other relation. All things being equal, however, the administration of the database will be simpler if one of the two is used consistently as a foreign key. This policy is just a convenience, however, and not a logical requirement for the design.

**Normalization Example 4**   For our last example, consider a relation that involves student data. Specifically, consider the following relation:

GRADE (ClassName, Section, Term, Grade, StudentNumber, StudentName, Professor, Department, ProfessorEmail)

Given the confused set of columns in this table, it does not seen well formed, and it appears that the table will have normalization problems. We can use the normalization process to find what they are and to remove them.

First, what are the candidate keys of this relation? No column by itself is a candidate key. One way to approach this is to realize that a grade is a combination of a class and a student. In this table, which columns identify classes and students? A particular class is identified by (ClassName, Section, Term), and a student is identified by StudentNumber. Possibly, then, a candidate key for this relation is:

(ClassName, Section, Term, StudentNumber)

This statement is equivalent to saying:

(ClassName, Section, Term, StudentNumber) →(Grade, StudentName, Professor, Department, ProfessorEmail)

| FIGURE 2-21 |
|---|
| **Normalized MEETING and CLIENT Relations and Data** |

| Attorney | ClientNumber | MeetingDate | Duration |
|---|---|---|---|
| Boxer | 1000 | 5/5/2006 | 2.00 |
| Boxer | 2000 | 5/5/2006 | 5.50 |
| James | 1000 | 5/7/2006 | 3.00 |
| Boxer | 1000 | 5/9/2006 | 4.00 |
| Wu | 3000 | 5/11/2006 | 7.00 |

| ClientNumber | ClientName |
|---|---|
| 1000 | ABC, Inc |
| 2000 | ZZZ Partners |
| 3000 | Malcomb Zoe |

This is a true statement as long as only one professor teaches a class section. For now, we will make that assumption and consider the alternate case later. If only one professor teaches a section, then (ClassName, Section, Term, StudentNumber) is the one and only candidate key.

Second, what are the additional functional dependencies? One involves student data and another involves professor data, specifically StudentNumber → StudentName and Professor → ProfessorEmail. We also need to ask if Professor determines Department. It will if a professor teaches in only one department. In that case, we have Professor → (Department, ProfessorEmail). Otherwise, Department must remain in the GRADE relation.

Assume that professors teach in just one department. Then we have:

StudentNumber → StudentName

and

Professor → (Department, ProfessorEmail)

If you examine the GRADE relation a bit further, however, you can find one other functional dependency. If only one professor teaches a class section, then:

(ClassName, Section, Term) → Professor

Thus, according to Step 3 of the normalization process, GRADE has normalization problems because the determinants StudentNumber, Professor, and (ClassName, Section, Term) are not candidate keys. Therefore, we form a table for each of these functional dependencies. As a result, we will have a STUDENT table, PROFESSOR table, and a CLASS_PROFESSOR table. After forming these tables, we then take the appropriate columns out of GRADE. Call the new version of the grade table GRADE_1. We now have the following design.

STUDENT (StudentNumber, StudentName)
PROFESSOR (Professor, Department, ProfessorEmail)
CLASS_PROFESSOR (ClassName, Section, Term, *Professor*)
GRADE_1 (*ClassName, Section, Term*, Grade, *StudentNumber*)

with the referential integrity constraints:

StudentNumber in GRADE_1 must exist in StudentNumber in STUDENT

Professor in CLASS_PROFESSOR must exist in Professor in PROFESSOR

(ClassName, Section, Term) in GRADE_1 must exist in (ClassName, Section, Term) of CLASS_PROFESSOR

Next, consider what happens if more than one professor teaches a section of a class. In that case, the only change is to make Professor part of the primary key of CLASS_PROFESSOR. Thus, the new relation is:

CLASS_PROFESSOR_1 (ClassName, Section, Term, Professor)

Class sections that have more than one professor will have multiple rows in this table—one row for each of the professors.

(In the interest of full disclosure, if professors can teach more than one class, then GRADE has what is called a **multivalued dependency**. We have not discussed such dependencies in this book. If you want to learn about them, see one of the more advanced texts mentioned on page 64 and also Exercise 2.40.)

This example shows how normalization problems can become more complicated than simple examples might indicate. For large commercial applications that potentially involve hundreds of tables, such problems can sometimes consume days or weeks of design time.

# THE ACCESS WORKBENCH

## Section 2

## Working with Multiple Tables in Microsoft Access

In Chapter 1's "The Access Workbench," we learned to create Microsoft Access databases, tables, forms, and reports. However, we limited ourselves to working with one table. In this section, we will cover the following objectives:

- Illustrate the modification problems that have been discussed in Chapters 1 and 2
- Learn how to work with multiple tables

We will continue to use the WMCRM database we created in "The Access Workbench: Section 1." At this point, we have created and populated (which means we've inserted the data) the CUSTOMER table. Figure AW-2-1 shows the actual contacts that have been made with each customer. Note that there is no customer with CustomerID number 2—this is because we deleted and reentered the data for Jessica Christman.

### Possible Modification Problems in the WMCRM Database

Now, we know from the topics covered in this chapter that we really need a separate table to store this data, but in order to illustrate modification problems in action, let's combine it in one table with the data already in CUSTOMER. This has been done, and is available in the file WMCRM-Combined-Data.mdb, which is available at the Web site for this book (**www.prenhall.com/kroenke**). Start Access and then open this file. Let's take a look at the WMCRM-Combined-Data database.

*Examining the Access Database WMCRM-Combined-Data*

1. Start Microsoft Access.
2. In the menu bar, click **File | Open**. The Open dialog box is displayed. Browse to the **WMCRM-Combined-Data.mdb** file, click the file name to highlight it, and then

### FIGURE AW-2-1

**Contact Data**

| CustomerID | Date | Type | Remarks |
|---|---|---|---|
| 1 | 7/7/2005 | Phone | General interest in a Gaea. |
| 1 | 7/7/2005 | Email | Sent general information. |
| 1 | 7/12/2005 | Phone | Set up an appointment. |
| 1 | 7/14/2005 | Meeting | Bought a HiStandard. |
| 3 | 7/19/2005 | Phone | Interested in a SUHi, set up an appointment. |
| 1 | 7/21/2005 | Email | Sent a standard follow-up message. |
| 4 | 7/27/2005 | Phone | Interested in a HiStandard, set up an appointment. |
| 3 | 7/27/2005 | Meeting | Bought a SUHi. |
| 4 | 8/2/2005 | Meeting | Talked up to a HiLuxury. Customer bought one. |
| 3 | 8/3/2005 | Email | Sent a standard follow-up message. |
| 4 | 8/10/2005 | Email | Sent a standard follow-up message. |
| 5 | 8/15/2005 | Phone | General interest in a Gaea. |

---

### FIGURE AW-2-2

**The Security Warning Dialog Box**

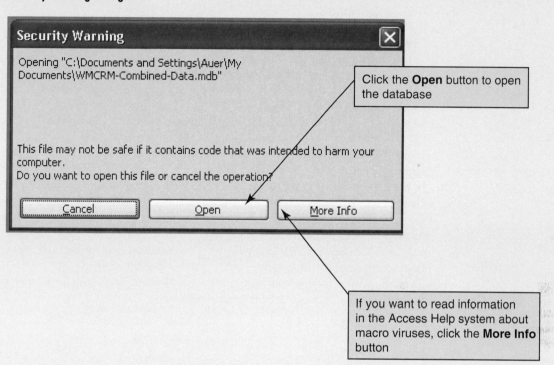

Click the **Open** button to open the database

If you want to read information in the Access Help system about macro viruses, click the **More Info** button

click the **Open** button. A Security Warning dialog box appears, as shown in Figure AW-2-2.

3. The Security Warning dialog box is now a standard message that appears when you open a database. It is a warning about macro viruses that may be present in a database. While this is a legitimate concern in general, databases that you create yourself (and those provided with this text) should not contain macro viruses. Click the **Open** button to open the database.

4. In the Tables objects pane, double-click the **CUSTOMER_CONTACT table object** to open it. The CUSTOMER_CONTACT table appears in data view as shown in Figure AW-2-3. Note that there is one line for each contact, which has resulted in

---

### FIGURE AW-2-3

**The CUSTOMER_CONTACT Table**

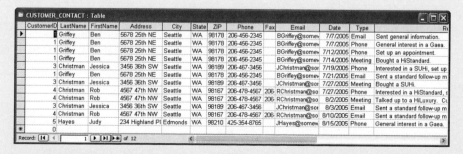

*(Continued)*

the duplication of basic customer data. For example, there are five sets of basic data for Ben Griffey.

5. Close the CUSTOMER_CONTACT table by clicking the **Close** button in the upper right corner of the CUSTOMER_CONTACT table window.

6. In the WMCRM: Database window, click **Forms** in the Objects pane to display the Forms pane.

7. In the Forms objects pane, double-click the **Customer-Contact Data Input form object** to open it. The Customer-Contact-Data-Input form appears as shown in Figure AW-2-4. Note that the form displays all the data for one record in the CUSTOMER_CONTACT table.

8. Close the Customer-Contact Data Input form by clicking the **Close** button in the upper right corner of the Customer-Contact Data Input form.

9. In the WMCRM: Database window, click **Reports** in the Objects pane to display the Reports pane.

10. In the Reports objects pane, double-click the **Wallingford Motors Customer Contact Report report object** to open it. After adjustment, the Wallingford Motors Customer Contact Reports appears as shown in Figure AW-2-5. Note that the form displays the data for all contacts in the CUSTOMER_CONTACT table, sorted by CustomerNumber and Date. For example, all the contact data for Ben Griffey (who has a CustomerID of 1) is grouped at the beginning of the report.

11. Close the Wallingford Motors Customer Contact Report by clicking the **Close** button in the upper right corner of the report window.

---

**FIGURE AW-2-4**

**The Customer-Contact Data Input Form**

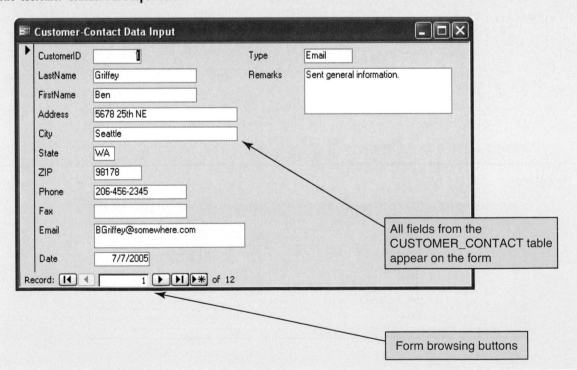

## FIGURE AW-2-5

**The Wallingford Motors Customer Contact Report**

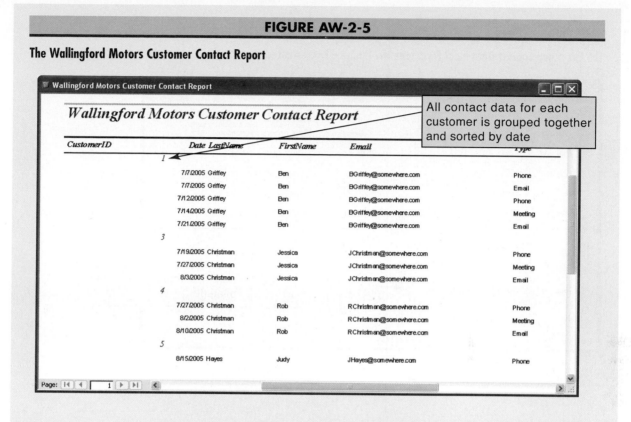

Now, let's assume that Ben Griffey has changed his email address from **BGriffey@somewhere.com** to **BGriffey@elsewhere.net**. In a well-formed relation, we would only have to make this change once, but a quick examination of Figures AW-2-3 through AW-2-5 shows that Ben Griffey's email address appears in multiple records. This means that we have to change it in every record to avoid an update problem. Unfortunately, it is easy to miss one or more records, especially in large tables.

### Updating Ben Griffey's Email Address

1. Start Microsoft Access.
2. In the WMCRM: Database window, click **Forms** in the Objects pane to display the Forms pane.
3. In the Forms objects pane, double-click the **Customer-Contact Data Input form object** to open it. Since Ben Griffey is the customer in the first record, his data is already in the form. Edit the **Email** address to read **BGriffey@elsewhere.net** as shown in Figure AW-2-6.
4. Click the **Next Record** button to move to the next record in the table. Again, the record shows Ben Griffey's data, so again edit the **Email** address to read **BGriffey@elsewhere.net**.
5. Click the **Next Record** button to move to the next record in the table. For the third time, the record shows Ben Griffey's data, so again edit the **Email** address to read **BGriffey@elsewhere.net**.
6. Click the **Next Record** button to move to the next record in the table. For the fourth time, the record shows Ben Griffey's data, so again edit the **Email** address to read **BGriffey@elsewhere.net**.

*(Continued)*

**FIGURE AW-2-6**

**The Customer-Contact Data Input Form with the Updated Email Address**

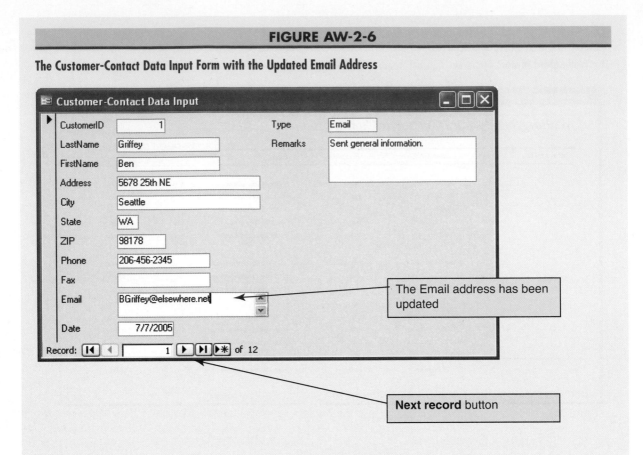

7. Click the **Next Record** button to move to the next record in the table. Finally, another customer's data appears in the form, so we will assume that we've made all the necessary updates to the database records.
8. Close the Customer-Contact Data Input form by clicking the **Close** button in the upper right corner of the Customer-Contact Data Input form.
9. In the WMCRM: Database window, click **Reports** in the Objects pane to display the Reports pane.
10. In the Reports objects pane, double-click the **Wallingford Motors Customer Contact Report report object** to open it. After adjustment, the Wallingford Motors Customer Contact Report now appears as shown in Figure AW-2-7. Note that the email addresses shown for Ben Griffey are inconsistent—we missed one record when we updated the table, and now we have inconsistent data. A modification error—in this case an update error—has occurred.
11. Close the Wallingford Motors Customer Contact Report by clicking the **Close** button in the upper right corner of the report window.

This simple example shows how easily modification problems can occur in tables that are not normalized. With a set of well-formed, normalized tables, this problem would never have occurred.

### Closing the WMCRM-Combined-Data Database

1. To close the WMCRM-Combined-Data: Database window, click the **Close** button in the upper right corner of the WMCRM-Combined-Data: Database window.

---

**FIGURE AW-2-7**

**The Updated Wallingford Motors Customer Contact Report**

*Wallingford Motors Customer Contact Report*

A modification problem has occurred. Not all records were updated with the new email address, and the database records are now inconsistent

| CustomerID | Date | LastName | FirstName | Email | |
|---|---|---|---|---|---|
| 1 | | | | | |
| | 7/7/2005 | Griffey | Ben | BGriffey@elsewhere.net | Phone |
| | 7/7/2005 | Griffey | Ben | BGriffey@elsewhere.net | Email |
| | 7/12/2005 | Griffey | Ben | BGriffey@elsewhere.net | Phone |
| | 7/14/2005 | Griffey | Ben | BGriffey@elsewhere.net | Meeting |
| | 7/21/2005 | Griffey | Ben | BGriffey@somewhere.com | Email |
| 3 | | | | | |
| | 7/19/2005 | Christman | Jessica | JChristman@somewhere.com | Phone |
| | 7/27/2005 | Christman | Jessica | JChristman@somewhere.com | Meeting |
| | 8/3/2005 | Christman | Jessica | JChristman@somewhere.com | Email |
| 4 | | | | | |
| | 7/27/2005 | Christman | Rob | RChristman@somewhere.com | Phone |
| | 8/2/2005 | Christman | Rob | RChristman@somewhere.com | Meeting |
| | 8/10/2005 | Christman | Rob | RChristman@somewhere.com | Email |
| 5 | | | | | |
| | 8/15/2005 | Hayes | Judy | JHayes@somewhere.com | Phone |

## Working with Multiple Tables

The table structure for the CUSTOMER_CONTACT table in the WMCRM-Combined-Data database is:

CUSTOMER_CONTACT (<u>CustomerID</u>, LastName, FirstName, Address, City, State, ZIP, Phone, Fax, Email, <u>Date</u>, <u>Type</u>, <u>Remarks</u>)

Applying the normalization process discussed in this chapter, we will have the following set of tables and referential integrity constraint:

CUSTOMER (<u>CustomerID</u>, LastName, FirstName, Address, City, State, ZIP, Phone, Fax, Email)

CONTACT (<u>ContactID</u>, *CustomerID*, Data, Type, Remarks)

CustomerID in CONTACT must exist in CustomerID in CUSTOMER

Our task now is to build and populate the CONTACT table, and then to establish the relationship and referential integrity constraint between the two tables.

First, we need to create and populate (insert data into) the CONTACT table, which will contain the columns shown in the table in Figure AW-2-8. As before, the table shows the column name and characteristics for each column.[5]

The CustomerID column appears again in CONTACT, this time designated as a foreign key. As discussed in this chapter, the term *foreign key* designates this column

*(Continued)*

---

[5]Although we are using it for simplicity in this example, a column such as Remarks can cause problems in a database. For a complete discussion, see David M. Kroenke, *Database Processing: Fundamentals, Design, and Implementation,* 10th Edition. (Upper Saddle River, NJ: Prentice Hall, 2006, pages 112–113.

---

**FIGURE AW-2-8**

**Database Column Characteristics for the CONTACT Table**

| Column Name | Type | Key | Required | Remarks |
|---|---|---|---|---|
| ContactID | AutoNumber | Primary Key | Yes | Surrogate Key |
| CustomerID | Number | Foreign Key | Yes | Long Integer |
| Date | Date/Time | No | Yes | Short Date |
| Type | Text(10) | No | Yes | Allowed values are Phone, Fax, Email and Meeting |
| Remarks | Memo | No | No | |

---

as the link to the CUSTOMER table. The value in the CustomerID column of CON-
TACT tells us which customer was contacted—all we have to do is look up the value
of CustomerID in the CUSTOMER table.

Note that when we build the CONTACT table itself, there is no "foreign key"
setting – we will see how to set up the actual database relationship between
CUSTOMER and CONTACT after we've completed building the CONTACT table.

Other things to note are:

- Some new data types are being used—Number, Data/Time, and Memo.
- CustomerID must be set as a Number and specifically as a Long Integer to
  match the data type Access creates for the AutoNumber data type in the
  CUSTOMER table.
- The Type column has only four allowed values—Phone, Fax, Email, and
  Meeting. For now, we will simply input only these data values. In "The
  Access Workbench: Section 3" we will learn how to enforce this data
  restriction for this column.

### Creating the CONTACT table

1. In the menu bar, click **File | Open**. The Open dialog box is displayed. Browse to the
   **WMCRM.mdb** file, click the file name to highlight it, and then click the **Open** button. When the Security Warning dialog box appears, click the **Open** button to open
   the database.
2. In the WRCRM: Database dialog box, click **Tables** in the Objects pane to select it.
3. Double-click **Create a table in Design view**. Using the steps we followed to create
   the CUSTOMER table in "The Access Workbench: Section 1," you should be able
   to create most of the CONTACT table. The steps below will detail only new information that you need to know to complete the CONTACT table.
4. When creating the ContactID column, be sure to set this column as the primary key.
5. When creating the CustomerID column, set the data type to **Number**. Note that the
   default Field Size for Number is Long Integer so that no change is necessary. Be
   sure to set the **Required** property to **Yes**.
6. When creating the Date column, set the data type to **Date/Time**, and set the
   Format to **Short Date** as shown in Figure AW-2-9. Be sure to set the **Required**
   property to **Yes**.
7. To name and save the CONTACT table, click the **Save** button in the Table Design
   toolbar.

### FIGURE AW-2-9

**Setting the Date Format**

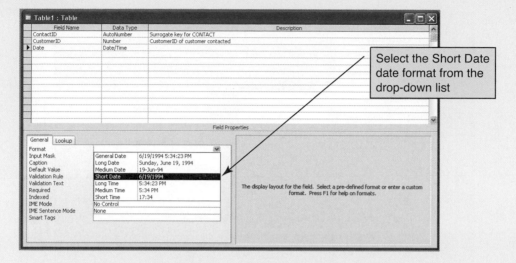

Select the Short Date date format from the drop-down list

8.  **Type** the table name *CONTACT* into the **Save As** dialog box text box, then click **OK**. The table is named and saved, and now appears with the table name CONTACT.
9.  To close the CONTACT table, click the **Close** button in the upper right corner of the CONTACT table window. The CONTACT table now appears as a table object in the WMCRM: Database window.

## Creating Relationships Between Tables

In Access, relationships between tables are built in the Relationships window. The Relationships window is accessed by using the Tools | Relationships. . . command on the Access main menu.

### Creating the Relationship Between the CUSTOMER and CONTACT Tables

1.  In the Access main menu, click **Tools** and then click **Relationships. . .** in the Tools menu as shown in Figure AW-2-10. The Relationships window appears with the Show Table dialog box open, as shown in Figure AW-2-11.
2.  In the Show Table dialog box, the CONTACT table is already selected. Click the **Add** button to add CONTACT to the Relationships window.
3.  In the Show Table dialog box, click the **CUSTOMER** table to select it. Click the **Add** button to add CUSTOMER to the Relationships window.
4.  In the Show Table dialog box, click the **Close** button to close the dialog box.
5.  You can rearrange and resize the table objects in the Relationships window using standard Windows drag-and-drop techniques. Rearrange the CUSTOMER and CONTACT table objects until they appear as shown in Figure AW-2-12. Now we are ready to create the relationship between the tables
    *   **NOTE:** A formal description of how to create a relationship between two tables is "In the Relationships window, drag a **primary key** column and drop it on top of the corresponding foreign key column." It is easier to understand this after you have actually done it!

*(Continued)*

**FIGURE AW-2-10**

**Opening the Relationships Window**

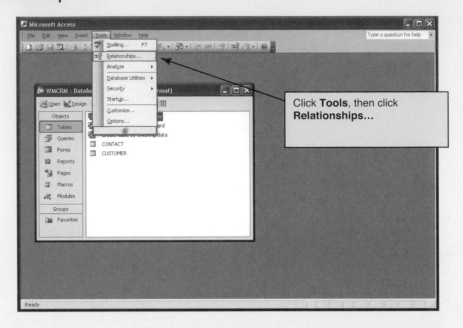

6. Click and hold the **column name CustomerID in the CUSTOMER table** object, and then drag it over the **column name CustomerID in the CONTACT table** object. The Edit Relationships dialog box appears as shown in Figure AW-2-13.
   - **NOTE:** In CUSTOMER, CustomerID is the primary key, while in CONTACT, CustomerID is the foreign key.

**FIGURE AW-2-11**

**Adding Tables to the Relationships Window**

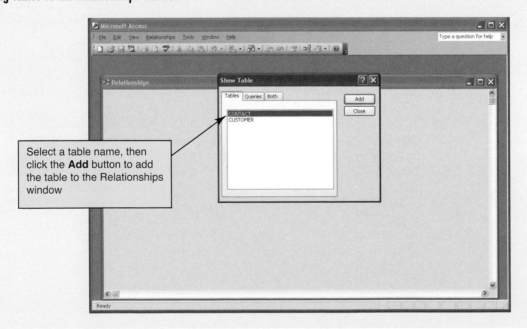

**FIGURE AW-2-12**

**The Table Objects in the Relationships Window**

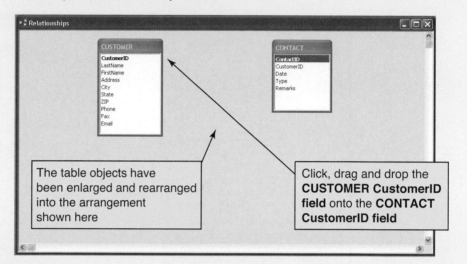

> The table objects have been enlarged and rearranged into the arrangement shown here

> Click, drag and drop the **CUSTOMER CustomerID field** onto the **CONTACT CustomerID field**

7. Click the **Enforce Referential Integrity** check box.
8. Click the **Create** button to create the relationship between CUSTOMER and CONTACT. The relationship between the tables now appears in the Relationships window as shown in Figure AW-2-14.
9. To close the Relationships window, click the **Close** button in the upper right corner of the Relationships window. An Access dialog box appears asking "Do you want to save changes to the layout of Relationships?" Click the **Yes** button to save the changes and close the window.

**FIGURE AW-2-13**

**The Edit Relationships Dialog Box**

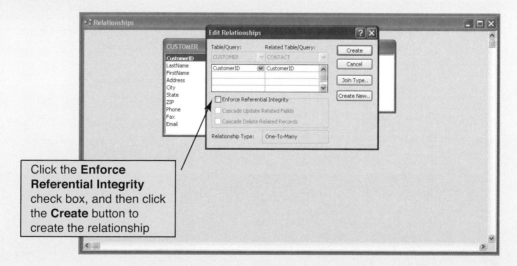

> Click the **Enforce Referential Integrity** check box, and then click the **Create** button to create the relationship

*(Continued)*

**FIGURE AW-2-14**

**The Completed Relationship**

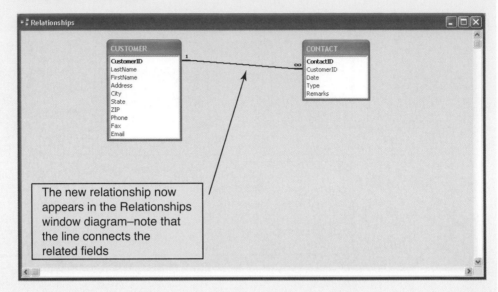

The new relationship now appears in the Relationships window diagram—note that the line connects the related fields

At this point, we need to add data on customer contacts to the CONTACT table. Using the CONTACT table in Datasheet View as we've already discussed, enter the data shown in Figure AW-2-1 into the CONTACT table. Note that there is no customer with CustomerID number 2—this is because we deleted and reentered the data for Jessica Christman in "The Access Workbench: Section 1." The CONTACT table with the data inserted appears as shown in Figure AW-2-15. Be sure to close the table after the data is entered.

**FIGURE AW-2-15**

**Data in the CONTACT Table**

CONTACT : Table

| | ContactID | CustomerID | Date | Type | Remarks |
|---|---|---|---|---|---|
| | 1 | 1 | 7/7/2005 | Phone | General interest in a Gaea. |
| | 2 | 1 | 7/7/2005 | Email | Sent general information. |
| | 3 | 1 | 7/12/2005 | Phone | Set up an appointment. |
| | 4 | 1 | 7/14/2005 | Meeting | Bought a HiStandard. |
| | 5 | 3 | 7/19/2005 | Phone | Interested in a SUHi, set up an appointment. |
| | 6 | 1 | 7/21/2005 | Email | Sent a standard follow-up message. |
| | 7 | 4 | 7/27/2005 | Phone | Interested in a HiStandard, set up an appointment. |
| | 8 | 3 | 7/27/2005 | Meeting | Bought a SUHi. |
| | 9 | 4 | 8/2/2005 | Meeting | Talked up to a HiLuxury.  Customer bought one. |
| | 10 | 3 | 8/3/2005 | Email | Sent a standard follow-up message. |
| | 11 | 4 | 8/10/2005 | Email | Sent a standard follow-up message. |
| | 12 | 5 | 8/15/2005 | Phone | General interest in a Gaea. |
| ▶ | (AutoNumber) | 0 | | | |

Record: |◄| |◄| 13 |►| |►I| |►*| of 13

## Using a Form That Includes Two Tables

In "The Access Workbench: Section 1," we created a data entry form for the CUSTOMER table. Now let's create an Access form that will let us work with the combined data from both tables.

### Creating a Form for Both the CUSTOMER and CONTACT Tables

1. In the WMCRM: Database window, click **Forms** in the Objects pane to display the Forms pane.
2. Double-click **Create form by using wizard**.
3. Select the **CUSTOMER table** in the Tables/Queries drop-down list. We will add all of the columns, so click the **right-facing double chevron** button to add all the columns, but do **NOT** click the **Next >** button yet!
4. Select the **CONTACT table** in the Tables/Queries drop-down list. Individually select and add the **Date, Type,** and **Remarks** columns to the Selected Fields list using the **right-facing chevron** button. Now, click the **Next >** button.
   - **NOTE:** We have just created a set of columns from two tables that we want to appear on one form.
5. We are now asked, "How do you want to view your data?" We will use the default By CUSTOMER selection since we want to see all contacts for each customer. We will also use the selected Forms with subforms option, which will treat the CONTACT data as a subform within the CUSTOMER form. Click the **Next >** button.
6. We are now asked, "What layout would you like for your subform?" We will use the default Datasheet layout, so click the **Next >** button.
7. We are now asked, "What style would you like?" We will use the default Standard style, so click the **Next >** button.
8. We are now asked, "What titles do you want for your forms?" **Type** the form tile *WMCRM Customer Contacts Form* in the **Form:** text box, and **Type** the form tile *Contact Data* in the **Subform:** text box. Click the **Finish** button. The completed form appears.
9. Unfortunately, the Access wizard again made the text boxes for Phone and Fax too small. Use the Design View to fix this, and then return to Form View. The result with the adjusted text boxes is shown in Figure AW-2-16.
10. Close the form window.

## Creating a Report That Includes Data from Two Tables

We can also create reports that include data from two or more tables. Let's create an Access report that will let us use the combined data from both the CUSTOMER and CONTACT tables.

### Creating a Report for Both the CUSTOMER and CONTACT Tables

1. In the WMCRM: Database window, click **Reports** in the Objects pane to display the Reports pane.
2. Double-click **Create report by using wizard.**
3. Select the **CUSTOMER table** in the Tables/Queries drop-down list. We will use only the following columns: **LastName, FirstName, Phone, Fax,** and **Email.** Click each column name to select it, then click the **right-facing chevron** button to add each column to the Selected Fields, but do **NOT** click the **Next >** button yet!
4. Select the **CONTACT table** in the Tables/Queries drop-down list. Individually select and add the **Date, Type,** and **Remarks** columns to the Selected Fields list using the **right-facing chevron** button. Now, click the **Next >** button.

*(Continued)*

**FIGURE AW-2-16**

**The Completed Form for CUSTOMER and CONTACT Data**

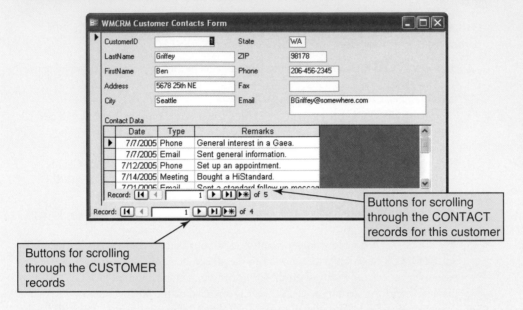

5. We are now asked, "How do you want to view your data?" We will use the default By CUSTOMER selection since we want to see all contacts for each customer. Click the **Next>** button.

6. We are now asked, "Do you want to add any grouping levels?" We'll use the default nongrouped column listing, so click the **Next>** button.

7. We are now asked, "What sort order do you want for detail records?" This is the sort order for the CONTACT information. The most useful sorting order is by Date in ascending order. Click the **sort field 1** drop-down list arrow and select **Date**. Leave the sort order button on its current setting of Ascending. Click the **Next** button.

8. We are now asked, "How would you like to lay out your report?" We will use the default setting of stepped layout, but click the **Landscape orientation** radio button to change the report orientation to landscape. Then click the **Next>** button.

9. Now we are asked, "What style would you like?" We will use the default setting of Corporate. Then click the **Next>** button.

10. Finally we are asked, "What title do you want for your report?" **Edit** the report title to read *Wallingford Motors Customer Contacts Report*. Leave the **Preview the report** radio button selected. Click the **Finish** button. The completed report is displayed.

11. Unfortunately, the Access form wizard made various data areas on the report too small. Use the report Design View to fix this—this works exactly the same as it does for the form Design View—and then return to Report View. The result with the adjusted Date fields is shown in Figure AW-2-17.

12. Click the **Close** button in the upper right corner of the Wallingford Motors Customer Contacts Report to close the report window.

### Closing the Database and Exiting Access

That completes the work we'll do in this section of "The Access Workbench." As usual, we will finish by closing the database and Access.

**FIGURE AW-2-17**

**The Completed Wallingford Motors Customer Contacts Report**

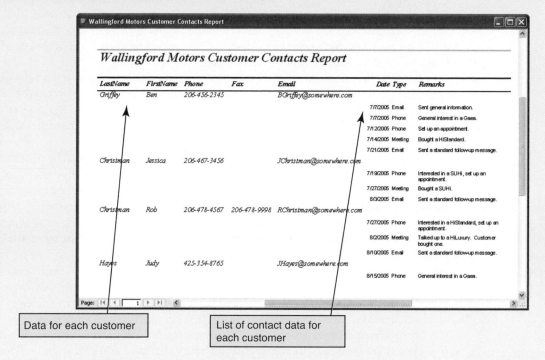

Data for each customer

List of contact data for each customer

### Closing the WMCRM Database

1. To close the WMCRM: Database window, click the **Close** button in the upper right corner of the WMCRM: Database window.

### Exiting Access

1. To exit Access, click the **Close** button in the upper right corner of the Microsoft Access window.

## SUMMARY

The relational model is the most important standard in database processing today. It was first published by E. F. Codd in 1970. Today, it is used for the design and implementation of almost every commercial database.

An entity is something of importance to a user that needs to be represented in a database.

A relation is a two-dimensional table that has the characteristics listed in Figure 2-1. In this book and in the database world in general, the term *table* is used synonymously with the term *relation*. Three sets of terminology are used for relational structures. The terms *table*, *row*, and *column* are used most commonly, but *file*, *record*, and *field* are sometimes used in traditional data processing. Theorists also use the terms *relation*, *tuple*, and *attribute* for the same three constructs. Sometimes these terms are mixed and matched. Strictly speaking, a relation may not have duplicate rows; however, sometimes this condition is relaxed because eliminating duplicates can be a time-consuming process.

A key is one or more columns of a relation that is used to identify a row. A unique key identifies a single row; a nonunique key identifies several rows. A composite key is a key that has two or more attributes. A relation has one primary key, which must be a unique key. A relation also may have additional unique keys called candidate keys. A primary key is used to represent the table in relationships, and many DBMS products use values of the primary key to organize table storage. In addition, an index normally is constructed to provide fast access via primary key values. An ideal primary key is short, numeric, and never changes.

A surrogate key is a unique, numeric value that is appended to a relation to serve as the primary key. Surrogate key values have no meaning to the user and normally are hidden on forms, queries, and reports.

A foreign key is an attribute that is placed in a relation to represent a relationship. A foreign key is the primary key of a table that is different from (foreign to) the table in which it is placed. Primary and foreign keys may have different names, but they must use the same sets of values. A referential integrity constraint specifies that the values of a foreign key be present in the primary key.

A null value occurs when no value has been given to an attribute. The problem with a null value is that its meaning is ambiguous. It can mean that no value is appropriate, that a value is appropriate but has not yet been chosen, or that a value is appropriate and has been chosen but is unknown to the user. Null values can be eliminated by requiring attribute values. Another problem with null values will be shown in the next chapter.

A functional dependency occurs when the value of one attribute (or set of attributes) determines the value of a second attribute (or set of attributes). The attribute on the left side of a functional dependency is called the determinant. One way to view the purpose of a relation is to state that the relation exists to store instances of functional dependencies. Another way to define a primary (and candidate) key is to state that such a key is an attribute that functionally determines all of the other attributes in a relation.

Normalization is the process of evaluating a relation and, when necessary, breaking the relation into two more relations that are better designed and said to be well formed. According to normalization theory, a relation is poorly structured if it has a functional dependency that does not involve the primary key. Specifically, in a well-formed relation, every determinant is a candidate key.

A process for normalizing relations is shown on page 68. According to this process, relations that have normalization problems are divided into two or more relations that do not have such problems. Foreign keys are established between the old and new relations, and referential integrity constraints are created.

## REVIEW QUESTIONS

**2.1**  Why is the relational model important?

**2.2**  Define the term *entity* and give an example.

**2.3**  List the characteristics a table must have to be considered a relation.

**2.4**  Give an example of a relation (other than the one in this chapter).

**2.5**  Give an example of a table that is not a relation (other than one from this chapter).

**2.6**  Under what circumstances can an attribute of a relation be of variable length?

**2.7**  Explain the use of the terms *file*, *record*, and *field*.

**2.8**  Explain the use of the terms *relation*, *tuple*, and *attribute*.

**2.9**  Under what circumstances can a relation have duplicate rows?

**2.10** Define the term *unique key* and give an example.

**2.11** Define the term *nonunique key* and give an example.

**2.12** Give an example of a relation with a unique composite key.

**2.13** Explain the difference between a primary key and a candidate key.

**2.14** Describe four uses of a primary key.

**2.15** What is a *surrogate key*, and under what circumstances would you use one?

**2.16** How do surrogate keys obtain their values?

**2.17** Why are the values of surrogate keys normally hidden from users on forms, queries, and reports?

**2.18** Explain the term *foreign key* and give an example.

**2.19** Explain how primary keys and foreign keys are denoted in this book.

**2.20** Define the term *referential integrity constraint* and give an example of one.

**2.21** Explain three possible interpretations of a null value.

**2.22** Give an example of a null value (other than one from this chapter), and explain each of the three possible interpretations for that value.

**2.23** Define the terms *functional dependency* and *determinant* using an example not in this book

**2.24** In the following equation, name the functional dependency and identify the determinant(s).

Area = Length × Width

**2.25** Explain the meaning of the following expression.

$A \rightarrow (B, C)$

Given this expression, tell if it is also true that:

$A \rightarrow B$

and

$A \rightarrow C$

**2.26** Explain the meaning of the following expression:

$(D, E) \rightarrow F$

Given this expression, tell if it is also true that:

$D \rightarrow F$

and

$E \rightarrow F$

**2.27** Explain the differences in your answers to questions 2.25 and 2.26.

**2.28** Define the term *primary key* in terms of functional dependencies.

**2.29** If we assume that a relation has no duplicate data, how do we know there is always at least one primary key?

**2.30** How does your answer to question 2.29 change if we allow a relation to have duplicate data?

**2.31** Using your own words, describe the nature and purpose of the normalization process.

**2.32** Examine the data in the Veterinary Office List in Figure 1-26 (see page 47), and state assumptions about functional dependencies in this table. What is the danger of making such conclusions on the basis of sample data?

**2.33** Using the assumptions you stated in your answer to question 2.32, what are the determinants of this relation? What attribute(s) can be the primary key of this relation?

**2.34** Describe a modification problem when changing data in the relation in question 2.32 and a second modification problem when deleting data in this relation.

**2.35** Examine the data in the Veterinary Office List—Version Two in Figure 1-27 (see page 48), and state assumptions about functional dependencies in this table.

**2.36** Using the assumptions you stated in your answer to question 2.35, what are the determinants of this relation? What attribute(s) can be the primary key of this relation?

**2.37** Explain a modification problem when changing data in the relation in question 2.35 and a second modification problem when deleting data in this relation.

**EXERCISES**

**2.38** Apply the normalization process to the Veterinary Office List relation shown in Figure 1-26 to develop a set of normalized relations. Show the results of each of the steps in the normalization process.

**2.39** Apply the normalization process to the Veterinary Office List—Version Two relation shown in Figure 1-27 to develop a set of normalized relations. Show the results of each of the steps in the normalization process.

**2.40** Consider the following relation.

STUDENT (<u>StudentNumber</u>, StudentName, <u>SiblingName</u>, Major)

Assume that the values of SiblingName are the names of all of a given student's brothers and sisters; also assume that students have at most one major.

**A.** Show an example of this relation for two students, one of whom has three siblings and the other of whom has only two siblings.

**B.** List the candidate keys in this relation.

**C.** State the functional dependencies in this relation.

**D.** Explain why this relation does not meet the relational design criteria set out in this chapter (i.e., why this is not a well-formed relation).

**E.** Divide this relation into a set of relations that do meet the relational design criteria (i.e., that are well formed).

**2.41** Alter question 2.39 to allow students to have multiple majors. In this case, the relational structure is:

STUDENT (<u>StudentNum</u>, StudentName, <u>SiblingName</u>, <u>Major</u>)

**A.** Show an example of this relation for two students, one of whom has three siblings and the other of whom has one sibling. Assume each student has a single major.

**B.** Show the data changes necessary to add a second major only for the first student.

**C.** Based on your answer to part B, show the data changes necessary to add a second major for the second student.

**D.** Explain the differences in your answers to questions parts B and C. Comment on the desirability of this situation.

**E.** Divide this relation into a set of well-formed relations.

**2.42** The text states that one can argue that "the only reason for having relations is to store instances of functional dependencies." Explain what this means in your own words.

**ACCESS WORKBENCH EXERCISES**

**AW.2.1** In the "Access Workbench Exercises" in Chapter 1, we created a database for the Wedgewood Pacific Corporation (WPC) of Seattle, Washington, and created and populated the EMPLOYEE table. In this exercise, we will build the rest of the tables needed for the database, create the referential integrity constraints between them, and populate the tables.

The full set of normalized tables for the WPC database is as follows:

DEPARTMENT (<u>DepartmentName</u>, BudgetCode, OfficeNumber, Phone)

EMPLOYEE (<u>EmployeeNumber</u>, FirstName, LastName, *Department*, Phone, Email)

PROJECT (<u>ProjectID</u>, Name, *Department*, MaxHours, StartDate, EndDate)

ASSIGNMENT (*<u>ProjectID</u>*, *<u>EmployeeNumber</u>*, HoursWorked)

The primary key of DEPARTMENT is DepartmentName, the primary key of EMPLOYEE is EmployeeNumber, and the primary key of PROJECT is ProjectID. Note that the EMPLOYEE table is the same as the table we have created, except that Department is now a foreign key. In EMPLOYEE and PROJECT, Department is a foreign key referencing DepartmentName in DEPARTMENT. Note that a foreign key does not need to have the same name as the primary key to which it refers. The primary key of ASSIGNMENT is the composite (ProjectID, EmployeeNumber). ProjectID is also a foreign key referencing ProjectID in PROJECT, and Employee-Number is a foreign key referencing EmployeeNumber in EMPLOYEE.

The referential integrity constraints are:

Department in EMPLOYEE must exist in DepartmentName in DEPARTMENT

Department in PROJECT must exist in DepartmentName in DEPARTMENT

ProjectID in ASSIGNMENT must exist in ProjectID in PROJECT

EmployeeNumber in ASSIGNMENT must exist in EmployeeNumber in EMPLOYEE

**A.** Figure 2-22 shows the column characteristics for the WPC DEPARTMENT table. Using the column characteristics, create the DEPARTMENT table in the WPC.mdb database.

**B.** Create a data input form for the DEPARTMENT table named WPC Department Data Form. Make any adjustments necessary to the form so that all data displays properly. Use this form to enter the data in the DEPARTMENT table shown in Figure 2-23 into your DEPARTMENT table.

**C.** Create the relationship and referential integrity constraint between DEPARTMENT and EMPLOYEE.

---

### FIGURE 2-22

**Column Characteristics for the DEPARTMENT Table**

| Column Name | Type | Key | Required | Remarks |
|---|---|---|---|---|
| DepartmentName | Text(35) | Primary Key | Yes | |
| BudgetCode | Text(30) | No | Yes | |
| OfficeNumber | Text(15) | No | Yes | |
| Phone | Text(12) | No | Yes | |

---

**FIGURE 2-23**

**WPC DEPARTMENT Data**

| Department Name | BudgetCode | OfficeNumber | Phone |
|---|---|---|---|
| Administration | BC-100-10 | BLDG01-300 | 360-285-8100 |
| Legal | BC-200-10 | BLDG01-200 | 360-285-8200 |
| Accounting | BC-300-10 | BLDG01-100 | 360-285-8300 |
| Finance | BC-400-10 | BLDG01-140 | 360-285-8400 |
| Human Resources | BC-500-10 | BLDG01-180 | 360-285-8500 |
| Production | BC-600-10 | BLDG02-100 | 360-287-8600 |
| Marketing | BC-700-10 | BLDG02-200 | 360-287-8700 |
| Info Systems | BC-800-10 | BLDG02-270 | 360-287-8800 |

---

**FIGURE 2-24**

**Column Characteristics for the PROJECT Table**

| Column Name | Type | Key | Required | Remarks |
|---|---|---|---|---|
| ProjectID | Number | Primary Key | Yes | Long Integer |
| Name | Text(50) | No | Yes | |
| Department | Text(35) | Foreign Key | Yes | |
| MaxHours | Number | No | Yes | Double |
| StartDate | Date/Time | No | No | |
| EndDate | Date/Time | No | No | |

**D.** Figure 2-24 shows the column characteristics for the WPC PROJECT table. Using the column characteristics, create the PROJECT table in the WPC.mdb database.

**E.** Create the relationship and referential integrity constraint between DEPARTMENT and PROJECT.

**F.** Create a data input form for the PROJECT table named *WPC Project Data Form*. Make any adjustments necessary to the form so that all data displays properly. Use this form to enter the data in the PROJECT table shown in Figure 2-25 into your PROJECT table.

**G.** When creating and populating the DEPARTMENT table, data was entered into the data before the referential integrity constraint with EMPLOYEE was created, but when creating and populating the PROJECT table, the referential integrity constraint was created before entering the data. Why did the order of the steps differ? Which order is normally the correct order to use?

**H.** Figure 2-26 shows the column characteristics for the WPC ASSIGNMENT table. Using the column characteristics, create the ASSIGNMENT table in the WPC.mdb database.

| FIGURE 2-25 |
| --- |

**WPC PROJECT Data**

| ProjectID | Name | Department | MaxHours | StartDate | EndDate |
| --- | --- | --- | --- | --- | --- |
| 1000 | 2005 Q3 Product Plan | Marketing | 135.00 | 10-MAY-05 | 15-JUN-05 |
| 1100 | 2005 Q3 Portfolio Analysis | Finance | 120.00 | 05-JUL-05 | 25-JUL-05 |
| 1200 | 2005 Q3 Tax Preparation | Accounting | 145.00 | 10-AUG-05 | 15-OCT-05 |
| 1300 | 2005 Q4 Product Plan | Marketing | 150.00 | 10-AUG-05 | 15-SEP-05 |
| 1400 | 2005 Q4 Portfolio Analysis | Finance | 140.00 | 05-OCT-05 | NULL |

| FIGURE 2-26 |
| --- |

**Column Characteristics for the ASSIGNMENT Table**

| Column Name | Type | Key | Required | Remarks |
| --- | --- | --- | --- | --- |
| ProjectID | Number | Primary Key, Foreign Key | Yes | Long Integer |
| EmployeeNumber | Number | Primary Key, Foreign Key | Yes | Long Integer |
| HoursWorked | Number | No | No | Double |

| FIGURE 2-27 |
| --- |

**WPC ASSIGNMENT Data**

| ProjectID | Employee Number | Hours Worked |
| --- | --- | --- |
| 1000 | 1 | 30.0 |
| 1000 | 8 | 75.0 |
| 1000 | 10 | 55.0 |
| 1100 | 4 | 40.0 |
| 1100 | 6 | 45.0 |
| 1200 | 1 | 25.0 |
| 1200 | 2 | 20.0 |
| 1200 | 4 | 45.0 |
| 1200 | 5 | 40.0 |
| 1300 | 1 | 35.0 |
| 1300 | 8 | 80.0 |
| 1300 | 10 | 50.0 |
| 1400 | 4 | 15.0 |
| 1400 | 5 | 10.0 |
| 1400 | 6 | 27.5 |

**I.** Create the relationship and referential integrity constraint between ASSIGN-MENT and PROJECT, and between ASSIGNMENT and EMPLOYEE.

**J.** Create a data input form for the ASSIGNMENT table named WPC Assignment Data Form. Make any adjustments necessary to the form so that all data displays properly. Use this form to enter the data in the ASSIGN-MENT table shown in Figure 2-27 into your ASSIGNMENT table.

**K.** Create a data input form for both the DEPARTMENT and EMPLOYEE tables named *WPC Department Employee Data Form*. This form should show all the employees in each department.

**L.** Create a report named *Wedgewood Pacific Corporation Department Employee Report* that presents the data contained in your DEPARTMENT and EMPLOYEE tables. The report should group employees by department. Print out a copy of this report.

## GARDEN GLORY PROJECT QUESTIONS

Figure 2-28 shows data that Garden Glory collects about properties and services.

**A.** Using these data, state assumptions about functional dependencies among the columns of data. Justify your assumptions on the basis of these sample data and also on the basis of what you know about service businesses.

**B.** Given your assumptions, comment on the appropriateness of the following designs.

**1.** PROPERTY (<u>PropertyName</u>, Type, Street, City, Zip, ServiceDate, Description, Amount)

**2.** PROPERTY (PropertyName, Type, Street, City, Zip, <u>ServiceDate</u>, Description, Amount)

**3.** PROPERTY (<u>PropertyName</u>, Type, Street, City, Zip, <u>ServiceDate</u>, Description, Amount)

**4.** PROPERTY (<u>PropertyID</u>, PropertyName, Type, Street, City, Zip, ServiceDate, Description, Amount)

**5.** PROPERTY (<u>PropertyID</u>, PropertyName, Type, Street, City, Zip, <u>ServiceDate</u>, Description, Amount)

**6.** PROPERTY (<u>PropertyID</u>, PropertyName, Type, Street, City, Zip, *ServiceDate*)

and

SERVICE (<u>ServiceDate</u>, Description, Amount)

**7.** PROPERTY (<u>PropertyID</u>, PropertyName, Type, Street, City, Zip, ServiceDate)

and

SERVICE (<u>ServiceID</u>, *ServiceDate*, Description, Amount)

| | | | | | | | |
|---|---|---|---|---|---|---|---|
| **FIGURE 2-28** | **Property Name** | **Type** | **Street** | **City** | **Zip** | **ServiceDate** | **Description** | **Amount** |

| Property Name | Type | Street | City | Zip | ServiceDate | Description | Amount |
|---|---|---|---|---|---|---|---|
| Eastlake Building | Office | 123 Eastlake | Seattle | 98119 | 5/5/06 | Lawn Mow | $42.50 |
| Elm St Apts | Apartment | 4 East Elm | Lynnwood | 98223 | 5/7/06 | Lawn Mow | $123.50 |
| Jefferson Hill | Office | 42 West 7th St | Bellevue | 98040 | 5/7/06 | Garden Service | $53.00 |
| Eastlake Building | Office | 123 Eastlake | Seattle | 98119 | 5/12/06 | Lawn Mow | $42.50 |
| Eastlake Building | Office | 123 Eastlake | Seattle | 98119 | 5/19/06 | Lawn Mow | $42.50 |
| Elm St Apts | Apartment | 4 East Elm | Lynnwood | 98223 | 5/14/06 | Lawn Mow | $123.50 |
| Eastlake Building | Office | 144 Eastlake | Bellevue | 98040 | 5/10/06 | Lawn Mow | $63.00 |

**Sample Data for Garden Glory**

8. PROPERTY (<u>PropertyID</u>, PropertyName, Type, Street, City, Zip, *ServiceID*)

   and

   SERVICE (<u>ServiceID</u>, ServiceDate, Description, Amount, *PropertyID*)

9. PROPERTY (<u>PropertyID</u>, PropertyName, Type, Street, City, Zip)

   and

   SERVICE (<u>ServiceID</u>, ServiceDate, Description, Amount, <u>*PropertyID*</u>)

**C.** Suppose Garden Glory decides to add the following table.

SERVICE_FEE (PropertyID, ServiceID, ServiceDate, Amount)

Add this table to what you consider to be the best design in your answer to question B. Modify the tables from question B as necessary to minimize the amount of duplicate data. Will this design work for the data in Figure 2-28? If not, modify the data so that this design will work. State the assumption implied by this design.

## JAMES RIVER JEWELRY PROJECT QUESTIONS

Figure 2-29 shows data that James River Jewelry collects for its frequent buyer program.

**A.** Using these data, state assumptions about functional dependencies among the columns of data. Justify your assumptions on the basis of these sample data and also on the basis of what you know about retail sales.

**B.** Given your assumptions, comment on the appropriateness of the following designs.

1. CUSTOMER (<u>Name</u>, Phone, Email, InvoiceNumber, Date, PreTaxAmount)

2. CUSTOMER (Name, Phone, Email, <u>InvoiceNumber</u>, Date, PreTaxAmount)

3. CUSTOMER (Name, Phone, <u>Email</u>, InvoiceNumber, Date, PreTaxAmount)

4. CUSTOMER (<u>CustomerID</u>, Name, Phone, Email, InvoiceNumber, Date, PreTax Amount)

5. CUSTOMER (<u>Name</u>, Phone, Email)

   and

   PURCHASE (<u>InvoiceNumber</u>, Date, PreTax Amount)

6. CUSTOMER (Name, Phone, <u>Email</u>)

   and

   PURCHASE (<u>InvoiceNumber</u>, Date, PreTax Amount, *Email*)

| | FIGURE 2-29 |
|---|---|

**Sample Data for James River Jewelry**

| Name | Phone | Email | InvoiceNumber | Date | PreTaxAmount |
|---|---|---|---|---|---|
| Elizabeth Stanley | 555-236-7789 | ES@somewhere.com | 1000 | 5/5/2006 | $155.00 |
| Fred Price | 555-236-0091 | FP@somewhere.com | 1010 | 5/7/2006 | $203.00 |
| Linda Becky | 555-236-0392 | LB@somewhere.com | 1020 | 5/11/2006 | $75.00 |
| Pamela Birch | 555-236-4493 | PB@somewhere.com | 1030 | 5/15/2006 | $67.00 |
| Ricardo Romez | 555-236-3334 | RB@somewhere.com | 1040 | 5/16/2006 | $330.00 |
| Elizabeth Stanley | 555-236-7789 | ES@somewhere.com | 1050 | 5/16/2006 | $25.00 |
| Linda Becky | 555-236-0392 | LB@somewhere.com | 1060 | 5/16/2006 | $45.00 |
| Elizabeth Stanley | 555-236-7789 | ES@somewhere.com | 1070 | 5/18/2006 | $445.00 |
| Samantha Jackson | 555-236-1095 | SJ@somewhere.com | 1080 | 5/19/2006 | $72.00 |

7. CUSTOMER (Name, <u>Email</u>)

and

PURCHASE (<u>InvoiceNumber</u>, Phone, Date, PreTax Amount, *Email*)

**C.** Modify what you consider to be the best design in question B to include a column called AwardPurchaseAmount. The purpose of this column is to keep a balance of the customers' purchases for award purposes. Assume that returns will be recorded with invoices having a negative PreTaxAmount.

**D.** Add a new AWARD table to your answer to question C. Assume that the new table will hold data concerning the date and amount of an award that is given after a customer has purchased 10 items. Ensure that your new table has appropriate primary and foreign keys.

## THE QUEEN ANNE CURIOSITY SHOP PROJECT QUESTIONS

Figure 2-30(a) shows typical sales data for the Queen Anne Curiosity Shop, and Figure 2-30(b) shows typical purchase data.

**A.** Using these data, state assumptions about functional dependencies among the columns of data. Justify your assumptions on the basis of these sample data and also on the basis of what you know about retail sales.

**B.** Given your assumptions, comment on the appropriateness of the following designs.
1. CUSTOMER (<u>LastName</u>, FirstName, Phone, Email, PurchaseDate, Item, Price, Tax, Total)
2. CUSTOMER (<u>LastName</u>, <u>FirstName</u>, Phone, Email, PurchaseDate, Item, Price, Tax, Total)
3. CUSTOMER (LastName, <u>FirstName</u>, <u>Phone</u>, Email, PurchaseDate, Item, Price, Tax, Total)
4. CUSTOMER (<u>LastName</u>, <u>FirstName</u>, Phone, Email, <u>PurchaseDate</u>, Item, Price, Tax, Total)
5. CUSTOMER (<u>LastName</u>, <u>FirstName</u>, Phone, Email, <u>PurchaseDate</u>, <u>Item</u>, Price, Tax, Total)
6. CUSTOMER (<u>LastName</u>, <u>FirstName</u>, Phone, Email)

   and

   SALE (<u>PurchaseDate</u>, Item, Price, Tax, Total)
7. CUSTOMER (<u>LastName</u>, <u>FirstName</u>, Phone, Email, *PurchaseDate*)

   and

   SALE (<u>PurchaseDate</u>, Item, Price, Tax, Total)
8. CUSTOMER (<u>LastName</u>, <u>FirstName</u>, Phone, Email)

   and

   SALE (<u>PurchaseDate</u>, <u>Item</u>, *LastName, FirstName,* Price, Tax, Total)

**C.** Modify what you consider to be the best design in question B to include surrogate ID columns called CustomerID and SaleID. How does this improve the design?

## FIGURE 2-30

**(a) Sample Sales Data for The Queen Anne Curiosity Shop**

| LastName | FirstName | Phone | PurchaseDate | Item | Price | Tax | Total |
|---|---|---|---|---|---|---|---|
| Shire | Robert | 206-524-2433 | 14-Dec-05 | Antique Desk | 3,000.00 | 249.00 | 3,249.00 |
| Shire | Robert | 206-524-2433 | 14-Dec-05 | Antique Desk Chair | 500.00 | 41.50 | 541.50 |
| Goodyear | Katherine | 206-524-3544 | 15-Dec-05 | Dining Table Linens | 1,000.00 | 83.00 | 1,083.00 |
| Bancroft | Chris | 425-635-9788 | 15-Dec-05 | Candles | 50.00 | 4.15 | 54.15 |
| Griffith | John | 206-524-4655 | 23-Dec-05 | Candles | 45.00 | 3.74 | 48.74 |
| Shire | Robert | 206-524-2433 | 5-Jan-06 | Desk Lamp | 250.00 | 20.75 | 270.75 |
| Tierney | Doris | 425-635-8677 | 10-Jan-06 | Dining Table Linens | 750.00 | 62.25 | 812.25 |
| Anderson | Donna | 360-538-7566 | 12-Jan-06 | Book Shelf | 250.00 | 20.75 | 270.75 |
| Goodyear | Katherine | 206-524-3544 | 15-Jan-06 | Antique Chair | 1,250.00 | 103.75 | 1,353.75 |
| Goodyear | Katherine | 206-524-3544 | 15-Jan-06 | Antique Chair | 1,750.00 | 145.25 | 1,895.25 |
| Tierney | Doris | 425-635-8677 | 25-Jan-06 | Antique Candle Holders | 350.00 | 29.05 | 379.05 |

---

**FIGURE 2-30**

**(b) Sample Purchase Data for The Queen Anne Curiosity Shop**

| Item | PurchasePrice | PurchaseDate | Vendor | Phone |
|------|---------------|--------------|--------|-------|
| Antique Desk | 1,800.00 | 7-Nov-05 | European Specialties | 206-325-7866 |
| Antique Desk | 1,750.00 | 7-Nov-05 | European Specialties | 206-325-7866 |
| Antique Candle Holders | 210.00 | 7-Nov-05 | European Specialties | 206-325-7866 |
| Antique Candle Holders | 200.00 | 7-Nov-05 | European Specialties | 206-325-7866 |
| Dining Table Linens | 600.00 | 14-Nov-05 | Linens and Things | 206-325-6755 |
| Candles | 30.00 | 14-Nov-05 | Linens and Things | 206-325-6755 |
| Floor Lamp | 300.00 | 14-Nov-05 | Lamps and Lighting | 206-325-8977 |
| Dining Table Linens | 450.00 | 21-Nov-05 | Linens and Things | 206-325-6755 |
| Candles | 27.00 | 21-Nov-05 | Linens and Things | 206-325-6755 |
| Book Shelf | 150.00 | 21-Nov-05 | Harrison Denise | 425-746-4322 |
| Antique Desk | 1,000.00 | 28-Nov-05 | Lee, Andrew | 425-746-5433 |
| Antique Desk Chair | 300.00 | 28-Nov-05 | Lee, Andrew | 425-746-5433 |
| Antique Chair | 750.00 | 28-Nov-05 | New York Brokerage | 206-325-9088 |
| Antique Chair | 1,050.00 | 28-Nov-05 | New York Brokerage | 206-325-9088 |

**D.** Modify the design in question C by breaking SALE into two relations named SALE and SALE_ITEM. Modify columns and add additional columns as you think necessary. How does this improve the design?

**E.** Given your assumptions, comment on the appropriateness of the following designs.

   **1.** PURCHASE (<u>Item</u>, PurchasePrice, PurchaseDate, Vendor, Phone)

   **2.** PURCHASE (<u>Item</u>, <u>PurchasePrice</u>, PurchaseDate, Vendor, Phone)

   **3.** PURCHASE (<u>Item</u>, PurchasePrice, <u>PurchaseDate</u>, Vendor, Phone)

   **4.** PURCHASE (<u>Item</u>, PurchasePrice, PurchaseDate, <u>Vendor</u>, Phone)

   **5.** PURCHASE (<u>Item</u>, PurchasePrice, <u>PurchaseDate</u>)

   and

   VENDOR (<u>Vendor</u>, Phone)

   **6.** PURCHASE (<u>Item</u>, PurchasePrice, <u>PurchaseDate</u>, *Vendor*)

   and

   VENDOR (<u>Vendor</u>, Phone)

**F.** Modify what you consider to be the best design in question E to include surrogate ID columns called PurchaseID and VendorID. How does this improve the design?

**G.** The relations in your design from question D and question F are not connected. Modify the database design so that sales data and purchase data are related.

# CHAPTER 3

# Structured Query Language

> Learn basic SQL statements for creating database structures
> Learn basic SQL statements to add data to a database
> Learn basic SQL SELECT statements and options for processing a single table
> Learn basic SQL SELECT statements for processing multiple tables with subqueries
> Learn basic SQL SELECT statements for processing multiple tables with joins
> Learn basic SQL statements to modify and delete data from a database
> Learn basic SQL statements to modify and delete database tables and constraints

This chapter describes and discusses **Structured Query Language (SQL)**. SQL is not a complete programming language but rather it is a **data sub-language**. SQL consists only of constructs for defining and processing a database. To obtain a full programming language, SQL statements must be embedded in scripting languages, such as VBScript, or in programming languages, such as Java or C#. SQL statements also can be submitted interactively using a DBMS-supplied command prompt.

SQL was developed by the IBM Corporation in the late 1970s and was endorsed as a national standard by the American National Standards Institute in 1992. The version presented here is based on that standard, sometimes referred to as SQL-92 or sometimes ANSI-92 SQL. A later version, SQL3, incorporates some object-oriented concepts. This later version has received little attention from commercial Database Management System (DBMS) vendors and at present is unimportant for practical database processing. We will not consider it here.

SQL is text oriented. It was developed long before graphical user interfaces and requires only a text processor. Today, Microsoft Access, SQL Server, Oracle, MySQL and other DBMS products provide graphic tools for performing many of the tasks that are performed using SQL. However, the key phrase in that last sentence is *many of*. You cannot do everything with graphic tools that you can do with SQL. Furthermore, to generate SQL statements dynamically in program code, you must use SQL.

You will learn how to use SQL with Microsoft Access in this chapter's "The Access Workbench." Access uses SQL but hides it behind the scenes, presenting a variant of the **Query By Example (QBE)** graphical user interface (GUI) for general use. Although knowledge of SQL is not a requirement for using Access, you will be a stronger and more effective Access developer if you know SQL.

SQL commands can be broken into two major categories: a **data definition language (DDL)**, which is used to define database structures, and a **data manipulation language (DML)**, which is used to query and modify database data. We will discuss each of these in turn.

## ▶ AN EXAMPLE DATEBASE

In this chapter, we will use an example database having the following four relations.

DEPARTMENT (<u>DepartmentName</u>, BudgetCode, OfficeNumber, Phone)
EMPLOYEE (<u>EmployeeNumber</u>, FirstName, LastName, *Department*, Phone, Email)
PROJECT (<u>ProjectID</u>, Name, *Department*, MaxHours, StartDate, EndDate)
ASSIGNMENT (*<u>ProjectID</u>*, *<u>EmployeeNumber</u>*, HoursWorked)

The primary key of DEPARTMENT is DepartmentName, the primary key of EMPLOYEE is EmployeeNumber, and the primary key of PROJECT is ProjectID. In EMPLOYEE and PROJECT, Department is a foreign key referencing DepartmentName in DEPARTMENT. Again, note that a foreign key does not need to have the same name as the primary key to which it refers. The primary key of ASSIGNMENT is the composite (ProjectID, EmployeeNumber). ProjectID is also a foreign key referencing ProjectID in PROJECT, and EmployeeNumber is a foreign key referencing EmployeeNumber in EMPLOYEE.

The referential integrity constraints are:

Department in EMPLOYEE must exist in DepartmentName in DEPARTMENT

Department in PROJECT must exist in DepartmentName in DEPARTMENT

ProjectID in ASSIGNMENT must exist in ProjectID in PROJECT

EmployeeNumber in ASSIGNMENT must exist in EmployeeNumber in EMPLOYEE

The database column characteristics for these tables are shown in Figure 3-1, and sample data for these relations is shown in Figure 3-2.

In this database, each row of DEPARTMENT is potentially related to many rows of EMPLOYEE and PROJECT. Similarly, each row of PROJECT is potentially related to

---

**FIGURE 3-1**

**Database Column Characteristics**

| ColumnName | Type | Key | Required | Remarks |
|---|---|---|---|---|
| Department Name | Text(35) | Primary Key | Yes | |
| BudgetCode | Text(30) | No | Yes | |
| OfficeNumber | Text(15) | No | Yes | |
| Phone | Text(12) | No | Yes | |

**(a) DEPARTMENT Table**

| ColumnName | Type | Key | Required | Remarks |
|---|---|---|---|---|
| EmployeeNumber | AutoNumber | Primary Key | Yes | Surrogate Key |
| FirstName | Text(25) | No | Yes | |
| Last Name | Text(25) | No | Yes | |
| Department | Text(35) | No | Yes | |
| Phone | Text(12) | No | No | |
| Email | Text(100) | No | Yes | |

**(b) EMPLOYEE Table**

| ColumnName | Type | Key | Required | Remarks |
|---|---|---|---|---|
| ProjectID | Number | Primary Key | Yes | Long Integer |
| Name | Text (50) | No | Yes | |
| Department | Text (35) | Foreign Key | Yes | |
| MaxHours | Number | No | Yes | Double |
| StartDate | Date/Time | No | No | |
| EndDate | Date/Time | No | No | |

**(c) PROJECT Table**

| Column Name | Type | Key | Required | Remarks |
|---|---|---|---|---|
| ProjectID | Number | Primary Key, Foreign Key | Yes | Long Integer |
| EmployeeNumber | Number | Primary Key, Foreign Key | Yes | Long Integer |
| HoursWorked | Number | No | No | Double |

**(d) ASSIGNMENT Table**

| FIGURE 3-2 | DepartmentName | BudgetCode | OfficeNumber | Phone |
|---|---|---|---|---|
| **Sample Data** | Administration | BC-100-10 | BLDG01-300 | 360-285-8100 |
| | Legal | BC-200-10 | BLDG01-200 | 360-285-8200 |
| | Accounting | BC-300-10 | BLDG01-100 | 360-285-8300 |
| | Finance | BC-400-10 | BLDG01-140 | 360-285-8400 |
| | Human Resources | BC-500-10 | BLDG01-180 | 360-285-8500 |
| | Production | BC-600-10 | BLDG02-100 | 360-287-8600 |
| | Marketing | BC-700-10 | BLDG02-200 | 360-287-8700 |
| | Info Systems | BC-800-10 | BLDG02-270 | 360-287-8800 |

**(a) DEPARTMENT Table**

| Employee Number | FirstName | LastName | Department | Phone | Email |
|---|---|---|---|---|---|
| 1 | Mary | Jacobs | Administration | 360-285-8110 | MJacobs@WPC.com |
| 2 | Rosalie | Jackson | Administration | 360-285-8120 | RJackson@WPC.com |
| 3 | Richard | Bandalone | Legal | 360-285-8210 | RBandalone@WPC.com |
| 4 | Tom | Caruthers | Accounting | 360-285-8310 | TCaruthers@WPC.com |
| 5 | Heather | Jones | Accounting | 360-285-8320 | HJones@WPC.com |
| 6 | Mary | Abernathy | Finance | 360-285-8410 | MAbernathy@WPC.com |
| 7 | George | Smith | Human Resources | 360-285-8510 | GSmith@WPC.com |
| 8 | Tom | Jackson | Production | 360-287-8610 | TJackson@WPC.com |
| 9 | George | Jones | Production | 360-287-8620 | GJones@WPC.com |
| 10 | Ken | Numoto | Marketing | 360-287-8710 | KNumoto@WPC.com |
| 11 | James | Nestor | Info Systems | | JNestor@WPC.com |
| 12 | Rick | Brown | Info Systems | 360-287-8820 | RBrown@WPC.com |

**(b) EMPLOYEE Table**

| ProjectID | Name | Department | MaxHours | StartDate | EndDate |
|---|---|---|---|---|---|
| 1000 | 2005 Q3 Product Plan | Marketing | 135.00 | 10-MAY-05 | 15-JUN-05 |
| 1100 | 2005 Q3 Portfolio Analysis | Finance | 120.00 | 05-JUL-05 | 25-JUL-05 |
| 1200 | 2005 Q3 Tax Preparation | Accounting | 145.00 | 10-AUG-05 | 15-OCT-05 |
| 1300 | 2005 Q4 Product Plan | Marketing | 150.00 | 10-AUG-05 | 15-SEP-05 |
| 1400 | 2005 Q4 Portfolio Analysis | Finance | 140.00 | 05-OCT-05 | |

**(c) PROJECT Table**

| ProjectID | Employee Number | HoursWorked |
|---|---|---|
| 1000 | 1 | 30.0 |
| 1000 | 8 | 75.0 |
| 1000 | 10 | 55.0 |
| 1100 | 4 | 40.0 |
| 1100 | 6 | 45.0 |
| 1200 | 1 | 25.0 |
| 1200 | 2 | 20.0 |
| 1200 | 4 | 45.0 |
| 1200 | 5 | 40.0 |
| 1300 | 1 | 35.0 |
| 1300 | 8 | 80.0 |
| 1300 | 10 | 50.0 |
| 1400 | 4 | 15.0 |
| 1400 | 5 | 10.0 |
| 1400 | 6 | 27.5 |

**(d) ASSIGNMENT Table**

many rows of ASSIGNMENT, and each row of EMPLOYEE is potentially related to many rows of ASSIGNMENT.

Finally, assume the following rules, which also are called **business rules**.

- If an EMPLOYEE row is to be deleted and that row is connected to any ASSIGNMENT, the EMPLOYEE row deletion will be disallowed.
- If a PROJECT row is deleted, then all the ASSIGNMENT rows that are connected to the deleted PROJECT row also will be deleted.

The business sense of these rules is the following:

- If an EMPLOYEE row is deleted (for example, the employee is transferred), then someone must take over that employee's assignments. Thus, the application needs someone to reassign assignments before deleting the employee row.
- If a PROJECT row is deleted, then the project has been canceled, and it is unnecessary to maintain records of assignments to that project.

These rules are typical business rules. You will learn more about such rules in Chapter 5.

## "Does Not Work With MS Access SQL"

If you have completed the end-of-chapter "Access Workbench Exercises" for Chapter 1 and Chapter 2, you will recognize this database as the Wedgewood Pacific Corporation database from those exercises. You can use that database to try out the SQL commands in this chapter. However, be warned that not all standard SQL syntax works in Access.

As previously discussed, the current standard version of SQL is ANSI SQL-92 (which Microsoft refers to as ANSI-92 SQL). Access, however, uses an earlier version of the ANSI standard—Microsoft calls it ANSI-89 SQL or Microsoft Jet SQL (after the Microsoft Jet DBMS used by Access). ANSI-89 SQL differs significantly from SQL-92, and, therefore, some features of the SQL-92 language will not work in Access.[1]

In the discussion that follows, we will use "Does Not Work With MS Access SQL" sections to identify SQL commands and clauses that will not work in Access ANSI-89 SQL. We will also identify workarounds when they are available.

> **B T W**
>
> **Each DBMS implements SQL in slightly different ways. The SQL statements in this chapter will run on Microsoft SQL Server (SQL Server 2005 Express Edition was used to obtain the output shown in this chapter) and will also run on MS Access with exceptions as noted. If you are running the SQL statements on a different DBMS, you may need to make adjustments—consult the documentation for the DBMS you are using.**

[1] MS Access 2003 does contain a setting that allows you to use SQL-92 instead of the default ANSI-89 SQL. For a particular Access database, use **Tools | Options** to open the Options dialog box, and then set the *SQL Server Compatible Syntax (ANSI-92)* property on the **Tables/Queries** tab. However, very few Access users are likely to do this, and, in this chapter, we will assume that Access is running in the default ANSI-89 SQL mode.

## ▶ SQL FOR DATA DEFINITION

The SQL DDL is used to create and alter database structures, such as tables, and to insert, modify, and delete data in the tables.

Before creating tables, you must create a database. Although there is an SQL statement for creating a database, most developers use graphical tools to create databases. The tools are DBMS specific. Creating a database in MS Access was demonstrated in Chapter 1's "The Access Workbench." For Microsoft SQL Server 2005 Express Edition, see Appendix A. For MySQL, see Appendix B. For all other DBMS products, consult the documentation.[2]

The SQL **CREATE TABLE statement** is used to create table structures. The essential format of this statement is:

CREATE TABLE *NewTableName* (

    three-part column definition,

    three-part column definition,

    three-part column definition,

    optional table constraints

    . . .

    );

The parts of the three-part column definition are the column name, the column data type, and, optionally, a constraint on column values. Thus, we can restate the CREATE TABLE format as:

CREATE TABLE *NewTableName* (

    ColumnName    DataType    OptionalConstraint,

    ColumnName    DataType    OptionalConstraint,

    ColumnName    DataType    OptionalConstraint,

    . . .

    );

Column constraints we will consider in this text are **PRIMARY KEY**, **NOT NULL**, **NULL**, and **UNIQUE**. In addition to these, there is also a **CHECK** column constraint, which is discussed with the ALTER statement at the end of this chapter. Finally, the **DEFAULT** keyword (DEFAULT is not considered a column constraint) can be used to set initial values.

---

### Does Not Work With MS Access SQL

MS Access SQL does not support the UNIQUE and CHECK column constraints, nor the DEFAULT keyword. However, equivalent constraints and initial values can be set in the table Design View. See "The Access Workbench" section later in this chapter for more details.

---

Consider the SQL Create Table statements for the DEPARTMENT, EMPLOYEE and PROJECT tables shown in Figure 3-3.

---

[2]Also see David M. Kroenke, *Database Processing: Fundamentals, Design, and Implementation* 10th Edition (Upper Saddle River, NJ: Prentice Hall, 2006), Chapter 10 for information on creating databases in Oracle 9i (and it works the same way in Oracle10g), and Chapter 11 for information on creating databases in SQL Server 2000.

**FIGURE 3-3**

**SQL CREATE TABLE**
**Statements**

```
CREATE   TABLE DEPARTMENT(
         DepartmentName    Char(35)       PRIMARY KEY
         BudgetCode        Char(30)       NOT NULL,
         OfficeNumber      Char(15)       NOT NULL,
         Phone             Char(12)       NOT NULL
         );


CREATE   TABLE EMPLOYEE(
         EmployeeNumber    Int            PRIMARY KEY,
         FirstName         Char(25)       NOT NULL,
         LastName          Char(25)       NOT NULL,
         Department        Char(35)       NOT NULL DEFAULT 'Human Resources',
         Phone             Char(12)       NULL,
         Email             VarChar(100)   NOT NULL UNIQUE
         );

CREATE   TABLE PROJECT(
         ProjectID         Int            PRIMARY KEY,
         Name              Char(50)       NOT NULL,
         Department        Char(35)       NOT NULL,
         MaxHours          Numeric(8,2)   NOT NULL DEFAULT 100,
         StartDate         DateTime       NULL,
         EndDate           DateTime       NULL
         );
```

The EMPLOYEE column EmployeeNumber has an Integer (abbreviated Int) data type, and has a PRIMARY KEY column constraint. The next column, FirstName, uses a Character (signified by Char) data type and is 25 characters in length. The column constraint NOT NULL indicates that a value must be supplied when a new row is created. The fifth column, Phone, uses a Char(12) data type (to store separators between the area code, prefix, and number) with a column constraint of NULL. NULL indicates that null values are allowed, which means that a row can be created without a value for this column.

The fourth column, Department, uses the Char(35) data type, a NOT NULL column constraint, and the DEFAULT keyword to set the department value to the Human Resources department if no department value is entered when a new row is created.

The sixth and final column Email uses the VarChar(100) data type and the NOT NULL and UNIQUE column constraints. VarChar means a variable-length character data type. Thus, Email contains character data values that vary in length from row to row, and the maximum length of an Email address is 100 characters. However, if an Email address value has only 14 characters, then only 14 characters will be stored.

As implied by the existence of VarChar, Char values are of fixed length. The Char(25) definition for FirstName means that 25 characters will be stored for every value of FirstName, regardless of the length of the value entered. FirstNames will be padded with blanks to fill the 25 spaces when necessary.

You might wonder, given the apparent advantage of VarChar, why it isn't used all the time. The reason is that extra processing is required for VarChar columns. A few extra bytes are required to store the length of the value, and the DBMS must go to some trouble to arrange variable-length values in memory and on disk. Vendors of DBMS products usually provide guidelines for when to use which type, and you should check the documentation for your specific DBMS product for more information.

The UNIQUE column constraint for Email means that there cannot be any duplicated values in the Email column. This ensures that each person has a different email address.

In the PROJECT table, the MaxHours column uses the Numeric (8, 2) data type. This means that MaxHours values consist of eight decimal numbers with two numbers assumed to the right of the decimal point. The decimal point is not stored, and does not count as one of the eight. Thus, the stored value 12345 would be displayed by the DBMS as 123.45. The DEFAULT keyword is used, and DEFAULT 100 means that when a new row is created, if no value is provided for MaxHours, the DBMS is to provide the value

100.00. Note that the input value does not assume that the last two numbers are to the right of the decimal place!

---

### Does Not Work With MS Access SQL

While MS Access SQL does support a Number data type, it does not support the (m, n) extension to specify the number of digits and the number of digits to the right of the decimal place. These values can be set in the table Design View after the column is created. See "The Access Workbench" later in this chapter for more details.

---

Also in the PROJECT table, the StartDate column uses the DateTime data type. This means that StartDate values will consist of dates (and actually, with this data type we could also specify a time if we wished). Various DBMS products handle date and time values in different ways, and again you should consult the documentation for your specific DBMS product. According to the SQL standard and as shown in Figure 3-3, every SQL statement should end with a semicolon. Although some DBMS products do not require the semicolon, it is good practice to learn to provide it. Also, as a matter of style, we place the ending parenthesis and the semicolon on a line of its own. This style blocks out the table definitions for easy reading.

The four data types shown in Figure 3-3 are the basic SQL data types, but DBMS vendors have added others to their products. Figure 3-4(a), 3-4(b), and 3-4(c) show some of the data types allowed by Microsoft SQL Server, by Oracle Corporation's Oracle, and by MySQL AB's MySQL, respectively.

---

Even when MS Access reads standard SQL, the results may be a bit different. For example, MS Access converts both Char and VarChar data types to a fixed Text data type.

---

## Defining Primary Keys with Table Constraints

Although primary keys can be defined as shown Figure 3-3, we prefer to define primary keys using a table constraint. Table constraints are identified by the **CONSTRAINT** keyword, and can be used to implement various constraints. Consider the CREATE TABLE statements shown in Figure 3-5, which shows how to define the primary key of a table using a table constraint.

First, the columns of the table are defined as usual, except that the column which will be the primary key must be given the column constraint NOT NULL. After the table columns are defined, a table constraint, identified by the word CONSTRAINT, is used to create the primary key. Every table constraint has a name followed by the definition of the constraint. Note that in the DEPARTMENT table, the DepartmentName column is now labeled as NOT NULL, and that a CONSTRAINT clause has been added at

| FIGURE 3-4 |
| --- |

**Common Data Types**

| Data Type | Description |
| --- | --- |
| Binary | Binary, length 0 to 8,000 bytes. |
| Char | Character, length 0 to 8,000 bytes. |
| Datetime | 8-byte datetime, Range from January 1, 1753, through December 31, 9999, with an accuracy of three-hundredths of a second. |
| Image | Variable length binary data. Maximum length 2,147,483,647 bytes. |
| Integer | 4-byte integer, Value range from −2,147,483,648 through 2,147,483,647. |
| Money | 8-byte money. Range from −922,337,203,685,477.5808 through +922,337,203,685,477.5807, with accuracy to a ten-thousandth of a monetary unit. |
| Numeric | Decimal—can set precision and scale. Range $-10_{38} + 1$ through $10_{38} -1$. |
| Smalldatetime | 4-byte datetime. Range from January 1, 1990, through June 6, 2079, with an accuracy of one minute. |
| Smallint | 2-byte integer. Range from −32,768 through 32,767. |
| Smallmoney | 4-byte money. Range from −214,748,3648 through +214,748.3647, with accuracy to a ten-thousandth of a monetary unit. |
| Text | Variable length text, maximum length 2,147,483,648 characters. |
| Tinyint | 1-byte integer. Range from 0 through 255. |
| Varchar | Variable-length character, length 0 to 8,000 bytes. |

**(a) SQL Server**

| Data Type | Description |
| --- | --- |
| BLOB | Binary large object. Up to 4 gigabytes in length. |
| CHAR(n) | Fixed length character field of length *n*. Maximum 2,000 characters. |
| DATE | 7-byte field containing both date and time. |
| INTEGER | Whole number of length 38. |
| NUMBER(n,d) | Numeric field of length *n*, *d* places to the right of the decimal. |
| VARCHAR(n) or VARCHAR2(n) | Variable length character field up to *n* characters long. Maximum value of *n* = 4,000. |

**(b) Oracle**

| Numeric Data Type | Description |
| --- | --- |
| BIT (M) | M = 1 to 64 |
| TINYINT | −128 to 127 |
| TINYINT UNSIGNED | 0 to 255 |
| BOOLEAN | 0 = FALSE; 1 = TRUE |
| SMALLINT | −32768 to 32767 |
| SMALLINT UNSIGNED | 0 to 65535 |
| MEDIUMINT | −8388608 to 8388607 |
| MEDIUMINT UNSIGNED | 0 to 16777215 |
| INT or INTEGER | −2147483648 to 2147483647 |
| INT UNSIGNED or INTEGER UNSIGNED | 0 to 4294967295 |
| BIGINT | −9223372036854775808 to 9223372036854775807 |
| BIGINT UNSIGNED | 0 to 1844674073709551615 |
| FLOAT (P) | P = Precision = 0 to 24 |

**FIGURE 3-4** *(Continued)*

| | |
|---|---|
| FLOAT (M, D) | Small (single-precision) floating point number:<br>M = Display width,<br>D = Number of significant digits |
| DOUBLE (M, B) | Normal (double-precision) floating point number:<br>M = display width,<br>B = Precision = (25 to 53) |
| DEC (M[,D]) or<br>DECIMAL (M[,D]) or<br>FIXED (M[,D]) | Fixed-point number:<br>M = Total number of digits,<br>D = Number of decimals |

| Date and Time Data Types | Description |
|---|---|
| DATE | YYYY-MM-DD<br>1000-01-01 to 9999-12-31 |
| DATETIME | YYYY-MM-DD HH:MM:SS<br>1000-01-01 00:00:00 to<br>9999-12-31 23:59:59 |
| TIMESTAMP | See documentation |
| TIME | HH:MM:SS<br>00:00:00 to 23:59:59 |
| YEAR (M) | M = 2 or 4 (default)<br>IF 2 = 1970 to 2069 (70 to 60)<br>IF 4 = 1901 to 2155 |

| String Data Types | Description |
|---|---|
| CHAR (M) | M = 0 to 255 |
| VARCHAR (M) | M = 1 to 255 |
| BLOB (M) | BLOB = Binary Large Object<br>Maximum 65535 characters |
| TEXT (M) | Maximum 65535 characters |
| TINYBLOB | See documentation |
| MEDIUMBLOB | See documentation |
| LONGBLOB | See documentation |
| TINYTEXT | See documentation |
| MEDIUMTEXT | See documentation |
| LONGTEXT | See documentation |
| ENUM ('value1', 'value2',. . . ) | An enumeration. Only one value,<br>but chosen form list.<br>See documentation |
| SET ('value1', 'value2',. . . ) | A set. Zero or more values, all<br>chosen from list.<br>See documentation |

### (c) MySQL

the end of the table definition. The constraint is named DEPARTMENT_PK, and it is defined by the keywords PRIMARY KEY(DepartmentName). The constraint name is selected by the developer, and the only naming restriction is that the constraint name must be unique in the database. Usually a standard naming convention is used. In this text, we name primary key constraints using the name of the table followed by an underscore and the letters *PK* (TABLENAME_PK).

Defining primary keys using table constraints offers three advantages. First, it is required for defining composite keys because the PRIMARY KEY column constraint

**FIGURE 3-5**

**Creating Primary Keys with Table Constraints**

```
CREATE   TABLE DEPARTMENT(
        DepartmentName    Char(35)        NOT NULL,
        BudgetCode        Char(30)        NOT NULL,
        OfficeNumber      Char(15)        NOT NULL,
        Phone             Char(12)        NOT NULL
        CONSTRAINT        DEPARTMENT_PK   PRIMARY KEY(DepartmentName)
        );

CREATE   TABLE EMPLOYEE(
        EmployeeNumber    Int             NOT NULL IDENTITY (1, 1),
        FirstName         Char(25)        NOT NULL,
        LastName          Char(25)        NOT NULL,
        Department        Char(35)        NOT NULL DEFAULT 'Human Resources',
        Phone             Char(12)        NULL,
        Email             VarChar(100)    NOT NULL UNIQUE,
        CONSTRAINT        EMPLOYEE_PK     PRIMARY KEY(EmployeeNumber),
        );

CREATE   TABLE PROJECT (
        ProjectID         Int             NOT NULL IDENTITY (1000, 100),
        Name              Char(50)        NOT NULL,
        Department        Char(35)        NOT NULL,
        MaxHours          Numeric(8,2)    NOT NULL DEFAULT 100,
        StartDate         DateTime        NULL,
        EndDate           DateTime        NULL,
        CONSTRAINT        PROJECT_PK      PRIMARY KEY(ProjectID),
        );

CREATE   TABLE ASSIGNMENT (
        ProjectID         Int             NOT NULL,
        EmployeeNumber    Int             NOT NULL,
        HoursWorked       Numeric(6,2)    NULL,
        CONSTRAINT        ASSIGNMENT_PK   PRIMARY KEY(ProjectID, EmployeeNumber),
        );
```

cannot be used on more than one column. It is not possible to declare the primary key of the ASSIGNMENT table using the technique in Figure 3-3, but Figure 3-5 (which now includes the ASSIGNMENT table) illustrates the declaration of the primary key ASSIGN-MENT_PK as PRIMARY KEY(ProjectID, EmployeeNumber). The second advantage is that by using table constraints, the developer is able to choose the name of the constraint that defines the primary key. Controlling the name of the constraint has advantages for administering the database, as you will see later when we discuss the DROP statement.

Finally, using a table constraint to define the primary key allows us to define easily surrogate keys in some DBMS products. Notice that in Figure 3-5, the EmployeeNumber column definition in EMPLOYEE and the ProjectID column definition in PROJECT now include the phrase **IDENTITY (M,N)**. This illustrates how surrogate keys are defined in Microsoft SQL Server. The keyword IDENTITY indicates that this is a surrogate key that will start a value M for the first row created and increase by increment N as each additional row is created. Thus, EmployeeNumber will start with the number 1 and increase by an increment of 1 (i.e., 1, 2, 3, 4, 5,. . . ). ProjectID will start with the number 1000 and increase by 100 (i.e., 1000, 1100, 1200,. . . ). The exact techniques used to

---

### Does Not Work With MS Access SQL

While MS Access SQL does support an AutoNumber data type, it *always* starts at 1 and increments by 1. Any other numbering system must be supported manually or by application code. Further, AutoNumber *cannot* be used as an SQL data type, but must be set manually after the table is created.

define surrogate key sequences vary extensively from DBMS to DBMS so consult the documentation for your specific product.

## Defining Foreign Keys with the Table Constraints

You may have noticed that none of the tables in Figure 3-3 or Figure 3-5 included any foreign key columns. We also can use table constraints to define foreign keys and their associated referential integrity constraints. Figure 3-6 shows the final SQL code for our tables, complete with the foreign key constraints.

EMPLOYEE has a table constraint named EMP_DEPART_FK that defines the foreign key relationship between the Department column in EMPLOYEE and the DepartmentName column in DEPARTMENT.

Notice the phrase ON UPDATE CASCADE. The **ON UPDATE** phrase shows what action should be taken if a value of the primary key DepartmentName in DEPARTMENT changes. The keyword **CASCADE** means that the same change should be made to the related Department column in EMPLOYEE. This means that if a department name *Marketing* is changed to *Sales and Marketing*, then the foreign key values should be updated to reflect this change. Since DepartmentName is not a surrogate key, the values could be changed and setting ON UPDATE CASCADE is reasonable.

**FIGURE 3-6**

**Creating Foreign Keys with Table Constraints**

```
CREATE   TABLE DEPARTMENT(
        DepartmentName   Char(35)         NOT NULL,
        BudgetCode       Char(30)         NOT NULL,
        OfficeNumber     Char(15)         NOT NULL,
        Phone            Char(12)         NOT NULL
        CONSTRAINT       DEPARTMENT_PK    PRIMARY KEY(DepartmentName)
        );

CREATE   TABLE EMPLOYEE(
        EmployeeNumber   Int              NOT NULL IDENTITY (1, 1),
        FirstName        Char(25)         NOT NULL,
        LastName         Char(25)         NOT NULL,
        Department       Char(35)         NOT NULL DEFAULT 'Human Resources',
        Phone            Char(12)         NULL,
        Email            VarChar(100)     NOT NULL UNIQUE,
        CONSTRAINT       EMPLOYEE_PK      PRIMARY KEY(EmployeeNumber),
        CONSTRAINT       EMP_DEPART_FK    FOREIGN KEY(Department)
                            REFERENCES DEPARTMENT(DepartmentName)
                                ON UPDATE CASCADE
        );

CREATE   TABLE PROJECT (
        ProjectID        Int              NOT NULL IDENTITY (1000, 100),
        Name             Char(50)         NOT NULL,
        Department       Char(35)         NOT NULL,
        MaxHours         Numeric(8,2)     NOT NULL DEFAULT 100,
        StartDate        DateTime         NULL,
        EndDate          DateTime         NULL,
        CONSTRAINT       PROJECT_PK       PRIMARY KEY(ProjectID),
        CONSTRAINT       PROJ_DEPART_FK FOREIGN KEY(Department)
                            REFERENCES DEPARTMENT(DepartmentName)
                                ON UPDATE CASCADE
        );

CREATE   TABLE ASSIGNMENT (
        ProjectID        Int              NOT NULL,
        EmployeeNumber   Int              NOT NULL,
        HoursWorked      Numeric(6,2)     NULL,
        CONSTRAINT       ASSIGNMENT_PK    PRIMARY KEY(ProjectID, EmployeeNumber),
        CONSTRAINT       ASSIGN_PROJ_FK FOREIGN KEY(ProjectID)
                            REFERENCES PROJECT (ProjectID)
                                ON UPDATE NO ACTION
                                ON DELETE CASCADE,
        CONSTRAINT       ASSIGN_EMP_FK    FOREIGN KEY(EmployeeNumber)
                            REFERENCES EMPLOYEE (EmployeeNumber)
                                ON UPDATE NO ACTION
                                ON DELETE NO ACTION
        );
```

The PROJECT table has a similar foreign key relationship with DEPARTMENT, and the same logic applies, except that here there will be two types of project: completed and in-process. The business rules dealing with this situation are explored in the end-of-chapter exercises.

For the ASSIGNMENT table, there are two foreign key constraints, one to EMPLOYEE and one to PROJECT. The first one defines the constraint ASSIGN_PROJ_FK (the name is up to the developer as long as it is unique) that specifies that ProjectID in ASSIGNMENT references the ProjectID column in PROJECT. Here the ON UPDATE phrase is set to **NO ACTION**. Recall that ProjectID is a surrogate key, and, thus, will never change. In this situation, there is no need to cascade updates to the referenced primary key.

Notice that there is also an **ON DELETE** phrase, which shows what action should be taken if a row in PROJECT is deleted. Here the phrase ON DELETE CASCADE means that when a PROJECT row is deleted, all rows in ASSIGNMENT that are connected to the deleted row in PROJECT also should be deleted. Thus, when a PROJECT row is deleted, all ASSIGNMENT rows for that PROJECT row will be deleted, as well. This action implements the second business rule on page 103.

The second foreign key table constraint defines the foreign key constraint ASSIGN_EMP_FK. This constraint indicates that the EmployeeNumber column references the EmployeeNumber column of EMPLOYEE. Again, the referenced primary key is a surrogate key so the phrase ON CASCADE NO ACTION is appropriate for this constraint. The phrase ON DELETE NO ACTION indicates to the DBMS that no EMPLOYEE row deletion should be allowed if that row is connected to an ASSIGNMENT row. This declaration implements the first business rule on page 103.

Because ON DELETE NO ACTION is the default, you can omit the ON DELETE expression, and the declaration will default to no action. However, specifying it makes better documentation.[3]

Table constraints can be used for purposes other than creating primary and foreign keys. One of the most important purposes is to define constraints on data values, and we will explore defining CHECK constraints in the end-of-chapter exercises. As always, see the documentation for your DBMS for more information on this topic.

---

### Does Not Work With MS Access SQL

MS Access does completely support foreign key CONSTRAINT phrases. While the basic constraint can be created using SQL, the ON UPDATE and ON DELETE clauses cannnot. ON UPDATE and ON DELETE actions can be specified manually, and this will be discussed in "The Access Workbench" later in this chapter.

---

[3]You may be wondering why we didn't use the ON DELETE phrase with the foreign key constraints between DEPARTMENT and EMPLOYEE and between DEPARTMENT and PROJECT. After all, there will probably be business rules defining what should be done with employees and projects if a department is deleted, However, enforcing those rules will be more complex than simply using an ON DELETE statement and is beyond the scope of this book. For a full discussion, see David M. Kroenke, *Database Processing: Fundamentals, Design, and Implementation* 10th Edition (Upper Saddle River, NJ: Prentice Hall, 2006) Chapter 7.

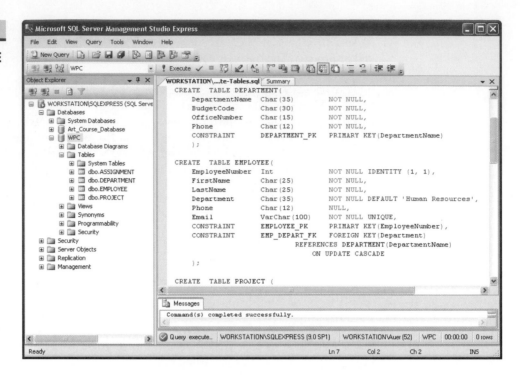

## Submitting SQL to the DBMS

After you have developed a text file with SQL statements like those in Figures 3-3, 3-5, and 3-6, you can submit them to the DBMS. The means by which this is done vary from DBMS to DBMS. With SQL Server 2005, you can type them into a query window in the Microsoft SQL Server 2005 Management Studio, or you can enter them via Visual Studio.Net. Oracle, DB2, and MySQL use other similar techniques. How to do this in MS Access is discussed in "The Access Workbench" at the end of this chapter.

Figure 3-7 shows the Microsoft SQL Server 2005 Management Studio Express windows after the SQL statements in Figure 3-6 have been entered and processed in SQL Server 2005 Express Edition.

The SQL code itself appears in a query window on the upper right, while the message "Command(s) completed successfully" in the Messages window on the lower right indicates that the SQL statements were processed correctly. The object icons representing the tables can be seen in the Object Explorer window on the left, where the name of each table is prefixed by *dbo*, which is an SQL Server convention standing for database owner.

Figure 3-8 shows the MySQL Query Browser windows after the SQL statements in Figure 3-6 [slightly modified to conform to MySQL syntax—note the AUTO_INCREMENT keyword instead of IDENTITY (1, 1)] that has been processed in MySQL.

The SQL code itself appears in a script tab window on the left, and the object icons representing the newly created tables can be seen in the Schemata window on the upper right.

---

### Does Not Work With MS Access SQL

Unlike SQL Server 2005 and My SQL, MS Access does not support SQL scripts. You can still create tables using the CREATE TABLE command and insert data using the INSERT command (discussed below), but you must do it one SQL command at a time.

---

FIGURE 3-8

**Processing the CREATE TABLE Statements Using MySQL**

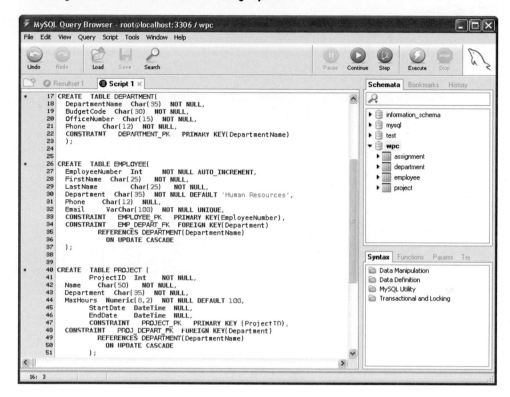

Some DBMS products can create database diagrams showing the tables and relationships in a database. We've already used the MS Access Relationships window in Chapter 2's "The Access Workbench." For SQL Server 2005, Figure 3-9 shows the WPC database structure in Microsoft SQL Server 2005 Management Studio Express.

## SQL FOR INSERTING RELATIONAL DATA

The SQL DML is used to query database and to modify data in the tables. We will first discuss using SQL to insert data into a database, then how to query the data, and finally how to change and delete the data.

There are three possible data modification operations: Insert, update, and delete. Since we need to populate our database tables, we will discuss how to insert data at this time. We will wait until later in the chapter, after we've learned some other SQL syntax that will be useful to us, to consider updating and deleting data.

### Inserting Data

Data can be added to a relation using the SQL **INSERT** command. This command has two forms, depending on whether or not data for all of the columns are supplied.

Consider the data shown in Figure 3-2(a) that will be put in the DEPARTMENT table. If the data for all columns is supplied, such as for the Administration department, then the following INSERT can be used.

**FIGURE 3-9**

**FIGURE 3-9**

**Database Diagram in SQL Server 2005 Management Studio Express**

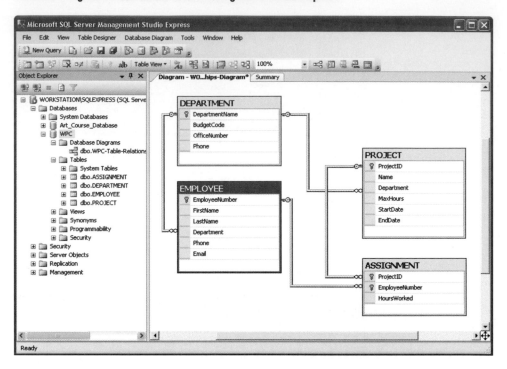

INSERT INTO DEPARTMENT VALUES('Administration',
     'BC-100-10', 'BLDG01-300', '360-285-8100');

If a surrogate key is being provided by the DBMS, then the primary key value does not need to be specified. Consider the data shown in Figure 3-2(c) that will be put in the PROJECT table. Since ProjectID is a surrogate key [specified as IDENTITY (1000, 100) in SQL Server 2005], the same type of INSERT statement can be used when data for all other columns is supplied. For example, to insert the data for the 2005 Q3 Product Plan, the following INSERT can be used:

INSERT INTO PROJECT VALUES('2005 Q3 Product Plan',
     'Marketing', 135.00, '10-MAY-05', '15-JUN-05');

Note that numbers such as that Integer and Numeric values are not enclosed in single quotes, but Char, VarChar and DateTime values are.

**B T W**

SQL is very fussy about those single quotes. It wants plain, nondirectional quotes found in basic text editors. The fancy, directional quotes produced by many word processors will produce errors. For example, the data value '2005 Q3 Product Plan' is correctly stated, but '2005 Q3 Product Plan' is not. Do you see the difference?

If data for some columns are missing, then the names of the columns for which data are provided must be listed. For example, consider the 2005 Q4 Portfolio Analysis project, which does not have an EndDate value. The correct INSERT statement for this data is:

INSERT INTO PROJECT(Name, Department, MaxHours, StartDate)
     VALUES('2005 Q4 Portfolio Analysis', 'Finance',
     140.00, '05-OCT-05');

A NULL value will be inserted for EndDate.

Three points should be made regarding the second version of the INSERT command. First, the order of the column names must match the order of the values. In the prior example, the order of the column names is Name, Department, MaxHours, StartDate, so the order of the values also must be Name, Department, MaxHours, StartDate.

**FIGURE 3-10**

**SQL INSERT Statements**

```
/*****   DEPARTMENT DATA   **************************************************/
INSERT INTO DEPARTMENT VALUES(
     'Administration', 'BC-100-10', 'BLDG01-300', '360-285-8100');
INSERT INTO DEPARTMENT VALUES(
     'Legal', 'BC-200-10', 'BLDG01-200', '360-285-8200');
INSERT INTO DEPARTMENT VALUES(
     'Accounting', 'BC-300-10', 'BLDG01-100', '360-285-8300');
INSERT INTO DEPARTMENT VALUES(
     'Finance', 'BC-400-10', 'BLDG01-140', '360-285-8400');
INSERT INTO DEPARTMENT VALUES(
     'Human Resources', 'BC-500-10', 'BLDG01-180', '360-285-8500');
INSERT INTO DEPARTMENT VALUES(
     'Production', 'BC-600-10', 'BLDG02-100', '360-287-8600');
INSERT INTO DEPARTMENT VALUES(
     'Marketing', 'BC-700-10', 'BLDG02-200', '360-287-8700');
INSERT INTO DEPARTMENT VALUES(
     'Info Systems', 'BC-800-10', 'BLDG02-270', '360-287-8800');

/*****    EMPLOYEE DATA    **************************************************/
INSERT INTO EMPLOYEE VALUES(
     'Mary', 'Jacobs', 'Administration', '360-285-8110', 'MJacobs@WPC.com');
INSERT INTO EMPLOYEE VALUES(
     'Rosalie', 'Jackson', 'Administration', '360-285-8120',
          'RJackson@WPC.com');
INSERT INTO EMPLOYEE VALUES(
     'Richard', 'Bandalone', 'Legal', '360-285-8210', 'RBanalone@WPC.com');
INSERT INTO EMPLOYEE VALUES(
     'Tom', 'Caruthers', 'Accounting', '360-285-8310',
          'TCaruthers@WPC.com');
INSERT INTO EMPLOYEE VALUES(
     'Heather', 'Jones', 'Accounting', '360-285-8320', 'HJones@WPC.com');
INSERT INTO EMPLOYEE VALUES(
     'Mary', 'Abernathy', 'Finance', '360-285-8410', 'MAbernathy@WPC.com');
INSERT INTO EMPLOYEE VALUES(
     'George', 'Smith', 'Human Resources', '360-285-8510',
          'GSmith@WPC.com');
INSERT INTO EMPLOYEE VALUES(
     'Tom', 'Jackson', 'Production', '360-287-8610', 'TJackson@WPC.com');
INSERT INTO EMPLOYEE VALUES(
     'George', 'Jones', 'Production', '360-287-8620', 'GJones@WPC.com');
INSERT INTO EMPLOYEE VALUES(
     'Ken', 'Numoto', 'Marketing', '360-287-8710', 'KMumoto@WPC.com');
```

**FIGURE 3-10  (*Continued*)**

```
INSERT INTO EMPLOYEE(FirstName, LastName, Department, Email)
      VALUES(
      'James', 'Nestor', 'Info Systems', 'JNestor@WPC.com');
INSERT INTO EMPLOYEE VALUES(
      'Rick', 'Brown', 'Info Systems', '360-287-8820', 'RBrown@WPC.com');


/*****   PROJECT DATA    *****************************************************/

INSERT INTO PROJECT VALUES(
      '2005 Q3 Product Plan', 'Marketing', 135.00, '10-MAY-05', '15-JUN-05');
INSERT INTO PROJECT VALUES(
      '2005 Q3 Portfolio Analysis', 'Finance', 120.00, '05-JUL-05',
         '25-JUL-05' );
INSERT INTO PROJECT VALUES(
      '2005 Q3 Tax Preparation', 'Accounting', 145.00, '10-AUG-05',
         '15-OCT-05');
INSERT INTO PROJECT VALUES(
      '2005 Q4 Product Plan', 'Marketing', 150.00, '10-AUG-05', '15-SEP-05');
INSERT INTO PROJECT (Name, Department, MaxHours, StartDate)
      VALUES(
      '2005 Q4 Portfolio Analysis', 'Finance', 140.00, '05-OCT-05');


/*****   ASSIGNMENT DATA    **************************************************/

INSERT INTO ASSIGNMENT VALUES(1000, 1, 30.0);
INSERT INTO ASSIGNMENT VALUES(1000, 8, 75.0);
INSERT INTO ASSIGNMENT VALUES(1000, 10, 55.0);
INSERT INTO ASSIGNMENT VALUES(1100, 4, 40.0);
INSERT INTO ASSIGNMENT VALUES(1100, 6, 45.0);
INSERT INTO ASSIGNMENT VALUES(1200, 1, 25.0);
INSERT INTO ASSIGNMENT VALUES(1200, 2, 20.0);
INSERT INTO ASSIGNMENT VALUES(1200, 4, 45.0);
INSERT INTO ASSIGNMENT VALUES(1200, 5, 40.0);
INSERT INTO ASSIGNMENT VALUES(1300, 1, 35.0);
INSERT INTO ASSIGNMENT VALUES(1300, 8, 80.0);
INSERT INTO ASSIGNMENT VALUES(1300, 10, 50.0);
INSERT INTO ASSIGNMENT VALUES(1400, 4, 15.0);
INSERT INTO ASSIGNMENT VALUES(1400, 5, 10.0);
INSERT INTO ASSIGNMENT VALUES(1400, 6, 27.5);
```

Second, although the order of the data must match the order of the column names, the order of column names does not have to match the order of the columns in the table. For example, the following insert, where Department is placed at the beginning of the column list, would also have worked:

```
INSERT INTO PROJECT(Department, Name, MaxHours, StartDate)
      VALUES('Finance', '2005 Q4 Portfolio Analysis',
      140.00, '05-OCT-05');
```

Finally, for the INSERT to work, values for all NOT NULL columns must be provided. We can omit the EndDate only because this column is defined as NULL.

The SQL INSERT statements needed to populate the WPC database tables created by the SQL CREATE TABLE statements in Figure 3-6 are shown in Figure 3-10. Note that the order in which the tables are populated does matter because of the foreign key referential integrity constraints.

---

**B T W**

Oracle and MySQL both handle surrogate keys in their own ways. Oracle uses Sequences (see the Oracle documentation), and MySQL treats the AUTO_INCREMENT value as a missing value so that you have to list all the other column names (see the MySQL documentation).

# ► SQL FOR RELATIONAL QUERY

After the tables have been defined and populated, you can use SQL DML to query data in many ways. You can also use it to change and delete data, but the SQL statements for these activities will be easier to learn if we begin with the query statements. For the following discussion, assume that the sample data shown in Figure 3-2 have been entered into the database.

## The SQL SELECT/FROM/WHERE Framework

The basic SQL framework for querying a single table in a database uses the SQL **SELECT command with FROM and WHERE clauses**.

SELECT      ColumnNames

FROM       TableName

WHERE     SomeConditionExists;

We will use and expand this framework as we work through examples in the following sections. All the examples will use the data in Figure 3-2 as the basis for the results of the queries.

## Reading Specified Columns from a Single Table

The following SQL statement will query (read) three of the six columns of the PROJECT table:

SELECT      Name, Department, MaxHours

FROM       PROJECT;

Notice that the names of the columns to be queried follow the keyword SELECT, and the name of the relation to use follows the keyword FROM. The result of this statement is:

| | Name | Department | MaxHours |
|---|---|---|---|
| 1 | 2005 Q3 Product Plan | Marketing | 135.00 |
| 2 | 2005 Q3 Portfolio Analysis | Finance | 120.00 |
| 3 | 2005 Q3 Tax Preparation | Accounting | 145.00 |
| 4 | 2005 Q4 Product Plan | Marketing | 150.00 |
| 5 | 2005 Q4 Portfolio Analysis | Finance | 140.00 |

To show you how the results look in actual DBMS management tools, Figure 3-11(a) shows the query as executed in SQL Server 2005 Express, and Figure 3-11(b) shows the query as executed in MySQL.

The result of an SQL SELECT statement is a relation. This is always true for SELECT statements. They start with one or more relations, manipulate them in some way, and then produce a relation. Even if the result of the manipulation is a single number, that number is considered to be a relation with one row and one column.

The order of the column names after the keyword SELECT determines the order of the columns in the resulting table. Thus, if we change the order of columns in the previous SELECT statement to:

SELECT      Name, MaxHours, Department

FROM       PROJECT;

FIGURE 3-11

SQL Query Results

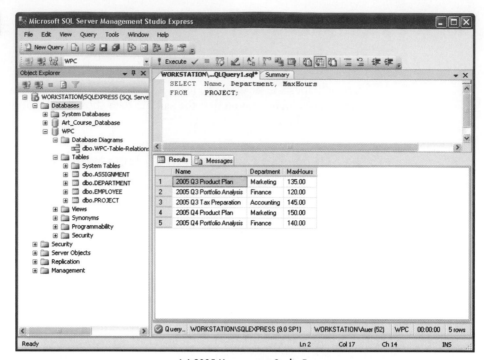

(a) 2005 Management Studio Express

(b) MySQL Query Browser

The result will be:

| | Name | MaxHours | Department |
|---|---|---|---|
| 1 | 2005 Q3 Product Plan | 135.00 | Marketing |
| 2 | 2005 Q3 Portfolio Analysis | 120.00 | Finance |
| 3 | 2005 Q3 Tax Preparation | 145.00 | Accounting |
| 4 | 2005 Q4 Product Plan | 150.00 | Marketing |
| 5 | 2005 Q4 Portfolio Analysis | 140.00 | Finance |

The next SQL statement obtains only the Department column from the PROJECT table.

SELECT      Department

FROM        PROJECT;

The result is:

| | Department |
|---|---|
| 1 | Marketing |
| 2 | Finance |
| 3 | Accounting |
| 4 | Marketing |
| 5 | Finance |

Notice that the first and fourth rows as well as the second and last rows of this table are duplicates. According to the definition of relation given in Chapter 2, such duplicate rows are prohibited. However, as also mentioned in Chapter 2, the process of checking for and eliminating duplicate rows is time-consuming. Therefore, by default, DBMS products do not check for duplication. Thus, in practice, duplicate rows can occur.

If the developer wants the DBMS to check for and eliminate duplicate rows, he or she must use the DISTINCT keyword as follows.

SELECT      DISTINCT Department

FROM        PROJECT;

The result of this statement is:

| | Department |
|---|---|
| 1 | Accounting |
| 2 | Finance |
| 3 | Marketing |

The duplicate rows have been eliminated as desired.

## Reading Specified Rows from a Single Table

In the previous SQL statements, we selected certain columns for all rows of a table. SQL statements also can be used for the reverse; that is, they can be used to select all the columns for certain rows. The rows to be selected are specified by using the SQL WHERE clause. For example, the following SQL statement will obtain all the columns of the PROJECT table for projects sponsored by the Finance department.

SELECT      ProjectID, Name, Department, MaxHours,

            StartDate, EndDate

FROM        PROJECT

WHERE     Department = 'Finance';

The result is:

| | ProjectID | Name | Department | MaxHours | StartDate | EndDate |
|---|---|---|---|---|---|---|
| 1 | 1100 | 2005 Q3 Portfolio Analysis | Finance | 120.00 | 2005-07-05 | 2005-07-25 |
| 2 | 1400 | 2005 Q4 Portfolio Analysis | Finance | 140.00 | 2005-10-05 | NULL |

---

**B T W**

The specific treatment of data and time values varies widely among DBMS products. Note that we input the StartDate for ProjectID 1100 as 05-JUL-05 (DD-MMM-YY) but the output above shows it as 2005-07-05 (YYYY-MM-DD). In fact, the StartDate value above is actually 2005-07-05 00:00:00:0000—a combination of the input date and time (since we didn't input a time, it shows up as all zeros). Since we don't care about the time, it is not displayed in the results in this book, but it may show up in actual DBMS output. As always, see the documentation for your DBMS product.

---

A second way to specify all the columns of a table is to use an asterisk (*) after the keyword SELECT. The following SQL statement is equivalent to the previous one.

SELECT          *

FROM          PROJECT

WHERE          Department = 'Finance';

The result is a table of all the columns of PROJECT for rows having a Department value of Finance:

| | ProjectID | Name | Department | MaxHours | StartDate | EndDate |
|---|---|---|---|---|---|---|
| 1 | 1100 | 2005 Q3 Portfolio Analysis | Finance | 120.00 | 2005-07-05 | 2005-07-25 |
| 2 | 1400 | 2005 Q4 Portfolio Analysis | Finance | 140.00 | 2005-10-05 | NULL |

As previously stated, the pattern SELECT/FROM/WHERE is the fundamental pattern of SQL SELECT statements. Many different conditions can be placed in a WHERE clause. For example, the query:

SELECT          *

FROM          PROJECT

WHERE          MaxHours > 135;

selects all columns from PROJECT where the value of the MaxHours column is greater than 135. The result is:

| | ProjectID | Name | Department | MaxHours | StartDate | EndDate |
|---|---|---|---|---|---|---|
| 1 | 1200 | 2005 Q3 Tax Preparation | Accounting | 145.00 | 2005-08-10 | 2005-10-15 |
| 2 | 1300 | 2005 Q4 Product Plan | Marketing | 150.00 | 2005-08-10 | 2005-09-15 |
| 3 | 1400 | 2005 Q4 Portfolio Analysis | Finance | 140.00 | 2005-10-05 | NULL |

Notice that when the column data type is Char or VarChar, comparison values must be placed in single quotes. If the column is Integer or Numeric, no quotes are necessary. Thus, we use the notation Department = 'Finance' for a WHERE condition of the VarChar column Department, but we use the notation MaxHours = 100 for the Numeric column MaxHours.

Values placed in quotations are case sensitive. WHERE Department = 'Finance' and WHERE Department = 'FINANCE' are not the same.

More than one condition can be placed in a WHERE clause by using the keyword AND as follows.

```
SELECT      *
FROM        PROJECT
WHERE       Department = 'Finance' AND MaxHours > 135;
```

The result of this statement is:

| | ProjectID | Name | Department | MaxHours | StartDate | EndDate |
|---|---|---|---|---|---|---|
| 1 | 1400 | 2005 Q4 Portfolio Analysis | Finance | 140.00 | 2005-10-05 | NULL |

## Reading Specified Columns and Specified Rows from a Single Table

We can combine the techniques just shown to select some columns and some rows from a table. For example, to obtain only the FirstName, LastName, Phone and Department values of employees in the accounting department, we use:

```
SELECT      FirstName, LastName, Phone, Department
FROM        EMPLOYEE
WHERE       Department ='Accounting';
```

The result is:

| | FirstName | LastName | Phone | Department |
|---|---|---|---|---|
| 1 | Tom | Caruthers | 360-285-8310 | Accounting |
| 2 | Heather | Jones | 360-285-8320 | Accounting |

We can combine two or more conditions in the WHERE clause by using the AND keyword and the OR keyword. If the **AND keyword** is used, only rows meeting *all* the conditions will be selected. If the **OR keyword** is used, rows meeting *any* of the conditions will be selected.

For example, the following query uses the AND keyword to ask for employees that work in Accounting *and* have the phone number 360-285-8310:

```
SELECT      FirstName, LastName, Phone, Department
FROM        EMPLOYEE
WHERE       Department ='Accounting'
            AND Phone = '360-285-8310';
```

The result is:

| | FirstName | LastName | Phone | Department |
|---|---|---|---|---|
| 1 | Tom | Caruthers | 360-285-8310 | Accounting |

On the other hand, this query uses the OR keyword to ask for employees that work in Accounting *or* have the phone number 360-285-8410:

SELECT      FirstName, LastName, Phone, Department

FROM        EMPLOYEE

WHERE       Department ='Accounting'

            OR Phone = '360-285-8410';

The result is:

|   | FirstName | LastName | Phone | Department |
|---|-----------|----------|-------|------------|
| 1 | Tom | Caruthers | 360-285-8310 | Accounting |
| 2 | Heather | Jones | 360-285-8320 | Accounting |
| 3 | Mary | Abernathy | 360-285-8410 | Finance |

Another use of the WHERE clause is to specify that a column should have one of a set of values by using the **IN keyword** as follows.

SELECT      FirstName, LastName, Phone, Department

FROM        EMPLOYEE

WHERE       Department IN ('Accounting', 'Finance',

            'Marketing');

In this query, a row will be displayed if it has a Department value equal to Accounting, Finance, or Marketing. The result is:

|   | FirstName | LastName | Phone | Department |
|---|-----------|----------|-------|------------|
| 1 | Tom | Caruthers | 360-285-8310 | Accounting |
| 2 | Heather | Jones | 360-285-8320 | Accounting |
| 3 | Mary | Abernathy | 360-285-8410 | Finance |
| 4 | Ken | Numoto | 360-287-8710 | Marketing |

To select rows that do not have a Department value with any of these, we would use the **NOT IN keywords** as follows.

SELECT      FirstName, LastName, Phone, Department

FROM        EMPLOYEE

WHERE       Department NOT IN ['Accounting', 'Finance',

            'Marketing'];

The result of this query is:

| | FirstName | LastName | Phone | Department |
|---|---|---|---|---|
| 1 | Mary | Jacobs | 360-285-8110 | Administration |
| 2 | Rosalie | Jackson | 360-285-8120 | Administration |
| 3 | Richard | Bandalone | 360-285-8210 | Legal |
| 4 | George | Smith | 360-285-8510 | Human Resources |
| 5 | Tom | Jackson | 360-287-8610 | Production |
| 6 | George | Jones | 360-287-8620 | Production |
| 7 | James | Nestor | NULL | Info Systems |
| 8 | Rick | Brown | 360-287-8820 | Info Systems |

Notice the essential difference between IN and NOT IN. When using IN, the column may equal *any* of the values in the list. When using NOT IN, the column must not be equal to *all* the values in the list.

## Ranges, Wildcards, and Nulls in WHERE Clauses

WHERE clauses also can refer to ranges of values and partial values. The BETWEEN keyword is used for ranges of values. For example, the statement:

SELECT     FirstName, LastName, Phone, Department

FROM       EMPLOYEE

WHERE     EmployeeNumber BETWEEN 2 AND 5;

| | FirstName | LastName | Phone | Department |
|---|---|---|---|---|
| 1 | Rosalie | Jackson | 360-285-8120 | Administration |
| 2 | Richard | Bandalone | 360-285-8210 | Legal |
| 3 | Tom | Caruthers | 360-285-8310 | Accounting |
| 4 | Heather | Jones | 360-285-8320 | Accounting |

will produce the following result.

This statement is equivalent to the following query, which uses the SQL **comparison operators** >= (greater than or equal to) and <= (less than or equal to):

SELECT     Name, Department

FROM       EMPLOYEE

WHERE     EmployeeNumber >= 2

              AND EmployeeNumber <= 5;

Thus, the end values of BETWEEN (here 2 and 5) are included in the selected range. The set of SQL comparison operators is shown in Figure 3-12. You can use any of them when creating WHERE clauses.

| | Operator | Indicates |
|---|---|---|
| **FIGURE 3-12** | = | Equal to |
| | > | Greater than |
| **SQL Comparison Operators** | < | Less than |
| | >= | Greater than or equal to |
| | <= | Less than or equal to |
| | <> | Not equal to |

The **LIKE keyword** is used in SQL expressions to select partial values. It is used with **wildcard characters**, which represent unknown characters in a pattern. The SQL wildcard characters are the **underscore symbol (_)**, which represents a single, unspecified character, and the **percent sign (%)**, which is used to represent a series of one or more unspecified characters.

In the following query, LIKE is used with the underscore symbol to find values that fit a pattern:

```
SELECT      *
FROM        PROJECT
WHERE       Name LIKE '2005 Q_ Portfolio Analysis';
```

The underscore means that any character can occur in the spot occupied by the underscore. The result of this statement is:

| | ProjectID | Name | Department | MaxHours | StartDate | EndDate |
|---|---|---|---|---|---|---|
| 1 | 1100 | 2005 Q3 Portfolio Analysis | Finance | 120.00 | 2005-07-05 | 2005-07-25 |
| 2 | 1400 | 2005 Q4 Portfolio Analysis | Finance | 140.00 | 2005-10-05 | NULL |

One underscore is used for each unknown character. To find all employees who have a Phone value that begins with 360-287-, we can use four underscores to represent any last four digits as follows.

```
SELECT      *
FROM        EMPLOYEE
WHERE       Phone LIKE '360-287-____';
```

The result is:

| | EmployeeNumber | FirstName | LastName | Department | Phone | Email |
|---|---|---|---|---|---|---|
| 1 | 8 | Tom | Jackson | Production | 360-287-8610 | TJackson@WPC.com |
| 2 | 9 | George | Jones | Production | 360-287-8620 | GJones@WPC.com |
| 3 | 10 | Ken | Numoto | Marketing | 360-287-8710 | KMumoto@WPC.com |
| 4 | 12 | Rick | Brown | Info Systems | 360-287-8820 | RBrown@WPC.com |

Since the percent sign represents one or more unknown characters, another way to write the query for employees having a phone number starting with 360-287- is the following.

```
SELECT      *
FROM        EMPLOYEE
WHERE       Phone LIKE '360-287-%';
```

The result is the same as in the previous example:

| | EmployeeNumber | FirstName | LastName | Department | Phone | Email |
|---|---|---|---|---|---|---|
| 1 | 8 | Tom | Jackson | Production | 360-287-8610 | TJackson@WPC.com |
| 2 | 9 | George | Jones | Production | 360-287-8620 | GJones@WPC.com |
| 3 | 10 | Ken | Numoto | Marketing | 360-287-8710 | KMumoto@WPC.com |
| 4 | 12 | Rick | Brown | Info Systems | 360-287-8820 | RBrown@WPC.com |

If we want to find all the employees who work in departments that end in *ing*, we could use the % character as follows.

```
SELECT      *
FROM        EMPLOYEE
WHERE       Department LIKE '%ing';
```

The result is:

| | EmployeeNumber | FirstName | LastName | Department | Phone | Email |
|---|---|---|---|---|---|---|
| 1 | 4 | Tom | Caruthers | Accounting | 360-285-8310 | TCaruthers@WPC.com |
| 2 | 5 | Heather | Jones | Accounting | 360-285-8320 | HJones@WPC.com |
| 3 | 10 | Ken | Numoto | Marketing | 360-287-8710 | KMumoto@WPC.com |

---

**B T W**

The NOT keyword, which we used previously as part of the NOT IN construction, can also be used with LIKE to form NOT LIKE phrases. For example, if we want to find all the employees who work in departments that do *not* end in *ing*, we could use the following SQL query:

```
SELECT      *
FROM        EMPLOYEE
WHERE       Department NOT LIKE '%ing';
```

---

**Does Not Work With MS Access SQL**

MS Access uses wildcards, but not the SQL-92 standard wildcards. MS Access uses a question mark (?) instead of an underscore to represent single characters, and an asterisk (*) instead of a percent sign to represent multiple characters. These symbols have their roots in the Microsoft MS-DOS operating system, where they appeared as equivalent wildcard characters.

Furthermore, MS Access can sometimes be fussy about stored trailing spaces in a text field. You may have problems with a WHERE clause like:

```
WHERE       Name LIKE '2005 Q? Portfolio Analysis';
```

But the clause will work if you use a trailing asterisk (*), which allows for the trailing spaces:

```
WHERE       Name LIKE '2005 Q? Portfolio Analysis*';
```

---

Another useful SQL keyword is the **IS NULL keyword**, which can be used in a WHERE clause to search for null values. The following SQL will find the names and departments of all employees having a null value for Phone.

SELECT      FirstName, LastName, Phone, Department

FROM        EMPLOYEE

WHERE      Phone IS NULL;

The result of this query is:

| | FirstName | LastName | Phone | Department |
|---|---|---|---|---|
| 1 | James | Nestor | NULL | Info Systems |

---

**B T W**

The NOT keyword can also be used with IS NULL to form IS NOT NULL phrases. For example, if we want to find all the employees who *do* have phone numbers, we could use the following SQL query:

SELECT      FirstName, LastName, Phone, Department

FROM        EMPLOYEE

WHERE      Phone IS NOT NULL;

---

## Sorting the Results

The order of rows in the result of a SELECT statement is somewhat arbitrary. If this is undesirable, the **ORDER BY clause** can be used to sort the rows. For example, the following will display the names, phone numbers, and departments of all employees sorted by Department:

SELECT      FirstName, LastName, Phone, Department

FROM        EMPLOYEE

ORDER BY   Department;

The result is:

| | FirstName | LastName | Phone | Department |
|---|---|---|---|---|
| 1 | Tom | Caruthers | 360-285-8310 | Accounting |
| 2 | Heather | Jones | 360-285-8320 | Accounting |
| 3 | Mary | Jacobs | 360-285-8110 | Administration |
| 4 | Rosalie | Jackson | 360-285-8120 | Administration |
| 5 | Mary | Abernathy | 360-285-8410 | Finance |
| 6 | George | Smith | 360-285-8510 | Human Resources |
| 7 | James | Nestor | NULL | Info Systems |
| 8 | Rick | Brown | 360-287-8820 | Info Systems |
| 9 | Richard | Bandalone | 360-285-8210 | Legal |
| 10 | Ken | Numoto | 360-287-8710 | Marketing |
| 11 | Tom | Jackson | 360-287-8610 | Production |
| 12 | George | Jones | 360-287-8620 | Production |

By default, SQL will sort in ascending order. The **ASC keyword** and **DESC keyword** can be used to specify ascending and descending order when necessary. Thus, to sort employees in descending order by Department, use:

SELECT      FirstName, LastName, Phone, Department

FROM        EMPLOYEE

ORDER BY    Department DESC;

The result is:

| | FirstName | LastName | Phone | Department |
|----|-----------|----------|-------------|------------------|
| 1 | Tom | Jackson | 360-287-8610 | Production |
| 2 | George | Jones | 360-287-8620 | Production |
| 3 | Ken | Numoto | 360-287-8710 | Marketing |
| 4 | Richard | Bandalone | 360-285-8210 | Legal |
| 5 | James | Nestor | NULL | Info Systems |
| 6 | Rick | Brown | 360-287-8820 | Info Systems |
| 7 | George | Smith | 360-285-8510 | Human Resources |
| 8 | Mary | Abernathy | 360-285-8410 | Finance |
| 9 | Mary | Jacobs | 360-285-8110 | Administration |
| 10 | Rosalie | Jackson | 360-285-8120 | Administration |
| 11 | Tom | Caruthers | 360-285-8310 | Accounting |
| 12 | Heather | Jones | 360-285-8320 | Accounting |

Two or more columns also can be used for sorting purposes. To sort the employee names and departments first in descending value of Department and then within Department by ascending value of Name, we would specify:

SELECT      FirstName, LastName, Phone, Department

FROM        EMPLOYEE

ORDER BY    Department DESC, LastName ASC;

The result is:

| | FirstName | LastName | Phone | Department |
|----|-----------|----------|-------------|------------------|
| 1 | Tom | Jackson | 360-287-8610 | Production |
| 2 | George | Jones | 360-287-8620 | Production |
| 3 | Ken | Numoto | 360-287-8710 | Marketing |
| 4 | Richard | Bandalone | 360-285-8210 | Legal |
| 5 | Rick | Brown | 360-287-8820 | Info Systems |
| 6 | James | Nestor | NULL | Info Systems |
| 7 | George | Smith | 360-285-8510 | Human Resources |
| 8 | Mary | Abernathy | 360-285-8410 | Finance |
| 9 | Rosalie | Jackson | 360-285-8120 | Administration |
| 10 | Mary | Jacobs | 360-285-8110 | Administration |
| 11 | Tom | Caruthers | 360-285-8310 | Accounting |
| 12 | Heather | Jones | 360-285-8320 | Accounting |

## SQL Built-In Functions and Calculations

SQL allows you to calculate values based on the data in the tables. You can use arithmetic formulas and you can also use built-in functions. SQL includes five built-in functions: **COUNT**, **SUM**, **AVG**, **MAX**, and **MIN**. These functions operate on the results of a SELECT statement. COUNT works regardless of column data type, but SUM, AVG, MAX, and MIN operate only on integer, numeric, and other number-oriented columns.

COUNT and SUM sound similar but are different. COUNT counts the number of rows in the result, while SUM totals the set of values of a numeric column. Thus, the following SQL statement will count the number of rows in the PROJECT table.

SELECT       COUNT(*)

FROM         PROJECT;

The result of this statement is the following relation:

| | (No column name) |
|---|---|
| 1 | 5 |

As stated earlier, the result of a SQL SELECT statement is always a relation. If, as is the case here, the result is a single number, that number is considered to be a relation that has only a single row and a single column.

Note that this result has no column name. A column name can be assigned to the result using the AS keyword:

SELECT       COUNT(*) AS NumberOfProjects

FROM         PROJECT;

Now the resulting number is identified by the column title:

| | NumberOfProjects |
|---|---|
| 1 | 5 |

Consider the following two SELECT statements.

SELECT       COUNT(Department) AS NumberOfDepartments

FROM         PROJECT;

and

SELECT       COUNT(DISTINCT Department) AS NumberOfDepartments

FROM         PROJECT;

The result of the first statement is the relation:

| | NumberOfDepartments |
|---|---|
| 1 | 5 |

and the result of the second is:

| | NumberOfDepartments |
|---|---|
| 1 | 3 |

The difference in answers occurs because duplicate rows were eliminated in the count of the departments in the second SELECT.

---

### Does Not Work With MS Access SQL

MS Access does not support the DISTINCT keyword as part of the COUNT expression, so while the first SQL command [with COUNT (Department)] will work, the second [with COUNT (DISTINCT Department)] will fail.

---

Another example of built-in functions is the following.

SELECT      MIN(MaxHours) AS MinmumMaxHours,

               MAX(MaxHours) AS MaximumMaxHours,

               SUM(MaxHours) AS TotalMaxHours

FROM        PROJECT

WHERE     ProjectID <= 1200;

The result is:

| | MinimumMaxHours | MaximumMaxHours | TotalMaxHours |
|---|---|---|---|
| 1 | 120.00 | 145.00 | 400.00 |

Standard mathematical calculations can also be done in SQL. For example, suppose that all employees at Wedgewood Pacific Corporation are paid $18.50 per hour. Given that each project has a MaxHours value, we want to calculate a *maximum project cost* value for each project that is equal to MaxHours multiplied by the hour wage rate. We can calculate the needed numbers using the following query:

SELECT      ProjectID, Name, MaxHours,

               (18.50 * MaxHours) AS MaxProjectCost

FROM        PROJECT;

The result of the query, which now shows the maximum project cost for each project, is:

| | ProjectID | Name | MaxHours | MaxProjectCost |
|---|---|---|---|---|
| 1 | 1000 | 2005 Q3 Product Plan | 135.00 | 2497.5000 |
| 2 | 1100 | 2005 Q3 Portfolio Analysis | 120.00 | 2220.0000 |
| 3 | 1200 | 2005 Q3 Tax Preparation | 145.00 | 2682.5000 |
| 4 | 1300 | 2005 Q4 Product Plan | 150.00 | 2775.0000 |
| 5 | 1400 | 2005 Q4 Portfolio Analysis | 140.00 | 2590.0000 |

Note that column names cannot be mixed with built-in functions, except as in certain uses of the SQL GROUP BY clause as discussed in the next section. Thus, the following is not allowed.

~~SELECT~~     ~~MaxHours, SUM(MaxHours)~~
~~FROM~~      ~~PROJECT~~
~~WHERE~~      ~~ProjectID <= 1200;~~

SQL Server 2005 returns the following error message if you attempt to run this query:

```
Msg 8120, Level 16, State 1, Line 1
Column 'PROJECT.MaxHours' is invalid in the select list because
it is not contained in either an aggregate function or the GROUP BY clause.
```

Also, DBMS products vary in the ways in which built-in functions can be used. Generally, built-in functions cannot be used in WHERE clauses. Thus, a WHERE clause such as the following is not normally allowed:

~~SELECT~~     ~~ProjectID, MaxHours~~
~~FROM~~      ~~PROJECT~~
~~WHERE~~      ~~MaxHours < AVG(MaxHours);~~

SQL Server 2005 returns the following error message if you attempt to run this query:

```
Msg 147, Level 15, State 1, Line 1
An aggregate may not appear in the WHERE clause unless it is in a subquery
contained in a HAVING clause or a select list,
and the column being aggregated is an outer reference.
```

## Built-In Functions and Grouping

In SQL, the **GROUP BY keyword** can be used to group rows by common values. This increases the utility of built-in functions because you can now apply them to groups of rows. For example, the following statement will count the number of employees in each department.

SELECT     Department, Count(*) AS NumberOfEmployees
FROM       EMPLOYEE
GROUP BY   Department;

The result is:

|   | Department | NumberOfEmployees |
|---|------------|-------------------|
| 1 | Accounting | 2 |
| 2 | Administration | 2 |
| 3 | Finance | 1 |
| 4 | Human Resources | 1 |
| 5 | Info Systems | 2 |
| 6 | Legal | 1 |
| 7 | Marketing | 1 |
| 8 | Production | 2 |

The GROUP BY keyword tells the DBMS to sort the table by the named column and then to apply the built-in function to groups of rows having the same value of the named column. When GROUP BY is used, the name of the grouping column and built-in functions may appear in the SELECT clause. This is the *only* time that a column name and a built-in function can appear together.

We can further restrict the results by using the **HAVING clause** to apply conditions to the groups that are formed. For example, if we want to consider only groups with more than two members, we could specify:

```
SELECT     Department, Count(*) AS NumberOfEmployees
FROM       EMPLOYEE
GROUP BY   Department
HAVING     COUNT(*) > 1;
```

The result of this SQL statement is:

| | Department | NumberOfEmployees |
|---|---|---|
| 1 | Accounting | 2 |
| 2 | Administration | 2 |
| 3 | Info Systems | 2 |
| 4 | Production | 2 |

It is possible to add WHERE clauses when using GROUP BY. However, an ambiguity results when this is done. If the WHERE condition is applied before the groups are formed, we will obtain one result. If, on the other hand, the WHERE condition is applied after the groups are formed, we will get a different result. To resolve this ambiguity, the SQL standard specifies that when WHERE and GROUP BY occur together, the WHERE condition will be applied first. For example, consider the following query.

```
SELECT     Department, Count(*) AS NumberOfEmployees
FROM       EMPLOYEE
WHERE      EmployeeNumber <= 6
GROUP BY   Department
HAVING     COUNT(*) > 1;
```

In this expression, first the WHERE clause is applied to select employees with an EmployeeNumber less than or equal to 6. Then the groups are formed, and finally the HAVING condition is applied. The result is:

| | Department | NumberOfEmployees |
|---|---|---|
| 1 | Accounting | 2 |
| 2 | Administration | 2 |

## Querying Multiple Tables with Subqueries

The queries we have considered so far have involved data from a single table. However, at times more than one table must be processed to obtain the desired information. For example, suppose we want to know the names of all employees who have worked more than

40 hours on any single assignment. The names of employees are stored in the EMPLOYEE table, but the hours they have worked are stored in the ASSIGNMENT table.

If we knew that employees with EmployeeNumber 8 and 10 have worked more than 50 hours on an assignment (which is true), we could obtain their names with the following expression.

```
SELECT      FirstName, LastName
FROM        EMPLOYEE
WHERE       EmployeeNumber IN (8, 10);
```

The result is:

| | FirstName | LastName |
|---|---|---|
| 1 | Tom | Jackson |
| 2 | Ken | Numoto |

But according to the problem description, we are not given the employee numbers. We can, however, obtain the appropriate employee numbers with the following query:

```
SELECT      DISTINCT EmployeeNumber
FROM        ASSIGNMENT
WHERE       HoursWorked > 50;
```

The result is:

| | EmployeeNumber |
|---|---|
| 1 | 8 |
| 2 | 10 |

Now, we can combine these two SQL statements using what is called a **subquery** as follows.

```
SELECT      FirstName, LastName
FROM        EMPLOYEE
WHERE       EmployeeNumber IN
            (SELECT   DISTINCT EmployeeNumber
            FROM      ASSIGNMENT
            WHERE     HoursWorked > 50);
```

The result of this expression is:

| | FirstName | LastName |
|---|---|---|
| 1 | Tom | Jackson |
| 2 | Ken | Numoto |

These are indeed the names of the employees who have worked more than 50 hours on any single assignment.

Subqueries can be extended to include three, four, or even more levels. Suppose, for example, we need to know the names of employees who have worked more than 40 hours on an assignment of a project that has been sponsored by the Accounting department.

We can obtain the ProjectIDs of projects sponsored by Accounting with:

| SELECT | ProjectID |
|---|---|
| FROM | PROJECT |
| WHERE | Department = 'Accounting'; |

The result is:

| | ProjectID |
|---|---|
| 1 | 1200 |

We can obtain the EmployeeNumbers of employees working more than 40 hours on those projects with:

| SELECT | DISTINCT EmployeeNumber |
|---|---|
| FROM | ASSIGNMENT |
| WHERE | HoursWorked > 40 |
| | AND ProjectID IN |
| | (SELECT ProjectID |
| | FROM PROJECT |
| | WHERE Department = 'Accounting'); |

The result is:

| | EmployeeNumber |
|---|---|
| 1 | 4 |

Finally, we can obtain the names of the employees in the above SQL statement with:

| SELECT | Name |
|---|---|
| FROM | EMPLOYEE |
| WHERE | EmployeeNumber IN |
| | (SELECT DISTINCT EmployeeNumber |
| | FROM ASSIGNMENT |
| | WHERE ProjectID IN |
| | (SELECT ProjectID |
| | FROM PROJECT |
| | WHERE Department = 'Accounting')); |

The final result is:

| | FirstName | LastName |
|---|---|---|
| 1 | Tom | Caruthers |

## Querying Multiple Tables with Joins

Subqueries are effective for processing multiple tables as long as the results come from a single table. If, however, we need to display data from two or more tables, subqueries will not work. We need to use a **join operation** instead.

The basic idea of a join is to form a new relation by connecting the contents of two or more other relations. Consider the following example.

SELECT     FirstName, LastName, HoursWorked

FROM       EMPLOYEE, ASSIGNMENT

WHERE     EMPLOYEE.EmployeeNumber = ASSIGNMENT.EmployeeNumber;

The function of this statement is to create a new table having the two columns Name and HoursWorked. Those columns are to be taken from the EMPLOYEE and ASSIGNMENT tables under the condition that EmployeeNumber in EMPLOYEE (written in the format *TABLENAME.ColumnName* as EMPLOYEE.EmployeeNumber) equals EmployeeNumber in ASSIGNMENT (written as ASSIGNMENT.Employee Number). Whenever there is ambiguity about which table the column data is coming from, the column name is always preceded with the table name in the format *TABLENAME.ColumnName.*

---

**B T W**

This ambiguity often happens (as in this case) because the primary key and foreign key column names are the same, but can happen in other situations. For example, both EMPLOYEE and DEPARTMENT have a Phone column, but Phone is not a primary key or foreign key in either table. If we wanted to list employees with both their own phone number and their department phone number, we would have to qualify the field names as EMPLOYEE.Phone and DEPARTMENT.Phone.

---

You can think of the join operation working as follows. Start with the first row in EMPLOYEE. Using the value of EmployeeNumber in this first row (1 for the data in Figure 3-2), examine the rows in ASSIGNMENT. When you find a row in ASSIGN-MENT where EmployeeNum is also equal to 1, join FirstName and LastName of the first row of EMPLOYEE with HoursWorked from the row you just found in ASSIGNMENT.

For the data in Figure 3-2, the first row of ASSIGNMENT has EmployeeNumber equal to 1, so we join FirstName and LastName from the first row of EMPLOYEE with HoursWorked from the first row in ASSIGNMENT to form the first row of the join. The result is:

| | FirstName | LastName | HoursWorked |
|---|---|---|---|
| 1 | Mary | Jacobs | 30.00 |

Now, still using the EmployeeNumber value of 1, look for a second row in ASSIGNMENT that has EmployeeNumber equal to 1. For our data, the sixth row of

ASSIGNMENT has such a value. So, join FirstName and LastName from the first row of EMPLOYEE to HoursWorked in the sixth row of ASSIGNMENT to obtain the second row of the join as follows:

|   | FirstName | LastName | HoursWorked |
|---|-----------|----------|-------------|
| 1 | Mary | Jacobs | 30.00 |
| 2 | Mary | Jacobs | 25.00 |

Continue in this way, looking for matches for the EmployeeNumber value of 1. There is one more in the tenth row, and we would add the data for that match to obtain the result:

|   | FirstName | LastName | HoursWorked |
|---|-----------|----------|-------------|
| 1 | Mary | Jacobs | 30.00 |
| 2 | Mary | Jacobs | 25.00 |
| 3 | Mary | Jacobs | 35.00 |

At this point, no more EmployeeNumber values of 1 appear in our sample data, so now we move to the second row of EMPLOYEE, obtain the new value of Employee Number (2), and begin searching for matches for it in the rows of ASSIGNMENT. In this case, the seventh row has such a match so we add FirstName, LastName, and HoursWorked to our result to obtain:

|   | FirstName | LastName | HoursWorked |
|---|-----------|----------|-------------|
| 1 | Mary | Jacobs | 30.00 |
| 2 | Mary | Jacobs | 25.00 |
| 3 | Mary | Jacobs | 35.00 |
| 4 | Rosalie | Jackson | 20.00 |

We continue until all rows of EMPLOYEE have been examined. The final result will be:

|    | FirstName | LastName | HoursWorked |
|----|-----------|----------|-------------|
| 1  | Mary | Jacobs | 30.00 |
| 2  | Mary | Jacobs | 25.00 |
| 3  | Mary | Jacobs | 35.00 |
| 4  | Rosalie | Jackson | 20.00 |
| 5  | Tom | Caruthers | 40.00 |
| 6  | Tom | Caruthers | 45.00 |
| 7  | Tom | Caruthers | 15.00 |
| 8  | Heather | Jones | 40.00 |
| 9  | Heather | Jones | 10.00 |
| 10 | Mary | Abernathy | 45.00 |
| 11 | Mary | Abernathy | 27.50 |
| 12 | Tom | Jackson | 75.00 |
| 13 | Tom | Jackson | 80.00 |
| 14 | Ken | Numoto | 55.00 |
| 15 | Ken | Numoto | 50.00 |

Actually, that is the theoretical result. But remember that row order in an SQL query can be arbitrary. To ensure that we get the results shown on the previous page, we need to add an ORDER BY clause to the query:

SELECT      FirstName, LastName, HoursWorked

FROM        EMPLOYEE, ASSIGNMENT

WHERE       EMPLOYEE.EmployeeNumber = ASSIGNMENT.EmployeeNumber

ORDER BY    EMPLOYEE.EmployeeNumber, ProjectID;

The actual result when the original query is run in SQL Server 2005 is:

| | FirstName | LastName | HoursWorked |
|---|---|---|---|
| 1 | Mary | Jacobs | 30.00 |
| 2 | Tom | Jackson | 75.00 |
| 3 | Ken | Numoto | 55.00 |
| 4 | Tom | Caruthers | 40.00 |
| 5 | Mary | Abernathy | 45.00 |
| 6 | Mary | Jacobs | 25.00 |
| 7 | Rosalie | Jackson | 20.00 |
| 8 | Tom | Caruthers | 45.00 |
| 9 | Heather | Jones | 40.00 |
| 10 | Mary | Jacobs | 35.00 |
| 11 | Tom | Jackson | 80.00 |
| 12 | Ken | Numoto | 50.00 |
| 13 | Tom | Caruthers | 15.00 |
| 14 | Heather | Jones | 10.00 |
| 15 | Mary | Abernathy | 27.50 |

The data results are the same, but the row order is definitely different!

A join is just another table so all the earlier SQL SELECT commands are available for use. We could, for example, group the rows of the join by employee and sum the hours they worked. The SQL for such a query is the following.

SELECT      FirstName, LastName,

            SUM(HoursWorked) AS TotalHoursWorked

FROM        EMPLOYEE AS E, ASSIGNMENT AS A

WHERE       E.EmployeeNumber = A.EmployeeNumber

GROUP BY    LastName, FirstName;

Note the new use of the **AS keyword** to assign aliases to table names and the use of these aliases in the WHERE clause. This makes it much easier to write queries with long table names. The result of this query is:

| | FirstName | LastName | TotalHoursWorked |
|---|---|---|---|
| 1 | Heather | Jones | 50.00 |
| 2 | Ken | Numoto | 105.00 |
| 3 | Mary | Abernathy | 72.50 |
| 4 | Mary | Jacobs | 90.00 |
| 5 | Rosalie | Jackson | 20.00 |
| 6 | Tom | Caruthers | 100.00 |
| 7 | Tom | Jackson | 155.00 |

Or, we could apply a WHERE clause during the process of creating the join as follows.

SELECT      FirstName, LastName, HoursWorked

FROM        EMPLOYEE AS E, ASSIGNMENT AS A

WHERE       E.EmployeeNumber = A.EmployeeNumber

          AND      HoursWorked > 50;

The result of this join is:

| | FirstName | LastName | HoursWorked |
|---|---|---|---|
| 1 | Tom | Jackson | 75.00 |
| 2 | Ken | Numoto | 55.00 |
| 3 | Tom | Jackson | 80.00 |

Now, suppose we want to join PROJECT to EMPOYEE and ASSIGNMENT to show the names of the projects that the employees worked on. We can use the same SQL statement structure as before, except for one complication—now we have to use two WHERE phrases combined by an AND to join the three tables:

SELECT      Name, FirstName, LastName, HoursWorked

FROM        EMPLOYEE AS E, PROJECT AS P, ASSIGNMENT AS A

WHERE       E.EmployeeNumber = A.EmployeeNumber

          AND      P.ProjectID = A.ProjectID

ORDER BY    P.ProjectID, A.EmployeeNumber;

The result of this query is:

| | Name | FirstName | LastName | HoursWorked |
|---|---|---|---|---|
| 1 | 2005 Q3 Product Plan | Mary | Jacobs | 30.00 |
| 2 | 2005 Q3 Product Plan | Tom | Jackson | 75.00 |
| 3 | 2005 Q3 Product Plan | Ken | Numoto | 55.00 |
| 4 | 2005 Q3 Portfolio Analysis | Tom | Caruthers | 40.00 |
| 5 | 2005 Q3 Portfolio Analysis | Mary | Abernathy | 45.00 |
| 6 | 2005 Q3 Tax Preparation | Mary | Jacobs | 25.00 |
| 7 | 2005 Q3 Tax Preparation | Rosalie | Jackson | 20.00 |
| 8 | 2005 Q3 Tax Preparation | Tom | Caruthers | 45.00 |
| 9 | 2005 Q3 Tax Preparation | Heather | Jones | 40.00 |
| 10 | 2005 Q4 Product Plan | Mary | Jacobs | 35.00 |
| 11 | 2005 Q4 Product Plan | Tom | Jackson | 80.00 |
| 12 | 2005 Q4 Product Plan | Ken | Numoto | 50.00 |
| 13 | 2005 Q4 Portfolio Analysis | Tom | Caruthers | 15.00 |
| 14 | 2005 Q4 Portfolio Analysis | Heather | Jones | 10.00 |
| 15 | 2005 Q4 Portfolio Analysis | Mary | Abernathy | 27.50 |

## The SQL JOIN. . . ON Syntax

An alternative join syntax uses the **JOIN. . . ON syntax**. Consider our original query example that used a join (with the ORDER BY clause for sorting the results):

SELECT     FirstName, LastName, HoursWorked

FROM       EMPLOYEE, ASSIGNMENT

WHERE     EMPLOYEE.EmployeeNumber =
            ASSIGNMENT.EmployeeNumber

ORDER BY   EMPLOYEE.EmployeeNumber, ProjectID;

    Using the JOIN. . . ON syntax, this query would be written as:

SELECT     FirstName, LastName, HoursWorked

FROM       EMPLOYEE JOIN ASSIGNMENT

          ON     EMPLOYEE.EmployeeNumber =
                 ASSIGNMENT.EmployeeNumber

ORDER BY   EMPLOYEE.EmployeeNumber, ProjectID;

    The result of the query, as we would expect, is:

| | FirstName | LastName | HoursWorked |
|---|---|---|---|
| 1 | Mary | Jacobs | 30.00 |
| 2 | Mary | Jacobs | 25.00 |
| 3 | Mary | Jacobs | 35.00 |
| 4 | Rosalie | Jackson | 20.00 |
| 5 | Tom | Caruthers | 40.00 |
| 6 | Tom | Caruthers | 45.00 |
| 7 | Tom | Caruthers | 15.00 |
| 8 | Heather | Jones | 40.00 |
| 9 | Heather | Jones | 10.00 |
| 10 | Mary | Abernathy | 45.00 |
| 11 | Mary | Abernathy | 27.50 |
| 12 | Tom | Jackson | 75.00 |
| 13 | Tom | Jackson | 80.00 |
| 14 | Ken | Numoto | 55.00 |
| 15 | Ken | Numoto | 50.00 |

    We can also use the JOIN. . . ON syntax for joins of more than two tables. Here is the previous query to combine data for EMPLOYEE, PROJECT, and ASSIGNMENT rewritten in the JOIN. . . ON style:

SELECT     Name, FirstName, LastName,HoursWorked

FROM       EMPLOYEE AS E JOIN ASSIGNMENT AS A

          ON E.EmployeeNumber = A.EmployeeNumber

             JOIN PROJECT AS P

                ON     A.ProjectID = P.ProjectID

ORDER BY   P.ProjectID, A.EmployeeNumber;

The result, as we would expect, is the same as we obtained with the query in the previous section.

| | Name | FirstName | LastName | HoursWorked |
|---|---|---|---|---|
| 1 | 2005 Q3 Product Plan | Mary | Jacobs | 30.00 |
| 2 | 2005 Q3 Product Plan | Tom | Jackson | 75.00 |
| 3 | 2005 Q3 Product Plan | Ken | Numoto | 55.00 |
| 4 | 2005 Q3 Portfolio Analysis | Tom | Caruthers | 40.00 |
| 5 | 2005 Q3 Portfolio Analysis | Mary | Abernathy | 45.00 |
| 6 | 2005 Q3 Tax Preparation | Mary | Jacobs | 25.00 |
| 7 | 2005 Q3 Tax Preparation | Rosalie | Jackson | 20.00 |
| 8 | 2005 Q3 Tax Preparation | Tom | Caruthers | 45.00 |
| 9 | 2005 Q3 Tax Preparation | Heather | Jones | 40.00 |
| 10 | 2005 Q4 Product Plan | Mary | Jacobs | 35.00 |
| 11 | 2005 Q4 Product Plan | Tom | Jackson | 80.00 |
| 12 | 2005 Q4 Product Plan | Ken | Numoto | 50.00 |
| 13 | 2005 Q4 Portfolio Analysis | Tom | Caruthers | 15.00 |
| 14 | 2005 Q4 Portfolio Analysis | Heather | Jones | 10.00 |
| 15 | 2005 Q4 Portfolio Analysis | Mary | Abernathy | 27.50 |

---

### Does Not Work With MS Access SQL

MS Access SQL supports the JOIN. . . ON only with a keyword specifying a standard (INNER) or nonstandard (OUTER) JOIN. OUTER joins are discussed next. The example JOIN. . . ON queries will run when written with the INNER keyword as:

```
SELECT      FirstName, LastName, HoursWorked

FROM        EMPLOYEE INNER JOIN ASSIGNMENT

            ON    EMPLOYEE.EmployeeNumber =
                      ASSIGNMENT.EmployeeNumber

ORDER BY    EMPLOYEE.EmployeeNumber, ProjectID;
```

Further, MS Access requires that the joins be grouped using parentheses when three or more tables are joined:

```
SELECT      Name, FirstName, LastName,HoursWorked

FROM        (EMPLOYEE AS E INNER JOIN ASSIGNMENT AS A

            ON    E.EmployeeNumber = A.EmployeeNumber)

            INNER JOIN PROJECT AS P

                ON      A.ProjectID = P.ProjectID

ORDER BY    P.ProjectID, A.EmployeeNumber;
```

---

Let's add a new project, the 2005 Q4 Tax Preparation project run by Accounting, to the PROJECT table:

INSERT INTO PROJECT(Name, Department, MaxHours, StartDate)

VALUES('2005 Q4 Tax Preparation', 'Accounting',

175.00, '10-DEC-05');

To see the updated PROJECT table, we use the query:

SELECT * FROM PROJECT;

The results are:

| | ProjectID | Name | Department | MaxHours | StartDate | EndDate |
|---|---|---|---|---|---|---|
| 1 | 1000 | 2005 Q3 Product Plan | Marketing | 135.00 | 2005-05-10 | 2005-06-15 |
| 2 | 1100 | 2005 Q3 Portfolio Analysis | Finance | 120.00 | 2005-07-05 | 2005-07-25 |
| 3 | 1200 | 2005 Q3 Tax Preparation | Accounting | 145.00 | 2005-08-10 | 2005-10-15 |
| 4 | 1300 | 2005 Q4 Product Plan | Marketing | 150.00 | 2005-08-10 | 2005-09-15 |
| 5 | 1400 | 2005 Q4 Portfolio Analysis | Finance | 140.00 | 2005-10-05 | NULL |
| 6 | 1500 | 2005 Q4 Tax Preparation | Accounting | 175.00 | 2005-12-10 | NULL |

Now, with the new project added to PROJECT, we'll rerun the previous query on EMPLOYEE, ASSIGNMENT, and PROJECT:

SELECT      Name, FirstName, LastName, HoursWorked

FROM        EMPLOYEE AS E JOIN ASSIGNMENT AS A

               ON E.EmployeeNumber = A.EmployeeNumber

                 JOIN PROJECT AS P

                    ON     A.ProjectID = P.ProjectID

ORDER BY   P.ProjectID, A.EmployeeNumber;

The results are:

| | Name | FirstName | LastName | HoursWorked |
|---|---|---|---|---|
| 1 | 2005 Q3 Product Plan | Mary | Jacobs | 30.00 |
| 2 | 2005 Q3 Product Plan | Tom | Jackson | 75.00 |
| 3 | 2005 Q3 Product Plan | Ken | Numoto | 55.00 |
| 4 | 2005 Q3 Portfolio Analysis | Tom | Caruthers | 40.00 |
| 5 | 2005 Q3 Portfolio Analysis | Mary | Abernathy | 45.00 |
| 6 | 2005 Q3 Tax Preparation | Mary | Jacobs | 25.00 |
| 7 | 2005 Q3 Tax Preparation | Rosalie | Jackson | 20.00 |
| 8 | 2005 Q3 Tax Preparation | Tom | Caruthers | 45.00 |
| 9 | 2005 Q3 Tax Preparation | Heather | Jones | 40.00 |
| 10 | 2005 Q4 Product Plan | Mary | Jacobs | 35.00 |
| 11 | 2005 Q4 Product Plan | Tom | Jackson | 80.00 |
| 12 | 2005 Q4 Product Plan | Ken | Numoto | 50.00 |
| 13 | 2005 Q4 Portfolio Analysis | Tom | Caruthers | 15.00 |
| 14 | 2005 Q4 Portfolio Analysis | Heather | Jones | 10.00 |
| 15 | 2005 Q4 Portfolio Analysis | Mary | Abernathy | 27.50 |

The results shown here are correct, but a surprising result occurs. What happened to the new 2005 Q4 Tax Preparation project? The answer is that it does not appear in the join results because its ProjectID value of 1500 had no match in the ASSIGNMENT table. Nothing is wrong with this result; you just need to be aware that unmatched rows will not appear in the result of a join.

## Outer Joins

We just saw in the last query of the previous section that data can be lost (or at least appear to be lost) when performing a join. In particular, if a row has a value that does not match the WHERE clause condition, then that row will not be included in the join result. The 2005 Q4 Tax Preparation did not appear in the previous join because no row in ASSIGNMENT matched its ProjectID value. This kind of loss is not always desirable so a special type of join called an **outer join** was created to avoid it.

Outer joins are not part of the SQL-92 specification, but most DBMS products today support them. The specific syntax for the outer join, however, varies by DBMS product.

---

**B T W**

The original join operation we discussed early is sometimes referred to as an equijoin or inner join.

---

Consider the following example, and notice the use of the JOIN. . . ON syntax—the **LEFT keyword** is simply added into the SQL query.

```
SELECT      Name, EmployeeNumber, HoursWorked
FROM        PROJECT LEFT JOIN ASSIGNMENT
            ON PROJECT.ProjectID = ASSIGNMENT.ProjectID;
```

The purpose of this join is to append rows of PROJECT to those of ASSIGNMENT as described previously, except that if any row in the table on the *left side* of the FROM clause (in this case, PROJECT) has no match, it is included in the results anyway. The result of this query is:

| | Name | EmployeeNumber | HoursWorked |
|---|---|---|---|
| 1 | 2005 Q3 Product Plan | 1 | 30.00 |
| 2 | 2005 Q3 Product Plan | 8 | 75.00 |
| 3 | 2005 Q3 Product Plan | 10 | 55.00 |
| 4 | 2005 Q3 Portfolio Analysis | 4 | 40.00 |
| 5 | 2005 Q3 Portfolio Analysis | 6 | 45.00 |
| 6 | 2005 Q3 Tax Preparation | 1 | 25.00 |
| 7 | 2005 Q3 Tax Preparation | 2 | 20.00 |
| 8 | 2005 Q3 Tax Preparation | 4 | 45.00 |
| 9 | 2005 Q3 Tax Preparation | 5 | 40.00 |
| 10 | 2005 Q4 Product Plan | 1 | 35.00 |
| 11 | 2005 Q4 Product Plan | 8 | 80.00 |
| 12 | 2005 Q4 Product Plan | 10 | 50.00 |
| 13 | 2005 Q4 Portfolio Analysis | 4 | 15.00 |
| 14 | 2005 Q4 Portfolio Analysis | 5 | 10.00 |
| 15 | 2005 Q4 Portfolio Analysis | 6 | 27.50 |
| 16 | 2005 Q4 Tax Preparation | NULL | NULL |

Notice that the last row of this table appends a null value to the 2005 Q4 Tax Preparation project.

Right outer joins operate similarly, except that the **RIGHT keyword** is used and that rows in the table on the right-hand side of the FROM clause are included. For example, we could join all three tables together with the following right outer join.

SELECT       Name, FirstName, LastName, HoursWorked

FROM          (PROJECT AS P JOIN ASSIGNMENT AS A

            ON P.ProjectID = A.ProjectID)

                RIGHT JOIN EMPLOYEE AS E

                    ON A.EmployeeNumber = E.EmployeeNumber

ORDER BY:    P.ProjectID, A.EmployeeNumber;

The result of this join, which now shows not only the employees assigned to projects but also those employees who are *not* assigned to any projects, is:

| | Name | FirstName | LastName | HoursWorked |
|---|---|---|---|---|
| 1 | NULL | Richard | Bandalone | NULL |
| 2 | NULL | George | Smith | NULL |
| 3 | NULL | George | Jones | NULL |
| 4 | NULL | James | Nestor | NULL |
| 5 | NULL | Rick | Brown | NULL |
| 6 | 2005 Q3 Product Plan | Mary | Jacobs | 30.00 |
| 7 | 2005 Q3 Product Plan | Tom | Jackson | 75.00 |
| 8 | 2005 Q3 Product Plan | Ken | Numoto | 55.00 |
| 9 | 2005 Q3 Portfolio Analysis | Tom | Caruthers | 40.00 |
| 10 | 2005 Q3 Portfolio Analysis | Mary | Abernathy | 45.00 |
| 11 | 2005 Q3 Tax Preparation | Mary | Jacobs | 25.00 |
| 12 | 2005 Q3 Tax Preparation | Rosalie | Jackson | 20.00 |
| 13 | 2005 Q3 Tax Preparation | Tom | Caruthers | 45.00 |
| 14 | 2005 Q3 Tax Preparation | Heather | Jones | 40.00 |
| 15 | 2005 Q4 Product Plan | Mary | Jacobs | 35.00 |
| 16 | 2005 Q4 Product Plan | Tom | Jackson | 80.00 |
| 17 | 2005 Q4 Product Plan | Ken | Numoto | 50.00 |
| 18 | 2005 Q4 Portfolio Analysis | Tom | Caruthers | 15.00 |
| 19 | 2005 Q4 Portfolio Analysis | Heather | Jones | 10.00 |
| 20 | 2005 Q4 Portfolio Analysis | Mary | Abernathy | 27.50 |

---

### Does Not Work With MS Access SQL

Even with the syntax as shown below, which is what has worked before in MS Access, the error message "*Join expression not supported*" is returned when the query is run.

SELECT       Name, FirstName, LastName, HoursWorked

FROM          (PROJECT AS P INNER JOIN ASSIGNMENT AS A

            ON P.ProjectID = A.ProjectID)

                RIGHT JOIN EMPLOYEE AS E

                    ON A.EmployeeNumber = E.EmployeeNumber

ORDER BY:    P.ProjectID, A.EmployeeNumber;

## ▶ SQL FOR RELATIONAL DATA MODIFICATION AND DELETION

The SQL DDL contains commands for the three possible data modification operations: Insert, modify, and delete. We have already discussed inserting data so now we will consider modifying and deleting data.

### Modifying Data

The values of existing data can be modified using the SQL **UPDATE. . . SET command**. However, this is a powerful command that needs to be used with care. Consider the EMPLOYEE table. We can see the current data in the table using the command:

SELECT * FROM EMPLOYEE;

The current data in the EMPLOYEE table looks like this:

|    | EmployeeNumber | FirstName | LastName | Department | Phone | Email |
|----|----------------|-----------|----------|------------|-------|-------|
| 1  | 1  | Mary    | Jacobs   | Administration  | 360-285-8110 | MJacobs@WPC.com |
| 2  | 2  | Rosalie | Jackson  | Administration  | 360-285-8120 | RJackson@WPC.com |
| 3  | 3  | Richard | Bandalone| Legal           | 360-285-8210 | RBanalone@WPC.com |
| 4  | 4  | Tom     | Caruthers| Accounting      | 360-285-8310 | TCaruthers@WPC.com |
| 5  | 5  | Heather | Jones    | Accounting      | 360-285-8320 | HJones@WPC.com |
| 6  | 6  | Mary    | Abernathy| Finance         | 360-285-8410 | MAbernathy@WPC.com |
| 7  | 7  | George  | Smith    | Human Resources | 360-285-8510 | GSmith@WPC.com |
| 8  | 8  | Tom     | Jackson  | Production      | 360-287-8610 | TJackson@WPC.com |
| 9  | 9  | George  | Jones    | Production      | 360-287-8620 | GJones@WPC.com |
| 10 | 10 | Ken     | Numoto   | Marketing       | 360-287-8710 | KMumoto@WPC.com |
| 11 | 11 | James   | Nestor   | Info Systems    | NULL         | JNestor@WPC.com |
| 12 | 12 | Rick    | Brown    | Info Systems    | 360-287-8820 | RBrown@WPC.com |

Note that James Nestor (EmployeeNumber = 11) has a NULL value for his phone number. Suppose that he has just gotten a phone with phone number 360-287-8810. We can change the value of the Phone column for his data row by using the UPDATE. . . SET statement as shown in the following SQL command:

UPDATE      EMPLOYEE

SET         Phone = '360-287-8810'

WHERE       EmployeeNumber = 11;

To see the result, we repeat the command:

SELECT * FROM EMPLOYEE;

|    | EmployeeNumber | FirstName | LastName | Department | Phone | Email |
|----|----------------|-----------|----------|------------|-------|-------|
| 1  | 1  | Mary    | Jacobs   | Administration  | 360-285-8110 | MJacobs@WPC.com |
| 2  | 2  | Rosalie | Jackson  | Administration  | 360-285-8120 | RJackson@WPC.com |
| 3  | 3  | Richard | Bandalone| Legal           | 360-285-8210 | RBanalone@WPC.com |
| 4  | 4  | Tom     | Caruthers| Accounting      | 360-285-8310 | TCaruthers@WPC.com |
| 5  | 5  | Heather | Jones    | Accounting      | 360-285-8320 | HJones@WPC.com |
| 6  | 6  | Mary    | Abernathy| Finance         | 360-285-8410 | MAbernathy@WPC.com |
| 7  | 7  | George  | Smith    | Human Resources | 360-285-8510 | GSmith@WPC.com |
| 8  | 8  | Tom     | Jackson  | Production      | 360-287-8610 | TJackson@WPC.com |
| 9  | 9  | George  | Jones    | Production      | 360-287-8620 | GJones@WPC.com |
| 10 | 10 | Ken     | Numoto   | Marketing       | 360-287-8710 | KMumoto@WPC.com |
| 11 | 11 | James   | Nestor   | Info Systems    | 360-287-8810 | JNestor@WPC.com |
| 12 | 12 | Rick    | Brown    | Info Systems    | 360-287-8820 | RBrown@WPC.com |

The revised data in the EMPLOYEE table with the new phone number now looks like this:

| | EmployeeNumber | FirstName | LastName | Department | Phone | Email |
|---|---|---|---|---|---|---|
| 1 | 1 | Mary | Jacobs | Administration | 360-287-8810 | MJacobs@WPC.com |
| 2 | 2 | Rosalie | Jackson | Administration | 360-287-8810 | RJackson@WPC.com |
| 3 | 3 | Richard | Bandalone | Legal | 360-287-8810 | RBanalone@WPC.com |
| 4 | 4 | Tom | Caruthers | Accounting | 360-287-8810 | TCaruthers@WPC.com |
| 5 | 5 | Heather | Jones | Accounting | 360-287-8810 | HJones@WPC.com |
| 6 | 6 | Mary | Abernathy | Finance | 360-287-8810 | MAbernathy@WPC.com |
| 7 | 7 | George | Smith | Human Resources | 360-287-8810 | GSmith@WPC.com |
| 8 | 8 | Tom | Jackson | Production | 360-287-8810 | TJackson@WPC.com |
| 9 | 9 | George | Jones | Production | 360-287-8810 | GJones@WPC.com |
| 10 | 10 | Ken | Numoto | Marketing | 360-287-8810 | KMumoto@WPC.com |
| 11 | 11 | James | Nestor | Info Systems | 360-287-8810 | JNestor@WPC.com |
| 12 | 12 | Rick | Brown | Info Systems | 360-287-8810 | RBrown@WPC.com |

Now consider why this command is dangerous. Suppose that while intending to make this update, you make an error and forget to include the WHERE clause. Thus, you submit the following to the DBMS.

UPDATE       EMPLOYEE

SET          Phone = '360-287-8810';

After this command has executed, the EMPLOYEE relation will appear as follows:
This is clearly not what you intended to do. Had you done this at a new job where there might be 10,000 rows in the EMPLOYEE table, you would experience a sinking feeling in the pit of your stomach and make plans to update your résumé that evening. The message here is: UPDATE is powerful and easy to use, but also capable of causing disasters.

The update command can modify more than one column value at a time as shown in the following statement. For example, if Heather Jones (EmployeeNumber = 5) is transferred to the Finance department from Accounting and given a new Finance phone number, the following command will update her data:

UPDATE       EMPLOYEE

SET          Department = 'Finance', Phone = '360-285-8420',

WHERE        EmployeeNumber = 5;

This command will change the values of Phone and Department for the indicated employee, and a SELECT command to display Heaather's data will now show the result is:

| | EmployeeNumber | FirstName | LastName | Department | Phone | Email |
|---|---|---|---|---|---|---|
| 1 | 5 | Heather | Jones | Finance | 360-285-8420 | HJones@WPC.com |

## Deleting Data

You can eliminate rows with the SQL **DELETE command**. However, the same warnings pertain to DELETE as pertain to UPDATE. DELETE is deceptively simple to use and easy to apply in unintended ways. The following, for example, will delete all projects sponsored by the marketing department.

DELETE

FROM        PROJECT

WHERE       Department = 'Marketing';

Given that we created an ON DELETE CASCADE referential integrity constraint, this DELETE operation will not only remove PROJECT rows, it also will remove any related ASSIGNMENT rows. For the WPC data in Figure 3-2, this DELETE operation will remove the projects with ProjectIDs 1000 (2005 Q3 Product Plan) and 1300 (2005 Q3 Product Plan), and six rows (rows one, two, and three for ProjectID 1000, and rows ten, eleven, and twelve for ProjectID 1300) of the ASSIGNMENT table.

As with UPDATE, if you forget to include the WHERE clause, disaster will ensue. For example, the SQL code

DELETE

FROM        PROJECT;

deletes *all* the rows in PROJECT (and because of the ON DELETE CASCADE constraint, *all* the ASSIGNMENT rows as well). This truly would be a disaster!

Observe how the referential integrity constraint differs with the EMPLOYEE table. Here, if we try to process the command

DELETE

FROM        EMPLOYEE

WHERE       EmployeeNumber = 1;

the DELETE operation will fail because rows in ASSIGNMENT depend on the EmployeeNumber value of 1 in EMPLOYEE. If you want to delete the row for this employee, you must first reassign or delete his or her rows in ASSIGNMENT.

## ▶ SQL FOR TABLE AND CONSTRAINT MODIFICATION AND DELETION

### The DROP TABLE and ALTER TABLE Statements

There are many data definition SQL statements that we have not yet described. Two of the most useful are the SQL **DROP TABLE** statement and the SQL **ALTER TABLE** statement. DROP TABLE, however, is also one of the most dangerous SQL statements because this statement drops the table's structure along with all of the table's data. For example, if you wanted to drop the ASSIGNMENT table and all its data, you would use the following SQL statement:

DROP TABLE ASSIGNMENT;

The DROP TABLE statement will not work if the table contains or could contain values needed to fulfill referential integrity constraints. EMPLOYEE, for example, contains values of EmployeeNumber needed by the foreign key constraint ASSIGN_EMP_FK. In this case, an attempt to issue the statement DROP TABLE EMPLOYEE will fail, and an error message will be generated.

If you want to drop the EMPLOYEE table, you must first drop the ASSIGNMENT table, or alternatively at least delete the foreign key constraint ASSIGN_EMP_FK. This is one place where the ALTER TABLE command is useful. The ALTER TABLE is used to add, modify, and drop columns and constraints. For example, we can use it to drop the ASSIGN_EMP_FK constraint with the statement:

ALTER TABLE ASSIGNMENT DROP CONSTRAINT ASSIGN_EMP_FK;

After either dropping the ASSIGNMENT table or the ASSIGN_EMP_FK foreign key constraint, you can then successfully drop the EMPLOYEE table.

---

**B T W**

Now you know why it is an advantage to control constraint names using the CONSTRAINT syntax. Since we create the foreign key constraint name ASSIGN_EMP_FK ourselves, we know what it is. This makes it easy to use when we need it.

---

## The CHECK Constraint

Alternatively, we can use the ALTER statement to add a constraint. For example, consider the PROJECT table, which has the columns StartDate and EndDate. Obviously, the StartDate must be earlier than the EndDate, but there is currently nothing in the table definition to enforce this. This is a perfect place to use a **CHECK** constraint. CHECK constraints are similar to WHERE clauses in SQL queries. They can contain the keywords IN, NOT IN, LIKE (for the specification of decimal places), and use less than ($<$) and greater than ($>$) signs for range checks.

---

**Does Not Work With MS Access SQL**

As discussed earlier, MS Access SQL does not support the CHECK column constraint. However, an equivalent constraint can be set in the table Design View. See "The Access Workbench" later in this chapter for more details.

---

To modify the PROJECT table with the needed constraint, we would use the following SQL statement:

ALTER TABLE PROJECT

    ADD CONSTRAINT PROJECT_Check_Dates

        CHECK (StartDate < EndDate);

The ALTER TABLE statement is handy when we need to add or drop columns. For example, suppose that we want to add a column to PROJECT to track how many hours have actually been worked on a project. If the name of this column is CurrentTotalHours, we can add it to the table with the SQL statement (note that the keyword COLUMN is *not* used in this command):

ALTER TABLE PROJECT

    ADD CurrentTotalHours Numeric(8,2) NULL;

Note that since we are adding a column to an existing table with data, we cannot add a NOT NULL column—this constraint would immediately be violated since there would be missing data in each row. If we want a column to be NOT NULL, we must create it as NULL, insert the needed data, and then modify the column to NOT NULL. For example, after putting the necessary date into CurrentTotalHours for the existing rows, we could convert it to NOT NULL (and supply a DEFAULT value at the same time) by using the SQL statement:

ALTER TABLE PROJECT

    ALTER COLUMN CurrentTotalHours Numeric(8,2) NOT NULL

        DEFAULT 1;

If we decided that this column was not needed, we could drop it from the PROJECT table using the SQL statement:

ALTER TABLE PROJECT

    DROP COLUMN CurrentTotalHours;

The ALTER TABLE statement can also be used to modify data types, but you have to be careful as this can result in a loss of data. Check your DBMS documentation carefully before attempting to modify data types.[4]

## ▶ SQL VIEWS

SQL contains a powerful tool known as a SQL view. A **SQL View** is a virtual table created by a DBMS-stored SELECT statement and, thus, can combine access to data in multiple tables and even in other views. SQL views are discussed in Appendix C.

## THE ACCESS WORKBENCH

### Section 3

### Working with Queries in Microsoft Access

In the previous sections of "The Access Workbench," we learned to create Microsoft Access databases, tables, forms, and reports in multiple table databases. In this section, we will cover the following objectives:

- Learn how to use Access SQL
- Learn run queries in single and multiple tables in using both SQL and Query By Example (QBE)
- Learn how to manually set table and relationship properties that Access SQL does not support

We will continue to use the WMCRM database we have been using. At this point, we have created and populated (which means we've inserted the data into) the CUSTOMER and CONTACT tables and set the referential integrity constraint between them.

*(Continued)*

---

[4]Also see David M. Kroenke, *Database Processing: Fundamentals, Design and Implementation*, 10th Edition (Upper Saddle River, NJ: Prentice Hall, 2006) Chapter 8.

### Working with Microsoft Access SQL

Work with Microsoft Access SQL is done in the SQL View of a Query window. Let's try a simple query to see how this works. We'll use the basic SQL query:

SELECT * FROM CUSTOMER;

*Opening an Access SQL Query Window and Running an Access SQL Query*

1. Start Microsoft Access.
2. In the menu bar, click **File | Open**. The Open dialog box is displayed. Browse to the **WMCRM.mdb** file, click the file name to highlight it, and then click the **Open** button. When the Security Warning dialog box appears, click the **Open** button to open the database.
3. In the WMCRM: Database window, click **Queries** in the Objects pane to display the Queries pane as shown in Figure AW-3-1.
4. In the Queries pane, double-click **Create query in Design view**. The Query1: Select Query window appears along with the Show Table dialog box as shown in Figure AW-3-2.
5. Click the **Close** button on the Show Table dialog box. The Query1: Select Query window appears as shown in Figure AW-3-3. This window is used for creating and editing Access queries in Design View, which is used with Access QBE, which we will discuss later in this section. The window name is composed of the *name* of the query, currently Query1, and the *type of query*, in this case a Select Query, separated by a colon (:). Note the SQL View button on the toolbar.
6. Click the **SQL View** button on the Query Design toolbar. The Query1: Select Query window switches to the SQL View, as shown in Figure AW-3-4. Note the basic SQL command of *SELECT;* in the window. This is an incomplete command, and running it will not produce any results

---

### FIGURE AW-3-1

**The Queries Pane**

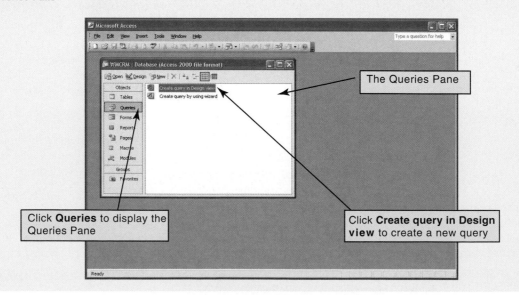

## FIGURE AW-3-2

**The Show Table Dialog Box**

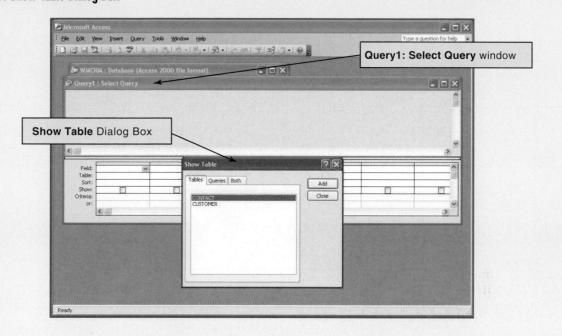

7. Edit the SQL SELECT command to read **SELECT \* FROM CUSTOMER;** as shown in Figure AW-3-5.
8. Click the **Run** button on the Query Design toolbar. The query results appear as shown in Figure AW-3-6.

## FIGURE AW-3-3

**The Query1: Select Query Window in Design View**

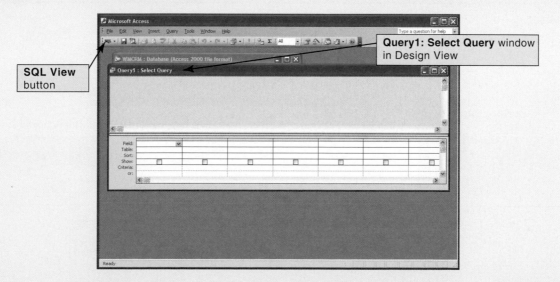

*(Continued)*

---

**FIGURE AW-3-4**

---

**The Query1: Select Query Window in SQL View**

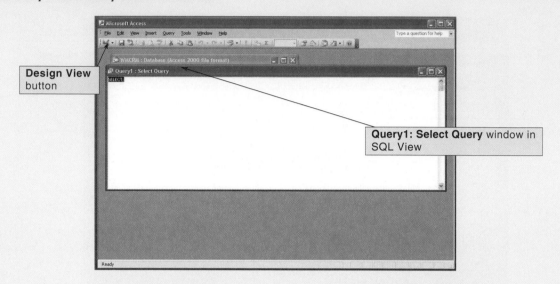

9. To save the query, click the **Save** button on the Query Design toolbar. The Save As dialog box appears as shown in Figure AW-3-7.

10. Type in the query name **SQLQuery-AW-3-01**, and then click the **OK** button. The query is saved, and the window is renamed with the query name as shown in Figure AW-3-8.

11. Close the Query-AW-3-01: Select Query query window by clicking the **Close** button in the upper right corner of the report window. Note that the SQLQuery-AW-3-01 query object now appears in the Queries pane as shown in Figure AW-3-9.

---

**FIGURE AW-3-5**

---

**The SQL Query**

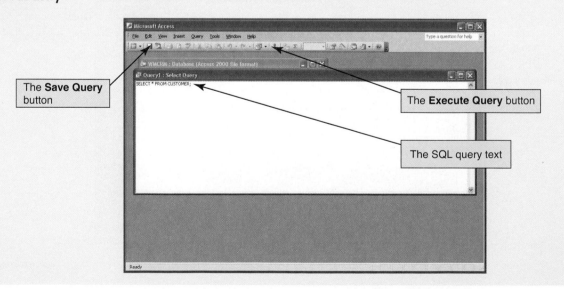

## FIGURE AW-3-6

### The Query Results

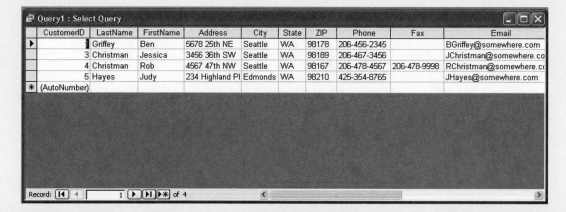

## FIGURE AW-3-7

### The Save As Dialog Box

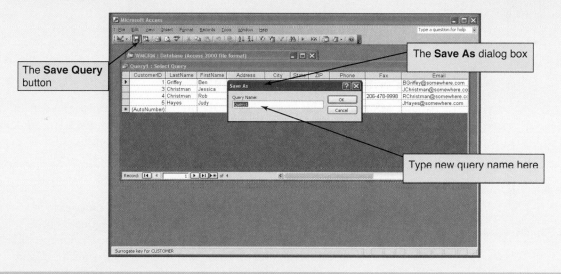

## FIGURE AW-3-8

### The SQLQuery-AW-3-01: Select Query Window

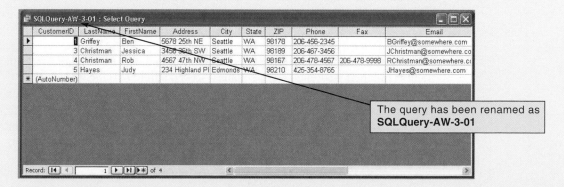

*(Continued)*

**FIGURE AW-3-9**

**The SQLQuery-AW-3-01 Object in the Queries Pane**

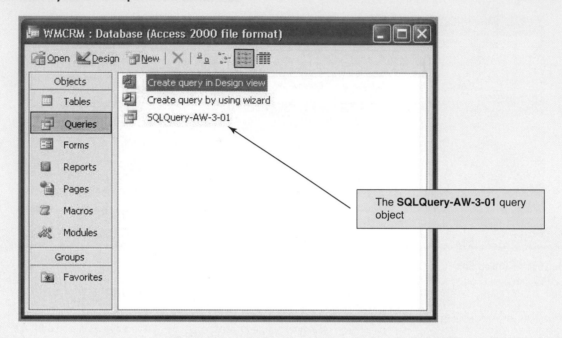

## Working with Microsoft Access QBE

By default, MS Access does not use the SQL interface. Instead it uses a version of Query By Example (QBE), which uses the Access GUI to build queries. To understand how this works, let's recreate the SQL query we just created using QBE.

### Creating and Running an Access QBE Query

1. You should still have the Queries pane open. If you don't, click **Queries** in the Objects pane of the WMCRM : Database window to display the Queries pane.
2. In the Queries pane, double-click **Create query in Design View**. The Query1: Select Query window appears along with the Show Table dialog box as shown in Figure AW-3-2.
3. Click **CUSTOMER** to select the CUSTOMER table. Click the **Add** button to add the CUSTOMER table to the query.
4. Click the **Close** button to close the Show Table dialog box.
5. You can rearrange and resize the query window objects in the Query1: Select Query window using standard Windows drag-and-drop techniques. Rearrange the window elements until they appear as shown in Figure AW-3-10.
6. Note the elements of the Query1: Select Query window shown in Figure AW-3-10: Tables (and their associated set of columns—called a **field list**) included in the query are shown in the upper pane, while the columns (fields) actually included in the query are shown in the lower pane. For each included column (field), we can set whether or not this column's data appears in the results, how the data is sorted, and the criteria for selecting which rows of data will be shown. Note that the first entry in the table's field list is the asterisk (*), which has its standard SQL meaning of *all columns in the table*.
7. Columns are included in the query by dragging them from the table's field list to a field column in the lower pane. Click and drag the **asterisk** in CUSTOMER to the

**FIGURE AW-3-10**

**The QBE Query1: Select Query Window**

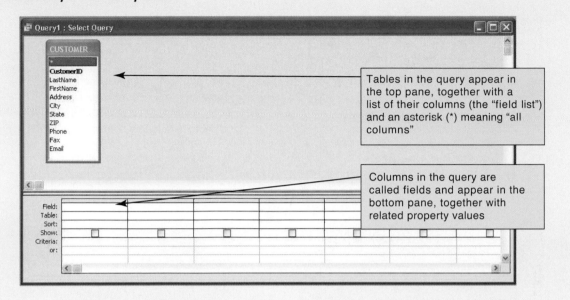

first field column as shown in Figure AW-3-11. Note that the column is entered as *CUSTOMER.*\* from the table CUSTOMER.

8. Click the **Run** button on the Query Design toolbar. The query results appear as shown in Figure AW-3-12. Note that these results are identical to the results shown in Figure AW-3-06.

**FIGURE AW-3-11**

**Adding Columns to the Query**

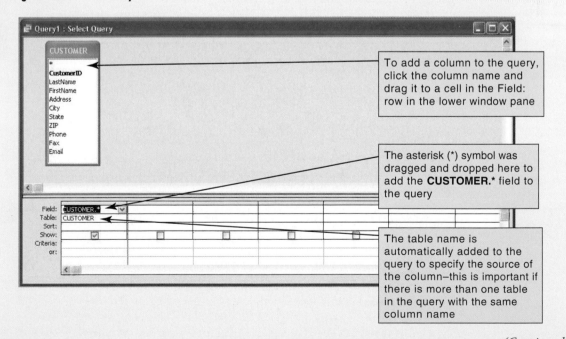

*(Continued)*

## FIGURE AW-3-12

**The Query Results**

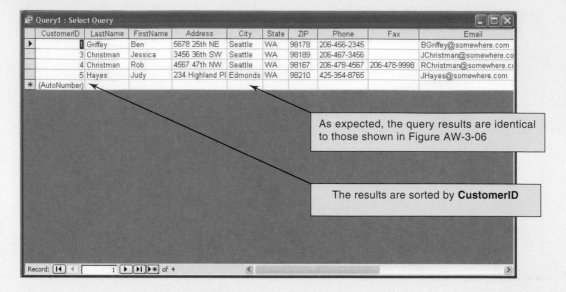

9. To save the query, click the **Save** button on the Query Design toolbar to display the Save As dialog box. Type in the query name **QBEQuery-AW-3-02**, and then click the **OK** button. The query is saved, and the window is renamed with the new query name.

10. Close the QBEQuery-AW-3-02: Note that the **QBEQuery-AW-3-02** query object now appears in the Queries pane.

This query is about as simple as they get, and we can use QBE for more complicated queries. For example, consider a query that uses only some of the columns in the table, includes the SQL WHERE clause, and also sorts data using the SQL ORDER BY clause:

SELECT        CustomerID, LastName, FirstName
FROM          CUSTOMER
WHERE         CustomerID > 2
ORDER BY      LastName DESC;

The QBE Query (named as QBEQuery-AW-3-03) is shown in Figure AW-3-13. Note that now we have included the specific columns that we want used in the query instead of the asterisk, used the Sort property for CustomerID, and included row selection conditions in the Criteria property for LastName.

### Creating and Running QBEQuery-AW-3-03

1. Using the previous instructions for QBEQuery-AW-3-02, create, run, and save the QBEQuery-AW-3-03 as described previously.

And, of course, we can use more than one table in a QBE query. We'll create the QBE version of this SQL query:

---

**FIGURE AW-3-13**

---

**The QBEQuery-AW-3-03: Select Query Window**

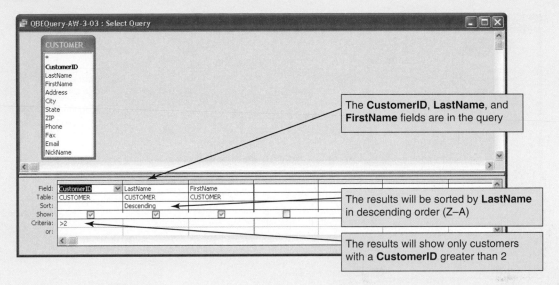

SELECT          LastName, FirstName, Date, Type, Remarks
FROM            CUSTOMER, CONTACT
WHERE           CUSTOMER.CustomerID = CONTACT.CustomerID
AND             CustomerID = 3
ORDER BY        Date;

Let's build this one step by step:

### Creating and Running an Access QBE Query with Multiple Tables

1. You should still have the Queries pane open. If you don't, click **Queries** in the Objects pane of the WMCRM : Database window to display the Queries pane.
2. In the Queries pane, double-click **Create query in Design View**. The Query1: Select Query window appears along with the Show Table dialog box.
3. Click **CUSTOMER** to select the CUSTOMER table. Click the **Add** button to add the CUSTOMER table to the query.
4. Click **CONTACT** to select the CONTACT table. Click the **Add** button to add the CONTACT table to the query.
5. Click the **Close** button to close the Show Table dialog box.
6. You can rearrange and resize the query window objects in the Query1: Select Query window using standard Windows drag-and-drop techniques. Rearrange the window elements until they appear as shown in Figure AW-3-14. Note that the relationship between the two tables is already included in the diagram—this implements the SQL clause

    WHERE CUSTOMER.CustomerID = CONTACT.CustomerID

7. From the CUSTOMER table, click and drag the **CustomerID, LastName,** and **FirstName** column names to the first three field columns in the lower pane.
8. From the CONTACT table, click and drag the **Date, Type,** and **Remarks** column names to the next three field columns in the lower pane.
9. In the field column for CustomerID, uncheck the **Show: check box** so that the data from this column is not included in the results display.

*(Continued)*

---
**FIGURE AW-3-14**
---

**The Query Window with the Two Tables**

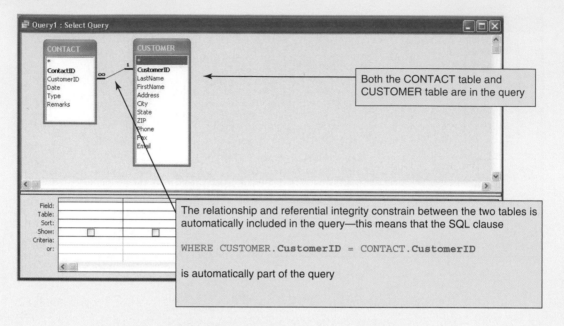

Both the CONTACT table and CUSTOMER table are in the query

The relationship and referential integrity constrain between the two tables is automatically included in the query—this means that the SQL clause

WHERE CUSTOMER.**CustomerID** = CONTACT.**CustomerID**

is automatically part of the query

10. In the field column for CustomerID, type the number **3** into the Criteria row.
11. In the field column for Date, set the Sort: setting to **Ascending**. The completed QBE query appears as shown in Figure AW-3-15.
12. Click the **Run** button on the Query Design toolbar. The query results appear as shown in Figure AW-3-16.

---
**FIGURE AW-3-15**
---

**The Completed Two-Table Query**

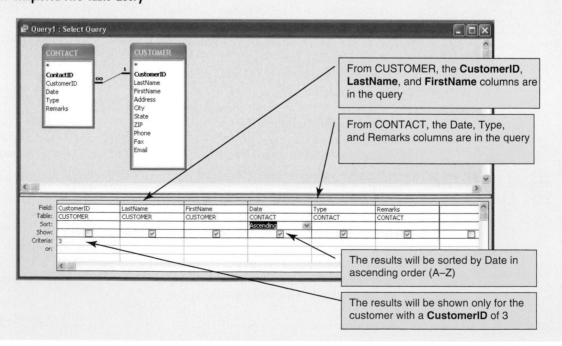

From CUSTOMER, the **CustomerID**, **LastName**, and **FirstName** columns are in the query

From CONTACT, the Date, Type, and Remarks columns are in the query

The results will be sorted by Date in ascending order (A–Z)

The results will be shown only for the customer with a **CustomerID** of 3

**FIGURE AW-3-16**

### The Two-Table Query Results

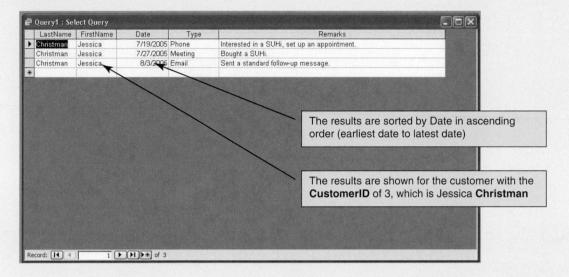

The results are sorted by Date in ascending order (earliest date to latest date)

The results are shown for the customer with the **CustomerID** of 3, which is Jessica **Christman**

13. To save the query, click the **Save** button on the Query Design toolbar to display the Save As dialog box. Type in the query name **QBEQuery-AW-3-04**, and then click the **OK** button. The query is saved, and the window is renamed with the new query name.
14. Close the QBEQuery-AW-3-04.

## Working with Microsoft Access Parameter Queries

Access allows us to construct queries that prompt the user for values to be used in the WHERE clause of the query. These are known as **parameterized queries**, where the word *parameter* refers to the column for which a value is needed. And since reports can be created that are based on queries, parameterized queries can be used as the basis of parameterized reports.

For an example of a parameterized query, we'll modify QBEQuery-AW-3-04 so that CustomerID is the parameter, and the user is prompted for the CustomerID value when the query is run.

### Creating and Running an Access Parameterized Query

1. You should still have the Queries pane open. If you don't, click **Queries** in the Objects pane of the WMCRM : Database window to display the Queries pane.
2. Click the **QBEQuery-AW-3-04** object to select it, and then click the **Design** button to open the query in Design View. Note that the CustomerID column, which was the first column in the query as shown in Figure AW-3-16, now appears as the last column in Design View. This occurred because we specified that the column would not be displayed.
3. Use the Access menu command **File | Save As. . .** to save a new copy of the query as **QBEQuery-AW-3-05**.
4. In the Criteria row of the CustomerID column, delete the current number and enter the text [**Enter the CustomerID Number:**] in its place. The QBEQuery-AW-3-05 : Select Query window now appears as shown in Figure AW-3-17.

*(Continued)*

**FIGURE AW-3-17**

**The Complete Parameterized Query**

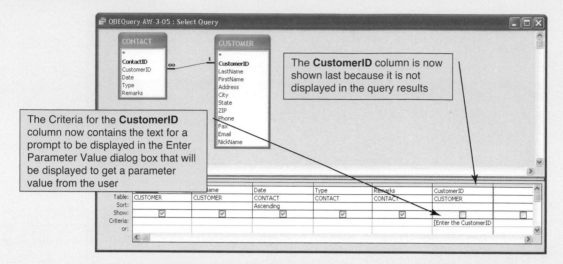

5. Click the **Run** button. The **Enter Parameter Value dialog box** appears as shown in Figure AW-3-18. Note that the text we entered in the Criteria row now appears as a prompt in the dialog box.
6. Enter the CustomerID number **3** as a parameter value, and then click the **OK** button. The query results appear—they are identical to those shown in Figure AW-3-16.
7. Click the **Save** button to save the changes to the design of the query and then close the query.

### Creating Tables with Microsoft Access SQL

Now let's try creating and populating a table using Microsoft Access SQL as done in the SQL View of a Query window. So far, our Wallingford Motors CRM has been for use by only a single salesperson. Now we'll add a SALESPERSON table. The sales staff members at Wallingford Motors are identified by a nickname. The nickname may be their actual first name or a true nickname, but it must be unique. We will assume that one salesperson is assigned to each customer, and that only that salesperson makes contact with the customer.

**FIGURE AW-3-18**

**The Enter Parameter Value Dialog Box**

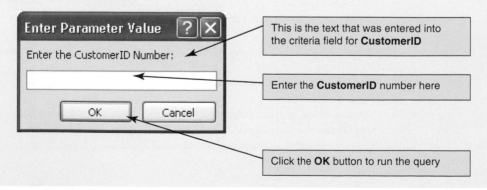

The full set of tables in the WMCRM database will now look like this:

SALESPERSON (<u>NickName</u>, LastName, FirstName, HireDate, WageRate, CommissionRate, Phone, Email)

CUSTOMER (<u>CustomerID</u>, LastName, FirstName, Address, City, State, ZIP, Phone, Fax, Email, *NickName*)

CONTACT (<u>ContactID</u>, *CustomerID*, Date, Type, Remarks)

The referential integrity constraints are:

NickName in CUSTOMER must exist in NickName in SALESPERSON

CustomerID in CONTACT must exist in CustomerID in CUSTOMER

The database column characteristics for SALESPERSON is shown in Figure AW-3-19, and SALESPERSON data is shown in Figure AW-3-20.

Note that adding the SALEPERSON TABLE will require alterations to our existing CUSTOMER table. We will need a new column for the foreign key NickName, a referential integrity constraint between CUSTOMER and SALESPERSON, and new data for the column.

---

### FIGURE AW-3-19

**Database Column Characteristics for the SALESPERSON Relation**

| ColumnName | Type | Key | Required | Remarks |
|---|---|---|---|---|
| NickName | Text (35) | Primary Key | Yes | |
| LastName | Text (25) | No | Yes | |
| FirstName | Text (25) | No | Yes | |
| HireDate | Date/Time | No | Yes | |
| WageRate | Number | No | Yes | Double, Default value = $12.50 |
| CommissionRate | Number | No | Yes | Double |
| Phone | Text (12) | No | Yes | |
| Email | Text (100) | No | Yes | Unique |

---

### FIGURE AW-3-20

**Data for the SALESPERSON Relation**

| Nick Name | Last Name | First Name | HireDate | WageRate | Commission Rate | Phone | Email |
|---|---|---|---|---|---|---|---|
| Tina | Smith | Tina | 10-AUG-04 | 15.50 | 12.5% | 206-287-7010 | Tina@WM.com |
| Big Bill | Jones | William | 25-SEP-04 | 15.50 | 12.5% | 206-287-7020 | BigBill@WM.com |
| Billy | Jones | Bill | 17-MAY-05 | 12.50 | 12.0% | 206-287-7030 | Billy@WM.com |

*(Continued)*

First, we'll build the SALEPERSON table. The correct SQL statement is:

```
CREATE TABLE SALESPERSON(
        NickName         Char(35)            NOT NULL,
        LastName         Char(25)            NOT NULL,
        FirstName        Char(25)            NOT NULL,
        HireDate         DateTime            NOT NULL,
        WageRate         Numeric(5,2)        NOT NULL
                                                DEFAULT(12.50),
        CommissionRate   Numeric(5,3)        NOT NULL,
        Phone            Char(12)            NOT NULL,
        Email            Varchar(100)        NOT NULL UNIQUE,
        CONSTRAINT       SALESPERSON_PK      PRIMARY KEY (NickName)
        );
```

This statement uses standard SQL data types (specifically SQL Server data types), but this is not a problem because Access will correctly read these and translate them into Access data types. However, from the SQL discussion in this chapter, we know that Access does not support the numeric data type with the (m,n) notation (where m = total number of digits, and n = number of digits to the right of the decimal). Further, Access does not support the UNIQUE constraint nor the DEFAULT keyword. Therefore, we have to create an SQL statement without these items, and then fine-tune the table after it is created by using the Access GUI.

The SQL that will run in Access is:

```
CREATE TABLE SALESPERSON(
        NickName         Char(35)            NOT NULL,
        LastName         Char(25)            NOT NULL,
        FirstName        Char(25)            NOT NULL,
        HireDate         DateTime            NOT NULL,
        WageRate         Numeric             NOT NULL,
        CommissionRate   Numeric             NOT NULL,
        Phone            Char(12)            NOT NULL,
        Email            Varchar(100)        NOT NULL,
        CONSTRAINT       SALESPERSON_PK      PRIMARY KEY (NickName)
        );
```

### Creating the SALESPERSON Table Using Access SQL

1. As described in the set of steps mentioned previously, open an Access query window in SQL View.
2. Type the SQL code into the query window. The query window now appears as shown in Figure AW-3-21.
3. Click the **Run** button on the Query Design toolbar. The statement runs, but since this statement creates a table, the only immediately visible results are that the query window title changes to Query1 : Data Definition Query.
4. Save the query as **Create-Table-SALESPERSON**, then close the query window. The Create-Table-SALESPERSON query object now appears in the Queries pane as shown in Figure AW-3-22.

**FIGURE AW-3-21**

**The CREATE TABLE SALESPERSON SQL Statement**

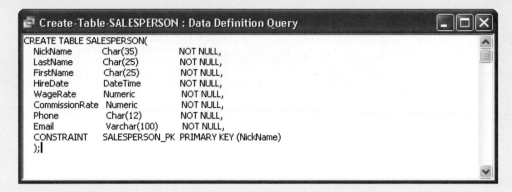

**FIGURE AW-3-22**

**The Create-Table-SALESPERSON Query in the Queries Pane**

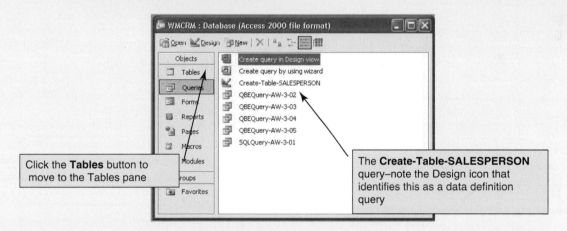

5.  Click the **Tables** Objects button to display the Tables pane. Note that the SALES-PERSON table now appears in the Tables pane as shown in Figure AW-3-23.

### Modifying Access Tables to Add Data Requirements Not Supported by Access SQL

To modify the SALESPERSON table to add the table requirements not supported by Access SQL, we use the Access table Design View.[5]

---

[5]Although we will not fully discuss the matter in this book, we should mention that Access SQL confounds the treatment of the SQL NOT NULL column constraint. When we use NOT NULL in defining a column, Access properly sets the column's **Required** field property to *Yes* (we discussed how to do this manually in "The Access Workbench: Section 1" when we created the CUSTOMER table). However, Access adds a second field property named **Allow Zero Length**, which it sets to *Yes*. To truly match NOT NULL, this value should be set to *No*. For a full discussion of setting the Allow Zero Length field property, see the MS Access help system.

*(Continued)*

---

**FIGURE AW-3-23**

**The SALESPERSON Table in the Tables Pane**

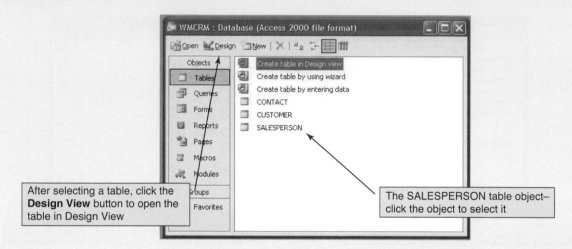

First, recall that Access SQL does not support the **numeric(m,n)** syntax, where *m* is the number of digits stored and *n* is the number of digits to the right of the decimal place. We can set the number of digits to some extent by setting the **Field Size** field property (which is as close as Access gets to setting the value of *m*). By default, Access sets a numeric value Field Size to *double*. We could change this, but a full discussion of this field property is beyond the scope of this book—see the MS Access help system discussion of the Field Size Property for more information.

We can, however, easily set the number of decimal places (which is the value of *n*) using the **Decimal Places** field property. In addition, MS Access does have the advantage of having a **Format** field property that allows us to apply formatting to a numeric value, so that the data appears as currency, a percentage, or in other formats. We will leave the default Field Size setting, and change the Format and Decimal Places property values.

Next, recall that Access SQL does not support the SQL **DEFAULT** keyword so we will have to add any needed default values. We can do this using the **Default Value** field property.

### Setting Number and Default Value Field Properties

1. To open the **SALESPERSON table** in Design View, click the SALESPERSON table object to select it, and then click the Design View button. The SALESPERSON table appears in Design View as shown in Figure AW-3-24.
2. Select the **WageRate** field. The WageRate field properties are displayed in the General tab as shown in Figure AW-3-25.
3. Click the **Format text field**. A drop-down list arrow appears on the right end of the text field as shown in Figure AW-3-26. Click the drop-down list arrow to display the list and select Currency.
    - **NOTE:** When you do this, a small icon will appear to the left of the text field. This is the Property Update Options drop-down list. Simply ignore it, and it will disappear when you take the next action. Then it will reappear for that action! In general, ignore it and keep working.
4. Click the **Decimal Places text field** (which is currently set to Auto). Again, a drop-down list arrow appears. Use the drop-down list to select **2 decimal places**.

**FIGURE AW-3-24**

**The SALESPERSON Table in Design View**

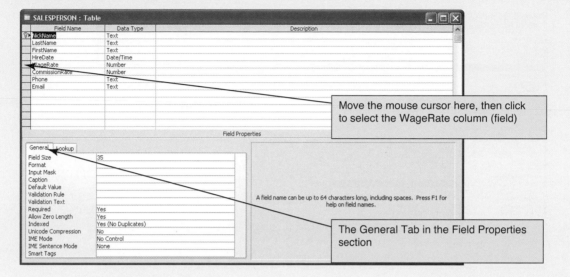

**FIGURE AW-3-25**

**The WageRate Field Properties**

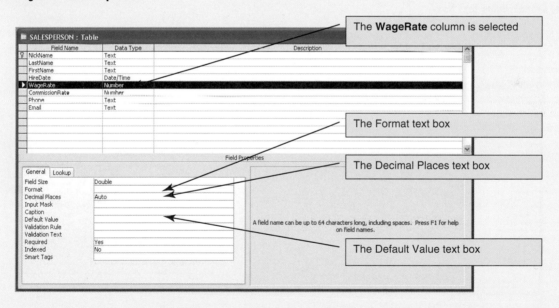

5. Click the **Default Value text box**. The Expression Builder icon appears as shown in Figure AW-3-27. We do not need to use the Expression Builder at this point. Type **12.50** into the Default Value text box. This completes setting the Field Property values for WageRate, and the final values are shown in Figure AW-3-28.
   - **NOTE:** Access will actually store this number as 12.5, which is the same value without the trailing zero. Just don't be alarmed if you look at these property values again and notice the missing zero!

*(Continued)*

**FIGURE AW-3-26**

**The Format Text Box**

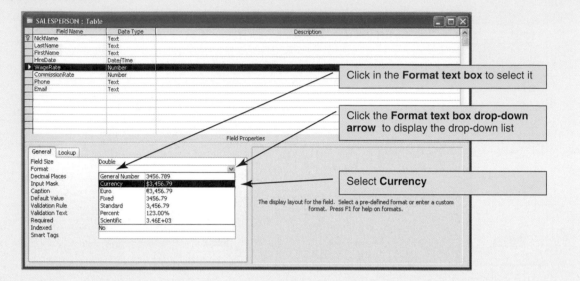

Click in the **Format text box** to select it

Click the **Format text box drop-down arrow** to display the drop-down list

Select **Currency**

**FIGURE AW-3-27**

**The Default Value Text Box**

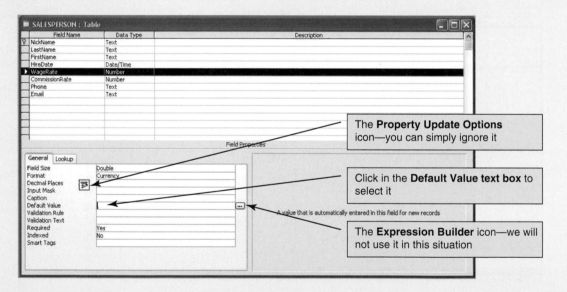

The **Property Update Options** icon—you can simply ignore it

Click in the **Default Value text box** to select it

The **Expression Builder** icon—we will not use it in this situation

6. Click the **Save** button to save the completed changes to the SALESPERSON table. Leave the SALESPERSON table in Design View.
7. Select the **CommissionRate** field. The CommissionRate field properties are displayed in the General tab.
8. Set the **Format** value to **Percent**.
9. Set the **Decimal Places** value to **3**.

---

**FIGURE AW-3-28**

**The Completed WageRate Field Properties**

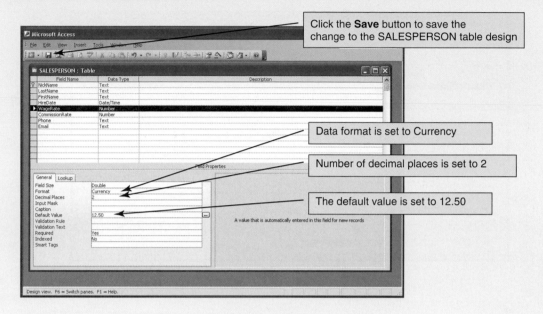

10. Click the **Save** button to save the completed changes to the SALESPERSON table.
11. Leave the SALESPERSON table open in Design View for more steps to follow.

The UNIQUE constraint is another SQL constraint that Access SQL does not support. To set a UNIQUE constraint in Access, we set the value of the **Indexed** field property. Access initially sets this value to *No*, which means that no index (a tool for making queries more efficient) is built for this column. The two other possible values of this property are *Yes (Duplicates OK)* and *Yes (No Duplicates)*. We enforce the UNIQUE constraint by setting the property value to **Yes (No Duplicates)**.

### Setting Indexed Field Properties

1. The **SALESPERSON table** should already be open in Design View. If not, open the table in Design View.
2. Select the **Email** field.
3. Click the **Indexed text field**. A drop-down list arrow appears on the right end of the text field as shown in Figure AW-3-29. Click the drop-down list arrow to display the list, and select **Yes (No Duplicates)**.
4. Click the **Save** button to save the completed changes to the SALESPERSON table.
5. **Close** the SALESPERSON table.

Finally, let's consider how to implement the SQL CHECK constraint. When we created the CONTACT table, we noted that the only allowed data types for the Type column were Phone, Fax, Email, and Meeting. The correct SQL statement to add this constraint to the CONTACT table would be:

*(Continued)*

---

**FIGURE AW-3-29**

**The Email Field Properties**

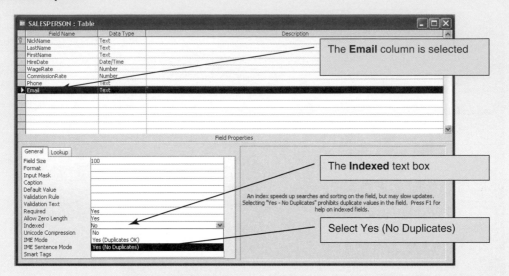

ALTER TABLE CONTACT
    ADD CONSTRAINT CONTACT_Check_Type
        CHECK (Type IN
            ('Phone', 'Fax', 'Email', 'Meeting'));

To implement the CHECK constraint in Access, we set the value of the Validation Rule for the Type column.

### Creating the CHECK Constraint for the CONTACT Table

1. Open the **CONTACT** table in Design View.
2. Select the **Type** column.
3. Click the Validation Rule text box and type **"Phone" Or "Fax" Or "Email" Or "Meeting"** as shown in Figure AW-3-30.
4. Save the CONTACT table. A warning dialog box will appear – read the message and then click the **No** button.
5. Close the CONTACT table.

### Inserting Data with Microsoft Access SQL

We can use Access SQL to enter the data shown in Figure AW-3-20 into the SALES-PERSON table. The only problem here is that Access will not handle multiple SQL commands in one query so each row of data must be input individually. The SQL commands to enter the data are:

INSERT INTO SALESPERSON
    VALUES('Tina', 'Smith', 'Tina', '10-AUG-04',
        15.50, .125, '206-287-7010', 'Tina@WM.com');

INSERT INTO SALESPERSON
    VALUES('Big Bill', 'Jones', 'William', '25-SEP-04',
        15.50, .125, '206-287-7020', 'BigBill@WM.com');

## FIGURE AW-3-30

**Specifying a Validation Rule**

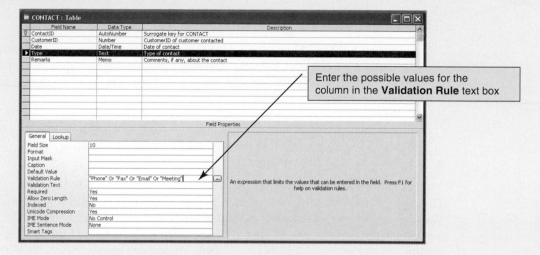

> Enter the possible values for the column in the **Validation Rule** text box

INSERT INTO SALESPERSON
    VALUES('Billy', 'Jones', 'Bill', '17-MAY-05',
    12.50, .120, '206-287-7030', 'Billy@WM.com');

*Inserting Data into the SALESPERSON Table Using Access SQL*

1. As described previously, open an Access query window in SQL View.
2. Type the SQL code for the first SQL INSERT statement into the query window.
3. Click the **Run** button on the Query Design toolbar. As shown in Figure AW-3-31, the query changes to Append Query and a dialog box appears asking you to confirm that you do want to insert the data.

## FIGURE AW-3-31

**Inserting Data into the SALESPERSON Table**

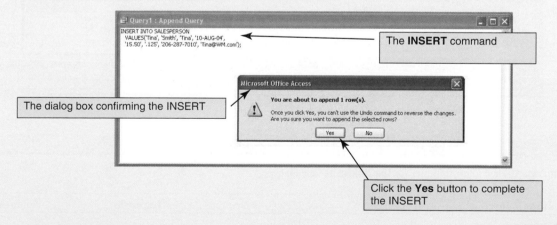

> The **INSERT** command

> The dialog box confirming the INSERT

> Click the **Yes** button to complete the INSERT

*(Continued)*

4. Click the **Yes** button in the dialog box. The data is inserted into the table.
5. Repeat Steps 2, 3, and 4 for the rest of the SQL INSERT statements for the SALES-PERSON data.
6. Close the Query1 : Append Query window. A dialog box will be displayed asking you if you want to save the query. Click the **No** button—there is no need to save this SQL statement.
7. Open the **SALESPERSON** table in Datasheet View. The table appears as shown in Figure AW-3-32. Note that the rows are sorted alphabetically ascending on the primary key (NickName) value—they do *not* appear in the order in which they were input.
   • **NOTE:** This is *not* typical of a SQL DBMS. Normally, if you ran a SELECT * FROM SALESPERSON query on the table, the data would appear in the order in which they were input unless you added an ORDER BY clause.
8. Close the **SALESPERSON** table.

Let's consider where we are in the process of adding the SALESPERSON table. The SALESPERSON table has been created and populated. We also know that at Wallingford Motors each customer is assigned to one and only one salesperson. Now, we need to create the relationship between SALESPERSON and CUSTOMER. This will require a foreign key in CUSTOMER to provide the needed link to SALESPERSON.

The problem is that the column needed for the foreign key—NickName—does not exist in CUSTOMER! Therefore, before creating the foreign key constraint, we must modify the CUSTOMER table by adding the NickName column and the appropriate data values.

Figure AW-3-33 shows the column characteristics for the NickName column in the CUSTOMER table, and Figure AW-3-34 shows the needed data for the column.

As shown in Figure AW-3-33, NickName is constrained as NOT NULL. As discussed in this chapter, however, adding a populated NOT NULL column requires multiple steps. First, the column must be added as a NULL column, then the column values must be added, and then the column must be altered to NOT NULL. We could do this using Access's GUI interface, but since we are working with Access SQL in this section, we will do these steps in SQL. The needed SQL statements are:

---

### FIGURE AW-3-32

**The Data in the SALESPERSON Table**

The data is sorted by **NickName** (the primary key value) in ascending order

---

### FIGURE AW-3-33

**Database Column Characteristics for the NickName Column**

| ColumnName | Type | Key | Required | Remarks |
|---|---|---|---|---|
| NickName | Text (35) | Foreign Key | Yes | |

## FIGURE AW-3-34

**CUSTOMER NickName Data**

| CustomerID | LastName | FirstName | . . . | NickName |
|---|---|---|---|---|
| 1 | Griffey | Ben | . . . | Big Bill |
| 3 | Christman | Jessica | . . . | Billy |
| 4 | Christman | Rob | . . . | Tina |
| 5 | Hayes | Judy | . . . | Tina |

```
ALTER TABLE CUSTOMER
        ADD NickName Char(35) NULL;
UPDATE CUSTOMER
SET         NickName = 'Big Bill'
WHERE       CustomerID = 1;
UPDATE CUSTOMER
SET         NickName = 'Billy'
WHERE       CustomerID = 3;
UPDATE CUSTOMER
SET         NickName = 'Tina'
WHERE       CustomerID = 4;
UPDATE CUSTOMER
SET         NickName = 'Tina'
WHERE         CustomerID = 5;
ALTER TABLE CUSTOMER
        ALTER COLUMN NickName Char(35) NOT NULL;
```

## FIGURE AW-3-35

**The Altered CUSTOMER Table**

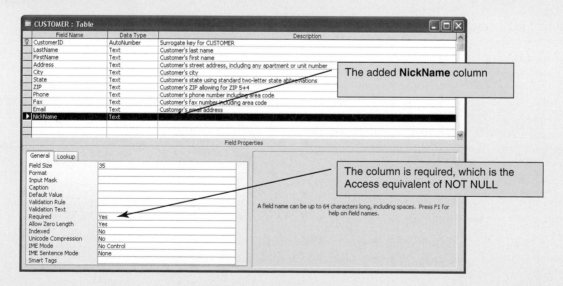

*(Continued)*

*Creating and Populating the NickName Column in the
CUSTOMER Table Using Access SQL*

1. As described previously, open an Access query window in SQL View.
2. Type the SQL code for the first SQL ALTER TABLE statement into the query window.
3. Click the **Run** button on the Query Design toolbar.
4. Type the SQL code for the first SQL UPDATE statement into the query window.
5. Click the **Run** button on the Query Design toolbar. When the dialog box appears asking you to confirm that you do want to insert the data, click the **Yes** button in the dialog box. The data is inserted into the table.
6. Repeat Steps 4 and 5 for the rest of the SQL UPDATE statements for the CUSTOMER data.
7. Type the SQL code for the second SQL ALTER TABLE statement into the query window.
8. Click the **Run** button on the Query Design toolbar.
9. Close the Query1 window. A dialog box will be displayed asking you if you want to save the query. Click the **No** button—there is no need to save this SQL statement.
10. Open the **CUSTOMER** table in Design View. The table appears as shown in Figure AW-3-35. Note the added NickName column.
11. Close the **CUSTOMER** table.

## Adding Referential Integrity Constraints Using Access SQL

Now that the NickName column is added and populated in the CUSTOMER Table, we can create the needed referential integrity constraint by adding a foreign key constraint between SALESPERSON and CUSTOMER. Since NickName is not a surrogate key, we will want any changed values of NickName in SALESPERSON to be updated in CUSTOMER. On the other hand, if a row is deleted from SALESPERSON, we do *not* want that deletion to cause the deletion of CUSTOMER data. Therefore, the needed constraint, written as an SQL ALTER TABLE statement, is:

```
ALTER TABLE CUSTOMER
        ADD CONSTRAINT CUSTOMER_SP_FK
            FOREIGN KEY(NickName)
            REFERENCES SALESPERSON(NickName)
                ON UPDATE CASCADE;
```

Unfortunately, as discussed in the chapter, Access SQL does not support ON UPDATE and ON DELETE clauses. Therefore, we will have to set ON UPDATE CASCADE manually after creating the basic constraint with the SQL statement:

```
ALTER TABLE CUSTOMER
        ADD CONSTRAINT CUSTOMER_SP_FK
            FOREIGN KEY(NickName)
            REFERENCES SALESPERSON(NickName);
```

*Creating the Referential Integrity Constraint Between
CUSTOMER and SALESPERSON Using Access SQL*

1. As described previously, open an Access query window in SQL View.
2. Type the SQL code for the SQL ALTER TABLE statement into the query window.

3. Click the **Run** button on the Query Design toolbar.
4. Close the Query1 window. A dialog box will be displayed asking you if you want to save the query. Click the **No** button—there is no need to save this SQL statement.

## Modifying Access Databases to Add Constraints Not Supported by Access SQL

The ON UPDATE CASCADE constraint will be set using the Relationships window and the Edit Relationships dialog box discussed in Section 2 of "The Access Workbench."

### Creating the Referential Integrity Constraint Between CUSTOMER and SALESPERSON Using Access SQL

1. In the Access main menu, click **Tools** and then click **Relationships . . .** in the Tools menu. The Relationships window appears as shown in Figure AW-3-36.
2. Click the **Show Table** button in the toolbar. The Show Table dialog box appears as shown in Figure AW-3-37.
3. In the Show Table dialog box, click **SALESPERSON** to select it, and then click the **Add** button to add SALESPERSON to the Relationships window.
4. In the Show Table dialog box, click the **Close** button to close the dialog box.
5. You can rearrange and resize the table objects in the Relationships window using standard Windows drag-and-drop techniques. Rearrange the SALESPERSON,

---

**FIGURE AW-3-36**

**The Relationships Window with the Current Relationship Diagram**

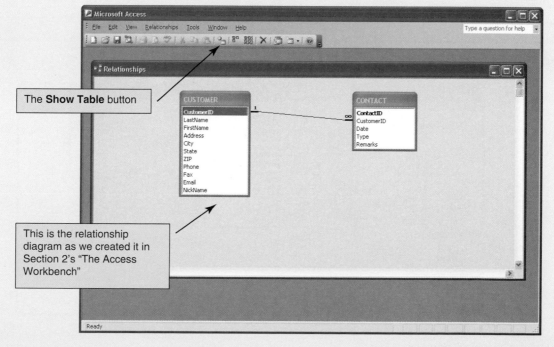

*(Continued)*

## FIGURE AW-3-37

**Adding the SALESPERSON Table to the Relationship Diagram**

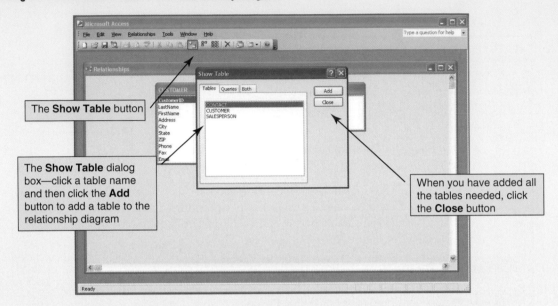

CUSTOMER, and CONTACT table objects until they appear as shown in Figure AW-3-38. Note that the relationship between SALESPERSON and CUSTOMER that we created using SQL is already shown in the diagram.

6. Right-click the **relationship line** between SALESPERSON and CUSTOMER, and then click **Edit Relationship** in the shortcut menu that appears. The **Edit Relationships dialog box** appears. Note that the **Enforce Referential Integrity**

## FIGURE AW-3-38

**The Updated Relationship Diagram**

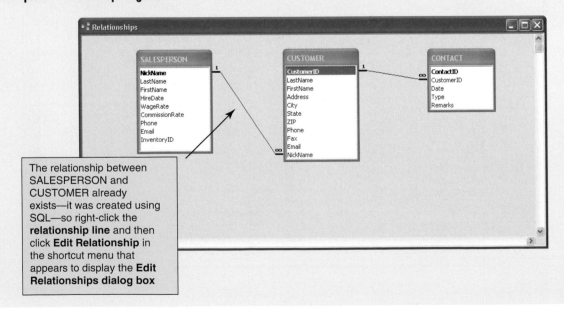

---

**FIGURE AW-3-39**

**The Completed Edit Relationships Dialog Box**

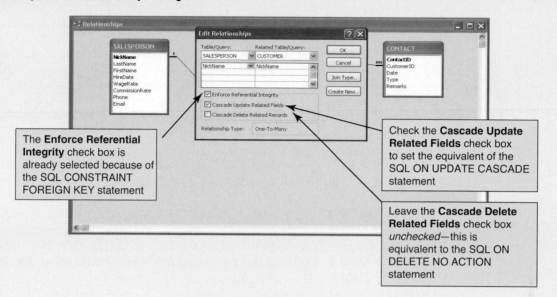

The **Enforce Referential Integrity** check box is already selected because of the SQL CONSTRAINT FOREIGN KEY statement

Check the **Cascade Update Related Fields** check box to set the equivalent of the SQL ON UPDATE CASCADE statement

Leave the **Cascade Delete Related Fields** check box *unchecked*—this is equivalent to the SQL ON DELETE NO ACTION statement

check box is already checked—this was set by the SQL ALTER TABLE statement that created the relationship between the two tables.

7. We need to set ON UPDATE CASCADE. To do this, click the **Cascade Update Related Fields** check box. The Edit Relationships dialog box now appears as shown in Figure AW-3-39. Click the **OK** Button to close the Edit Realitionships dialog box.

8. To close the Relationships window, click the **Close** button in the upper right corner of the Relationships window. An Access dialog box appears asking "Do you want to save changes to the layout of 'Relationships'?" Click the **Yes** button to save the changes and close the window.

## Closing the Database and Exiting Access

Now we're done adding the SALESPERSON table to the database. We created the SALESPERSON table, added data, altered the CUSTOMER data with a new column and foreign key values, and created the referential integrity constraint between the two tables. In the process, we saw where Access SQL does not support the standard SQL language, and learned how to use the Access GUI to compensate for the lacking SQL language features.

That completes the work we'll do in this section's "The Access Workbench." As usual, we will finish by closing the database and Access.

### Closing the WMCRM Database

1. To close the WMCRM : Database window, click the **Close** button in the upper right corner of the WMCRM : Database window.

### Exiting Access

1. To exit Access, click the **Close** button in the upper right corner of the Microsoft Access window.

## SUMMARY

Structured Query Language (SQL) is a data sublanguage that has constructs for defining and processing a database. SQL has two components: a data definition language (DDL), which is used for creating database tables and other structures, and a data manipulation language (DML), which is used to query and modify database data. SQL can be embedded into scripting languages, such as VBScript, or programming languages, such as Java and C#. SQL statements also can be processed from a command window. SQL was developed by IBM and was endorsed as a national standard known as SQL-92 by the American National Standards Institute in 1992. A later version, SQL3, has not gained acceptance in the industry and is not considered here. Modern DBMS products provide graphical facilities for accomplishing many of the tasks that SQL does. Use of SQL is mandatory for programmatically creating SQL statements.

Microsoft Access uses a variant of SQL known as ANSI-89 SQL or Microsoft Jet SQL, which differs significantly from SQL-92. Not all SQL statements written in SQL-92 will run in Access.

The CREATE TABLE statement is used for creating relations. Each column is described in three parts: the column name, data type, and optional column constraints. Column constraints considered in this chapter are PRIMARY KEY, NULL, NOT NULL, and UNIQUE. The DEFAULT keyword (not considered a constraint) is also considered. If a no column constraint is specified, the column is set to NULL.

Standard data types are Char, VarChar, Integer, Numeric and DateTime. These types have been supplemented by DBMS vendors. Figure 3-4 shows some of the additional data types for SQL Server, Oracle, and MySQL.

If a primary key has only one column, it can be defined using the primary key constraint. Another way to define a primary key is to use the table constraint. Such constraints can be used to define single and multicolumn primary keys, and they also can be used to implement referential integrity constraint by defining foreign keys. Foreign key definitions can specify that updates and deletions should cascade.

After the tables and constraints are created, data can be added using the INSERT command, and data can be queried using the SELECT command. The basic format of the SQL SELECT command is SELECT (column names or the asterisk symbol *), FROM (table names, separated by commas if there is more than one), WHERE (conditions). SELECT can be used to obtain specific columns, specific rows, or both.

Conditions after the WHERE require single quotes around values for Char and VarChar columns, but no single quotes for Integer and Numeric columns. Compound conditions can be specified with AND and OR. Sets of values can be used with IN (match any in the set) and NOT IN (not match any in the set). The wildcard symbols _ and % (? and * in MS Access) can be used with LIKE to specify a single unknown character or multiple unknown characters, respectively. IS NULL can be used to test for null values.

Results can be sorted using the ORDER BY command. The five SQL built-in functions are COUNT, SUM, MAX, MIN, and AVG. SQL can also perform mathematical calculations. Groups can be created using GROUP BY, and groups can be limited using HAVING. If the keywords WHERE and HAVING both occur in a SQL statement, WHERE is applied before HAVING.

Multiple tables can be queried using either subqueries or joins. If all the result data come from a single table, then subqueries can be used. If results come from two or more tables, then joins must be used. The JOIN . . . ON syntax may be used for joins. Rows that do not match the join conditions will not appear in the result. Outer joins can be used to ensure that all rows from a table appear in the result.

Data can be modified using UPDATE and deleted using DELETE. UPDATE and DELETE can easily cause disasters so the commands must be used with great care.

Tables (and their data) can be removed from a database using DROP TABLE. Constraints can be removed using the ALTER TABLE DROP CONSTRAINT command. Tables and constraints can be modified using the ALTER TABLE command. The CHECK constraint can be used to validate data values.

## REVIEW QUESTIONS

**3.1** What does SQL stand for?

**3.2** What is a data sublanguage?

**3.3** Explain the importance of SQL-92.

**3.4** Why is it important to learn SQL?

**3.5** Describe in your own words the purpose of the two business rules listed on page 103.

**3.6** Why won't some standard SQL-92 statements run successfully in Microsoft Access?

Use the following tables for your answers to questions 3.7 through 3.50. Sample data for these tables is shown in Figure 1-27 on page 48. For each SQL statement you write, show the results based on this data.

PET_OWNER (OwnerID, Name, Phone, Email)

PET (PetID, Name, Type, Breed, DOB, OwnerID)

If possible, run the statements you write in the questions that follow in an actual DBMS as appropriate (don't delete tables or data you'll need later!) to obtain your results. Use data types consistent with the DBMS you are using. If you are not using an actual DBMS, consistently represent data types using either the SQL Server, Oracle, or MySQL data types shown in Figure 3-4.

**3.7** Write a SQL CREATE TABLE statement to create the PET_OWNER table. Justify your choices of column properties.

**3.8** Write a SQL CREATE TABLE statement to create the PET table. Justify your choices of column properties. Why not make every column NOT NULL?

**3.9** Create a referential integrity constraint on OwnerID in PET. Assume that deletions should not cascade.

**3.10** Create a referential integrity constraint on OwnerID in PET. Assume that deletions should cascade.

**3.11** Write the required SQL statements for the following alternative version of the PET table.

PET_2 (Name, Type, Breed, DOB, OwnerID)

**3.12** Is PET or PET_2 a better design? Explain your rationale.

**3.13** Write the SQL statements necessary to remove the PET_OWNER table from the database. Assume that the referential integrity constraint is to be removed.

**3.14** Write the SQL statements necessary to remove the PET_OWNER table from the database. Assume that the PET table is also to be removed.

**3.15** Write a SQL statement to display all columns of all rows of PET. Do not use the asterisk (*) notation.

**3.16** Write a SQL statement to display all columns of all rows of PET. Use the asterisk (*) notation.

**3.17** Write a SQL statement to display the Breed and Type of all pets.

**3.18** Write a SQL statement to display the Breed, Type, and DOB of all pets having the Type Dog.

**3.19** Write a SQL statement to display the Breed column of PET.

**3.20** Write a SQL statement to display the Breed column of PET. Do not show duplicates.

**3.21** Write a SQL statement to display the Breed, Type, and DOB for all pets having the Type Dog and the Breed Std. Poodle.

**3.22** Write a SQL statement to display the Name, Breed, and Type for all pets that are not of Type Cat, Dog, or Fish.

**3.23** Write a SQL statement to display the PetID, Breed, and Type for all pets having a four-character Name starting with D.

**3.24** Write a SQL statement to display the Name and Email of all owners who have an email address ending with somewhere.com. Assume that email account names can be any number of characters.

**3.25** Write a SQL statement to display the Name of any owner who has a NULL value for Phone.

**3.26** Write a SQL statement to display the Name and Breed of all pets sorted by Name.

**3.27** Write a SQL statement to display the Name and Breed of all pets sorted by Breed in ascending order and by Name in descending order within Breed.

**3.28** Write a SQL statement to count the number of pets.

**3.29** Write a SQL statement to count the number of distinct breeds.

**3.30** Write the required SQL statements for the following alternative version of the PET table. Assume Weight is Numeric(4,1). Create your own weight data.

PET_3 (PetID, Name, Type, Breed, Weight, *OwnerID*)

Write a SQL statement to display the minimum, maximum, and average Weight of dogs.

**3.31** For the PET_3 table, write a SQL statement to group the data by Breed and display the average Weight per breed.

**3.32** Answer question 3.31, but consider only breeds for which five or more pets are included in the database.

**3.33** Answer question 3.32, but do not consider any pet having the breed *Spinone Italiano*. (Italian pets consider their weight to be personal data!)

**3.34** Write a SQL statement to display the Name and Email of any owners of cats. Use a subquery.

**3.35** Write a SQL statement to display the Name and Email of any owners of cats with the name Teddy. Use a subquery.

**3.36** Suppose the following new table is added to the pet database.

BREED (BreedName, MinWeight, MaxWeight, AverageLifeExpectancy)

Assume that Breed in PET is a foreign key that matches the primary key BreedName in BREED. Create your own data for BREED as necessary. Write a SQL statement to display Name and Email of any owner of a pet that has an AverageLifeExpectancy greater than 15. Use a subquery.

**3.37** Answer question 3.34, but use a join.

**3.38** Answer question 3.35, but use a join.

**3.39** Answer question 3.36, but use joins.

**3.40** Answer question 3.34, but use a left outer join. How will your results differ from those in your answer to question 3.37?

**3.41** Write a SQL statement to add three new rows to the PET_OWNER table. Assume OwnerID is a surrogate key, and the DBMS will provide a value for it. Otherwise, assume you have all the data. Create the necessary data for this question.

**3.42** Write a SQL statement to add three new rows to the PET_OWNER table. Assume OwnerID is a surrogate key, and the DBMS will provide a value for it. Otherwise, you have only Name and Phone; assume Email is NULL. Create the necessary data for this question.

**3.43** Write a SQL statement to change the value of Std. Poodle in Breed of PET to Poodle, Std.

**3.44** Explain what will happen if you leave the WHERE clause off your answer to question 3.43.

**3.45** Write a SQL statement to delete all rows of pets of Type Anteater. What will happen if you forget to code the WHERE clause in this statement?

**3.46** Write a SQL statement to add a Weight column like the one in PET_2 to the PET table, given that this column is NULL. Again, assume Weight is Numeric(4,1).

**3.47** Write SQL statements to insert data into the Weight column you created in question 3.46. Create your own weight data.

**3.48** Write SQL statements to add a Weight column like the one in PET_2 to the PET table, given that this column is NOT NULL. Again, assume Weight is Numeric(4,1). Use the same weight data you created in question 3.47.

**3.49** Write a SQL statement to add a CHECK constraint to the PET table so that the weight data recorded in the Weight column you added to the table in either question 3.46 or 3.48 is less than 250.

**3.50** Write a SQL statement to drop the Weight column you added to the PET table in either question 3.46 or 3.48.

## EXERCISES

Below is a set of tables for the Art Course database shown in Figure 1-10. For the data for these tables, use the data shown in Figure 1-10.

CUSTOMER (<u>CustomerNumber</u>, CustomerName, Phone)

COURSE (<u>CourseNumber</u>, Course, CourseDate, Fee)

ENROLLMENT (*<u>CustomerNumber</u>*, *<u>CourseNumber</u>*, AmountPaid)

where

CustomerNumber in ENROLLMENT must exist in CustomerNumber in CUSTOMER

CourseNumber in ENROLLMENT must exist in CourseNumber in COURSE

CustomerNumber and CourseNumber are surrogate keys. Therefore, these numbers will never be modified, and there is no need for cascading updates. No customer data is ever deleted so there is no need to cascade deletions. Courses can be deleted, and if there are enrollment entries for that class, they should also be deleted.

These tables, referential integrity constraints, and data are used as the basis for the SQL statements you will create in the exercises that follow. If possible, run these statements in an actual DBMS as appropriate to obtain your results—name your database ART_COURSE_DATABASE. For each SQL statement you write, show the results based on this data. Use data types consistent with the DBMS you are using. If you are not using an actual DBMS, consistently represent data types using either the SQL Server, Oracle, or MySQL data types shown in Figure 3-4.

**3.51** Write and run the SQL statements necessary to create the tables and their referential integrity constraints.

**3.52** Populate the tables with data.

**3.53** Write and run a SQL query to list all occurrences of Adv. Pastels. Include all associated data for each occurrence of the class.

**3.54** Write and run a SQL query to list all students and courses they are registered for. Include, in this order, CustomerNumber, CustomerName, Phone, CourseNumber, and AmountPaid.

**3.55** Write and run a SQL query to list all students registered in the Adv. Pastels starting on October 1, 2006. Include, in this order, the CourseName, CourseDate, Fee, CustomerName, and Phone.

**3.56** Write and run an SQL query to list all students registered in the Adv. Pastels starting on October 1, 2006. Include in this order, the CourseName, CourseDate, CustomerName, Phone, Fee, and AmountPaid. Use a join.

**3.57** Modify your query to include all students regardless of whether or not they registered in the Adv. Pastels starting on October 1, 2006. Include, in this order, CustomerName, Phone, CourseName, CourseDate, Fee, and AmountPaid.

**3.58** Write a set of SQL statements (Hint: Use the SQL ALTER TABLE command) to add a FullFeePaid column to ENROLLMENT and populate the column, assuming that the column is NULL. The only possible values for this column are *Yes* and *No* (compare COURSE.Fee to ENROLLMENT.AmountPaid to determine data values).

**3.59** Write a set of SQL statements (Hint: Use the SQL ALTER TABLE command) to add a FullFeePaid column to ENROLLMENT and populate the column, assuming that the column is NOT NULL. The only possible values for this column are *Yes* and *No* (compare COURSE.Fee to ENROLLMENT.AmountPaid to determine data values). What is the difference between your answer to question 3.58 and this question?

**3.60** Write an ALTER TABLE statement to add a CHECK constraint to the ENROLLMENT table to ensure that the value of FullFeePaid is either *Yes* or *No*.

The following exercises are intended for use with a DBMS other than MS Access. If you are using MS Access, see the equivalent questions in the "Access Workbench Exercises" that follow.

**3.61** If you haven't done so, create the WPC database, tables, and relationships as described in this chapter using the SQL DBMS of your choice. This includes populating the tables with the data shown in Figure 3-2.

**3.62** Using the SQL DBMS of your choice, create and run queries to answer the questions in Access Workbench Exercise AW.3.1.

**3.63** Using the SQL DBMS of your choice, complete steps A through E in Access Workbench Exercise AW.3.3—*exclude step F.*

## ACCESS WORKBENCH EXERCISES

In the "Access Workbench Exercises" in Chapters 1 and 2, we created a database for the Wedgewood Pacific Corporation (WPC) of Seattle, Washington. In this set of exercises, we will:

- create and run queries against the database using Access SQL,
- create and run queries against the database using Access QBE,
- create tables and relationships using Access SQL, and
- populate tables using Access SQL.

**AW.3.1**  Using Access SQL, create and run queries to answer the questions that follow. Save each query using the query name format SQLQuery-AWE-3-1-## where the ## sign is replaced by the letter designator of the question. For example, the first query will be saved as SQLQuery-AWE-3-1-A.

**A.**  What projects are in the PROJECT table? Show all information for each project.

**B.**  What are the ProjectID, Name, StartDate, and EndDate values of projects in the PROJECT table?

**C.**  What projects in the PROJECT table started before August 1, 2005? Show all the information for each project.

**D.**  What projects in the PROJECT table have not been completed? Show all the information for each project.

**E.**  Who are the employees assigned to each project? Show the ProjectID, EmployeeID, LastName, FirstName, and Phone.

**F.**  Who are the employees assigned to each project? Show the ProjectID, Name, and Department. Show the EmployeeID, LastName, FirstName, and Phone.

**G.**  Who are the employees assigned to each project? Show the ProjectID, Name, Department, and Department Phone. Show the EmployeeID, LastName, FirstName, and Employee Phone. Sort by ProjectID in ascending order.

**H.**  Who are the employees assigned to projects run by the Marketing Department? Show the ProjectID, Name, Department, and Department Phone. Show the EmployeeID, LastName, FirstName, and Employee Phone. Sort by ProjectID in ascending order.

**I.**  How many projects are being run by the Marketing Department?

**J.**  What is the total MaxHours of projects being run by the Marketing Department?

**K.**  What is the average MaxHours of projects being run by the Marketing Department?

**L.**  How many projects are being run by each department?

*(Continued)*

**AW.3.2** Using Access QBE, create and run new queries to answer the questions in exercise AW.3.1. Save each query using the query name format QBEQuery-AWE-3-1-## where the ## sign is replaced by the letter designator of the question. For example, the first query will be saved as QBEQuery-AWE-3-1-A.

**AW.3.3** WPC has decided to keep track of computers used by the employees. In order to do this, two new tables will be added to the database. The schema for these tables as related to the existing EMPLOYEE table is:

EMPLOYEE (EmployeeNumber, FirstName, LastName, *Department*, Phone, Email)

COMPUTER (SerialNumber, Make, Model, ProcessorType, ProcessorSpeed, MainMemory, DiskSize)

COMPUTER_ASSIGNMENT (*SerialNumber*, *EmployeeNumber*, DateAssigned)

The referential integrity constraints are:

SerialNumber in COMPUTER_ASSIGNMENT must exist in SerialNumber in COMPUTER

EmployeeNumber in COMPUTER_ASSIGNMENT must exist in EmployeeNumber in EMPLOYEE

EmployeeNumber is a surrogate key and never changes. Employee records are never deleted from the database. SerialNumber is not a surrogate key since it is not generated by the database. However, a computer's SerialNumber never changes, and, therefore, there is no need to cascade updates. When a computer is at its end of life, the record in COMPUTER for that computer and all associated records in COMPUTER_ASSIGNMENT are deleted from the database.

**A.** Figure 3-13 shows the column characteristics for the WPC COMPUTER table. Using the column characteristics, use Access SQL to create the COMPUTER table and its associated constraints in the WPC.mdb database. Are there any table characteristics that cannot be created in SQL? If so, what are they? Use the Access GUI to finish setting table characteristics if necessary.

**FIGURE 3-13**

**Column Characteristics for the COMPUTER Table**

| Column Name | Type | Key | Required | Remarks |
|---|---|---|---|---|
| SerialNumber | Number | Primary Key | Yes | Long Integer |
| Make | Text (18) | No | Yes | Must be "Dell" or "Gateway" or "HP" or "Other" |
| Model | Text (18) | No | Yes | |
| ProcessorType | Text (18) | No | No | |
| ProcessorSpeed | Number | No | Yes | Double [3,2], Between 1.0 and 5.0 |
| MainMemory | Text (10) | No | Yes | |
| DiskSize | Text (10) | No | Yes | |

---

**FIGURE 3-14**

---

**WPC COMPUTER Data**

| Serial Number | Make | Model | Processor Type | Processor Speed | Main Memory | DiskSize |
|---|---|---|---|---|---|---|
| 9871234 | HP | Compaq DC5100 | Intel Pentium 4 | 3.0 | 512 MBytes | 40 GByte |
| 9871245 | HP | Compaq DC5100 | Intel Pentium 4 | 3.0 | 512 MBytes | 40 GByte |
| 9871256 | HP | Compaq DC5100 | Intel Pentium 4 | 3.0 | 512 MBytes | 40 GByte |
| 9871267 | HP | Compaq DC5100 | Intel Pentium 4 | 3.0 | 512 MBytes | 40 GByte |
| 9871278 | HP | Compaq DC5100 | Intel Pentium 4 | 3.0 | 512 MBytes | 40 GByte |
| 9871289 | HP | Compaq DC5100 | Intel Pentium 4 | 3.0 | 512 MBytes | 40 GByte |
| 6541001 | Dell | OptiPlex GX620 | Intel Pentium 4 | 3.2 | 1024 MBytes | 80 GByte |
| 6541002 | Dell | OptiPlex GX620 | Intel Pentium 4 | 3.2 | 1024 MBytes | 80 GByte |
| 6541003 | Dell | OptiPlex GX620 | Intel Pentium 4 | 3.2 | 1024 MBytes | 80 GByte |
| 6541004 | Dell | OptiPlex GX620 | Intel Pentium 4 | 3.2 | 1024 MBytes | 80 GByte |
| 6541005 | Dell | OptiPlex GX620 | Intel Pentium 4 | 3.2 | 1024 MBytes | 80 GByte |
| 6541006 | Del | OptiPlex GX620 | Intel Pentium 4 | 3.2 | 1024 MBytes | 80 GByte |

**B.** The data for the COMPUTER table is in Figure 3-14. Use Access SQL to enter this data into your COMPUTER table.

**C.** Figure 3-15 shows the column characteristics for the WPC COMPUTER table. Using the column characteristics, use Access SQL to create the COMPUTER table and the associated constraints in the WPC.mdb database. Are there any table or relationship settings or characteristics that cannot be created in SQL? If so, what are they? Use the Access GUI to finish setting table characteristics and relationship settings if necessary

**D.** The data for the COMPUTER_ASSIGNMENT table is in Figure 3-16. Use Access SQL to enter this data into your COMPUTER_ASSIGNMENT table.

**E.** Who currently is using which computer at WPC? Create an appropriate SQL query to answer this question. Show the SerialNumber, Make, and Model. Show the EmployeeID, LastName, FirstName, Department, and Employee Phone. Sort first by Department and then by employee LastName. Save this query using the query naming rules in AW.3.1.

---

**FIGURE 3-15**

---

**Column Characteristics for the COMPUTER_ASSIGNMENT Table**

| Column Name | Type | Key | Required | Remarks |
|---|---|---|---|---|
| SerialNumber | Number | Primary Key, Foreign Key | Yes | Long Integer |
| EmployeeNumber | Number | Primary Key, Foreign Key | Yes | Long Integer |
| DateAssigned | Date/Time | No | Yes | |

*(Continued)*

## FIGURE 3-16

**WPC COMPUTER_ASSIGNMENT Data**

| SerialNumber | EmployeeNumber | DateAssigned |
|---|---|---|
| 9871234 | 11 | 15-Sep-05 |
| 9871245 | 12 | 15-Sep-05 |
| 9871256 | 4 | 15-Sep-05 |
| 9871267 | 5 | 15-Sep-05 |
| 9871278 | 8 | 15-Sep-05 |
| 9871289 | 9 | 15-Sep-05 |
| 6541001 | 11 | 21-Oct-05 |
| 6541002 | 12 | 21-Oct-05 |
| 6541003 | 1 | 21-Oct-05 |
| 6541004 | 2 | 21-Oct-05 |
| 6541005 | 3 | 21-Oct-05 |
| 6541006 | 6 | 21-Oct-05 |
| 9871234 | 7 | 05-Nov-05 |
| 9871245 | 10 | 05-Nov-05 |

**F.** Who currently is using which computer at WPC? Create an appropriate QBE query to answer this question. Show the SerialNumber, Make, Model, ProcessorType, and ProcessorSpeed. Show the EmployeeID, LastName, FirstName, Department, and Employee Phone. Sort first by Department and then by employee LastName. Save this query using the query naming rules in AW.3.2.

## GARDEN GLORY PROJECT QUESTIONS

Assume that Garden Glory designs a database with the following tables.

OWNER (<u>OwnerID</u>, OwnerName, Email, Type)

PROPERTY (<u>PropertyID</u>, PropertyName, Street, City, State, Zip, *OwnerID*)

EMPLOYEE (<u>Initials</u>, Name, CellPhone, ExperienceLevel)

SERVICE (*<u>PropertyID</u>*, *<u>Initials</u>*, <u>Date</u>, HoursWorked)

where

OwnerID in PROPERTY must exist in OwnerID in OWNER

PropertyID in SERVICE must exist in PropertyID in PROPERTY

Initials in SERVICE must exist in Initials in EMPLOYEE

Assume that OwnerID in OWNER and PropertyID in PROPERTY are surrogate keys with values as follows:

| OwnerID | Start at 1 | Increment by 1 |
|---|---|---|
| PropertyID | Start at 1 | Increment by 1 |

Some sample data is shown in Figure 2-28, but you will need to create additional data to populate the tables (alternately, your instructor may provide you with a data set). Type is either Individual or Corporation, and ExperienceLevel is one of Junior, Senior, Master, or SuperMaster. These tables, referential integrity constraints, and data are used as the basis for the SQL statements you will create in the exercises that follow. If possible, run these statements in an actual DBMS as appropriate to obtain your results—name your database GARDEN_GLORY.

Use data types consistent with the DBMS you are using. If you are not using an actual DBMS, consistently represent data types using either the SQL Server, Oracle, or MySQL data types shown in Figure 3-4. For each SQL statement you write, show the results based on your data.

Write SQL statements and answer questions for this database as follows:

**A.** Write CREATE TABLE statements for each of these tables.

**B.** Write foreign key constraints for the relationships in each of these tables. Make your own assumptions regarding cascading updates and deletions and justify those assumptions. (Hint: You can combine the SQL for your answers to A and B)

**C.** Write SQL statements to insert at least three rows of data into each of these tables. Assume that any surrogate key value will be supplied by the DBMS. Use the data in Figure 2-28 as appropriate.

**D.** Write SQL statements to list all columns for all tables.

**E.** Write a SQL statement to list the Name and CellPhone for all employees having an experience level of Master.

**F.** Write a SQL statement to list the Name and CellPhone for all employees having an experience level of Master and a Name that begins with the letter *J*.

**G.** Write a SQL statement to list the Name of employees who have worked on a property in New York. Use a subquery.

**H.** Answer question G but use a join.

**I.** Write a SQL statement to list the Name of employees who have worked on a property owned by a Corporation. Use a subquery.

**J.** Answer question I but use a join.

**K.** Write a SQL statement to show the Name and sum of HoursWorked for each employee.

**L.** Write a SQL statement to show the sum of HoursWorked for each ExperienceLevel of EMPLOYEE. Sort the results by ExperienceLevel in descending order.

**M.** Write a SQL statement to show the sum of HoursWorked for each Type of OWNER but exclude services of employees who have an ExperienceLevel of Junior and exclude any Type with less than three members.

**N.** Write a SQL statement to modify all EMPLOYEE rows with an ExperienceLevel of Master to SuperMaster.

**O.** Write a SQL statement to switch the values of ExperienceLevel so that all rows currently having the value Junior will have the value Senior, and all rows currently having the value Senior will have the value Junior.

**P.**  Given your assumptions about cascading deletions in your answer to question B, write the fewest number of DELETE statements possible to remove all the data in your database but leave the table structures intact. Do *not* run these statements if you are using an actual database!

## JAMES RIVER JEWELRY PROJECT QUESTIONS

Assume that James River designs a database with the following tables.

> CUSTOMER (<u>CustomerID</u>, LastName, FirstName, Phone, Email)
>
> PURCHASE (<u>InvoiceNumber</u>, Date, PreTaxAmount, *CustomerID*)
>
> PURCHASE_ITEM (*<u>InvoiceNumber</u>*, *<u>ItemNumber</u>*, RetailPrice)
>
> ITEM (<u>ItemNumber</u>, Description, Cost, ArtistName)

where

> CustomerID in PURCHASE must exist in CustomerID in CUSTOMER
>
> InvoiceNumber in PURCHASE_ITEM must exist in InvoiceNumber in PURCHASE
>
> ItemNumber in PURCHASE_ITEM must exist in ItemNumber in ITEM

Assume that CustomerID of CUSTOMER, ItemNumber of ITEM, InvoiceNumber of PURCHASE, and ItemNumber of PURCHASE_ITEM are all surrogate keys with values as follows:

| | | |
|---|---|---|
| CustomerID | Start at 1 | Increment by 1 |
| ItemNumber | Start at 1 | Increment by 1 |
| InvoiceNumber | Start at 1 | Increment by 1 |
| ItemNumber | Start at 1 | Increment by 1 |

Some sample data is shown in Figure 2-29, but you will need to create additional data to populate the tables (alternately, your instructor may provide you with a data set). These tables, referential integrity constraints, and data are used as the basis for the SQL statements you will create in the exercises that follow. If possible, run these statements in an actual DBMS as appropriate to obtain your results—name your database JAMES_RIVER_JEWELRY.

Use data types consistent with the DBMS you are using. If you are not using an actual DBMS, consistently represent data types using either the SQL Server, Oracle, or MySQL data types shown in Figure 3-4. For each SQL statement you write, show the results based on your data.

Write SQL statements and answer questions for this database as follows:

**A.**  Write SQL CREATE TABLE statements for each of these tables.

**B.**  Write foreign key constraints for the relationships in each of these tables. Make your own assumptions regarding cascading deletions and justify those assumptions. (Hint: You can combine the SQL for your answers to A and B)

**C.**  Write SQL statements to insert at least three rows of data into each of these tables. Assume that surrogate key column values will be supplied by the DBMS. Use the data in Figure 2-29 as appropriate.

**D.**   Write SQL statements to list all columns for all tables.

**E.**   Write a SQL statement to list the ItemNumber and Description for all items that cost more than $100.

**F.**   Write a SQL statement to list the ItemNumber and Description for all items that cost more than $100 and were produced by an artist with a name ending with the letters *son*.

**G.**   Write a SQL statement to list the LastName and FirstName of customers who have made at least one purchase with PreTaxAmount greater than $200. Use a subquery.

**H.**   Same as question G but use a join.

**I.**   Write a SQL statement to list the LastName and FirstName of customers who have purchased an item that costs more than $50. Use a subquery.

**J.**   Same as question I but use a join.

**K.**   Write a SQL statement to list the LastName and FirstName of customers who have purchased an item that was created by an artist with a name that begins with the letter *J*. Use a subquery.

**L.**   Same as question K but use a join.

**M.**   Write a SQL statement to show the Name and sum of PreTaxAmount for each customer.

**N.**   Write a SQL statement to show the sum of PreTaxAmount for each ArtistName. Sort the results by ArtistName in descending order.

**O.**   Write a SQL statement to show the sum of PreTaxAmount for each ArtistName but exclude any items that were part of purchases with a PreTaxAmount less than $25.

**P.**   Write a SQL statement to modify all ITEM rows with a name of Baker to Rex Baker.

**Q.**   Write SQL statements to switch the values of ArtistName so that all rows currently having the value Baker will have the value Baxter, and all rows currently having the value Baxter will have the value Baker.

**R.**   Given your assumptions about cascading deletions in your answer to question B, write the fewest number of DELETE statements possible to remove all the data in your database, but leave the table structures intact. Do *not* run these statements if you are using an actual database!.

## THE QUEEN ANNE CURIOSITY SHOP PROJECT QUESTIONS

Assume that The Queen Anne Curiosity Shop designs a database with the following tables.

CUSTOMER (<u>CustomerID</u>, LastName, FirstName, Address, City, State, ZIP, Phone, Email)

EMPLOYEE (<u>EmployeeID</u>, LastName, FirstName, Phone, Email)

VENDOR (<u>VendorID</u>, CompanyName, ContactLastName, ContactFirstName, Address, City, State, ZIP, Phone, Fax, Email)

ITEM (<u>ItemID</u>, ItemDescription, PurchaseDate, ItemCost, ItemPrice, *VendorID*)

SALE (<u>SaleID</u>, *CustomerID*, *EmployeeID*, SaleDate, SubTotal, Tax, Total)

SALE_ITEM (<u>*SaleID*</u>, <u>SaleItemID</u>, *ItemID*, ItemPrice)

where

VendorID in ITEM must exist in VendorID in VENDOR

CustomerID in SALE must exist in CustomerID in CUSTOMER

EmployeeID in SALE must exist in EmployeeID in EMPLOYEE

SaleID in SALE_ITEM must exist in SaleID in SALE

ItemID in SALE_ITEM must exist in ItemID in ITEM

Assume that CustomerID of CUSTOMER, EmployeeID of EMPLOYEE, ItemID of ITEM, and SaleID of SALE are all surrogate keys with values as follows:

| | | |
|---|---|---|
| CustomerID | Start at 1 | Increment by 1 |
| EmployeeID | Start at 1 | Increment by 1 |
| VendorID | Start at 1 | Increment by 1 |
| ItemID | Start at 1 | Increment by 1 |
| SaleID | Start at 1 | Increment by 1 |

A vendor may be an individual or a company. If the vendor is an individual, the CompanyName field is left blank, while the ContactLastName and ContactFirstName fields must have data values. If the vendor is a company, the company name is recorded in the CompanyName field, and the name of the primary contact at the company is recorded in the ContactLastName and ContactFirstName fields.

Some sample data is shown in Figures 2-30(a) and 2-30(b), but you will need to create additional data to populate the tables (alternately, your instructor may provide you with a data set). These tables, referential integrity constraints, and data are used as the basis for the SQL statements you will create in the exercises that follow. If possible, run these statements in an actual DBMS as appropriate to obtain your results—name your database QACS.

Use data types consistent with the DBMS you are using. If you are not using an actual DBMS, consistently represent data types using either the SQL Server, Oracle, or MySQL data types shown in Figure 3-4. For each SQL statement you write, show the results based on your data.

Write SQL statements and answer questions for this database as follows:

**A.** Write SQL CREATE TABLE statements for each of these tables.

**B.** Write foreign key constraints for the relationships in each of these tables. Make your own assumptions regarding cascading deletions and justify those assumptions. (Hint: You can combine the SQL for your answers to A and B.)

**C.** Write SQL statements to insert at least three rows of data into each of these tables. Assume that all surrogate key column values will be supplied by the DBMS. Use the data in Figures 2-30(a) and 2-30(b) as appropriate.

**D.** Write SQL statements to list all columns for all tables.

**E.** Write a SQL statement to list the ItemID and ItemDescription for all items that cost $1000 or more.

**F.** Write a SQL statement to list the ItemNumber and Description for all items that cost $1000 or more and were purchased from a vendor whose CompanyName starts with the letters *New*.

**G.** Write a SQL statement to list the LastName, FirstName, and Phone of the customer who made the purchase with SaleID 1. Use a subquery.

**H.** Same as question G but use a join.

**I.** Write a SQL statement to list the LastName, FirstName, and Phone of the customers who made the purchase with SaleIDs 1, 2, and 3. Use a subquery.

**J.** Same as question I but use a join.

**K.** Write a SQL statement to list the LastName, FirstName, and Phone of customers who have made at least one purchase with SubTotal greater than $500. Use a subquery.

**L.** Same as question K but use a join.

**M.** Write a SQL statement to list the LastName, FirstName, and Phone of customers who have purchased an item that has an ItemPrice of $500 or more. Use a subquery.

**N.** Same as question M but use a join.

**O.** Write a SQL statement to list the LastName, FirstName, and Phone of customers who have purchased an item that was supplied by a vendor with a CompanyName that begins with the letter *L*. Use a subquery.

**P.** Same as question O but use a join.

**Q.** Write a SQL statement to show the sum of SubTotal for each customer. List CustomerID, LastName, FirstName, Phone, and the calculated result. Name the sum of SubTotal as SumOfSubTotal, and sort the results by CustomerID in descending order.

**R.** Write a SQL statement to modify all the vendor CompanyName of *Linens and Things* to *Linens and Other Stuff*.

**S.** Write SQL statements to switch the values of vendor CompanyName so that all rows currently having the value *Linens and Things* will have the value *Lamps and Lighting*, and all rows currently having the value *Lamps and Lighting* will have the value *Linens and Things*.

**T.** Given your assumptions about cascading deletions in your answer to question B, write the fewest number of DELETE statements possible to remove all the data in your database but leave the table structures intact Do *not* run these statements if you are using an actual database!

# PART II

# Database Design and Management

**S**o far, you have been introduced to the fundamental concepts and techniques of relational database management. In Chapter 1, you learned that databases consist of related tables, and you learned the major components of a database system. Chapter 2 introduced you to the relational model, and you learned the basic ideas of functional dependencies and normalization. In Chapter 3, you learned how to use SQL statements to create and process a database.

All this material gives you a background for understanding the nature of database management and the basic tools and techniques. However, you do not yet know how to apply all this technology to solve a business problem. Imagine, for example, that you walk into a small business—for example, a bookshop—and are asked to build a database to support a frequent buyer program. How would you proceed? So far, we have assumed that the database design already exists. How would you go about creating the design of the database? Furthermore, once the database exists, what tasks need to be done to manage it over time?

The next four chapters address these important topics. We begin Chapter 4 with an overview of the database design process, and then we describe data modeling—a technique for representing database requirements. In Chapter 5, you will learn how to transform a data model into a relational database design. Finally, in Chapter 6, you will learn about database management. Here, you also will be introduced to many of the problems that occur when a database is concurrently processed by more than one user. Finally, Chapter 7 will conclude the book by surveying important advanced database concepts, including the use of databases to support Web sites. After completing these chapters, you will have surveyed all the basic database technology. This knowledge will give you the necessary background to learn more in the area of your interests or job requirements. For example, you will be able to learn more about SQL, or to learn to use a particular DBMS product, such as SQL Server, Oracle, or MySQL, or to learn to publish databases using Internet technology.

# CHAPTER 4

# Data Modeling and the Entity-Relationship Model

> - Learn the basic stages of database development
> - Understand the purpose and role of a data model
> - Know the principal components of the E-R data model
> - Understand how to interpret traditional E-R diagrams
> - Understand how to interpret Information Engineering (IE) Crow's Foot E-R diagrams
> - Learn to construct E-R diagrams
> - Know how to represent 1:1, 1:N, N:M, and binary relationships with the E-R model
> - Understand two types of weak entities and know how to use them
> - Understand nonidentifying and identifying relationships and know how to use them
> - Know how to represent subtype entities with the E-R model
> - Know how to represent recursive relationships with the E-R model
> - Learn how to create an E-R diagram from source documents

The process of developing a database system consists of three major stages: requirements, design, and implementation. During the **requirements stage**, system users are interviewed and sample forms, reports, queries, and descriptions of update activities are obtained. These system requirements are used to create a **data model**, which is a representation of the content, relationships, and constraints of the data needed to support the requirements. Often, prototypes, or working demonstrations of selected portions of the future system, are created during the requirements phase. Such prototypes are used to obtain feedback from the system users.

During the **design stage**, the data model is transformed into a **database design**. Such a design consists of tables, relationships, and constraints. The design includes the table names and the names of all table columns. The design also includes the data types and properties of the columns, as well as a description of primary and foreign keys. Data constraints consist of limits on data values (e.g., part numbers are seven-digit numbers starting with the number three), referential integrity constraints, and business rules. An example of a business rule for a manufacturing company is that every purchased part will have a quotation from at least two suppliers.

The last stage of database development is the **implementation stage**. During this stage, the database is constructed and filled with data; queries, forms, and reports are created; application programs are written; and all these are tested. Finally, during this stage users are trained, documentation is written, and the system is installed for use.

In this chapter, we will consider the requirements stage in general and data modeling in particular. You will learn about an important tool, the entity-relationship data model, and you will learn how to apply this tool to represent the data requirements for a small business. Our goal here is to focus only on the database aspects of information systems development. The design and development of other components of an information system are outside the scope of this text; they are the subject matter of a systems development class.

## ▶ THE REQUIREMENTS STAGE

Sources of user requirements are listed in Figure 4-1. As you will learn in your systems development class, the general practice is to identify the users of the new information system and to interview them. During the interviews, examples of existing forms, reports, and queries are obtained. In addition, the users are asked about the need for changes to existing forms, reports, and queries and also about the need for new forms, reports, and queries.

**FIGURE 4-1**

Sources of
Requirements for a
Database Application

> User Interviews
> Forms
> Reports
> Queries
> Use Cases
> Business Rules

**Use cases** are descriptions of the ways users will employ the features and functions of the new information system. A use case consists of a description of the roles users will play when utilizing the new system, together with descriptions of activities' scenarios. Inputs provided to the system and outputs generated by the system are defined. Sometimes dozens of such use cases are necessary. Use cases provide sources of requirements and also can be used to validate the data model, design, and implementation.

In addition to these requirements, the development team needs to document characteristics of data items. For each data item in a form, report, or query, the team needs to determine its data type, properties, and limits on values.

Finally, during the process of establishing requirements, system developers need to document business rules that constrain actions on database activity. Generally, such rules arise from business policy and practice. For example, the following business rules could pertain to an academic database.

- Students must declare a major before enrolling in any class.
- Graduate classes can be taken by juniors or seniors with a grade point average of 3.70 or greater.
- No adviser may have more than 25 advisees.
- Students may declare one or two majors, but no more.

## ► THE ENTITY-RELATIONSHIP DATA MODEL

The system requirements described in the prior section, although necessary and important as a first step, are not sufficient for designing a database. In addition, the requirements must be transformed into a data model. When writing application programs, program logic must first be documented in flowcharts or object diagrams; this is also the case with a database—data requirements must first be documented in a **data model.**

A number of different techniques can be used to create data models. By far the most popular is the **entity-relationship (E-R) model**, so this book will focus on it. The E-R model was first published by Peter Chen[1] in 1976. Chen's basic model was extended to create the **extended entity-relationship (E-R) model**. Today, when we say *E-R model*, we mean the extended E-R model, and we will use it in this text.

There are several versions of the E-R model in use today. We begin with the traditional E-R model. Later in the chapter, after the basic principles of E-R models have been covered, we will introduce and use another version of the E-R model.

The most important elements of the E-R model are entities, attributes, identifiers, and relationships. We will consider each of these in turn.

### Entities

An **entity** is something that users want to track. Examples of entities are CUSTOMER John Doe, PURCHASE 12345, PRODUCT A4200, SALES-ORDER 1000, SALESPERSON John Smith, and SHIPMENT 123400. Entities of a given type are grouped into an

---

[1]Peter P. Chen, "The Entity-Relationship Model—Towards a Unified View of Data," *ACM Transactions on Database Systems* (January 1976): 9–36.

**entity class**. Thus, the EMPLOYEE entity class is the collection of all EMPLOYEE entities. In this text, entity classes are shown in capital letters.

An **entity instance** of an entity class is the occurrence of a particular entity, such as CUSTOMER 12345. It is important to understand the differences between an entity class and an entity instance. An entity class is a collection of entities and is described by the structure of the entities in that class. There are usually many instances of an entity in an entity class. For example, within the class CUSTOMER, there are many instances—one for each customer represented in the database. The ITEM entity class and two of its instances are shown in Figure 4-2.

When developing a data model, the developers analyze the forms, reports, queries, and other system requirements. Entities are usually the subject of one or more forms or reports, or are a major section in one or more forms or reports. For example, a form entitled PRODUCT Data Entry Form indicates the likelihood of an entity class called PRODUCT. Similarly, a report entitled CUSTOMER PURCHASE Summary indicates that most likely the business has CUSTOMER and PURCHASE entities.

## Attributes

Entities have attributes. **Attributes** describe the entity's characteristics. Examples of attributes include EmployeeName, DateOfHire, and JobSkillCode. In this text, attributes are printed in a combination of uppercase and lowercase letters. The E-R model assumes that all instances of a given entity class have the same attributes. For example, in Figure 4-2 the ITEM entity has the attributes ItemNumber, Description, Cost, ListPrice and QuantityOnHand.

Attributes have a data type and properties that are determined from the requirements. Typical data types are character, numeric, date, currency, and the like. Properties specify whether the attribute is required, whether it has a default value, whether its value has limits, and any other constraint.

## Identifiers

Entity instances have identifiers. **Identifiers** are attributes that name, or identify, entity instances. For example, the ITEM entity in Figure 4-2 uses ItemNumber as an identifier. Similarly, EMPLOYEE instances could be identified by SocialSecurityNumber, by

**FIGURE 4-2**

**Two Entity Instances**

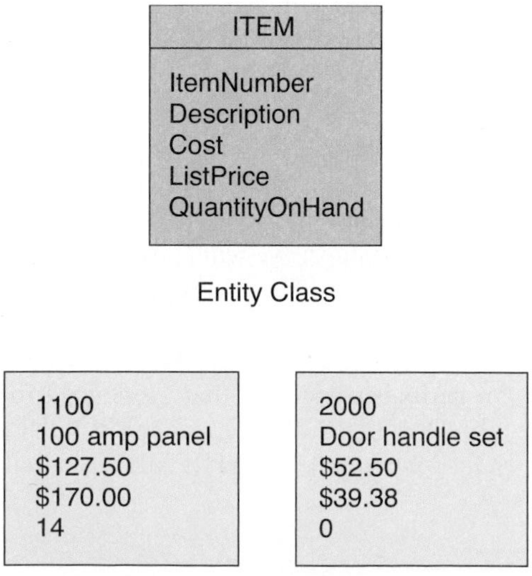

| ITEM |
| --- |
| ItemNumber |
| Description |
| Cost |
| ListPrice |
| QuantityOnHand |

Entity Class

| 1100 | | 2000 |
| --- | --- | --- |
| 100 amp panel | | Door handle set |
| $127.50 | | $52.50 |
| $170.00 | | $39.38 |
| 14 | | 0 |

Two Entity Instances

EmployeeNumber, or by EmployeeName. EMPLOYEE instances are not likely to be identified by attributes such as Salary or DateOfHire because these attributes normally are not used in a naming role. CUSTOMER instances could be identified by CustomerNumber or CustomerName, and SALES-ORDER instances could be identified by OrderNumber.

The identifier of an entity instance consists of one or more of the entity's attributes. Identifiers that consist of two or more attributes are called **composite identifiers**. Examples are (AreaCode, LocalNumber), (ProjectName, TaskName), and (FirstName, LastName, PhoneExtension).

An identifier may be either **unique** or **nonunique**. The value of a unique identifier will identify one, and only one, entity instance. On the other hand, the value of a nonunique identifier will identify a set of instances. EmployeeNumber is normally a unique identifier, but EmployeeName is most likely a nonunique identifier (more than one John Smith might be employed by the company, for example).

---

**B T W**

As you can tell from these definitions, identifiers are similar to keys in the relational model, but with two important differences. First, an identifier is a logical concept—it is one or more attributes that users think of as a name of the entity. Such identifiers might or might not be represented as keys in the database design. Second, primary and candidate keys must be unique, whereas identifiers might or might not be unique.

---

As shown in Figure 4-3, entities are portrayed in three levels of detail in a data model. Sometimes the entity and all its attributes are displayed. In such cases, the identifier of the attribute is shown at the top of the entity and a horizontal line is drawn after the identifier as shown in Figure 4-3(a). In a large data model, so much detail can make the data model diagrams unwieldy. In those cases, the entity diagram is abbreviated by showing just the identifier as in Figure 4-3(b), or by showing just the name of the entity in a rectangle as shown in Figure 4-3(c).

## Relationships

Entities can be associated with one another in **relationships**. The E-R model contains relationship classes and relationship instances. **Relationship classes** are associations among entity classes, and **relationship instances** are associations among entity instances. In the original specification of the E-R model, relationships could have attributes. In modern practice, that feature is not used and only entities have attributes.

A relationship class can involve many entity classes. The number of entity classes in the relationship is known as the **degree** of the relationship. In Figure 4-4(a), the

**FIGURE 4-3**

Level of Entity
Attribute Display

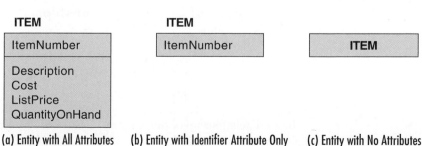

(a) Entity with All Attributes    (b) Entity with Identifier Attribute Only    (c) Entity with No Attributes

**FIGURE 4-4**

**Example Relationships**

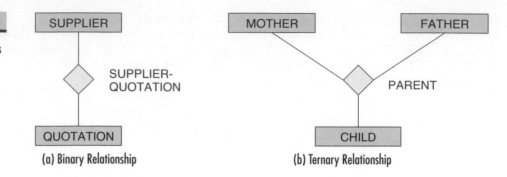

(a) Binary Relationship     (b) Ternary Relationship

SUPPLIER-QUOTATION relationship is of degree two because it involves two entity classes, SUPPLIER and QUOTATION. The PARENT relationship in Figure 4-4(b) is of degree three, because it involves three entity classes: MOTHER, FATHER, and CHILD. Relationships of degree two, which are the most common, are called **binary relationships**. Similarly, relationships of degree three are called **ternary relationships**.

---

**B T W**

You may be wondering "what's the difference between an entity and a table?" They may seem like different terms for the same thing. *The principle difference between an entity and a table is that you can express a relationship between entities without using foreign keys.* In the E-R model, you can specify a relationship just by drawing a line connecting two entities. Because you are doing *logical data modeling,* and not physical database design, you need not worry about primary and foreign keys, referential integrity constraints, and the like.

This characteristic makes entities easier to work with than tables, especially early in a project when entities and relationships are fluid and uncertain. You can show relationships between entities before you even know what the identifiers are. For example, you can say that a DEPARTMENT relates to many EMPLOYEEs before you know any of the attributes of either EMPLOYEE or DEPARTMENT. This characteristic allows you to work from the general to the specific. When you are creating a data model, first identify the entities, then think about the relationships, and finally determine the attributes.

---

**Three Types of Binary Relationships**   Figure 4-5 shows the three types of binary relationships:

- The one-to-one (1:1) relationship
- The one-to-many (1:N) relationship
- The many-to-many (N:M) relationship

In a 1:1 relationship, a single entity instance of one type is related to a single entity instance of another type. In Figure 4-5(a), the LOCKER-ASSIGNMENT relationship

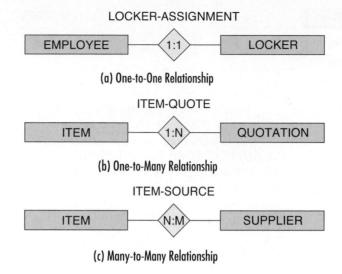

**FIGURE 4-5**

**Three Types of Binary Relationships**

associates a single EMPLOYEE with a single LOCKER. According to this diagram, no employee has more than one locker assigned, and no locker is assigned to more than one employee.

Figure 4-5(b) shows a 1:N binary relationship. In this relationship, which is called the ITEM-QUOTE relationship, a single instance of ITEM relates to many instances of QUOTATION. According to this sketch, an item has many quotations, but a quotation has only one item.

Think of the diamond as representing the relationship. The position of the 1 indicates that the relationship has one ITEM; the position of the N indicates that it also has many QUOTATION entities. Thus, each instance of the relationship consists of one ITEM and many QUOTATIONS. Notice that if the 1 and the N were reversed and the relationship were written N:1, each instance of the relationship would have many ITEMs and one QUOTATION.

When discussing 1:N relationships, the terms parent and child are sometimes used. The **parent** is the entity on the one side of the relationship and the **child** is the entity on the many side of the relationship. Thus, in the 1:N relationship between ITEM and QUOTATION, ITEM is the parent and QUOTATION is the child.

Figure 4-5(c) shows the N:M binary relationship. This relationship is named ITEM-SOURCE, and it relates instances of ITEM to instances of SUPPLIER. In this case, an item can be supplied by many suppliers, and a supplier can supply many items.

**Maximum Cardinality**  The three relationships are named and classified by their **cardinality**, which is a word that means *count*. In each of the relationships in Figure 4-5, the numbers inside the relationship diamond show the *maximum* number of entity instances that can occur on each side of the relationship. These numbers are called the relationship's **maximum cardinality**, which is the maximum number of entity instances that may participate in a relationship instance.

The ITEM-QUOTE relationship in Figure 4-5(b), for example, is said to have a maximum cardinality of 1:N. However, the cardinalities are not restricted to the values shown here. It is possible, for example, for the maximum cardinality to be other than 1 and N. The relationship between BASKETBALL-TEAM and PLAYER, for example, could be 1:5, indicating that a basketball team has at most five players.

**Minimum Cardinality**  Relationships also have a **minimum cardinality**, which is the minimum number of entity instances that *must* participate in a relationship instance. Minimum cardinality can be shown in several different ways. One way, illustrated in Figure 4-6, is to place a *hash mark* across the relationship line to indicate that an

**FIGURE 4-6**

**Relationship with
Minimum Cardinalities**

ITEM-SOURCE

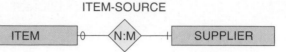

entity must exist in the relationship, and to place an *oval* across the relationship line to indicate that an entity might or might not be in the relationship.

Accordingly, Figure 4-6 shows that an ITEM must have a relationship with at least one SUPPLIER, but that a SUPPLIER is not required to have a relationship with an ITEM. The complete relationship restrictions are that an ITEM has a minimum cardinality of one and a maximum cardinality of many SUPPLIER entities. A SUPPLIER has a minimum cardinality of zero and a maximum cardinality of many ITEM entities.

If the minimum cardinality is zero, the entity's participation in the relationship is **optional**. If the minimum cardinality is one, the entity's participation in the relationship is **mandatory**.

---

**B T W**

Interpreting minimum cardinalities in diagrams like Figure 4-6 is often one of the most difficult parts of E-R models. It's very easy to become confused about which entity is optional and which is required (mandatory). An easy way to clarify this situation is to imagine that you are standing in the diamond, on the relationship line, and looking toward one of the entities. If you see an oval in that direction, then that entity is optional; if you see a hash mark, then that entity is required. Thus, in Figure 4-6, if you stand on the diamond and look toward SUPPLIER, you see a hash mark. This means that SUPPLIER is required in the relationship.

---

## ▶ ENTITY-RELATIONSHIP DIAGRAMS

The sketches in Figures 4-5 and 4-6 are called **entity-relationship diagrams**. Such diagrams are standardized, but only loosely. According to this standard, entity classes are shown by rectangles, relationships are shown by diamonds, the maximum cardinality of the relationship is shown inside the diamond, and the minimum cardinality is shown by the oval or hash mark next to the entity. The name of the entity is shown inside the rectangle, and the name of the relationship is shown near the diamond. You will still see examples of such E-R diagrams, and it is important for you to be able to interpret them.

---

**B T W**

Relationships like those in Figures 4-5 and 4-6 are sometimes called HAS-A relationships. The term is used because each entity instance has a relationship to a second entity instance. An employee has a badge, and a badge has an employee. If the maximum cardinality is greater than one, then each entity has a set of other entities. An employee has a set of skills, for example, and a skill has a set of employees who have that skill.

For two reasons, however, this original notation is seldom used today. First, there are a number of different versions of the E-R model, and those versions use different symbols. Second, data modeling software products use different techniques. For example, Computer Associates' product ERwin uses one set of symbols and Microsoft Visio uses a second set.

## Variations of the E-R Model

There are at least three different versions of the E-R model in use today. One of them, called **Information Engineering (IE)** was developed by James Martin in 1990. This model uses "crow's feet" to show the many side of a relationship, and it is sometimes called the **crow's foot model**. It is easy to understand, and we will use it in this text.

Other significant variations include the IDEF1X version and the Unified Modeling Language (UML) version of the E-R model.[2] In 1993, the National Institute of Standards and Technology announced that the **IDEF1X**, or **Integrated Definition 1, Extended**[3] version of the E-R model would be a national standard. This standard incorporates the basic ideas of the E-R model, but uses different graphical symbols which, unfortunately, make it difficult to understand and use. Still, it is a national standard used in government work and, therefore, may be important to you. Meanwhile, to add further complication, a new object-oriented development methodology called the **Unified Modeling Language (UML)** adopted the E-R model, but introduced its own symbols while putting an object-oriented programming spin on the model. UML also has begun to receive widespread use among object-orient programming (OOP) practitioners, and you may encounter UML notation in systems development courses.

## E-R Variations in Data Modeling Products

In addition to differences due to different versions of the E-R model, there are also differences due to software products. For example, two products that both implement the crow's foot model may do so in different ways. Thus, when creating a data model diagram, you need to know not just the version of the E-R model you are using, but also the idiosyncrasies of the data modeling product you use.

Figure 4-7 shows two versions of a 1:N, optional to mandatory relationship. Figure 4-7(a) shows the original E-R model version. Figure 4-7(b) shows the crow's foot model using common crow's foot symbology. Notice that the line representing the

**FIGURE 4-7**

Two Versions of a 1:N
Relationship

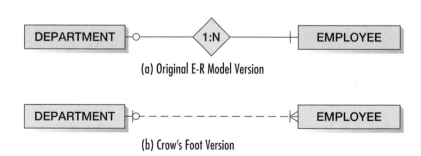

(a) Original E-R Model Version

(b) Crow's Foot Version

---

[2]For more information on these models, see David M. Kroenke, *Database Processing: Fundamentals, Design, and Implementation* 10th Edition (Upper Saddle River: Prentice-Hall, 2006) Appendix B (IDEF1X) and Appendix C (UML).

[3]*Integrated Definition for Information Modeling (IDEF1X)*. Federal Information Processing Standards Publication 184, 1993.

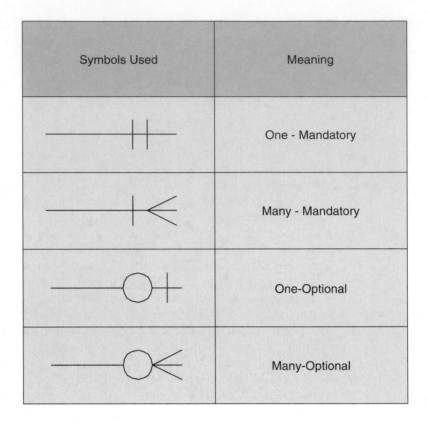

| Symbols Used | Meaning |
|---|---|
| | One - Mandatory |
| | Many - Mandatory |
| | One-Optional |
| | Many-Optional |

relationship is drawn as a dashed line. The reason for this will be explained later in this chapter. Notice the **crow's foot symbol** used to show the many side of the relationship.

The crow's foot model uses the notation shown in Figure 4-8 to indicate relationship cardinality. The symbol closest to the entity shows the maximum cardinality, and other symbol shows the minimum cardinality. A hash mark indicates one (and therefore also mandatory), a circle indicates zero (and thus optional), and the crow's foot indicates many. Thus, the diagram in Figure 4-7(b) means that a DEPARTMENT has one or more EMPLOYEEs (the symbol shows many and mandatory), and an EMPLOYEE belongs to zero or one DEPARTMENT (the symbol shows one and optional).

A 1:1 relationship would be drawn in a similar manner, but the line connecting to each entity should be similar to the connection shown for the one side of the 1:N relationship in Figure 4-7(b).

Figure 4-9 shows two versions of an N:M, optional to mandatory relationship. According to the original E-R model diagram shown in Figure 4-9(a), an EMPLOYEE must have at least one SKILL and may have several. At the same time, although a particular SKILL may not be held by any EMPLOYEE, a SKILL may also be held by several

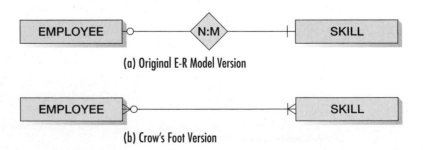

(a) Original E-R Model Version

(b) Crow's Foot Version

EMPLOYEEs. The crow's foot version in Figure 4-9(b) shows the N:M cardinalities using the notation in Figure 4-8. The crow's foot symbols again indicate the minimum cardinalities for the relationship.

For the rest of this text, we will use the crow's foot model for E-R diagrams. There are no completely standard symbols for the crow's foot notation, and we explain our symbols and notation when we first use it. You can obtain various modeling products that will produce crow's foot models, and they are easily understood and related to the original E-R model. Be aware that those other products may use the oval, hash mark, crow's foot and other symbols in slightly differently ways.

---

**B T W**

There are a number of modeling products that you can try—each will have its own idiosyncrasies. Although it is better at creating database designs (discussed in Chapter 5) than data models, Microsoft's Visio is a possibility. Computer Associates produces ERwin, a commercial data modeling product. You can download a free trial version from the Computer Associates Web site at www3.ca.com/solutions/Product.aspx?ID=260. Look for AllFusion ERwin Data Modeler 4.1.4 under Downloads and Trials. You can use ERwin to produce either crow's foot or IDEF1X. DBDesigner 4 from fabForce at fabforce.net/dbdesigner4 is a free open-source data modeling tool. It is designed to be used with MySQL as the DBMS, but it can be used for data modeling even if you're not using MySQL. Finally, MySQL AB, the company that created MySQL, is now developing a data modeling tool named the MySQL Workbench that is downloaded as part of the MySQL GUI Tools Bundle (see Appendix B). At this writing it is still in the early development stage, but more mature versions will become available. These are just a few of the many data modeling products available.

---

## Weak Entities

The E-R model also defines another special type of entity called a weak entity. A **weak entity** is an entity that cannot exist in a database unless another type of entity also exists in that database. An entity that is *not* weak is called a **strong entity**.

## ID-Dependent Entities

The E-R model includes a special type of weak entity called an **ID-dependent entity**. Such an entity is one in which the identifier of one entity includes the identifier of another entity. Consider the entities BUILDING and APARTMENT shown in Figure 4-10(a).

As we would expect, the identifier of BUILDING is a single attribute, in this case BuildingName. The identifier of APARTMENT, however, is *not* the single attribute ApartmentNumber, but rather the composite identifier (BuildingName, Apartment Number). This happens because logically and physically, an APARTMENT simply cannot exist unless a BUILDING exists for that APARTMENT to be part of. Whenever this type of situation occurs, an **ID-dependent entity** exists. In this case, APARTMENT is ID-dependent on BUILDING. The identifier of an ID-dependent entity will always be a composite that includes the identifier of the entity that the ID-dependent entity depends on for its existence.

**FIGURE 4-10**

Example ID-Dependent Entities

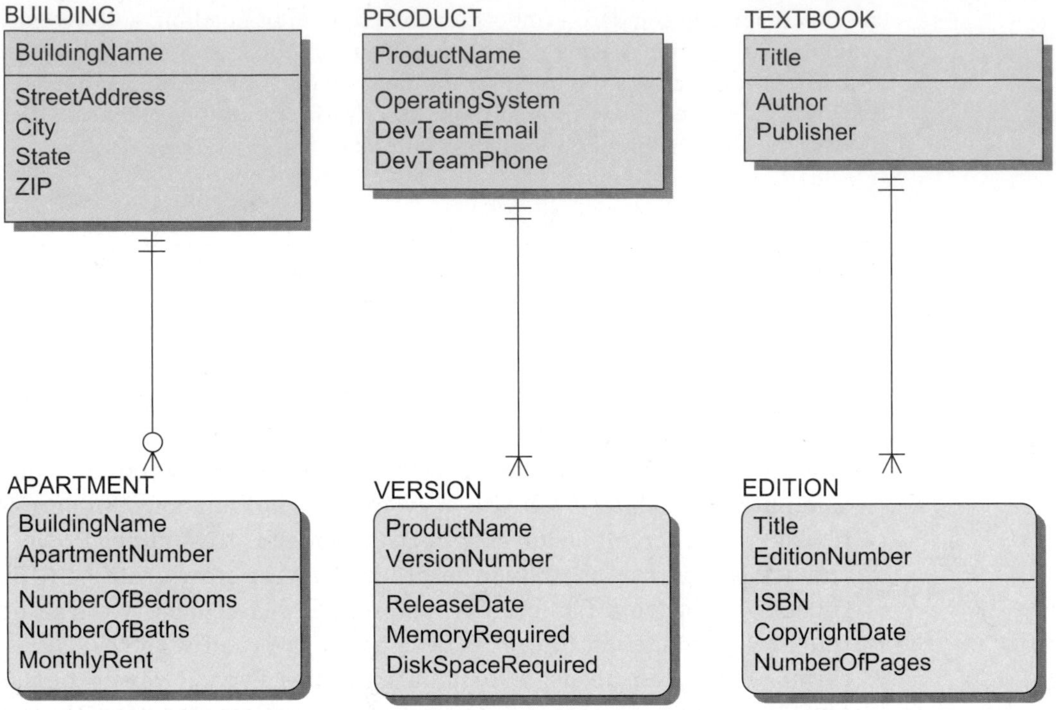

(a) APARTMENT is ID-Dependent on BUILDING   (b) VERSION is ID-Dependent on PRODUCT   (c) EDITION is ID-Dependent on TEXTBOOK

As shown in Figure 4-10, in our E-R models we will use an entity with rounded corners to represent the ID-dependent entity. We will also use a solid line to represent the relationship between the ID-dependent entity and its parent. This type of a relationship is called an **identifying relationship**. A relationship drawn with the dashed line as we saw in Figure 4-7 is used between strong entities, and is called a **nonidentifying relationship** since there are no ID-dependent entities in the relationship.

ID-dependent entities are common. Another example is shown in Figure 4-10(b), where the entity VERSION is ID-dependent on the entity PRODUCT. Here, PRODUCT is a software product and VERSION is a release of that software product. The identifier of PRODUCT is ProductName, and the identifier of VERSION is (ProductName, VersionNumber). A third example is shown in Figure 4-10(c), where EDITION is ID-dependent on TEXTBOOK. The identifier of TEXTBOOK is Title, and the identifier of EDITION is (Title, EditionNumber). In each of these cases, the ID-dependent entity cannot exist unless the parent (the entity on which it depends) also exists. Thus, the minimum cardinality from the ID-dependent entity to the parent is always one.

On the other hand, whether the parent is required to have an ID-dependent entity depends on business requirements. In Figure 4-10(a), the database can contain a BUILDING, such as a store or warehouse, so APARTMENT is optional. In Figure 4-10(b), every PRODUCT made by this company has versions (including version 1.0), so VERSION is mandatory. Similarly, in Figure 4-10(c), every TEXTBOOK has an EDITION number (including the first edition), which makes EDITION mandatory. Those restrictions arise from the nature of each business and its applications and not from any logical requirement.

Finally, notice that we cannot add an ID-dependent entity instance until the parent entity instance is created, and when we delete the parent entity instance, we must delete all the ID-dependent entity instances, as well.

## Non–ID-Dependent Weak Entities

All ID-dependent entities are weak entities. But there are other entities that are weak but not ID-dependent. To understand weak entities, consider the relationship between the AUTO_MODEL and VEHICLE entity classes in the database of a car manufacturer, such as Ford or Honda, as shown in Figure 4-11.

In Figure 4-11(a), each VEHICLE is assigned a sequential number as it is manufactured. So, for the "Super SUV" AUTO_MODEL, the first VEHICLE manufactured gets a ManufacturingSeqNumber of 1, the next gets a ManufacturingSeqNumber of 2, and so on. This is clearly an ID-dependent relationship because the ManufacturingSeqNumber is based on the Manufacturer and Model.

But now let's assign VEHICLE an identifier that is independent of the Manufacturer and Model. We'll use a VIN (Vehicle Identification Number), as shown in Figure 4-11(b). Now, the VEHICLE has a unique identifier of its own and does not need to be identified by its relation to AUTO-MODEL.

This is an interesting situation. The VEHICLE has an identity of its own, therefore, it is not ID-dependent. Yet, the VEHICLE is an AUTO_MODEL, and if that particular AUTO_MODEL did not exist, the VEHICLE itself would never have existed. Therefore, VEHICLE is now a *weak, but non–ID-dependent entity*.

Consider *your* car—let's say it's a Ford Mustang just for the sake of this discussion. Your individual Mustang is a VEHICLE, and it exists as a physical object and is identified by the VIN that is required for each licensed automobile. It is *not* ID-dependent on AUTO_MODEL, which in this case is Ford Mustang, for its identity. But on the other hand, if the Ford Mustang had never been created as an AUTO_MODEL—a logical concept that was first designed on paper—your car would never have been built since *no* Ford Mustangs would ever have been built! Therefore, your physical individual VEHICLE would not exist without a logical AUTO_MODEL of Ford Mustang, and in a data model (which *is* what we're talking about), a VEHICLE cannot exist without a related AUTO-MODEL. This makes VEHICLE a weak, but non–ID-dependent entity.

**FIGURE 4-11**

**Example Weak Entity**

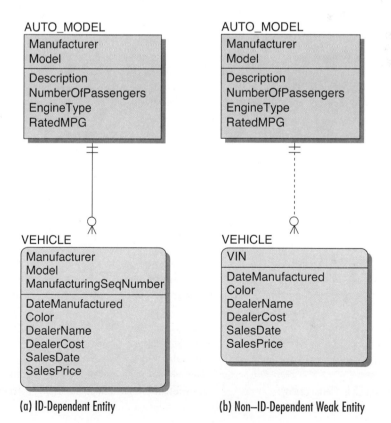

(a) ID-Dependent Entity          (b) Non–ID-Dependent Weak Entity

Unfortunately, an ambiguity is hidden in the definition of weak entity, and this ambiguity is interpreted differently by different database designers (as well as different textbook authors). The ambiguity is this: In a strict sense, if a weak entity is defined as any entity whose presence in the database depends on another entity, then any entity that participates in a relationship having a minimum cardinality of one to a second entity is a weak entity. Thus, in an academic database, if a STUDENT must have an ADVISER, then STUDENT is a weak entity because a STUDENT entity cannot be stored without an ADVISER.

This interpretation seems too broad to some people. A STUDENT is not physically dependent on an ADVISER (unlike an APARTMENT to a BUILDING), and a STUDENT is not logically dependent on an ADVISER (despite how it might appear to either the student or the adviser), and, therefore, STUDENT should be considered a strong entity.

To avoid such situations, some people interpret the definition of weak entity more narrowly. To be a weak entity, an entity must logically depend on another entity. According to this definition, APARTMENT is a weak entity, but STUDENT is not. An APARTMENT cannot exist without a BUILDING in which it is located. However, a STUDENT can logically exist without an ADVISER, even if a business rule requires it.

To illustrate this interpretation, consider the examples shown in Figure 4-12. Suppose a data model includes the relationship between an ORDER and a SALESPERSON, as shown in Figure 4-12(a). Although we might state that an ORDER must have a SALESPERSON, it does not necessarily require one for its existence. (The ORDER could be a cash sale in which the salesperson is not recorded.) Hence, the minimum cardinality of one arises from a business rule, not from logical necessity. Thus, ORDER requires a SALESPERSON but is not existence-dependent on it, and, thus, ORDER is a strong entity.

Now, consider ASSIGNMENT in Figure 4-12(b), which is ID-dependent on PROJECT, and the identifier of ASSIGNMENT contains the identifier of PROJECT. Here,

---

**FIGURE 4-12**

**Examples of Required Entities**

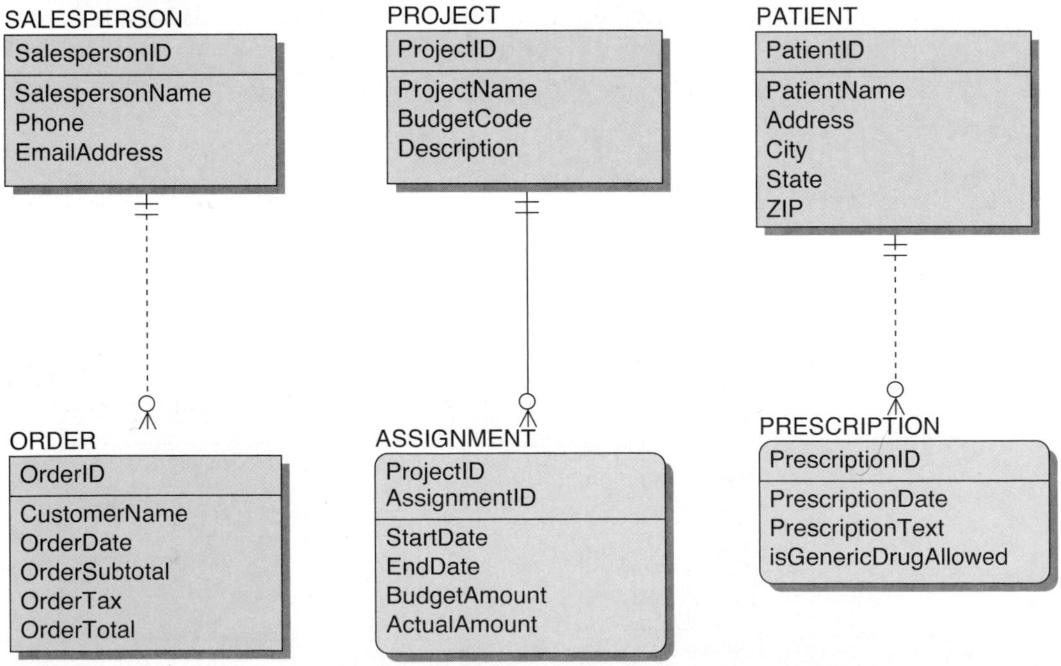

(a) ORDER is a Strong Entity  (b) ASSIGNMENT is an ID-Dependent Entity  (c) PRESCRIPTION is a Non-ID-Dependent Weak Entity

not only does ASSIGNMENT have a minimum cardinality of one, and not only is ASSIGNMENT existence-dependent on PROJECT, but ASSIGNMENT is also ID-dependent on PROJECT because its identifier requires the key of the parent entity. Thus, ASSIGNMENT is a weak entity that is ID-dependent.

Finally, consider the relationship of PATIENT and PRESCRIPTION in Figure 4-12(c). Here, a PRESCRIPTION cannot logically exist without a PATIENT. Hence, not only is the minimum cardinality one, but also the PRESCRIPTION is existence-dependent on PATIENT. Thus, PRESCRIPTION is a weak entity.

We will define weak entities as those that logically depend on another entity. Hence, not all entities that have a minimum cardinality of one in relation to another entity are weak. Only those that are logically dependent are weak. This definition implies that all ID-dependent entities are weak. In addition, every weak entity has a minimum cardinality of one on the entity on which it depends, but every entity that has a minimum cardinality of one is not necessarily weak.

As illustrated in Figures 4-11 and 4-12, in our E-R models we will again use an entity with rounded corners to represent the non-ID-dependent entity, but we will also use a dashed line to represent the nonidentifying relationship between the non-ID-dependent entity and its parent.

## Subtype Entities

The extended E-R model introduced the concept of subtypes. A **subtype** entity is a special case of another entity called its **supertype**. Students, for example, may be classified as undergraduate or graduate students. In this case, STUDENT is the supertype and UNDERGRADUATE and GRADUATE are the subtypes. Figure 4-13 shows these subtypes for a student database. Note that the identifier of the supertype is also the identifier of the subtypes.

Alternatively, a student could be classified as a freshman, sophomore, junior, or senior. In that case, STUDENT would the supertype and FRESHMAN, SOPHOMORE, JUNIOR, and SENIOR would be the subtypes.

As illustrated in Figure 4-13, in our E-R models we will use a circle with a line under it as a subtype symbol to indicate a supertype/subtype relationship. Think of this as a symbol for an optional (the circle) 1:1 (the line) relationship. We will also use a solid line to represent an ID-dependent subtype entity, since each subtype is ID-dependent on the supertype. Also note that there none of the line end symbols shown in Figure 4-8 are used on the connecting lines.

---

## FIGURE 4-13

**Example Subtype Entities**

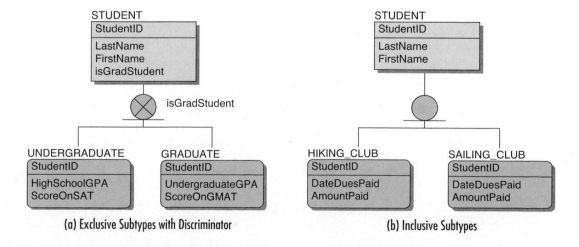

(a) Exclusive Subtypes with Discriminator        (b) Inclusive Subtypes

In some cases, an attribute of the supertype indicates which of the subtypes is appropriate for a given instance. An attribute that determines which subtype is appropriate is called a **discriminator**. In Figure 4-13, the attribute isGradStudent (which has only the values *Yes* or *No*) is the discriminator. In our E-R diagrams, the discriminator is shown next to the subtype symbol as illustrated in Figure 4-13(a). Not all supertypes have a discriminator. If not, application code must be written to create the appropriate subtype.

Subtypes can be exclusive or inclusive. If **exclusive**, the supertype relates to at most one subtype. If **inclusive**, the supertype can relate to one or more subtypes. In Figure 4-13(a), the *X* in the circle means that the UNDERGRADUATE and GRADUATE subtypes are exclusive. Thus, a STUDENT can be either an UNDERGRADUATE or a GRADUATE, but not both.

Figure 4-13(b) shows a STUDENT can join either the HIKING_CLUB or the SAILING_CLUB or both—these subtypes are inclusive (note there is no *X* in the circle). Because a supertype may relate to more than one subtype, inclusive subtypes do not have a discriminator.

Subtypes are used in a data model to avoid inappropriate NULL values. Undergraduate students take the SAT exam and report that score, while graduate students take the GMAT and report their score on that exam. Thus, the SAT score would be NULL in all STUDENT entities for graduates, while the GMAT score would be NULL for all undergraduates. Such null values can be avoided by creating subtypes.

> **B T W**
>
> The relationships that connect supertypes and subtypes are called IS-A relationships because a subtype is the same entity as the supertype. Because this is so, the identifier of a supertype and all of its subtypes must be the same; they all represent different aspects of the same entity. Contrast this term with HAS-A relationships in which an entity has a relationship to another entity, but the identity of the two entities is different.

## Recursive Relationships

It is possible for an entity to have a relationship to itself. Figure 4-14 shows a CUSTOMER entity in which one customer can refer many other customers. This is called a

**FIGURE 4-14**

**Example Recursive Relationship**

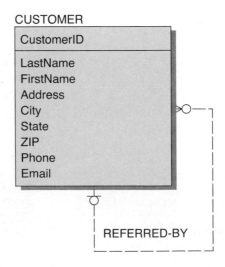

**recursive relationship**. As with binary relationships, recursive relationships can be 1:1, 1:N (shown in Figure 4-14), and N:M. We will discuss each of these three types further in Chapter 5.

## DEVELOPING AN EXAMPLE E-R DIAGRAM

The best way to gain proficiency with data modeling is to do it. In this section, we will examine a set of documents used by a small business and create a data model from those documents. After you have read this section, you should practice creating data models with one or more of the projects at the end of the chapter.

### Heather Sweeney Designs

Heather Sweeney is an interior designer who specializes in home kitchen design. She offers a variety of seminars at home shows, kitchen and appliance stores, and other public locations. The seminars are free; she offers them as a way of building her customer base. She earns revenue by selling books and videos that instruct people on kitchen design. She also offers custom-design consulting services.

After someone attends a seminar, Heather wants to leave no stone unturned in attempting to sell that person one of her products or services. Accordingly, she would like to develop a database to keep track of customers, the seminars they have attended, the contacts she has made with them, and the purchases they have made. She wants to use this database to continue to contact her customers and offer them products and services.

### The Seminar Customer List

Figure 4-15 shows the seminar customer list that Heather or her assistant fills out at seminars. It includes basic data about the seminar as well as the name, phone, and email address of all the attendees at the seminar. If we examine this list in terms of a data model, two potential entities are found: SEMINAR and CUSTOMER.

From the form in Figure 4-15, we can conclude that a SEMINAR relates to many CUSTOMERs, and we can make the initial E-R diagram shown in Figure 4-16(a).

| **FIGURE 4-15** |
|---|

**Example Seminar Customer List**

*Heather Sweeney Designs*
*Seminar Customer List*

| Date: | Oct. 11, 2005 | Location: | San Antonio Convention Center |
|---|---|---|---|
| Time: | 11 AM | Title: | Kitchen on a Budget |

| Name | Phone | Email Address |
|---|---|---|
| Nancy Jacobs | 817-871-8123 | NJ@somewhere.com |
| Chantel Jacobs | 817-871-8234 | CJ@somewhere.com |
| Ralph Able | 210-281-7687 | RA@somewhere.com |
| Etc. | | |
| 27 names in all | | |

However, from this single document a number of facts *cannot* be determined. As shown in the figure, we are not sure about cardinalities. Currently, we show a 1:N relationship with both entities required in the relationship, but we are not certain about this. Neither do we know what to use for the identifier of each entity.

Having missing facts is typical during the data-modeling process. We examine documents and conduct user interviews, then create a data model with the data that we have. We also note where data are missing and supply that data later as we learn more. Thus, there is no need to stop data modeling when something is unknown; we just note that it is unknown and keep going with the goal of supplying missing information at some later point.

Suppose we talk with Heather and determine that customers can attend as many seminars as they would like, but that she would like to be able to record customers even if they have not been to a seminar ("Frankly, I'll take a customer wherever I can find one!" was her actual response). Also, she never offers a seminar to fewer than 10 attendees. Given this information, we can fill out more of the E-R diagram as shown in Figure 4-16(b).

Before continuing, consider the minimum cardinality of the relationship from SEMINAR to CUSTOMER in Figure 4-16(b). The notation says that a seminar must have at least 10 customers, which is what we were told. However, this means that we cannot add a new SEMINAR to the database unless it already has 10 customers. This is incorrect. When Heather first schedules a seminar, it probably has no customers at all, but she still would like to record it in the database. Therefore, even though she has a business policy of requiring at least 10 customers at a seminar, we cannot place this limit as a constraint in the data model.

## FIGURE 4-16

**Initial E-R Diagram for Heather Sweeney Designs**

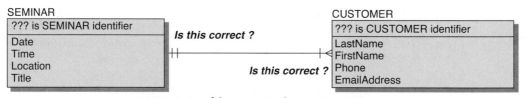

(a) First Version of the SEMINAR and CUSTOMER E-R Diagram

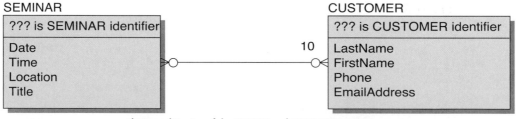

(b) Second Version of the SEMINAR and CUSTOMER E-R Diagram

(c) Third Version of the SEMINAR and CUSTOMER E-R Diagram

In Figure 4-16(b), neither of the entities has an identifier. For SEMINAR, the composites (Date, Time, Location) and (Date, Time, Title) are probably unique and could be the identifier. However, identifiers will become table keys during database design, and these will be large character keys. A surrogate key is probably a better idea here, so we will add one. Also, looking at our data and thinking about the nature of email addresses, we can reasonably suppose that EmailAddress can be the identifier of CUSTOMER. All these decisions are shown for the E-R diagram in Figure 4-16(c).

## The Customer Form Letter

Figure 4-17 shows a form letter that Sweeney Designs uses.

---

### FIGURE 4-17

**Heather Sweeney Designs Customer Form Letter**

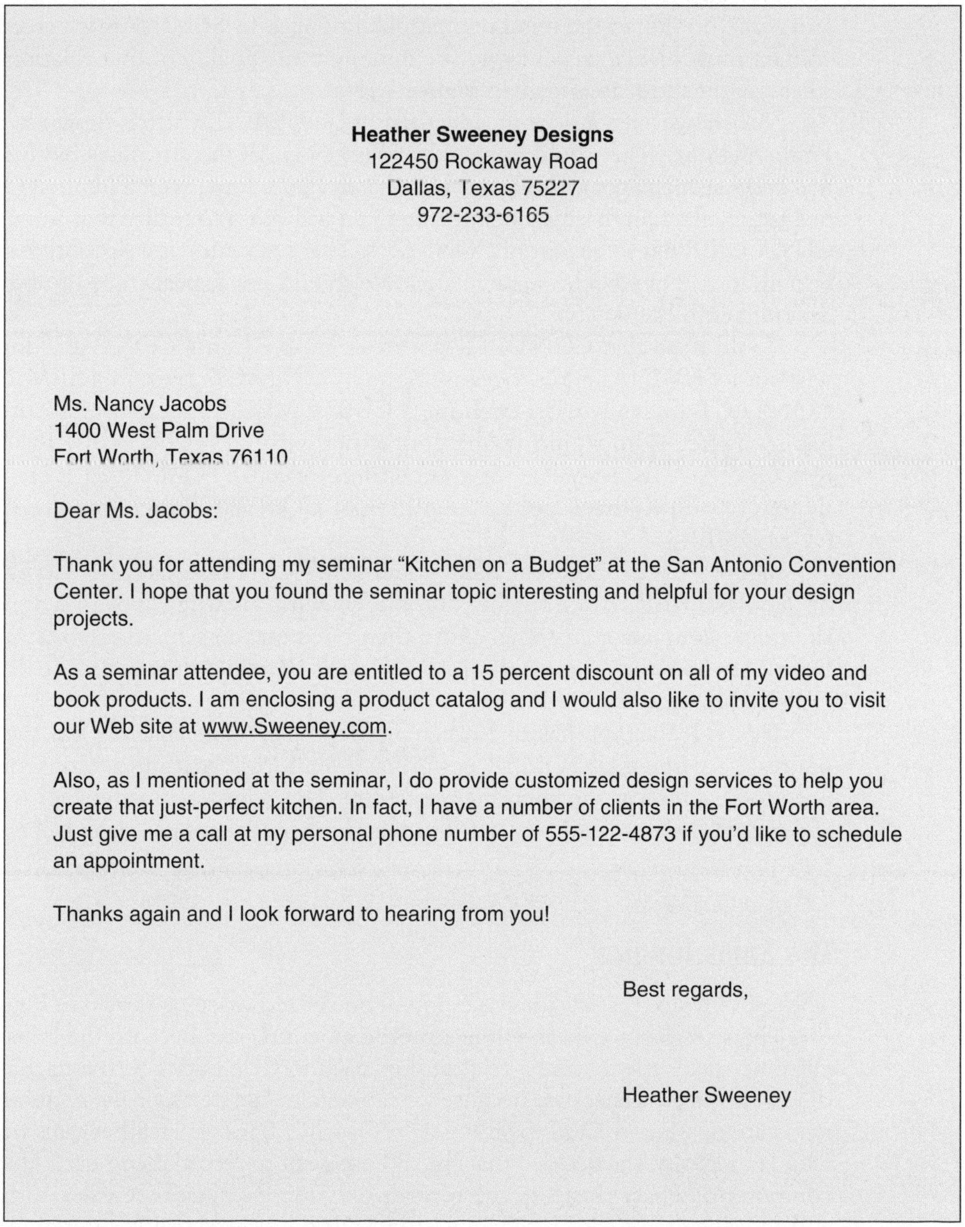

**Heather Sweeney Designs**
122450 Rockaway Road
Dallas, Texas 75227
972-233-6165


Ms. Nancy Jacobs
1400 West Palm Drive
Fort Worth, Texas 76110

Dear Ms. Jacobs:

Thank you for attending my seminar "Kitchen on a Budget" at the San Antonio Convention Center. I hope that you found the seminar topic interesting and helpful for your design projects.

As a seminar attendee, you are entitled to a 15 percent discount on all of my video and book products. I am enclosing a product catalog and I would also like to invite you to visit our Web site at www.Sweeney.com.

Also, as I mentioned at the seminar, I do provide customized design services to help you create that just-perfect kitchen. In fact, I have a number of clients in the Fort Worth area. Just give me a call at my personal phone number of 555-122-4873 if you'd like to schedule an appointment.

Thanks again and I look forward to hearing from you!

Best regards,


Heather Sweeney

Eventually, Heather would like to send messages like this via email, as well. Accordingly, we will represent this form letter with an entity called CONTACT, which could be a letter, an email, or some other form of customer contact. She uses several different form letters (and, in the future, emails); Heather refers to each one by a number. Thus, she has form letter 1, form letter 2, and so forth. For now, we will represent the attributes of CONTACT as ContactNumber and Type, where Type can be either Form Letter or, in the future Email or some other type.

Reading the form letter, we see that it refers to a seminar and a customer. Therefore, we will add it to the E-R diagram with relationships to both of these entities as shown in Figure 4-18.

As shown in the design in Figure 4-18(a), a seminar can result in many contacts, and a customer may receive many contacts so the maximum cardinality of these relationships is N. However, neither a customer nor a seminar need generate a contact so the minimum cardinality of these relationships is zero.

Working from CONTACT back to SEMINAR and CUSTOMER, we can determine that the contact is for a single CUSTOMER and refers to a single SEMINAR so the maximum cardinality in that direction is one. Also, some of the form letters refer to seminars and some do not so the minimum cardinality back to SEMINAR is zero. However, a contact must have a customer so the minimum cardinality of that relationship is one. These cardinalities are shown in Figure 4-18(a).

Now, however, consider the identifier of CONTACT, which is shown as unknown in Figure 4-18(a). What could be the identifier? None of the attributes by themselves suffice because many contacts will have the same values for ContactNumber, ContactType, or Date. Reflect on this for a minute, and you will begin to realize that some attribute of CUSTOMER has to be part of CONTACT. That realization is a signal that something is wrong. In a data model, the same attribute should not logically need to be part of two different entities.

Could it be that CONTACT is a weak entity? Can a CONTACT logically exist without a SEMINAR? Yes, because not all CONTACTs refer to a SEMINAR. Can a CONTACT logically exist without a CUSTOMER? The answer to that question has to be no. Who would we be contacting without a CUSTOMER? Aha! That's it: CONTACT is a weak entity, depending on CUSTOMER; in fact, it is an ID-dependent entity because the identifier of CONTACT includes the identifier of CUSTOMER.

Figure 4-18(b) shows the data model with CONTACT as an ID-dependent entity on CUSTOMER. After further interviews with Heather, it was determined that she never contacts a customer more than once on the same day, so (EmailAddress, Date) can be the identifier of CONTACT (EmailAddress is the identifier of CUSTOMER).

This E-R diagram has one other problem. The contact letter has the customer's address, but the CUSTOMER entity has no address attributes. Consequently, they need to be added as shown in Figure 4-18(c). This adjustment is typical; as more forms and reports are obtained, new attributes and other changes will need to be made to the data model.

## The Sales Invoice

The sales invoice that Heather uses to sell books and videos is shown in Figure 4-19.

The sales invoice itself will need to be an entity, and because the sales invoice has customer data, it will have a relationship back to CUSTOMER. (Note that we do not duplicate the customer data because we can obtain data items via the relationship; if data items are missing, we add them to CUSTOMER.) Because Heather runs her computer with lax security, she decided that she did not want to record credit card numbers in her computer database. Instead, she records only the PaymentType value in the database and files the credit card receipts in a (locked) physical file with a notation that relates them back to an invoice number.

**FIGURE 4-18**

Heather Sweeney Designs Data Model with CONTACT

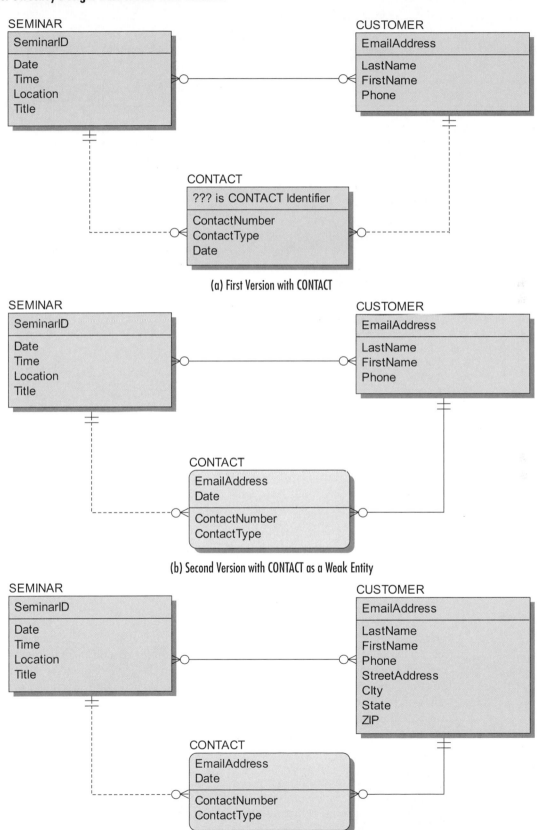

(a) First Version with CONTACT

(b) Second Version with CONTACT as a Weak Entity

(c) Third Version with Modified CUSTOMER

**FIGURE 4-19**

**Heather Sweeney Designs Sales Invoice**

| | |
|---|---|
| *Heather Sweeney Designs*<br>*122450 Rockaway Road*<br>*Dallas, Texas 75227* | Invoice No.     35000 |

**INVOICE**

**Customer**

| | | | |
|---|---|---|---|
| Name | Ralph Able | | |
| Address | 123 Elm Street | | |
| City | San Antonio | State TX | ZIP 78214 |
| Phone | 210-281-7987 | | |

**Misc**

| | |
|---|---|
| Date | 10/15/05 |
| Order No. | |
| Rep | |
| FOB | |

| Qty | Description | Unit Price | TOTAL |
|---|---|---|---|
| 1 | Kitchen Remodeling Basics - Video | $ 14.95 | $ 14.95 |
| 1 | Kitchen Remodeling Basics - Video Companion | $ 7.99 | $ 7.99 |

| | | |
|---|---|---|
| Subtotal | $ | 22.94 |
| Shipping | $ | 5.95 |
| Tax Rate(s) 5.70% | $ | 1.31 |
| **TOTAL** | $ | 30.20 |

**Payment**    Credit

| | |
|---|---|
| Comments | Visa |
| Name | Ralph J. Able |
| CC # | xxxx xxx xxx xxxxxx |
| Expires | May-08 |

Office Use Only

Figure 4-20 shows the completion of the Heather Sweeney Designs data model. Figure 4-20(a) shows a first cut at the data model with INVOICE. This diagram is missing data about the line items on the order. Because there are multiple line items, the line item data cannot be stored in INVOICE. Instead, an ID-dependent entity LINE_ITEM must be defined. The need for an ID-dependent entity is typical for documents that contain a group of repeating data. If the repeating group is not logically independent, then it must be made into an ID-dependent weak entity. Figure 4-20(b) shows the adjusted design.

Because LINE_ITEM belongs to an identifying relationship from INVOICE, it needs an attribute that can be used to identify a particular LINE_ITEM within an INVOICE. The identifier we will use for LINE_ITEM will be the composite (InvoiceNumber, LineNumber), where the InvoiceNumber is the identifier of INVOICE and the LineNumber attribute identifies the line within the INVOICE on which an item appears.

**FIGURE 4-20**

**Final Data Model for Heather Sweeney Designs**

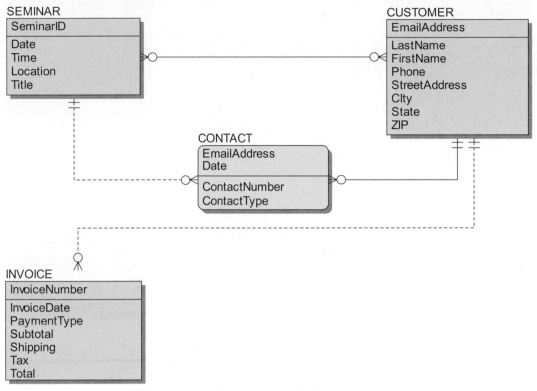

(a) Version with INVOICE

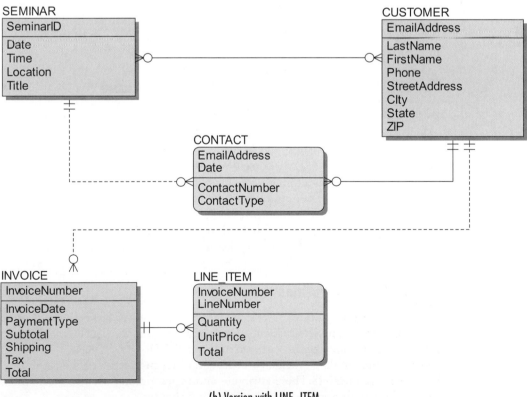

(b) Version with LINE_ITEM

**FIGURE 4-20** *(Continued)*

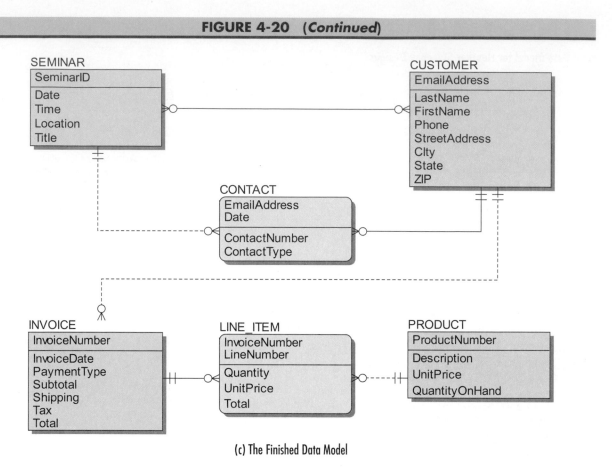

(c) The Finished Data Model

We need to make one more correction to this data model. Heather sells standard products—her books and videos have standardized names and prices. She does not want the person who fills out an order to be able to use nonstandard names or prices. Accordingly, we need to add a PRODUCT entity and relate it to LINE_ITEM as shown in Figure 4-20(c).

Observe that UnitPrice is an attribute of both PRODUCT and LINE_ITEM. This was done so that Heather can update UnitPrice without impacting the recorded orders. At the time a sale is made, UnitPrice in LINE_ITEM is set equal to UnitPrice in PRODUCT. The LINE_ITEM UnitPrice never changes. However, as time passes and Heather changes prices for her products, she can update UnitPrice in PRODUCT. If UnitPrice were not copied into LINE_ITEM, when the PRODUCT price changes, the price in already-stored LINE_ITEMs would change as well, and Heather does not want this to occur. This means that although two attributes are named UnitPrice, they are different attributes used for different purposes.

Also note in Figure 4-20(c) that based on interviews with Heather, we have added ProductNumber and QuantityOnHand to PRODUCT. These attributes do not appear in any of the documents, but they are known by Heather and are important to her.

## Attribute Specifications

The data model in Figure 4-20(c) shows entities, attributes, and entity relationships, but it does not document details about attributes. To do that, the development team needs to create a set of tables like those shown in Figure 4-21.

Here, the data type, default values, and other properties of the attributes of each entity are documented. These attributes and properties are used to create the tables in the database design, as you will see in the next chapter.

**FIGURE 4-21**

**Heather Sweeney Designs Attribute Specifications**

| Column Name | DataType (Length) | Key | Required | Default Value | Remarks |
|---|---|---|---|---|---|
| SeminarID | AutoNumber | Primary Key | Yes | DBMS supplied | Surrogate Key: Initial value =1 Increment = 1 |
| Date | Date | No | Yes | None | As: mm/dd/yy |
| Time | Time | No | Yes | None | As: ##:##(AM/PM) |
| Location | Varchar (100) | No | Yes | None | |
| Title | Varchar (100) | No | Yes | None | |

**(a) SEMINAR**

| Column Name | DataType (Length) | Key | Required | Default Value | Remarks |
|---|---|---|---|---|---|
| EmailAddress | Varchar(100) | Primary Key | Yes | None | |
| LastName | Char (25) | No | Yes | None | |
| FirstName | Char (25) | No | Yes | None | |
| Phone | Char (12) | No | Yes | None | As: (###)###-#### |
| Street | Char (35) | No | No | None | |
| City | Char (35) | No | No | Dallas | |
| State | Char (2) | No | No | TX | As: SS |
| ZIP | Char (10) | No | No | 75201 | As: #####-#### |

**(b) CUSTOMER**

| Column Name | DataType (Length) | Key | Required | Default Value | Remarks |
|---|---|---|---|---|---|
| EmailAddress | Varchar(100) | Primary Key | Yes | None | REF: CUSTOMER |
| Date | Date | Primary Key | Yes | None | As: mm/dd/yy |
| ContactNumber | Integer | No | Yes | None | |
| ContactType | Char(15) | No | Yes | None | |

**(c) CONTACT**

| Column Name | DataType (Length) | Key | Required | Default Value | Remarks |
|---|---|---|---|---|---|
| InvoiceNumber | AutoNumber | Primary Key | Yes | DBMS supplied | Surrogate Key: Initial value = 35000 Increment = 1 |
| InvoiceDate | Date | No | Yes | None | As: mm/dd/yy |
| PaymentType | Char (25) | No | Yes | Cash | |
| Subtotal | Numeric (9,2) | No | No | None | |
| Shipping | Numeric (9,2) | No | No | None | |
| Tax | Numeric (9,2) | No | No | None | |
| Total | Numeric (9,2) | No | No | None | |

**(d) INVOICE**

**FIGURE 4-21** *(Continued)*

| Column Name | DataType (Length) | Key | Required | Default Value | Remarks |
|---|---|---|---|---|---|
| InvoiceNumber | Integer | Primary Key | Yes | None | REF: INVOICE |
| LineNumber | Integer | Primary Key | Yes | None | This is not quite a Surrogate Key—for *each* InvoiceNumber: Initial value = 1 Increment = 1 Application logic will be needed to supply the correct value |
| Quantity | Integer | No | No | None | |
| UnitPrice | Numeric (9,2) | No | No | None | |
| Total | Numeric (9,2) | No | No | None | |

**(e) LINE_ITEM**

| Column Name | DataType (Length) | Key | Required | Default Value | Remarks |
|---|---|---|---|---|---|
| ProductNumber | AutoNumber | Primary Key | Yes | DBMS supplied | Surrogate Key: Initial value = 100 Increment = 1 |
| Description | Varchar (100) | No | Yes | None | |
| UnitPrice | Numeric (9,2) | No | Yes | None | |
| QuantityOnHand | Integer | No | Yes | 0 | |

**(f) PRODUCT**

## Business Rules

While creating the data model, the development team needs to be on the lookout for business rules that constrain data values and the processing of the database. We encountered such a business rule with regard to CONTACT, when Heather stated that no more than one form letter or email per day is to be sent to a customer.

In more complicated data models, many such business rules would exist. These rules are generally too specific or too complicated to be enforced by the DBMS. Rather, application programs or other forms of procedural logic need to be developed to enforce such rules.

## Validating the Data Model

After the data model has been completed, it needs to be validated. The most common way to do this is to show it to the users and obtain their feedback. However, a large, complicated data model is off-putting to many users so often the data model needs to be broken into sections and validated piece by piece or expressed in some other terms that are more understandable.

As mentioned earlier in this chapter, prototypes are sometimes constructed for users to review. This is because prototypes are easier for users to understand and evaluate than data models. Prototypes can be developed that show the consequences of data model design decisions without requiring the users to learn E-R modeling. For example, showing a form with room for only one customer is a way of indicating that the maximum cardinality of a relationship is one. If the users respond to such a form with the question "But where do I put the second customer?" you know that the maximum cardinality is greater than one.

It is relatively easy to create mock-ups of forms and reports using Microsoft Access wizards. Such mock-ups are often developed even in situations where Access is not going to be used as the operational DBMS. The mock-ups are used to demonstrate the consequences of data-modeling decisions.

Finally, the data model needs to be evaluated against all use cases. For each use case, the development team needs to verify that all the data and relationships necessary to support the use case are present and accurately represented in the data model.

Data model validation is exceedingly important. It is far easier and cheaper to correct errors at this stage than it is to correct them after the database has been designed and implemented. Changing a cardinality in a data model is a simple adjustment to a document, but changing the cardinality later might require the construction of new tables, new relationships, new queries, new forms, new reports, and so forth. So, every minute spent validating a data model will pay great dividends down the line.

## THE ACCESS WORKBENCH

### Section 4

### Prototyping Using Microsoft Access

In the presentation of data modeling concepts and techniques, the idea of building a prototype database for users to review as a model validation technique was mentioned. Prototypes are easier for users to understand and evaluate than data models in one of the E-R modeling methodologies. Prototypes can be used to show the consequences of data-model design decisions.

Since it is relatively easy to create mock-ups of forms and reports using Microsoft Access wizards, such mock-ups are often developed even in situations where Access is not going to be used as the operational DBMS. The mock-ups are used as a prototyping tool to demonstrate the consequences of data modeling decisions.

In this section, we will cover the following objectives:

- Illustrate how to use Access as a prototyping tool

We will continue to use the WMCRM database. At this point, we have created and populated the CONTACT, CUSTOMER, and SALESPERSON tables. We have also learned how to create forms, reports, and queries in the preceding chapters, and how to create and use view equivalent queries in Appendix C.

Let's start by considering what the WMCRM database looks like from a data-modeling point of view. Figure AW-4-1 shows the WMCRM database as an IE Crow's Foot E-R model.

Now, this model is based on the business rule that each CUSTOMER works with one and only one SALESPERSON. Therefore, we have a 1:N relationship between SALESPERSON and CUSTOMER, which shows that each SALESPERSON can work with many CUSTOMERs, but that each CUSTOMER is attended to by only one SALESPERSON. Further, since there is no doubt about which SALESPERSON is involved in each CONTACT with a CUSTOMER, the connection to CONTACT is a 1:N relationship to CUSTOMER.

*(Continued)*

## FIGURE AW-4-1

**The WMCRM Database as a Data Model**

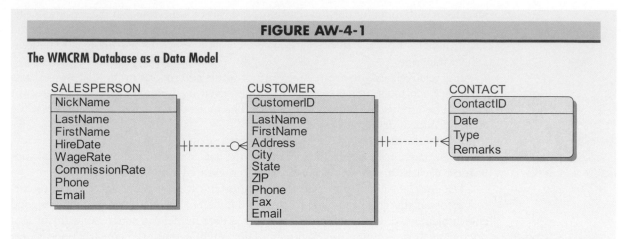

But all this would change if the business rule was that any CUSTOMER could work with more than one SALESPERSON. This would allow any SALESPERSON to contact the CUSTOMER as needed, rather than relying on just one SALESPERSON to be available whenever needed for work with a particular CUSTOMER. Each CONTACT would now need to be linked to the CUSTOMER contacted and the SALEPERSON making the CONTACT. This results in a data model as shown in Figure AW-4-2.

Here we have a 1:N relationship between SALESPERSON and CONTACT instead of between SALESPERON and CUSTOMER, while the 1:N relationship between CUSTOMER and CONTACT remains the same. CONTACTs for one CUSTOMER can now be linked to various SALESPERSONs.

## FIGURE AW-4-2

**The Modified WMCRM Data Model**

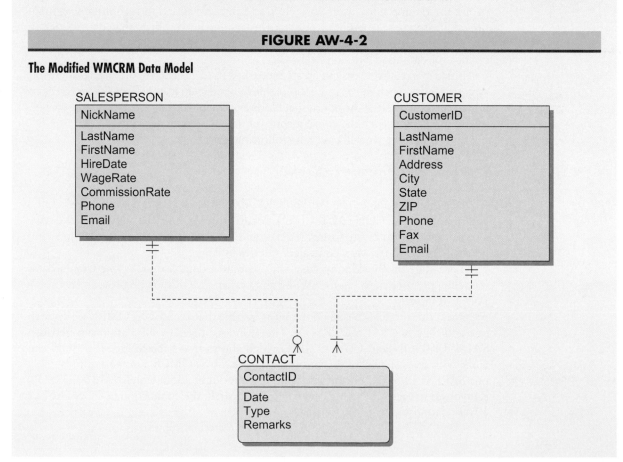

Imagine that you have been hired as a consultant to create the WMCRM database. You now have two alternative data models that you need to show to the Wallingford Motors management so that they can make a decision about which model they want to use.

But they don't understand E-R data modeling.

How can you illustrate the differences of the two approaches? One way is to generate some mock-up prototype forms and reports in MS Access. Forms and reports are much more easily understood by the users than your abstract E-R model.

### Creating a Prototype Form for the Original Data Model

We'll start by creating a sample form in our current version of the WRCRM database, which we are treating here as a prototype we created to illustrate our first data model (this includes populating the database with sample data). The database structure for this database is shown in the Relationships window in Figure AW-4-3.

You already know how to create forms that use more than one table, and the only difference in this form will be that it uses three tables instead of two. The basic table is SALESPERSON, with CUSTOMER as the second table added to the form, finally followed by the CONTACT table. Various choices of design options in the Form Wizard will lead to different appearances of the final form. One possible design (using subforms in tabular layout) of the WMCRM Salesperson Contacts form is shown in Figure AW-4-4.

In this form, there are three distinct sections—the top section shows SALEPERSON data, the middle section shows selectable CUSTOMER data, and the bottom section shows the CONTACT data for the current CUSTOMER. It should be fairly easy to explain this form to the Wallingford Motors management and users.

---

**FIGURE AW-4-3**

**The Original WMCRM Database**

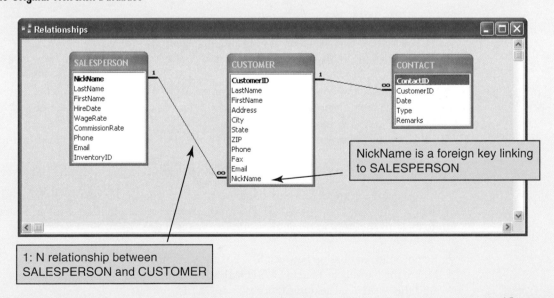

*(Continued)*

---

### FIGURE AW-4-4

**The WMCRM Salesperson Contacts Form**

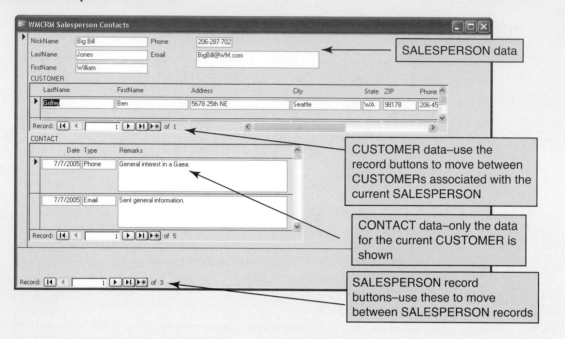

- SALESPERSON data
- CUSTOMER data–use the record buttons to move between CUSTOMERs associated with the current SALESPERSON
- CONTACT data–only the data for the current CUSTOMER is shown
- SALESPERSON record buttons–use these to move between SALESPERSON records

## Creating a Prototype Form for the Modified Data Model

Before we can create the equivalent WMCRM Salesperson Contacts form for the second data model, we must prototype the resulting database in MS Access. Fortunately, we do not need to create a new database from scratch—we can simply make a copy of the existing Access database. This is one of the nice features of Access—each database is stored in one *.mdb file. For example, recall that our original database was named (in Section 1) as WMCRM.mdb and stored in the My Documents folder. We can make renamed copies of this file as the basis for prototyping other data models.

### Copying the WMCRM.mdb Database

1. Click **Start | My Documents** to open the My Documents folder.
2. Right-click the **WMCRM.mdb file object** to display the shortcut menu, then click **Copy**.
3. Right-click anywhere in the empty area of the My Documents window to display the shortcut menu, then click **Paste**. A file object named **copy of WMCRM.mdb** appears in the My Documents window.
4. Right-click the **copy of WMCRM.mdb file object** to display the shortcut menu, then click **Rename**.
5. Edit the file name to read **WMCRM-AW04-v02.mdb**, and then press the **Enter** key.

Now we need to modify this database file. Our goal is the set of database relationships shown in Figure AW-4-5. The modifications are straightforward, and we've done most of the steps in previous sections. We need to:

- Remove the relationship between SALESPERSON and CUSTOMER (this is new)
- Delete the NickName field in CUSTOMER (this is new)
- Add the NickName field to CONTACT as NULL
- Populate the NickName field in CONTACT

---

**FIGURE AW-4-5**

**The Modified WMCRM Database**

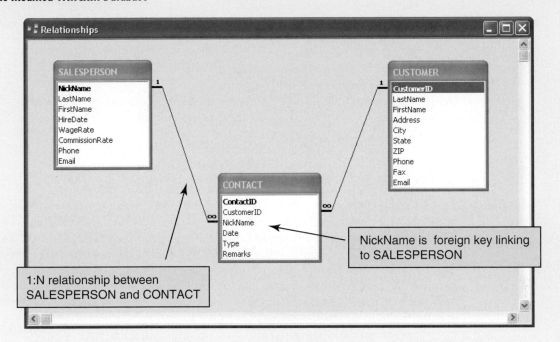

- Modify the NickName field in CONTACT to NOT NULL
- Create the relationship between SALESPERSON and CONTACT

The only new steps are deleting a relationship and deleting a field from a table.

### Deleting the SALESPERSON to CUSTOMER Relationship

1. Start Microsoft Access.
2. In the menu bar, click **File | Open**. The Open dialog box is displayed. Browse to the **WMCRM-AW04-v02.mdb** file, click the file name to highlight it, and then click the **Open** button. When the Security Warning dialog box appears, click the **Open** button to open the database.
3. Click **Tools | Relationships. . .** to display the Relationships window shown in Figure AW-4-3.
4. Right-click on the **relationship line** between SALESPERSON and CUSTOMER to display the shortcut menu, then click **Delete**.
5. A dialog box will be displayed with the message "Are you sure you want to permanently delete the selected relationship from your database?" Click the **Yes** button.
6. Click the **X** button in the upper right corner of the Relationships window to close the window.
7. If a dialog box is displayed with the message "Do you want to save the changes to the layout of 'Relationships'?", then click the **Yes** button. This dialog box will only appear if you moved a table object or otherwise reorganized the relationships diagram.

*(Continued)*

### Deleting a Column (Field) in an Access Table

1. Open the **CUSTOMER table** in **Design View**.
2. Select the **NickName** column (field).
3. Right-click anywhere in the row containing data about the selected row to display the shortcut menu. Click **Delete Rows**.
   - **NOTE:** There is also a Delete Rows button on the Table Design Toolbar currently displayed under the Access menu. You can use this button instead of the shortcut menu if you want to.
4. A dialog box will be displayed with the message "Do you want to permanently delete the selected field(s) and all the data in the field(s)?" Click the **Yes** button.
5. Click the **Save** button on the Table Design toolbar currently displayed under the Access menu to save the changes to the table design.
6. Close the **CUSTOMER** table.

The other steps needed to modify the database are the same ones we used when we added the SALESPERSON table to the database in Section 3's "The Access Workbench." Following the instructions in that section, we can add the NickName column to CONTACT, populate it, and create the relationship between SALESPERSON and CONTACT. Note that Figure 4-5 shows NickName inserted as the third column (field) in the table—it could just as easily be added as the last column in the table. In a relational table, column order doesn't matter—we use the one that makes it easier for us as database developers to read!

With these modifications done, we now create another version of the WMCRM Salesperson Contacts form. This version is shown in Figure AW-4-6. In this form, there are only two distinct sections—the top section shows SALEPERSON data, while the bottom section shows that the data for each CONTACT also contains the data for the contacted CUSTOMER. This form is distinctively different from the form based on the first data model, but again it should be fairly easy to explain this form to the Wallingford Motors management and users. Given the two forms, management and users will be able to decide how they want the data presented, and this decision will then determine which data model should be used.

---

### FIGURE AW-4-6

**The WMCRM Salesperson Contacts Form for the Modified Database**

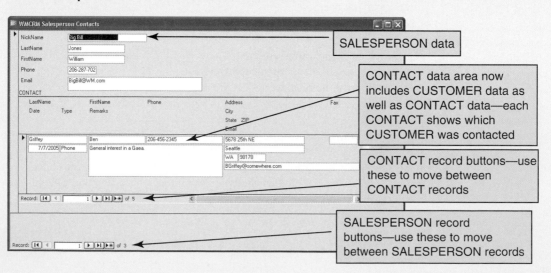

### The Access Banded Form and Report Editors

The form in Figure AW-4-6 has extensively rearranged labels and data text boxes in the CONTACT section of the form. Access uses **banded form and report editors**, where each element of the form or report is displayed in its own band such as Header, Detail, or Footer, which makes such rearranging very easy to do. The form shown in Figure AW-4-6 is shown in Design View in Figure AW-4-7.

Note that the form and the CONTACT subform each have their own Form Header, Detail, and Form Footer sections. These can be resized as necessary, as can the size of the entire form itself and the size and position of the subform area within the form. The labels and text boxes that display the data can be moved or resized using standard windows drag-and-drop actions. Label text can be edited, and additional labels or other text added. Although this figure shows a form, report formats can be edited exactly the same way.

### Closing the Database and Exiting Access

This completes the work we'll do in this section of "The Access Workbench." As usual, we will finish by closing the database and Access.

#### Closing the WMCRM-AW04-v02 Database

1. To close the WMCRM-AW04-v02 : Database window, click the **Close** button in the upper right corner of the WMCRM-AW04-v02 : Database window.

#### Exiting Access

1. To exit Access, click the **Close** button in the upper right corner of the Microsoft Access window.

---

### FIGURE AW-4-7

**The Access Banded Form Editor**

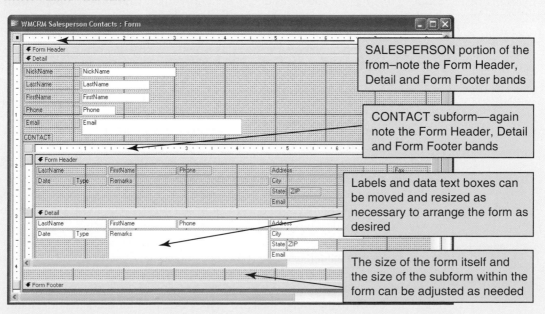

The process of developing a database system consists of three stages: requirements, design, and implementation. During the requirements stage, users are interviewed, systems requirements are documented, and a data model is constructed. Often, prototypes of selected portions of the future system are created. During the design phase, the data model is transformed into a relational database design. During the implementation stage, the database is constructed and filled with data, and queries, forms, reports, and application programs are created.

In addition to a data model, the development team also must determine data-item data types, properties, and limits on data values. Business rules that constrain database activity also need be documented.

The entity-relationship (E-R) model is the most popular tool used to develop a data model. With the E-R model, entities—which are identifiable things of importance to the users—are defined. All of the entities of a given type form an entity class. A particular entity is called an instance. Attributes describe the characteristics of entities, and one or more attributes identify an entity. Identifiers can be unique or nonunique.

Relationships are associations among entities. The E-R model explicitly defines relationships. Each relationship has a name, and there are relationship classes as well as relationship instances. According to the original specification of the E-R model, relationships may have attributes; however, this is not common in contemporary data models.

The degree of a relationship is the number of entities participating in the relationship. Most relationships are binary. The three types of binary relationships are 1:1, 1:N, and N:M. A recursive relationship occurs when an entity has a relationship to itself.

In traditional E-R diagrams, such as the traditional E-R model, entities are shown in rectangles, and relationships are shown in diamonds. The maximum cardinality of a relationship is shown inside the diamond. The minimum cardinality is indicated by a hash mark or an oval.

A weak entity is one whose existence depends on another entity; an entity that is not weak is called a strong entity. In this text, we further define a weak entity as an entity that logically depends on another entity. An entity can have a minimum cardinality of one in a relationship with another entity and not necessarily be a weak entity. ID-dependent entities must include the identifier of the entity upon which the ID-dependent entity depends as part of the identifier of the ID-dependent entity.

The extended E-R model introduced the concept of subtypes. A subtype entity is a special case of another entity known as its supertype. In some cases, an attribute of the supertype, called a discriminator, indicates which of the subtypes is appropriate for a given instance. Subtypes can be exclusive, where the supertype relates to at most one subtype, or inclusive, where the supertype can relate to one or more subtypes. The identifier of the subtype is the identifier of the supertype.

This text uses the Information Engineering Crow's Foot E-R model in the E-R diagrams shown in the book. You should be familiar with diagrams of that style, but you also should realize that when creating a database design, no fundamental difference exists between the traditional style and this style.

In addition to E-R diagrams, a data model includes attribute specifications. The development team also needs to document business rules that constrain database activity while creating a data model.

After E-R models are completed, they must be evaluated. The development team can show the data model, or portions of the data model, directly to the users for evaluation. This requires the users to learn how to interpret an E-R diagram. Sometimes, instead of the data model, prototypes that demonstrate the consequences of the data model are shown to the users. Such prototypes are easier for users to understand.

**4.1** Name the three stages in the process of developing database systems. Summarize the tasks in each.

**4.2** What is a *data model*, and what is its purpose?

**4.3** What is a *prototype*, and what is its purpose?

**4.4** What is a *use case*, and what is its purpose?

**4.5** Give an example of a data constraint.

**4.6** Give an example of a business rule that would need to be documented in a database development project.

**4.7** Define the term *entity* and give an example other than those used in this book.

**4.8** Explain the difference between an entity class and an entity instance.

**4.9** Define the term *attribute* and give examples for the entity you created in question 4.7.

**4.10** Define the term *identifier*, and indicate which attribute defined in your answer to question 4.9 identifies the *entity*.

**4.11** Define the term *composite identifier* and give an example other than those used in this book.

**4.12** Define the term *relationship* and give an example other than those used in this book.

**4.13** Explain the difference between a relationship class and a relationship instance.

**4.14** Define the term *degree of relationship*. Give an example, other than one in this text, of a relationship greater than degree two.

**4.15** List and give an example of the three types of binary relationships other than the ones used in this book. Draw both a traditional E-R diagram and an IE Crow's Foot E-R diagram for each.

**4.16** Define the terms *maximum cardinality* and *minimum cardinality*.

**4.17** Draw an IE Crow's Foot E-R diagram for the entities DEPARTMENT and EMPLOYEE and the 1:N relationship between them. Assume that a DEPARTMENT does not need to have an EMPLOYEE, but that every EMPLOYEE is assigned to a DEPARTMENT. Include appropriate identifiers and attributes for each entity.

**4.18** Define the term *ID-dependent entity* and give an example other than one in this text. Draw an IE Crow's Foot E-R diagram for your example.

**4.19** Define the term *weak entity* and give an example other than the one used in this text. Draw an IE Crow's Foot E-R diagram for your example.

**4.20** Explain the ambiguity in the definition of the term *weak entity*. Explain how this book interprets this term.

**4.21** Define the terms *supertype, subtype,* and *discriminator*.

**4.22** What is an exclusive subtype relationship? Give an example other than one shown in this chapter. Draw an IE Crow's Foot E-R diagram for your example.

**4.23** What is an inclusive subtype relationship? Give an example other than one shown in this chapter. Draw an IE Crow's Foot E-R diagram for your example.

**4.24** Give an example of a recursive relationship other than the one shown in this chapter. Draw an IE Crow's Foot E-R diagram for your example.

**4.25** List important attribute properties that need to be developed as part of a data model.

**4.26** Create example properties for the attributes in your E-R diagram for DEPART-MENT and EMPLOYEE in question 4.18.

**4.27** Give an example of a business rule for your work for question 4.18.

**4.28** Describe why it is important to evaluate a data model.

**4.29** Summarize one technique for evaluating a data model, and explain how that technique could be used to evaluate the data model in Figure 4-20.

## EXERCISES

**4.30** Suppose that Heather Sweeney wants to include records of her consulting services in her database. Extend the data model in Figure 4-20(c) to include CONSULTING_PROJECT and DAILY_PROJECT_HOURS entities. CONSULTING_PROJECT contains data about a particular project for one of her customers, and DAILY_PROJECT_HOURS contains data about the hours spent and a description of the work accomplished on a particular day for a particular project. Use strong and/or weak entities as appropriate. Specify minimum and maximum cardinalities. Use the IE Crow's Foot E-R model for your E-R diagrams.

**4.31** Extend your work for question 4.30 to include supplies that Heather uses on a project. Assume that she wants to track the description, price, and amount used of each supply. Supplies are used on multiple days of a project. Use the IE Crow's Foot E-R model for your E-R diagrams.

**4.32** Using recursive relationships as appropriate, develop a data model of the boxcars on a railway train. Use the IE Crow's Foot E-R model for your E-R diagrams.

**4.33** Develop a data model of a genealogical diagram. Model only biological parents; do not model stepparents. Use the IE Crow's Foot E-R model for your E-R diagrams.

**4.34** Develop a data model of a genealogical diagram. Model all parents, including stepparents. Use the IE Crow's Foot E-R model for your E-R diagrams.

## ACCESS WORKBENCH EXERCISES

"The Access Workbench" in this chapter described how to create two prototype databases and example forms. Some of the steps, steps that were new, were detailed in the section, but most were not because you've done them before. In this set of exercises, we will:

- create prototype forms, and
- create prototype reports.

**AW.4.1** We've built an extensive database for the Wedgewood Pacific Corporation (**WPC.mdb**) in the previous chapters. We'll use it to build some prototype forms and reports so that the users at WPC. In this case, there is no need to restructure the database.

    **A.** Create a form that allows users to view and edit employee data. The form should show information about the employee, the department that he or she works for, and which projects the employee is assigned to.

**B.** Create a report that displays the employee information shown on the form you created in A. The report should show this information for all users, sorted alphabetically in ascending order by LastName.

**C.** Create a form that allows users to view and edit project data. The form should show information about the project, the department that is responsible for the project, and list all employees who are assigned to work on that project.

**D.** Create a report that displays the project information shown on the form you created in C. The report should show this information for all projects, sorted in ascending order by ProjectID.

## GARDEN GLORY PROJECT QUESTIONS

Garden Glory wants to expand its database applications beyond the recording of property services. The company still wants to maintain data on owners, properties, employees, and services, but it wants to include other data as well. Specifically, Garden Glory wants to track equipment, how it is used during services, and equipment repairs. In addition, employees need to be trained before using certain equipment, and management wants to be able to determine who has obtained training on which equipment.

With regard to properties, Garden Glory has determined that most of the properties it services are too large and complex to be described in one record. The company wants the database to allow for many subproperty descriptions of a property. Thus, a particular property might have subproperty descriptions of Front Garden, Back Garden, Second-Level Courtyard, and so on. For better accounting to the customers, services are to be related to the subproperties rather than to the overall property.

**A.** Draw an E-R data model for the Garden Glory database schema shown in Chapter 3's "Garden Glory Project Questions." Use the IE Crow's Foot E-R model for your E-R diagrams. Justify the decisions you make regarding minimum and maximum cardinality.

**B.** Extend and modify the E-R data model to meet Garden Glory's new requirements. Use the IE Crow's Foot E-R model for your E-R diagrams. Create appropriate identifiers and attributes for each entity. Justify the decisions you make regarding minimum and maximum cardinality.

**C.** Specify data properties for the attributes in your E-R diagram in question B.

**D.** Describe how you would go about validating the model in question B.

## JAMES RIVER JEWELRY PROJECT QUESTIONS

James River Jewelry wants to expand its database applications beyond the recording of purchases and purchase awards (see the description of the award program in Chapter 1's "James River Jewelry Project Questions"). The company still wants to maintain data on customers, purchases, and awards, but it wants to include other data as well. Specifically, James River Jewelry wants to record artists and styles and keep track of which customers are interested in which artists and styles.

Also, most of the jewelry is sold on consignment so the company does not pay the artist of a piece of jewelry until it is sold. Typically, the company pays artists 60 percent of the sales price, but the terms are negotiated separately for each item. For some items, the artists earn a larger percentage, and for others they earn less. Artists and James River Jewelry personnel agree on the initial sales price at the time the item is brought to the shop. When an item has been in the shop for some time, James River Jewelry may reduce the price; sometimes it renegotiates the sales percentage.

**A.** Draw an E-R data model for the James River Jewelry database schema shown in Chapter 3's "James River Jewelry Project Questions." Use the IE Crow's Foot E-R model for your E-R diagrams. Justify the decisions you make regarding minimum and maximum cardinality.

**B.** Extend and modify the E-R data model to show the James River Jewelry's award program. Use the IE Crow's Foot E-R model for your E-R diagrams. Create appropriate identifiers and attributes for each entity. Justify the decisions you make regarding minimum and maximum cardinality.

**C.** Extend and modify the E-R data model in question B to meet James River Jewelry's new requirements. Use the IE Crow's Foot E-R model for your E-R diagrams. Create appropriate identifiers and attributes for each entity. Justify the decisions you make regarding minimum and maximum cardinality.

**D.** Specify data properties for the attributes in your E-R diagram in question C.

**E.** Describe how you would go about validating the data model in question C.

## THE QUEEN ANNE CURIOSITY SHOP PROJECT QUESTIONS

The Queen Anne Curiosity Shop wants to expand its database applications beyond the current recording of sales. The company still wants to maintain data on customers, employees, vendors, sales, and items, but it wants to (a) modify the way it handles inventory, and (b) simplify the storage of customer and employee data.

Currently, each item is considered unique, which means that the item must be sold as a whole, and that multiple units of the item in stock must be treated as separate items in the ITEM table. The Queen Anne Curiosity Shop management wants the database modified to include an inventory system that will allow multiple units of an item to be stored under one ItemID. The system should allow for a quantity on hand, a quantity on order, and an order due date. If the same identical item is stocked by multiple vendors, the item should be orderable from any of these vendors. The SALE_ITEM table should then include Quantity and ExtendedPrice columns to allow for sales of multiple units of an item.

It has not escaped notice of the Queen Anne Curiosity Shop management that some of the fields in CUSTOMER and EMPLOYEE store similar data. Under the current system, when an employee buys something at the store, their data has to be reentered in the CUSTOMER table! The managers would like to have have the CUSTOMER and EMPLOYEE tables redesigned using subtypes.

**A.** Draw an E-R data model for the Queen Anne Curiosity Shop database schema shown in Chapter 3's "Queen Anne Curiosity Shop Project Questions." Use the IE Crow's Foot E-R model for your E-R diagrams. Justify the decisions you make regarding minimum and maximum cardinality.

**B.** Extend and modify the E-R data model to meet only the Queen Anne Curiosity Shop's inventory system requirements. Use the IE Crow's Foot E-R model for your E-R diagrams. Create appropriate identifiers and attributes for each entity. Justify the decisions you make regarding minimum and maximum cardinality.

**C.** Extend and modify the E-R data model to meet only the Queen Anne Curiosity Shop's need for more efficient storage of CUSTOMER and EMPLOYEE data. Use the IE Crow's Foot E-R model for your E-R diagrams. Create appropriate identifiers and attributes for each entity. Justify the decisions you make regarding minimum and maximum cardinality.

**D.** Combine the E-R data models from questions B and C to meet all the Queen Anne Curiosity Shop's new requirements, making additional modifications if any are needed. Use the IE Crow's Foot E-R model for your E-R diagrams.

**E.** Specify data properties for the attributes in your E-R diagram in question D.

**F.** Describe how you would go about validating your data model in question D.

# CHAPTER 5

# Database Design

> Learn how to transform E-R data models into relational designs

> Practice applying the normalization process from Chapter 2

> Understand the need for denormalization

> Learn how to represent weak entities with the relational model

> Know how to represent 1:1, 1:N, and N:M binary relationships

> Know how to represent 1:1, 1:N, and N:M recursive relationships

> Learn SQL statements for creating joins over binary and recursive relationships

> Understand the nature and background of normalization theory

**T**his chapter describes a process for converting E-R data models into relational designs. We begin by explaining how entities are expressed as relations (or tables). We then apply the role of the normalization process that you learned in Chapter 2 and describe normalization in more detail. Next, we show how to represent relationships using foreign keys, including how to use these techniques for representing recursive relationships. Finally, we apply all these techniques to design a database for the data model of Heather Sweeney Designs, developed in Chapter 4.

> **B T W**
>
> As you learned in Chapter 2, the technically correct term for the representation of an entity in a relational model is *relation.* However, the use of the synonym *table* is common, and we will use it in the chapter. Just remember that the two terms mean the same thing when used to discuss databases.

# ▷ TRANSFORMING A DATA MODEL INTO A DATABASE DESIGN

The steps for transforming a data model into a database design are shown in Figure 5-1. First, we create a table for each entity in the data model. Then, we make sure that each of the tables is properly normalized. Finally, we create the relationships between the tables.[1]

# ▷ REPRESENTING ENTITIES WITH THE RELATIONAL MODEL

The representation of entities using the relational model is direct and straightforward. First, define a table for each entity and give that table the same name as the entity. Make the primary key of the relation the identifier of the entity. Then, create a column in the relation for each attribute in the entity. Finally, apply the normalization process described in Chapter 2 to remove any normalization problems. To understand this process, we will consider three examples.

**FIGURE 5-1**

**The Steps for Transforming a Data Model into a Database Design**

1. Create a table for each entity
   - Specify primary key (consider surrogate keys as appropriate)
   - Specify properties for each column
     - Data type
     - Null status
     - Default value (if any)
     - Specify data constraints (if any)
   - Verify normalization

2. Create relationships by placing foreign keys
   - Strong entity relationships (1:1, 1:N, N:M)
   - ID-dependent and non-ID-dependent weak entity relationships
   - Subtypes
   - Recursive (1:1, 1:N, N:M)

---

[1]The transformation is actually a bit more complex than this when the need to enforce minimum cardinalities is considered. Although the referential integrity constraints (with ON UPDATE and ON DELETE) handle some parts of this, application logic is required to handle other parts, and that is beyond the scope of this book. See David M. Kroenke, *Database Processing: Fundamentals, Design, and Implementation*, 10th Edition (Upper Saddle River: Pearson/Prentice-Hall, 2006), Chapter 6.

## Representing the ITEM Entity

Consider the ITEM entity shown in Figure 5-2(a), which contains the attributes ItemNumber, Description, Cost, ListPrice, and QuantityOnHand.

To represent this entity with a table, we define a table named ITEM and place the attributes in it as columns in the relation. ItemNumber is the identifier of the entity and becomes the primary key of the table. The result is shown in Figure 5-2(b), and can also be written as:

ITEM (<u>ItemNumber</u>, Description, Cost, ListPrice, QuantityOnHand)

Note that in Figure 5-(2)b, a key symbol identifies the primary key, and that in the table notation above the primary key of the table is underlined.

**Surrogate Keys**   The ideal primary key is short, numeric, and nonchanging. ItemNumber meets these criteria. However, if the primary key does not meet these criteria, a DBMS-generated **surrogate key** should be used. Surrogate key values are numeric, unique within a table, and never change. These keys are assigned when a row is created and deleted when the row is deleted—the numbers are never reused. They would be the ideal primary key except for a couple of considerations.

First, the numbers generated have no intrinsic meaning. When you look at ItemNumbers, you cannot interpret them in a meaningful way. Second, although the surrogate key values may not be duplicated within a table, they may not be unique between two databases. Consider two databases that each has an ITEM table with the surrogate ID of ItemNumber. If the data from these databases is ever shared, this may present a problem.

Nonetheless, surrogate keys are very useful and are commonly used as ID numbers in tables.

**Column Properties**   Note that each attribute in the ITEM entity has become a column in the ITEM table. We need to specify certain properties for each column, as was mentioned in the discussion of attributes at the end of Chapter 4. These include data type, null status, default values, and any constraints on the values.

**Data Types**   Each DBMS specifies certain data types that it supports. Data types for SQL Server 2005, MySQL, and Access were discussed in Chapter 3. For each column, we will indicate exactly what type of data will be stored in this column. Data types are usually set when the table is actually created in the database as discussed in Chapter 3.

**NULL Values**   Next, we will decide which column must have data values entered when a new row is created in the table. If a column *must* have a data value entered, then this column will be designated NOT NULL—if the value can be left empty, then the column will be designated as NULL. We have to be careful here. If we specify columns as NOT NULL when we may not know the data value at the time the row is being created, we will not be able to create the row. For this reason, some columns that may appear to you as needing to be NOT NULL may actually be specified as NULL. This data will be entered but not at the exact moment the row is created in the table.

For the ITEM table, we will set only ListPrice as NULL. This is a number that may not have been determined by management at the time data on an ITEM is entered into the database. All other columns should have known values at the time a row is created and will be NOT NULL. NULL or NOT NULL is usually set when the table is actually created in the database as discussed in Chapter 3.

**FIGURE 5-2**

The ITEM Entity and Table

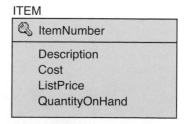

(a) The ITEM Entity

(b) The ITEM Table

**Default Values** A **default value** is a value automatically supplied by the DBMS when a new row is created. The default value may be a static value, or one calculated by application logic. In this book, we will deal with only static values. In the ITEM table, we will specify a default of 0 (zero) for QuantityOnHand. This will indicate that the ITEM is out of stock until this value is updated. Default values are usually set when the table is actually created in the database as discussed in Chapter 3.

**Data Constraints** The data values in some columns may be subject to restrictions on the values that can exist in those columns. Such limitations are called data constraints. An example we have already seen is the referential integrity constraint, which states that the only values allowed in a foreign key column are values already existing in the corresponding primary key column in the related table.

In the ITEM table, one needed data constraint is that (ListPrice > Cost) to ensure that we do not inadvertently sell an ITEM for less than we paid for it. Data constraints are usually set when the table is actually created in the database as discussed in Chapter 3.

**Verifying Normalization** Finally, we need to verify that the ITEM table is properly normalized—the table results from converting an entity in this way might have normalization problems. Therefore, the next step is to apply the normalization process from Chapter 2. In the case of ITEM, the only candidate key is the primary key, which is ItemNumber, and no other functional dependencies exist. Therefore, the ITEM table is normalized to BCNF. The final ITEM table with column types, surrogate key indicator, and NULL/NOT NULL constraints indicated is shown in Figure 5-3. Generally, we will not show this much detail in the illustrations of the tables in this chapter, but note that it is available in commercial database design programs and can usually be displayed as needed.

## Representing the CUSTOMER Entity

To understand an entity that gives rise to normalization problems, consider the CUSTOMER entity in Figure 5-4(a). If we transform the entity as just described, we obtain the table shown in Figure 5-4(b). This can be written as:

CUSTOMER (<u>CustomerNumber</u>, CustomerName, StreetAddress, City, State, ZIP, ContactName, Phone)

CustomerNumber is the key of the relation, and we will assume that we have done all the necessary work on column definition.

---

**FIGURE 5-3**

**The ITEM Table**

ITEM

| ITEM |
|------|
| 🔑 ItemNumber: int IDENTITY(10000,1) |
| Description: varchar(100) NOT NULL<br>Cost: numeric(9,2) NOT NULL<br>ListPrice: numeric(9,2) NULL<br>QuantityOnHand: int NOT NULL |

---

**FIGURE 5-4**

**The CUSTOMER Entity and Table**

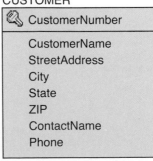

| CUSTOMER |
|------|
| CustomerNumber |
| CustomerName<br>StreetAddress<br>City<br>State<br>ZIP<br>ContactName<br>Phone |

(a) The CUSTOMER Entity

| CUSTOMER |
|------|
| 🔑 CustomerNumber |
| CustomerName<br>StreetAddress<br>City<br>State<br>ZIP<br>ContactName<br>Phone |

(b) The CUSTOMER Table

According to the normalization process (page 68), we need to check for functional dependencies besides those involving the primary key. At least one exists, namely:

ZIP→(City, State)

The only candidate key in CUSTOMER is CustomerNumber. ZIP is *not* a candidate key for this relation, and, therefore, this relation is not normalized. Furthermore, there is another possible functional dependency involving Phone. Is Phone the phone number of the CUSTOMER, or is it the phone number of the contact? If PhoneNumber is the phone number of the CUSTOMER, then

CustomerNumber→Phone

and no additional normalization problem exists. However, if the PhoneNumber is that of the contact, then

ContactName→Phone

and because ContactName is not a candidate key, there are normalization problems here as well.

The answer to the question about "whose phone number is it?" can be resolved by asking the users. Assume that we do that, and the users say that indeed it is the phone number of the contact. Thus:

ContactName→Phone

Given these facts, we will proceed to normalize the CUSTOMER table. According to the normalization process, we pull the attributes of the functional dependencies out of the tables while leaving a copy of their determinants in the original relation as foreign keys. The result is the three relations as seen in Figure 5-5 and below:

CUSTOMER (<u>CustomerNumber</u>, LastName, FirstName, Address, *ZIP*, *ContactName*)

ZIP (<u>Zip</u>, City, State)

CONTACT (<u>ContactName</u>, Phone)

with the referential integrity constraints:

ZIP in CUSTOMER must exist in ZIP in ZIP

ContactName in CUSTOMER must exist in ContactName in CONTACT

**FIGURE 5-5**

**The Normalized CUSTOMER and Associated Tables**

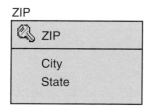
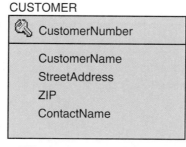
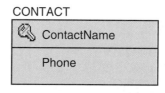

ZIP
is a foreign key referencing
ZIP in ZIP

ContactName
is a foreign key referencing
ContactName in CONTACT

These three relations are now normalized, and we can continue with the design process. However, before we proceed, let's consider another perspective on normalization.

**Denormalization**   It is possible to take normalization too far. Most practitioners would consider the construction of a separate ZIP table to be going too far. People are accustomed to writing their city, state, and ZIP as a group, and breaking City and State away from Zip will make the design hard to use. It also will mean that the DBMS has to read two separate tables just to get the customer's address. Therefore, even though it results in normalization problems, a better overall design would result by leaving Zip, City, and State in the CUSTOMER relation. This is an example of **denormalization**.

What are the consequences of this decision to denormalize? To answer that question, consider the three basic operations: insert, update, and delete. If we leave ZIP, City, and State in CUSTOMER, then we will not be able to insert data for a new ZIP code until a customer has that zip code. However, we will never want to do that. We only care about ZIP code data when one of our customers has that ZIP code. Therefore, leaving the ZIP data in CUSTOMER does not pose problems when inserting.

What about modifications? If a city changes its ZIP code, then we might have to change multiple rows in CUSTOMER. How frequently do cities change their ZIP codes though? Because the answer is almost never, updates in the denormalized relation are not a problem. Finally, what about deletes? If only one customer has the ZIP data (80210, Denver, Colorado), then if we delete that customer, we will lose the fact that 80210 is in Denver. This does not really matter though because when another customer with this ZIP code is inserted, that customer also will provide the city and state.

Therefore, denormalizing CUSTOMER by leaving the attributes ZIP, City, State in the relation will make the design easier to use and not cause modification problems. The denormalized design is better, and our final design is shown in Figure 5-6 and below.

CUSTOMER (CustomerNumber, LastName, FirstName, Address, City, State, ZIP, *ContactName*)

CONTACT (ContactName, Phone)

with the referential integrity constraint:

ContactName in CUSTOMER must exist in ContactName in CONTACT

The need for denormalization also can arise for reasons such as security and performance. If the cost of the modification problems is low (like for zip code) and if other factors cause denormalized relations to be preferred, then denormalizing is a good idea.

---

**FIGURE 5-6**

**The Denormalized CUSTOMER and Associated CONTACT Tables**

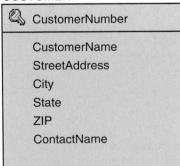

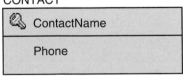

CUSTOMER

| 🔑 CustomerNumber |
| --- |
| CustomerName |
| StreetAddress |
| City |
| State |
| ZIP |
| ContactName |

CONTACT

| 🔑 ContactName |
| --- |
| Phone |

ContactName
is a foreign key referencing
ContactName in CONTACT

## A Relational Design for the SALES-COMMISSION Entity

To summarize the discussion so far, when representing an entity with the relational model, the first step is to construct a table that has all the entity's attributes as columns. The identifier of the entity becomes the primary key of the table, and we define our column constraints. Then, the table is normalized. There may be reason for leaving parts of a table denormalized.

By proceeding in this way, we always consider the normalized design. If we make a decision to denormalize, we are doing so from a position of knowledge and not from ignorance.

To reinforce these ideas, consider a third example—that for the SALES-COMMISSION entity in Figure 5-7(a). First, we create a relation having all the attributes as columns as shown in Figure 5-7(b) and below:

SALES_COMMISSION (SalespersonNumber, SalespersonLastName, SalespersonFirstName, Phone, <u>CheckNumber</u>, CheckDate, CommissionPeriod, TotalCommissionSales, CommissionAmount, BudgetCategory)

As shown, the primary key of the table is CheckNumber, the identifier of the entity. The attributes of the relation have two additional functional dependencies:

SalespersonNumber→
(SalespersonLastName, SalespersonFirstName, Phone, BudgetCategory)

and

(SalespersonNumber, CommissionPeriod)→(TotalCommissionSales, CommissionAmount)

According to the normalization process, we extract the attributes of these functional dependencies from the original table and make the determinants the primary keys of the new tables. We also leave a copy of the determinants in the original table as foreign keys. The only complication in this case is that the name of the original table actually makes more sense when used for one of the new tables that has been created! The original table, given the primary key of CheckNumber, should actually be called COMMISSION_CHECK, and has been renamed as such in the normalization results shown in Figure 5-8 and which can be written as:

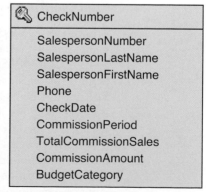

| FIGURE 5-7 | SALES_COMMISSION | SALES_COMMISSION |
|---|---|---|

**The SALES_ COMMISSION Entity and Table**

SALES_COMMISSION

| CheckNumber |
|---|
| SalespersonNumber |
| SalespersonLastName |
| SalespersonFirstName |
| Phone |
| CheckDate |
| CommissionPeriod |
| TotalCommissionSales |
| CommissionAmount |
| BudgetCategory |

(a) The SALES_COMMISSION Entity

SALES_COMMISSION

| 🔍 CheckNumber |
|---|
| SalespersonNumber |
| SalespersonLastName |
| SalespersonFirstName |
| Phone |
| CheckDate |
| CommissionPeriod |
| TotalCommissionSales |
| CommissionAmount |
| BudgetCategory |

(b) The SALES_COMMISSION Table

**FIGURE 5-8**

**The Normalized SALES_COMMISSION and Associated Tables**

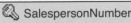

SALESPERSON (SalespersonNumber, SalespersonLastName, SalespersonFirstName, Phone)

SALES_COMMISSION (*SalespersonNumber*, CommissionPeriod, TotalCommissionSales, CommissionAmount)

COMMISSION_CHECK (CheckNumber, CheckDate, *SalespersonNumber*, *CommissionPeriod*)

with referential integrity constraints:

SalespersonNumber in COMMISSION_CHECK must exist in SalespersonNumber in SALESPERSON

(SalespersonNumber, CommissionPeriod) in COMMISSION_CHECK must exist in (SalespersonNumber, CommissionPeriod) in SALESPERSON_SALES

Now consider denormalization. Is there any reason not to create these new relations? Is the design better if we leave them in the COMMISSION_CHECK relation (the renamed SALES_COMMISSION relation)? In this case, there is no reason to denormalize so we leave the normalized relations alone.

## Representing Weak Entities

This process works for all entity types, but weak entities sometimes require special treatment. Recall that a weak entity logically depends on another entity. In Figure 5-8, SALES_COMMISSION is an ID-dependent weak entity that depends upon SALESPERSON for its existence—in this model, there are no SALES_COMMISSIONs without a SALESPERSON. On the other hand, note that in Figure 5-8, COMMISSION_CHECK is a strong entity because COMMISSION_ CHECKs exist (as blank checks) regardless of whether or not a commission has been earned.

If a weak entity is not ID-dependent, it can be represented as a table using the techniques just described. The dependency needs to be recorded in the relational design so that no application will create a weak entity without its proper parent (the entity on which the weak entity depends). Finally, a business rule will need to be implemented so that when the parent is deleted, the weak entity also is deleted. These rules are part of the relational design, and, in this case, will take the form of an ON DELETE CASCADE constraint on the weak, non–ID-dependent table.

The situation is slightly different if a weak entity is also ID-dependent. This is the case in the dependence of SALES_COMMISSION on SALESPERSON since SALES_COMMISSIONs are identified by the SALESPERSON who made the sales. When creating a table for an ID-dependent entity, we must ensure that the identifier of the parent and the identifier of the ID-dependent weak entity itself appear in the table. For example, consider what would happen if we established the table for SALES_ COMMISSION without including the key of SALESPERSON. What would be the key of this table? It would be just CommissionPeriod, but because SALES_COMMISSION is ID-dependent, this is not a complete key. In fact, without the needed reference to SALESPERSON included, CommissionPeriod by itself cannot be the primary key because this table would likely have duplicate rows. (This would happen if two occurrences of a specific CommissionPeriod had the same TotalCommissionSales—which could happen because this table records data for more than one SALESPERSON.) Thus, for an ID-dependent weak entity, it is necessary to add the primary key of the parent entity to the weak entity's table, and this added attribute becomes part of that table's key. In Figure 5-8, note that SALES_COMMISSION has the correct composite primary key (SalespersonNumber, CommissionPeriod).

For another example, consider Figure 5-9(a), where LINE_ITEM is an ID-dependent weak entity. It is weak because its logical existence depends on INVOICE, and it is ID-dependent because its identifier contains the identifier of INVOICE. Again, consider what would happen if we established a relation for LINE_ITEM without including the key of INVOICE. What would be the key of this relation? It would be just LineNumber, but because LINE_ITEM is ID-dependent, this cannot be a complete key. Without the needed reference to ITEM included, LINE_ITEM, like SALEPSERSON_SALES in the previous example, would likely have duplicate rows. (This would happen if two invoices had the same quantity of the same item on the same line.) Figure 5-9(b) shows LINE_ITEM with the correct composite primary key (InvoiceNumber, LineNumber).

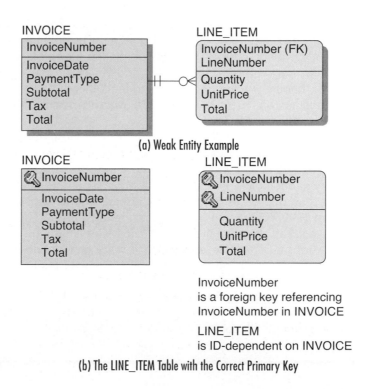

**FIGURE 5-9**

**Relational Representation of a Weak Entity**

(a) Weak Entity Example

InvoiceNumber is a foreign key referencing InvoiceNumber in INVOICE

LINE_ITEM is ID-dependent on INVOICE

(b) The LINE_ITEM Table with the Correct Primary Key

# Normal Forms

A table and a spreadsheet are very similar in that you can think of both as having rows, columns, and cells. Edgar Frank Codd, the father of the relational model, defined three normal forms in an early paper on the relational model. He defined any table that meets the definition of a relation (see Figure 2-1 on page 54) as being in **first normal form (1NF)**.

Codd pointed out that such tables can have anomalies, and he defined a **second normal form (2NF)** that eliminated some of those anomalies. A relation is in 2NF if and only if (1) it is in 1NF, and (2) all non-key attributes are determined by the entire primary key. This means that if the primary key is a composite primary key, no non-key attribute can be determined by an attribute or attributes that make up only part of the key. Thus, if we have a relation **(A, B, N, O, P)** with the composite key **(A, B)**, then none of the non-key attributes **N, O,** or **P** can be determined by *just* **A** or *just* **B**.

However, the conditions of 2NF did not eliminate all the anomalies so he defined **third normal form (3NF)**. A relation is in 3NF if and only if (a) it is in 2NF, and (b) there are no non-key attributes determined by another non-key attribute. Technically, the situation described by the last condition is called a **transitive dependency**. Thus, in our relation **(A, B, N, O, P), none** of the non-key attributes **N, O,** or **P** can be determined by **N, O** or **P** or any combination of them.

Not long after Codd published his paper on normal forms, it was pointed out to him that even relations in 3NF could have anomalies. As a result, he and R. Boyce defined **Boyce-Codd Normal Form (BCNF)**, which eliminated the anomalies that had been found with 3NF. As we stated in Chapter 2, a relation is in BCNF if and only if every determinant is a candidate key. This is summed up in a widely known phrase: "I swear to construct my tables so that all non-key columns are dependent on the key, the whole key, and nothing but the key, so help me Codd!"

All these definitions were made in such a way that a relation in a higher normal form is defined to be in all lower normal forms. Thus, a relation in BCNF is automatically in 3NF, a relation in 3NF is automatically in 2NF, and a relation in 2NF is automatically in 1NF.

There the matter rested until others discovered another kind of dependency called a **multivalued dependency**. Such dependencies were discussed in Exercises 2.40 and 2.41 at the end of Chapter 2. To eliminate such dependencies, **fourth normal form (4NF)** was defined. To put tables into 4NF, the initial table must be split into tables such that the multiple values of any multivalued attribute are moved into the new tables. These are then accessed by 1:N relationships between the original table and the tables holding the multiple values.

A little later, another kind of anomaly involving tables that can be split apart but not correctly joined back together was identified, and **fifth normal form (5NF)** was defined to eliminate that type of anomaly.

You can see how the knowledge evolved; none of these normal forms were perfect—each one eliminated certain anomalies, and none asserted that it was vulnerable to no anomaly at all. At this stage, in 1981, R. Fagin took a different approach and asked why, rather than just chipping away at anomalies, we don't look for conditions that would have to exist in order for a relation to have no anomalies at all. He did just this and in the process defined **domain/key normal form (DK/NF)**. Fagin proved that a relation in DK/NF can have no anomalies, and he further proved that a relation that has no anomalies is also in DK/NF.

For some reason, DK/NF never caught the fancy of the general database population, but it should have. As you can tell, no one should brag that their relations are in 3NF; instead, we all should brag that our relations are in DK/NF. But for some reason (perhaps because there is fashion in database theory, just as there is fashion in clothes), it just isn't done.

You're probably wondering what the conditions of DK/NF are. Without getting into the details, DK/NF requires that all the constraints on data values be logical implications of the definition of domains and keys. To the level of detail of this text, and to the level of detail experienced by 99 percent of all database practitioners, this can be restated as follows: Every determinant of a functional dependency must be a candidate key. This is exactly where we started, and what we've defined as BCNF.

You can broaden this statement a bit to include multivalued dependencies and say that every determinant of a functional or multivalued dependency must be a candidate key. The trouble with this statement is that as soon as one constrains a multivalued dependency in this way, it is transformed into a functional dependency. Our original statement is fine. It is like saying that good health comes to overweight people who lose weight until they are of an appropriate weight. As soon as they lose their excess weight, they are no longer overweight. Hence, good health comes to people who have appropriate weight.

So, as Paul Harvey says, now you know the rest of the story. Just ensure that every determinant of a functional dependency is a candidate key (BCNF), and you can claim that your relations are fully normalized. You do not want to say they are in DK/NF until you learn more about it though because someone might ask you what that means. However, for most practical purposes, your relations are in DK/NF as well.

For more information on normal forms, see David Kroenke, *Database Processing: Fundamentals, Design, and Implementation* 9th Edition (Upper Saddle River, NJ: Prentice Hall, 2006) pages 125–137; and David Kroenke, *Database Processing: Fundamentals, Design, and Implementation* 10th Edition (Upper Saddle River, NJ: Prentice Hall, 2006) pages 81–94.

## ▶ REPRESENTING RELATIONSHIPS

So far, you have learned how to create a relational design for the entities in an E-R model. However, to convert a data model to a relational design, we also must represent the relationships.

The techniques used to represent E-R relationships depend on the maximum cardinality of the relationships. As you saw in the last chapter, three relationship possibilities exist: one-to-one (1:1), one-to-many (1:N), and many-to-many (M:N). A fourth possibility, many-to-one (N:1), is represented in the same way as 1:N so we need not consider it as a separate case. In general, we create relationships by placing foreign keys in tables. The following sections will consider various types of relationships.

### Relationships Among Strong Entities

The easiest relationships to work with are relationships among strong entities. We will start with these, and then consider other types of relationships.

**Representing 1:1 Strong Entity Relationships** The simplest form of binary relationship is a 1:1 relationship, in which an entity of one type is related to at most one entity of another type. In Figure 5-10(a), the same 1:1 relationship that was used in Figure 4-5(a) between EMPLOYEE and LOCKER is shown in IE Crow's Foot notation. According to this diagram, an employee is assigned at most one locker, and a locker is assigned to at most one employee.

Representing a 1:1 relationship with the relational model is straightforward. First, each entity is represented with a table as just described, and then the key of one of the tables is placed in the other as a foreign key. In Figure 5-10(b), the key of LOCKER is stored in EMPLOYEE as a foreign key, and we create the referential integrity constraint

LockerNumber in EMPLOYEE must exist in LockerNumber in LOCKER

**FIGURE 5-10**

1:1 Strong Entity
Relationships

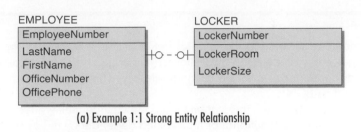

(a) Example 1:1 Strong Entity Relationship

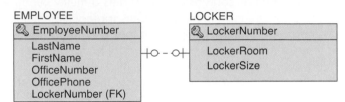

(b) Placing the Primary Key of LOCKER into EMPLOYEE

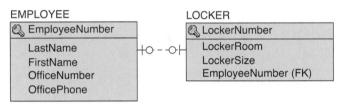

(c) Placing the Primary Key of EMPLOYEE into LOCKER

In Figure 5-10(c), the key of EMPLOYEE is stored in LOCKER as a foreign key, and we create the referential integrity constraint

EmployeeNumber in LOCKER must exist in EmployeeNumber in EMPLOYEE

In general, for a 1:1 relationship, the key of either table can be placed as a foreign key in the other table. To verify that this is so, consider both cases in Figure 5-10. Suppose that for the design in Figure 5-10(b), we have an employee and want the locker assigned to that employee. To get the employee data, we use EmployeeNumber to obtain the employee's row in EMPLOYEE. From this row, we obtain the LockerNumber of the locker assigned to that employee. We then use this number to look up the locker data in LOCKER.

Now consider the other direction. Assume that we have a locker and want to know which employee is assigned to that locker. Using the design in Figure 5-10(b), we access the EMPLOYEE table and look up the row that has the given LockerNumber. The data of the employee who has been assigned that locker appears in that row.

We take similar actions to travel in either direction for the alternative design in which the foreign key of EmployeeNumber is placed in LOCKER as shown in Figure 5-10(c). Using this design, to go from EMPLOYEE to LOCKER, we go directly to the LOCKER table and look up the row in LOCKER that has the given employee's number as its value of EmployeeNumber. To travel from LOCKER to EMPLOYEE, we look up the row in LOCKER having a given LockerNumber. From this row, we extract the EmployeeNumber and use it to access the employee data in EMPLOYEE.

In this situation, we are using the term *look up* to mean "to find a row given a value of one of its columns." Another way to view this is in terms of joins. For the relations in Figure 5-10(b), we can form the following join.

SELECT          *

FROM            EMPLOYEE, LOCKER

WHERE           EMPLOYEE.LockerNumber = LOCKER.LockerNumber;

Because the relationship is 1:1, the result of this join will have a single row for a given combination of employee and locker. The row will have all columns from both tables.

For the relations in Figure 5-10(c), we can join the two tables on EmployeeNumber as follows.

SELECT          *

FROM            EMPLOYEE, LOCKER

WHERE           EMPLOYEE.EmployeeNumber = LOCKER.EmployeeNumber;

Again, one row will be found for each combination of employee and locker. In both of these joins, neither unassigned employees nor unassigned lockers will appear.

Although the two designs in Figures 5-10(b) and 5-10(c) are equivalent in concept, they may differ in performance. For instance, if a query in one direction is more common than a query in the other, we might prefer one design to the other. Also, depending on underlying structures, if an index for EmployeeNumber is in both tables but no index on LockerNumber is in either table, then the first design is better. In addition, considering the join operation, if one table is much larger than the other, then one of these joins might be faster to perform than the other.

Another example of a 1:1 strong entity relationship is the relationship between the CUSTOMER and CONTACT tables shown in Figure 5-6. For each CUSTOMER, there is one and only one CONTACT, and based on the normalization we did, we have used the primary key of CONTACT as the foreign key in CUSTOMER. The resulting relationship is shown in Figure 5-11.

**Representing 1:N Strong Entity Relationships**   The second type of binary relationship, known as 1:N, is a relationship in which an entity of one type can be related to many entities of another type. In Figure 5-12(a), the 1:N relationship that was used in Figure 4-5(b) between ITEM and QUOTATION is shown in IE Crow's Foot notation. According to this diagram, we have received from zero to several quotations for each item in the database.

The terms **parent** and **child** are sometimes applied to relations in 1:N relationships. The parent relation is on the *one* side of the relationship, and the child relation is on the *many* side. In Figure 5-12(a), ITEM is the parent entity, and QUOTATION is the child entity.

Representing 1:N relationships is simple and straightforward. First, each entity is represented by a table as described, and then the key of the table representing the *parent entity* is placed in the table representing the *child entity* as a foreign key. Thus, to represent the relationship in Figure 5-12(a), we place the primary key of ITEM, which is ItemNumber, into the QUOTATION table as shown in Figure 5-12(b), and we create the referential integrity constraint.

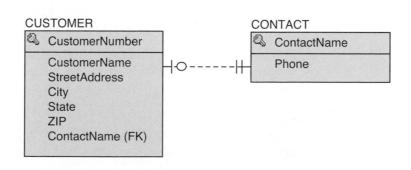

**FIGURE 5-11**

**1:1 Strong Entity Relationship Between CUSTOMER and CONTACT**

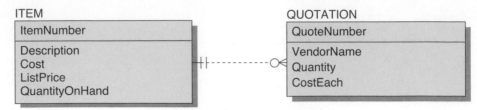

(a) Example 1:N Strong Entity Relationship

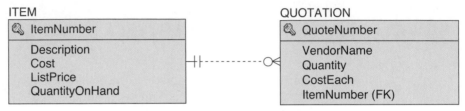

(b) Placing the Primary Key of ITEM into QUOTATION

ItemNumber in QUOTATION must exist in ItemNumber in ITEM

Notice that with ItemNumber stored as a foreign key in QUOTATION, we can process the relationship in both directions. Given a QuoteNumber, we can look up the appropriate row in QUOTATION and get the ItemNumber of the item from the row data. To obtain the rest of the ITEM data, we use the ItemNumber obtained from QUOTATION to look up the appropriate row in ITEM. To determine all the quotes associated with a particular item, we look up all rows in QUOTATION that have the item's ItemNumber as a value for ItemNumber. Quotation data are then taken from those rows.

In terms of joins, we can obtain the item and quote data in one table with the following.

SELECT          *

FROM            ITEM, QUOTATION

WHERE           ITEM.ItemNumber = QUOTATION.ItemNumber;

Contrast this 1:N relationship design strategy with that for 1:1 relationships. In both cases, we store the key of one relation as a foreign key in the second relation. In a 1:1 relationship, we can place the key of either relation in the other. In a 1:N relationship, however, the key of the parent relation *must* be placed in the child relation.

To understand this better, notice what would happen if we tried to put the key of the child into the parent relation (placing QuoteNumber in ITEM). Because attributes in a relation can have only a single value, each ITEM record has room for only one QuoteNumber. Consequently, such a structure cannot be used to represent the many sides of the 1:N relationship. Hence, to represent a 1:N relationship, we must always place the key of the parent relation in the child relation.

**Representing N:M Strong Entity Relationships**   The third and final type of binary relationship is N:M, in which an entity of one type corresponds to many entities of the second type, and an entity of the second type corresponds to many entities of the first type.

Figure 5-13(a) presents an E-R diagram of the N:M relationship between students and classes. A STUDENT entity can correspond to many CLASS entities, and a CLASS

**FIGURE 5-13**

**N:M Strong Entity
Relationships**

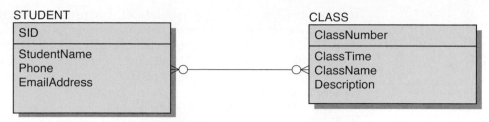

(a) N:M Strong Entity Relationship Example

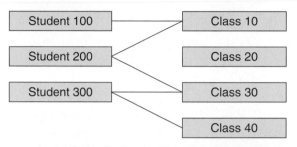

(b) Sample Data for the STUDENT to CLASS Relationship

entity can correspond to many STUDENT entities. Notice that both participants in the relationship are optional: A student does not need to be enrolled in a class, and a class does not need to have any students. Figure 5-13(b) gives sample data.

N:M relationships cannot be represented directly by relations in the same way that 1:1 and 1:N relationships are represented. To understand why this is so, try using the same strategy as for 1:1 and 1:N relationships—placing the key of one relation as a foreign key into the other relation. First, define a relation for each of the entities; call them STUDENT and CLASS. Then, try to put the primary key of STUDENT, which is SID, into CLASS. Because multiple values are not allowed in the cells of a relation, we have room for only one StudentNumber so we have no place to record the StudentNumber of the second and subsequent students.

A similar problem will occur if we try to put the primary key of CLASS, which is ClassNumber, into STUDENT. We can readily store the identifier of the first class in which a student is enrolled, but we have no place to store the identifier of additional classes.

Figure 5-14 shows another (but incorrect) strategy. In this case, we have stored a row in the CLASS relation for each STUDENT enrolled in one class so we have two

**FIGURE 5-14**

**Incorrect
Representation of an
N:M Relationship**

| SID | Other STUDENT Data |
|-----|--------------------|
| 100 | . . . |
| 200 | . . . |
| 300 | . . . |

STUDENT

| ClassNumber | ClassTime | Other CLASS Data | SID |
|-------------|-----------|------------------|-----|
| 10 | 10:00 MWF | . . . | 100 |
| 10 | 10:00 MWF | . . . | 200 |
| 30 | 3:00 TH | . . . | 200 |
| 30 | 3:00 TH | . . . | 300 |
| 40 | 8:00 MWF | . . . | 300 |

CLASS

records for Class 10 and two for Class 30. The problem with this scheme is that we duplicate the class data and create modification anomalies. Many rows will need to be changed if, for example, the schedule for Class 10 is modified. Also, consider the insertion and deletion anomalies: How can we schedule a new class until a student has enrolled? In addition, what will happen if Student 300 drops out of Class 40? This strategy is unworkable.

The solution to this problem is to create a third table called an **intersection table** that represents the relationship itself. We will define a table named STUDENT_CLASS as shown in Figure 5-15(a) and below:

STUDENT (<u>SID</u>, StudentName, Phone, EmailAddress)

CLASS (<u>ClassNumber</u>, ClassTime, ClassName, Description)

STUDENT_CLASS (<u>SID</u>, <u>*ClassNumber*</u>)

where

SID in STUDENT_CLASS must exist in SID in STUDENT

ClassNumber in STUDENT_CLASS must exist in ClassNumber in CLASS

Some instances of this relation are shown in Figure 5-15(b). Such relations are called intersection tables because each row documents the intersection of a particular student with a particular class. Notice in Figure 5-15(b) that the intersection relation has one row for each line between STUDENT and CLASS as in Figure 5-13(b).

In Figure 5-15(a), notice that the relationship from STUDENT to STUDENT_CLASS is 1:N, and the relationship from CLASS to STUDENT_CLASS is also 1:N.

---

**FIGURE 5-15**

**Representing an N:M Strong Entity Relationship**

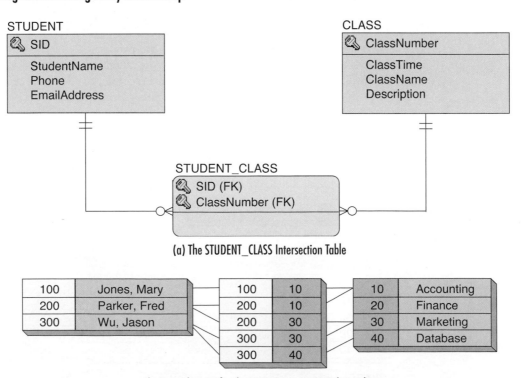

(a) The STUDENT_CLASS Intersection Table

(b) Example Data for the STUDENT to CLASS Relationship

In essence, we have decomposed the M:N relationship into two 1:N relationships. The key of STUDENT_CLASS is (SID, ClassNumber), which is the combination of the primary keys of both of its parents. The key for an intersection table is *always* the combination of parent keys. Note that the parent relations are *both* required because a parent now must exist for each key value in the intersection relation.

Finally, notice that STUDENT_CLASS is an ID-dependent weak entity, which is ID-dependent on both STUDENT and CLASS. In order to create a database design for an N:M *strong entity* relationship, we have had to introduce an ID-dependent *weak entity*! We will have more to say about relationships with weak entities in the next section.

We can obtain data about students and classes using the following SQL statement.

```
SELECT      *
FROM        STUDENT, CLASS, STUDENT_CLASS
WHERE       STUDENT.SID = STUDENT_CLASS.SID
AND         STUDENT_CLASS.ClassNumber = CLASS.ClassNumber;
```

The result of this SQL statement is a table with all columns for a student and the classes the student takes. The student data will be repeated in the table for as many classes as the student takes, and the class data will be repeated in the relation for as many students as are taking the class.

## Relationships Using Weak Entities

Since weak entities exist, they are bound to end up as tables in relationships! We've just seen one place where this occurs—an ID-dependent entity becomes the table that represents an N:M relationship. Note that the intersection table that is formed in this case has only the columns that make up its composite primary key. In the STUDENT_CLASS table, this key was (SID, ClassNumber).

Another ID-dependent weak entity occurs when we take an intersection table and add entity attributes (table columns) beyond those in the composite primary key. For example, Figure 5-16 shows the table and relationship structure of Figure 5-15(a) but with one new attribute (column)—Grade—added to STUDENT CLASS.

---

**FIGURE 5-16**

**The Association Relationship**

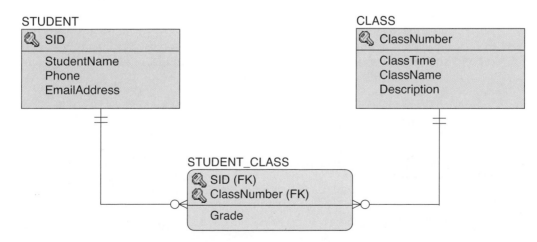

---

**FIGURE 5-17**

---

**Example Mixed Entity Relationship**

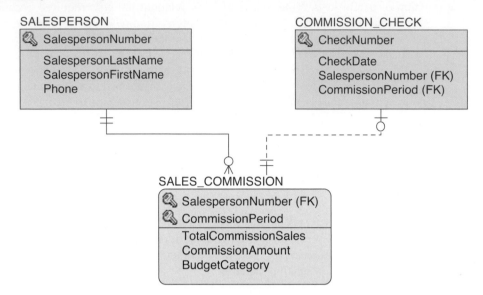

STUDENT_CLASS as an entity is now called an **associative entity**, and this entity has been converted into the new STUDENT_CLASS table. Note that while it stills connects STUDENT and CLASS (and is still ID-dependent on both of these tables), it now has data that is uniquely its own. This pattern is called an **association relationship**.

Finally, let's take another look at the tables shown in Figure 5-8, where we normalized SALES_COMMISSION into three related tables. Figure 5-17 shows these tables with their correct relationships.

Note the 1:N identifying relationship between SALESPERSON and the ID-dependent table SALES_COMMISSION, which correctly uses the primary key of SALESPERSON as part of the composite primary key of SALES_COMMISSION. Also note the 1:1 relationship between SALES_COMMISSION and COMMISSION_CHECK. Since SALES_COMMISSION is a strong entity and has its own unique primary key, this is a nonidentifying relationship. This set of tables and relationships illustrates a **mixed entity pattern**.[2]

## Relationships with Subtypes

Since the identifier of a subtype entity is the identifier of the associated supertype entity, creating relationships between these tables is simple. The identifier of the subtype becomes the primary key of the subtype *and* the foreign key linking the subtype to the supertype. Figure 5-18(a) shows the E-R model in Figure 4-13(a), while Figure 5-18(b) shows the equivalent database design.

## Representing Recursive Relationships

A recursive relationship is a relationship among entities of the same class. Recursive relationships are not fundamentally different from other relationships and can be repre-

---

[2]For more information on mixed entity patterns, see David Kroenke, *Database Processing: Fundamentals, Design, and Implementation* 10th Edition (Upper Saddle River, NJ: Prentice Hall, 2006) pages 147–150, 185–188.

**FIGURE 5-18**

**Representing Subtypes**

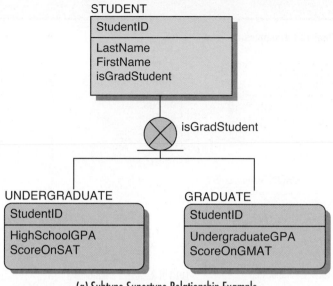

(a) Subtype-Supertype Relationship Example

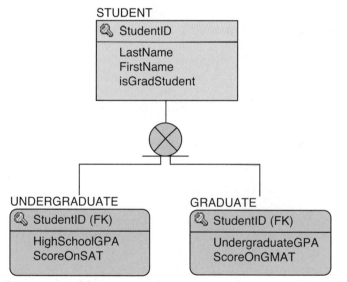

(b) The Primary Key of the Supertype as the Primary Key and Foreign Key of the Subtype

sented using the same techniques. As with nonrecursive relationships, three types of recursive relationships are possible: 1:1, 1:N, and N:M. Figure 5-19 shows an example of each of these three types.

Let's start by considering the 1:1 recursive SPONSORED_BY relationship in Figure 5-19(a). As with a regular 1:1 relationship, one person can sponsor another person, and each person is sponsored by no more than one person. Figure 5-20(a) shows sample data for this relationship.

To represent 1:1 recursive relationships, we take an approach nearly identical to that for regular 1:1 relationships; that is, we can place the key of the person being sponsored in the row of the sponsor, or we can place the key of the sponsor in the row of the person

**FIGURE 5-19**

**Recursive Relationships Examples**

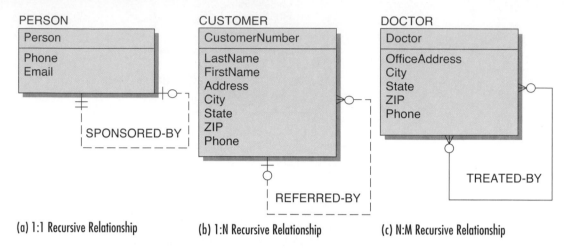

(a) 1:1 Recursive Relationship     (b) 1:N Recursive Relationship     (c) N:M Recursive Relationship

being sponsored. Figure 5-20(b) shows the first alternative, and Figure 5-20(c) shows the second. Both work.

This technique is identical to that for nonrecursive 1:1 relationships, except that the child and parent rows reside in the same table. You can think of the process as follows: Pretend that the relationship is between two different tables. Determine where the key goes, and then combine the two tables into a single one.

We also can use SQL joins to process recursive relationships; to do so, however, we need to introduce additional SQL syntax. In the FROM clause, it is possible to assign a synonym for a table name. For example, the expression FROM CUSTOMER A assigns the synonym A to the table CUSTOMER. Using this syntax, we can create a join on a recursive relationship for the design in Figure 5-20(b) as follows.

SELECT          *

FROM            PERSON1 A, PERSON1 B

WHERE           A.Person = B.PersonSponsored;

The result will be a table with one row for each person. It will have all the columns of the person and also of the person they sponsor.

Similarly, to create a join of the recursive relationship shown in Figure 5-20(c), we would use:

SELECT          *

FROM            PERSON2 A, PERSON2 B

WHERE           A.Person = B.PersonSponsoredBy;

The result will be a table with a row for each person. It will have all the columns of the person and also of the sponsoring person.

Now consider the 1:N recursive relationship REFERRED-BY in Figure 5-19(b). This is a 1:N relationship, as shown in the sample data in Figure 5-21(a). When these data are placed in a table, one row represents the referrer, and the other rows represent those who have been referred. The referrer row takes the role of the parent, and the

**FIGURE 5-20**

1:1 Recursive
Relationship Example

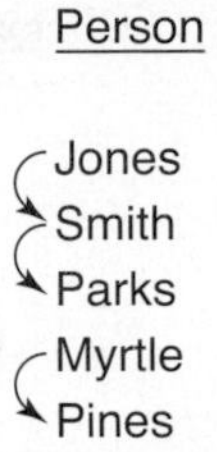

Person

Jones
Smith
Parks
Myrtle
Pines

(a) Sample Data for a 1:1 Recursive Relationship

PERSON1 Relation

| Person | PersonSponsored |
|--------|-----------------|
| Jones | Smith |
| Smith | Parks |
| Parks | null |
| Myrtle | Pines |
| Pines | null |

Referential integrity constraint:
PersonSponsored in PERSON1
must exist in Person in PERSON1

(b) First Alternative for Representing a 1:1 Recursive Relationship

PERSON2 Relation

| Person | PersonSponsoredBy |
|--------|-------------------|
| Jones | null |
| Smith | Jones |
| Parks | Smith |
| Myrtle | null |
| Pines | Myrtle |

Referential integrity constraint:
PersonSponsoredBy PERSON2
must exist in Person in PERSON2

(c) Second Alternative for Representing a 1:1 Recursive Relationship

referred rows take the role of the child. As with all 1:N relationships, we place the key of the parent in the child. In Figure 5-21(b), we place the CustomerNumber of the referrer in all the rows for people who have been referred.

We can join the 1:N recursive relationship with:

SELECT          *

FROM          CUSTOMER A, CUSTOMER B

WHERE          A.CustomerNumber = B.ReferredBy;

The result will be a row for each customer that is joined to the data for the customer who referred the person.

Finally, let's consider N:M recursive relationships. The TREATED-BY relationship in Figure 5-19(c) represents a situation in which doctors give treatments to each other. Sample data are shown in Figure 5-22(a).

As with other N:M relationships, we must create an intersection table that shows pairs of related rows. The name of the doctor in the first column is the one who provided the treatment, and the name of the doctor in the second column is the one who received the treatment. This structure is shown in Figure 5-22(b). We can join the N:M relationship with:

**FIGURE 5-21**

**1:N Recursive
Relationship Example**

| Customer Number | Referred These Customers |
|---|---|
| 100 | 200, 400 |
| 300 | 500 |
| 400 | 600, 700 |

(a) Sample Data for a 1:N Recursive Relationship

CUSTOMER Relation

| CustomerNumber | CustomerData | ReferredBy |
|---|---|---|
| 100 | . . . | null |
| 200 | . . . | 100 |
| 300 | . . . | null |
| 400 | . . . | 100 |
| 500 | . . . | 300 |
| 600 | . . . | 400 |
| 700 | . . . | 400 |

Referential integrity constraint:
  ReferredBy in CUSTOMER must exist in
  CustomerNumber in CUSTOMER

(b) Representing a 1:N Recursive Relationship Within a Table

**FIGURE 5-22**

**N:M Recursive
Relationship Example**

| Provider | Receiver |
|---|---|
| Jones | Smith |
| Parks | |
| Smith | Abernathy |
| Abernathy | Jones |
| Franklin | Franklin |

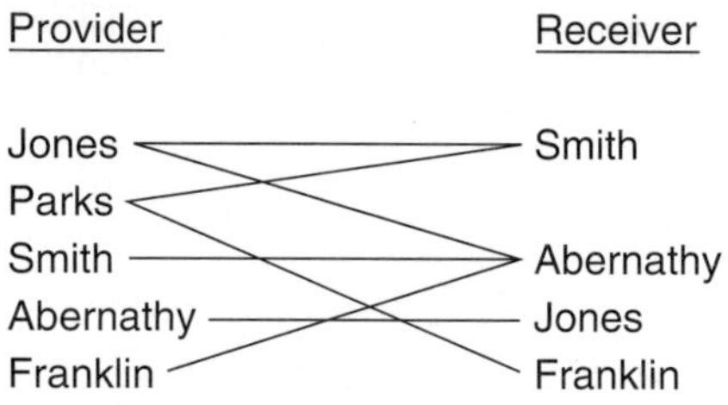

(a) Sample Data for an N:M Recursive Relationship

DOCTOR Relation

| Name | Other Attributes |
|---|---|
| Jones | . . . |
| Parks | . . . |
| Smith | . . . |
| Abernathy | . . . |
| O'Leary | . . . |
| Franklin | . . . |

TREATMENT-INTERSECTION Relation

| Physician | Patient |
|---|---|
| Jones | Smith |
| Parks | Smith |
| Smith | Abernathy |
| Abernathy | Jones |
| Parks | Franklin |
| Franklin | Abernathy |
| Jones | Abernathy |

Referential integrity constraints:
  Physician in TREATMENT-INTERSECTION
  must exist in Name in DOCTOR

  Patient in TREATMENT-INTERSECTION
  must exist in Name in DOCTOR

(b) Representing an N:M Recursive Relationship Using Tables

| SELECT | * |
|---|---|
| FROM | DOCTOR A, TREATMENT-INTERSECTION, DOCTOR B |
| WHERE | A.Name = TREATMENT-INTERSECTION.Physician |
| AND | TREATMENT-INTERSECTION.Patient = B.Name; |

The result of this will be a table having rows of doctor (as treatment provider) joined to doctor (as patient). The doctor data will be repeated once for every patient treated and once for every time the doctor was treated.

Recursive relationships are thus represented in the same way as are other relationships; however, the rows of the tables can take two different roles. Some are parent rows, and others are child rows. If a key is supposed to be a parent key and the row has no parent, its value will be NULL. If a key is supposed to be a child key and the row has no child, its value will be NULL.

# ▶ DATABASE DESIGN AT HEATHER SWEENEY DESIGNS

Figure 5-23 shows the final E-R diagram for Heather Sweeney Designs, the database example discussed in Chapter 4. To transform this E-R diagram into a relational design, we follow the process described in the last sections. First, represent each entity with a relation of its own, as shown in the following database schema.

---

**FIGURE 5-23**

---

**Final Data Model for Heather Sweeney Designs**

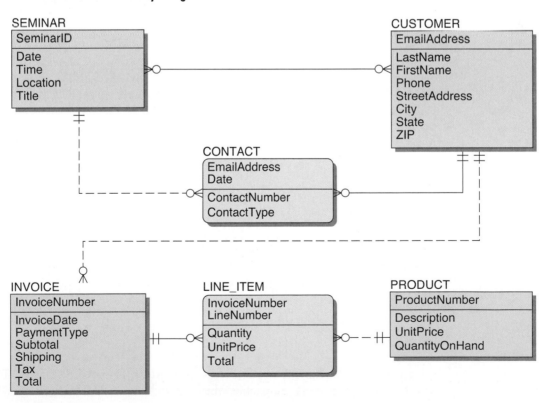

SEMINAR (<u>SeminarID</u>, Date, Time, Location, Title)

CUSTOMER (<u>EmailAddress</u>, Name, Phone, Street, City, State, Zip)

CONTACT (*<u>EmailAddress</u>*, <u>Date</u>, ContactNumber, ContactType)

PRODUCT (<u>ProductNumber</u>, Description, UnitPrice, QuantityOnHand)

INVOICE (<u>InvoiceNumber</u>, Date, PaymentType, SubTotal, Tax, Total)

LINE_ITEM (*<u>InvoiceNumber</u>*, <u>LineNumber</u>, Quantity, UnitPrice, Total)

Next, apply the normalization process to each of these tables. Do any of them have a functional dependency that does not involve the primary key? From what we know so far, the only such functional dependency is:

Zip→(City, State)

However, for the reasons explained before, we will choose not to place Zip into its own table.

One possible functional dependency concerns locations, dates, times, or titles. If, for example, Heather offers seminars only at certain times in some locations, or if she only gives certain seminar titles in some locations, then a functional dependency would exist with Location as its determinant. It would be important for the design team to check this out, but for now assume that no such dependency exists.

## Weak Entities

There are two weak entities in this model, and they both are ID-dependent. CONTACT is a weak entity, and its identifier depends in part on the identifier of CUSTOMER. Thus, we have placed the key of CUSTOMER, which is EmailAddress, into CONTACT. Similarly, LINE_ITEM is a weak entity, and its identifier depends on the identifier of INVOICE. Consequently, we have placed the key of INVOICE in LINE_ITEM

Note that CONTACT.EmailAddress and LINE_ITEM.InvoiceNumber are underlined and italicized because they are part of a primary key and also a foreign key.

## Relationships

Now, considering the relationships in this diagram, 1:N relationships exist between SEMINAR and CONTACT, between CUSTOMER and INVOICE, and between PRODUCT and LINE_ITEM. For each of these, we place the key of the parent in the child as a foreign key. Thus, we will place the key of SEMINAR in CONTACT, the key of CUSTOMER in INVOICE, and the key of PRODUCT in LINE_ITEM. The relations are now as follows.

SEMINAR (<u>SeminarID</u>, Date, Time, Location, Title)

CUSTOMER (<u>EmailAddress</u>, Name, Phone, Street, City, State, Zip)

CONTACT (*<u>EmailAddress</u>*, <u>Date</u>, ContactNumber, ContactType, *SeminarID*)

PRODUCT (<u>ProductNumber</u>, Description, UnitPrice, QuantityOnHand)

INVOICE (<u>InvoiceNumber</u>, Date, PaymentType, SubTotal, Tax, Total, *EmailAddress*)

LINE_ITEM (*<u>InvoiceNumber</u>*, <u>LineNumber</u>, Quantity, UnitPrice, Total, *ProductNumber*)

Finally, one N:M relationship exists between SEMINAR and CUSTOMER. To represent it, we create an intersection table, which we will name SEMINAR_CUSTOMER.

As with all intersection tables, its columns are the keys of the two tables involved in the N:M relationship. The final set of tables is:

SEMINAR (<u>SeminarID</u>, Date, Time, Location, Title)

CUSTOMER (<u>EmailAddress</u>, Name, Phone, Street, City, State, Zip)

SEMINAR_CUSTOMER (*<u>SeminarID</u>*, *<u>EmailAddress</u>*)

CONTACT (*<u>EmailAddress</u>*, <u>Date</u>, ContactNumber, ContactType, *SeminarID*)

PRODUCT (<u>ProductNumber</u>, Description, UnitPrice, QuantityOnHand)

INVOICE (<u>InvoiceNumber</u>, Date, PaymentType, SubTotal, Tax, Total, *EmailAddress*)

LINE_ITEM (*<u>InvoiceNumber</u>*, <u>LineNumber</u>, Quantity, UnitPrice, Total, *ProductNumber*)

where referential integrity constraints will be created as discussed next.

Now, to express the minimum cardinalities of children back to their parents, we need to decide whether or not foreign keys are required. In Figure 5-23, we see that an INVOICE is required to have a CUSTOMER, and that LINE_ITEM is required to have a PRODUCT. Thus, we will make INVOICE.EmailAddress and LINE_ITEM. ProductNumber required. CONTACT.SeminarID will not be required because a contact is not required to refer to a seminar. The final design is shown in the data structure diagram in Figure 5-24.

---

**FIGURE 5-24**

---

**Database Design for Heather Sweeney Designs**

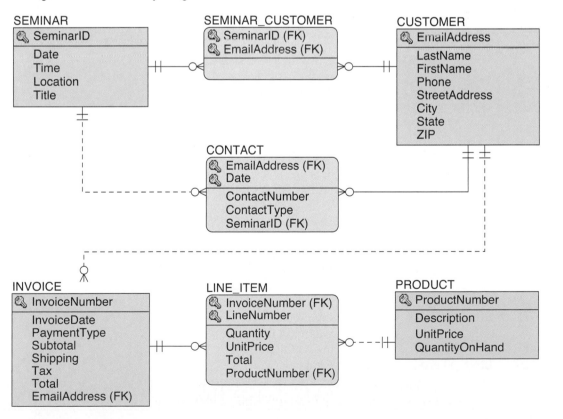

## Enforcing Referential Integrity

Figure 5-25 summarizes the relationship enforcement for Heather Sweeney Designs. SeminarID is a surrogate key so no cascading update behavior will be necessary for any of the relationships that it carries. Similarly, InvoiceNumber in INVOICE is an unchanging value so its relationships do not need cascading updates either. However, updates of EmailAddress and ProductNumber do need to cascade through their relationships.

With regard to cascading deletions, rows in the intersection table require a SEMINAR and a CUSTOMER parent. Therefore, when a user attempts to cancel a seminar or to remove a customer record, the deletion must either cascade or be prohibited. The development team must discuss this issue with Heather and her employees and determine whether they want users to be able to remove seminars that have customers enrolled or to remove customers that have enrolled in a seminar. As shown in Figure 5-25, the team decided that removing such seminar or customer records would be permitted; hence, both of these relationships have cascading deletions.

Other decisions reached by the design team are shown in this figure. The deletion of a seminar will not cascade to contact so any seminar that has a contact record cannot be deleted. However, the deletion of a CUSTOMER row will trigger a cascading deletion of CONTACT. These decisions make sense. The cancellation of a seminar should not cause

---

### FIGURE 5-25

**Referential Integrity Constraint Enforcement for Heather Sweeney Designs**

| Relationship | | Referential Integrity Constraint | Cascading Behavior | |
| --- | --- | --- | --- | --- |
| **PARENT** | **CHILD** | | **ON UPDATE** | **ON DELETE** |
| SEMINAR | SEMINAR_CUSTOMER | SeminarID in SEMINAR_CUSTOMER must exist in SeminarID in SEMINAR | No | Yes |
| CUSTOMER | SEMINAR_CUSTOMER | EmailAddress in SEMINAR_CUSTOMER must exist in EmailAddress in CUSTOMER | Yes | Yes |
| SEMINAR | CONTACT | SeminarID in CONTACT must exist in SeminarID in SEMINAR | No | No |
| CUSTOMER | CONTACT | EmailAddress in CONTACT must exist in EmailAddress in CUSTOMER | Yes | Yes |
| CUSTOMER | INVOICE | EmailAddress in INVOICE must exist in EmailAddress in CUSTOMER | Yes | No |
| INVOICE | LINE_ITEM | InvoiceNumber in LINE_ITEM must exist in InvoiceNumber in INVOICE | No | Yes |
| PRODUCT | LINE_ITEM | ProductNumber in LINE_ITEM must exist in ProductNumber in PRODUCT | Yes | No |

the deletion of the record of a customer contact. In fact, because a contact has occurred with a customer about a seminar, it is important for Heather to keep a record of what the seminar was. On the other hand, if a customer record is deleted, all the contacts for the customer should be deleted, as well.

As shown in Figure 5-25, an attempt to delete a CUSTOMER with one or more ORDERs will fail because the relationship is required. The deletion will not cascade, but the deletion of an INVOICE will cause the deletion of related LINE_ITEMs. Finally, an attempt to delete a PRODUCT that is related to one or more LINE_ITEMs will fail; cascading the deletion here would cause LINE_ITEMs to disappear out of ORDERs, a situation that cannot be allowed.

At this point, the design of the database for Heather Sweeney is complete enough to create tables, columns, relationships, and referential integrity constraints using a DBMS. Before going on, the team would need to document any additional business rules to be enforced by application programs or other DBMS techniques. After this, the database can be created using the SQL statements we discussed in Chapter 3.

## THE ACCESS WORKBENCH

### Section 5

### Relationships in Microsoft Access

At this point, we have created and populated the CONTACT, CUSTOMER, and SALESPERSON tables in the Wallingford Motors CRM database. We have also learned how to create forms, reports, and queries in the preceding sections, and how to create and use view equivalent queries in Appendix C.

However, all the tables we've used so far have had 1:N relationships, which raises the question: How are 1:1 and N:M relationships managed in Access? In this section, we will cover the following objectives:

- Understand 1:1 relationships in Access
- Understand N:M relationships in Access

### N:M Relationships in Access

We'll start by discussing N:M relationships. This is actually a nonissue, because pure N:M relationships occur in data modeling. Remember that when a data model is transformed into a database design, an N:M relationship is broken down into two 1:N relationships. Each 1:N relationship is between a table resulting from one of the original entities in the N:M relationship and a new intersection table. If this doesn't make sense to you, then review the chapter section "Representing N:M Strong Entity Relationships" and see Figures 5-13 and 5-15 for an illustration of how N:M relationships are converted to two 1:N relationships.

Since databases are built in DBMSs, such as Access, from the database design, Access only deals with the resulting 1:N relationships—as far as Access is concerned, there are no N:M relationships!

### 1:1 Relationships in Access

1:1 relationships, however, are another matter—they definitely exist in Access. Since our current WMCRM database doesn't contain a 1:1, let's add one to it. We'll let each

*(Continued)*

**FIGURE AW-5-1**

**The WMCRM Database Design with VEHICLE**

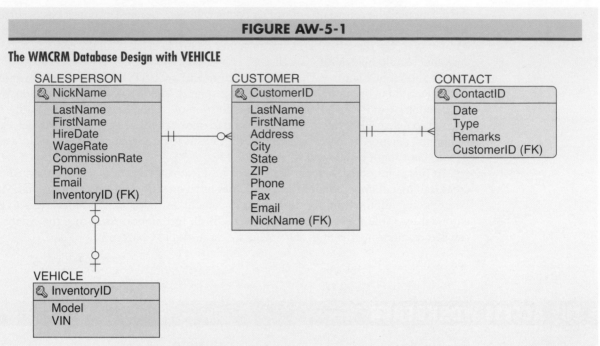

SALESPERSON use one and only one car from the Wallingford Motors inventory as a demo vehicle. Our database design with this addition is shown in Figure AW-5-1.

Note that both SALESPERSON and VEHICLE are optional in this relationship. First, a VEHICLE does not have to be assigned to a SALESPERSON, which makes sense since there will be a lot of cars in inventory and only a few SALESPERSONs. Second, a SALESPERSON does not have to take a demo car and may choose not to (yeah, right!). Also note that we have chosen to put the foreign key in SALESPER-SON. This is a case where there is an advantage to putting the foreign key in one table or the other because if we'd put it in VEHICLE, the foreign key column (which would have been NickName) would have been NULL for every car except the few used as demo vehicles. Finally, this is a table we're using just to illustrate a 1:1 relationship—a functional VEHICLE table would have a lot more columns.

The column characteristics for the VEHICLE table are shown in Figure AW-5-2, and the data for the table is shown in Figure AW-5-3.

We already know how to create a table and populate it with data, so we'll go ahead and add the VEHICLE table and its data to the WMCRM.mdb database. Now, we need to modify SALESPERSON by adding the InventoryID column and populating it with data. The column characteristics for the new InventoryID column in the SALEPERSON table are shown in Figure AW-5-4, and the data for the column is shown in Figure AW-5-5 (Tina and Big Bill are driving the HiLuxury model, while Billy opted for a SUHi).

There is nothing here that we don't know how to do—we altered the CUS-TOMER table in a similar way in Section 3's "The Access Workbench"—so we will go ahead and add the InventoryID column and its data to the SALESPERSON table. This is an easier table alteration to make than the one we made to CUSTOMER

**FIGURE AW-5-2**

**Database Column Characteristics for the VEHICLE Table**

| Column Name | Type | Key | Required | Remarks |
|---|---|---|---|---|
| Inventory ID | AutoNumber | Primary Key | Yes | Surrogate Key |
| Model | Text(25) | No | Yes | |
| VIN | Text(35) | No | Yes | |

**FIGURE AW-5-3**

**Wallingford Motors VEHICLE Data**

| InventoryID | Model | VIN |
|---|---|---|
| [AutoNumber] | HiStandard | G06HS123400001 |
| [AutoNumber] | HiStandard | G06HS123400002 |
| [AutoNumber] | HiStandard | G06HS123400003 |
| [AutoNumber] | HiLuxury | G06HL234500001 |
| [AutoNumber] | HiLuxury | G06HL234500002 |
| [AutoNumber] | HiLuxury | G06HL234500003 |
| [AutoNumber] | SUHi | G06HU345600001 |
| [AutoNumber] | SUHi | G06HU345600002 |
| [AutoNumber] | SUHi | G06HU345600003 |
| [AutoNumber] | HiElectra | G06HE456700001 |

because the InventoryID column in SALESPERSON is NOT NULL so we do not have to set it to NULL after entering the data.

Now, we're ready to establish the relationship between the two tables.

*Creating the Relationship Between SALESPERSON and VEHICLE*

1. In the Access main menu, click **Tools** and then click **Relationships. . .** in the Tools menu.
   - **NOTE:** WARNING! We are about to encounter another peculiarity of Access. The next steps lead to that situation, not the final outcome that we want. Remember that we want a 1:1 relationship and see if you can figure out what's happening as we go along.
2. Click the **Show Table** button in the toolbar.
3. In the Show Table dialog box, click **VEHICLE** to select it, and then click the **Add** button to add VEHICLE to the Relationships window.
4. In the Show Table dialog box, click the **Close** button to close the dialog box.
5. You can rearrange and resize the table objects in the Relationships window using standard Windows drag-and-drop techniques. Rearrange the SALESPERSON,

**FIGURE AW-5-4**

**Database Column Characteristics for the InventoryID Column**

| Column Name | Type | Key | Required | Remarks |
|---|---|---|---|---|
| InventoryID | Int | Foreign Key | No | |

**FIGURE AW-5-5**

**SALESPERSON InventoryID Data**

| NickName | LastName | FirstName | . . . | InventoryID |
|---|---|---|---|---|
| Tina | Smith | Tina | . . . | 4 |
| Big Bill | Jones | William | . . . | 5 |
| Billy | Jones | Bill | . . . | 7 |

*(Continued)*

## FIGURE AW-5-6

**The Relationships Window with the Current Relationship Diagram**

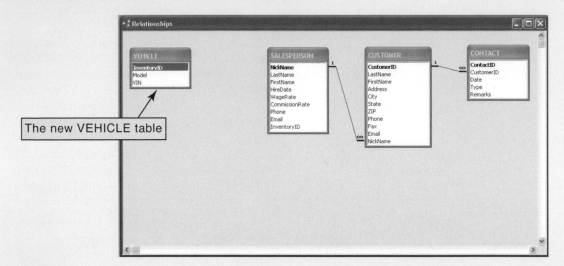

The new VEHICLE table

CUSTOMER, CONTACT, and VEHICLE table objects until they appear as shown in Figure AW-5-6.

* **NOTE:** Remember that we create a relationship between two tables in the Relationships window by dragging a *primary key* column and dropping it on top of the *corresponding foreign key* column.

6. Click and hold the **column name InventoryID** in the **VEHICLE** table object, and then drag it over the **column name InventoryID** in the **SALECUSTOMER** table. The Edit Relationships dialog box appears.
7. Click the **Enforce Referential Integrity** check box.
8. Click the **Create** button to create the relationship between VEHICLE and SALES-PERSON.
9. Right-click the **relationship line** between SALESPERSON and CUSTOMER, and then click **Edit Relationship** in the shortcut menu that appears. The **Edit Relationships dialog box** appears.
10. The relationship between the tables now appears in the Relationships window as shown in Figure AW-5-7.

## FIGURE AW-5-7

**The Completed VEHICLE to SALESPERSON Relationship**

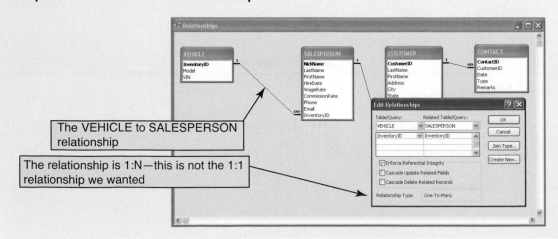

The VEHICLE to SALESPERSON relationship

The relationship is 1:N—this is not the 1:1 relationship we wanted

But now we have a serious problem—the relationship that was created is a 1:N relationship, not the 1:1 relationship that we wanted. Let's fix it—there *must* be a way to fix the relationship somewhere on the Edit Relationship dialog box! Unfortunately, there isn't—go ahead and try everything you can think of, it won't work. This is the peculiarity of Access that we mentioned.

So just what is the trick to creating a 1:1 relationship in Access? The trick is setting the **indexed** property of the foreign key column (InventoryID in SALESPERSON in this case) as *Indexed (no duplicates)* as shown in Figure AW-5-8. As long as the same value can occur more than once in the foreign key column, Access will create a 1:N relationship instead of the desired 1:1 relationship.

To create the 1:1 relationship, we will need to delete the existing relationship, modify the InventoryID property in SALESPERSON, and create a new relationship between the tables.

### Deleting the Incorrect Relationship Between SALESPERSON and VEHICLE

1. Click the **OK** button on the Edit Relationships dialog box.
2. Right-click on the **relationship line** between VEHICLE and SALESPERSON to display the shortcut menu, then click **Delete**.
3. A dialog box will be displayed with the message "Are you sure you want to permanently delete the selected relationship from your database?" Click the **Yes** button.
4. Click the **X** button in the upper right corner of the Relationships window to close the window.
5. A dialog box will be displayed with the message "Do you want to save the changes to the layout of 'Relationships'?" Click the **Yes** button.

### Setting the Indexed Property of the InventoryID Column in SALEPERSON

1. Open the **SALESPERSON table** in Design View.
2. Select the **InventoryID** field. The InventoryID field properties are displayed in the General tab.

## FIGURE AW-5-8

**Setting the Indexed Property Value in the SALESPERSON Table**

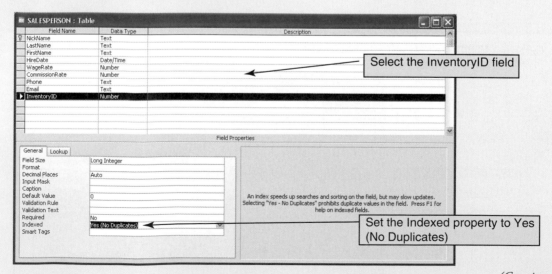

*(Continued)*

3. Click the **Indexed text field**. A drop-down list arrow appears on the right end of the text field. Click the drop-down list arrow to display the list, and select **Yes (No Duplicates)**. The result appears as shown in Figure AW-5-8.
4. Click the **Save** button to save the completed changes to the SALESPERSON table.
5. Close the SALESPERSON table.

*Creating the Correct 1:1 Relationship Between SALESPERSON and VEHICLE*

1. In the Access main menu, click **Tools** and then click **Relationships. . .** in the Tools menu.
2. Click and hold the **column name InventoryID** in the **VEHICLE** table object, and then drag it over the **column name InventoryID** in the **SALECUSTOMER** table. The Edit Relationships dialog box appears.
3. Click the **Enforce Referential Integrity** check box.
4. Click the **Create** button to create the relationship between VEHICLE and SALES-PERSON.
5. Right-click the **relationship line** between SALESPERSON and CUSTOMER, and then click **Edit Relationship** in the shortcut menu that appears. The **Edit Relationships dialog box** appears.
6. The relationship between the tables now appears in the Relationships window as shown in Figure AW-5-9.
7. Click the **Cancel** button on the Edit Relationships dialog box.
8. Click the **X** button in the upper right corner of the Relationships window to close the window.
9. If a dialog box is displayed with the message "Do you want to save the changes to the layout of 'Relationships'?" then click the **Yes** button.

We have successfully created the 1:1 relationship that we wanted—we just had to learn the Access way of doing it!

### Closing the Database and Exiting Access

That completes the work we'll do in this section of "The Access Workbench." As usual, we will finish by closing the database and Access.

---

### FIGURE AW-5-9

**The Correct 1:1 VEHICLE to SALESPERSON Relationship**

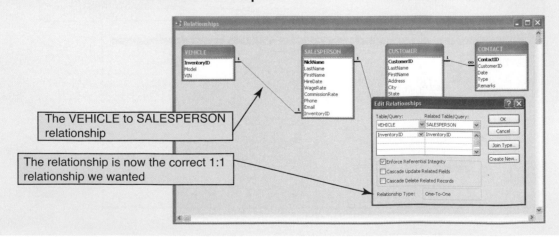

### Closing the WMCRM Database

1. To close the WMCRM: Database window, click the **Close** button in the upper right corner of the WMCRM: Database window.

### Exiting Access

1. To exit Access, click the **Close** button in the upper right corner of the Microsoft Access window.

## SUMMARY

To transform an E-R data model into a relational database design, a table is created for each entity. The attributes of the entity become the columns of the table, and the identifier of the entity becomes the primary key of the table. For each column, we must define data types, null status, default values (if any) and data constraints (if any). The normalization process is then applied to each table, and additional tables are created if necessary. In some cases, tables are denormalized. If so, the table will have insertion, update, and deletion problems. Denormalization makes sense if the benefit of not normalizing outweighs the possible problems that could be caused by such modification problems.

Weak entities are represented by a table. ID-dependent entities must include the key columns of the tables upon which they depend, as well as of the identifiers of the entities themselves. Non-ID-dependent entities must have their existence dependence recorded as business rules.

Supertypes and subtypes are each represented by separate tables. The identifier of the supertype entity becomes the primary key of the supertype table, and the identifiers of the subtype entities become the primary keys of the subtype tables. The primary key of each subtype is also the same primary key that is used for the supertype, and the primary key of each subtype serves as a foreign key linking to the the subtype back to the supertype

The E-R model has three types of binary relationships: 1:1, 1:N, and N:M. To represent a 1:1 relationship, we place the key of one table into the other table. To represent a 1:N relationship, we place the key of the parent table in the child table. Finally, to represent an M:N relationship, we create an intersection table that contains the keys of the other two tables.

Recursive relationships are relationships in which the participants in the relationship arise from the same entity class. The three types of recursive relationships are 1:1, 1:N, and N:M. These types of relationships are represented in the same way as are their equivalent nonrecursive relationships. For 1:1 and 1:N relationships, we add a foreign key to the relation that represents the entity. For an N:M recursion, we create an intersection table that represents the M:N relationship.

## REVIEW QUESTIONS

**5.1** Explain how entities are transformed into tables.

**5.2** Explain how attributes are transformed into columns. What column properties do we take into account when making the transformations?

**5.3** Why is it necessary to apply the normalization process to the tables created according to your answer to question 5.1?

**5.4** What is denormalization?

**5.5** When is denormalization justified?

**5.6** Explain the problems that unnormalized tables have for insert, update, and delete actions.

**5.7** Explain how the representation of weak entities differs from the representation of strong entities.

**5.8** Explain how the supertype and subtype entities are transformed into tables.

**5.9** List the three types of binary relationships and give an example of each. Do not use the examples given in this text.

**5.10** Define the term *foreign key* and give an example.

**5.11** Show two different ways to represent the 1:1 relationship in your answer to question 5.9. Use IE Crow's Foot E-R diagrams.

**5.12** For your answers to question 5.11, describe a method for obtaining data about one of the entities, given the key of the other. Describe a method for obtaining data about the second entity, given the key of the first. Describe methods for both of your alternatives in question 5.11.

**5.13** Code SQL statements to create a join having all data about both tables from your work for question 5.11.

**5.14** Define the terms *parent* and *child* as they apply to tables in a database design, and give an example of each.

**5.15** Show how to represent the 1:N relationship in your answer to question 5.9. Use an IE Crow's Foot E-R diagram.

**5.16** For your answer to question 5.15, describe a method for obtaining data for all the children, given the key of the parent. Describe a method for obtaining data for the parent, given a key of the child.

**5.17** For your answer to question 5.15, code a SQL statement that creates a table having all data from both tables.

**5.18** For a 1:N relationship, explain why you must place the key of the parent table in the child table, rather than placing the key of the child table in the parent table.

**5.19** Give examples of binary 1:N relationships, other than those in this text, for (a) an optional-to-optional relationship, (b) an optional-to-mandatory relationship, (c) a mandatory-to-optional relationship, and (d) a mandatory-to-mandatory relationship. Illustrate your answer using IE Crow's Foot E-R diagrams.

**5.20** Show how to represent the N:M relationship in your answer to question 5.9. Use an IE Crow's Foot E-R diagram.

**5.21** Explain the meaning of the term *intersection table*.

**5.22** Explain how the terms *parent table* and *child table* relate the tables in your answer to question 5.20.

**5.23** For your answers to questions 5.20, 5.21, and 5.22, describe a method for obtaining the children for one of the entities in the original data model, given the primary key of the table based on the second entity. Also, describe a method for obtaining the children for the second entity, given the primary key of the table based on the first entity.

**5.24** For your answer to question 5.20, code a SQL statement that creates a relation having all data from all tables.

**5.25** Why is it not possible to represent N:M relationships with the same strategy used to represent 1:N relationships?

**5.26** What is an associative entity? What is an association relationship? Give an example of an association relationship other than one shown in this text. Illustrate your answer using an IE Crow's Foot E-R diagram.

**5.27** Give an example of a 1:N relationship with an ID-dependent weak entity, other than one shown in this text. Illustrate your answer using an IE Crow's Foot E-R diagram.

**5.28** Give an example of a supertype–subtype relationship, other than one shown in this text. Illustrate your answer using an IE Crow's Foot E-R diagram.

**5.29** Define the three types of recursive binary relationships, and give an example of each, other than the ones shown in this text.

**5.30** Show how to represent the 1:1 recursive relationship in your answer to question 5.29. How does this differ from the representation of 1:1 nonrecursive relationships?

**5.31** Code a SQL statement that creates a table with all columns from the parent and child tables in your answer to question 5.30.

**5.32** Show how to represent the 1:N recursive relationship in your answer to question 5.29. How does this differ from the representation of 1:N nonrecursive relationships?

**5.33** Code a SQL statement that creates a table with all columns from the parent and child tables in your answer to question 5.32.

**5.34** Show how to represent the M:N recursive relationship in your answer to question 5.29. How does this differ from the representation of M:N nonrecursive relationships?

**5.35** Code a SQL statement that creates a table with all columns from the parent and child tables in your answer to question 5.34. Code a SQL statement using a left outer join that creates a table with all columns from the parent and child tables. Explain the difference between these two SQL statements.

## EXERCISES

**5.36** Consider the following table that holds data about employee project assignments:

ASSIGNMENT (<u>EmployeeNumber</u>, <u>ProjectNumber</u>, ProjectName, HoursWorked)

Assume that ProjectNumber determines ProjectName, and explain why this relation is not normalized. Demonstrate an insertion anomaly, a modification anomaly, and a deletion anomaly. Apply the normalization process to this relation. State the referential integrity constraint.

**5.37** Consider the following relation that holds data about employee assignments:

ASSIGNMENT (<u>EmployeeNumber</u>, ProjectNumber, ProjectName, HoursWorked)

Assume that ProjectNumber determines ProjectName, and explain why this relation is not normalized. Demonstrate an insertion anomaly, a modification anomaly, and a deletion anomaly. Apply the normalization process to this relation. State the referential integrity constraint.

**5.38** Explain the difference between the two ASSIGNMENT tables in questions 5.36 and 5.37. Under what circumstances is the table in question 5.36 more correct? Under what circumstances is the table in question 5.37 more correct?

**5.39** Create a relational database design for the data model you developed for question 4.30.

**5.40** Create a relational database design for the data model you developed for question 4.31.

**5.41** Create a relational database design for the data model you developed for question 4.32.

**5.42** Create a relational database design for the data model you developed for question 4.33.

**5.43** Create a relational database design for the data model you developed for question 4.34.

## ACCESS WORKBENCH EXERCISES

**AW.5.1** Using an IE Crow's Foot E-R diagram, draw a database design for the Wedgewood Pacific Corporation (WPC) database as completed at the end of Section 3's "The Access Workbench."

**AW.5.2** This chapter's "The Access Workbench" described how to create 1:1 relationships in Access. In particular, we added the business rule that each salesperson at Wallingford Motors can have one and only one vehicle as a demo car. Suppose that the rule has been changed so that each salesperson can have one or more cars as demo vehicles.

**A.** Using an IE Crow's Foot E-R diagram, redraw the database design in Figure AW-5-1 to show the new relationship between VEHICLE and SALESPERSON. Which table(s) is (are) the parent(s) in the relationship? Which table(s) is (are) the child(ren)? In which table(s) do you place a foreign key?

**B.** Start with the Wallingford Motors database that you've created so far (**WMCRM.mdb**) as it exists after working through all the steps in this chapter's section of "The Access Workbench" (If you haven't completed these actions, do so now). Copy the **WMCRM.mdb** database and rename the copy as **WMCRM-AW05-v02.mdb**. Modify the WMCRM-AW05-v02.mdb to implement the new relationship between VEHICLE and SALESPERSON (Note: Copying an Access database is discussed in Section 4's "The Access Workbench").

**AW.5.3** This chapter's "The Access Workbench" described how to create 1:1 relationships in Access. In particular, we added the business rule that each salesperson at Wallingford Motors can have one and only one vehicle as a demo car. Suppose that the rule has been changed so that (1) each salesperson can have one or more cars as demo vehicles, and (2) each demo vehicle can be shared by two or more salespersons.

**A.** Using an IE Crow's Foot E-R diagram, redraw the database design in Figure AW-5-1 to show the new relationship between VEHICLE and SALESPERSON. Which table(s) is (are) the parent(s) in the relationship? Which table(s) is (are) the child(ren)? In which table(s) do you place a foreign key?

**B.** Start with the Wallingford Motors database that you've created so far (**WMCRM.mdb**) as it exists after working through all the steps in this chapter's section of "The Access Workbench" (If you haven't completed these actions, do so now). Copy the **WMCRM.mdb** database and rename the copy as **WMCRM-AW05-v03.mdb**. Modify the WMCRM-AW05-v03.mdb to implement the new relationship between VEHICLE and SALESPERSON (NOTE: Copying an Access database is discussed in Section 4's "The Access Workbench").

## GARDEN GLORY PROJECT QUESTIONS

Using the data model you constructed for Garden Glory in Question B at the end of Chapter 4 (or, alternatively, your instructor may provide a data model for you to use), convert that data model into a relational database design for Garden Glory. Document your database design as follows.

**A.** Specify tables, primary keys, and foreign keys.

**B.** Describe how you have represented weak entities if any exist.

**C.** Describe how you have represented supertype and subtype entities if any exist.

**D.** Create a Crow's Foot E-R diagram similar to that in Figure 5-24.

**E.** Document referential integrity constraint enforcement; use Figure 5-25 as a guide.

**F.** Document any business rules that you think might be important.

**G.** Describe how you would validate that your design is a good representation of the data model upon which it is based.

## JAMES RIVER JEWELRY PROJECT QUESTIONS

Using the data model you constructed for James River Jewelry in Question C at the end of Chapter 4 (or, alternatively, your instructor may provide a data model for you to use), convert that data model into a relational database design for James River Jewelry. Document your database design as follows.

**A.** Specify tables, primary keys, and foreign keys.

**B.** Describe how you have represented weak entities if any exist.

**C.** Describe how you have represented supertype and subtype entities if any exist.

**D.** Create a Crow's Foot E-R diagram similar to that in Figure 5-24.

**E.** Document referential integrity constraint enforcement; use Figure 5-25 as a guide.

**F.** Document any business rules that you think might be important.

**G.** Describe how you would validate that your design is a good representation of the data model upon which it is based.

## THE QUEEN ANNE CURIOSITY SHOP PROJECT QUESTIONS

Using the data model you constructed for The Queen Anne Curiosity Shop in Question D at the end of Chapter 4 (or, alternatively, your instructor may provide a data model for you to use), convert that data model into a relational database design for The Queen Anne Curiosity Shop. Document your database design as follows.

**A.** Specify tables, primary keys, and foreign keys.

**B.** Describe how you have represented weak entities if any exist.

**C.** Describe how you have represented supertype and subtype entities if any exist.

**D.** Create a Crow's Foot E-R diagram similar to that in Figure 5-24.

**E.** Document referential integrity constraint enforcement; use Figure 5-25 as a guide.

**F.** Document any business rules that you think might be important.

**G.** Describe how you would validate that your design is a good representation of the data model upon which it is based.

# Database Administration

> Understand the need for and importance of database administration

> Learn different ways of processing a database

> Understand the need for concurrency control, security, and backup and recovery

> Learn typical problems that can occur when multiple users process a database concurrently

> Understand the use of locking and the problem of deadlock

> Learn the difference between optimistic and pessimistic locking

> Know the meaning of *ACID transaction*

> Learn the four 1992 ANSI standard isolation levels

> Understand the need for security and specific tasks for improving database security

> Know the difference between recovery via reprocessing and recovery via rollback/rollforward

> Understand the nature of the tasks required for recovery using rollback/rollforward

> Know basic administrative and managerial DBA functions

> Understand distributed database processing

> Understand the concept of object-relational databases

This chapter describes the major tasks of an important business function called database administration (DBA). This function involves managing a database so that its value to an organization is maximized. Usually, this means balancing the conflicting goals of protecting the database and maximizing its availability and benefit to users. Both the terms **data administration** and **database administration** are used in the industry. In some cases, the terms are considered synonymous; in other cases, they have different meanings. Most commonly, the term *data administration* refers to a function that applies to an entire organization; it is a management-oriented function that concerns corporate data privacy and security issues. The term *database administration* refers to a more technical function that is specific to a particular database, including the applications that process that database. This chapter addresses database administration.

Databases vary considerably in size and scope: from a single-user personal database to a large interorganizational database, such as an airline reservation system. All these databases have a need for database administration, although the tasks to be accomplished vary in complexity. For a personal database, for example, individuals follow simple procedures for backing up their data, and they keep minimal records for documentation. In this case, the person who uses the database also performs the DBA functions, even though he or she is probably unaware of it.

For multi-user database applications, database administration becomes both more important and more difficult. Consequently, it generally has formal recognition. For some applications, one or two people are given this function on a part-time basis. For large Internet or intranet databases, database administration responsibilities are often too time-consuming and too varied to be handled even by a single full-time person. Supporting a database with dozens or hundreds of users requires considerable time as well as both technical knowledge and diplomatic skills, and usually is handled by an office of database administration. The manager of the office is often known as the **database administrator**; in this case, the acronym **DBA** refers to either the office or the manager.

The overall responsibility of the DBA is to facilitate the development and use of the database. Usually, this means balancing the conflicting goals of protecting the database and maximizing its availability and benefit to users. The DBA is responsible for the development, operation, and maintenance of the database and its applications.

In this chapter, we will describe three important database administration functions: concurrency control, security, and backup and recovery. Then, we will summarize the need for configuration change management. Finally, we will look at two advanced database topics: distributed databases and object-oriented database systems.

But before we do any of this, we'll create the Heather Sweeney Designs database that we've discussed in the previous database modeling and design chapters as an example database for our discussion both in this chapter and in Chapter 7.

## ▶ THE HEATHER SWEENEY DESIGNS DATABASE

The SQL statements to create the Heather Sweeney Designs (which we will name HSD) database are shown in Figure 6-1 in SQL Server 2005 syntax. The SQL statements are built from the HSD database design in Figure 5-24, the column constraints follow the attribute specifications in Figure 4-21, and the referential integrity constraint specifications outlined in Figure 5-25.

The SQL statements to populate the HSD database are shown in Figure 6-2, again in SQL Server 2005 syntax. Finally, the completed HSD database is shown in SQL Server 2005 Express Edition in Figure 6-3.

---

### FIGURE 6-1

**SQL Statements to Create the HSD Database**

```
CREATE TABLE SEMINAR(
        SeminarID          Int              NOT NULL IDENTITY (1, 1),
        [Date]             DateTime         NOT NULL,
        [Time]             DateTime         NOT NULL,
        Location           VarChar(100)     NOT NULL,
        Title              VarChar(100)     NOT NULL,
        CONSTRAINT         SEMINAR_PK       PRIMARY KEY(SeminarID)
        );

CREATE TABLE CUSTOMER(
        EmailAddress       VarChar(100)     NOT NULL,
        LastName           Char(25)         NOT NULL,
        FirstName          Char(25)         NOT NULL,
        Phone              Char(12)         NOT NULL,
        Address            Char(35)         NULL,
        City               Char(35)         NULL DEFAULT 'Dallas',
        State              Char(2)          NULL DEFAULT 'TX',
        ZIP                Char(10)         NULL DEFAULT '75201',
        CONSTRAINT         CUSTOMER_PK      PRIMARY KEY(EmailAddress)
        );

CREATE TABLE SEMINAR_CUSTOMER(
        SeminarID          Int              NOT NULL,
        EmailAddress       VarChar(100)     NOT NULL,
        CONSTRAINT         S_C_PK PRIMARY KEY(SeminarID,EmailAddress),
        CONSTRAINT         S_C_SEMINAR_FK   FOREIGN KEY(SeminarID)
                              REFERENCES SEMINAR(SeminarID)
                                 ON UPDATE NO ACTION
                                 ON DELETE CASCADE,
        CONSTRAINT         S_C_CUSTOMER_FK  FOREIGN KEY(EmailAddress)
                              REFERENCES CUSTOMER(EmailAddress)
                                 ON UPDATE CASCADE
                                 ON DELETE CASCADE
        );
```

## FIGURE 6-1 (Continued)

```
CREATE TABLE CONTACT(
        EmailAddress    VarChar(100)    NOT NULL,
        [Date]          DateTime        NOT NULL,
        ContactNumber   Int             NOT NULL,
        ContactType     Char(15)        NOT NULL,
        SeminarID       Int             NULL,
        CONSTRAINT      CONTACT_PK      PRIMARY KEY(EmailAddress, [Date]),
        CONSTRAINT      CONTACT_SEMINAR_FK FOREIGN KEY(SeminarID)
                            REFERENCES SEMINAR(SeminarID)
                                ON UPDATE NO ACTION
                                ON DELETE NO ACTION,
        CONSTRAINT      CONTACT_CUSTOMER_FK FOREIGN KEY(EmailAddress)
                            REFERENCES CUSTOMER(EmailAddress)
                                ON UPDATE CASCADE
                                ON DELETE CASCADE
        );

CREATE TABLE PRODUCT(
        ProductNumber   Char(35)        NOT NULL,
        Description     VarChar(100)    NOT NULL,
        UnitPrice       Numeric(9,2)    NOT NULL,
        QuantityOnHand  Int             NOT NULL DEFAULT 0,
        CONSTRAINT      PRODUCT_PK      PRIMARY KEY(ProductNumber)
        );

CREATE TABLE INVOICE(
        InvoiceNumber   Int             NOT NULL IDENTITY (35000, 1),
        [Date]          DateTime        NOT NULL,
        PaymentType     Char(25)        NOT NULL DEFAULT 'Cash',
        SubTotal        Numeric(9,2)    NULL,
        Shipping        Numeric(9,2)    NULL,
        Tax             Numeric(9,2)    NULL,
        Total           Numeric(9,2)    NULL,
        EmailAddress    VarChar(100)    NOT NULL,
        CONSTRAINT      INVOICE_PK      PRIMARY KEY (InvoiceNumber),
        CONSTRAINT      INVOICE_CUSTOMER_FK FOREIGN KEY(EmailAddress)
                            REFERENCES Customer(EmailAddress)
                                ON UPDATE CASCADE
                                ON DELETE NO ACTION
        );

CREATE TABLE LINE_ITEM(
        InvoiceNumber   Int             NOT NULL,
        LineNumber      Int             NOT NULL,
        Quantity        Int             NOT NULL,
        UnitPrice       Numeric(9,2)    NOT NULL,
        Total           Numeric(9,2)    NULL,
        ProductNumber   Char(35)        NOT NULL,
        CONSTRAINT      LINE_ITEM_PK PRIMARY KEY(InvoiceNumber, LineNumber),
        CONSTRAINT      L_I_INVOICE_FK  FOREIGN KEY(InvoiceNumber)
                            REFERENCES INVOICE(InvoiceNumber)
                                ON UPDATE NO ACTION
                                ON DELETE CASCADE,
        CONSTRAINT      L_I_PRODUCT_FK  FOREIGN KEY(ProductNumber)
                            REFERENCES PRODUCT(ProductNumber)
                                ON UPDATE CASCADE
                                ON DELETE NO ACTION
        );
```

**FIGURE 6-2**

**SQL Statements to Populate the HSD Database**

```
/*****    SEMINAR DATA    *****/


INSERT INTO SEMINAR VALUES(
    '11-OCT-2005', '11:00 AM', 'San Antonio Convention Center',
    'Kitchen on a Budget');
INSERT INTO SEMINAR VALUES(
    '25-OCT-2005', '04:00 PM', 'Dallas Convention Center',
    'Kitchen on a Big D Budget');
INSERT INTO SEMINAR VALUES(
    '01-NOV-2005', '08:30 AM', 'Austin Convention Center',
    'Kitchen on a Budget');
INSERT INTO SEMINAR VALUES(
    '22-MAR-2006', '11:00 AM', 'Dallas Convention Center',
    'Kitchen on a Big D Budget');


/*****    CUSTOMER DATA    *****/


INSERT INTO CUSTOMER VALUES(
    'NJ@somewhere.com', 'Jacobs', 'Nancy', '817-871-8123',
    '1440 West Palm Drive', 'Fort Worth', 'TX', '76110');
INSERT INTO CUSTOMER VALUES(
    'CJ@somewhere.com', 'Jacobs', 'Chantel', '817-871-8234',
    '1550 East Palm Drive', 'Fort Worth', 'TX', '76112');
INSERT INTO CUSTOMER VALUES(
    'RA@somewhere.com', 'Able', 'Ralph', '210-281-7987',
    '123 Elm Street', 'San Antonio', 'TX', '78214');
INSERT INTO CUSTOMER VALUES(
    'SB@elsewhere.com', 'Baker', 'Susan', '210-281-7876',
    '456 Oak Street', 'San Antonio', 'TX', '78216');
INSERT INTO CUSTOMER VALUES(
    'SE@elsewhere.com', 'Eagleton', 'Sam', '210-281-7765',
    '789 Pine Street', 'San Antonio', 'TX', '78218');
INSERT INTO CUSTOMER VALUES(
    'KF@somewhere.com', 'Foxtrot', 'Kathy', '972-233-6234',
    '11023 Elm Street', 'Dallas', 'TX', '75220');
INSERT INTO CUSTOMER VALUES(
    'SG@somewhere.com', 'George', 'Sally', '972-233-6345',
    '12034 San Jacinto', 'Dallas', 'TX', '75223');
INSERT INTO CUSTOMER VALUES(
    'SH@elsewhere.com', 'Hullett', 'Shawn', '972-233-6456',
    '13045 Flora', 'Dallas', 'TX', '75224');
INSERT INTO CUSTOMER VALUES(
    'BP@elsewhere.com', 'Pearson', 'Bobbi', '512-974-3344',
    '43 West 23rd Street', 'Auston', 'TX', '78710');
INSERT INTO CUSTOMER VALUES(
    'TR@somewhere.com', 'Ranger', 'Terry', '512-974-4455',
    '56 East 18th Street', 'Auston', 'TX', '78712');
INSERT INTO CUSTOMER VALUES(
    'JT@somewhere.com', 'Tyler', 'Jenny', '972-233-6567',
    '14056 South Ervay Street', 'Dallas', 'TX', '75225');
INSERT INTO CUSTOMER VALUES(
    'JW@elsewhere.com', 'Wayne', 'Joan', '817-871-8245',
    '1660 South Aspen Drive', 'Fort Worth', 'TX', '76115');


/*****    SEMINAR_CUSTOMER DATA    *****/


INSERT INTO SEMINAR_CUSTOMER VALUES(1, 'NJ@somewhere.com');
INSERT INTO SEMINAR_CUSTOMER VALUES(1, 'CJ@somewhere.com');
INSERT INTO SEMINAR_CUSTOMER VALUES(1, 'RA@somewhere.com');
INSERT INTO SEMINAR_CUSTOMER VALUES(1, 'SB@elsewhere.com');
INSERT INTO SEMINAR_CUSTOMER VALUES(1, 'SE@elsewhere.com');
INSERT INTO SEMINAR_CUSTOMER VALUES(2, 'KF@somewhere.com');
```

**FIGURE 6-2   (Continued)**

```
INSERT INTO SEMINAR_CUSTOMER VALUES(2, 'SG@somewhere.com');
INSERT INTO SEMINAR_CUSTOMER VALUES(2, 'SH@elsewhere.com');
INSERT INTO SEMINAR_CUSTOMER VALUES(3, 'BP@elsewhere.com');
INSERT INTO SEMINAR_CUSTOMER VALUES(3, 'TR@somewhere.com');
INSERT INTO SEMINAR_CUSTOMER VALUES(4, 'KF@somewhere.com');
INSERT INTO SEMINAR_CUSTOMER VALUES(4, 'SG@somewhere.com');
INSERT INTO SEMINAR_CUSTOMER VALUES(4, 'JT@somewhere.com');
INSERT INTO SEMINAR_CUSTOMER VALUES(4, 'JW@elsewhere.com');


/*****   CONTACT DATA   *****/

INSERT INTO CONTACT VALUES(
     'NJ@somewhere.com', '11-OCT-2005', 1, 'Seminar', 1);
INSERT INTO CONTACT VALUES(
     'CJ@somewhere.com', '11-OCT-2005', 1, 'Seminar', 1);
INSERT INTO CONTACT VALUES(
     'RA@somewhere.com', '11-OCT-2005', 1, 'Seminar', 1);
INSERT INTO CONTACT VALUES(
     'SB@elsewhere.com', '11-OCT-2005', 1, 'Seminar', 1);
INSERT INTO CONTACT VALUES(
     'SE@elsewhere.com', '11-OCT-2005', 1, 'Seminar', 1);

INSERT INTO CONTACT (EmailAddress, [Date], ContactNumber, ContactType)
     VALUES(
     'NJ@somewhere.com', '16-OCT-2005', 2, 'FormLetter01');
INSERT INTO CONTACT (EmailAddress, [Date], ContactNumber, ContactType)
     VALUES(
     'CJ@somewhere.com', '16-OCT-2005', 2, 'FormLetter01');
INSERT INTO CONTACT (EmailAddress, [Date], ContactNumber, ContactType)
     VALUES(
     'RA@somewhere.com', '16-OCT-2005', 2, 'FormLetter01');
INSERT INTO CONTACT (EmailAddress, [Date], ContactNumber, ContactType)
     VALUES(
     'SB@elsewhere.com', '16-OCT-2005', 2, 'FormLetter01');
INSERT INTO CONTACT (EmailAddress, [Date], ContactNumber, ContactType)
     VALUES(
     'SE@elsewhere.com', '16-OCT-2005', 2, 'FormLetter01');

INSERT INTO CONTACT VALUES(
     'KF@somewhere.com', '25-OCT-2005', 1, 'Seminar', 2);
INSERT INTO CONTACT VALUES(
     'SG@somewhere.com', '25-OCT-2005', 1, 'Seminar', 2);
INSERT INTO CONTACT VALUES(
     'SH@elsewhere.com', '25-OCT-2005', 1, 'Seminar', 2);

INSERT INTO CONTACT (EmailAddress, [Date], ContactNumber, ContactType)
     VALUES(
     'KF@somewhere.com', '30-OCT-2005', 2, 'FormLetter01');
INSERT INTO CONTACT (EmailAddress, [Date], ContactNumber, ContactType)
     VALUES(
     'SG@somewhere.com', '30-OCT-2005', 2, 'FormLetter01');
INSERT INTO CONTACT (EmailAddress, [Date], ContactNumber, ContactType)
     VALUES(
     'SH@elsewhere.com', '30-OCT-2005', 2, 'FormLetter01');

INSERT INTO CONTACT VALUES(
     'BP@elsewhere.com', '01-NOV-2005', 1, 'Seminar', 3);
INSERT INTO CONTACT VALUES(
     'TR@somewhere.com', '01-NOV-2005', 1, 'Seminar', 3);


INSERT INTO CONTACT (EmailAddress, [Date], ContactNumber, ContactType)
     VALUES(
     'BP@elsewhere.com', '06-NOV-2005', 2, 'FormLetter01');
INSERT INTO CONTACT (EmailAddress, [Date], ContactNumber, ContactType)
     VALUES(
     'TR@somewhere.com', '06-NOV-2005', 2, 'FormLetter01');
INSERT INTO CONTACT (EmailAddress, [Date], ContactNumber, ContactType)
     VALUES(
     'KF@somewhere.com', '20-FEB-2006', 3, 'FormLetter02');
```

**FIGURE 6-2  (Continued)**

```
INSERT INTO CONTACT (EmailAddress, [Date], ContactNumber, ContactType)
     VALUES(
     'SG@somewhere.com', '20-FEB-2006', 3, 'FormLetter02');
INSERT INTO CONTACT (EmailAddress, [Date], ContactNumber, ContactType)
     VALUES(
     'SH@elsewhere.com', '20-FEB-2006', 3, 'FormLetter02');

INSERT INTO CONTACT VALUES(
     'KF@somewhere.com', '22-MAR-2006', 4, 'Seminar', 4);
INSERT INTO CONTACT VALUES(
     'SG@somewhere.com', '22-MAR-2006', 4, 'Seminar', 4);
INSERT INTO CONTACT VALUES(
     'JT@somewhere.com', '22-MAR-2006', 1, 'Seminar', 4);
INSERT INTO CONTACT VALUES(
     'JW@elsewhere.com', '22-MAR-2006', 1, 'Seminar', 4);


/*****   PRODUCT DATA   *****/


INSERT INTO PRODUCT VALUES(
     'VK001', 'Kitchen Remodeling Basics - Video', 14.95, 50);
INSERT INTO PRODUCT VALUES(
     'VK002', 'Advanced Kitchen Remodeling - Video', 14.95, 35);
INSERT INTO PRODUCT VALUES(
     'VK003', 'Kitchen Remodeling Dallas Style - Video', 19.95, 25);
INSERT INTO PRODUCT VALUES(
     'VK004', 'Heather Sweeny Seminar Live in Dallas on 25-OCT-05 -
     Video', 24.95, 20);
INSERT INTO PRODUCT VALUES(
     'VB001', 'Kitchen Remodeling Basics - Video Companion', 7.99, 50);
INSERT INTO PRODUCT VALUES(
     'VB002', 'Advanced Kitchen Remodeling - Video Companion', 7.99, 35);
INSERT INTO PRODUCT VALUES(
     'VB003', 'Kitchen Remodeling Dallas Style - Video Companion',
     9.99, 25);
INSERT INTO PRODUCT VALUES(
     'BK001', 'Kitchen Remodeling Basics For Everyone - Book', 24.95, 75);
INSERT INTO PRODUCT VALUES(
     'BK002', 'Advanced Kitchen Remodeling For Everyone  Book', 24.95,
     75);


/*****   INVOICE DATA   *****/


INSERT INTO INVOICE VALUES(
     '15-Oct-05', 'VISA', 22.94, 5.95, 1.31, 30.20, 'RA@somewhere.com');
INSERT INTO INVOICE VALUES(
     '25-Oct-05',.'MasterCard', 47.89, 5.95, 2.73, 56.57,
     'SB@elsewhere.com');
INSERT INTO INVOICE VALUES(
     '20-Dec-05', 'VISA', 24.95, 5.95, 1.42, 32.32, 'SG@somewhere.com');
INSERT INTO INVOICE VALUES(
     '25-Mar-06', 'MasterCard', 64.85, 5.95, 3.70, 74.50,
     'SB@elsewhere.com');


/*****   LINE_ITEM DATA   *****/


INSERT INTO LINE_ITEM VALUES(35000, 1, 1, 14.95, 14.95, 'VK001');
INSERT INTO LINE_ITEM VALUES(35000, 2, 1, 7.99, 7.99, 'VB001');
INSERT INTO LINE_ITEM VALUES(35001, 1, 1, 14.95, 14.95, 'VK001');
INSERT INTO LINE_ITEM VALUES(35001, 2, 1, 7.99, 7.99, 'VB001');
INSERT INTO LINE_ITEM VALUES(35001, 3, 1, 24.95, 24.95, 'BK001');
INSERT INTO LINE_ITEM VALUES(35002, 1, 1, 24.95, 24.95, 'VK004');
INSERT INTO LINE_ITEM VALUES(35003, 1, 1, 14.95, 14.95, 'VK002');
INSERT INTO LINE_ITEM VALUES(35003, 2, 1, 24.95, 24.95, 'BK002');
INSERT INTO LINE_ITEM VALUES(35003, 3, 1, 24.95, 24.95, 'VK004');
```

**FIGURE 6-3**

**The HSD Database in SQL Server 2005 Express Edition**

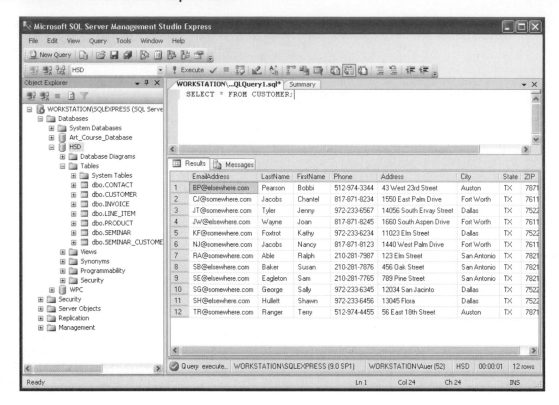

## The Need for Control, Security, and Reliability

Databases vary considerably in size and scope, from single-user databases to large, interorganizational databases, such as an airline reservation system. As shown in Figure 6-4, they also vary in the way they are processed.

We will define and discuss the various pieces of the environment shown in Figure 6-4 in detail in Chapter 7 when we discuss database processing applications. For now, just realize that it is possible for every one of the application elements in Figure 6-4 to be operating at the same time. Queries, forms, and reports can be generated while Web pages [Active Server Pages (ASPs) and Java Server Pages (JSPs)] access the database, possibly invoking stored procedures. Traditional application programs running in COBOL, C#, and other programming languages can be processing transactions on the database. All this activity can cause pieces of programming code stored in the DBMS—which are known as triggers and stored procedures and which will be discussed in Chapter 7—to be invoked. While all this is occurring, constraints, such as those on referential integrity, must be enforced. Finally, hundreds or even thousands of people might be using the system, and they might want to process the database 24 hours a day, seven days a week.

Three database administration functions are necessary to bring order to this potential chaos. First, the actions of concurrent users must be controlled to ensure that results are consistent with what is expected. Second, security measures must be in place and enforced so that only authorized users can take authorized actions at appropriate times. Finally, backup and recovery techniques and procedures must be operating to protect the database in case of failure and to recover it as quickly and accurately as possible when necessary. We will consider each of these in turn, and we will see some of them in use in Chapter 7 when we use Web applications to access databases.

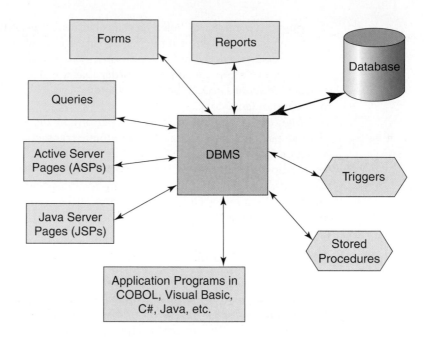

**FIGURE 6-4**

The Database
Processing
Environment

## CONCURRENCY CONTROL

The purpose of concurrency control is to ensure that one user's work does not inappropriately influence another user's work. In some cases, these measures ensure that a user gets the same result when processing with other users as that person would have received if processing alone. In other cases, it means that the user's work is influenced by other users but in an anticipated way.

For example, in an order-entry system, a user should be able to enter an order and get the same result regardless of whether there are no other users or hundreds of other users. On the other hand, a user who is printing a report of the most current inventory status might want to obtain in-process data changes from other users, even if those changes might later be canceled.

Unfortunately, no concurrency control technique or mechanism is ideal for all circumstances; they all involve trade-offs. For example, a user can obtain strict concurrency control by locking the entire database, but while that person is processing, no other user will be able to do anything. This is robust protection, but it comes at a high cost. As you will see, other measures are available that are more difficult to program and enforce but that allow more throughput. Still other measures are available that maximize throughput but for a low level of concurrency control. When designing multi-user database applications, developers need to choose among these trade-offs.

### The Need for Atomic Transactions

In most database applications, users submit work in the form of **transactions**, which are also known as **logical units of work (LUWs)**. A transaction (or LUW) is a series of actions to be taken on a database such that all of them are performed successfully or none of them are performed at all, in which case the database remains unchanged. Such a transaction is sometimes called **atomic**, because it is performed as a unit. Consider the following sequence of database actions that could occur when recording a new order.

1. Change the customer record, increasing the value of Amount Owed.
2. Change the salesperson record, increasing the value of Commission Due.
3. Insert the new order record into the database.

Suppose the last step failed, perhaps because of insufficient file space. Imagine the confusion that would ensue if the first two changes were made but the third one was not. The customer would be billed for an order that was never received, and a salesperson would receive a commission on an order that was never sent to the customer. Clearly, these three actions need to be taken as a unit—either all of them should be done or none of them should be done.

Figure 6-5 compares the results of performing these activities as a series of independent steps [Figure 6-5(a)] and as an atomic transaction [Figure 6-5(b)]. Notice that when the steps are carried out atomically and one fails, no changes are made in the database. Also note that the commands Start Transaction, Commit Transaction, or Rollback Transaction must be issued by the application program to mark the boundaries of the transaction logic. The particular form of these commands varies from one DBMS product to another.

## Concurrent Transaction Processing

When two transactions are being processed against a database at the same time, they are termed **concurrent transactions**. Although it might appear to the users that concurrent transactions are being processed simultaneously, this cannot be true because the central processing unit (CPU) of the machine processing the database can execute only one instruction at a time. Usually transactions are interleaved, which means the operating

---

**FIGURE 6-5**

**Comparison of the Results of Applying Serial Actions Versus a Multiple-Step Transaction**

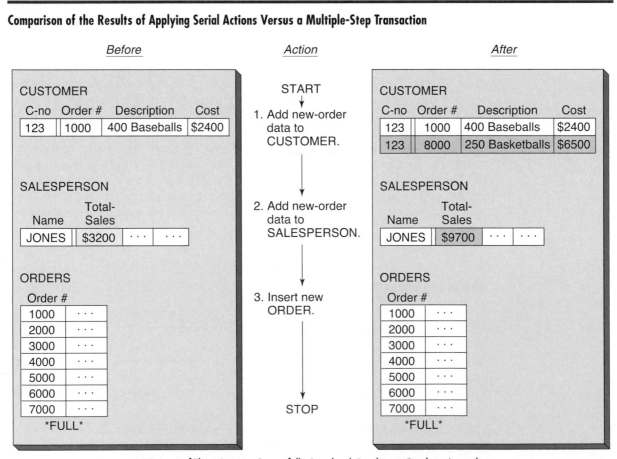

(a) Two out of Three Activities Successfully Completed, Resulting in Database Anomalies

**FIGURE 6-5** *(Continued)*

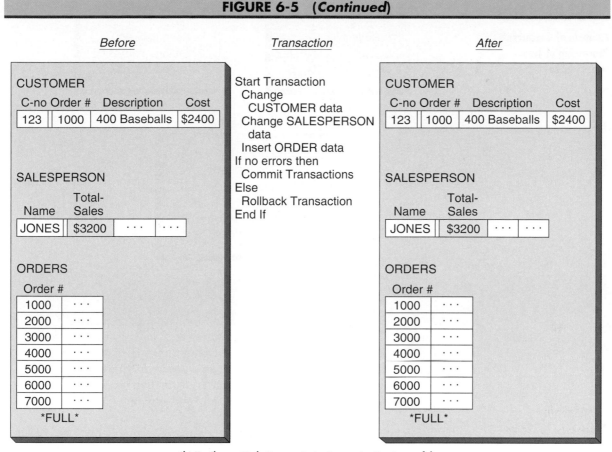

| Before | Transaction | After |
|---|---|---|

Start Transaction
 Change
  CUSTOMER data
 Change SALESPERSON
  data
 Insert ORDER data
If no errors then
 Commit Transactions
Else
 Rollback Transaction
End If

**CUSTOMER**

| C-no | Order # | Description | Cost |
|---|---|---|---|
| 123 | 1000 | 400 Baseballs | $2400 |

**SALESPERSON**

| Name | Total-Sales | | |
|---|---|---|---|
| JONES | $3200 | · · · | · · · |

**ORDERS**

| Order # | |
|---|---|
| 1000 | · · · |
| 2000 | · · · |
| 3000 | · · · |
| 4000 | · · · |
| 5000 | · · · |
| 6000 | · · · |
| 7000 | · · · |
| *FULL* | |

(b) No Change Made Because Entire Transaction Not Successful

system switches CPU services among tasks so that some portion of each of them is carried out in a given interval. This switching among tasks is done so quickly that two people seated at browsers side by side, processing against the same database, might believe that their two transactions are completed simultaneously. However, in reality the two transactions are interleaved.

Figure 6-6 shows two concurrent transactions. User A's transaction reads Item 100, changes it, and rewrites it in the database. User B's transaction takes the same actions but on Item 200. The CPU processes User A's transaction until the CPU must wait for a read or write operation to complete or for some other action to finish. The operating system then shifts control to User B. The CPU processes User B's transaction until a similar interruption in the transaction processing occurs, at which point the operating system passes control back to User A. Again, to the users, the processing appears to be simultaneous, but in reality it is interleaved, or concurrent.

## The Lost Update Problem

The concurrent processing illustrated in Figure 6-6 poses no problems because the users are processing different data. Now suppose both users want to process Item 100. For example, User A wants to order 5 units of Item 100, and User B wants to order 3 units of Item 100.

Figure 6-7 illustrates the problem. User A reads Item 100's record, which is transferred into a user work area. According to the record, 10 items are in inventory. Then, User B reads Item 100's record, and it goes into another user work area. Again,

**FIGURE 6-6**

**Example of Concurrent Processing of Two Users' Tasks**

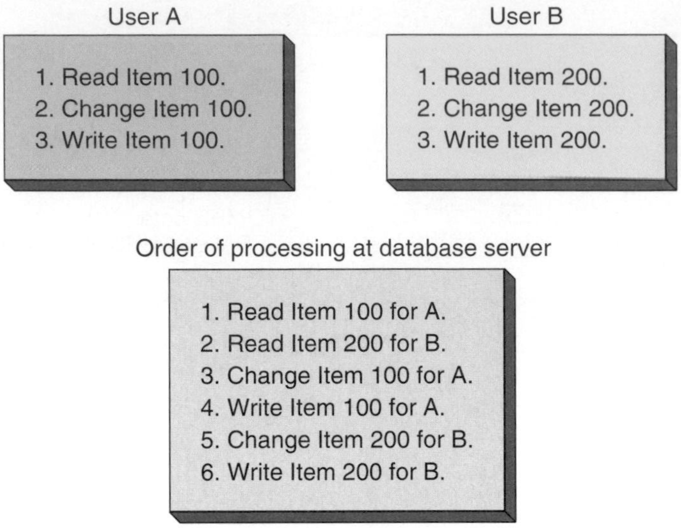

User A

1. Read Item 100.
2. Change Item 100.
3. Write Item 100.

User B

1. Read Item 200.
2. Change Item 200.
3. Write Item 200.

Order of processing at database server

1. Read Item 100 for A.
2. Read Item 200 for B.
3. Change Item 100 for A.
4. Write Item 100 for A.
5. Change Item 200 for B.
6. Write Item 200 for B.

according to the record, 10 items are in inventory. Now, User A takes 5 of them, decrements the count of items in its user work area to 5, and rewrites the record for Item 100. Then, User B takes 3, decrements the count in its user work area to 7, and rewrites the record for Item 100. The database now shows, incorrectly, that 7 units of Item 100 remain in inventory. To review, we started with 10 in inventory, then User A took 5, User B took 3, and the database wound up showing that 7 were left in inventory. Clearly, this is a problem.

Both users obtained data that were correct at the time they obtained it. However, when User B read the record, User A already had a copy that it was about to update. This situation is called the **lost update problem**, or the **concurrent update problem**. Another similar problem is called the **inconsistent read problem**. In this situation, User A reads data that have been processed by only a portion of a transaction from User B. As a result, User A reads incorrect data.

**FIGURE 6-7**

**Example of a Lost Update Problem**

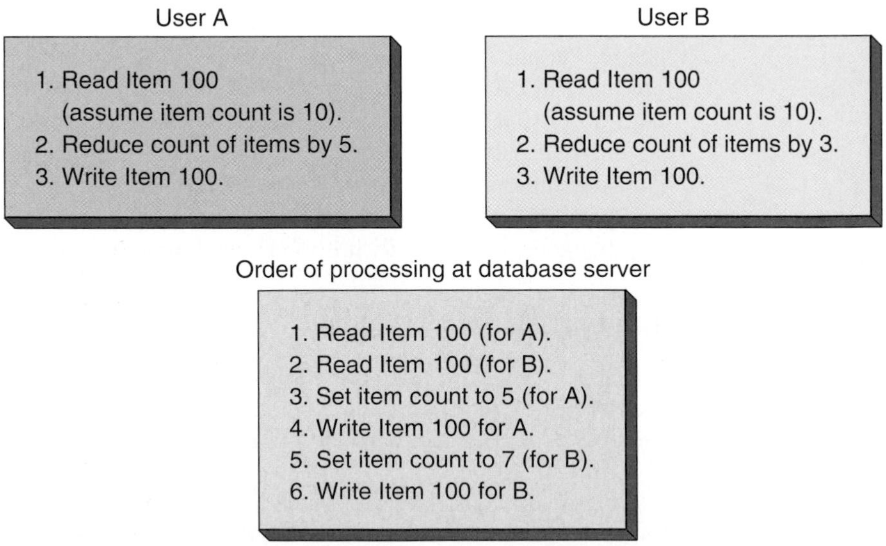

User A

1. Read Item 100
   (assume item count is 10).
2. Reduce count of items by 5.
3. Write Item 100.

User B

1. Read Item 100
   (assume item count is 10).
2. Reduce count of items by 3.
3. Write Item 100.

Order of processing at database server

1. Read Item 100 (for A).
2. Read Item 100 (for B).
3. Set item count to 5 (for A).
4. Write Item 100 for A.
5. Set item count to 7 (for B).
6. Write Item 100 for B.

Note: The change and write in Steps 3 and 4 are lost.

## Concurrency Problems: Dirty Reads, Nonrepeatable Reads, and Phantom Reads

The problems that can occur due to concurrent processing have standardized names: dirty read, nonrepeatable read, and phantom read. A **dirty read** occurs when one transaction reads a changed record that has not been committed to the database. This can occur, for example, if one transaction reads a row changed by a second transaction, and this second transaction later cancels its changes. A **nonrepeatable read** occurs when a transaction rereads data it has previously read and finds modifications or deletions caused by another transaction. A **phantom read** occurs when a transaction rereads data and finds new rows that were inserted by a different transaction since the prior read.

## Resource Locking

One remedy for the inconsistencies caused by concurrent processing is to prevent multiple applications from obtaining copies of the same rows or tables when those rows or tables are about to be changed. This remedy is called **resource locking** and it prevents concurrent processing problems by disallowing sharing by locking data that are retrieved for update. Figure 6-8 shows the order of processing using a lock command.

Because of the lock, User B's transaction must wait until User A is finished with the Item 100 data. Using this strategy, User B can read Item 100's record only after User A has completed the modification. In this case, the final item count stored in the database is 2, which is what it should be. (We started with 10, then A took 5 and B took 3, leaving 2.)

Locks can be placed automatically by the DBMS or by a command issued to the DBMS from the application program or query user. Locks placed by the DBMS are called **implicit locks**; those placed by command are called **explicit locks**.

In the preceding example, the locks were applied to rows of data; however, not all locks are applied at this level. Some DBMS products lock at the page level, some at the table level, and some at the database level. The size of a lock is referred to as the **lock granularity**. Locks with large granularity are easy for the DBMS to administer but

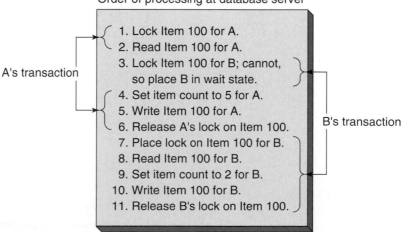

**FIGURE 6-8**

**Example of Concurrent Processing with Explicit Locks**

User A
1. Lock Item 100.
2. Read Item 100.
3. Reduce count by 5.
4. Write Item 100.

User B
1. Lock Item 100.
2. Read Item 100.
3. Reduce count by 3.
4. Write Item 100.

Order of processing at database server

A's transaction
1. Lock Item 100 for A.
2. Read Item 100 for A.
3. Lock Item 100 for B; cannot, so place B in wait state.
4. Set item count to 5 for A.
5. Write Item 100 for A.
6. Release A's lock on Item 100.
7. Place lock on Item 100 for B.
8. Read Item 100 for B.
9. Set item count to 2 for B.
10. Write Item 100 for B.
11. Release B's lock on Item 100.

B's transaction

frequently cause conflicts. Locks with small granularity are difficult to administer (the DBMS has many more details to keep track of and check), but conflicts are less common.

Locks also vary by type. An **exclusive lock** locks an item from access of any type. No other transaction can read or change the data. A **shared lock** locks an item from being changed but not from being read. That is, other transactions can read the item as long as they do not attempt to alter it.

## Serializable Transactions

When two or more transactions are processed concurrently, the results in the database should be logically consistent with the results that would have been achieved had the transactions been processed in an arbitrary serial fashion. A scheme for processing concurrent transactions in this way is said to be **serializable**.

Serializability can be achieved by a number of different means. One way is to process the transaction using **two-phased locking**. With this strategy, transactions are allowed to obtain locks as necessary, but once the first lock is released, no other lock can be obtained. Transactions have a growing phase in which the locks are obtained, and a shrinking phase in which the locks are released.

A special case of two-phased locking is used with a number of DBMS products. With it, locks are obtained throughout the transaction, but no lock is released until the COMMIT or ROLLBACK command is issued. This strategy is more restrictive than two-phase locking requires, but it is easier to implement.

Consider an order-entry transaction that involves processing data in the CUSTOMER, SALESPERSON, and ORDER table. To make sure the database will suffer no anomalies due to concurrency, the order-entry transaction issues locks on CUSTOMER, SALESPERSON, and ORDER as needed; makes all the database changes; and then releases all its locks.

## Deadlock

Although locking solves one problem, it causes another. Consider what might happen when two users want to order two items from inventory. Suppose User A wants to order some paper, and if she can get the paper, she also wants to order some pencils. Suppose also that User B wants to order some pencils, and if he can get the pencils, he also wants to order some paper. An example of the possible order of processing is shown in Figure 6-9.

**FIGURE 6-9**

**Example of Deadlock**

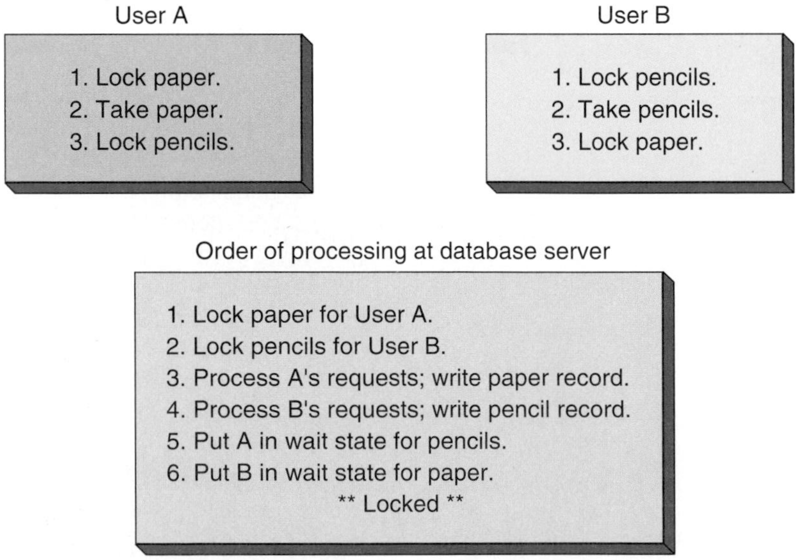

User A

1. Lock paper.
2. Take paper.
3. Lock pencils.

User B

1. Lock pencils.
2. Take pencils.
3. Lock paper.

Order of processing at database server

1. Lock paper for User A.
2. Lock pencils for User B.
3. Process A's requests; write paper record.
4. Process B's requests; write pencil record.
5. Put A in wait state for pencils.
6. Put B in wait state for paper.
        ** Locked **

In this Figure, Users A and B are locked in a condition known as **deadlock**, sometimes called the **deadly embrace**. Each is waiting for a resource that the other person has locked. Two common ways of solving this problem are preventing the deadlock from occurring or allowing the deadlock to occur and then breaking it.

Deadlock can be prevented in several ways. One way is to allow users to issue only one lock request at a time; in essence, users must lock all the resources they want at once. If User A in the illustration had locked both the paper and the pencil records at the beginning, the deadlock would not have occurred. A second way to prevent deadlock is to require all application programs to lock resources in the same order.

Almost every DBMS has algorithms for detecting deadlock. When deadlock occurs, the normal solution is to roll back one of the transactions to remove its changes from the database.

## Optimistic Versus Pessimistic Locking

Locks can be invoked in two basic styles. With **optimistic locking**, the assumption is made that no conflict will occur. Data are read, the transaction is processed, updates are issued, and then a check is made to see if conflict occurred. If not, the transaction is finished. If so, the transaction is repeated until it processes with no conflict. With **pessimistic locking**, the assumption is made that conflict will occur. First locks are issued, then the transaction is processed, and then the locks are freed.

Figure 6-10 and 6-11 show examples of both styles of locking for a transaction that is reducing the quantity of the pencil row in the PRODUCT table by five. Figure 6-10 shows optimistic locking. First, the data are read and the current value of Quantity of pencils is saved in the variable OldQuantity. The transaction is then processed, and assuming that all is okay, a lock is obtained on PRODUCT. The lock might be only for the pencil row, or it might be at a larger level of granularity. In any case, a SQL statement is issued to update the pencil row with a WHERE condition that the current value of Quantity equals OldQuantity. If no other transaction has changed the Quantity of the

**FIGURE 6-10**

**Example of Optimistic Locking**

```
SELECT    PRODUCT.Name, PRODUCT.Quantity
FROM      PRODUCT
WHERE     PRODUCT.Name = 'Pencil'

OldQuantity = PRODUCT.Quantity

Set NewQuantity = PRODUCT.Quantity – 5

{process transaction – take exception action if NewQuantity < 0, etc.

Assuming all is OK: }

LOCK PRODUCT {at some level of granularity}

UPDATE    PRODUCT
SET       PRODUCT.Quantity = NewQuantity
WHERE     PRODUCT.Name = 'Pencil'
     AND  PRODUCT.Quantity = OldQuantity

UNLOCK    PRODUCT

{check to see if update was successful;
if not, repeat transaction}
```

**FIGURE 6-11**

**Example of Pessimistic Locking**

```
LOCK        PRODUCT {at some level of granularity}

SELECT      PRODUCT.Name, PRODUCT.Quantity
FROM        PRODUCT
WHERE       PRODUCT.Name = 'Pencil'

Set NewQuantity = PRODUCT.Quantity – 5

{process transaction – take exception action if NewQuantity < 0, etc.

Assuming all is OK: }

UPDATE      PRODUCT
SET         PRODUCT.Quantity = NewQuantity
WHERE       PRODUCT.Name = 'Pencil'

UNLOCK      PRODUCT

{no need to check if update was successful}
```

pencil row, then this UPDATE will be successful. If another transaction has changed the Quantity of the pencil row, the UPDATE will fail and the transaction will need to be repeated.

Figure 6-11 shows the logic for the same transaction using pessimistic locking. In this case, a lock is obtained on PRODUCT (at some level of granularity) before any work is begun. Then, values are read, the transaction is processed, the UPDATE occurs, and PRODUCT is unlocked.

The advantage of optimistic locking is that the lock is obtained only after the transaction has processed. Thus, the lock is held for less time than with pessimistic locking. If the transaction is complicated or if the client is slow (due to transmission delays or to the user doing other work, getting a cup of coffee, or shutting down without exiting the application), the lock will be held for considerably less time. This advantage will be even more important if the lock granularity is large—for example, the entire PRODUCT table.

The disadvantage of optimistic locking is that if a lot of activity occurs on the pencil row, the transaction might have to be repeated many times. Thus, transactions that involve a lot of activity on a given row (purchasing a popular stock, for example) are poorly suited for optimistic locking.

## Declaring Lock Characteristics

Concurrency control is a complicated subject; some of the decisions about lock types and strategy have to be made on the basis of trial and error. For this and other reasons, database application programs generally do not explicitly issue locks. Instead, the programs mark transaction boundaries and then declare the type of locking behavior they want the DBMS to use. In this way, if the locking behavior needs to be changed, the application need not be rewritten to place locks in different locations in the transaction. Instead, the lock declaration is changed.

Figure 6-12 shows the pencil transaction with transaction boundaries marked with BEGIN TRANSACTION, COMMIT TRANSACTION, and ROLLBACK TRANSACTION statements. These boundaries provide the essential information that the DBMS needs in order to enforce different locking strategies. If the developer later declares (via a system parameter or similar means) a desire for optimistic locking, the DBMS will implicitly set the locks in the correct place for that locking style. If the developer changes tactics

```
BEGIN TRANSACTION:

SELECT      PRODUCT.Name, PRODUCT.Quantity
FROM        PRODUCT
WHERE       PRODUCT.Name = 'Pencil'

Old Quantity = PRODUCT.Quantity

Set NewQuantity = PRODUCT.Quantity – 5

{process part of transaction – take exception action if NewQuantity < 0, etc.}

UPDATE      PRODUCT
SET         PRODUCT.Quantity = NewQuantity
WHERE       PRODUCT.Name = 'Pencil'

{continue processing transaction} . . .



IF transaction has completed normally      THEN

        COMMIT TRANSACTION

ELSE

        ROLLBACK TRANSACTION

END IF

Continue processing other actions not part of this transaction . . .
```

again and requests pessimistic locking, then the DBMS will implicitly set the locks in a different place.

## Consistent Transactions

Sometimes the acronym **ACID** is applied to transactions. An **ACID transaction** is one that is *atomic, consistent, isolated,* and *durable.* Atomic and durable are easy to define. An **atomic** transaction is one in which all of the database actions occur or none of them do. A **durable** transaction is one in which all committed changes are permanent. The DBMS will not remove such changes, even in the case of failure. If the transaction is durable, the DBMS will provide facilities to recover the changes of all committed actions when necessary.

The terms *consistent* and *isolated* are not as definitive as the terms *atomic* and *durable.* Consider the following SQL update command.

UPDATE   CUSTOMER

SET       AreaCode = '425'

WHERE    ZipCode = '98050';

Suppose the CUSTOMER table has 500,000 rows, and 500 of them have a ZipCode value equal to 98050. It will take some time for the DBMS to find all 500 rows. During that time, will other transactions be allowed to update the AreaCode or ZipCode fields of CUSTOMER? If the SQL statement is **consistent**, such updates will be disallowed. The update will apply to the set of rows as they existed at the time the SQL statement started. Such consistency is called **statement level consistency**.

Now consider a transaction that contains two SQL update statements.

BEGIN TRANSACTION

UPDATE CUSTOMER

SET AreaCode = '425'

WHERE ZipCode = '98050';

...

{other transaction work}

...

UPDATE CUSTOMER

SET Discount = 0.05

WHERE AreaCode = '425';

...

{other transaction work}

...

COMMIT TRANSACTION

In this context, what does consistent mean? Statement level consistency means that each statement independently processes consistent rows, but changes from other users to these rows might be allowed during the interval between the two SQL statements. **Transaction level consistency** means that all rows impacted by either of the SQL statements are protected from changes during the entire transaction.

However, observe that for some implementations of transaction level consistency, a transaction will not see its own changes. In this example, the second SQL statement might not see rows changed by the first SQL statement.

Thus, when you hear the term *consistent*, look further to determine which type of consistency is intended. Be aware as well of the potential trap of transaction-level consistency. The situation is even more complicated for the term *isolated*, which we will consider next.

## Transaction Isolation Level

The 1992 ANSI SQL standard defines four isolation levels that specify which of the concurrency control problems are allowed to occur. These isolation levels are shown in Figure 6-13.

---

**FIGURE 6-13**

**Summary of Isolation Levels**

| Problem Type | | Isolation Level | | | |
|---|---|---|---|---|---|
| | | Read Uncommitted | Read Committed | Repeatable Read | Serializable |
| Problem Type | Dirty Read | Possible | Not Possible | Not Possible | Not Possible |
| | Nonrepeatable Read | Possible | Possible | Not Possible | Not Possible |
| | Phantom Read | Possible | Possible | Possible | Not Possible |

The goal of having four isolation levels is to allow the application programmer to declare the type of isolation level desired and then to have the DBMS manage locks to achieve that level of isolation. As shown in Figure 6-13, **read uncommitted isolation** allows dirty reads, nonrepeatable reads, and phantom reads to occur. With **read committed isolation**, dirty reads are disallowed. The **repeatable reads isolation** level disallows both dirty reads and nonrepeatable reads. The **serializable isolation level** will not allow any of these three.

Generally, the more restrictive the level is, the less throughput occurs, though much depends on the workload and how the application programs were written. Moreover, not all DBMS products support all these levels. Products also vary in the manner in which they are supported and in the burden they place on the application programmer.

# ▶ CURSOR TYPES

A cursor is a pointer into a set of rows that are the result set from an SQL SELECT statement, and cursors are usually defined using SELECT statements. For example, the following statement defines a cursor named TransCursor that operates over the set of rows indicated by this SELECT statement:

DECLARE CURSOR TransCursor AS

     SELECT    *

     FROM     [TRANSACTION]

     WHERE    PurchasePrice > '10000';

After an application program opens a cursor, it can place the cursor somewhere in the result set. Most commonly, the cursor is placed on the first or last row, but other possibilities exist.

A transaction can open several cursors—either sequentially or simultaneously. Additionally, two or more cursors may be open on the same table; either directly on the table or through a SQL view on that table. Because cursors require considerable memory, having many cursors open at the same time (for example, for a thousand concurrent transactions) will consume considerable memory. One way to reduce cursor burden is to define reduced-capability cursors and use them when a full capability cursor is not needed.

Figure 6-14 lists four cursor types used in the Windows environment (cursor types for other systems are similar). The simplest cursor is the **forward only cursor**. With it, the application can only move forward through the records. Changes made by other cursors in this transaction and by other transactions will be visible only if they occur to rows ahead of the cursor.

The next three types of cursors are called **scrollable cursors** because the application can scroll forward and backward through the records. A **static cursor** takes a snapshot of a relation and processes that snapshot. Changes made using this cursor are visible; changes from other sources are not visible.

A **dynamic cursor** is a fully featured cursor. All inserts, updates, deletions, and changes in row order are visible to a dynamic cursor. Unless the isolation level of the transaction is a dirty read, only committed changes are visible.

**Keyset cursors** combine some features of static cursors with some features of dynamic cursors. When the cursor is opened, a primary key value is saved for each row. When the application positions the cursor on a row, the DBMS uses the key value to read the current value of the row. Inserts of new rows by other cursors (in this transaction or in other transactions) are not visible. If the application issues an update on a row that has been deleted by a different cursor, the DBMS creates a new

**FIGURE 6-14**

Summary of Cursor
Types

| CursorType | Description | Comments |
|---|---|---|
| Forward only | Application can only move forward through the recordset. | Changes made by other cursors in this transaction or in other transactions will be visible only if they occur on rows ahead of the cursor. |
| Static | Application sees the data as they were at the time the cursor was opened. | Changes made by this cursor are visible. Changes from other sources are not visible. Backward and forward scrolling allowed. |
| Keyset | When the cursor is opened, a primary key value is saved for each row in the recordset. When the application accesses a row, the key is used to fetch the current values for the row. | Updates from any source are visible. Inserts from sources outside this cursor are not visible (there is no key for them in the keyset). Inserts from this cursor appear at the bottom of the recordset. Deletions from any source are visible. Changes in row order are not visible. If the isolation level is dirty read, then committed updates and deletions are visible; otherwise only committed updates and deletions are visible. |
| Dynamic | Changes of any type and from any source are visible. | All inserts, updates, deletions, and changes in recordset order are visible. If the isolation level is dirty read, then uncommitted changes are visible. Otherwise, only committed changes are visible. |

row with the old key value and places the updated values in the new row (assuming that all required fields are present). As with dynamic cursors, unless the isolation level of the transaction is a dirty read, only committed updates and deletions are visible to the cursor.

The amount of overhead and processing required to support a cursor is different for each type. In general, the cost goes up as we move down the cursor types shown in Figure 6-14. In order to improve DBMS performance, therefore, the application developer should create cursors that are just powerful enough to do the job. It is also very important to understand how a particular DBMS implements cursors and whether cursors are located on the server or on the client. In some cases, it might be better to place a dynamic cursor on the client than to have a static cursor on the server. No general rule can be stated because performance depends on the implementation used by the DBMS product and the application requirements.

A word of caution: If you do *not* specify the isolation level of a transaction or do not specify the type of cursors you open, the DBMS will use a default level and types. These defaults may be perfect for your application, but they also may be terrible. Thus, even though these issues can be ignored, the consequences of them cannot be avoided. You must learn the capabilities of your DBMS product.

## ▶ DATABASE SECURITY

The goal of database security is to ensure that only authorized users can perform authorized activities at authorized times. This goal is usually broken into two parts: authentication, which makes sure the user has the basic right to use the system in the first place, and authorization, which assigns the authenticated user specific rights or permissions to do specific activities on the system. As shown in Figure 6-15, user authentication is achieved by requiring the user to log in to the system with a password (or other means of positive identification, such as a biometric scan of a finger print) while user authorization is achieved by granting DBMS specific permissions.

Note that authentication (user logs in to the system) by itself is not sufficient for use of the database—unless the user has been granted permissions, he or she cannot access the database or take any actions that use it.

The goal of database security is difficult to achieve, and to make any progress at all, the database development team must determine (1) which users should be able to use the database (authentication), and (2) the processing rights and responsibilities of each user. These security requirements can then be enforced using the security features of the DBMS, as well as the additions to those features written into the application programs.

### User Accounts

Consider, for example, the database security needs of Heather Sweeney Designs. There must be some means of controlling which employees can have access to the database. This is accomplished by creating user accounts for each of these employees. Figure 6-16 shows the creation of the user login HSD-User at the DBMS security level in SQL Server 2005.

This step creates the initial user account in the DBMS—*not* a specific database. The password being assigned is "HSD-User+password," which we will also need for the HSD Web pages in Chapter 7. Note that in the Windows environment, there are two choices for controlling authentication: We can use the Windows operating system to control authentication, or we can create an SQL Server internal user account with its own login name and password. For other DBMS products that are not as operating-system specific as SQL Server, only the second option of internal user accounts can be used.

User accounts and passwords should be managed carefully. The exact terminology, features, and functions of DBMS account and password security depend on the DBMS product used.

### User Processing Rights and Responsibilities

All major DBMS products provide security tools that limit certain actions on certain objects to certain users. A general model of DBMS security is shown in Figure 6-17.

According to Figure 6-17, a user can be assigned to one or more roles (groups), and a role can have one or more users. Users, roles, and objects (used in a generic sense) have

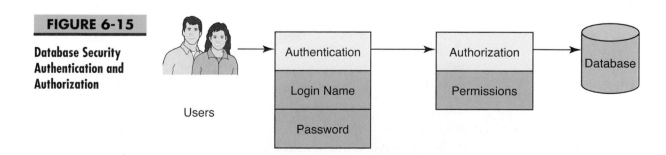

**FIGURE 6-15**

**Database Security Authentication and Authorization**

Users → Authentication [Login Name, Password] → Authorization [Permissions] → Database

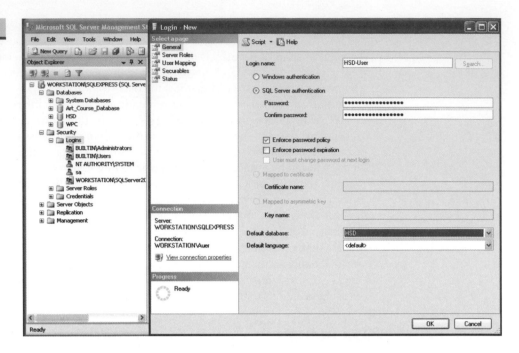

many permissions. Each permission is assigned to one user or role and one object. Once a user is authenticated by the DBMS, the DBMS limits the person's actions to the defined permissions for that user and to the permissions for roles to which that user has been assigned.

Now, let's consider user authorization at Heather Sweeney Designs. The company has three types of users: administrative assistants, management (Heather and others), and a systems administrator (Heather's consultant). Figure 6-18 summarizes the processing rights that Heather determined were appropriate for her business.

Administrative assistants can read, insert, and change data in all tables. However, they can delete data only from SEMINAR_CUSTOMER and LINE_ITEM. This means that administrative assistants can disenroll customers from seminars and can remove items from an order. Management can take all actions on all tables except delete CUSTOMER data. Heather believes that for as hard as she works to get a customer, she does not want to ever run the risk that she could accidentally delete one.

Finally, the system administrator can modify the database structure and grant rights (assign permissions) to other users but can take no action on data. The system administrator is not a user and so should not be allowed access to user data. This limitation might

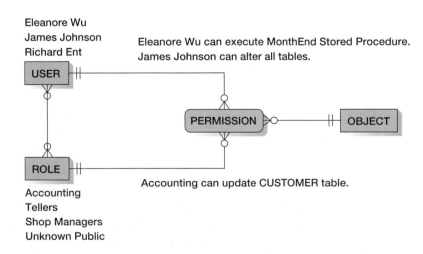

Eleanore Wu
James Johnson
Richard Ent

Eleanore Wu can execute MonthEnd Stored Procedure.
James Johnson can alter all tables.

USER

PERMISSION — OBJECT

ROLE

Accounting can update CUSTOMER table.

Accounting
Tellers
Shop Managers
Unknown Public

**FIGURE 6-18**

**Processing Rights at Heather Sweeney Designs**

| | DATABASE RIGHTS GRANTED | | |
|---|---|---|---|
| Table | Administrative Assistants | Management | System Administrator |
| SEMINAR | Read, Insert, Change | Read, Insert, Change, Delete | Grant Rights, Modify Structure |
| CUSTOMER | Read, Insert, Change | Read, Insert, Change, Delete | Grant Rights, Modify Structure |
| SEMINAR_CUSTOMER | Read, Insert, Change, Delete | Read, Insert, Change, Delete | Grant Rights, Modify Structure |
| CONTACT | Read, Insert, Change | Read, Insert, Change, Delete | Grant Rights, Modify Structure |
| INVOICE | Read, Insert, Change | Read, Insert, Change, Delete | Grant Rights, Modify Structure |
| LINE_ITEM | Read, Insert, Change, Delete | Read, Insert, Change, Delete | Grant Rights, Modify Structure |
| PRODUCT | Read, Insert, Change | Read, Insert, Change, Delete | Grant Rights, Modify Structure |

seem weak. After all, if the system administrator can assign permissions, he or she can get around the security system by changing the permissions to take whatever action is desired, make the data changes, and then change the permissions back. This is true, but it would leave an audit trail in the DBMS logs. That coupled with the need to make the security system changes will dissuade the administrator from unauthorized activity. It is certainly better than allowing the administrator to have user data access permissions with no effort.

A very important principle of database security administration (and of network administration) is that the types of permissions shown in this table are given to user *groups* (also known as user *roles*) and *not* to individual users unless absolutely necessary. There may be some cases where specific users need to be assigned permissions within the database, but we will avoid this whenever possible. Note that since groups or roles are used, it is necessary to have a means for assigning users to groups or roles. When Heather Sweeney signs onto the computer, some means must be available to determine which group or groups she belongs to.

Now, we will make role and permission assignments in the HSD database. HSD-User is one of Heather's administrative assistants and, therefore, needs the ability to read, insert, and change data in all tables. First, we need to grant HSD-User permission to use the HSD database within the DBMS. Figure 6-19 shows the creation of the *database level user* named *HSD Database User* at the HSD database security level in SQL Server 2005. Note that this user is being created specifically for the HSD database but is based on the already created DBMS login name. Also note that in SQL Server 2005, no password is assigned at the database security level, only at the DBMS security level.

Figure 6-20 shows the fixed database roles in SQL Server 2005 and their associated permissions. Since HSD Database User needs the ability to read, insert, and change data in all tables in the HSD database, we will assign HSD Database User to the roles of *db_datareader* and *db_datawriter*. Figure 6-21 shows HSD Database User being added to the db_datawriter role.

We will cover this further in the next section.

In this discussion, we have used the phrase *processing rights and responsibilities*. As this phrase implies, responsibilities go with processing rights. If, for example, the systems administrator deletes CUSTOMER data, it is that person's responsibility to ensure that these deletions do not adversely impact the company's operation, accounting, and so forth.

**FIGURE 6-19**

**Creating the Database User Name**

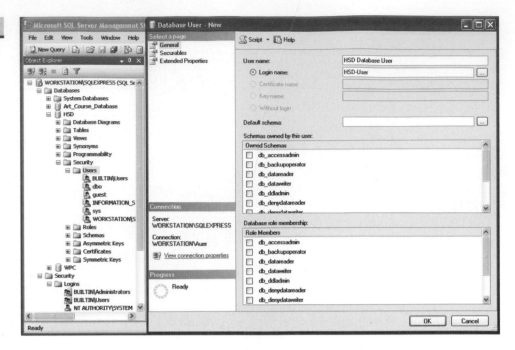

## FIGURE 6-20

### SQL Server 2005 Fixed Database Roles

| Fixed Database Role | Database Specific Permissions | DBMS Server Permissions |
|---|---|---|
| db_accessadmin | Permissions granted:<br>ALTER ANY USER, CREATE SCHEMA<br>Permissions granted with GRANT option:<br>CONNECT | Permissions granted:<br>VIEW ANY DATABASE |
| db_backupoperator | Permissions granted:<br>BACKUP DATABASE, BACKUP LOG,<br>CHECKPOINT | Permissions granted:<br>VIEW ANY DATABASE |
| db_datareader | Permissions granted:<br>SELECT | Permissions granted:<br>VIEW ANY DATABASE |
| db_datawriter | Permissions granted:<br>DELETE, INSERT, UPDATE | Permissions granted:<br>VIEW ANY DATABASE |
| db_ddladmin | Permissions granted:<br>*See SQL Server 2005 documentation* | Permissions granted:<br>VIEW ANY DATABASE |
| db_denydatareader | Permissions denied:<br>SELECT | Permissions granted:<br>VIEW ANY DATABASE |
| db_denydatawriter | Permissions *denied:*<br>DELETE, INSERT, UPDATE | Permissions granted:<br>VIEW ANY DATABASE |
| db_owner | Permissions granted with GRANT option:<br>CONTROL | Permissions granted:<br>VIEW ANY DATABASE |
| db_securityadmin | Permissions granted:<br>ALTER ANY APPLICATION ROLE, ALTER ANY<br>ROLE, CREATE SCHEMA, VIEW DEFINITION | Permissions granted:<br>VIEW ANY DATABASE |

Note: For the definitions of each of the SQL Server 2005 permissions shown in the table, consult the SQL Server 2005 documentation.

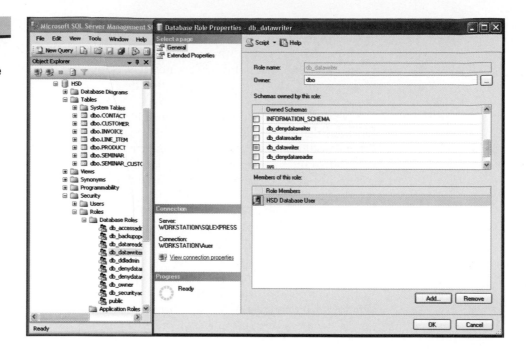

**FIGURE 6-21**

Assigning HSD
Database User to the
*db_datawriter* Role

Processing responsibilities cannot be enforced by the DBMS or the database applications. Responsibilities are, instead, encoded in manual procedures and explained to users during systems training. These are topics of a systems development book, and we will not consider them further here except to reiterate that responsibilities go with rights. Such responsibilities must be documented and enforced.

The DBA has the task of managing processing rights and responsibilities. As this implies, these rights and responsibilities will change over time. As the database is used and as changes are made to the applications and to the DBMS's structure, the need for new or different rights and responsibilities will arise. The DBA is a focal point for the discussion of such changes and for their implementation.

After processing rights have been defined, they can be implemented at many levels: operating system, network directory service, Web server, DBMS, and application. The next two sections will consider the DBMS and application aspects. The others are beyond the scope of this book.

## DBMS Level Security

Security guidelines for the DBMS are shown in Figure 6-22. First, the DBMS should be run behind a firewall. In most cases, no communication with the DBMS or database applications should be allowed to be initiated from outside the organization's network. However, if the DBMS supports e-commerce applications, then this rule cannot be followed. In this case though, the DBMS should support only the e-commerce applications. All other database applications should be managed by a different DBMS on a different machine behind a firewall.

**FIGURE 6-22**

DBMS Security
Guidelines

- Run the DBMS behind a firewall
- Apply the latest operating system and DBMS service packs and fixes
- Limit DBMS functionality to needed features
- Protect the computer that runs the DBMS
- Manage accounts and passwords

Second, service packs and fixes for the operating system and the DBMS must be applied as soon as possible. In the spring of 2003, the slammer worm exploited a security hole in SQL Server, bringing major organizational database applications to their knees. Microsoft had published a patch that eliminated the hole prior to the release of the slammer worm, so any organization that applied that patch was not affected by the worm.

A third protection is to limit the capabilities of the DBMS to only those features and functions that the applications need. For example, Oracle can support many different communications protocols. To improve security, any Oracle-supported protocol that is not used should be removed or disabled. Similarly, every DBMS ships with hundreds of system-stored procedures. Any procedure that is not used should be removed from operational databases.

Another important security measure is to protect the computer that runs the DBMS. No users should be allowed to work on the DBMS computer, and that computer should reside in a separate facility behind locked doors. Visits to the room housing the DBMS should be logged with date and time.

A user can enter a name and password, or in some applications, the name and password is entered on behalf of the user. For example, as we saw in Figure 6-16, the Windows XP operating system user name and password can be passed directly to SQL Server. In other cases, an application program provides the user name and password.

Internet applications usually define a group, such as Unknown Public, and assign anonymous users to that group when they sign on. In this way, companies that conduct e-commerce with unknown customers do not need to enter every such customer into their security system by name and password.

The security systems used by SQL Server, MySQL, Oracle, and DB2 are variations on the model shown in Figure 6-17. The terminology used might vary from this, but the essence of their security systems is the same.

## Application Level Security

Although DBMS products, such as SQL Server, MySQL, Oracle, and DB2, do provide substantial database security capabilities, they are generic by their very nature. If the application requires specific security measures, such as disallowing users to view a row of a table or of a join of a table that has an employee name other than the user's own, the DBMS facilities will not be adequate. In these cases, the security system must be augmented by features in database applications.

For example, application security in Internet applications often is provided on the Web server computer. Executing application security on this server means that sensitive security data does not need to be transmitted over the network.

To understand this better, suppose an application is written such that when users click a particular button on a browser page, the following query is sent to the Web server and then to the DBMS.

```
SELECT    *
FROM      EMPLOYEE;
```

This statement will return all EMPLOYEE rows. If the application security allows employees to access only their own data, then a Web server could add the following WHERE clause to this query.

```
SELECT    *
FROM      EMPLOYEE
WHERE     EMPLOYEE.Name = '<%SESSION("EmployeeName")%>';
```

As you will learn when you study Internet applications technology, an expression like this will cause the Web server to fill in the employee's name for the WHERE clause. For a user signed on under the name Benjamin Franklin, the following statement results from this expression.

SELECT    *

FROM      EMPLOYEE

WHERE     EMPLOYEE.Name = 'Benjamin Franklin';

Because the name is inserted by a program on the Web server, the browser user does not know it is occurring and cannot interfere with it. Such security processing can be done as shown here on a Web server, but it also can be done within the application programs themselves, or written as code stored within the DBMS to be executed by the DBMS at the appropriate times.

This idea can be extended by storing additional data in a security database that is accessed by the Web server and also by stored DBMS code. That security database could contain, for example, the identities of users paired with additional values of WHERE clauses. For example, suppose the users in the personnel department can access more than just their own data. The predicates for appropriate WHERE clauses could be stored in the security database, read by the application program, and appended to SQL SELECT statements as necessary.

Many other possibilities exist for extending DBMS security with application processing. In general, you should use the DBMS security features first. Only if they are inadequate for the requirements should you add to them with application code. The closer the security enforcement is to the data, the less chance there is for infiltration. Also, using the DBMS security features is faster, cheaper, and probably produces higher-quality results than if you develop your own.

## ▶ DATABASE BACKUP AND RECOVERY

Computer systems fail. Hardware breaks. Programs have bugs. Procedures written by humans contain errors, and people make mistakes. All these failures can and do occur in database applications. Because a database is shared by many people, and because it often is a key element of an organization's operations, it is important to recover it as soon as possible.

Several problems must be addressed. First, from a business standpoint, business functions must continue. For example, customer orders, financial transactions, and packing lists must be completed manually. Later, when the database application is operational again, the new data can be entered. Second, computer operations personnel must restore the system to a usable state as quickly as possible and as close as possible to what it was when the system crashed. Third, users must know what to do when the system becomes available again. Some work might need to be reentered, and users must know how far back they need to go.

When failures occur, it is impossible simply to fix the problem and resume processing. Even if no data are lost during a failure (which assumes that all types of memory are nonvolatile—an unrealistic assumption), the timing and scheduling of computer processing are too complex to be accurately recreated. Enormous amounts of overhead data and processing would be required for the operating system to be able to restart processing precisely where it was interrupted. It is simply not possible to roll back the clock and put all the electrons in the same configuration they were in at the time of the failure. However, two other approaches are possible: **recovery via reprocessing** and **recovery via rollback/rollforward**.

## Recovery via Reprocessing

Because processing cannot be resumed at a precise point, the next-best alternative is to go back to a known point and reprocess the workload from there. The simplest form of this type of recovery involves periodically making a copy of the database (called a database save) and keeping a record of all transactions that were processed since the save. Then, when failure occurs, the operations staff can restore the database from the save and reprocess all the transactions.

Unfortunately, this simple strategy normally is not feasible. First, reprocessing transactions takes the same amount of time as processing them did in the first place. If the computer is heavily scheduled, the system might never catch up. Second, when transactions are processed concurrently, events are asynchronous. Slight variations in human activity, such as a user reading an email message before responding to an application prompt, could change the order of the execution of concurrent transactions. Therefore, whereas Customer A got the last seat on a flight during the original processing, Customer B might get the last seat during reprocessing. For these reasons, reprocessing is normally not a viable form of recovery from failure in multi-user systems.

## Recovery via Rollback and Rollforward

A second approach involves periodically making a copy of the database (the database save) and keeping a log of the changes made by transactions against the database since the save. Then, when a failure occurs, one of two methods can be used. In the first method, called **rollforward**, the database is restored using the saved data, and all valid transactions since the save are reapplied. Note that we are not reprocessing the transactions, as the application programs are not involved in the rollforward. Instead, the processed changes, as recorded in the log, are reapplied.

The second method is called **rollback**, in which we correct mistakes caused by erroneous or partially processed transactions by undoing the changes they made in the database. Then, the valid transactions that were in process at the time of the failure are restarted.

As stated, both of these methods require that a **log** of the transaction results be kept. This log contains records of the data changes in chronological order. Note that transactions must be written to the log before they are applied to the database. That way, if the system crashes between the time a transaction is logged and the time it is applied, then at worst there is a record of an unapplied transaction. If transactions were applied before being logged, it would be possible (and undesirable) to change the database without having a record of the change. If this happens, an unwary user might reenter an already-completed transaction.

In the event of a failure, the log is used to undo and redo transactions, as shown in Figure 6-23. To undo a transaction, shown in Figure 6-23(a), the log must contain a copy of every database record before it was changed. Such records are called **before-images**. A transaction is undone by applying before-images of all its changes to the database.

To redo a transaction, shown in Figure 6-23(b), the log must contain a copy of every database record (or page) after it was changed. These records are called **after-images**. A transaction is redone by applying after-images of all its changes to the database. Possible data items of a transaction log are shown in Figure 6-24.

For this example log, each transaction has a unique name for identification purposes. Furthermore, all images for a given transaction are linked together with pointers. One pointer points to the previous change made by this transaction (the reverse pointer), and the other points to the next change made by this transaction (the forward pointer). A zero in the pointer field means that this is the end of the list. The DBMS recovery subsystem uses these pointers to locate all records for a particular transaction. Figure 6-24 shows an example of the linking of log records.

**FIGURE 6-23**

**Undo and Redo Transactions**

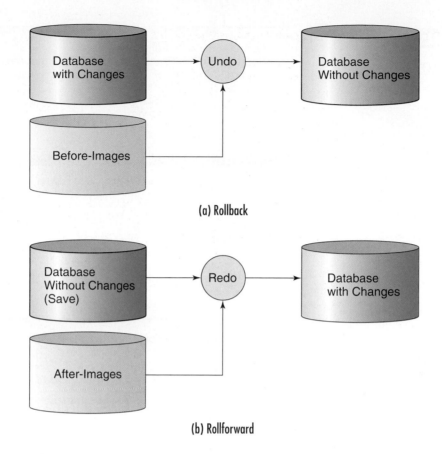

(a) Rollback

(b) Rollforward

Other data items in the log are: (1) the time of the action, (2) the type of operation, (3) the object acted upon (such as record type and identifier), and (4) the before-images and after-images. Note that *START* marks the beginning of a transaction and *COMMIT* terminates a transaction which release all locks that were in place.

Given a log with before-images and after-images, the undo and redo actions are straightforward. Figure 6-25 shows how recovery for a system crash is accomplished.

**FIGURE 6-24**

**Example Transaction Log**

| Relative Record Number | Transaction ID | Reverse Pointer | Forward Pointer | Time | Type of Operation | Object | Before-Image | After-Image |
|---|---|---|---|---|---|---|---|---|
| 1 | OT1 | 0 | 2 | 11:42 | START | | | |
| 2 | OT1 | 1 | 4 | 11:43 | MODIFY | CUST 100 | (old value) | (new value) |
| 3 | OT2 | 0 | 8 | 11:46 | START | | | |
| 4 | OT1 | 2 | 5 | 11:47 | MODIFY | SP AA | (old value) | (new value) |
| 5 | OT1 | 4 | 7 | 11:47 | INSERT | ORDER 11 | | (value) |
| 6 | CT1 | 0 | 9 | 11:48 | START | | | |
| 7 | OT1 | 5 | 0 | 11:49 | COMMIT | | | |
| 8 | OT2 | 3 | 0 | 11:50 | COMMIT | | | |
| 9 | CT1 | 6 | 10 | 11:51 | MODIFY | SP BB | (old value) | (new value) |
| 10 | CT1 | 9 | 0 | 11:51 | COMMIT | | | |

**FIGURE 6-25**

**Recovery Example**

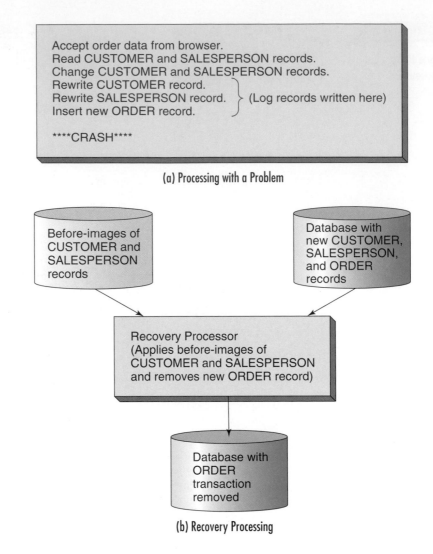

Accept order data from browser.
Read CUSTOMER and SALESPERSON records.
Change CUSTOMER and SALESPERSON records.
Rewrite CUSTOMER record.
Rewrite SALESPERSON record.  } (Log records written here)
Insert new ORDER record.

****CRASH****

(a) Processing with a Problem

Before-images of CUSTOMER and SALESPERSON records

Database with new CUSTOMER, SALESPERSON, and ORDER records

Recovery Processor (Applies before-images of CUSTOMER and SALESPERSON and removes new ORDER record)

Database with ORDER transaction removed

(b) Recovery Processing

To undo the transaction in Figure 6-25(a), the recovery processor simply replaces each changed record with its before-image as shown in Figure 6-25(b). When all before-images have been restored, the transaction is undone. To redo a transaction, the recovery processor starts with the version of the database at the time the transaction started and applies all after-images. This action assumes that an earlier version of the database is available from a database save.

Restoring a database to its most recent save and reapplying all transactions might require considerable processing. To reduce the delay, DBMS products sometimes use checkpoints. A **checkpoint** is a point of synchronization between the database and the transaction log. To perform a checkpoint, the DBMS refuses new requests, finishes processing outstanding requests, and writes its buffers to disk. The DBMS then waits until the operating system notifies it that all outstanding write requests to the database and to the log have been completed successfully. At this point, the log and the database are synchronized. A checkpoint record is then written to the log. Later, the database can be recovered from the checkpoint, and only after-images for transactions that started after the checkpoint need to be applied.

Checkpoints are inexpensive operations, and it is feasible to make three or four (or more) per hour. In this way, no more than 15 or 20 minutes of processing needs to be recovered. Most DBMS products perform automatic checkpoints, making human intervention unnecessary.

You will need to learn more about backup and recovery if you work in database administration using products such as SQL Server, MySQL, Oracle, or DB2. For now, you just need to understand the basic ideas and to realize that it is the responsibility of the DBA to ensure that adequate backup and recovery plans have been developed, and that database saves and logs are generated as required.

### Additional DBA Responsibilities

Concurrency control, security, and reliability are the three major concerns of database administration. However, other administrative and managerial DBA functions are also important.

For one, the DBA needs to ensure that a system exists to gather and record user-reported errors and other problems. A means needs to be devised to prioritize those errors and problems and to ensure that they are corrected accordingly. In this regard, the DBA works with the development team not only to resolve these problems but also to evaluate features and functions of new releases of the DBMS.

As the database is used and as new requirements develop and are implemented, requests for changes to the structure of the database will occur. Changes to an operational database need to be made with great care and thoughtful planning. Because databases are shared resources, a change to the structure of a database to implement features desired by one user or group can be detrimental to the needs of other users or groups.

Therefore, the DBA needs to create and manage a process for controlling the database configuration. Such a process includes procedures for recording change requests, conducting user and developer reviews of such requests, and creating projects and tasks for implementing changes that are approved. All these activities need to be conducted with a community-wide view.

Finally, the DBA is responsible for ensuring that appropriate documentation is maintained about database structure, concurrency control, security, backup and recovery, applications use, and a myriad of other details that concern the management and use of the database. Some vendors provide tools for recording such documentation. At a minimum, the DBMS will have its own metadata that it uses to process the database. Some products augment these metadata with facilities for storing and reporting application metadata, as well as operational procedures.

The DBA has significant responsibilities in the management and administration of a database. These responsibilities vary with the database type and size, the number of users, and the complexity of applications. However, the responsibilities are important for all databases. You should know about the need for DBA services and consider the material in this chapter even for the smallest, most personal database.

To finish this chapter, we'll take a look at two advanced types of databases—distributed databases and object-relational databases.

## ▶ DISTRIBUTED DATABASE PROCESSING

A **distributed database** is a database that is stored and processed on more than one computer. Depending on the type of database and the processing that is allowed, distributed databases can present significant problems. Let's consider the types of distributed databases.

### Types of Distributed Databases

A database can be distributed by **partitioning**, which means to break the database into pieces and to store the pieces on multiple computers; by **replication**, which means to

**FIGURE 6-26**

**Types of Distributed Databases**

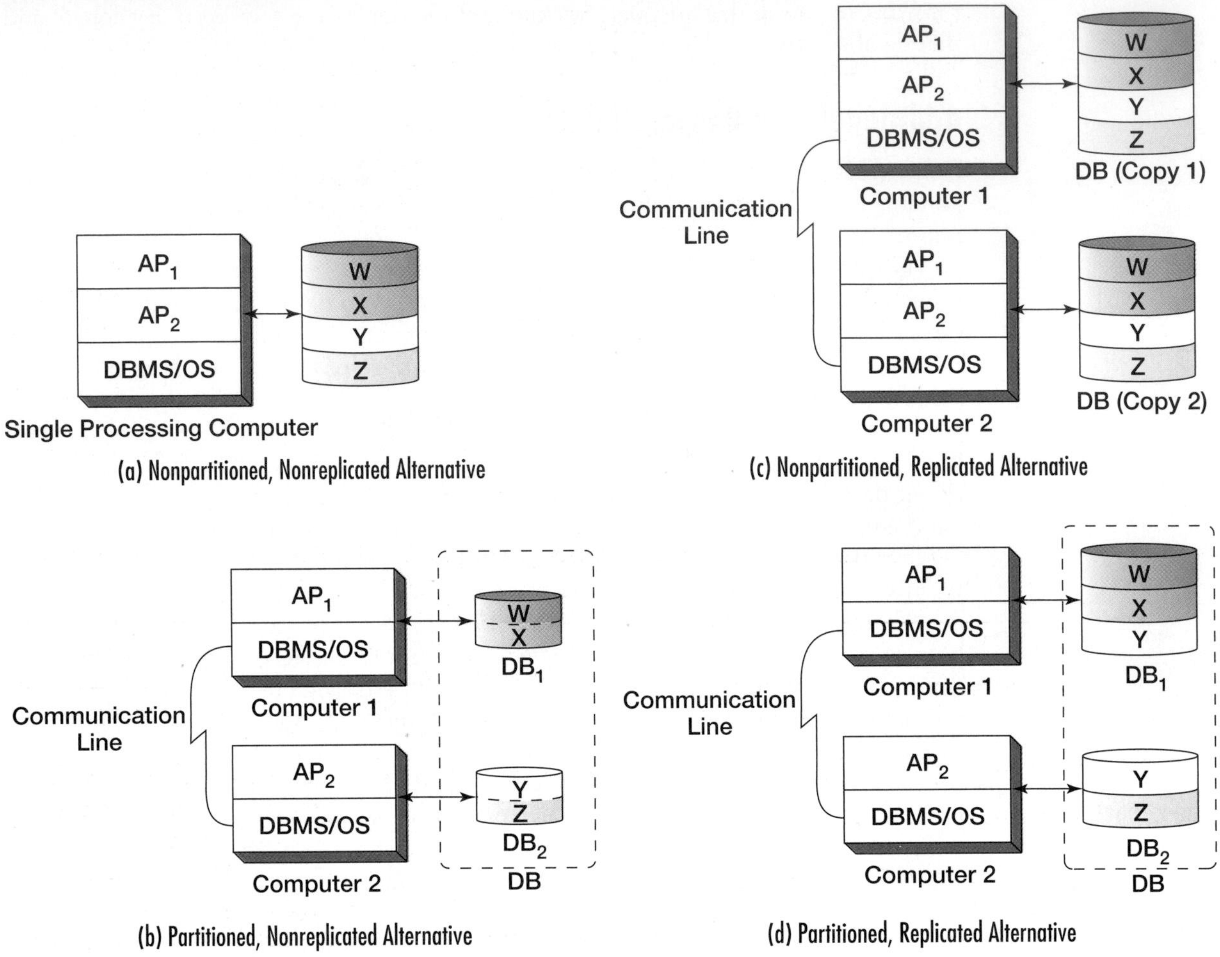

(a) Nonpartitioned, Nonreplicated Alternative

(b) Partitioned, Nonreplicated Alternative

(c) Nonpartitioned, Replicated Alternative

(d) Partitioned, Replicated Alternative

store the copies of the database on multiple computers; or by both replication and partitioning combined.

Figure 6-26 illustrates these alternatives. Figure 6-26(a) shows a nondistributed database with four pieces labeled W, X, Y, and Z. In Figure 6-26(b), the database has been partitioned but not replicated. Portions W and X are stored and processed on Computer 1, and portions Y and Z are stored and processed on Computer 2. Figure 6-26(c) shows a database that has been replicated but not partitioned. The entire database is stored and processed on Computers 1 and 2. Finally, Figure 6-26(d) shows a database that is partitioned and replicated. Portion Y of the database is stored and processed on Computers 1 and 2.

The portions to be partitioned or replicated can be defined in many different ways. A database that has five tables (for example, CUSTOMER, SALESPERSON, INVOICE, LINE_ITEM, and PART) could be partitioned by assigning CUSTOMER to portion W, SALESPERSON to portion X, INVOICE and LINE_ITEM to portion Y, and PART to portion Z. Alternatively, different rows of each of these five tables could be assigned to different computers, or different columns of each of these tables could be assigned to different computers.

Databases are distributed for two major reasons: performance and control. Having the database on multiple computers can improve throughput, either because multiple computers are sharing the workload or because communications delays can be reduced by placing the computers closer to their users. Distributing the database can improve control by segregating different portions of the database to different computers, each of which can have its own set of authorized users and permissions.

## Challenges of Distributed Databases

Significant challenges must be overcome when distributing a database, and those challenges depend on the type of distributed database and on the activity that is allowed. In the case of a fully replicated database, if only one computer is allowed to make updates on one of the copies, then the challenges are not too great. All update activity occurs on that single computer, and copies of that database are sent periodically to the replication sites. The challenge is to ensure that only a logically consistent copy of the database is distributed (no partial or uncommitted transactions, for example), and to ensure that the sites understand that they are processing data that might not be current, because changes could have been made to the updated database after the local copy was made.

If multiple computers can make updates to a replicated database, then difficult problems arise. Specifically, if two computers are allowed to process the same row at the same time, they can cause three types of error: They can make inconsistent changes— one computer can delete a row that another computer is updating, or the two computers can make changes that violate uniqueness constraints.

To prevent these problems, some type of record locking is required. Because multiple computers are involved, standard record locking will not work. Instead, a far more complicated locking scheme, called **distributed two-phase locking**, must be used. The specifics of that scheme are beyond the scope of this discussion; however, implementing this algorithm is difficult and expensive. For now, simply be aware that if multiple computers can process multiple replications of a distributed database, then significant problems must be solved.

If the database is partitioned but not replicated [Figure 6-26(b)], then problems will occur if any transaction updates data that span two or more distributed partitions. For example, suppose the CUSTOMER and SALESERSON tables are placed on a partition on one computer and that INVOICE, LINE_ITEM, and PART tables are placed on a second computer. Further suppose that when recording a sale, all five tables are updated in an atomic transaction. In this case, a transaction must be started on both computers, and it can be allowed to commit on one computer only if it can be allowed to commit on both computers. In this case, distributed two-phase locking also must be used.

If the data are partitioned in such a way that no transaction requires data from both partitions, then regular locking will work. However, in this case, the databases are actually two separate databases, and some would argue that they should not be considered a distributed database.

If the data are partitioned in such a way that no transaction updates data from both partitions but that one or more transactions read data from one partition and update data on a second partition, then problems might or might not result with regular locking. If dirty reads are possible, then some form of distributed locking will be required; otherwise, regular locking should work.

If the database is partitioned and at least one of those partitions is replicated, then locking requirements are a combination of those just described. If the replicated portion is updated, if transactions span the partitions, or if dirty reads are possible, then distributed two-phase locking is required; otherwise, regular locking might suffice.

Distributed processing is complicated and can create substantial problems. Except for replicated, read-only databases, only experienced teams with a substantial budget and significant time to invest should attempt distributed databases. Such databases also require data communications expertise. Distributed databases are not for the faint of heart.

# OBJECT-RELATIONAL DATABASES

**Object-oriented programming (OOP)** is a technique for designing and writing computer programs. Today, most new program development is done using OOP techniques. Java, C++, C#, and VisualBasic.Net are object-oriented computer programs.

**Objects** have **methods**, which are computer programs that perform some task, and **properties**, which are data items particular to that object. All objects of a given class have the same methods, but each has its own set of data items. When using an OOP, the properties of the object are created and stored in main memory. Storing the values of properties of an object is called **object persistence**. Many different techniques have been used for object persistence. One of them is to use some variation of database technology.

Although relational databases can be used for object persistence, doing so requires substantial work on the part of the programmer. The problem is that, in general, object data structures are more complicated than the row of a table. Typically, several or even many rows of several different tables are required to store object data. This means the OOP programmer must design a minidatabase just to store objects. Many objects usually are involved in an information system so many different minidatabases need to be designed and processed. That prospect is so undesirable that it is seldom used.

In the early 1990s, several vendors developed special-purpose DBMS products for storing object data. These products, which were called **object-oriented DBMS (OODBMS)**, never achieved commercial success. The problem was that by the time they were introduced, billions of bytes of data already were stored in relational DBMS format, and no organization wanted to convert their data to OODBMS format to be able to use an OODBMS. Consequently, such products failed in the marketplace.

However, the need for object persistence did not disappear. Some vendors, most notably Oracle, added features and functions to their relational database DBMS products. These features and functions are basically add-ons to a relational DBMS that facilitate object persistence. Using them, object data can be stored more readily than with a pure relational database. However, an object-relational database still can process, at the same time, relational data.

If you wish to learn more about object-relational databases, take a look at Oracle's Web site at www.Oracle.com. Also, search for OODBMS and ODBMS on the Web.

## THE ACCESS WORKBENCH

### Section 6

### Database Administration in Microsoft Access

At this point, we have created and populated the CONTACT, CUSTOMER, SALESPERSON, and VEHICLE tables in the Wallingford Motors CRM database. We have learned how to create forms, reports, and queries in the preceding sections, and how to create and use view equivalent queries in Appendix C. We've also studied how 1:1, 1:N, and N:M relationships are created and managed in Access.

The proceeding chapter dealt with database administration topics, and in this section of "The Access Workbench" we'll look at database security in Access. In this section, we will cover the following objectives:

- Understand database security in Access
- Understand the role of the workgroup information file in Access security
- Use the Access Security Wizard to implement basic database security
- Use other Access security tools to manage database security

### Database Security in Access

Access has a built-in database security system, and although you haven't known it, you've been running within the security system all the time you've been using Access. Access stores the default security settings in a **workgroup information file** named *system.mwb*, located in the Windows system files as *C:\WINDOWS\system32\ system.mwb*. Other workgroup information files (*.mwb* files) can be created to secure individual or groups of databases, but before this is done—before any of the steps in this section of "The Access Workbench" are done—**make a backup copy of the original system.mwb file!** If this file gets corrupted or otherwise messed up, you will have real problems using Access. All you need to do is copy the *system.mwb* file to your *My Documents* folder.

You can see some of the default contents of the default workgroup information file by using the **Tools | Security | User and Group Accounts** menu command.

#### Viewing the Default Security Settings

*   **NOTE:** WARNING! Have you made a backup copy of the *system.mwb file? If not, do it now!* Copy it to your My Documents folder.

1.  Start Access, but do *not* open a database.
2.  In the Access main menu click **Tools,** then click **Security,** and then select **User and Group Accounts. . .** in the Tools menu. The User and Group Accounts dialog box appears, as shown in Figure AW-6-1.
3.  Click the **Name: drop-down list arrow**. Note that there is only one user account in the System—Admin.

---

**FIGURE AW-6-1**

**The User and Group Accounts Dialog Box**

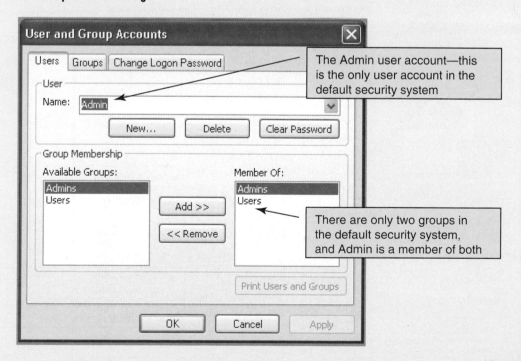

*(Continued)*

4. Note that there are two groups—Admins and Users—and that Admin is already a member of both.
5. Click the **OK** button to close the dialog box.

Although you haven't known it, you have been running Access as Admin *with no password* and, thus, have had full administrator privileges in Access. Since the Admin account hasn't had a password, a login hasn't been required. If you assigned Admin a password at this point (note the Change Login Password tab in the dialog box in Figure AW-6-1), you would have to log in as Admin with that password every time you started Access—every database would be affected.

So Access has the ability to handle user authentication by the use of user login and password. Access also has user authorization capability at the DBMS level. Further, Access authentication and authorization security settings can also be applied to individual databases. While this can be done manually, it is easier to set up database security and to learn the abilities of the security system by using the Access Security Wizard. This Wizard is inconsistently named within Access and the Wizard itself as the *Security Wizard*, the *User-Level Security Wizard*, and the *One-step Security Wizard*. We'll generally refer to is as the *Security Wizard* or just *Wizard*, but watch out for the other names in the steps that follow! So, let's secure the WMCRM database with the Wizard (by whichever name it is calling itself at the moment), and see what we encounter.

### Securing the WMCRM Database

- **NOTE:** *LAST WARNING!* Have you made that backup copy of the *system.mwb file*? If you haven't done it yet, do it now!

1. Open the **WMCRM** database.

---

## FIGURE AW-6-2

**The User and Group Accounts Dialog Box**

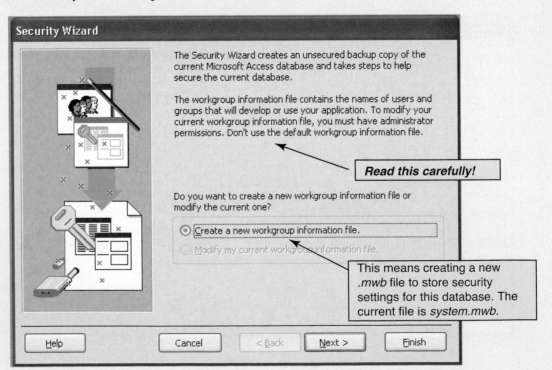

2. In the Access main menu click **Tools,** then click **Security** and then select **User Level Security Wizard . . .** in the Tools menu. The Security Wizard dialog box appears, as shown in Figure AW-6-2.

3. Read the messages on the Security Wizard dialog box page carefully—we are going to create a new *workgroup information file* (*.mwb* file) for this database. Access will secure the database but also make and store an unsecured copy as a backup.

4. Click the **Next** button to move to the next page of the Wizard.

5. As shown in Figure AW-6-3, we next create the new workgroup information file. The default file name and location (the filename will be *Security.mwb* and it will be located in your *My Documents* folder) are fine so we'll use them. Similarly, we'll use the WID that Access generated. Type the company name **Wallingford Motors** into the **Company text box.**

6. Note that we can assign the new workgroup information file as the default for all Access databases, or just use it with this database. We want to use it with this database only. The Wizard will create a desktop shortcut icon to open the WMCRM database using the new workgroup information file.

7. Click the **Next** button to move to the next page of the Wizard.

8. As shown in Figure AW-6-4, we next specify which database objects we want secured. By default, Access secures all objects—both those already existing and any new ones created after the database is secured. This is exactly what we want so there's no need to change anything on this page.

9. Click the **Next** button to move to the next page of the Wizard.

10. As shown in Figure AW-6-5, Access has predefined security groups that can be included in our security settings. A summary of the permissions associated with each group is shown in Figure AW-6-6.

---

### FIGURE AW-6-3

**Creating the Workgroup Information File**

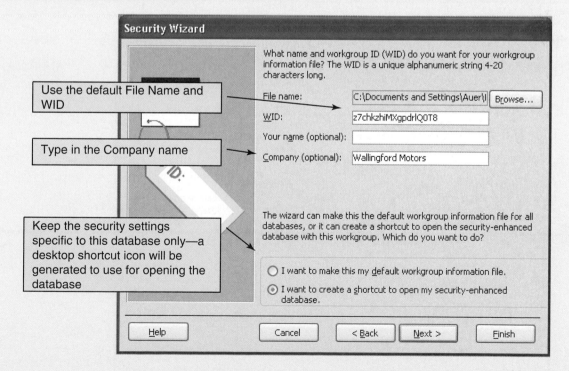

*(Continued)*

## FIGURE AW-6-4

### Specifying the Included Database Objects

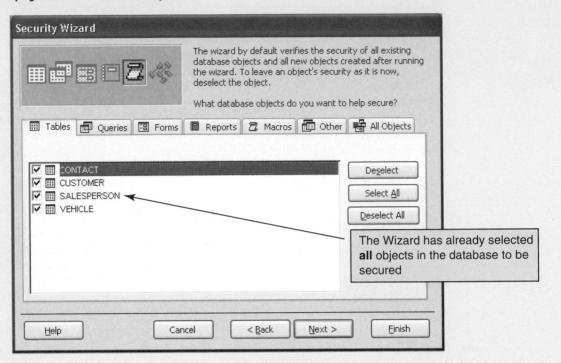

## FIGURE AW-6-5

### Specifying the Included Security Groups

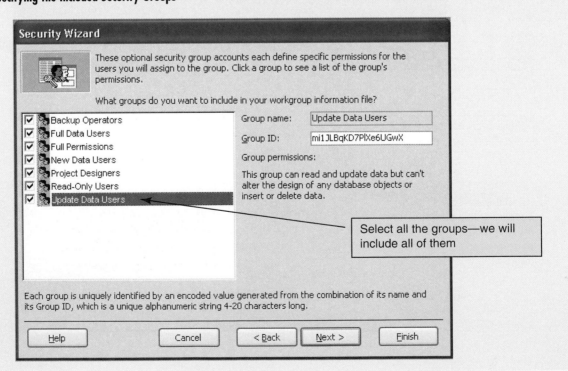

## FIGURE AW-6-6

**Access Security Group Permissions Summary**

| Group | Group Permissions Granted |
|-------|---------------------------|
| Backup Operators | The group can open the database exclusively for backup operations and compacting the database, but it can't see any database objects |
| Full Data Users | The group has full permissions to edit database data, but it can't alter the design of any database objects |
| Full Permissions | The group has full permissions on all database objects, but it can't assign database permissions to other users |
| New Data Users | The group can read and insert data, but it can't alter the design of any database object nor delete or update database data |
| Project Designers | The group has full permissions to edit database data and all database objects, but it can't alter the database tables or the relationships between them |
| Read-Only Users | The group can read database data, but it can't alter the design of any database object nor insert, delete, or update database data |
| Update Data Users | The group can read and update database data, but it can't alter the design of any database object nor insert or delete database data |

11. We will include all these groups, so click the **check box** of each group to select it.
12. Click the **Next** button to move to the next page of the Wizard.
13. As shown in Figure AW-6-7 the Security Wizard gives us the option of assigning permissions to workstation users. Note that the workstation users group is the

## FIGURE AW-6-7

**Setting Permissions for the Workstation Users Group**

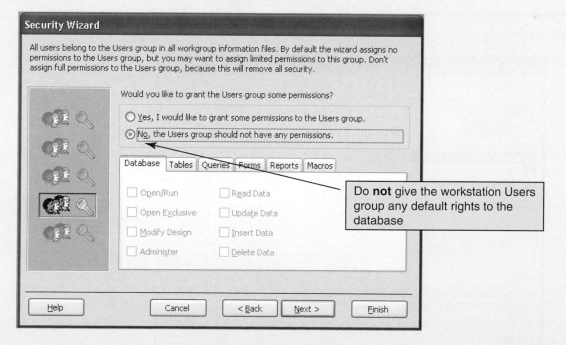

*(Continued)*

Windows operating system group that automatically includes all user accounts on the workstation. Giving permissions to this group gives rights to use the database to anyone with a user account on the workstation. We will not grant such access to the WMCRM database—we want only very specific users to have rights to use this database. Click the **Next** button to move to the next page of the Wizard.

14. Next, we create our database user accounts. This is shown in Figure AW-6-8. We will use the user's WMCRM *NickName* as their login, and assign a password of the user's initials and the word *password* connected by a plus (+) sign. For example, Tina Smith's User Name will be her NickName of *Tina*, and her password will be *TS+password*. Create user accounts for all three of the Wallingford Motors sales staff.

15. Create a user account for the Wallingford Motors database administrator. Use the User Name *WM-Admin* and the nonstandard (it differs from *our password creation rule*) password *Admin+password*. We have to use this password because Access only allows password of up to 14 characters.

16. Finally, note the user named *Auer* in the list of users. When the Security Wizard runs, it automatically creates an account with full administrator privileges for the developer running the Wizard. Since I'm running the Wizard, it created an account for me using my Windows workstation operating system login name of *Auer*. When you run the Wizard, you will automatically have a User account created for *you*, and *your user name* will show up in the list!

17. Click the **Next** button to move to the next page of the Wizard.

18. Now, it's time to assign group memberships. The rule here is that users are assigned to groups, and groups are granted permissions. Permissions should never be assigned directly to a user if a group can be used for the assignment. You are not limited to the default users groups—you can create your own groups as needed manually. Group membership can be assigned in two ways—users can be assigned to groups, or groups can be assigned users as members. The method of assigning users

**FIGURE AW-6-8**

**Creating Users**

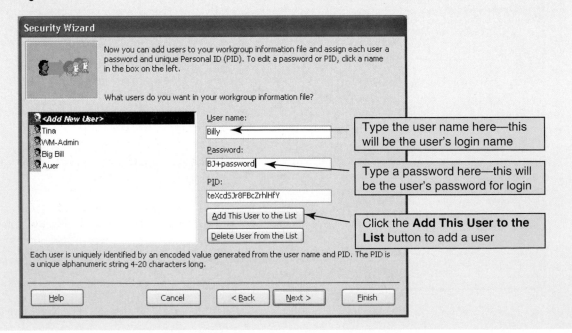

**FIGURE AW-6-9**

**Assigning Group Membership to a User**

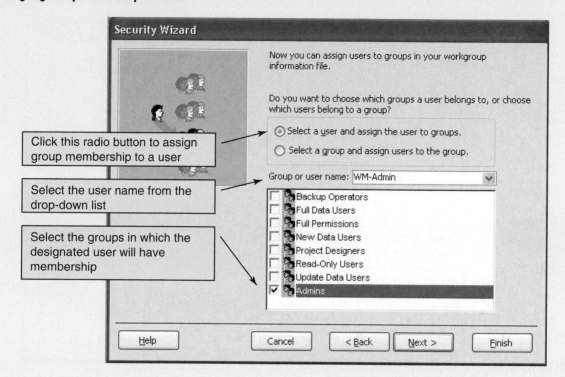

Click this radio button to assign group membership to a user

Select the user name from the drop-down list

Select the groups in which the designated user will have membership

to groups is shown in Figure AW-6-9. Note that the Admins group, which has full administrative rights to the database, did not appear in the previous list of groups in Figures AW-6-5 and AW-6-7. Admins is an Access group, not a database specific group, and is always included in each set of security assignments. Assign **WM-Admin** to the **Admins** group.

19. While still on the same page of the Wizard, click the **Select a group and assign user to the group** radio button. Now the page appears as shown in Figure AW-6-10. Here, we select a group from the drop-down list and then assign users to it. Select the **Full Data Users** group, and assign **Tina**, **Big Bill,** and **Billy** to the group.

20. Click the **Next** button to move to the next page of the Wizard.

21. This is the last page of the Security Wizard. It asks you for your preferred name (and location) for the unsecured backup copy of the database. The default name of the backup copy will be *WMCRM.bak*—the same name as the original database with the *.bak* extension—and the default location will be the *My Documents* folder. There is no need to change this name or location.

22. The Wizard page also warns you that a report documenting the security work that was done will be displayed. Click the **Finish** button to complete the Security Wizard.

23. At this point, the One-step Security Wizard Report appears in the Security Wizard window. You can print the report at this point if you want to—use the **Print** button on the Print Preview toolbar or the **File | Print . . .** menu command. However, there's a better way to do this so close the Security Wizard window. When you close it, the Security Wizard warning shown in Figure AW-6-11 appears asking you if you want to save this report as a Snapshot (.snp) file.

*(Continued)*

## FIGURE AW-6-10

**Assigning User Members to a Group**

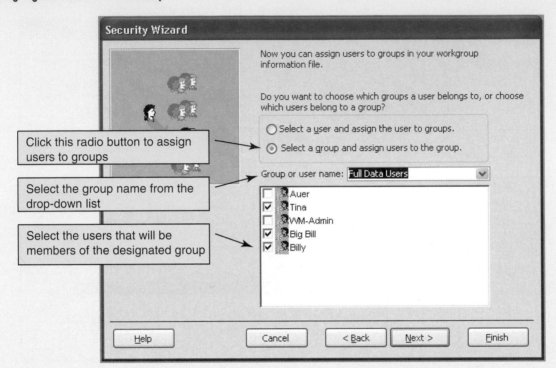

Click this radio button to assign users to groups

Select the group name from the drop-down list

Select the users that will be members of the designated group

24. Click the **Yes** button on the Security Wizard warning dial box. The One-step Security Wizard Report file for the WMCRM will be named *WMCRM.snp*, saved in the *My Documents* folder and displayed in the Snapshot Viewer as shown in Figure AW-6-12.
25. Print the One-step Security Wizard Report by either clicking the **Print** button on the Scroll Bar at the bottom of the window or by using the **File | Print** menu command.
26. Close the **Snapshot Viewer**.
27. The Security Wizard is displaying an informational warning dialog box telling us that in order to use the secured database we must use it in conjunction with the new workgroup information file (the security.mwb file in My Documents). In order to do this, we have to close Access and restart it. Click the **OK** button to close the dialog box.

## FIGURE AW-6-11

**The Security Wizard Warning Dialog Box**

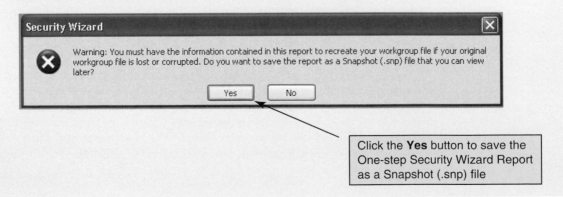

Click the **Yes** button to save the One-step Security Wizard Report as a Snapshot (.snp) file

---

**FIGURE AW-6-12**

**The One-step Security Wizard Report**

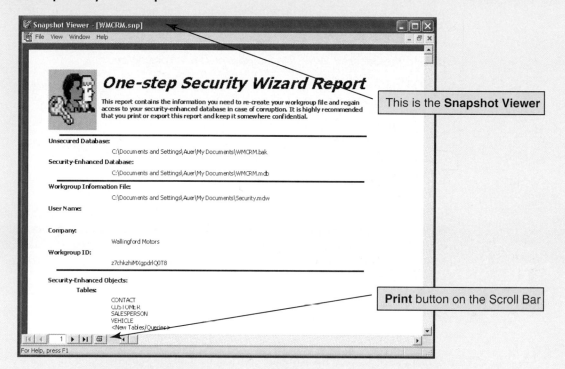

28. Close Access.
    - **NOTE:** *ANOTHER WARNING!* We are about to backup another critical file—*do the following steps now*!
29. Note the **WMCRM.mdb shortcut icon** that the Security Wizard has placed on the Windows desktop. We need to make a backup copy of this shortcut icon, so right-click the **WMCRM.mdb shortcut icon** and click **Copy**.
30. Click **Start | My Documents** to open the My Documents window (this is the Windows XP command using the Windows XP Start menu). Right-click anywhere in the blank window to display the shortcut menu, then click **Paste Shortcut**. The **WMCRM.mdb shortcut icon** is copied to the My Documents window.
    - **NOTE:** This backup was needed to protect the new shortcut icon. It is particularly critical in computer lab settings. In computer labs, it is common to *dynamically create* a workstation user account when the user logs in and then to *delete* the user account from the workstation when the user logs out. In this case, the desktop shortcut icon will be deleted along with all other account information. In such situations, the user's My Documents folder is usually stored on a network server so the backup copy we just made will be safe. Check with your instructor about the proper procedures for your computer lab.

### Using the Secured Database

Now that we've used the Security Wizard to secure the WMCRM database, we'll use the secured database. However, this is not necessarily as straightforward as it sounds. Note that the Security Wizard created a shortcut icon on the Windows desktop named

*(Continued)*

WMCRM.mdb (the name of the Access database file). The properties of this icon have been set to automatically use the correct workgroup information file (*security.mwb*) when the database is opened. But the Access program itself is still using the original system.mwb workgroup information file! Watch what happens if we try to open the WMCRM database in Access itself instead of using the shortcut icon.

### Opening the Secured WMCRM Database: The Wrong Way

- **NOTE:** LAST, LAST WARNING! You <u>did</u> backup the <u>*system.mwb file, didn't you?*</u> If you still haven't done it, do it now!

1. Open Access.
2. Attempt to open the **WMCRM** database—the anxiety-provoking error message shown in Figure AW-6-13 is displayed.
3. Click the **OK** button to close the dialog box.
4. Close Access.

The error message is generated because the permissions in the system.mwb workgroup information file being used by Access itself are not the permissions needed to run the WMCRM database—those permissions are in the *security.mwb* workgroup information file in My Documents.

Now, let's use the shortcut icon to open the WMCRM database.

### Opening the Secured WMCRM Database: The Right Way

- **NOTE:** Need I ask?

1. Double-click the **WMCRM.mdb shortcut icon** on the Windows Desktop.
2. The Access Login dialog box as shown in Figure AW-6-14 is displayed.

---

**FIGURE AW-6-13**

**The "You Don't Have the Necessary Permissions to Use This File" Dialog Box**

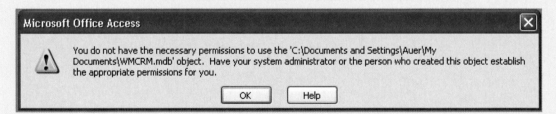

---

**FIGURE AW-6-14**

**The Access Login Dialog Box**

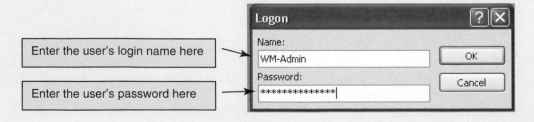

3. Enter the user login **WM-Admin** in the Name text box.
4. Enter the password **Admin+password** in the Password text box.
5. Click the **OK** button.
6. The usual **Security Warning** dialog box is displayed. Click the **Open** button.
7. The WMCRM database is opened in Access.
8. Close the WMCRM database.

It is possible to manually connect Access itself to the *security.mwb* workgroup information file in My Documents used by the WMCRM database,[1] but then every database used in Access will run under those security settings. Since we have databases we're working on that we don't want to use with these security settings, we will not change the default workgroup information file.

### Secured Database Administration

We can manually make changes to the WMCRM security settings if we need to. User accounts and group memberships are administered by using the **Tools | Security | User and Group Accounts . . .** menu command. This displays the User and Group Account dialog box we saw earlier (see Figure AW-6-1). User and group permissions are administered by using the **Tools | Security | User and Group Permissions . . .** menu command. This displays the User and Group Permissions dialog box, which is shown in Figure AW-6-15.

### Closing the Database and Exiting Access

That completes the work we'll do in this section of "The Access Workbench." As usual, we will finish by closing the database and Access.

#### Closing the WMCRM Database

1. If the WMCRM database is still open, then click the **Close** button in the upper right corner of the WMCRM : Database window.

#### Exiting Access

1. To exit Access, click the **Close** in the upper right corner of the Microsoft Access window.

---

### FIGURE AW-6-15

**The User and Group Permissions Dialog Box**

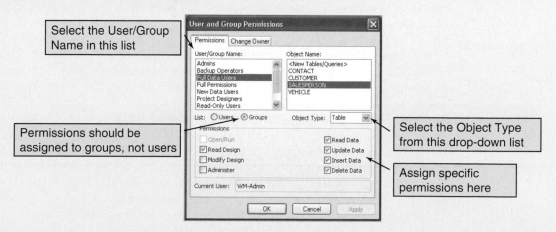

---

## SUMMARY

Database administration is a business function that involves managing a database in a way that maximizes its value to an organization. The conflicting goals of protecting the database and maximizing its availability and benefit to users must be balanced via good administration.

All databases need database administration. The database administration for small, personal databases is informal; database administration for large, multi-user databases can involve an office and many people. The acronym *DBA* can stand for database administration or database administrator. Three basic database administration functions are necessary: concurrency control, security, and backup and recovery.

The goal of concurrency control is to ensure that one user's work does not inappropriately influence another user's work. No single concurrency control technique is ideal for all circumstances. Trade-offs need to be made between the level of protection and data throughput.

A transaction, or logical unit of work, is a series of actions taken against a database that occur as an atomic unit; either all of them occur or none of them do. The activity of concurrent transactions is interleaved on the database server. In some cases, updates can be lost if concurrent transactions are not controlled. Another concurrency problem concerns inconsistent reads.

A dirty read occurs when one transaction reads a changed record that has not been committed to the database. A nonrepeatable read occurs when one transaction rereads data it has previously read and finds modifications or deletions caused by another transaction. A phantom read occurs when a transaction rereads data and finds new rows that were inserted by a different transaction.

To avoid concurrency problems, database elements are locked. Implicit locks are placed by the DBMS; explicit locks are issued by the application program. The size of the locked resource is called lock granularity. An exclusive lock prohibits other users from reading the locked resource; a shared lock allows other users to read the locked resource, but they cannot update it.

Two transactions that run concurrently and generate results that are consistent with the results that would have occurred if the transactions had run separately are referred to as serializable transactions. Two-phased locking, in which locks are acquired in a growing phase and released in a shrinking phase, is one scheme for serializability. A special case of two-phase locking is to acquire locks throughout the transaction but not to free any lock until the transaction is finished.

Deadlock, or *the deadly embrace*, occurs when two transactions are each waiting on a resource that the other transaction holds. Deadlock can be prevented by requiring transactions to acquire all locks at the same time. Once deadlock occurs, the only way to cure it is to abort one of the transactions and back out partially completed work.

Optimistic locking assumes that no transaction conflict will occur and then deals with the consequences if it does. Pessimistic locking assumes that conflict will occur and so prevents it ahead of time with locks. In general, optimistic locking is preferred for the Internet and for many intranet applications.

Most application programs do not explicitly declare locks. Instead, they mark transaction boundaries with BEGIN, COMMIT, and ROLLBACK transaction statements and declare the concurrent behavior they want. The DBMS then places locks for the application that will result in the desired behavior. An ACID transaction is one that is atomic, consistent, isolated, and durable. Durable means that database changes are permanent. Consistency can mean either statement level or transaction level consistency. With transaction level consistency, a transaction may not see its own changes.

The 1992 SQL standard defines four transaction isolation levels: read uncommitted, read committed, repeatable read, and serializable. The characteristics of each are summarized in Figure 6-13.

A cursor is a pointer into a set of records. Four cursor types are prevalent: forward only, static, keyset, and dynamic. Developers should select isolation levels and cursor types that are appropriate for their application workload and for the DBMS product in use.

The goal of database security is to ensure that only authorized users can perform authorized activities at authorized times. To develop effective database security, the processing rights and responsibilities of all users must be determined.

DBMS products provide security facilities. Most involve the declaration of users, groups, objects to be protected, and permissions or privileges on those objects. Almost all DBMS products use some form of user name and password security. DBMS security can be augmented by application security.

In the event of system failure, the database must be restored to a usable state as soon as possible. Transactions in process at the time of the failure must be reapplied or restarted. Although in some cases recovery can be done by reprocessing, the use of logs and before-images and after-images with rollback and rollforward is almost always preferred. Checkpoints can be taken to reduce the amount of work that needs to be done after a failure.

In addition to concurrency control, security, and backup and recovery, the DBA needs to ensure that a system exists to gather and record errors and problems. The DBA works with the development team to resolve such problems on a prioritized basis and also to evaluate features and functions of new releases of the DBMS. Additionally, the DBMS needs to create and manage a process for controlling the database configuration so that changes to the database structure are made with a community-wide view. Finally, the DBA has the responsibility of ensuring that appropriate documentation is maintained about database structure, concurrency control, security, backup and recovery, and other details that concern the management and use of the database.

A distributed database is a database that is stored and processed on more than one computer. A replicated database is one in which multiple copies of some or all of the database are stored on different computers. A partitioned database is one in which different pieces of the database are stored on different computers. A distributed database can be replicated and distributed.

Distributed databases pose processing challenges. If the database is updated on a single computer, then the challenge is simply to ensure that the copies of the database are logically consistent when they are distributed. However, if updates are to be made on more than one computer, the challenges become significant. If the database is partitioned and not replicated, then challenges occur if transactions span data on more than one computer. If the database is replicated and if updates occur to the replicated portions, then some form of a special locking algorithm called distributed two-phase locking is required. Implementing this algorithm can be difficult and expensive.

Objects consist of methods and properties or data values. All objects of a given class have the same methods, but they have different property values. Object persistence is the process of storing object property values. Relational databases are difficult to use for object persistence. Some specialized products called object-oriented DBMS were developed in the 1990s but never received commercial acceptance. Oracle and others have extended the capabilities of their relational DBMS products to provide support for object persistence. Such databases are referred to as object-relational databases. In the future, XML is likely to be used for object persistence and probably will replace the use of object-relational databases.

## REVIEW QUESTIONS

**6.1** What is the purpose of database administration?

**6.2** Explain how database administration tasks vary with the size and complexity of the database.

**6.3** What are two interpretations of the acronym *DBA*?

**6.4** What is the purpose of concurrency control?

**6.5** What is the goal of a database security system?

**6.6** Explain the meaning of the word *inappropriately* in the phrase "one user's work does not inappropriately influence another user's work."

**6.7** Explain the trade-off that exists in concurrency control.

**6.8** Describe what an atomic transaction is, and explain why atomicity is important.

**6.9** Explain the difference between concurrent transactions and simultaneous transactions. How many CPUs are required for simultaneous transactions?

**6.10** Give an example, other than the one in this text, of the lost update problem.

**6.11** Define the terms *dirty read*, *nonrepeatable read*, and *phantom read*.

**6.12** Explain the difference between an explicit and an implicit lock.

**6.13** What is lock granularity?

**6.14** Explain the difference between an exclusive lock and a shared lock.

**6.15** Explain two-phased locking.

**6.16** How does releasing all locks at the end of a transaction relate to two-phase locking?

**6.17** What is deadlock? How can it be avoided? How can it be resolved once it occurs?

**6.18** Explain the difference between optimistic and pessimistic locking.

**6.19** Explain the benefits of marking transaction boundaries, declaring lock characteristics, and letting the DBMS place locks.

**6.20** Explain the use of the BEGIN, COMMIT, and ROLLBACK TRANSACTION statements.

**6.21** Explain the meaning of the expression ACID transaction.

**6.22** Describe statement level consistency.

**6.23** Describe transaction level consistency. What disadvantage can exist with it?

**6.24** What is the purpose of transaction isolation levels?

**6.25** Explain what read uncommitted isolation level is. Give an example of its use.

**6.26** Explain what read committed isolation level is. Give an example of its use.

**6.27** Explain what repeatable read isolation level is. Give an example of its use.

**6.28** Explain what serializable isolation level is. Give an example of its use.

**6.29** Explain the term *cursor*.

**6.30** Explain why a transaction may have many cursors. Also, how is it possible that a transaction may have more than one cursor on a given table?

**6.31** What is the advantage of using different types of cursors?

**6.32** Explain forward only cursors. Give an example of their use.

**6.33** Explain static cursors. Give an example of their use.

**6.34** Explain keyset cursors. Give an example of their use.

**6.35** Explain dynamic cursors. Give an example of their use.

**6.36** What happens if you do not declare transaction isolation level and cursor type to the DBMS? Is this good or bad?

**6.37** Explain the necessity of defining processing rights and responsibilities. How are such responsibilities enforced?

**6.38** Explain the relationships of users, groups, permission, and objects for a generic database security system.

**6.39** Describe the advantages and disadvantages of DBMS-provided security.

**6.40** Describe the advantages and disadvantages of application-provided security.

**6.41** Explain how a database could be recovered via reprocessing. Why is this generally not feasible?

**6.42** Define the terms *rollback* and *rollforward.*

**6.43** Why is it important to write to the log before changing the database values?

**6.44** Describe the rollback process. Under what conditions should rollback be used?

**6.45** Describe the rollforward process. Under what conditions should rollforward be used?

**6.46** What is the advantage of taking frequent checkpoints of a database?

**6.47** Summarize the DBA's responsibilities for managing database user problems.

**6.48** Summarize the DBA's responsibilities for configuration control.

**6.49** Summarize the DBA's responsibilities for documentation.

**6.50** Define *distributed database.*

**6.51** Explain one way to partition a database that has three tables: T1, T2, and T3.

**6.52** Explain one way to replicate a database that has three tables: T1, T2, and T3.

**6.53** Explain what must be done when fully replicating a database but allowing only one computer to process updates.

**6.54** If more than one computer can update a replicated database, what three problems can occur?

**6.55** What solution is used to prevent the problems in question 6.54?

**6.56** Explain what problems can occur in a distributed database that is partitioned but not replicated.

**6.57** What organizations should consider using a distributed database?

**6.58** Explain the meaning of the term *object persistence.*

**6.59** In general terms, explain why relational databases are difficult to use for object persistence.

**6.60** What does *OODBMS* stand for and what is its purpose?

**6.61** According to this chapter, why were OODBMSs not successful?

**6.62** What is an object-relational database?

## EXERCISES

**6.63** To respond to the following, open Microsoft Access and search in Access Help for "sharing an Access database."

**A.** Summarize the ways in which an Access database can be shared.

**B.** Summarize Access locking facilities.

**C.** Summarize the facilities for setting options on shared Access databases.

**D.** Search in Help for "backup and restore." Summarize the backup and recovery options available with Microsoft Access.

**6.64** If you have access to SQL Server, search its Help site to answer the following questions.

**A.** Does SQL Server support both optimistic and pessimistic locking?

**B.** What levels of transaction isolation are available?

    **C.** What types of cursors, if any, are used by SQL Server?

    **D.** How does the security model for SQL Server differ from that shown in Figure 6-17?

    **E.** Summarize the types of SQL Server backup.

    **F.** Summarize the SQL Server recovery models.

**6.65** If you have access to MySQL, search its Help site to answer the following questions.

    **A.** How does MySQL use read locks and write locks?

    **B.** What, if any, levels of transaction isolation are available in MySQL?

    **C.** What types of cursors, if any, are used by MySQL?

    **D.** How does the security model for MySQL differ from that shown in Figure 6-17?

    **E.** Summarize the backup capabilities of MySQL.

    **F.** Summarize the recovery capabilities of MySQL.

**6.66** Search the Web for the term *distributed two-phase locking*. Find a tutorial on that topic and explain, in general terms, how this locking algorithm works.

**6.67** Go to www.Oracle.com and search for tutorial information on object-relational databases. Explain the terms *column object*, *nested tables*, and *row objects*.

## ACCESS WORKBENCH EXERCISES

**AW.6.1** Having completed the steps in Section 6's "The Access Workbench," you now have five files related to the WMCRM database itself (not counting variants with modified names that we've used in other sections) in your My Documents folder. What are they, and what is the function of each one?

**AW.6.2** Using a spreadsheet, document the permissions that each of the Access security groups shown in Figure AW-6-6 has to the tables, queries, forms, and reports in the WMCRM database.

**AW.6.3** As members of the WMCRM Full Data Users group, the permissions that the Wallingford Motors sales staff currently has in the WMCRM database are excessive. For example, they can currently modify data in the SALES-PERSON table, which will let them change their own WageRate and CommissionRate values! Create a new security group named *Contact Data Users*. This group should have the same permissions to the CONTACT and CUSTOMER tables and their related forms and reports that the Full Data Users group currently has. However, the new group should only have the ability to read the data in the SALESPERSON and VEHICLE tables. The new group should have rights to run existing queries, but not to create a new one, nor to modify or delete existing queries. After you create the group, add the sales staff to it, and remove them from Full Data Users.

**AW.6.4** Using the Wedgewood Pacific Corporation that has been developed in previous sections of "The Access Workbench":

**A.** Analyze the data in the tables in WPC database tables (particularly DEPARTMENT and EMPLOYEE), and create a database security plan using Figure 6-18 as an example.

**B.** Run the Access Security Wizard on the WPC database. Store the new workgroup information file in My Documents, and name it *WPCsecurity.mdw*. Create user accounts for James Nestor, Rick Brown, Mary Abernathy, Tom Caruthers, and Heather Jones. Use the naming scheme of *FirstInitialLastName* to create the login names. For example, James Nestor will have a login name of *JNestor*. For passwords, use *Initials+password*. Thus, James Nestor's password will be *JN+password*. Put all the users in the Full Data Users group. Print out the One-step Security Wizard Report so that you have documentation of the security setup.

**C.** After the Security Wizard is complete, there will be a shortcut icon on your desktop named WPC.mdb. Place a copy of this file in your My Documents folder.

**D.** Compare the database permissions you planned in step A with the permissions assigned to the Full Data Users group. How well do they match? If they do not match well, create your own set of one or more security groups to implement your security plan and reassign users as necessary to the groups. Document your work in a written memo so that you have a record of how many groups were created, which users were assigned to them, and which permissions have been granted to each security group.

## GARDEN GLORY PROJECT QUESTIONS

The Garden Glory database design that was used in Chapter 3 was:

OWNER (<u>OwnerID</u>, OwnerName, Email, Type)

PROPERTY (<u>PropertyID</u>, PropertyName, Street, City, State, Zip, *OwnerID*)

EMPLOYEE (<u>Initials</u>, Name, CellPhone, ExperienceLevel)

SERVICE (<u>PropertyID</u>, *<u>Initials</u>*, Date, HoursWorked)

Garden Glory has modified the EMPLOYEE table by adding a TotalHoursWorked column as follows:

EMPLOYEE (<u>Initials</u>, Name, CellPhone, ExperienceLevel, TotalHoursWorked)

The office personnel at Garden Glory use a database application to record services and related data changes in this database. For a new service, the service-recording application reads a row from the PROPERTY table to get the PropertyID. It then creates a new row in SERVICE and updates TotalHoursWorked in EMPLOYEE by adding the HoursWorked value in the new SERVICE record to TotalHoursWorked. This operation is referred to as a Service Update Transaction.

In some cases, the employee record does not exist before the service is recorded. In this case, a new EMPLOYEE row is created and then the service is recorded. This is called a Service Update for New Employee Transaction.

**A.** Explain why it is important for the changes made by the Service Update Transaction to be atomic.

**B.** Describe a scenario in which an update of TotalHoursWorked could be lost during a Service Update Transaction.

**C.** Assume that many Service Update Transactions and many Service Update for New Employee Transactions are processed concurrently. Describe a scenario for a nonrepeatable read and a scenario for a phantom read.

**D.** Explain how locking could be used to prevent the lost update in your answer to question B.

**E.** Is it possible for deadlock to occur between two Service Update Transactions? Why or why not? Is it possible for deadlock to occur between a Service Update Transaction and a Service Update for New Employee Transaction? Why or why not?

**F.** Do you think optimistic or pessimistic locking would be better for the Service Update Transactions?

**G.** Suppose Garden Glory identifies three groups of users: managers, administrative personnel, and system administrators. Suppose further that the only job of administrative personnel is to make Service Update Transactions. Managers can make Service Update Transactions and Service Updates for New Employee Transactions. System administrators have unrestricted access to the tables. Describe processing rights that you think would be appropriate for this situation. Use Figure 6-18 as an example. What problems might this security system have?

**H.** Garden Glory has developed the following procedure for backup and recovery. The company backs up the database from the server to a second computer on its network each night. Once a month, it copies the database to a CD and stores it at a manager's house. It keeps paper records of all services provided for an entire year. If it ever loses its database, it plans to restore it from a backup and reprocess all service requests. Do you think this backup and recovery program is sufficient for Garden Glory? What problems might occur? What alternatives exist? Describe any changes you think the company should make to this system.

## JAMES RIVER JEWELRY PROJECT QUESTIONS

The James River Jewelry database design that was used in Chapter 3 was:

CUSTOMER (<u>CustomerID</u>, LastName, FirstName, Phone, Email)

PURCHASE (<u>InvoiceNumber</u>, Date, PreTaxAmount, *CustomerID*)

PURCHASE_ITEM (<u>*InvoiceNumber*</u>, <u>*ItemNumber*</u>, RetailPrice)

ITEM (<u>ItemNumber</u>, Description, Cost, ArtistName)

James River Jewelry has modified the database by adding two tables—OWNER and JEWELRY_ITEM—as shown below:

OWNER (<u>OwnerID</u>, Name, Phone, Email, AmountOwed)

JEWELRY_ITEM (<u>*ItemNumber*</u>, DateReceived, DateSold, NegotiatedSalesPrice, ActualSalesPrice, CommissionPercentage, *OwnerID*) where

OwnerID in JEWELRY_ITEM must exist in OwnerID in OWNER

ItemNumber in JEWELRY_ITEM must exist in ItemNumber in ITEM

The tables are used to record data and maintain owner data about jewelry accepted on consignment. JEWELRY_ITEM (which is a subtype of ITEM—note the referential integrity constraint) is used to record the negotiated sales price, the commission percentage, and the actual sales price for each item of consigned jewelry.

Assume that office personnel at James River Jewelry use a database application to record consignment data. When an item is received on consignment, owner data are stored in OWNER if the owner is new; otherwise existing owner data are used. New ITEM and JEWELRY_ITEM rows are created. In ITEM, ItemNumber and Description are recorded, Cost is set to $0.00, and if there is an artist associated with the piece, ArtistName is entered. For JEWELRY_ITEM, data are stored for all columns except DateSold and ActualSalesPrice. James River Jewelry personnel refer to these actions as an Acceptance Transaction. Later, if the jewelry item does not sell, the NegotiatedSalesPrice and CommissionPercentage values may be reduced. This is called a Price Adjustment Transaction. Finally, when an item sells, the DateSold and ActualSalesPrice fields for the item are given values, and the AmountOwed value in OWNER is updated by increasing AmountOwed by the owner's percentage of the ActualSalesPrice value. This third transaction is called a Sales Transaction.

**A.** Explain why it is important for the changes made by each of these transactions to be atomic.

**B.** Describe a scenario in which an update of AmountOwed could be lost.

**C.** Describe a scenario for a nonrepeatable read and a scenario for a phantom read.

**D.** Explain how locking could be used to prevent the lost update in your answer to question B.

**E.** Is it possible for deadlock to occur between two Acceptance Transactions? Why or why not? Is it possible for deadlock to occur between two Sales Transactions? Why or why not? Is it possible for deadlock to occur between an Acceptance Transaction and a Sales Transaction? Why or why not?

**F.** For each of these three types of transaction, describe whether you think optimistic or pessimistic locking would be better. Explain the reasons for your answer.

**G.** Suppose James River Jewelry identifies three groups of users: managers, administrative personnel, and system administrators. Suppose further that managers and administrative personnel can perform Acceptance Transactions and Sales Transactions, but only managers can perform Price Adjustment Transactions. Describe processing rights that you think would be appropriate for this situation. Use Figure 6-18 as an example.

**H.** James River Jewelry has developed the following procedure for backup and recovery. The company backs up the database from the server to a second computer on its network each night. Once a month, it copies the database to a CD and stores it at a manager's house. It keeps paper records of all services provided for an entire year. If it ever loses its database, it plans to restore it from a backup and reprocess all service requests. Do you think this backup and recovery program is sufficient for James River Jewelry? What problems might occur? What alternatives exist? Describe any changes you think the company should make to this system.

The Queen Anne Curiosity Shop database design that was used in Chapter 3 was:

> CUSTOMER (CustomerID, LastName, FirstName, Address, City, State, ZIP, Phone, Email)
>
> EMPLOYEE (EmployeeID, LastName, FirstName, Phone, Email)
>
> VENDOR (VendorID, CompanyName, ContactLastName, ContactFirstName, Address, City, State, ZIP, Phone, Fax, Email)
>
> ITEM (ItemID, ItemDescription, PurchaseDate, ItemCost, ItemPrice, VendorID)
>
> SALE (SaleID, CustomerID, EmployeeID, SaleDate, SubTotal, Tax, Total)
>
> SALE_ITEM (SaleID, SaleItemID, ItemID, ItemPrice)

The Queen Anne Curiosity Shop has modified the ITEM and SALE_ITEM tables are follows:

> ITEM (ItemID, ItemDescription, UnitCost, UnitPrice, QuantityOnHand, VendorID)
>
> SALE_ITEM (SaleID, SaleItemID, ItemID, Quantity, ItemPrice, Extended Price)

These changes allow the sales system to handle non-unique items that can be bought and sold in quantity. When new items arrive at the Queen Anne Curiosity Shop from vendors, the office personnel unpack the items, put them in the stock room and run an Item Quantity Received Transaction that adds the quantity received to QuantityOnHand. At the same time, another transaction called an Item Price Adjustment Transaction will be run if necessary to adjust UnitCost and UnitPrice. Sales may occur at anytime, and when a sale occurs, the Sale Transaction is run. Every time a SALE_ITEM line is entered, the input Quantity is subtracted from QuantityOnHand in ITEM and the ItemPrice is set to the UnitPrice.

**A.** Explain why it is important for the changes made by each of these transactions to be atomic.

**B.** Describe a scenario in which an update of QuantityOnHand could be lost.

**C.** Describe a scenario for a nonrepeatable read and a scenario for a phantom read.

**D.** Explain how locking could be used to prevent the lost update in your answer to question B.

**E.** Is it possible for deadlock to occur between two Sale Transactions? Why or why not? Is it possible for deadlock to occur between a Sale Transaction and a Quantity Received Transaction? Why or why not?

**F.** For each of these three types of transaction, describe whether you think optimistic or pessimistic locking would be better. Explain the reasons for your answer.

**G.** Suppose that the Queen Anne Curiosity Shop identifies four groups of users: sales personnel, managers, administrative personnel, and system administrators. Suppose further that managers and administrative personnel can perform Item Quantity Received Transactions, but only managers can perform

Item Price Adjustment Transactions. Describe processing rights that you think would be appropriate for this situation. Use Figure 6-18 as an example.

**H.**   The Queen Anne Curiosity Shop has developed the following procedure for backup and recovery. The company backs up the entire database from the server to tape every Saturday night. The tapes are taken to a safety deposit box at a local bank on the following Thursday. Printed paper records of all sales are kept for five years. If the database is ever lost, the plan is to restore the database from the last full backup and reprocess all the sales records. Do you think this backup and recovery program is sufficient for the Queen Anne Curiosity Shop? What problems might occur? What alternatives exist? Describe any changes you think the company should make to this system.

# CHAPTER 7

# Database Processing Applications and Business Intelligence

> Understand and be able to set up Web database processing
> Learn the basic concepts of Extensible Markup Language (XML)
> Learn the basic concepts of business intelligence (BI) systems
> Learn the basic concepts of OLAP and data mining

This chapter introduces topics that build on the fundamentals you learned in the prior six chapters. Now that we have designed and built our database, we are ready to put it to work. In this chapter, we will look at some of the various applications that use database processing, with our primary focus on Web-based database processing. We will also look at Extensible Markup Language (XML), which is rapidly expanding what can be done with Web-based applications. Finally, we will briefly look at business intelligence (BI) applications, particularly OLAP and data mining.

For our work in this chapter, we will continue to use the Heather Sweeney Designs database that we modeled in Chapter 4, designed in Chapter 5, and created in Chapter 6. The name of the database is HSD, and an SQL Server 2005 database diagram for the HSD database is shown in Figure 7-1.

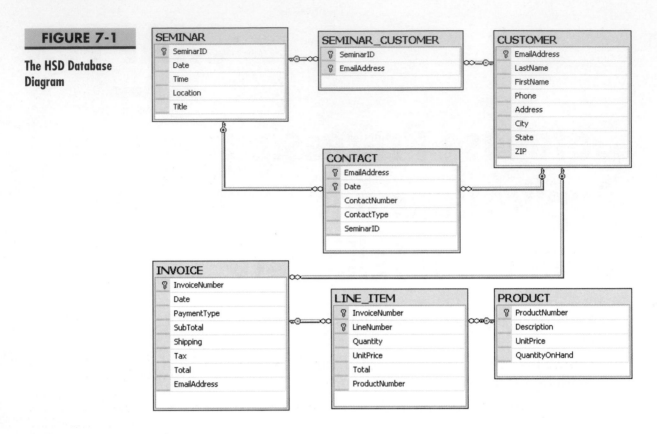

## THE DATABASE PROCESSING ENVIRONMENT

Databases vary considerably in size and scope, from single-user databases to large, interorganizational databases, such as an airline reservation system. As shown in Figure 7-2, which repeats Figure 6-4, they also vary in the way they are processed.

Some databases have only a few forms and reports. Others are processed by applications using Internet technology such as **Active Server Pages (ASPs)** and **Java Server Pages (JSPs)**. Still others are processed by ancient COBOL application programs or by more recent programs coded in Visual Basic .NET, Java, C#, or another language. Still other databases are processed by stored procedures and triggers. We'll consider each of these types of database processing in this chapter.

### Queries, Forms, and Reports

This book has focused on the use of a DBMS to build and process databases. For example, it has covered the need to specify rules, such as cascading updates or deletions. Applications are built to use the databases managed by the DBMS, and queries, forms, and reports are the basis of applications. Query, form and report generators can be built into a database product, such as Access, or they can be run as separate products. It is possible to use Access for its query, form, and report features while connecting to a database in another DBMS, such as SQL Server (Access files created for this function use the *.adp* extension). In this way, the Access "database" actually runs as an application that uses an attached, but distinct, database. Figure 7-3 shows an Access **project** (application) running

**FIGURE 7-2**

**The Database
Processing
Environment**

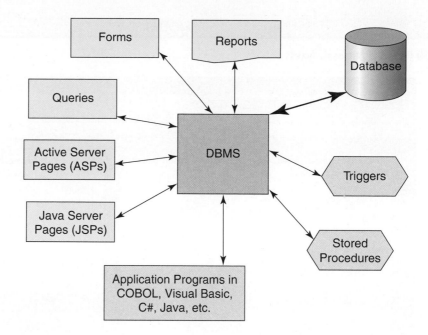

against the HSD database in SQL Server 2005 Express shown in Figure 6-3 and diagrammed in Figure 7-1.[1]

Note that in Figure 7-3 the HSD tables stored in SQL Server 2005 are shown in the table object in the Tables window, and that a Customer data input form created and stored in the Access HSD project file allows users to work with data in the CUSTOMER table.

Now, let's think about some of the tasks that the DBMS—for example, Access—needs to be doing in the background to implement the database processing commands. Suppose, for example, that you create a delete query on a table that has a 1:N relationship to a second table with On Delete Cascade permission. Suppose further that the second table has a 1:N relationship to a third table having Enforce Referential Integrity but without On Delete Cascade. When running your delete query, Access needs to delete rows from the first and second tables consistent with these relationship properties.

The situation is even more complicated if a second user is creating a report on these three tables as your delete query is operating. What should Access do? Should it show the report with whatever data remain as your query runs? Or should Access protect the report from your deletions and not make any of them until the report is finished? Should it deny your query, or do something else completely?

For a simpler example, suppose you create a form that has data from one table in the main section and data from a second table in a subform. Now, suppose a user makes changes in five rows in the subform, then makes changes to some of the data in the first form, then presses the Escape key. Which of these changes will actually be made to the database? None? Changes to the subform data only? Or some other option?

Even in the case of simple queries, forms, and reports, management of the background functions is complex. You can change properties in your database to govern some of Access's behavior in these cases, but you need to know the implications of such

---

[1]Before you can connect an Access project to an SQL Server 2005 database, you must start the SQL Server Browser. Use **Start | Programs | Microsoft SQL Server 2005 | Configuration Tools | SQL Server Configuration Manager** command to run the SQL Server Configuration Manager. Look under SQL Server 2005 Services to find the SQL Server Browser, and use the SQL Server Browser properties to (1) start the service and (2) set it to Automatic start mode. Additionally, users must have appropriate permissions for database use—this was discussed in Chapter 6.

**FIGURE 7-3**

**The HSD Project in Microsoft Access**

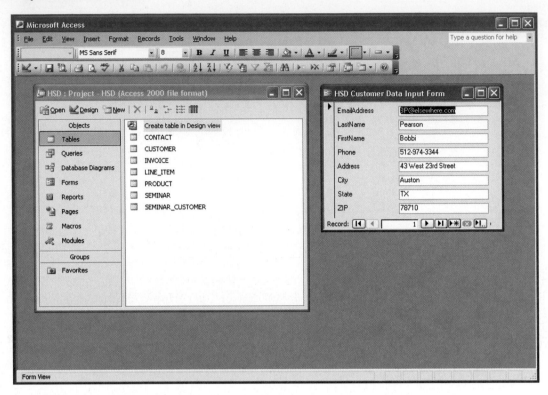

changes. Organizational DBMS products, such as SQL Server, MySQL, Oracle, and DB2, provide many more features and functions that let the developer change DBMS behavior for such cases. Many of these were discussed in the concurrency control section in Chapter 6.

## Client/Server and Traditional Application Processing

Organizational database processing began in the early 1970s. Since then, thousands, if not millions, of databases have been processed by application programs written in COBOL, Basic, C, C++, Visual Basic, Java, and C#. All these languages embed SQL statements or their equivalent into programs written in these standard languages.

For example, to process an online order, an application needs to perform the following functions.

- Communicate with a user to obtain customer and salesperson identifiers.
- Read CUSTOMER data.
- Read SALESPERSON data.
- Present an order entry form to a user.
- Obtain ordered ITEMs and quantities.
- Verify stock levels for ITEMs.
- Remove ITEMs from inventory.
- Schedule backorders as necessary.
- Schedule inventory picking and shipping.
- Update CUSTOMER, SALESPERSON, ORDER, and LINE_ITEM data.

The application will be written to respond to exceptions, such as data not present, data in error, communication failure, and dozens of other potential problems.

In addition, an order-processing application program will be written so that it can be used by many users concurrently. We addressed this issue in Chapter 6 when we discussed concurrency control. Based on that discussion, you should understand how, for example, 50 to 100 users trying to run such an application at the same time would be able to do so.

## Stored Procedures and Triggers

Enterprise-class DBMS products, such as SQL Server, Oracle, MySQL, and DB2, include features to allow developers to create modules of logic and database actions called triggers and stored procedures. Triggers and stored procedures are written in languages provided by the DBMS.[2] For example, SQL Server has a language called TRANSACT-SQL (T-SQL), while Oracle has developed a language called PL/SQL. Programmers can embed SQL statements in these programming languages.

A **trigger** is a program stored within the database that is executed by the DBMS when specific events occur. The events are typically SQL commands using the INSERT, UPDATE, or DELETE statements. These events are then handled with BEFORE, AFTER, or INSTEAD OF trigger logic. Thus, we will find such trigger combinations as BEFORE DELETE, INSTEAD OF UPDATE, and AFTER INSERT (note that these are examples—there are nine possible combinations of trigger logic and SQL statements).

Different DBMS products support different sets of triggers. For example, Oracle supports BEFORE, AFTER, and INSTEAD OF triggers. MySQL 5.0 supports only BEFORE and AFTER triggers. SQL Server 2000 supported only BEFORE and AFTER triggers, but SQL Server 2005 trigger support has been extended beyond the nine trigger combinations described previously.

A **stored procedure** is similar to a computer program subroutine or function, but it is stored within the database that performs database activity. An example for the HSD database would be a stored procedure to update the columns of INVOICE for a particular InvoiceNumber as LINE_ITEMs are added to the INVOICE. Application programs, Web applications, and interactive query users can invoke the stored procedure, pass parameters to it, and receive results.

## ▶ WEB DATABASE PROCESSING

The environment in which today's Internet technology database applications reside is rich and complicated. As shown in Figure 7-4, a typical Web server needs to publish applications that involve data of many different data types. In this text, we have considered only relational databases, but there are many other data types as well.

Several standard interfaces have been developed for accessing database servers. Every DBMS product has an **application program interface (API)**. An API is a collection of objects, methods, and properties for executing DBMS functions from program code. Unfortunately, each DBMS has its own API, and APIs vary from one DBMS product to another. To save programmers from having to learn to use many different interfaces, the computer industry has developed standards for database access.

The **Open Database Connectivity (ODBC)** standard was developed in the early 1990s to provide a DBMS-independent means for processing relational database data. In the mid-1990s, Microsoft announced **OLE DB**, which is an object-oriented interface that encapsulates data-server functionality. OLE DB was designed not just for access to relational databases, but also for accessing many other types of data as well. As a COM

---

[2]For more information on triggers, stored procedures, and their uses, see David M. Kroenke, *Database Processing: Fundamentals, Design, and Implementation* 10th Edition (Upper Saddle River, NJ: Prentice-Hall, 2006) Chapters 7, 10, and 11.

**FIGURE 7-4**

**The Web Database Processing Environment**

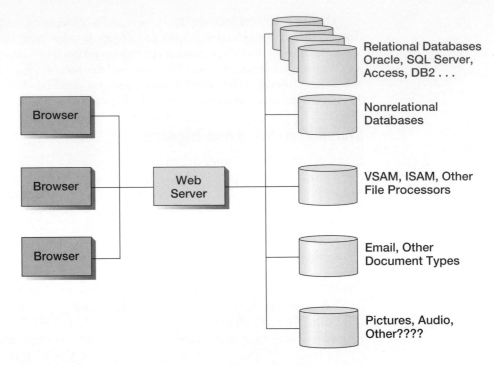

interface, OLE DB is readily accessible to programmers using such programming languages as C, C#, and Java. However OLE DB is not as accessible to users of Visual Basic and scripting languages. Therefore, Microsoft developed **Active Data Objects (ADO)**, which is a set of objects for utilizing OLE DB that is designed for use by any language, including VB, VBScript, and JScript. ADO has now been followed by **ADO.NET**, which is an improved version of ADO developed as part of Microsoft's .NET initiative. In this text, we'll look at ODBC and ADO and how we can use them to write Web-based database applications, and use ASP technology and techniques. ASPs are combinations of HTML and VBScript or JScript that can read and write database data and transmit it over public and private networks using Internet protocols. ASPs run on Microsoft's Web Server product, which is named **Internet Information Server (IIS)**. The roles of ODBC, OLE DB, and ADO are illustrated in Figure 7-5.

Figure 7-2 also shows JSP technology. JSPs are similar combinations of HTML and Java that accomplish the same function by compiling pages into Java servlets. JSPs are often used on the open-source **Apache** Web Server. Another favorite combination of

**FIGURE 7-5**

**ODBC, OLE DB, and ADO in the Web Database Processing Environment**

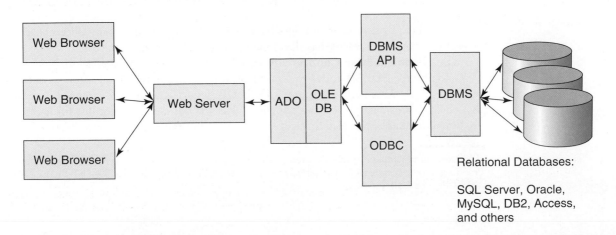

Web developers is the Apache Web Server with the MySQL database and either the Pearl or PHP language. This combination is called **AMP** (Apache-MySQL-PHP/Pearl). When running on the Linux operating system, it's referred to as **LAMP**; when running on the Windows operating system, it's referred to as **WAMP**.[3]

In a Web-based database processing environment, if the Web server and the DBMS can run on the same computer, the system has **two-tier architecture**. (One tier is for the browsers and one is for the Web server/DBMS computer.) Alternatively, the Web server and DBMS can run on different computers in which the system has **three-tier architecture**. High-performance applications might use many Web server computers, and in some systems, several computers can run the DBMS, as well. In the latter case, if the DBMS computers are processing the same databases, the system is referred to as a distributed database. (Distributed databases were discussed in Chapter 6.)

## ODBC

The Open Database Connectivity (ODBC) standard allows programmers to code instructions to various DBMS products using ODBC standard statements. These instructions are passed to an ODBC driver, which translates them into the API of the particular DBMS in use. The driver receives results back from the DBMS and translates those results into a form that is part of the ODBC standard.

**ODBC Architecture** The basic ODBC architecture in a three-tier Web server environment—*but before OLE DB and ADO*—is shown in Figure 7-6. The application program, the **ODBC driver manager**, and the **ODBC DBMS driver** (a multi-tier driver in this case) all reside on the Web server. The DBMS driver sends requests to data sources, which reside on the database server. According to the ODBC standard, a **data source** is the database, its associated DBMS, operating system, and network platform.

The application issues requests to create a connection with a data source; to issue SQL statements and receive results; to process errors; and to start, commit, and roll back transactions. ODBC provides a standard means for each of these requests, and it defines a standard set of error codes and messages.

The driver manager serves as an intermediary between the application and the DBMS drivers. When the application requests a connection, the driver determines the type of DBMS that processes a given ODBC data source and loads that driver in memory (if it is not already loaded).

A **driver** processes ODBC requests and submits specific SQL statements to a given type of data source. There is a different driver for each data source type. It is the responsibility of the driver to ensure that standard ODBC commands execute correctly. The driver also converts data source error codes and messages into the ODBC standard codes and messages.

---

### FIGURE 7-6

**ODBC Three-tier Web Server Architecture**

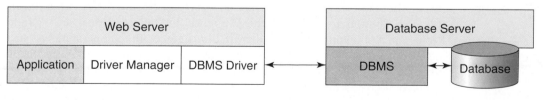

SQL Commands

---

[3]For information on JSPs, JDBC, and related technology and tools, see David M. Kroenke, *Database Processing: Fundamentals, Design, and Implementation* 10th Edition (Upper Saddle River, NJ: Prentice-Hall, 2006) Chapter 14.

ODBC identifies two types of drivers: single tier and multiple tier. A **single-tier** driver processes both ODBC calls and SQL statements. A **multiple-tier** driver processes ODBC calls, but passes the SQL requests directly to the database server. Although it may reformat an SQL request to conform to the dialect of a particular data source, it does not process the SQL.

**Establishing an ODBC Data Source Name**   A **data source** is an ODBC data structure that identifies a database and the DBMS that processes it. There are three types of data sources: file, system, and user. A **file data source** is a file that can be shared among database users. The only requirement is that the users have the same DBMS driver and privilege to access the database. A **system data source** is one that is local to a single computer. The operating system and any user on that system (with proper permissions) can use a system data source. A **user data source** is available only to the user who created it. Each created data source is given a **data source name (DSN)** that is used to reference the data source.

In general, the best choice for Internet applications is to create a system data source on the Web server. Browser users then access the Web server, which in turn uses a system data source to set up a connection with the DBMS and the database.

We will need a system data source for the Heather Sweeney Designs HSD database so that we can use it in a Web database processing application. To create a system data source in the Windows XP operating system, use the **ODBC Data Source Administrator**.

Opening the ODBC Data Source Administrator:

1. Open the Windows Control Panel by clicking the **Start** button and then clicking **Control Panel**.
2. In the Control Panel window, double-click the **Administrative Tools** icon.
3. In the Administrative Tools window, double-click the **Data Sources (ODBC)** shortcut icon.

Creating a system data source named HSD:

1. In the ODBC Data Source Administrator, click the **System DSN** tab, and then click the **Add button**.
2. In the Create New Data Source dialog box, select **SQL Native Client** as shown in Figure 7-7, and then click the **Finish** button.
3. In the Create New Data Source to SQL Server dialog box, enter the information shown in Figure 7-8—note that the database server is selected from the Server drop-down list—and then click the **Next** button.
4. Continue through the configuration. Set the authentication to use HSD-User, and set the default database to HSD. The completed HSD system data source is shown in Figure 7-9. Click the **OK** button to close the ODBC Data Source Administrator.

## Web Processing with IIS

Now that we have our ODBC data source created, let's take a look at Web processing using Microsoft's Internet Information Server (IIS) and ASPs. One advantage of this combination for users of the Windows 2000 Professional and Windows XP Professional operating systems is that IIS is included with the operating system. It is not installed by default but can be easily installed at another time. This means that any user can practice creating and using Web pages on their own workstation. When IIS is installed, it creates an *Inetpub* folder on the C: drive as C:\Inetpub. Within the *Inetpub* folder is a subfolder named *wwwroot*, which is where IIS stores the most basic Web pages used by the Web server. Figure 7-10 shows this directory structure after IIS has been installed, with the files in the *wwwroot* folder displayed in the file pane.

IIS is managed using a program called simply **Internet Information Services**. To open Internet Information Services, open **Control Panel** and then open

**FIGURE 7-7**

The Create New Data
Source Dialog Box

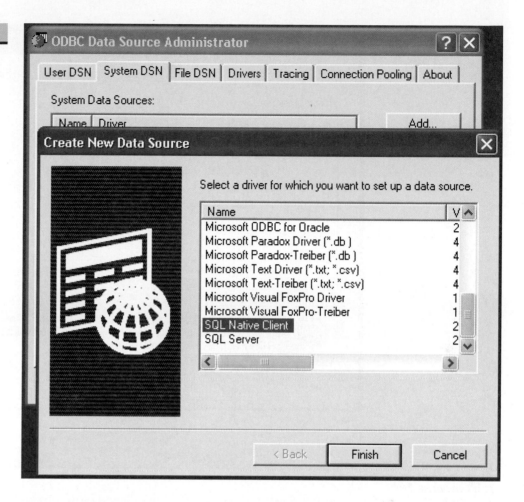

**FIGURE 7-8**

The Create New Data
Source to SQL Server
Dialog Box

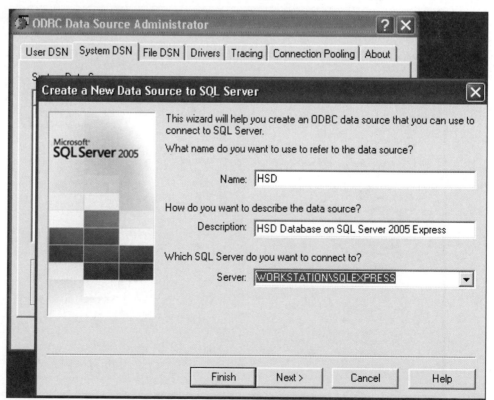

**FIGURE 7-9**

**The Completed HSD System Data Source**

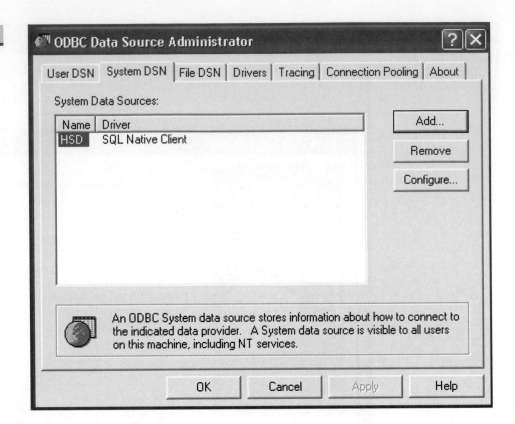

**FIGURE 7-10**

**The IIS wwwroot Folder**

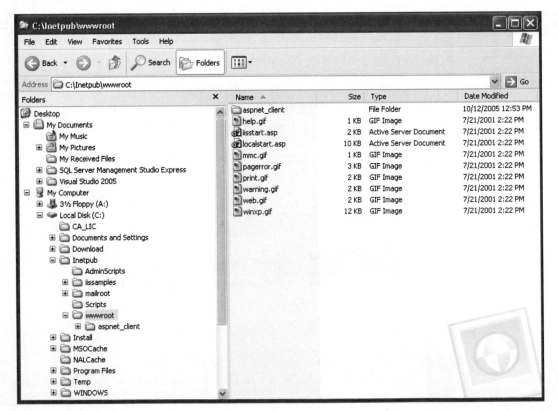

---

**FIGURE 7-11**

The Internet Information Services Management Program

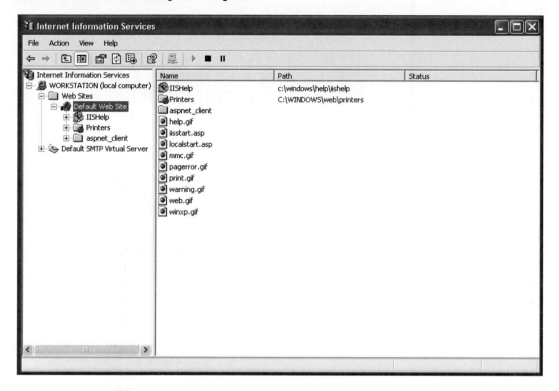

**Administrative Tools**. The shortcut icon for Internet Information Services is located in Administrative Tools, and Figure 7-11 shows the Internet Information Services management window.

Note that the files shown in the *Default Web Site* folder in Figure 7-11 are the same files that are in the *wwwroot* folder in Figure 7-10—they are the default files created by IIS when it is installed. The file *iisstart.asp* generates the Web page that Internet Explorer (or any other Web browser) contacting this Web server over the Internet will see displayed. When you contact the Web from the workstation running ISS, the *iisstart.asp* file calls the file *localstart.asp* which provides a special Web page for Web server administrator. To test the Web server installation, open your Web browser, type in the URL http://localhost, and press the **Enter** key. The Web page generated by *localstart.asp* shown in Figure 7-12 should be displayed—if it isn't, your Web server is not properly installed.

IIS processes HTTP and provides other features and functions that support server programs. We'll set up a small Web site that can be used for Web database processing of the Heather Sweeney Designs HSD database.

First, we'll create two new folders under the wwwroot folder—*DBC* and *ADO-Files*. The *DBC* (Database Concepts) folder will be used to hold all the Web pages developed from chapter discussions or exercises in this book. The *ADO-Files* folder will be used to hold a special file we'll need for our work with ASPs. The file we want is named *adovbs.inc*, and in Window XP, it is located in the *C:\Program Files\Common Files\System\ado* folder (if you don't find it there, search for it by name on the C: drive). We'll simply copy *adovbs.inc* to the *ADO-Files* folder.

Second, we'll create one more new folder. This one will be a subfolder of DBC and will be named *HSD*. This folder will hold the Heather Sweeney Designs HSD Web site.

**FIGURE 7-12**

The IIS Localstart
Web Page

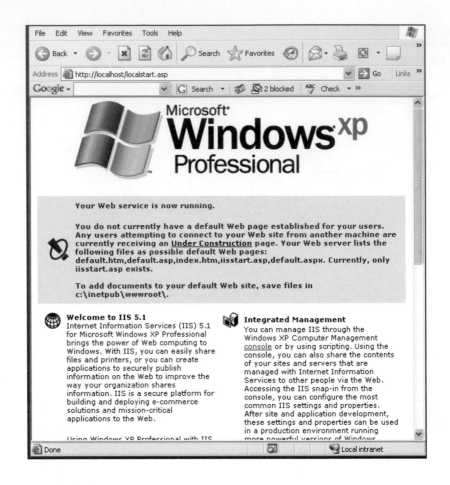

Next, we'll create a simple HTML home page for the Heather Sweeney Designs Web site, and place it in the *HSD* folder.[4] The name of this file is *Default.htm*, which is a special name as far as Web services are concerned. It is one of a few file names that the Web server automatically displays when a URL request is made without a specific file reference. It will become the new default display page for our Web server. The code for *Default.htm*, which consists entirely of basic HTML statements,[5] is shown in Figure 7-13. If we now use the URL http://localhost/DBC/HSD, we get the Web page shown in Figure 7-14.

## Active Server Pages (ASPs)

Now that we have our basic Web site set up, we'll start using ASPs. Let's consider an example that we can use for this discussion. The ASP code for *ReadSeminar.asp*, which is located in the *HSD* folder, is shown in Figure 7-15.

---

[4]There are numerous Web page editors available, but all you need to create Web pages is a simple text editor. The work on the pages in this chapter was done using the Microsoft Notepad ASCII text editor, which is supplied with the Windows operating system.

[5]To learn more about HTML, go to the Web site of the World Wide Web Consortium (W3C) at http://www.w3.org. For good HTML tutorials, see David Raggett's *Getting Started with HTML* tutorial at http://www.w3.org/MarkUp/Guide, his *More Advanced Features* tutorial at http://www.w3.org/MarkUp/Guide/Advanced.html, and his *Adding a Touch of Style* tutorial at http://www.w3.org/MarkUp/Guide/Style.html.

**FIGURE 7-13**

The HTML Code for the
*Default.htm* File in the
*HSD* Folder

```
<html>
    <head>
        <meta http-equiv="Content-Type" content="text/html; charset=windows-1252">
        <title>Heather Sweeney Designs Demonstration Pages Home Page</title>
    </head>
    <body>
        <P align="center">
            <font face="" color="#0000ff" size="6">
                Database Concepts (3rd Edition)
            </font>
        </P>
        <p align="center">
            <b>David M. Kroenke (University of Washington)</b>
        </p>
        <p align="center">
            <b>David J. Auer (Western Washington University)</b>
        </p>
        <hr>
        <p align="center">
            <font size="5">
                Welcome to the Heather Sweeney Designs Home Page
            </font>
        </p>
        <hr>
        <p>Chapter 7 Demonstration Pages from Figures in the Text:</p>
        <p>Example 1:   
            <a href="ReadSeminar.asp">
                Display the SEMINAR Table (No surrogate key)
            </a>
        </p>
        <hr>
    </body>
</html>
```

Now if we use the URL http://localhost/DBC/HSD and then click on *Display the Seminar Table (No surrogate key)* we get the Web page shown in Figure 7-16.

The *ReadSeminar.asp* page runs the query

SELECT * FROM SEMINAR;

and displays the result of the query, without the surrogate key of SeminarID, in a Web page. The *ReadSeminar.asp* ASP code blends HTML (that are executed on the user's workstation) and VBScript program statements (that are executed on the Web server).

**FIGURE 7-14**

The *Default.htm* Web
Page in HSD

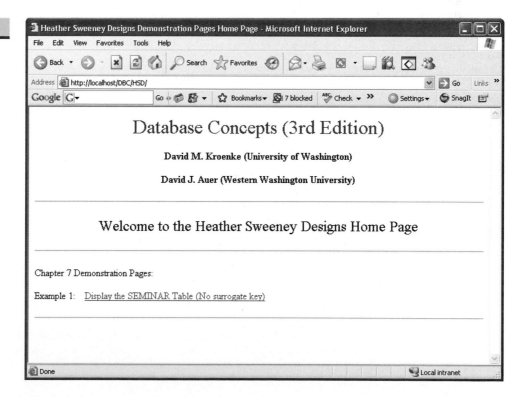

**FIGURE 7-15**

**The ASP Code for *ReadSeminar.asp***

```
<HTML>
    <HEAD>
        <META HTTP-EQUIV="Content-Type" CONTENT="text/html;charset=windows-1252">
        <TITLE>Seminar</TITLE>
    </HEAD>
<!--#include virtual="ADO-Files/adovbs.inc"-->
<BODY>
<%
    Dim objConn, objRecordSet, objField
    Dim varNumCols, varI, varSql

    Set objConn = Server.CreateObject("ADODB.connection")    'get connection

    objConn.open "HSD", "HSD-User", "HSD-User+password"
    objConn.IsolationLevel = adXactReadCommitted              'Use ADOVBS
    Set Session("_conn") = objConn

    Set objRecordSet = Server.CreateObject("ADODB.Recordset")

    varSQL = "SELECT * FROM SEMINAR"

    objRecordSet.Open varSql, objConn, adOpenStatic , adLockReadOnly
                                            'static cursor with read only lock
%>

    <p align="center">
        <font size="5">
            The Heather Sweeney Designs SEMINAR Table
        </font>
    </p>
    <hr>
    <TABLE BORDER=1 BGCOLOR=#ffffff CELLSPACING=5>
        <FONT FACE="Arial" COLOR=#000000>
            <B>SEMINAR</B>
        </FONT>
    <THEAD>
        <TR>
<%
    varNumCols = objRecordSet.Fields.Count
    For varI = 0 to varNumCols - 1
        Set objField = objRecordSet.Fields(varI)
            ' objField.Name now has the name of the field
            ' objField.Value now has the value of the field
        If objField.Name <> "SeminarID" Then                  ' omit surrogate key
%>

            <TH BGCOLOR=#c0c0c0 BORDERCOLOR=#000000 >
                <FONT SIZE=2 FACE="Arial" COLOR=#000000>
                    <%=objField.Name%>
                </FONT>
                 
            </TH>
<%
        End If
    Next
%>
        </TR>
    </THEAD>
    <TBODY>
<%
    On Error Resume Next
    objRecordSet.MoveFirst
    do while Not objRecordSet.eof
%>
        <TR VALIGN=TOP>
<%
    varNumCols = objRecordSet.Fields.Count
    For varI = 0 to varNumCols - 1
    Set objField = objRecordSet.Fields(varI)
    If objField.Name <> "SeminarID" Then     ' omit surrogate key
%>
            <TD BORDERCOLOR=#c0c0c0 >
                <FONT SIZE=2 FACE="Arial" COLOR=#000000>
                    <%=Server.HTMLEncode(objField.Value)%>
                    <BR>
                </FONT>
            </TD>
<%
    End If
    Next
%>
        </TR>
```

**FIGURE 7-15** *(Continued)*

```
<%
    objRecordSet.MoveNext
    loop
%>

    </TBODY>
    <TFOOT></TFOOT>
</TABLE>
<p></p>
<hr>
<p align="center">
    <a href="../HSD/Default.htm">Return to Heather Sweeney Designs Home Page</a>
</p>
<hr>
</BODY>
</HTML>
```

In Figure 7-15, the statements included between <% and %>—and shown in red in the figure—are program code that is to be executed on the Web server computer. All the rest of the ASP code is HTML that is generated and sent to the browser client. In Figure 7-15, the statements:

> <HTML>
>
> > <HEAD>
> >
> > > <META HTTP-EQUIV="Content-Type" CONTENT="text/html;charset=windows-1252">
> > >
> > > <TITLE>Seminar</TITLE>
> >
> > </HEAD>
> >
> > <!--#include virtual="ADO-Files/adovbs.inc"-->
> >
> > <BODY>

are normal HTML code. When sent to the browser, they set the title of the browser window to Artist and cause other HTML-related actions. The next group of statements are

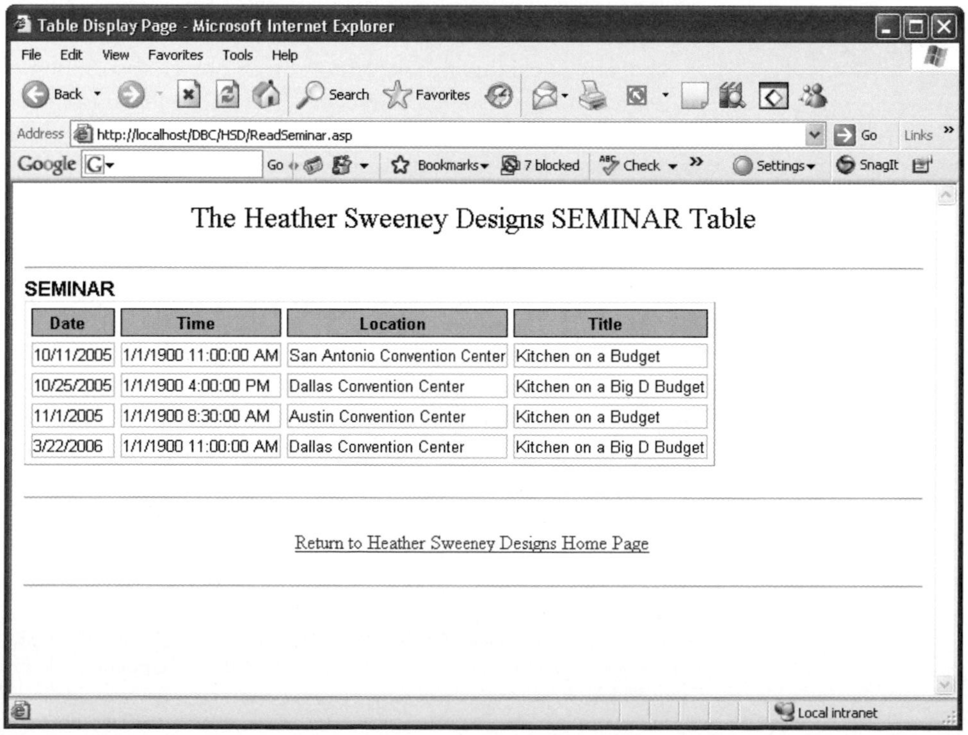

**FIGURE 7-16**

**Result of *ReadSeminar.asp* in Figure 7-15**

The Heather Sweeney Designs SEMINAR Table

SEMINAR

| Date | Time | Location | Title |
|------|------|----------|-------|
| 10/11/2005 | 1/1/1900 11:00:00 AM | San Antonio Convention Center | Kitchen on a Budget |
| 10/25/2005 | 1/1/1900 4:00:00 PM | Dallas Convention Center | Kitchen on a Big D Budget |
| 11/1/2005 | 1/1/1900 8:30:00 AM | Austin Convention Center | Kitchen on a Budget |
| 3/22/2006 | 1/1/1900 11:00:00 AM | Dallas Convention Center | Kitchen on a Big D Budget |

Return to Heather Sweeney Designs Home Page

included between <% and %> and, thus, are code that will be executed by IIS on the Web server computer. To understand these statements, we need to learn some more about ADO.

## Active Data Objects (ADO)

**ADO** is a simple object model that overlies the more complex OLE DB object model. ADO can be called from scripting languages, such as JScript and VBScript, and from more powerful languages, such as Visual Basic .NET, Java, C#, and C++. Because ADO is easier to understand and use than OLE DB, ADO is more frequently used for database applications.

**The ADO Object Model** The ADO object model is built on top of the OLE DB object model, but it isn't necessary to go into the specifics of the OLE DB object to understand ADO.[6] We do, however, need to learn some basic concepts of object-oriented programming that are common to OLE DB and ADO.

In particular, we need to understand abstractions, methods, properties, and collections. An **abstraction** is a generalization of something. For example, ODBC interfaces are abstractions of native DBMS access methods.

When we abstract something, we lose detail, but we gain the ability to work with a broader range of types. For example, a **recordset** is an abstraction of a table (relation). In this abstraction, a recordset is defined to have certain characteristics that will be common to all recordsets. Every recordset, for instance, has a set of columns, which are *Fields*. Thus, the goal of abstraction is to capture everything important, but omit details that are not needed by users of the abstraction. Therefore, SQL Server tables may have some characteristic that is not represented in a recordset, and the same might be true for tables in MySQL, Oracle, DB2, and other DBMS products. These unique characteristics will be lost in the abstraction, but if the abstraction is a good one, no one will care.

An object-oriented programming **object** is an abstraction that is defined by its properties and methods. **Properties** represent characteristics or attributes of the object. **Methods** are actions that the object can perform. For example, a recordset object has an *AllowEdits* property, a *RecordsetType* property and an *EOF* (End of File) property. A recordset object also has methods, such as *Open*, *MoveFirst*, *MoveNext*, and *Close*.

Strictly speaking, the definition of an object abstraction is called an **object class**, or just class. An instance of an object class, such as a particular recordset, is called an object. All objects of a class have the same properties and the same methods, but the values of the properties vary from object to object.

The last term we need to address is collection. A **collection** is an object that contains a group of other objects. A recordset has a collection of other objects called Fields. The collection, being an object, also has properties and methods. One of the properties of all collections is *Count*, which is the number of objects in the collection. Thus, *recordset.Fields.Count* is the number of fields in the collection.

In ADO and OLE DB, collections are named as the plural of the objects they collect. Thus, there is a Fields collection of Field objects, an Errors collection of Error objects, a Parameters collection of Parameters, and so forth. An important method of a collection is an **iterator**, which is a method that can be used to pass through or otherwise identify the items in the collection.

---

[6]For a complete discussion of the OLE DB, see David M. Kroenke, *Database Processing: Fundamentals, Design, and Implementation* 10th Edition (Upper Saddle River, NJ: Prentice-Hall, 2006) Chapter 12.

**FIGURE 7-17**

**The ADO Object Model**

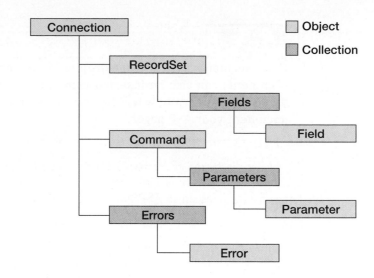

If you're getting frustrated and somewhat confused with all these definitions, don't give up—you will see the practical use of these concepts as we continue our discussion of ADO!

The ADO object model is shown in Figure 7-17.

The **Connection object** is the first ADO object to be created and is the basis for the others. From a connection, a developer can create one or more **RecordSet objects** and one or more **Command objects**. In the process of creating or working with any of these objects, ADO will place any errors (**error objects**) that are generated in the **Errors collection**.

Each RecordSet object has a **Fields collection**; each **Field element** corresponds to a column in the recordset. In addition, each Command object has a **Parameters Collection** that contains **Parameter objects** which are the parameters needed by the command.

**The Connection Object**   In the ASP code in Figure 7-15, the following VBScript code is embedded in the ASP to create a connection object. After it runs, the variable *objConn* will point to an object that is connected to the ODBC data source HSD.

```
<%

Dim objConn, objRecordSet, objField

Dim varNumCols, varI, varSql

Set objConn = Server.CreateObject("ADODB.connection")   'get connection

objConn.open "HSD", "HSD-User", "HSD-User+password"
objConn.IsolationLevel = adXactReadCommitted              'Use ADOVBS
Set Session("_conn") = objConn
```

In this code, variables that will be needed are declared using *Dim* statements, then the statement *Server.CreateObject* invokes the CreateObject method of the ASP server object. The type of object, here *ADODB.connection*, is passed as a parameter. After this statement executes, the variable *objConn* points to the new connection object.

> **B T W**
>
> Code segments with the apostrophe (') in front of them are comments. Comments can also be inserted using the symbols <!-- and -->. Any text between those symbols will be considered a comment. Use comments to document your ASP pages.

In our discussion of database administration in Chapter 6, we discussed the concurrency control topics of isolation levels, cursor types, and lock types. Now, we will see some of these in use in an ASP. Note the line in Figure 7-15 that reads:

```
objConn.IsolationLevel = adXactReadCommitted ' Use ADOVBS
```

This line sets the isolation level of this connection by using the *adovbs.inc* that we copied into the *ADO-Files* folder. The *adovbs.inc* file is a set of constants that are used by ADO to set concurrency control levels, and these ADO constants are shown in Figure 7-18.

The *adovbs.inc* file is made available to the ASP script with the *include* statement shown in Figure 7-15:

```
<!--#include virtual ="ADO-Files/adovbs.inc"-->
```

This statement must be part of the ASP file, but *outside* of the <% %> designators.

In the last statement, the open method of the connection is used to open the HSD ODBC data source. Here, the user ID of *HSD-User* and the password of *HSD-User+password* that we created in Chapter 6 are being used to authenticate to the DBMS. For the Windows operating system, an alternative would be to use the statement:

```
objConn.Open "HSD"
```

Here, instead of using a user ID and password, the database will be opened using an authenticated name provided by the operating system. By default, ASP will use the name *IUSR_machine-name*, or in this case, IUSR_WORKSTATION. If this method is used, this account must be set up in SQL Server 2005 with privileges to read and update the VRG user tables. However, since *IUSR_machine-name* is the name of any anonymous Web user, this is not a secure way to run a Web database processing application. For our purposes in this book, however, it could be used for learning purposes. Other drivers, such as the Oracle ODBC, do not allow a null password to be passed. For such drivers, we must provide a user ID and password.

At this point, a connection has been established to the DBMS via the ODBC data source, and the database is open. The *objConn* pointer can be used to refer to any other methods for a connection (see Figure 7-18), including the creation and use of RecordSet and Command objects. The Errors collection can be processed as well.

**The RecordSet Object**   Given the connection with an open database, the following code segment from Figure 7-15 will create a RecordSet object:

```
Set objRecordSet = Server.CreateObject("ADODB.Recordset")
varSQL = "SELECT * FROM SEMINAR"
objRecordSet.Open varSql, objConn, adOpenStatic , adLockReadOnly
'static cursor with read only lock
%>
```

These statements cause the SQL statement in varSQL to be executed using a static, read-only cursor. Only the Date, Time, Location, and Title columns of the SEMINAR table will be included as fields in the recordset.

**FIGURE 7-18**

**ADO Constants**

| Isolation Level | Const Name | Value |
|---|---|---|
| Dirty reads | adXactReadUncommitted | 256 |
| Read committed | adXactReadCommitted | 4096 |
| Repeatable read | adXactRepeatableRead | 65536 |
| Serializable | adXactSerializable | 1048576 |

(a) Isolation Levels

| Cursor Type | Const Name | Value |
|---|---|---|
| Forward only | adOpenForwardOnly | 0 |
| Keyset | adOpenKeyset | 1 |
| Dynamic | adOpenDynamic | 2 |
| Static | adOpenStatic | 3 |

(b) Cursor Types

| Lock Type | Const Name | Value |
|---|---|---|
| Read only | adLockReadOnly | 1 |
| Pessimistic locking | adLockPessimistic | 2 |
| Optimistic locking | adLockOptimistic | 3 |
| Optimistic with batch updates | adBatchOptimistic | 4 |

(c) Lock Types

**B  T  W**

There is a "gotcha" lurking here. With SQL Server, if a table name has spaces or odd characters or is a SQL Server reserved word, you enclose the name in brackets, []. To Oracle, however, a table name enclosed in brackets is illegal. For oddly named tables in Oracle, you enclose the name in quotes. Thus, if your database has such tables, you have to write different code, depending on whether you are using an SQL Server, Oracle, or some other DBMS.

**Fields Collection**   After the recordset has been created, its Fields collection is instantiated. We can process that collection with the following:

```
<%
    varNumCols = objRecordSet.Fields.Count
    For varI = 0 to varNumCols - 1
        Set objField = objRecordSet.Fields(varI)
            ' objField.Name now has the name of the field
            ' objField.Value now has the value of the field
        If objField.Name <> "SeminarID" Then ' omit surrogate key
%>
        <TH BGCOLOR=#c0c0c0 BORDERCOLOR=#000000 >
        <FONT SIZE=2 FACE="Arial" COLOR=#000000>
            <%=objField.Name%>
        </FONT>
         
        </TH>
<%
        End If
    Next
%>
```

In the first statement, *varNumCols* is set to the number of columns in the recordset by accessing the Count property of the Fields collection. Then, a loop is executed to iterate over this collection. The property *Fields(0)* refers to the first column of the recordset, so the loop needs to run from 0 to Count −1.

Next, *objField.Name* is used to print the names of the columns. *objField.Value* is used in a following section to print the data values.

**Errors Collection**   Whenever an error occurs, ADO instantiates an Errors collection. It must be a collection because more than one error can be generated by a single ADO statement. This collection can be processed in a manner similar to that for the Fields collection. The ReadSeminar.asp code contains only the single line:

```
<%
On Error Resume Next
```

However, we could insert more complete error handling, such as:

```
Dim varI, varErrorCount, objError
On Error Resume Next
varErrorCount = objConn.Errors.Count
If varErrorCount = 0 Then
```

```
For varI = 0 to varErrorCount −1

    Set objError = objConn.Errors(varI)

        ' objError.Description contains

        ' a description of the error

    Next

End If
```

In the loop in this example (*not* in *ReadSeminar.asp*) *objError* is set to *objConn. Errors(varI)*. Note that this collection belongs to *objConn*, not to *objRecordSet*. Also the Description property of *objError* can be used to display the error to the user.

Unfortunately, VBScript has quite limited error processing. The code for checking errors (starting with *On Error Resume Next*) must be placed after every ADO object statement that might cause an error. Because this can bulk up the code undesirably, it would be better to write an error-handling function and call it after every ADO object invocation.

**The Command Object** The ADO command object is used to execute queries and stored procedures that are stored with the database. The parameters collection of Command is used to pass parameters to the stored procedures. This topic is beyond the scope of this book—you should return to it when you study stored procedures in detail and start using them in your databases.

ASPs can contain only scripting language statements. However, such scripts can call COM objects written in languages like C# and C++. Thus, some Web database applications are a mixture of logic encoded in scripting languages along with calls to compiled objects.

The latest Web server offering from Microsoft is ASP.NET. This is a new version of ASP; with it, Web pages are blends of HTML and object-oriented programming statements. Whereas ASP pages are interpreted, ASP.NET pages are compiled. Therefore, ASP.NET pages are faster than ASP pages. ASP.NET pages also segregate HTML from programming statements so they are easier to understand and maintain.

## Challenges for Web Database Processing

Web database application processing is complicated by an important characteristic of HTTP. Specifically, HTTP is stateless; it has no provision for maintaining sessions between requests. Using HTTP, a client at a browser makes a request of a Web server. The server services the client request, sends results back to the browser, and forgets about the interaction with that client. A second request from that same client is treated as a new request from a new client. No data are kept to maintain a session or connection with the client.

This characteristic poses no problem for serving content, either static Web pages or responses to queries of a database. However, it is not acceptable for applications that require multiple database actions in an atomic transaction. Recall from Chapter 6 that in some cases, a group of database actions needs be grouped into a transaction with all of them committed to the database or none of them committed to the database. In this case, the Web server or other program must augment the base capabilities of HTTP.

For example, IIS provides features and functions for maintaining data about sessions between multiple HTTP requests and responses. Using these features and functions, the application program on the Web server can save data to and from the browser. A particular session will be associated with a particular set of data. In this way, the application program can start a transaction, conduct multiple interactions with the user at the browser, make intermediate changes to the database, and finally, commit or roll back all changes when ending the transaction.

Other means are used to provide for sessions and session data with Apache. In some cases, the application programs must create their own methods for tracking session data. PHP4 includes limited support for sessions that will likely be extended in the future.

The particulars of session management are beyond the scope of the present discussion. However, you should be aware that HTTP is stateless, and regardless of the Web server, additional code must be added to database applications to enable transaction processing.

## ▶ DATABASE PROCESSING AND XML

The **extensible markup language (XML)** is becoming a standard means for defining the structure of documents and for transmitting documents from one computer to another. XML is important for database processing because it provides a standardized means of submitting data to a database and for receiving results back from the database. XML is a large, complicated subject that requires several books to explain fully. Here, we will touch on the fundamentals and further explain why XML is important for database processing.

An example of an XML document for the HSD database is shown in Figure 7-19. XML is a markup language like HTML, but it is much more, as well. Consider the XML document in Figure 7-19, which contains data about an HSD seminar. Like HTML, it has tags that identify content. For example, the tag <Location> . . . </Location> identifies the data item San Antonio Convention Center. The tag <Title> . . . </Title> identifies the data value Kitchen on a Budget. Other tags identify the SeminarID, date and time.

### XML Schema Documents

HTML has a fixed set of tags that was determined by the developers of that language. In contrast, with XML, the author of a document type can create his or her own set of tags. That is the meaning of the term *extensible* in Extensible Markup Language—the developer can extend the basic XML tags. The author of a document type can declare the relationships the tags have to one another. Thus, with XML, Heather Sweeney Designs can declare that a document called INVOICE will have a tag named Customer. Within that tag, there could be a Name and a Phone number; within Name, there could be a LastName and a FirstName, and within Phone, there could be an AreaCode and a LocalNumber.

The allowable tags and their relationships to one another are defined in an XML schema document. Figure 7-20 shows an XML Schema document that defines the structure of the document in Figure 7-19. Without worrying about the particulars, notice the relationship of the tags in Figure 7-19 to their definition in Figure 7-20.

An XML document can declare the name and location of the schema document that defines the tags it uses. When this is done, a validation program can verify that the document does conform to its schema. Every browser today, as well as hundreds of other programs, contains a schema validation program. You can submit an XML document

**FIGURE 7-19**

**Example of an XML Document**

```
<?xml version="1.0" encoding="UTF-8"?>
<Seminar xmlns:xsi="http://www.w3.org/2001/XMLSchema-instance"
xsi:noNamespaceSchemaLocation="C:\Documents and Settings\Auer\My Documents\DBC-e03-Figure-
07-20.xsd">
    <SeminarID>1</SeminarID>
    <Date>10/11/2005</Date>
    <Time>11:00</Time>
    <Location>San Antonio Convention Center</Location>
    <Title>Kitchen on a Budget</Title>
</Seminar>
```

**FIGURE 7-20**

**XML Schema Document for the XML Document in Figure 7-19**

```
<?xml version="1.0" encoding="UTF-8"?>
<xs:schema xmlns:xs="http://www.w3.org/2001/XMLSchema" elementFormDefault="qualified"
attributeFormDefault="unqualified">
    <xs:element name="Seminar">
        <xs:complexType>
            <xs:sequence>
                <xs:element name="SeminarID"/>
                <xs:element name="Date"/>
                <xs:element name="Time"/>
                <xs:element name="Location"/>
                <xs:element name="Title"/>
            </xs:sequence>
        </xs:complexType>
    </xs:element>
</xs:schema>
```

and its schema to Internet Explorer, for example, and it will verify whether the document conforms to its schema or is a schema-valid document.

XML schema documents are themselves XML documents. This means that they, too, can be validated against their schema, which is a schema of schemas. That document is maintained by the World Wide Web Consortia (W3C) on its Web site at http://www.w3.org. That Web site contains much more information as well, including a number of excellent tutorials.

The ability of an automated process to validate documents means enormous cost savings. For example, a large corporation, such as Wal-Mart, can publish XML schemas for all the documents that it exchanges with its vendors. In particular, suppose they publish an XML schema for invoice documents. Any vendor that wishes to submit an invoice to Wal-Mart can first obtain the schema (from a publicly accessible location on the Web) to determine how to prepare the invoice. The vendor can then prepare an invoice accordingly and can check its work by validating the invoice before sending it. When Wal-Mart receives the invoice, it validates it against the schema to ensure that the vendor sent a correctly formatted invoice. Thus, once the document has been created, the validation is automated. This might not sound important, but it can save thousands of clerical hours for a corporation like Wal-Mart.

## XML and Database Processing

What does all this have to do with database processing? Notice the next-to-last sentence in the prior paragraph: "Once the document has been created, the validation is automated." How are the XML documents to be generated in the first place? In addition, once a company has received and validated a document, how does it place the data in that document into its database?

The answer is to use database applications. Such applications can be written to generate XML documents that conform to an XML schema document, and they can be written to accept such documents and extract that data for storage in the database.

The means by which this is done is currently under development. One way is to extend SQL to cause the results from a SQL statement to be produced in XML format. For example, Figure 7-21 shows the following SQL statement, which uses the SQL FOR XML clause, run on SQL Server 2005 Express Edition.

SELECT    *

FROM      SEMINAR

          FOR XML AUTO, ELEMENTS;

Note that in Figure 7-21 the output (which is all in one cell in this format) in the Messages window is a hyperlink. Clicking the hyperlink produces the XML output shown in Figure 7-22.

This output was then saved as a file named SEMINAR.XML, and edited (the <MyData> . . . </MyData> tags were added) into the text output shown in Figure 7-23.

**FIGURE 7-21**

**SQL FOR XML Query**

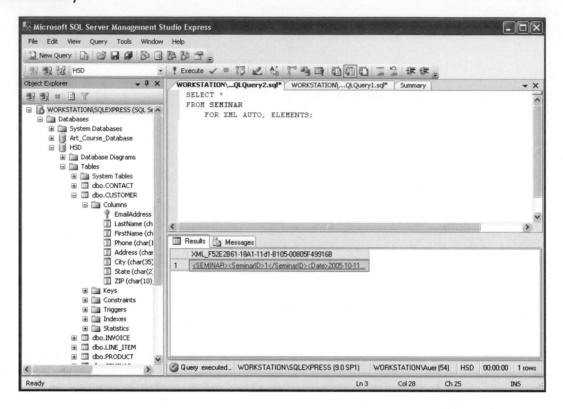

**FIGURE 7-22**

**Results of the SQL FOR XML Query**

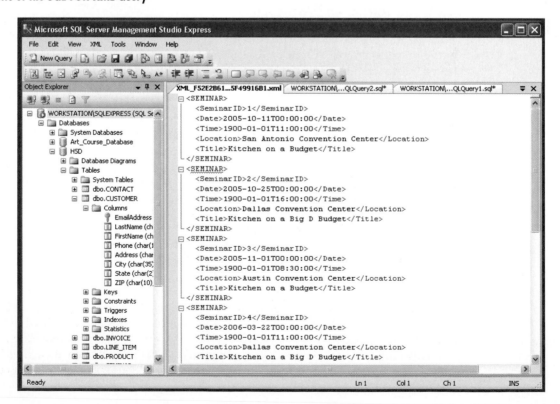

**FIGURE 7-23**

**Text Output from the
SQL FOR XML Query**

```
<MyData>
    <SEMINAR>
        <SeminarID>1</SeminarID>
        <Date>2005-10-11T00:00:00</Date>
        <Time>1900-01-01T11:00:00</Time>
        <Location>San Antonio Convention Center</Location>
        <Title>Kitchen on a Budget</Title>
    </SEMINAR>
    <SEMINAR>
        <SeminarID>2</SeminarID>
        <Date>2005-10-25T00:00:00</Date>
        <Time>1900-01-01T16:00:00</Time>
        <Location>Dallas Convention Center</Location>
        <Title>Kitchen on a Big D Budget</Title>
    </SEMINAR>
    <SEMINAR>
        <SeminarID>3</SeminarID>
        <Date>2005-11-01T00:00:00</Date>
        <Time>1900-01-01T08:30:00</Time>
        <Location>Austin Convention Center</Location>
        <Title>Kitchen on a Budget</Title>
    </SEMINAR>
    <SEMINAR>
        <SeminarID>4</SeminarID>
        <Date>2006-03-22T00:00:00</Date>
        <Time>1900-01-01T11:00:00</Time>
        <Location>Dallas Convention Center</Location>
        <Title>Kitchen on a Big D Budget</Title>
    </SEMINAR>
</MyData>
```

This solution is not satisfactory for a number of reasons. It works for certain data structures but not for all. Other means are currently being developed by Oracle, Microsoft, and additional companies. ADO.NET, for example, is Microsoft's leading solution for the transformation of XML documents to and from databases.

## XML Web Services

The use of XML for the transmission of database data is even more important because of the development of a new standard called XML Web Services. XML Web Services involves several new standards including SOAP, WSDL, UDDI, and others. In essence, XML Web Services is a means for exposing elements of program functionality over the Web.

For example, suppose you have created a database application that converts currencies. Your program will receive the amount of money stated in one currency and convert it into a second currency. You can convert U.S. dollars into Mexican pesos, or Japanese yen into euros, and so on. Using XML Web Services, you can publish your database application over the Web in such a way that other programs can consume your program as if it were on their own machine. It will appear to them as if they are using a local program even though your program might be on the other side of the world.

Perhaps you have heard the statement "The Internet is the computer." That statement becomes a reality when different computers, connected via Internet plumbing, can share programs as if they are all on the same machine.

When database applications are written as XML Web Services, any computer in the world can access the database applications using standard interfaces, and it will appear as if the applications are local to the machine that uses those applications. Thus, Wal-Mart can publish its ordering application as an XML Web Service, and its vendors can write programs to consume that ordering application. The particulars are beyond the scope of this discussion. Realize, however, that Web Services are going to be important in the future, and learning about them could be advantageous.

# ▶ BUSINESS INTELLIGENCE SYSTEMS

**Business intelligence (BI)** systems are information systems that assist managers and other professionals in the analysis of current and past activities and in the prediction of future events. Unlike transaction processing systems, they do not support operational activities, such as the recording and processing of orders, but rather support management assessment, analysis, planning, and control.

BI systems fall into two broad categories: reporting and data mining. **Reporting systems** sort, filter, group, and make elementary calculations on operational data. **Data mining applications**, on the other hand, perform sophisticated analyses on data, analyses that usually involve complex statistical and mathematical processing.

Figure 7-24 summarizes the relationship among operational and business intelligence systems. Operational systems, such as order entry, purchasing, manufacturing, and inventory support primary business activities. They use the DBMS to both read data from and store data in the operational database.

BI systems support management and management activities. They obtain data from three possible sources. First, they read and process data from the operational database. They use the operational DBMS to obtain data, but they do not insert, modify, or delete operational data. Second, BI systems process data that is extracted from operational databases. In this situation, they manage the extracted database using a BI DBMS, which may be the same or different from the operational DBMS. Finally, BI systems read data that is purchased from data vendors.

## OLAP and Data Mining

Two popular BI applications are OLAP and data mining. We will briefly consider each.

**OLAP**  **OnLine Analytical Processing (OLAP)** is a technique for slicing and dicing database data in a dynamic fashion. OLAP is a tool to use when you don't know the second question to ask until you see the answer to the first question.

Figure 7-25 shows an OLAP analysis of student project data.

---

**FIGURE 7-24**

**The Relationship Among Operational and BI Applications**

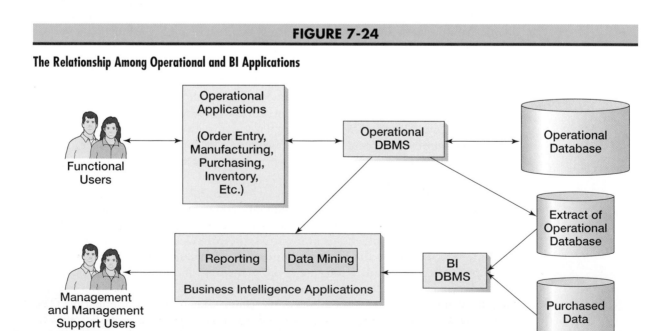

**FIGURE 7-25**

**OLAP Analysis of Student Assignment Scores**

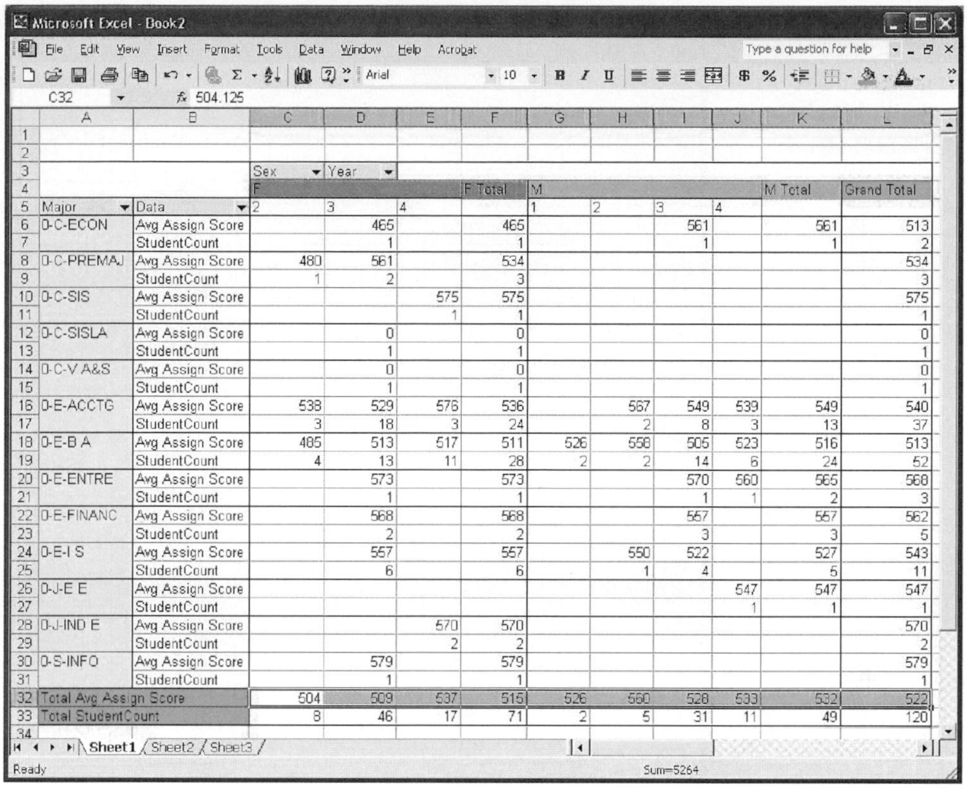

| Major | Data | F: 2 | F: 3 | F: 4 | F Total | M: 1 | M: 2 | M: 3 | M: 4 | M Total | Grand Total |
|---|---|---|---|---|---|---|---|---|---|---|---|
| 0-C-ECON | Avg Assign Score | | 465 | | 465 | | | 561 | | 561 | 513 |
| | StudentCount | | 1 | | 1 | | | 1 | | 1 | 2 |
| 0-C-PREMAJ | Avg Assign Score | 480 | 561 | | 534 | | | | | | 534 |
| | StudentCount | 1 | 2 | | 3 | | | | | | 3 |
| 0-C-SIS | Avg Assign Score | | | 575 | 575 | | | | | | 575 |
| | StudentCount | | | 1 | 1 | | | | | | 1 |
| 0-C-SISLA | Avg Assign Score | | 0 | | 0 | | | | | | 0 |
| | StudentCount | | 1 | | 1 | | | | | | 1 |
| 0-C-V A&S | Avg Assign Score | | 0 | | 0 | | | | | | 0 |
| | StudentCount | | 1 | | 1 | | | | | | 1 |
| 0-E-ACCTG | Avg Assign Score | 538 | 529 | 576 | 536 | | 567 | 549 | 539 | 549 | 540 |
| | StudentCount | 3 | 18 | 3 | 24 | | 2 | 8 | 3 | 13 | 37 |
| 0-E-B A | Avg Assign Score | 485 | 513 | 517 | 511 | 526 | 558 | 505 | 523 | 516 | 513 |
| | StudentCount | 4 | 13 | 11 | 28 | 2 | 2 | 14 | 6 | 24 | 52 |
| 0-E-ENTRE | Avg Assign Score | | 573 | | 573 | | | 570 | 560 | 565 | 568 |
| | StudentCount | | 1 | | 1 | | | 1 | 1 | 2 | 3 |
| 0-E-FINANC | Avg Assign Score | | 568 | | 568 | | | 557 | | 557 | 562 |
| | StudentCount | | 2 | | 2 | | | 3 | | 3 | 5 |
| 0-E-I S | Avg Assign Score | | 557 | | 557 | | 550 | 522 | | 527 | 543 |
| | StudentCount | | 6 | | 6 | | 1 | 4 | | 5 | 11 |
| 0-J-E E | Avg Assign Score | | | | | | | | 547 | 547 | 547 |
| | StudentCount | | | | | | | | 1 | 1 | 1 |
| 0-J-IND E | Avg Assign Score | | | 570 | 570 | | | | | | 570 |
| | StudentCount | | | 2 | 2 | | | | | | 2 |
| 0-S-INFO | Avg Assign Score | | 579 | | 579 | | | | | | 579 |
| | StudentCount | | 1 | | 1 | | | | | | 1 |
| Total Avg Assign Score | | 504 | 509 | 537 | 515 | 526 | 560 | 528 | 533 | 532 | 522 |
| Total StudentCount | | 8 | 46 | 17 | 71 | 2 | 5 | 31 | 11 | 49 | 120 |

The body of the table shows the **measures** of the analysis, which in this case are the average of student project scores and the total number of students. If you look in the bottom, right-hand corner of this table, you can see that the average total points for all students was 522. You also can see that the analysis was performed on a total of 120 students.

A **dimension** in an OLAP analysis is a characteristic associated with the measures. Figure 7-25 shows three measures: Major (shown in rows), Sex, and Year (shown in columns). The values of the majors are coded; the user of this analysis knows the meanings of these values. For your interpretation, the value *O-E-ACCTG* means a business college accounting major, the value *O-E-B A* means a general business administration major, the value *O-E I S* means a business college information systems major, and so forth.

The values of the Sex dimension are *F* (female) and *M* (male), and the values of the Year dimension are *1* (freshman), *2* (sophomore), *3* (junior), and *4* (senior). If you examine this table, you can see the results of average project scores broken down by the dimensions. Looking along the right-hand margin, you can see, for example, that a total of 37 accounting students averaged 540 points on the projects. The 52 business administration students averaged 513 points.

Looking along the bottom of the grid you can see that a total of 71 females and 49 males are counted in the data, including 8 sophomore females, 46 junior females, and 17 senior females. You can see the average for each of these categories, as well.

One of the advantages of OLAP is that the dimensions can easily be switched and combined in different ways. Figure 7-26 shows the same data, but this time broken down first by grade level and second by sex.

The analysis in Figure 7-25 was changed to that in Figure 7-26 by simply dragging and dropping the Year label on top of the Sex label. Using the analysis in Figure 7-26, you can now see, for example, that the average scores and number of students for freshmen, sophomores, juniors, and seniors were, respectively (526, 2), (525, 13), (516, 77),

**FIGURE 7-26**

Alternative OLAP Analysis of Student Assignment Scores

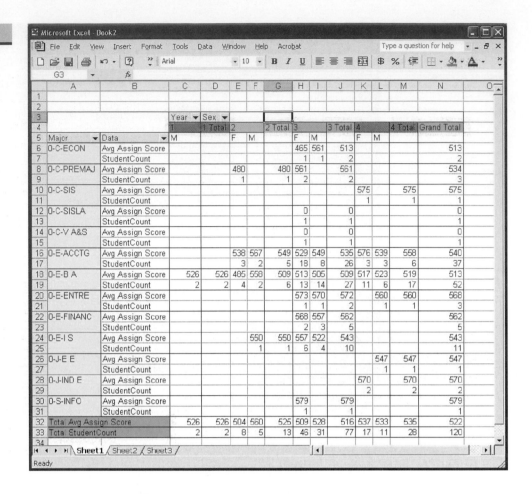

and (535, 28). Other breakouts on this data would be to show Major with Year, Year within Major, Major within Sex, and Sex within Major.

Figures 7-25 and 7-26 show an analysis with three dimensions. The number of dimensions in an OLAP analysis is unlimited. It is possible to have as many dimensions as are available from the underlying data.

Figure 7-27 shows the Cube Editor window for the Analysis Services (OLAP) processor that is part of the SQL Server. The right-hand pane shows the structure of the two tables used to generate Figures 7-25 and 7-26. The Sex, Year, and Major columns of STUDENT were used for the dimensions. The TotalGrade column of AssignmentGrade6 (which is actually a join and not a table in the underlying database) was used to provide the measure. If desired, other columns of STUDENT could generate other dimensions. LabSection, for example, would make a good dimension.

Figures 7-25 and 7-26 are two-dimensional projections of the three dimensions of data. If this table were shown as a cube, it would include a Major axis, a Year axis, and a Sex axis. If a LabSection dimension were included, then we would have a four-dimensional display.

Because a cube has three dimensions and because three dimensions are the most that can be shown in a display, an OLAP analysis like that in Figure 7-25 is called an **OLAP cube**. Such terminology is misleading because the display is a table, and the table is not restricted to three dimensions; regardless, such displays are called OLAP cubes. Hence, the display in Figure 7-27 is called the Cube Editor.

OLAP is a powerful analytical tool that is easy to learn, at least for basic analyses. Much untapped information undoubtedly lies in operational databases. Learning to use OLAP could be an excellent career builder for you.

**FIGURE 7-27**

OLAP Cube Editor for Data Used in Figures 7-25 and 7-26

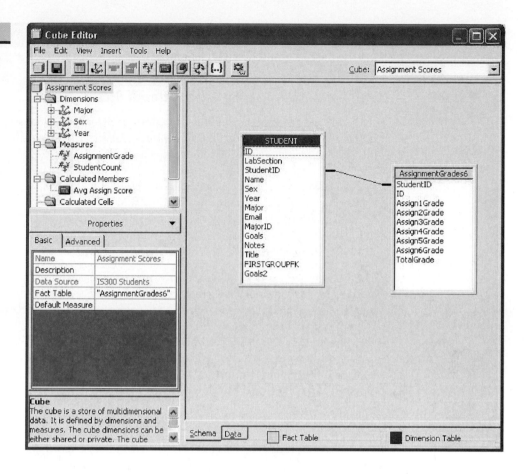

**Data Mining**  Data mining is another form of analysis of database data. Whereas OLAP consists of the analysis of sums, averages, and other simple arithmetic measures, data mining involves the statistical processing of data, usually involving complicated mathematical and statistical techniques.

Cluster analysis is one form of data mining. With it, the underlying data are processed to search for non-normal (in the statistical sense, as in a non-Gaussian distribution) groupings in the data. For example, the data shown in Figure 7-26 might be analyzed to determine that junior, female accounting majors and senior, male information systems majors have a similar, non-normal pattern of project scores. A cluster analysis is so named because it results in descriptions of the data points that tend to cluster together.

Other forms of data mining involve regression analysis, time-series analysis, factor analysis, and more sophisticated fitting techniques, such as nonparametric Monte Carlo analysis. Each of these techniques is used to search for patterns in the database data.

Data mining is used increasingly in science, where it is causing some debate and consternation among traditional scientists. When using data mining, researchers gather data and use statistical techniques to find patterns. After those patterns are found, the researchers look for explanations in science. This flies in the face of traditional research, in which hypotheses are formed and then experiments are designed to test those hypotheses. Traditional scientists would say that using data mining is allowing the throw of the dice to determine the theory. On the contrary, proponents of data mining say that data mining is just a way of using the immense computational power of the modern computer to facilitate the growth in scientific knowledge.

**THE ACCESS WORKBENCH**

## Section 7

### Web Database Processing Using Microsoft Access

Now that we've built the Wallingford Motors CRM database it's time to develop a Web application to allow Wallingford Motors sales staff to access it over the Web. In this section, we will cover the following objectives:

- Build a Web home page for Wallingford Motors
- Create an ODBC data source to access the WMCRM database
- Build a Web page to display data about customer contacts

### A Web Home Page for Wallingford Motors

The actions we need to take here are the same discussed for Heather Sweeney Designs in the chapter. We'll create a folder to hold the Web site files, and build a home page named *Default.htm* in that folder. The HTML code for the WM Default.htm page is shown in Figure AW-7-1.

This code can be used in any text editor or Web page editor, but the simplest one to use for our purposes is the Microsoft Notepad ASCII text editor. Notepad is not fancy, but it does the job, produces clean HTML (what we type in and only what we type in), and comes with Windows.

#### Creating the Wallingford Motors Web Site

1. Click **Start | All Programs | Accessories | Windows Explorer** to open Windows Explorer. Expand the **C:** drive in **My Computer** so that the *wwwroot* folder is displayed. See Figure 7-10 in the chapter for this display.
2. Expand the *wwwroot* folder to display the **DBC** folder.
3. Click the **DBC** folder object to display the folder and files in the *DBC* folder.
4. Right-click anywhere in the file pane to display the shortcut menu.

### FIGURE AW-7-1

**The HTML Code for the *Default.htm* File in the *WM* Folder**

```
<html>
    <head>
        <meta http-equiv="Content-Type" content="text/html; charset=windows-1252">
        <title>Wallingford Motors CRM Demonstration Pages Home Page</title>
    </head>
    <body>
        <P align="center">
            <font face="" color="#0000ff" size="6">
                Database Concepts (3rd Edition)
            </font>
        </P>
        <hr>
        <p align="center">
            <font size="5">
                Welcome to the Wallingford Motors Home Page
            </font>
        </p>
        <hr>
        <p>The Access Workbench Section 7 Web Pages:</p>
        <p>Report 1:   
            <a href="CustomerContacts.asp">
                Display the Customer Contacts List (viewCustomerContacts)
            </a>
        </p>
        <hr>
    </body>
</html>
```

5. Click **New**, then click **Folder**.
6. Name the new folder **WM**.
7. Click the new **WM folder** object to display the folder and files in the *DBC* folder—this will be empty.
8. Right-click anywhere in the file pane to display the shortcut menu.
9. Click **New**, then click **Text Document**.
10. Name the new Text Document **Default.htm.**
11. Right-click the **Default.htm** file to display the shortcut menu.
12. Click **Open With**, then click **Notepad**.
13. Enter the text shown into the open Default.htm file in Notepad. The completed text is shown in Figure AW-7-2.
14. Use the Notepad **File | Save** menu command to save the *Default.htm* file.
15. Close Notepad.
16. Open Windows Explorer or whatever Web browser you use.
17. Type the URL *http://DBC/WM* into the Address text box and press the **Enter** key. The WM home page appears in the Web browser as shown in Figure AW-7-3.
18. Close the Web browser.

### Selecting the Database File

In Section 6's "The Access Workbench," we secured the WMCRM database. In this section, however, we will be running with the *unsecured* version of the WMCRM database, and we're going to put the WMCRM on the WM Web site itself.

If you did *not* work through Section 6's "The Access Workbench," put a copy of the WMCRM.mdb file from your My Documents folder in the WM Web site folder. If you *did* work through it, put a copy of the WMCRM.bak file (this is the unsecured copy of WMCRM.mdb that the Security Wizard created) from your My Documents

---

**FIGURE AW-7-2**

**The *Default.htm* file in Notepad**

```
Default.htm - Notepad
File  Edit  Format  View  Help
<html>
        <head>
                <meta http-equiv="Content-Type" content="text/html; charset=windows-1252">
                <title>wallingford Motors CRM Demonstration Pages Home Page</title>
        </head>
        <body>

                <P align="center">
                        <font face="" color="#0000ff" size="6">
                                Database Concepts (3rd Edition)
                        </font>
                </P>
                <hr>
                <p align="center">
                        <font size="5">
                                Welcome to the wallingford Motors Home Page
                        </font>
                </p>
                <hr>
                <p>The Access workbench Section 7 Web Pages:</p>
                <p>Report 1:   
                        <a href="CustomerContacts.asp">
                                Display the Customer Contacts List (viewCustomerContacts)
                        </a>
                </p>
                <hr>
        </body>
</html>
```

*(Continued)*

## FIGURE AW-7-3

**The Wallingford Motors Home Page**

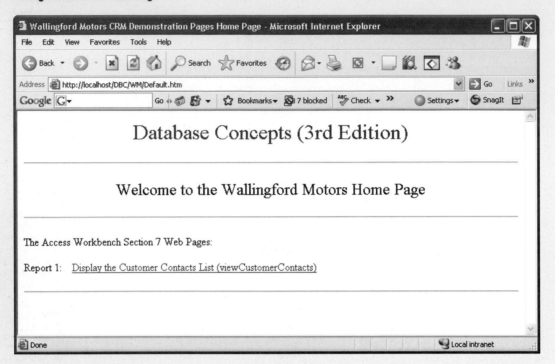

folder in the WM Web site folder, and then *rename* the copy of the WMCRM.bak in the WM folder to WMCRM.mdb.

### Creating an ODBC Data Source

We've got the basic Wallingford Motors Web site set up. Now, we need to create an OBDC data source. Again, we follow the same steps outlined in the chapter.

*Creating the WM System Data Source*

1. Open the Windows Control Panel by clicking the **Start** button and then clicking **Control Panel**.
2. In the Control Panel window, click **Administrative Tools**.
3. In the Administrative Tools window, click the **Data Sources (ODBC)** shortcut icon.
4. In the ODBC Data Source Administrator, click the **System DSN** tab, and then click the **Add** button.
5. In the **Create New Data Source** dialog box, select **Microsoft Access Driver** as shown in Figure AW-7-4, and then click the **Finish** button.
6. The ODBC Microsoft Access Setup dialog box appears. In the Data Source Name text box type **WM**. In the Description text box type **Wallingford Motors CRM on Access 2003**.
7. Click the **Database: Select** button and then select the **WMCRM.mdb** database in the Select Database dialog box as shown in Figure AW-7-5.
8. Click the **OK** button to close the Select Database dialog box.
9. Click the **OK** button to close the ODBC Microsoft Access Setup dialog box.
10. Click the **OK** button to close the ODBC Data Source Administrator.

**FIGURE AW-7-4**

**Selecting the Microsoft Access Driver**

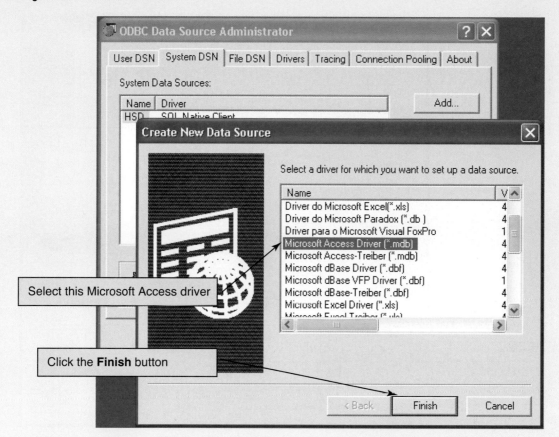

## Creating the Customer Contacts View

We want to display a list of customer contacts. The list will contain a combination of data from the CONTACT and CUSTOMER tables. To simplify the process, we'll define a view named viewCustomerContacts. SQL views are discussed in Appendix C, and if you haven't studied that material, take a few minutes to read Appendix C. In Access, a view is simply a saved query. Figure AW-7-6 shows the details of the viewCustomerContacts query.

There is nothing new here. We know how to create Access QBE queries, so we'll create and save the viewCustomerContacts query. After we're done, we'll close both the WMCRM database and Access at this time.

## Creating the ASP Page

All that's left to do is to create an ASP that we will name *CustomerContacts.asp*. This is the ASP that will query the database and display the returned data. The code for the *CustomerContacts.asp* is shown in Figure AW-7-7.

At this point, we know how to use Microsoft Notepad ASCII to create a text file, so we'll use it to create the *CustomerContacts.asp* file and store it in the *WM* folder.

*(Continued)*

---

**FIGURE AW-7-5**

**Selecting the WMCRM.mdb Database**

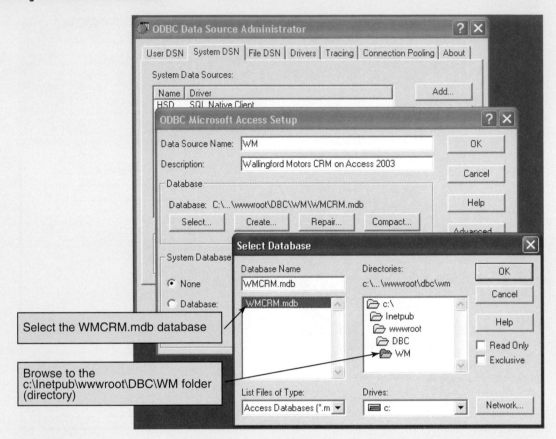

---

**FIGURE AW-7-6**

**The viewCustomerContacts Query**

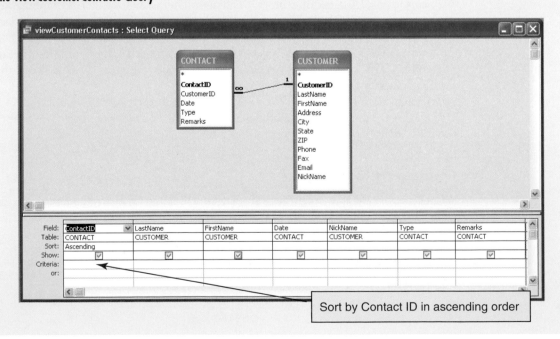

## The ASP Code for *CustomerContacts.asp*

```
<HTML>
    <HEAD>
        <META HTTP-EQUIV=" Content-Type" CONTENT="text/html;charset=windows-1252">
        <TITLE>WMCRM Customer Contacts Page</TITLE>
    </HEAD>
<!--#include virtual="ADO-Files/adovbs.inc"-->
<BODY>
<%
    Dim objConn, objRecordSet, objField
    Dim varNumCols, varI, varSql


    Set objConn = Server.CreateObject("ADODB.connection") ' get connection
    objConn.open "WM"
    objConn.IsolationLevel = adXactReadCommitted          ' avoid dirty reads
    Set Session("_conn") = objConn

    Set objRecordSet = Server.CreateObject("ADODB.Recordset")

    varSQL = "SELECT * FROM viewCustomerContacts"

    objRecordSet.Open varSql, objConn, adOpenStatic , adLockReadOnly
                                         ' static cursor with read only lock
%>
    <p align="center">
        <font size="5">
            The Wallingford Motors CRM Customer Contacts List
        </font>
    </p>
    <hr>

    <TABLE BORDER=1 BGCOLOR=#ffffff CELLSPACING=5>
        <FONT FACE="Arial" COLOR=#000000>
            <B>viewCustomerContacts</B>
        </FONT>
    <THEAD>
        <TR>
<%
    varNumCols = objRecordSet.Fields.Count
    For varI = 0 to varNumCols - 1
    Set objField = objRecordSet.Fields(varI)
%>


        <TH BGCOLOR=#c0c0c0 BORDERCOLOR=#000000 >
            <FONT SIZE=2 FACE="Arial" COLOR=#000000>
                <%=objField.Name%>
            </FONT>
             
        </TH>
<%
    Next
%>
        </TR>
    </THEAD>
    <TBODY>
<%
    On Error Resume Next
    objRecordSet.MoveFirst
    do while Not objRecordSet.eof
%>
        <TR VALIGN=TOP>
<%
    varNumCols = objRecordSet.Fields.Count
    For varI = 0 to varNumCols - 1
    Set objField = objRecordSet.Fields(varI)
%>
            <TD BORDERCOLOR=#c0c0c0 >
                <FONT SIZE=2 FACE="Arial" COLOR=#000000>
                    <%=Server.HTMLEncode(objField.Value)%>
                    <BR>
                </FONT>
            </TD>
<%
    Next
%>
        </TR>
```

*(Continued)*

---

```
<%
   objRecordSet.MoveNext
   loop
%>
      </TBODY>
      <TFOOT></TFOOT>
   </TABLE>

   <p></p>
   <hr>
   <p align="center"><a href="../WM/Default.htm">Return to Wallingford Motors Home Page</a></p>
   <hr>

   </BODY>
   </HTML>
```

### Running the ASP Page

We're done, so let's try out the *CustomerContacts.asp.*

### Using the CustomerContacts.asp

1. Open Windows Explorer or whatever Web browser you use.
2. Type the URL *http://DBC/WM* into the Address text box and press the **Enter** key. The WM home page appears in the Web browser.
3. Click the Report hyperlink labeled "Display the Customer Contacts List (viewCustomerContacts)." The Web page is displayed as shown in Figure AW-7-8.
4. Close the Web browser.

---

Result of the *CustomerContacts.asp*

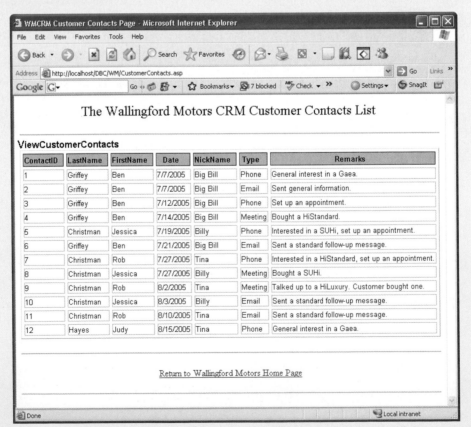

### In Closing

Our work is done. Neither the WMCRM database nor Access is open, so we don't have to close them.

In "The Access Workbench," we have covered the essentials of working with Microsoft Access. We haven't covered everything, but now you know how to create and populate Access databases; build and use Access queries (including view equivalent queries), forms, and reports; how to secure an Access database; and how to connect to an Access database from a Web page. And that should give you a solid foundation to build on, which was, after all, the overall goal of "The Access Workbench."

## SUMMARY

This chapter introduces five advanced topics: Web database processing, XML and database processing, distributed database processing, OLAP and data mining, and object-relational database management.

Databases vary not only in size and scope and in their number of users, but also in the way they are processed. Some databases are processed just by queries, forms, and reports; some are processed by ASPs and JSPs that use Internet technology to publish database applications; some are processed by traditional application programs; and some are processed by stored procedures and triggers. Other databases are processed by all of these types of applications, with hundreds or thousands of concurrent users.

Web database processing systems consist of users who employ browsers that connect via HTTP to a Web server that processes communications and database applications. The database applications process the database via the DBMS. In a two-tiered system, the Web server and DBMS reside on the same computer. In a three-tiered system, the Web server and DBMS reside on different computers. Higher-capacity systems employ more than one Web server.

If the Web server host runs Windows, the Web server software is usually IIS. IIS processes the HTTP protocol and Active Server Pages. These pages are blends of HTML and scripting code. HTML is processed and sent to the users' browsers. Any scripting code enclosed in <% . . . %> is executed on the Web server. Database application logic is often processed using such scripts. Scripts also can call COM objects written in full programming languages. If the Web server host runs Linux or Unix, then the Web server software is normally Apache.

Every DBMS has it own API. The Open Database Connectivity (ODBC) standard provides an interface by which database applications can access and process relational data sources in a DBMS-independent manner. ODBC involves applications program, driver manager, DBMS driver, and data source components. Single-tier and multiple-tier drivers are defined. There are three types of data source names: file, system, and user. System data sources are recommended for Web servers. The process of defining a system data source name involves specifying the type of driver and the identity of the database to be processed.

Key object terms are abstraction, methods, properties, and collections. Objects are defined by properties that specify their characteristics and methods that are actions they can perform. A collection is an object that contains a group of other objects.

ADO is a simple object model used by OLE DB data consumers. It can be used from any language supported by Microsoft. The ADO object model has Connection, RecordSet, Command, and Errors collection objects. Recordsets have a Fields collection, and Commands have a Parameters collection.

A Connection object establishes a connection to a data provider and data source. Connections have an isolation mode. Once a connection is created, it can be used to create RecordSet and Command objects. RecordSet objects represent cursors; they have both CursorType and LockType properties. RecordSets can be created with SQL statements. The Fields collection of a RecordSet can be processed to individually manipulate fields.

The Errors collection contains one or more error messages that result from an ADO operation. The command object is used to execute stored parameterized queries or stored procedures.

Microsoft's latest Web server offering is ASP.NET. With it, object-oriented programming languages like VisualBasic.Net, C#, and C++ can be used. ASP.NET pages are compiled and not interpreted.

Web database processing is complicated by the fact that HTTP is stateless. When processing atomic transactions, application programs must include logic to provide for session state. The means by which this is done depends on the Web server and language in use.

XML is becoming a standard means for defining documents and transmitting them from one computer to another. Increasingly, it is used to transmit data to and from database applications. XML tags are not fixed but can be extended by document designers. An XML schema is a document that defines the structure of another document. XML schema documents are themselves XML documents; their structure is defined by a schema document at http://www.w3.org. A document that conforms to its schema is a schema-valid document. Hundreds of programs are available that can determine schema validity. The ability to use automated means to verify document correctness means substantial labor savings to organizations.

Database applications can create XML documents. One means for doing this is via extensions to SQL like the FOR XML expression in SQL Server, and ADO.NET is another.

XML Web Services include several standards that enable program functionality to be published, or consumed, over the Web. Using XML Web Services, a database application can be used by computer programs across the Web as if those programs were on the local machine. XML Web Services enable the Internet to become one large computer.

BI applications obtain data from three sources: operational databases, extracts of operational databases, and purchased data. BI systems sometimes have their own DBMS, which can be the same or different from the operational DBMS. Common BI applications are of reporting and data mining applications.

OLAP is a reporting application. With OLAP, measures of data are summed and averaged, and other simple arithmetic operations are performed. The measures are broken down by dimensions in the data. Exchanging the dimensions is easily done, and OLAP provides a flexible analytic tool.

Data mining involves the statistical processing of data, usually involving complicated mathematical and statistical techniques. Cluster analysis searches for groupings in the data. Data mining tools also include regression analysis, time-series analysis, factor analysis, and other more sophisticated techniques. The use of data mining has increased in science, where it is used to identify patterns and trends in data. Data mining flies in the face of traditional hypothesis testing, and its use is causing debate among scientists.

## REVIEW QUESTIONS

**7.1**  Describe five different ways databases can be processed (use Figure 7-2).

**7.2**  Summarize the issues involved in processing a form as described in this chapter.

**7.3**  Describe, in your own words, the nature of traditional database processing applications.

**7.4**  What is a trigger and how is it used?

**7.5**  Name three types of triggers.

**7.6**  What is a stored procedure and how is it used?

**7.7**  Describe why the data environment is complicated.

**7.8**  Name the three major components of a Web database application.

**7.9**  As explained in this chapter, what are the two major functions of the Web server?

**7.10**  Explain the difference between two-tier and three-tier architecture.

**7.11**  What is IIS and what functions does it serve?

**7.12**  What do the acronyms *ASP* and *JSP* stand for?

**7.13**  What is ASP and what functions does it serve?

**7.14**  What is the significance of the symbols <% and %> in an ASP?

**7.15**  What languages are used in ASPs?

**7.16**  What is ASP.NET?

**7.17**  In the Windows world, what type of Web pages are interpreted and what type are compiled?

**7.18**  What is Apache and what functions does it serve?

**7.19**  Explain the relationship of ODBC, OLE DB, and ADO.

**7.20**  Name the components of the ODBC standard.

**7.21**  What role does the driver manager serve?

**7.22**  What role does the DBMS driver serve?

**7.23**  What is a single-tier driver?

**7.24**  What is a multiple-tier driver?

**7.25**  Explain the differences between the three types of ODBC data sources.

**7.26**  Which ODBC data source type is recommended for Web servers?

**7.27**  Define *abstraction*.

**7.28**  Define *object properties* and *methods*.

**7.29**  What is the difference between an object class and an object?

**7.30**  What is an API?

**7.31**  What languages can use ADO?

**7.32**  List the objects in the ADO object model and explain their relationships.

**7.33**  What is the function of the Connection object?

**7.34**  Show a snippet of VBScript for creating a Connection object.

**7.35**  What is the function of the recordset object?

**7.36**  Show a snippet of VBScript for creating a recordset object.

**7.37**  What does the Fields collection contain? Explain a situation in which you would use it.

**7.38**  Show a snippet of VBScript for processing the Fields collection.

**7.39**  What does the Errors collection contain? Explain a situation in which you would use it.

**7.40**  Show a snippet of VBScript for processing the Errors collection.

**7.41**  What is the purpose of the Command object?

**7.42**  Explain the purpose of the <% and %> tags in ASP.

**7.43**  With respect to HTTP, what does *stateless* mean?

**7.44**  Under what circumstances does statelessness pose a problem for database processing?

**7.45**  In general terms, how are sessions managed by database applications when using HTTP?

**7.46** What does *XML* stand for?

**7.47** How does XML differ from HTML?

**7.48** Explain why XML is extensible.

**7.49** What is the purpose of an XML schema document?

**7.50** How is an XML document validated?

**7.51** How is an XML schema document validated?

**7.52** Explain an advantage of automated schema validation.

**7.53** In general terms, explain why XML is important for database processing.

**7.54** What is the purpose of the FOR XML expression in a SQL statement?

**7.55** What is the purpose of XML Web Services?

**7.56** Explain how XML Web Services enable the Internet to be the computer.

**7.57** What are BI systems?

**7.58** How do BI systems differ from transaction processing systems?

**7.59** Name and describe the two main categories of BI systems.

**7.60** What does *OLAP* stand for and what is its purpose?

**7.61** Give an example of a measure of an OLAP analysis.

**7.62** Give three examples of a dimension of an OLAP analysis.

**7.63** Explain the essential difference between the OLAP cube in Figure 7-25 and Figure 7-26.

**7.64** Explain the meaning of the term *OLAP cube*.

**7.65** How does data mining differ from OLAP?

**7.66** What is the purpose of cluster analysis?

**7.67** Summarize the philosophical problem when using data mining for scientific research.

## EXERCISES

**7.68** This exercise will create a Web home page in the DBC folder and link it to the HSD Home page in the HSD folder.

   **A.** Figure 7-28 shows the HTML code for a Web home page for the DBC folder. Note that the page is called *Default.htm*, the same name as the Web home page in the HSD folder. This is not a problem since the files are in different folders. Create the *Default.htm* in the DBC folder.

   **B.** Figure 7-29 shows some additional HTML to be added near the end of code for the HSD Web home page in the file *Default.htm* in the HSD folder. The new lines are shown in red. Update that file with the code.

   **C.** Try out the pages. Type http://localhost/DBC into your Web browser to display the DBC home page. From there, you should be able to move back and forth between the two pages by using the hyperlinks on each page. Note: You may need to hit the Refresh button on you Web browser when using the HDS home page to get the hyperlink back to the DBC home page to work properly.

**7.69** Create a Web page for Heather Sweeney Designs to display all the data in the CUSTOMER table. Add a hyperlink to the HSD home page to access the page.

**FIGURE 7-28**

The HTML Code for the
*Default.htm* File in the
DBC Folder

```
<html>
    <head>
        <meta http-equiv="Content-Type" content="text/html; charset=windows-1252">
        <title>DBC-e03 Home Page</title>
    </head>
    <body>
        <P align="center">
            <font face="" color="#ff0066" size="6">
                <b>Database Concepts (3rd Edition) Home Page</b>
            </font>
        </P>
        <hr>
        <p>
            <FONT size="4">
                Use this page to access Web-based materials from Chapter 7 of:
            </FONT>
        </p>
        <p align="center">
            <font color="#0000ff" face="" size="6">Database Concepts (3rd Edition)</font>
        </p>
        <p align="center">
            <b>David M. Kroenke (University of Washington)</b>
        </p>
        <p align="center">
            <b>David J. Auer (Western Washington University)</b>
        </p>
        <hr>
        <p align="left">
            <font color="#0000ff" face="" size="4">Chapter 7 Demonstration Pages: </font>
        </p>
            <p>
                <a href="HSD/Default.htm">Heather Sweeney Design Demonstration Pages</a>
            </p>
            <p>
                <a href="WM/Default.htm">Wallingford Motors CRM Demonstration Pages</a>
            </p>
        <P></P>
        <hr>
    </body>
</html>
```

**7.70** Create a Web page for Heather Sweeney Designs to display the EmailAddress, LastName, FirstName, and Phone of customers in the CUSTOMER table. Add a hyperlink to the HSD home page to access the page.

**7.71** Create a Web page for Heather Sweeney Designs to display the data in the SEMINAR_CUSTOMER table. Add a hyperlink to the HSD home page to access the page.

**7.72** Create a Web page for Heather Sweeney Designs to display the data in the SEMINAR_CUSTOMER table for the SEMINAR with SeminarID = 3. Add a hyperlink to the HSD home page to access the page.

**7.73** Create a Web page for Heather Sweeney Designs to display data in the SEMINAR, SEMINAR_CUSTOMER, and CUSTOMER tables to list the SEMINAR data and the EmailAddress, LastName, FirstName, and Phone of any CUSTOMER who attended the SEMINAR with SeminarID = 3. Add a hyperlink to the HSD home page to access the page.

**7.74** Go to http://www.w3.org and read tutorials on XML and XML schema. Develop an XML schema for a document that uses the data in the HSD

**FIGURE 7-29**

The HTML
Modifications for the
*Default.htm* File in the
DBC Folder

```
<p>Example 1:   
    <a href="ReadSeminar.asp">
            Display the SEMINAR Table (No Surrogate Key)
    </a>
</p>
<hr>
<p align="center">
    <a href="../Default.htm">
            Return to Database Concepts Home Page
    </a>
</p>
<hr>
    </body>
</html>
```

SEMINAR, SEMINAR_CUSTOMER and CUSTOMER tables. Give an example XML document for your schema. Use Internet Explorer (or any other program you find) to validate your three XML documents against your schema document.[7]

**7.75** Search the Web for the terms *ADO Tutorial* and *ADO.NET Tutorial*. Find out the purposes of ADO and ADO.NET. How are they similar, and how are they different?

**7.76** If you have an OLAP software product available to you, it should have tutorials to help you get started. Work through enough early tutorials that you understand how to create an OLAP cube. Explain, in general terms, the process for creating an OLAP cube.

## ACCESS WORKBENCH EXERCISES

**AW 7.1** If you haven't completed Exercise 7.68, do it now.

**AW 7.2** Link the WM home page to the DBC home page.

**AW 7.3** Using the WMCRM database, code an ASP to display the data in SALESPERSON. Add a hyperlink on the WM home page to access the page. Using your database, demonstrate that your page works.

**AW 7.4** Using the WMCRM database, code an ASP to display the data in VEHICLE. Add a hyperlink on the WM home page to access the page. Using your database, demonstrate that your page works.

**AW 7.5** Using the WMCRM database, create a view named viewSalespersonVehicle, which should include all the columns in both the SALESPERSON and VEHICLE tables. Code an ASP to display viewSalespersonVehicle. Add a hyperlink on the WM home page to access the page. Using your database, demonstrate that your page works.

## GARDEN GLORY PROJECT QUESTIONS

If you have not already implemented the Garden Glory database shown in Chapter 3 in a DBMS product, create and populate the GARDEN_GLORY database now in the DBMS of your choice (or as assigned by your instructor).

**A.** Create a user named *GG-User* with the password *GG-User+password*. Assign this user to database roles so that the user can read, insert, delete, and modify data.

**B.** If you haven't completed Exercise 7.68, do it now.

**C.** Add a new folder to the DBC Web site named *GG*. Create a Web home page for Garden Glory in this folder—use the file name *Default.htm*. Link this page to the DBC home page.

**D.** Create an appropriate ODBC data source for your database.

---

[7]XMLSpy Home Edition is available for free download at **http://www.altova.com/download_components .html**. This is an excellent program for XML work.

**E.** Code an ASP to display the data in PROPERTY. Add a hyperlink on the GG home page to access the page. Using your database, demonstrate that your page works.

**F.** Code an ASP to display the data in SERVICE. Add a hyperlink on the GG home page to access the page. Using your database, demonstrate that your page works.

**G.** Create a view named Property_Service_View that displays PROPERTY. PropertyID, PropertyName, SERVICE.Initials, Date, HoursWorked. Code an ASP to display the data in Property Service_View. Add a hyperlink to the GG home page to access the page. Using your database, demonstrate that your page works.

## JAMES RIVER JEWELRY PROJECT QUESTIONS

If you have not already implemented the James River Jewelry database shown in Chapter 3 in a DBMS product, create and populate the JAMES_RIVER_JEWELRY database now in the DBMS of your choice (or as assigned by your instructor).

**A.** Create a user named JRJ-*User* with the password JRJ-*User+password*. Assign this user to database roles so that the user can read, insert, delete, and modify data.

**B.** If you haven't completed Exercise 7.68, do it now.

**C.** Add a new folder to the DBC Web site named *JRJ*. Create a Web home page for James River Jewelry in this folder—use the file name *Default.htm*. Link this page to the DBC home page.

**D.** Create an appropriate ODBC data source for your database.

**E.** Code an ASP to display the data in PURCHASE. Add a hyperlink on the JRJ home page to access the page. Using your database, demonstrate that your page works.

**F.** Code an ASP to display the data in ITEM. Add a hyperlink on the JRJ home page to access the page. Using your database, demonstrate that your page works.

**G.** Create a view named Purchase_Item_Item_View that displays PURCHASE. InvoiceNumber, PURCHASE_ITEM.ItemNumber, PURCHASE.Date, ITEM. Description, and PURCHASE_ITEM.RetailPrice. Code an ASP to display the data in Purchase_Item_Item_View. Add a hyperlink to the JRJ home page to access the page. Using your database, demonstrate that your page works.

## THE QUEEN ANNE CURIOSITY SHOP PROJECT QUESTIONS

If you have not already implemented the Queen Anne Curiosity Shop database shown in Chapter 3 in a DBMS product, create and populate the QACS database now in the DBMS of your choice (or as assigned by your instructor).

**A.** Create a user named QACS-*User* with the password QACS-*User+password*. Assign this user to database roles so that the user can read, insert, and modify data.

**B.** If you haven't completed Exercise 7.68, do it now.

**C.** Add a new folder to the DBC Web site named *QACS*. Create a Web home page for the Queen Anne Curiosity Shop in this folder—use the file name *Default.htm*. Link this page to the DBC home page.

**D.** Create an appropriate ODBC data source for your database.

**E.** Code an ASP to display the data in PURCHASE. Add a hyperlink on the QACS home page to access the page. Using your database, demonstrate that your page works.

**F.** Code an ASP to display the data in ITEM. Add a hyperlink on the QACS home page to access the page. Using your database, demonstrate that your page works.

**G.** Create a view named Sale_Item_Item_View that displays SALE.SaleID, SALE_ITEM.SaleItemID, SALE.SaleDate, ITEM.ItemDescription, and SALE_ITEM.SalePrice. Code an ASP to display the data in Sale_Item_Item_View. Add a hyperlink to the QACS home page to access the page. Using your database, demonstrate that your page works.

# APPENDIX A

# Getting Started with Microsoft SQL Server 2005 Express Edition

> Learn how to create a database
> Learn how to submit SQL commands to create table structures
> Learn how to submit SQL commands to insert database data
> Learn how to submit SQL commands to query a database

**M**icrosoft's SQL Server is an enterprise class DBMS that has been around for many years. In November 2005, SQL Server 2005 was released, including the new SQL Server 2005 Express Edition. The Express Edition seems to be designed to compete with MySQL (see Appendix B). MySQL, while not having as many features as SQL Server, is an open-source database that has had the advantage of being available for free via downloads over the Internet. It has become widely used and very popular as a DBMS supporting Web sites running the Apache Web server.

Microsoft has released several versions of SQL Server 2005. SQL Server 2005 Express is the least powerful version, but it is intended for general use and can be downloaded for free from the Microsoft SQL Server home page at http://www.microsoft.com/sql/ default.mspx. You will need to download four programs:[1]

1. Microsoft SQL Server 2005 Express Edition
2. Microsoft SQL Server 2005 Management Studio Express Edition—this is the graphical management utility for SQL Server 2005 Express. SQL Server 2005 is a text command line oriented program. The SQL Server 2005 Management Studio makes it much easier to work with SQL Server 2005.
3. Microsoft .NET Framework 2.0
4. Microsoft Core XML Services (MSXML) (currently 6.0)

Read the installation requirements carefully. Before installing either of the SQL Server 2005 products, you should install the Microsoft .NET Framework 2.0 and the Microsoft Core XML Services (MSXML).

Be aware that SQL Server 2005 is an enterprise-class DBMS and, as such, is much more complex than Microsoft Access. Further, it does not include application development tools, such as form and report generators. For more information on the Microsoft Express series of products, a good place to start is http://msdn.microsoft.com/vstudio/express/support/faq.

## ▶ WHY SHOULD I LEARN TO USE SQL SERVER 2005 EXPRESS EDITION?

The most important reason in terms of this book is that SQL Server 2005 really handles SQL well. All the SQL results shown in Chapter 3 and Appendix C were created in SQL Server 2005 Express Edition. All the SQL commands and keywords in Chapter 3 marked "Does Not Work With MS Access SQL" will work with SQL Server 2005.

## ▶ WHAT WILL THIS APPENDIX TEACH ME?

As the name implies, this appendix is designed to get you started creating databases and running SQL commands using SQL Server 2005.

## ▶ WHAT WON'T THIS APPENDIX TEACH ME?

The material in this appendix does not go beyond what is necessary to get you started. There are many important SQL Server 2005 topics not covered here, including stored procedures, triggers, backup and restore, and database security. These topics are covered in David M. Kroenke's *Database Processing: Fundamentals, Design, and Implementation,* 10th Edition (Upper Saddle River, NJ: Prentice-Hall, 2006).

---

[1]You will also need Windows Installer 3.0 if you are not running Windows XP SP2 (or higher) or Windows Server 2003 SP1 (or higher). See the installation instructions at the Microsoft site.

## ▶ STARTING SQL SERVER 2005 MANAGEMENT STUDIO EXPRESS EDITION

To start working with SQL Server 2005 Express, click **Start | Programs | Microsoft SQL Server 2005 | SQL Server Management Studio Express**.[2] The Microsoft SQL Server Management Studio Express **Connect to Server** dialog box appears as shown in Figure A-1. Using the default Windows Authentication method, you will be authenticated using your current Windows user name and password, so just click the **Connect** button. Having completed your login, the **Microsoft SQL Server Management Studio Express** window now appears as shown in Figure A-2.

**FIGURE A-1**

**The Connect to Server Dialog Box**

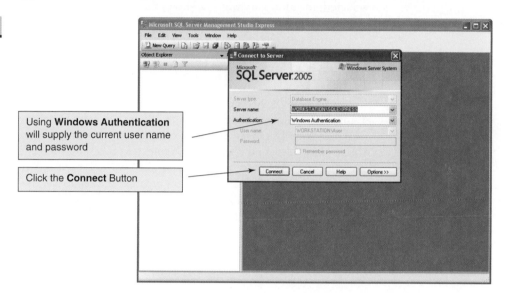

Using **Windows Authentication** will supply the current user name and password

Click the **Connect** Button

**FIGURE A-2**

**The Microsoft SQL Server Management Studio Express Window**

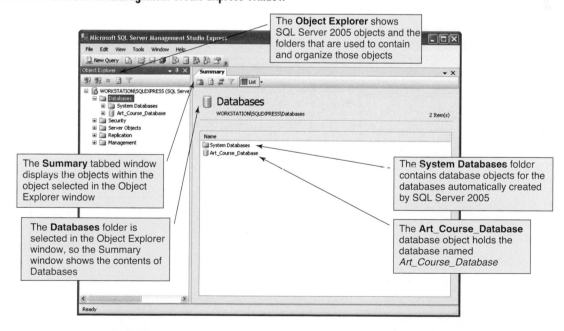

The **Object Explorer** shows SQL Server 2005 objects and the folders that are used to contain and organize those objects

The **Summary** tabbed window displays the objects within the object selected in the Object Explorer window

The **Databases** folder is selected in the Object Explorer window, so the Summary window shows the contents of Databases

The **System Databases** folder contains database objects for the databases automatically created by SQL Server 2005

The **Art_Course_Database** database object holds the database named *Art_Course_Database*

[2]Alternatively, you may start SQL Server Management Studio Express Edition from a desktop icon if you created one during installation.

In Figure A-2, we can see that there is an **Object Explorer** window on the left side of the Microsoft SQL Server Management Studio Express window, and a tabbed window labeled **Summary** on the right side. The Object Explorer displays SQL Server 2005 objects (such as databases and tables) and the folders (with labels such as **Databases** and **Security**) that are used to organize the presentation of the objects. The folders are considered to be objects, and, therefore, the window contains an expandable set of objects. In Figure A-2, the Databases folder has been expanded to show that it contains a folder named *System Databases* and a database named *Art_Course_Database*.

The contents of whichever object is selected (highlighted) in the Object Explorer window is displayed in the **Summary** tabbed window. Since the Databases folder is selected, the Summary window shows the objects in the Databases object. Again, we see a folder named *System Databases* and a database named *Art_Course_Database*.

## ▶ CREATING A DATABASE IN SQL SERVER 2005 EXPRESS EDITION

To create an SQL Server 2005 database, right-click the **Databases** object in the Object Explorer to display the shortcut menu, then click **New Database** as shown in Figure A-3.

The **New Database** dialog box appears as shown in Figure A-4. Type the name of the new database in the **Database Name:** text box, and then click the **OK** button to create the new database. In this example, we are creating the **Wedgewood Pacific Corporation (WPC)** database. After creating the database, the new database name will now appear in the Databases folder object. Figure A-5 shows the **WPC database object** selected and expanded to show the objects within the database.

---

**FIGURE A-3**

**The New Database Command**

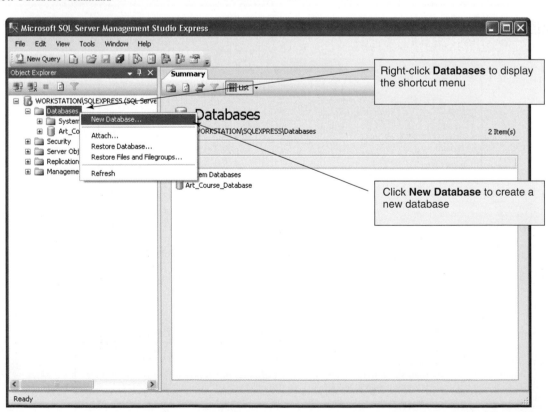

## FIGURE A-4

**Naming the New Database**

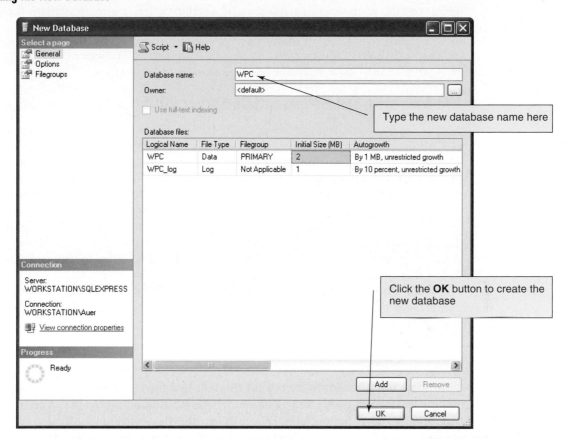

## FIGURE A-5

**The New Database In the Object Explorer**

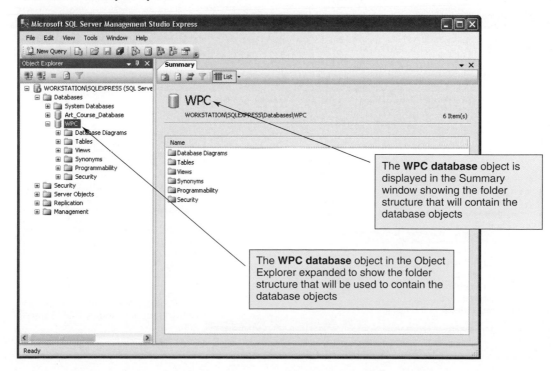

## ▶ WORKING WITH SQL STATEMENTS IN SQL SERVER 2005

In SQL Server 2005, SQL statements can be run individually or as part of a related group of SQL statements that is known as a **script**. Scripts are more efficient for processing groups of SQL statements such as:

- A set of CREATE TABLE commands to build a new database structure.
- A set of INSERT commands when data needs to be added to a table.

### Working with SQL Scripts in SQL Server 2005

Scripts can be created in SQL Server 2005 Management Studio Express or in any other ASCII text editor. In the Windows operating system, the **Notepad** text editor is a good choice. Regardless of which text editor you use, save your scripts with the file extension *.sql* so that they are recognizable by SQL Server 2005. By default, SQL Server 2005 Management Studio Express looks for scripts in a special folder that was created in the user's My Documents folder (on a personal workstation) when the program was installed. The folder structure created by the installation process is shown in Figure A-6 (in Microsoft Windows Explorer). Note that a folder named *SQL Server Management Studio Express* was created in My Documents, and four additional folders were created below that one. SQL scripts are stored in the *Projects* folder.

**SQL Commands to Create Table Structures**   The SQL statements to create the WPC database shown in Figure 3-6 *are* SQL Server 2005 SQL commands. We will use them with two modifications.

---

**B T W**

The first modification is based on the fact that Server 2005 is very sensitive about SQL keywords used as table or column names. Avoid keywords such as *name*, *date*, and *transaction*. Use modified versions of such words whenever possible—*ProjectName*, *StartDate*, *ItemTransaction*. If you must use unmodified keywords, then enclose them in square brackets ( [ ] ) to distinguish your name from the keyword.

---

**FIGURE A-6**

**The Projects Folder**

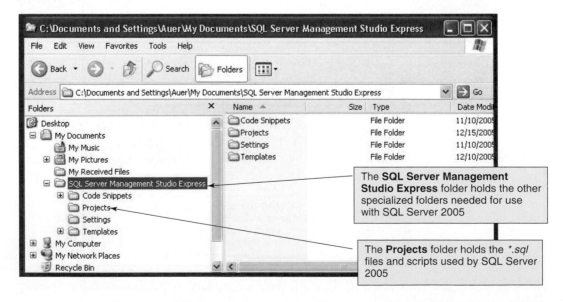

The **SQL Server Management Studio Express** folder holds the other specialized folders needed for use with SQL Server 2005

The **Projects** folder holds the *.sql* files and scripts used by SQL Server 2005

**FIGURE A-7**

**The WPC SQL Statements in Notepad**

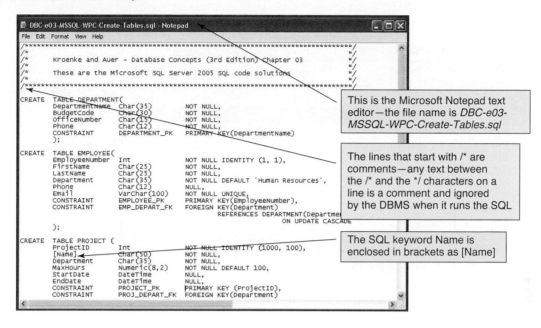

First, note that in the SQL statements for the PROJECT table, the column name *Name* is an SQL keyword, so we will enclose it in square brackets as *[Name]*. The SQL statements are shown in the Microsoft Notepad text editor in Figure A-7.

Second, we will add some comments to the script file to label and document the file. In Figure A-7, the seven lines at the top of the file that start with the characters /* (blackslash, asterisk) identify comments, and any text between that symbol and the */ (asterisk, backslash) characters that end the same line is treated as a comment.

To open a script in SQL Server Management Studio Express, use the **File | Open | File . . .** menu command. When the **Open File** dialog box shown in Figure A-8 appears, select the **script file name** and the click the **Open** button.

At this point, SLQ Server 2005 will ask you to authenticate again. A dialog box identical to the one shown in Figure A-1 except that it is named **Connect to Database Engine** will appear, and you will have to click the **Connect** button.

The script appears in a tabbed window labeled with the name of the script, as shown in Figure A-9. To run the script, first specify that the **WPC database** is being used, and then click the **Execute** button in the **SQL Editor toolbar**.

As shown in Figure A-10, after the script is executed, a **Message** window appears below the script window indicating success (or displaying appropriate error messages). The objects representing the table that were created are shown in the expanded Tables folder in the Object Explorer.

**SQL Commands to Insert Database Data**   The SQL statements needed to insert the data into these tables are the same as those shown in Figure 3-10. This data set should be put into a script file and then run as an SQL script.

## Working with SQL Queries in SQL Server 2005

Now that we've created and populated the WPC database, we can run SQL queries against the data. While scripts are good for large sets of SQL commands that need to be run together, most SQL queries are run as single commands. To run a query, be sure the Databases folder in the Object Browser is expanded so that you can see the database names,

## FIGURE A-8

**The Open File Dialog Box**

Use the **File | Open | File...** menu command to use an already created *.sql* script file

Select the **file name** of the *.sql* script to be run

Click the **Open button** to open the selected *.sql* script file

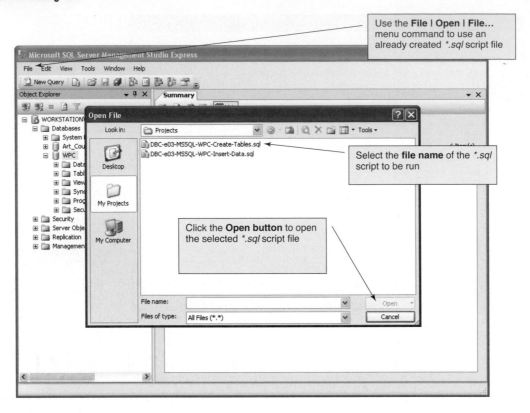

## FIGURE A-9

**The Script Window**

Click the **Execute** button in the **SQL Editor toolbar** to run the script

You have to specify which database is being used when the script is run—select **WPC** from the drop down list before executing the script

The tabbed script window with the open script displayed—to close this window after the script is run click the **X** symbol to the right of this tab

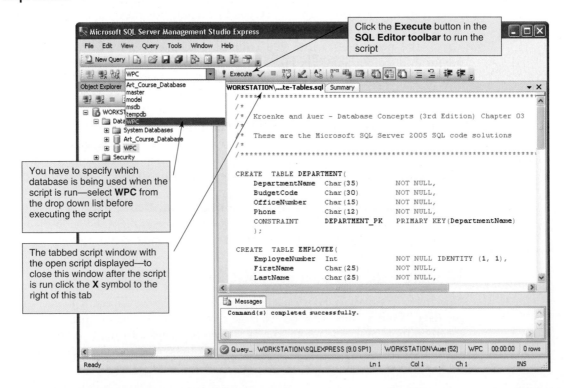

## FIGURE A-10

**The Script Results**

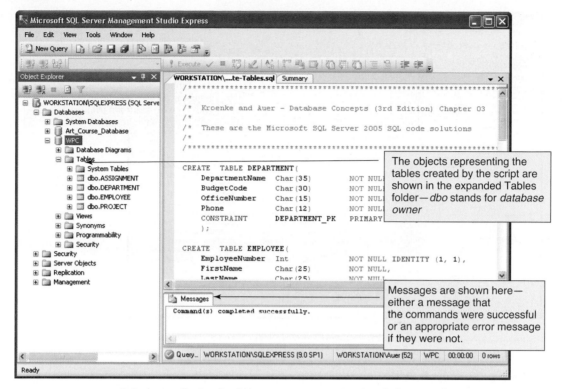

and then specify the database you want to query by clicking on the database name to select it. Next, click the **New Query** button in the **Standard toolbar** as shown in Figure A-11. A tabbed window will appear along with the SQL Editor toolbar—both of these can also be seen in Figure A-11. In the new window, type the text of the SQL query you want to run, then click the **Execute** button in the SQL Editor toolbar. The results appear in a tabbed **Results** window below the query window in a spreadsheet style display as shown in Figure A-12. The size of the query window and the results window can be adjusted, and the col-

## FIGURE A-11

**Creating an SQL Query in the Microsoft SQL Server Management Studio Express Edition**

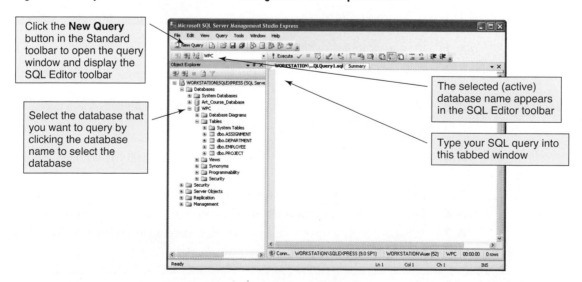

## FIGURE A-12

**The Query Results**

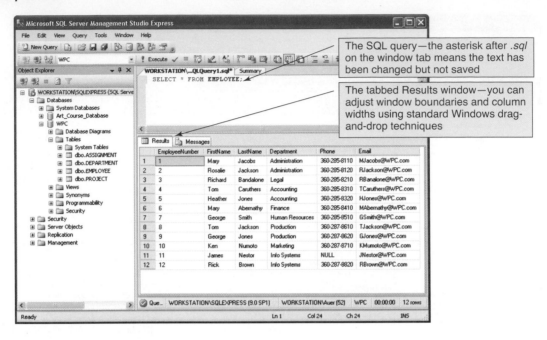

The SQL query—the asterisk after *.sql* on the window tab means the text has been changed but not saved

The tabbed Results window—you can adjust window boundaries and column widths using standard Windows drag-and-drop techniques

umn widths in the results display can be modified using standard Windows drag-and-drop techniques to help make more data visible. You can run multiple queries at the same time—clicking the New Query button again will open another tabbed query window.

## ADDITIONAL DOCUMENTATION FOR SQL SERVER 2005 EXPRESS

To get access to SQL Server 2005 documentation, use the Microsoft Download Center at http://www.microsoft.com/downloads/Search.aspx?displaylang=en and search for "SQL Server 2005 Express Edition Documentation."

## REVIEW QUESTIONS

**A.1**  What is SQL Server 2005 Express Edition?

**A.2**  What is the primary advantage of using SQL Server 2005 Express Edition instead of Microsoft Access?

**A.3**  What are the four Microsoft programs that are recommended as a necessary set of SQL Server 2005 Express Edition software products? In what order should these products be installed?

**A.4**  What is the purpose of the Microsoft SQL Server 2005 Management Studio Express Edition?

**A.5**  How do you create a new database in SQL Server 2005 Express Edition?

**A.6**  How do you specify the active database in SQL Server 2005 Express Edition?

**A.7**  What is a SQL script? What types of SQL statements and commands can be run more efficiently as scripts?

**A.8**   What tool(s) can be used to create a script?

**A.9**   What file extension should be used with SQL Server 2005 Express Edition scripts?

**A.10**   How do you open and run a script in SQL Server 2005 Express Edition?

**A.11**   How do you create and run an SQL query in SQL Server 2005 Express Edition?

## EXERCISES

**A.12**   If you haven't already done so, download and install SQL Server 2005 Express Edition and the SQL Server 2005 Management Studio Express Edition. Use the default settings for each installation.

**A.13**   If you haven't already done so, work through the steps described in this appendix to create and populate the WPC database.

**A.14**   Use SQL Server 2005 Express Edition and SQL Server 2005 Management Studio Express Edition to run the SQL queries in the SQL for Relational Query section of Chapter 3. Save each query as follows:
- Create and run each query in SQL Server 2005 Management Studio Express Edition.
- After you have run the query, use the **File | Save SQLQuery#.sql As. . .** command to save the query (the # sign in the name will change as you create different queries). By default, SQL Server 2005 will save each file as an SQL File with the file extension *.sql*. Use this default setting unless your instructor tells you to use a different extension. Name your queries in *numerical sequence* starting with the file name *MSSQL-SQLQuery01.sql*.

**A.15**   Use the SQL Server 2005 Management Studio Express Edition to run one or more of the saved SQL queries you created in A.15:
- Open a query with the **File | Open | File. . .** menu command. Note that the query is opened in a tabbed query window and that you will have to re-authenticate to the SQL Server 2005 database engine. Run the query.
- Use the **File | Open | File. . .** menu command to open and run another query in another tabbed window.
- Experiment with opening and closing windows and running various queries in these windows.

**A.16**   Complete Exercise 3.62 using SQL Server 2005 Express Edition and the SQL Server 2005 Management Studio Express Edition. Preface each saved query name with *MSSQL-* and use the default *.sql* file extension. Thus, the first saved query name will be *MSSQL-SQLQuery-AWE-3-1-A.sql*.

**A.17**   Complete Exercise 3.63 using SQL Server 2005 Express Edition and the SQL Server 2005 Management Studio Express Edition. Preface each saved query name with *MSSQL-* and use the default *.sql* file extension. Thus, the saved query name will be *MSSQL-SQLQuery-AWE-3-3-E.sql*.

# APPENDIX B

# Getting Started with MySQL

> Learn how to create a database
> Learn how to submit SQL commands to create table structures
> Learn how to submit SQL commands to insert database data
> Learn how to submit SQL commands to query a database

**M**ySQL is an open source, freely downloadable, enterprise-class DBMS that has been around for many years. In November 2005, MySQL 5.0 was released. MySQL, while not having as many features as SQL Server, has become widely used and very popular as a DBMS supporting Web sites running the Apache Web server. And the MySQL Community Server version is free.

MySQL runs on Linux, Unix, NetWare, and even on the Microsoft Windows operating systems. The various versions of Microsoft SQL Server 2005 (including the free SQL Server 2005 Express Edition discussed in Appendix A, "Getting Started with Microsoft SQL Server 2005 Express Edition"), like all Microsoft products, run only on Microsoft operating systems. If you are not using a Microsoft operating system, MySQL is an obvious contender for your DBMS of choice. MySQL is intended for general use and can be downloaded from the MySQL home page at http://www.mysql.com. You will need to download at least the first two of the following three programs, but we recommend that you download all three:

1. MySQL Community Server 5.0 (download the version for your operating system)
2. MySQL Query Browser (the version for your operating system). This program is contained in the MySQL GUI Tools Bundle, and is the graphical SQL command utility for MySQL. MySQL is a text command line oriented program, and the MySQL Query Browser makes it much easier to work with MySQL.
3. MySQL Adminstrator. This program is contained in the MySQL GUI Tools Bundle, and, although it is not needed for simple SQL work, this is the graphical administration utility for MySQL. MySQL is a text command line oriented program, and the MySQL Adminstrator utility really helps with administration issues, such as backup, restore, and user rights administration (all of which are beyond the scope of this section).

MySQL and its associated utilities are very easy to install. Install MySQL 5.0, then the MySQL Query Browser and (optionally) MySQL Administrator from the MySQL GUI Tools bundle.

Be aware that MySQL 5.0 is an enterprise-class DBMS and, as such, is much more complex than Microsoft Access. Further, it does not include application development tools, such as form and report generators.

## ▶ WHY SHOULD I LEARN TO USE MYSQL?

The most important reason, in terms of this book, is that MySQL really handles SQL well. All the SQL commands and keywords in Chapter 3 marked "Does Not Work With MS Access SQL" will work with MySQL 5.0. There will still be minor variations in some SQL statements, but this is typical of *all* DBMS products

## ▶ WHAT WILL THIS APPENDIX TEACH ME?

As the name implies, this appendix is designed to get you started creating databases and running SQL commands and scripts (which are related groups of SQL commands) in MySQL.

## ▶ WHAT WON'T THIS APPENDIX TEACH ME?

The material in this appendix does not go beyond what is necessary to get you started. There are many important MySQL topics not covered here, including stored procedures, triggers, backup and restore, and database security. Some of these topics are covered in David M. Kroenke's *Database Processing: Fundamentals, Design, and Implementation* 10th Edition (Upper Saddle River, NJ: Prentice-Hall, 2006), and all these topics will be covered in the future editions of that text.

## ▶ STARTING MYSQL

To start MySQL, click **Start | Programs | MySQL | MySQL Query Browser**.[1] The MySQL Query Browser **Connect to MySQL Server Instance** dialog box appears as shown in Figure B-1. Enter your user name (it is easiest to run as Root[2] to begin with) and the associated password, then click the **OK** button.

---

[1]Alternatively, you may start the MySQL Query Brower from a desktop icon if you created one during installation.

[2]**Root** is the name of the default MySQL administrator account. You are prompted for a password for this account during the installation of MySQL. The user name *Root* itself comes from the UNIX and LINUX operating systems, where it is the name of the default system administrator account.

At this point, you will see the **Connection Dialog – No Default Schema Specified** dialog box, as shown in Figure B-2. **Schema** is MySQL's term for database. The dialog box is telling you that you have not specified a default database—the database you want to work with during this session. Don't worry, you don't have to. You will select the default schema later. Click the **Ignore** button to proceed.

Having completed your login, the MySQL Query Browser window now appears as shown in Figure B-3. In Figure B-3, note the MySQL Query Browser **Query Toolbar** with the text box for entering SQL statements, the **Resultset** window, and the **Schemata** pane. The set of existing databases (schemas) is listed in the Schemata pane.

---

**FIGURE B-1**

The Connect to MySQL Server Instance Dialog Box

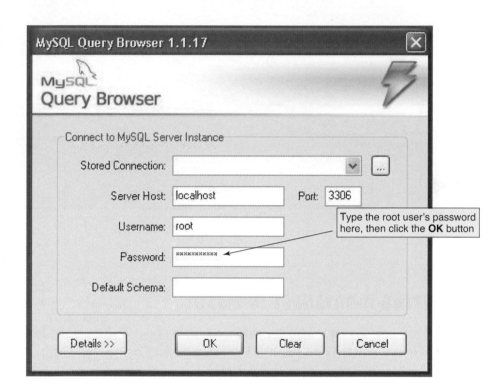

---

**FIGURE B-2**

The Connection Dialog – No Default Schema Specified Dialog Box

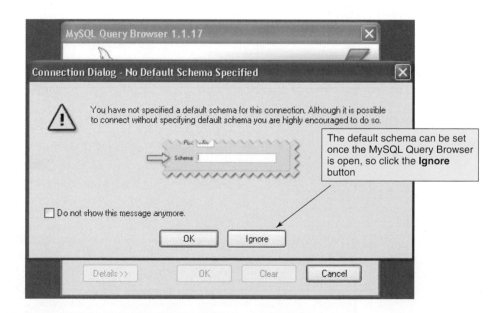

**FIGURE B-3**

**The MySQL Query Browser Window**

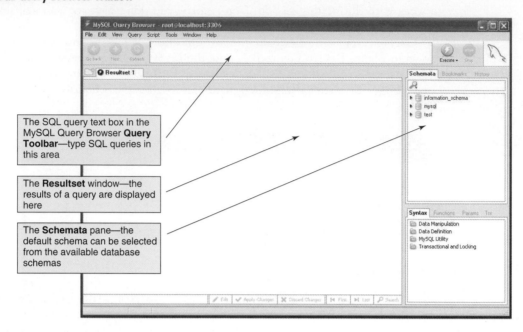

The SQL query text box in the MySQL Query Browser **Query Toolbar**—type SQL queries in this area

The **Resultset** window—the results of a query are displayed here

The **Schemata** pane—the default schema can be selected from the available database schemas

# CREATING A DATABASE IN MYSQL

To create a MySQL database, right-click anywhere in the Schemata pane to display the schemata shortcut menu, then click **Create New Schema** as shown in Figure B-4.

**FIGURE B-4**

**The Create New Schema Command**

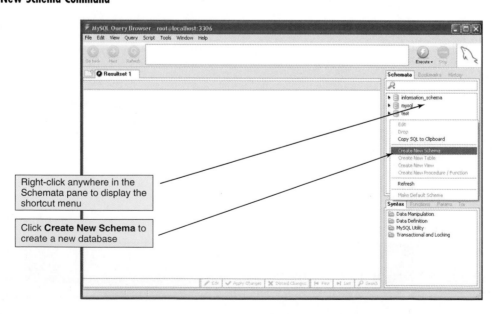

Right-click anywhere in the Schemata pane to display the shortcut menu

Click **Create New Schema** to create a new database

The **Create New Schema** dialog box appears as shown in Figure B-5. Type the name of the new database in the **Schema Name:** text box, and then click the **OK** button to create the new database. In this example, we are creating the Wedgewood Pacific Corporation (WPC) database. After creating the database, the new database (schema) name will now appear in the Schemata list.

**FIGURE B-5**

Naming the New Database

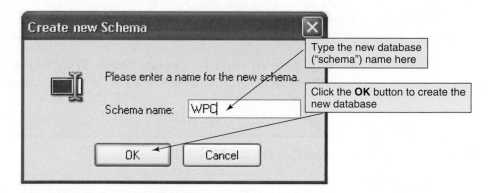

### SELECTING A DATABASE IN MYSQL

To work with a MySQL database, you must select it as the active database. In MySQL terms, this is called the **default schema**. To set the default schema, right-click the name of the database that you want to work with in the Schemata pane to display the schemata shortcut menu, then click **Set Default Schema** as shown in Figure B-6.

### WORKING WITH SQL STATEMENTS IN MYSQL

In MySQL, SQL statements can be run individually or as part of a related group of SQL statements that is known as a **script**. Scripts are more efficient for processing groups of

**FIGURE B-6**

Setting the Default Schema

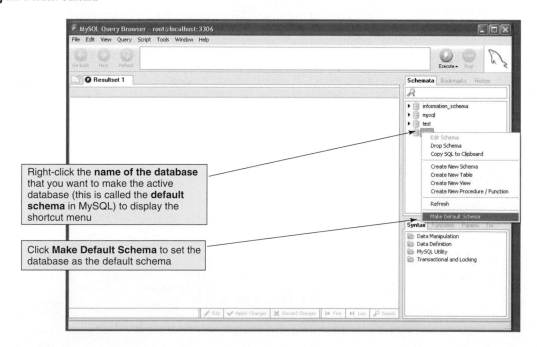

SQL statements, such as:

- A set of CREATE TABLE commands to build a new database structure.
- A set of INSERT commands when data needs to be added to a table.

## Working with SQL Scripts in MySQL

Scripts can be created in MySQL or in any other ASCII text editor. In Windows OS, the Notepad text editor is a good choice. Regardless of which text editor you use, save your scripts with the file extension *.sql* so that they are recognizable by MySQL. By default, MySQL looks for scripts in the user's My Documents folder on a personal workstation.

**SQL Commands to Create Table Structures**    Figure B-7 shows the MySQL version of the SQL statements to create the WPC database shown in Figure 3-6

---

### FIGURE B-7

**WPC Database Structure SQL Statements in MySQL**

```
CREATE  TABLE DEPARTMENT(
    DepartmentName      Char(35)        NOT NULL,
    BudgetCode          Char(30)        NOT NULL,
    OfficeNumber        Char(15)        NOT NULL,
    Phone               Char(12)        NOT NULL,
    CONSTRAINT          DEPARTMENT_PK   PRIMARY KEY(DepartmentName)
    );


CREATE  TABLE EMPLOYEE(
    EmployeeNumber      Int             NOT NULL AUTO_INCREMENT,
    FirstName           Char(25)        NOT NULL,
    LastName            Char(25)        NOT NULL,
    Department          Char(35)        NOT NULL DEFAULT 'Human Resources',
    Phone               Char(12)        NULL,
    Email               VarChar(100)    NOT NULL UNIQUE,
    CONSTRAINT          EMPLOYEE_PK     PRIMARY KEY(EmployeeNumber),
    CONSTRAINT          EMP_DEPART_FK   FOREIGN KEY(Department)
                            REFERENCES DEPARTMENT(DepartmentName)
                                ON UPDATE CASCADE
    );


CREATE  TABLE PROJECT (
    ProjectID           Int             NOT NULL,
    Name                Char(50)        NOT NULL,
    Department          Char(35)        NOT NULL,
    MaxHours            Numeric(8,2)    NOT NULL DEFAULT 100,
    StartDate           DateTime        NULL,
    EndDate             DateTime        NULL,
    CONSTRAINT          PROJECT_PK      PRIMARY KEY (ProjectID),
    CONSTRAINT          PROJ_DEPART_FK FOREIGN KEY(Department)
                            REFERENCES DEPARTMENT(DepartmentName)
                                ON UPDATE CASCADE
    );


CREATE  TABLE ASSIGNMENT (
    ProjectID           Int             NOT NULL,
    EmployeeNumber      Int             NOT NULL,
    HoursWorked         Numeric(6,2)    NULL,
    CONSTRAINT          ASSIGNMENT_PK  PRIMARY KEY (ProjectID, EmployeeNumber),
    CONSTRAINT          ASSIGN_PROJ_FK FOREIGN KEY (ProjectID)
                            REFERENCES PROJECT (ProjectID)
                                ON UPDATE NO ACTION
                                ON DELETE CASCADE,
    CONSTRAINT          ASSIGN_EMP_FK  FOREIGN KEY (EmployeeNumber)
                            REFERENCES EMPLOYEE (EmployeeNumber)
                                ON UPDATE NO ACTION
                                ON DELETE NO ACTION
    );
```

[and MySQL data types are shown in Chapter 3 in Figure 3-4(c)]. Comparing the two versions of these SQL statements will help you understand any differences in how SQL is used in MySQL. The same statements are shown in the Microsoft Notepad text editor in Figure B-8.

---

### B T W

MySQL uses the AUTO_INCREMENT keyword to set surrogate key values. The default values for AUTO_INCREMENT are an initial value of 1 and an increment of 1. After the table is created, the initial value can be modified using an ALTER TABLE statement. For example, in the WPC database, the PROJECT table has a surrogate key that starts at 1000 and increments by 100. We could set the correct initial value using the SQL statement:

ALTER TABLE PROJECT AUTO_INCREMENT=1000;

Unfortunately, the MySQL increment of 1 cannot be modified. So for cases such as the ProjectID values in PROJECT, the correct values must be inserted manually in MySQL.

---

To open a script in MySQL Query Browser, use the menu command **File | Open Script . . .** as shown in Figure B-9. When the Open Script Files dialog box shown in Figure B-10 appears, select the **script file name** and then click the **Open** button. The script appears in a tabbed **Script** window, as shown in Figure B-11. To run the script,

---

### FIGURE B-8

**The WPC SQL Statements in Notepad**

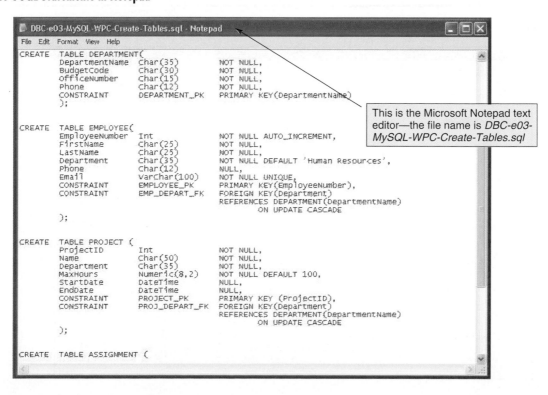

click the **Execute** button. After the script executes, the WPC Schema icon can be expanded to display the tables created by the script. To close the script window, click the **X** symbol on the script window tab.

**SQL Commands to Insert Database Data**   The SQL statements needed to insert the data into these tables is shown in Figure B-12. Note the differences between these and the SQL statements shown in Figure 3-10. In particular, note the way the date values are formatted. This data set should be put into a script file and then run as a MySQL script.

## Working with SQL Queries in MySQL

Now that we've created and populated the WPC database, we can run SQL queries against the data. While scripts are good for large sets of SQL commands that need to be run together, most SQL queries are run as single commands. As shown in Figure B-13, these are entered into the **SQL text box** (which functions as a text editor) in the **Query toolbar** and then executed by clicking the **Execute** button. The results appear in a tabbed **Resultset** window in a spreadsheet-style display. The column widths in the results display can be modified using standard Windows drag-and-drop techniques to help make more data visible. You can run multiple queries at the same time by using multiple Resultset windows. Additional Resultset windows can be opened by using the **File | New Resultset Tab** command as shown in Figure B-14.

### FIGURE B-9

**Opening a MySQL Script**

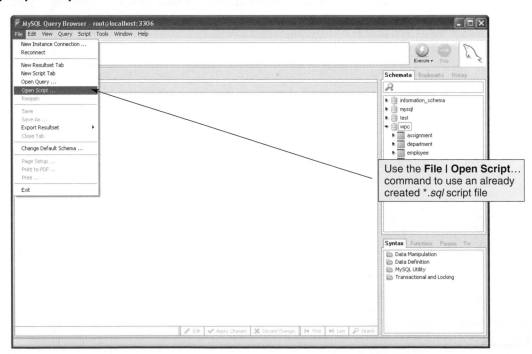

Use the **File | Open Script**... command to use an already created *.sql* script file

## FIGURE B-10

**The Open Script File Dialog Box**

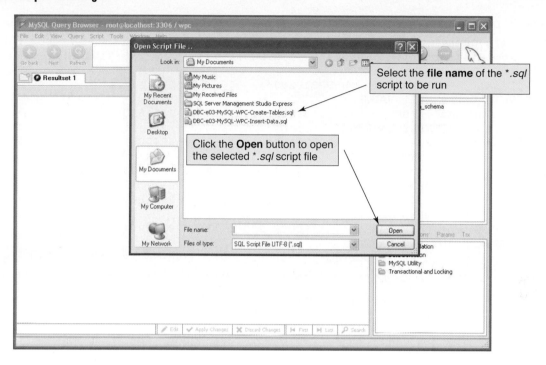

Select the **file name** of the *\*.sql* script to be run

Click the **Open** button to open the selected *\*.sql* script file

## FIGURE B-11

**The Script 1 Window**

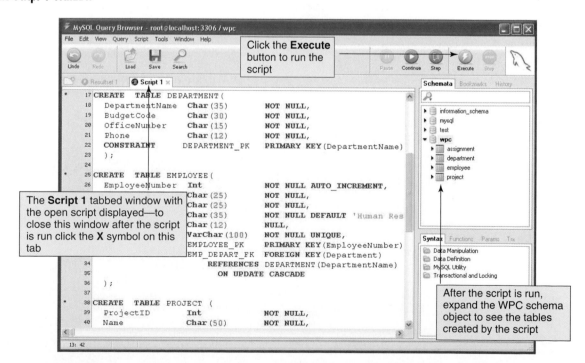

Click the **Execute** button to run the script

The **Script 1** tabbed window with the open script displayed—to close this window after the script is run click the **X** symbol on this tab

After the script is run, expand the WPC schema object to see the tables created by the script

## FIGURE B-12

**WPC Database SQL INSERT Statements in MySQL**

```
/*****    DEPARTMENT DATA    ***************************************************/
INSERT INTO DEPARTMENT VALUES(
      'Administration', 'BC-100-10', 'BLDG01-300', '360-285-8100');
INSERT INTO DEPARTMENT VALUES(
      'Legal', 'BC-200-10', 'BLDG01-200', '360-285-8200');
INSERT INTO DEPARTMENT VALUES(
      'Accounting', 'BC-300-10', 'BLDG01-100', '360-285-8300');
INSERT INTO DEPARTMENT VALUES(
      'Finance', 'BC-400-10', 'BLDG01-140', '360-285-8400');
INSERT INTO DEPARTMENT VALUES(
      'Human Resources', 'BC-500-10', 'BLDG01-180', '360-285-8500');
INSERT INTO DEPARTMENT VALUES(
      'Production', 'BC-600-10', 'BLDG02-100', '360-287-8600');
INSERT INTO DEPARTMENT VALUES(
      'Marketing', 'BC-700-10', 'BLDG02-200', '360-287-8700');
INSERT INTO DEPARTMENT VALUES(
      'Info Systems', 'BC-800-10', 'BLDG02-270', '360-287-8800');
/*****    EMPLOYEE DATA    *****************************************************/
INSERT INTO EMPLOYEE (FirstName, LastName, Department, Phone, Email)
   VALUES(
   'Mary', 'Jacobs', 'Administration', '360-285-8110', 'MJacobs@WPC.com');
INSERT INTO EMPLOYEE (FirstName, LastName, Department, Phone, Email)
   VALUES(
   'Rosalie', 'Jackson', 'Administration', '360-285-8120',
   'RJackson@WPC.com');
INSERT INTO EMPLOYEE (FirstName, LastName, Department, Phone, Email)
   VALUES(
   'Richard', 'Bandalone', 'Legal', '360-285-8210', 'RBanalone@WPC.com');
INSERT INTO EMPLOYEE (FirstName, LastName, Department, Phone, Email)
   VALUES(
   'Tom', 'Caruthers', 'Accounting', '360-285-8310', 'TCaruthers@WPC.com');
INSERT INTO EMPLOYEE (FirstName, LastName, Department, Phone, Email)
   VALUES(
   'Heather', 'Jones', 'Accounting', '360-285-8320', 'HJones@WPC.com');
INSERT INTO EMPLOYEE (FirstName, LastName, Department, Phone, Email)
   VALUES(
   'Mary', 'Abernathy', 'Finance', '360-285-8410', 'MAbernathy@WPC.com');
INSERT INTO EMPLOYEE (FirstName, LastName, Department, Phone, Email)
   VALUES(
   'George', 'Smith', 'Human Resources', '360-285-8510', 'GSmith@WPC.com');
INSERT INTO EMPLOYEE (FirstName, LastName, Department, Phone, Email)
   VALUES(
   'Tom', 'Jackson', 'Production', '360-287-8610', 'TJackson@WPC.com');
INSERT INTO EMPLOYEE (FirstName, LastName, Department, Phone, Email)
   VALUES(
   'George', 'Jones', 'Production', '360-287-8620', 'GJones@WPC.com');
INSERT INTO EMPLOYEE (FirstName, LastName, Department, Phone, Email)
   VALUES(
   'Ken', 'Numoto', 'Marketing', '360-287-8710', 'KMumoto@WPC.com');
INSERT INTO EMPLOYEE(FirstName, LastName, Department, Email)
   VALUES(
   'James', 'Nestor', 'Info Systems', 'JNestor@WPC.com');
INSERT INTO EMPLOYEE (FirstName, LastName, Department, Phone, Email)
   VALUES(
   'Rick', 'Brown', 'Info Systems', '360-287-8820', 'RBrown@WPC.com');
```

## FIGURE B-12 (Continued)

**WPC Database SQL INSERT Statements in MySQL**

```
/*****    PROJECT DATA    ****************************************************/

INSERT INTO PROJECT
    VALUES(1000, '2005 Q3 Product Plan', 'Marketing', 135.00,
    '2005-05-10', '2005-06-15');
INSERT INTO PROJECT
    VALUES(1100, '2005 Q3 Portfolio Analysis', 'Finance', 120.00,
    '2005-07-05', '2005-07-25' );
INSERT INTO PROJECT
    VALUES(1200, '2005 Q3 Tax Preparation', 'Accounting', 145.00,
    '2005-08-10', '2005-10-15');
INSERT INTO PROJECT
    VALUES(1300, '2005 Q4 Product Plan', 'Marketing', 150.00,
    '2005-08-10', '2005-09-15');
INSERT INTO PROJECT (ProjectID, Name, Department, MaxHours, StartDate)
    VALUES(
    1400, '2005 Q4 Portfolio Analysis', 'Finance', 140.00, '2005-10-05');


/*****    ASSIGNMENT DATA    *************************************************/

INSERT INTO ASSIGNMENT VALUES(1000, 1, 30.0);
INSERT INTO ASSIGNMENT VALUES(1000, 8, 75.0);
INSERT INTO ASSIGNMENT VALUES(1000, 10, 55.0);
INSERT INTO ASSIGNMENT VALUES(1100, 4, 40.0);
INSERT INTO ASSIGNMENT VALUES(1100, 6, 45.0);
INSERT INTO ASSIGNMENT VALUES(1200, 1, 25.0);
INSERT INTO ASSIGNMENT VALUES(1200, 2, 20.0);
INSERT INTO ASSIGNMENT VALUES(1200, 4, 45.0);
INSERT INTO ASSIGNMENT VALUES(1200, 5, 40.0);
INSERT INTO ASSIGNMENT VALUES(1300, 1, 35.0);
INSERT INTO ASSIGNMENT VALUES(1300, 8, 80.0);
INSERT INTO ASSIGNMENT VALUES(1300, 10, 50.0);
INSERT INTO ASSIGNMENT VALUES(1400, 4, 15.0);
INSERT INTO ASSIGNMENT VALUES(1400, 5, 10.0);
INSERT INTO ASSIGNMENT VALUES(1400, 6, 27.5);
```

## FIGURE B-13

**An SQL Query in the MySQL Query Browser**

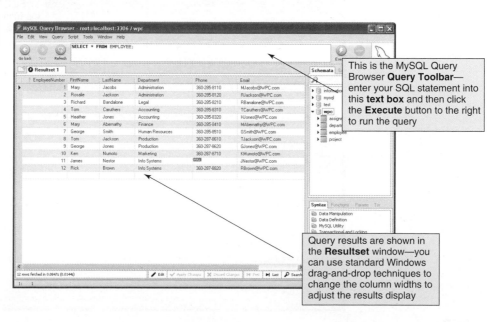

This is the MySQL Query Browser **Query Toolbar**— enter your SQL statement into this **text box** and then click the **Execute** button to the right to run the query

Query results are shown in the **Resultset** window—you can use standard Windows drag-and-drop techniques to change the column widths to adjust the results display

**Opening Additional Query Results Windows**

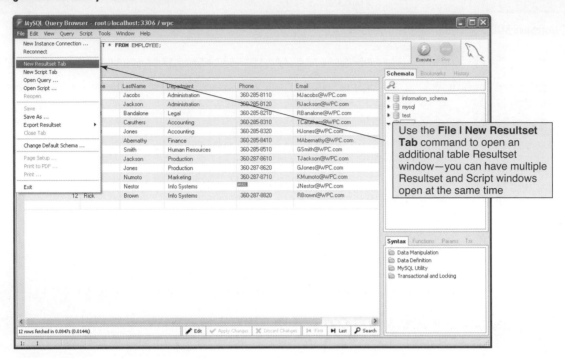

Use the **File | New Resultset Tab** command to open an additional table Resultset window—you can have multiple Resultset and Script windows open at the same time

## ADDITIONAL DOCUMENTATION FOR MYSQL

To get access to MySQL documentation, use the **Help | Online Docs** command. Documentation in the MySQL Reference Manual and other sources available at the MySQL Web site will be displayed in an **Inline Help** window within the MySQL Query Browser as shown in Figure B-15. This is another tabbed window that can be used like any other tabbed window. This window can be left open while you are using other tabbed windows, and then closed when you no longer need it.

**FIGURE B-15**

**The MySQL Query Browser Inline Help Window**

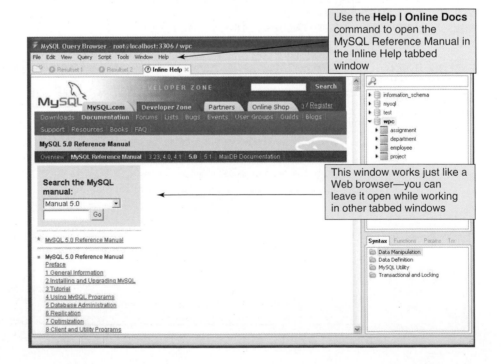

Use the **Help | Online Docs** command to open the MySQL Reference Manual in the Inline Help tabbed window

This window works just like a Web browser—you can leave it open while working in other tabbed windows

## REVIEW QUESTIONS

**B.1** What is MySQL?

**B.2** What is the primary advantage of using MySQL instead of SQL Server Express Edition?

**B.3** What are the three MySQL programs that are recommended as a useful set of MySQL software products?

**B.4** What is the purpose of the MySQL Query Browser?

**B.5** What is a MySQL schema?

**B.6** How do you create a new database in MySQL?

**B.7** What is a MySQL default schema? How do you specify the default schema?

**B.8** What is a MySQL script? What types of SQL statements and commands can be run more efficiently as scripts?

**B.9** What tool(s) can be used to create a script?

**B.10** What file extension should be used with MySQL scripts?

**B.11** How do you open and run a script in MySQL?

**B.12** How does MySQL use the AUTO_INCREMENT keyword? What limitations are there on the use of the AUTO_INCREMENT keyword?

**B.13** How do you create and run a SQL query in the MySQL?

**B.14** How do you obtain online help when using the MySQL Query Browser? Where is the help information displayed?

**B.15** Summarize the types of tabbed windows used in the MySQL Query Browser. How do you open each of these types of tabbed windows? How many tabbed windows can be open at once?

## EXERCISES

**B.16** If you haven't already done so, download and install MySQL, the MySQL Query Browser utility and the MySQL Administrator utility. Use the default settings for each installation. You will be asked for a password for the Root user account. Be sure to create a password for this user account.

**B.17** If you haven't already done so, work through the steps described in this appendix to create and populate the WPC database.

**B.18** Use MySQL and the MySQL Query Browser to run the SQL queries in the "SQL for Relational Query" section of Chapter 3. Save each query as follows:
- Create and run each query in the MySQL Query Browser.
- After you have run the query, use the **File | Save As. . .** command to save the query. By default, MySQL will save each file as a UTF-8 Query File with the file extension *.qbquery*. Use this default setting unless your instructor tells you to use a different extension. Name your queries in *numerical sequence* starting with the file name **MySQL-SQLQuery01.qbquery**.

**B.19** Use MySQL and the MySQL Query Browser to run one or more of the saved SQL queries you created in B.18:
- At this point, you should have only one **Resultset** window open (the **Resultset1** window that is opened by default when you start the MySQL Query Browser). Open a query with the **File | Open Query. . .** command. Note that the query is opened in the active **Resultset** window.

- Use the **File | New Resultset Tab** command to open a new **Resultset** window. With this window active, use the **File | Open Query. . .** command to open and run another query in this window.
- Experiment with opening and closing Resultset windows and running various queries in these windows.

**B.20** Complete Exercise 3.62 using MySQL. Preface each saved query name with MySQL- and use the default .qbquery files extension. Thus, the first saved query name will be MySQL-SQLQuery-AWE-3-1-A.qbquery.

**B.21** Complete Exercise 3.63 using MySQL. Preface the saved query name with MySQL- and use the default .qbquery files extension. Thus, the saved query name will be MySQL-SQLQuery-AWE-3-3-E.qbquery.

# APPENDIX C

# SQL Views

> Learn basic SQL statements for creating views
> Learn basic SQL statements for using views
> Understand the reasons for using views

In Chapter 3, we discussed SQL in depth. We classified SQL statements into two categories: data definition language (DDL) statements, which are used for creating tables, relationships, and other structures, and data manipulation language (DML) statements, which are used for querying and modifying data. This appendix describes and illustrates SQL views, a tool that extends the DML capabilities of SQL.

# CREATING SQL VIEWS

A SQL **view** is a virtual table that is constructed from other tables or views. A view has no data of its own, but uses data stored in tables or other views. Views are created using SQL SELECT statements, and then used in other SELECT statements just like they are in any other table. The only limitation on the SQL statements that create the views is that they may not contain an ORDER BY clause.[1] If the results of a query using a view need to be sorted, the sort order must be provided by the SELECT statement that processes the view.

---

### Does Not Work With MS Access SQL

Unfortunately, MS Access does not support views. However, Access allows you to create a query, name it, and then save it, which is not supported in a standard SQL implementation. You can then process Access-saved queries in the same ways that we process views in the following discussion. See "The Access Workbench" at the end of this appendix for more details.

---

We will use the WPC database that we created in Chapter 3 as the example database for our discussion of views. The SQL **CREATE VIEW statement** is used to create view structures. The essential format of this statement is:

CREATE VIEW *ViewName* AS

    {SQL SELECT statement};

The following statement defines a view named EmployeePhoneView on the EMPLOYEE table:

CREATE VIEW EmployeePhoneView AS

    SELECT      FirstName, LastName, Phone AS EmployeePhone

    FROM       EMPLOYEE;

Figure C-1 shows the view being created in the SQL Server 2005 Management Studio Express Edition, and Figure C-2 shows the view creation in the MySQL Query Browser.

---

### B T W

SQL Server 2005 and most other DBMSs process the CREATE VIEW statements as written here without difficulty. However, the previous version of SQL Server (SQL Server 2000) will not run such statements unless you *remove the semicolon* at the end of the CREATE VIEW statement. We have no idea why SQL Server 2000 works this way, but if you are using SQL Server 2000 be aware of this peculiarity.

---

[1]This limitation appears in the SQL-92 standard. Some DBMSs modify this limitation in their implementation of SQL. For example, Oracle allows views to include ORDER BY and SQL Server 2005 will allow ORDER BY in very limited circumstances.

**FIGURE C-1**

Creating a View in the
SQL Server 2005
Management Studio
Express Edition

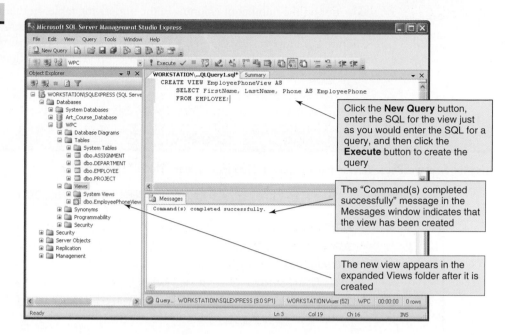

**FIGURE C-2**

Creating a View in the
MySQL Query Browser

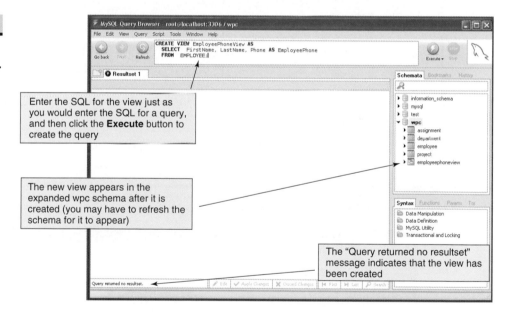

Once the view is created, it can be used in the FROM clause of SELECT statements just like a table. The following obtains a list of employee names and phone numbers sorted by the employee's last name:

```
SELECT      *
FROM        EmployeePhoneView
ORDER BY  LastName;
```

Figure C-3 shows this SQL statement run in the SQL Server 2005 Management Studio Express Edition, and Figure C-4 shows it run in the MySQL Query Browser. Note that the number of columns returned depends on the number of columns in the view, not on the number of columns in the underlying table. In this example, SELECT * produces just three columns because the view has just three columns. Also notice that the column Name in the EMPLOYEE table has been renamed to EmployeePhone in the view so that the DBMS uses the label EmployeePhone when producing results.

---

**FIGURE C-3**

**Using the EmployeePhoneView in the SQL Server 2005 Management Studio Express Edition**

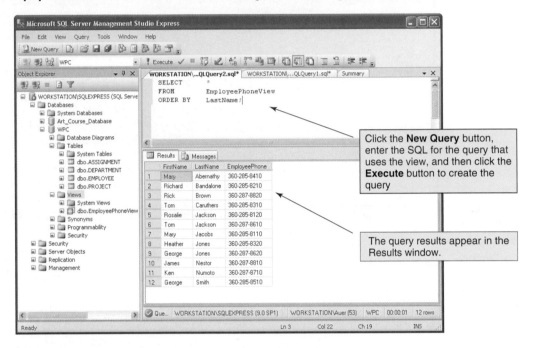

---

**FIGURE C-4**

**Using the EmployeePhoneView in the MySQL Query Browser**

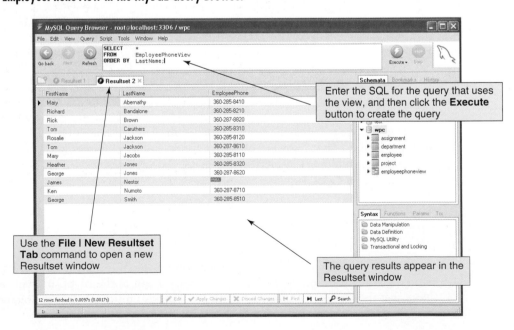

> **B T W**
>
> If you ever need to modify the SQL view you have created, use the ALTER VIEW *ViewName* AS statement. This works exactly the same as the CREATE VIEW *ViewName* AS statement except that it replaces the existing view definition with the new one. This statement is very useful when you are trying to fine-tune your view definitions.
>
> And should you ever want to delete a view, simply use the SQL statement DROP VIEW *ViewName*; to do so.

## ▶ USING SQL VIEWS

Figure C-5 lists some of the uses for views.[2] They can hide columns or rows. They also can be used to display the results of computed columns, to hide complicated SQL syntax, and to layer the use of built-in functions to create results that are not possible with a single SQL statement. We will give examples of each of these uses.

### Using Views to Hide Columns and Rows

Views can be used to hide columns to simplify results or to prevent the display of sensitive data. For example, suppose the users at WPC Ridge want a simplified list of departments that has just the department names and phone numbers. One use for such a view would be to populate a Web page. The following statement defines a view, BasicDepartmentDataView, that will produce that list:

CREATE VIEW BasicDepartmentDataView AS

        SELECT      DepartmentName, Phone AS DepartmentPhone

        FROM       DEPARTMENT;

The results of a SELECT * sorted by DepartmentName on this view are:

| | DepartmentName | DepartmentPhone |
|---|---|---|
| 1 | Accounting | 360-285-8300 |
| 2 | Administration | 360-285-8100 |
| 3 | Finance | 360-285-8400 |
| 4 | Human Resources | 360-285-8500 |
| 5 | Info Systems | 360-287-8800 |
| 6 | Legal | 360-285-8200 |
| 7 | Marketing | 360-287-8700 |
| 8 | Production | 360-287-8600 |

### FIGURE C-5

**Some Uses for SQL Views**

- Hide columns or rows
- Display results of computations
- Hide complicated SQL syntax
- Layer built-in functions

---

[2]Additional uses of SQL views are discussed in David M. Kroenke, *Database Processing: Fundamentals, Design, and Implementation,* 10th Edition (Upper Saddle River, NJ: Prentice Hall, 2006) Chapter 7.

Views also can hide rows by providing a WHERE clause in the view definition. The next SQL statement defines a view of WPC projects in the Marketing department:

CREATE VIEW MarkingDepartmentProjectView AS

SELECT          ProjectID, Name AS ProjectName, MaxHours,

StartDate, EndDate

FROM            PROJECT

WHERE           Department = 'Marketing';

The results of a SELECT * sorted by ProjectID on this view are:

|   | ProjectID | ProjectName | MaxHours | StartDate | EndDate |
|---|-----------|-------------|----------|-----------|---------|
| 1 | 1000 | 2005 Q3 Product Plan | 135.00 | 2005-05-10 ... | 2005-06-15 ... |
| 2 | 1300 | 2005 Q4 Product Plan | 150.00 | 2005-08-10 ... | 2005-09-15 ... |

As desired, only the Marketing department projects are shown in this view. This limitation is not obvious from the results because Department is not included in the view. This characteristic is good or bad, depending on the use of the view. It is good if this view is used in a setting in which only Marketing department projects matter; it is bad if the view indicates that these projects are the only WPC projects currently underway.

## Using Views to Display Results of Computed Columns

Another use of views is to show the results of computed columns without requiring the user to enter the computation expression. For example, the following view allows the user to compare the maximum hours allocated for each WPC project to the total hours worked to date on the project:

CREATE VIEW ProjectHoursToDateView AS

SELECT          PROJECT.ProjectID,

Name AS ProjectName,

MaxHours AS ProjectMaxHours,

SUM(HoursWorked) AS ProjectHoursWorkedToDate

FROM            PROJECT, ASSIGNMENT

WHERE           PROJECT.ProjectID = ASSIGNMENT.ProjectID

GROUP BY  PROJECT.ProjectID;

When the view user enters:

SELECT          *

FROM            ProjectHoursToDateView

ORDER BY  PROJECT.ProjectID;

these results will be displayed:

|   | ProjectID | ProjectName | ProjectMaxHours | ProjectHoursWorkedToDate |
|---|-----------|-------------|-----------------|--------------------------|
| 1 | 1000 | 2005 Q3 Product Plan | 135.00 | 160.00 |
| 2 | 1100 | 2005 Q3 Portfolio Analysis | 120.00 | 85.00 |
| 3 | 1200 | 2005 Q3 Tax Preparation | 145.00 | 130.00 |
| 4 | 1300 | 2005 Q4 Product Plan | 150.00 | 165.00 |
| 5 | 1400 | 2005 Q4 Portfolio Analysis | 140.00 | 52.50 |

Placing computations in views has two major advantages. First, it saves users from having to know or remember how to write an expression to get the results they want. Second, it ensures consistent results. If each developer who uses a computation writes his or her own SQL expression, they may write it differently and obtain inconsistent results.

---

**B T W**

SQL Server 2005 requires that any column specified in the SELECT phrase must be used in either an SQL built-in function or in the GROUP BY phrase. The previous SQL statement is correct SQL-92 syntax and will run in MySQL as written. However SQL Server 2005 requires us to write:

CREATE VIEW ProjectHoursToDateView AS

    SELECT    PROJECT.ProjectID,

             [Name] AS ProjectName,

             MaxHours AS ProjectMaxHours,

             SUM(HoursWorked) AS ProjectHoursWorkedToDate

    FROM    PROJECT AS P, ASSIGNMENT AS A

    WHERE    PROJECT.ProjectID = ASSIGNMENT.ProjectID

    GROUP BY    P.ProjectID, [Name], MaxHours;

Note the use of the extra column names in the GROUP BY clause. These are necessary to create the view, but have no practical effect on the results.

---

## Using Views to Hide Complicated SQL Syntax

Another use of views is to hide complicated SQL syntax. Using a view, developers do not need to enter a complex SQL statement when they want a particular result. Also, such views give the benefits of complicated SQL statements to developers who do not know how to write such statements. This use of views also ensures consistency.

For example, suppose that WPC users need to know which employees are assigned to which project and how many hours that employee has worked on that project. To display these interests, two joins are necessary: one to join EMPLOYEE to ASSIGNMENT and another to join that result to PROJECT. We have already seen the SQL statement to do this in Chapter 3, and it is:

SELECT    Name, FirstName, LastName, HoursWorked

FROM    EMPLOYEE AS E JOIN ASSIGNMENT AS A

        ON    E.EmployeeNumber = A.EmployeeNumber

            JOIN PROJECT AS P

               ON    A.ProjectID = P.ProjectID

ORDER BY    P.ProjectID, A.EmployeeNumber;

Now, we need to make it into a view named EmployeeProjectHoursWorkedView. Remember that we cannot include the ORDER BY clause in the view. If we want to sort the output, we'll need to do this when we use the view:

```
CREATE VIEW EmployeeProjectHoursWorkedView AS
        SELECT  Name, FirstName, LastName, HoursWorked
        FROM    EMPLOYEE AS E JOIN ASSIGNMENT AS A
                ON   E.EmployeeNumber = A.EmployeeNumber
                JOIN PROJECT AS P
                    ON   A.ProjectID = P.ProjectID;
```

This is a complicated SQL statement to write, but once the view is created, the results of this statement can be obtained with a simple SELECT statement. When the user uses:

```
SELECT * FROM EmployeeProjectHoursWorkedView;
```

these results will be displayed:

| | Name | FirstName | LastName | HoursWorked |
|---|---|---|---|---|
| 1 | 2005 Q3 Product Plan | Mary | Jacobs | 30.00 |
| 2 | 2005 Q3 Product Plan | Tom | Jackson | 75.00 |
| 3 | 2005 Q3 Product Plan | Ken | Numoto | 55.00 |
| 4 | 2005 Q3 Portfolio Analysis | Tom | Caruthers | 40.00 |
| 5 | 2005 Q3 Portfolio Analysis | Mary | Abernathy | 45.00 |
| 6 | 2005 Q3 Tax Preparation | Mary | Jacobs | 25.00 |
| 7 | 2005 Q3 Tax Preparation | Rosalie | Jackson | 20.00 |
| 8 | 2005 Q3 Tax Preparation | Tom | Caruthers | 45.00 |
| 9 | 2005 Q3 Tax Preparation | Heather | Jones | 40.00 |
| 10 | 2005 Q4 Product Plan | Mary | Jacobs | 35.00 |
| 11 | 2005 Q4 Product Plan | Tom | Jackson | 80.00 |
| 12 | 2005 Q4 Product Plan | Ken | Numoto | 50.00 |
| 13 | 2005 Q4 Portfolio Analysis | Tom | Caruthers | 15.00 |
| 14 | 2005 Q4 Portfolio Analysis | Heather | Jones | 10.00 |
| 15 | 2005 Q4 Portfolio Analysis | Mary | Abernathy | 27.50 |

Clearly, using the view is much simpler than constructing the join syntax. Even developers who know SQL well will appreciate having a simpler view with which to work.

## Layering Computations and Built-in Functions

Recall from Chapter 3 that you cannot use a computation or a built-in function as part of a WHERE clause. You can, however, construct a view that computes a variable and then write an SQL statement on that view that uses the computed variable in a WHERE clause. To understand this, consider the ProjectHoursToDateView definition we created previously:

```
CREATE VIEW ProjectHoursToDateView AS
        SELECT  PPOJECT.ProjectID,
                Name AS ProjectName,
                MaxHours AS ProjectMaxHours,
                SUM(HoursWorked) AS ProjectHoursWorkedToDate
        FROM    PROJECT, ASSIGNMENT
        WHERE   PROJECT.ProjectID = ASSIGNMENT.ProjectID
        GROUP BY  PROJECT.ProjectID;
```

The view definition contains the maximum allocated hours for each project and the total hours actually worked on the project to date as ProjectHoursWorkedToDate. Now, we can use ProjectHoursWorkedToDate in both an additional calculation and in the WHERE clause as follows:

```
SELECT      ProjectID, ProjectName, ProjectMaxHours,
            ProjectHoursWorkedToDate
FROM        ProjectHoursToDateView
WHERE       ProjectHoursWorkedToDate > ProjectMaxHours;
ORDER BY    ProjectID;
```

Here, we are using the result of a computation in a WHERE clause, something that is not allowed in a single SQL statement. This allows users to determine which projects have exceeded the number of hours allocated to them by producing the result:

|   | ProjectID | ProjectName | ProjectMaxHours | ProjectHoursWorkedToDate |
|---|-----------|-------------|-----------------|--------------------------|
| 1 | 1000 | 2005 Q3 Product Plan | 135.00 | 160.00 |
| 2 | 1300 | 2005 Q4 Product Plan | 150.00 | 165.00 |

Such layering can be continued over many levels. We can turn this SELECT statement into another view named ProjectsOverAllotedMaxHoursView (again without the ORDER BY clause):

```
CREATE VIEW ProjectsOverAllotedMaxHoursView AS
        SELECT  ProjectID, ProjectName, ProjectMaxHours,
                ProjectHoursWorkedToDate
        FROM    ProjectHoursToDateView
        WHERE   ProjectHoursWorkedToDate > ProjectMaxHours;
```

Now, we can use ProjectsOverAllotedMaxHoursView in a further calculation—this time to find the number of hours that each project has overrun its allocated hours:

```
SELECT      ProjectID, ProjectName, ProjectMaxHours,
            ProjectHoursWorkedToDate,
            (ProjectHoursWorkedToDate − ProjectMaxHours)
                AS HoursOverMaxAllocated
FROM        ProjectsOverAllotedMaxHoursView
ORDER BY  ProjectID;
```

Here are the results:

| | ProjectID | ProjectName | ProjectMaxHours | ProjectHoursWorkedToDate | HoursOverMaxAllocated |
|---|---|---|---|---|---|
| 1 | 1000 | 2005 Q3 Product Plan | 135.00 | 160.00 | 25.00 |
| 2 | 1300 | 2005 Q4 Product Plan | 150.00 | 165.00 | 15.00 |

These SQL views are a very useful tool for database developers and application programmers.

## THE ACCESS WORKBENCH

### Section 3

### Working with Views in Microsoft Access

In Section 3's "The Access Workbench," we learned to work with Microsoft Access SQL and QBE. In this section, we will cover the following objective:

- Learn how to create the Access equivalent of SQL views.

We will continue to use the WMCRM database we have been using. At this point, we have created and populated (which means we've inserted the data into) the CUSTOMER, CONTACT, and SALESPERSON tables, and set the referential integrity constraints between them.

### Working with SQL Views in Microsoft Access

Although a view is a virtual table, it is can also be represented as a stored query. While most DBMSs do not allow queries to be saved in a database, Access does. Access allows us to run queries against tables or against saved queries. This gives us a way to implement the equivalent of a view in Access—we will simply save the SELECT query that would be used to create the SQL view and use it as we would an SQL view in other queries.

Here is an SQL CREATE VIEW statement that would be used to list Customer data from the WMCRM database if we were creating a standard SQL view:

```
CREATE VIEW CustomerPhoneView AS
    SELECT    FirstName, LastName, Phone
    FROM      CUSTOMER;
```

In Access, we will create a query—using either Access SQL or QBE—based on the SELECT portion of this statement. Then, we will choose a query name that indicates to us that this query is intended to be used as an SQL view. Our naming convention will be to put the word *view* at the beginning of any such query name. Thus, we will name this query as *viewCustomerPhone*.

#### Creating an Access Query as a View Equivalent

1. Start Microsoft Access.
2. In the menu bar, click **File | Open**. The Open dialog box is displayed. Browse to the **WMCRM.mdb** file, click the file name to highlight it, and then click the **Open** button. When the Security Warning dialog box appears, click the **Open** button to open the database.

3.  In the WMCRM : Database window, click **Queries** in the Objects pane to display the Queries pane.
4.  From the Queries pane, use either the SQL or QBE technique of creating the SELECT query shown in "The Access Workbench: Section 3."
5.  Save the query, naming it as **viewCustomerPhone**.
6.  Close the query. The viewCustomerPhone query object now appears in the Queries pane as shown in Figure AW-C-1.

---
**FIGURE AW-C-1**
---

**The viewCustomerPhone Query in the Queries Pane**

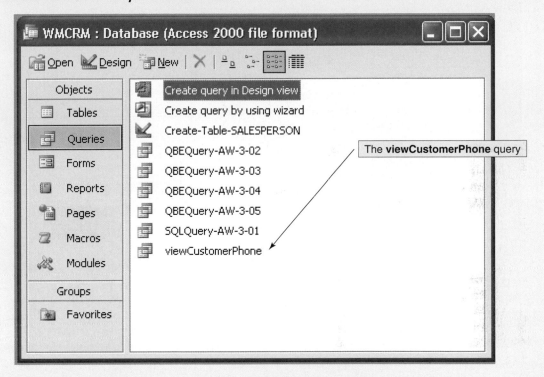

Now, we can use this query just as we would any other SQL view (or Access saved query). For example, let's implement the following SQL statement:

SELECT        FirstName, LastName, Phone

FROM          viewCustomerPhone

ORDER BY   LastName;

We'll use Access QBE in this example.

*Using an Access Query in Another Access Query*

1.  You should still have the Queries pane open. If you don't, click **Queries** in the Objects pane of the WMCRM : Database window to display the Queries pane.
2.  In the Queries pane, double-click **Create query in Design View**. The Query1: Select Query window appears along with the Show Table dialog box.
3.  In the Show Table dialog box, click the Queries tab to select it. The list of all saved queries appears as shown in Figure AW-C-2.

*(Continued)*

## FIGURE AW-C-2

**Queries Displayed in the Show Table Dialog Box**

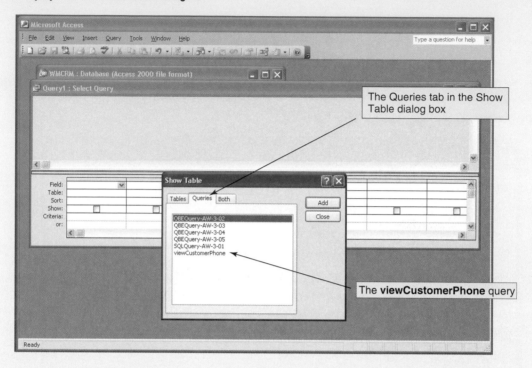

The Queries tab in the Show Table dialog box

The **viewCustomerPhone** query

4. Click **viewCustomerPhone** to select the viewCustomerPhone query. Click the **Add** button to add the viewCustomerPhone query to the new query.
5. Click the **Close** button to close the Show Table dialog box.
6. From the viewCustomerPhone query, click and drag the **LastName**, **FirstName**, and **Phone** column names to the first three field columns in the lower pane.
7. In the field column for LastName, set the Sort: setting to **Ascending**. The completed QBE query appears as shown in Figure AW-C-3 (The objects have been resized so that complete labels are shown in the figure).
8. Click the **Run** button on the Query Design toolbar. The query results appear as shown in Figure AW-C-4.

## FIGURE AW-C-3

**The Completed Query**

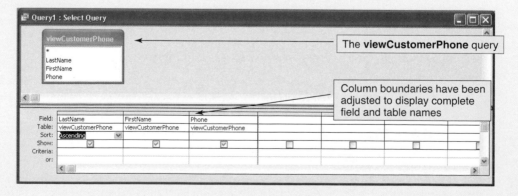

The **viewCustomerPhone** query

Column boundaries have been adjusted to display complete field and table names

## FIGURE AW-C-4

**The Query Results**

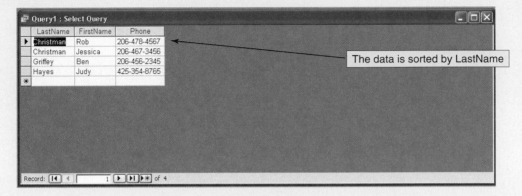

9. Save the query as **QBEQuery-AW-C-01**.
10. Close the QBEQuery-AW-C-01.

Now, we can use the equivalent of SQL views in Access by using one query as the source for additional queries. That completes the work we'll do in this section of "The Access Workbench," so we will finish by closing the database and Access.

### Closing the WMCRM Database

1. To close the WMCRM : Database window, click the **Close** button in the upper right corner of the WMCRM : Database window.

### Exiting Access

1. To exit Access, click the **Close** button in the upper right corner of the Microsoft Access window.

## SUMMARY

A SQL view is a virtual table that is constructed from other tables and views. An SQL SELECT statement is used as part of a CREATE VIEW *ViewName* statement to define a view. However, view definitions may not include ORDER BY clauses. Once defined, view names are used in SELECT statements the same way table names are used.

There are several uses for views. Views are used (a) to hide columns or rows, (b) to show the results of computed columns, (c) to hide complicated SQL syntax, and (d) to layer computations and built-in functions.

## REVIEW QUESTIONS

**C.1**  What is a SQL view? What purposes do views serve?

**C.2**  What SQL statements are used to create SQL views?

**C.3**  What is the limitation on SELECT statements used in SQL views?

**C.4**  How are views handled in Microsoft Access?

Use the following tables for your answers to questions C.5 through C.18. These are the same tables that are used in the Review Questions for Chapter 3, and sample data for these tables is shown in Figure 1-27 on page 48. For each SQL statement you write, show the results based on this data.

PET_OWNER (<u>OwnerID</u>, Name, Phone, Email)

PET (<u>PetID</u>, Name, Type, Breed, DOB, *OwnerID*)

If possible, run the statements you write in the questions that follow in an actual DBMS, as appropriate, to obtain your results.

**C.5**  Code a SQL statement to create a view named *OwnerPhoneView* that shows PET_OWNER.Name and Phone.

**C.6**  Code a SQL statement that displays the data in *OwnerPhoneView* sorted alphabetically by PET_OWNER.Name.

**C.7**  Code an SQL statement to create a view named *DogBreedView* that shows PetID, PET.Name, Breed, and DOB for Dogs.

**C.8**  Code a SQL statement that displays the data in *DogBreedView* sorted alphabetically by PET.Name.

**C.9**  Code a SQL statement to create a view named *CatBreedView* that shows PetID, PET.Name, Breed, and DOB for Cats.

**C.10**  Code a SQL statement that displays the data in *CatBreedView* sorted alphabetically by PET.Name.

**C.11**  Code a SQL statement to create a view named *PetOwnerView* that shows PetID, PET.Name, Type, OwnerID, PET_OWNER.Name, Phone, and Email.

**C.12**  Code a SQL statement that displays the data in *PetOwnerView* sorted alphabetically by OWNER.Name and PET.Name.

**C.13**  Code a SQL statement to create a view named *OwnerPetView* that shows OwnerID, PET_OWNER.Name, PetID, PET.Name, Type, Breed, and DOB.

**C.14**  Code a SQL statement that displays the data in *OwnerPetView* sorted alphabetically by PET_OWNER.Name and PET.Name.

**C.15**  Code a SQL statement to create a view named *PetCountView* that shows each type (i.e., dog or cat) and the number of each type (i.e., how many dogs and how many cats) in the database.

**C.16**  Code a SQL statement that displays the data in *PetCountView* sorted alphabetically by Type.

**C.17**  Code a SQL statement to create a view named *DogBreedCountView* that shows each Breed of Dog and the number of each Breed in the database.

**C.18**  Code a SQL statement that displays the data in *DogBreedCountView* sorted alphabetically by Breed.

## EXERCISES

If you haven't created the Art Course database described in Chapter 3's exercises, create it now—complete exercises 3.51 and 3.52. Use the Art Course database for answering exercises C.19 through C.26.

**C.19**  Code a SQL statement to create a view named *CourseView* that shows unique Course names and Fee.

**C.20**  Code a SQL statement that displays the data in *CourseView* sorted alphabetically by Course.

**C.21**  Code a SQL statement to create a view named *CourseEnrollmentView* that shows CourseNumber, Course, CourseDate, CustomerNumber, CustomerName, and Phone.

**C.22** Code a SQL statement that displays the data in *CourseEnrollmentView* for the Advanced Pastels course starting on 10/01/06. Sort the data alphabetically by CustomerName.

**C.23** Code a SQL statement that displays the data in *CourseEnrollmentView* for the Beginning Oils course starting on 10/15/06. Sort the data alphabetically by CustomerName.

**C.24** Code a SQL statement to create a view named *CourseFeeOwedView* that shows CourseNumber, Course, CourseDate, CustomerNumber, CustomerName, Phone, Fee, AmountPaid, and the calculated column (Fee – AmountPaid) renamed as AmountOwed.

**C.25** Code a SQL statement that displays the data in *CourseFeeOwedView* sorted alphabetically by CustomerName.

**C.26** Code a SQL statement that displays the data in *CourseFeeOwedView* sorted alphabetically by CustomerName for any customer that still owes money for a course fee.

## ACCESS WORKBENCH EXERCISES

In each of the following "Access Workbench Exercises," questions A and B use the WMCRM database that we used in this section of "The Access Workbench." Questions C and D use the Wedgewood Pacific Corporation (WPC) database that we created in the "Access Workbench Exercises"in Chapters 1, 2, and 3.

**AW.C.1** Using Access QBE or SQL create and run view equivalent queries to answer the questions that follow. Save each query using the query name format *viewViewQueryName* where the *ViewQueryName* is the name specified in the question.

**A.** Create an Access view equivalent query named *CustomerContact* that shows CUSTOMER.CustomerID, LastName, FirstName, Date, Type, and Remarks.

**B.** Create an Access view equivalent query named *SalespersonCustomerContact* that shows SALESPERSON.NickName, SALESPERSON.LastName, SALESPERSON.FirstName, CUSTOMER.CustomerID, CUSTOMER.LastName, CUSTOMER.FirstName, Date, Type, and Remarks.

**C.** Create an Access view equivalent query named *Computer* that shows Make, Model, SerialNumber, ProcessorType, ProcessorSpeed, MainMemory, and DiskSize.

**D.** Create an Access view equivalent query named *EmployeeComputer* that uses *viewComputer* for question C above to show EMPLOYEE.EmployeeNumber, LastName, FirstName, and the data about the computer assigned to that employee including Make, Model, SerialNumber, ProcessorType, ProcessorSpeed, MainMemory, and DiskSize.

**AW.C.2** Using Access QBE, create and run the queries that follow. Save each query using the query name format QBEQuery-AWE-C-1-## where the ## sign is replaced by the letter designator of the question. For example, the first query will be saved as QBEQuery-AWE-C-1-A.

> **A.** Create an Access QBE query to display the data in *viewCustomerContact* sorted alphabetically by LastName.
>
> **B.** Create an Access QBE query to display the data in *viewSalespersonCustomer Contact* sorted alphabetically by SALESPERSON.LastName.
>
> **C.** Create an Access QBE query to display the data in *viewComputer* sorted alphabetically by Make and Model and then numerically by SerialNumber.
>
> **D.** Create an Access QBE query to display the data in *viewEmployeeComputer*. Sort the results alphabetically by LastName, FirstName, Make, and Model and then numerically by SerialNumber.

## GARDEN GLORY PROJECT QUESTIONS

These questions are based on Chapter 3's Garden Glory Project Questions. Base your answers to the questions that follow on the Garden Glory database as described there. If possible, run your SQL statements in an actual DBMS to validate your work.

**A.** Create (and run) the following SQL view statements:

   **1.** Create a SQL view named *OwnerPropertyView* that shows OWNER.OwnerID, OwnerName, Type, PropertyID, PropertyName, Street, City, and Zip.

   **2.** Create a SQL view named *PropertyServiceView* that shows PROPERTY. PropertyID, PropertyName, Street, City, Zip, Date, and HoursWorked.

**B.** Create (and run) the following SQL queries:

   **1.** Create a SQL statement to run *OwnerPropertyView*, with the results sorted alphabetically by OwnerName.

   **2.** Create a SQL statement to run *PropertyServiceView* with the results sorted alphabetically by Zip, State, and City.

## JAMES RIVER JEWELRY PROJECT QUESTIONS

These questions are based on Chapter 3's James River Jewelry Project Questions. Base your answers to the questions that follow on the James River Project database as described there. If possible, run your SQL statements in an actual DBMS to validate your work.

**A.** Create (and run) the following SQL view statements:

   **1.** Create an SQL view named *CustomerPurchaseView* that shows CUSTOMER.CustomerID, LastName, FirstName, InvoiceNumber, Date, and PreTaxAmount.

   **2.** Create a SQL view named *PurchaseItemItemView* that shows InvoiceNumber, ItemNumber, ArtistName, Description, Cost, and RetailPrice.

**B.** Create (and run) the following SQL queries:

1. Create a SQL statement to run *CustomerPurchaseView*, with the results sorted alphabetically by LastName and FirstName.

2. Create a SQL statement to run *PurchaseItemItemView* with the results sorted by InvoiceNumber and ItemNumber.

3. Create a SQL query that uses the *PurchaseItemItemView* to calculate and display the sum of Cost as TotalItemCost and the sum of RetailPrice as TotalRetailSales.

## THE QUEEN ANNE CURIOSITY SHOP PROJECT QUESTIONS

These questions are based on Chapter 3's Queen Anne Curiosity Shop Project Questions. Base your answers to the questions that follow on the Queen Anne Curiosity Shop Project database as described there. If possible, run your SQL statements in an actual DBMS to validate your work.

**A.** Create (and run) the following SQL view statements:

1. Create a SQL view named *BasicCustomerView* that shows each customer's CustomerID, LastName, FirstName, Phone, and Email.

2. Create a SQL view named *SaleItemItemView* that shows SaleID, SaleItemID, SALE_ITEM.ItemID, SaleDate, ItemDescription, ItemCost, ITEM.ItemPrice as ListItemPrice, and SALE_ITEM.ItemPrice as ActualItemPrice.

**B.** Create (and run) the following SQL queries:

1. Create a SQL statement to run *BasicCustomerView*, with the results sorted alphabetically by LastName and FirstName.

2. Create a SQL statement to run *SaleItemItemView* with the results sorted by SaleID and SaleItemID.

3. Create an SQL query that uses the *SaleItemItemView* to calculate and display the sum of SALE_ITEM.ItemPrice (which is relabeled as ActualItemPrice) as TotalPretaxRetailSales.

# Glossary

**ACID transaction:** An acronym that stands for *atomic, consistent, isolated,* and *durable*. An atomic transaction is one in which all of a set of database changes are committed as a unit; either all of them are completed or none of them are. A consistent transaction is one in which all actions are taken against rows in the same logical state. An isolated transaction is one that is protected from changes by other users. A durable transaction is one that, once committed to a database, is permanent regardless of subsequent failure. There are different levels of consistency and isolation. See **Transaction level consistency** and **Statement level consistency**. Also see **Transaction isolation level**.

**Active Server Page (ASP):** A combination of HTML and scripting language statements. Any statement included in <%. . . %> is processed on the server. Used with Internet Information server (IIS).

**After-image:** A record of a database entity (normally a row or a page) after a change. Used in recovery to perform rollforward.

**Anomaly:** An undesirable consequence of a data modification; the term is used primarily in discussions of normalization. With an insertion anomaly, facts about two or more different themes must be added to a single row of a relation. With a deletion anomaly, facts about two or more themes are lost when a single row is deleted.

**Application metadata:** Data dictionary; data concerning the structure and contents of application menus, forms, and reports.

**Application program interface (API):** The set of objects, methods, and properties that is used to access the functionality of a program such as a DBMS.

**Atomic:** A set of actions that is completed as a unit. Either all actions are completed or none are.

**Atomic transaction:** A group of logically related database operations that are performed as a unit. Either all of the operations are performed or none of them are.

**Attribute:** (1) A value that represents a characteristic of an entity. (2) A column of a relation.

**Band:** The section of a report definition that contains the format of a report section. Bands normally are included for the report heading and footing, page heading and footing, and the detail line of a report. Bands also are created for group or break points within a report.

**Banded report writer:** A report writer in which the sections of reports are defined by bands. See **Band**.

**Before-image:** A record of a database entity (normally a row or a page) before a change. Used in recovery to perform rollback.

**Binary relationship:** A relationship between exactly two entities or tables.

**Boyce-Codd normal form (BCNF):** A relation in third normal form in which every determinant is a candidate key.

**Built-in function:** In SQL, any of the functions COUNT, SUM, AVG, MAX, or MIN.

**Business rule:** A statement of a policy in a business that restricts the ways in which data can be inserted, updated, or deleted in the database.

**Candidate key:** An attribute or group of attributes that identifies a unique row in a relation. One of the candidate keys is chosen to be the primary key.

**Cardinality:** In a binary relationship, the maximum or minimum number of elements allowed on each side of the relationship. The maximum cardinality can be 1:1, 1:N, N:1, or N:M. The minimum cardinality can be optional/optional, optional/mandatory, mandatory/optional, or mandatory/mandatory.

**Cascading deletion:** A property of a relationship that indicates that when one row is deleted, related rows should be deleted, as well.

**Checkpoint:** The point of synchronization between a database and a transaction log. All buffers are written to external storage. This is the standard definition of checkpoint, but this term is sometimes used in other ways by DBMS vendors.

**Child:** A row, record, or node on the "many" side of a one-to-many relationship.

**Cluster analysis:** A form of data mining that uses statistical techniques to identify groups of similar data.

**Column:** A logical group of bytes in a row of a relation or a table. The meaning of a column is the same for every row of the relation.

**Commit:** A command issued to the DBMS to make database modifications permanent. After the command has been processed, the changes are written to the database and to a log in such a way that they will survive system crashes and other failures. A commit usually is used at the end of an atomic transaction. Contrast this with **rollback**.

**Composite identifier:** An identifier of an entity that consists of two or more attributes.

**Composite key:** A key of a relation that consists of two or more columns.

**Computed value:** A column of a table that is computed from other column values. Values are not stored but are computed when they are to be displayed.

**Concurrency:** A condition in which two or more transactions are processed against a database at the same time. In a single CPU system, the changes are interleaved; in a multi-CPU system, the transactions can be processed simultaneously, and the changes on the database server are interleaved.

**Concurrent update problem:** An error condition in which one user's data changes are overwritten by another user's data changes. Also called *lost update problem*.

**Constraint:** A rule concerning the allowed values of attributes whose truth can be evaluated. A constraint usually does not include dynamic rules such as "SalespersonPay can never decrease" or "Salary now must be greater than Salary last quarter."

**CRUD:** An acronym representing *create, read, update, delete*, which are the four actions that can be performed on a database table.

**Cube:** In OLAP a set of measures and dimensions normally arranged in the format of a table.

**Data administration:** The enterprise-wide function that concerns the effective use and control of an organization's data assets. It can be performed by a person but more often is performed by a group. Specific functions include setting data standards and policies, and providing a forum for conflict resolution. See **Database administration**.

**Database:** A self-describing collection of integrated records. In a relational database, a self-describing collection of related tables.

**Database administration (DBA):** The function that concerns the effective use and control of a particular database and its related applications.

**Database administrator:** The person or group responsible for establishing policies and procedures to control and protect a database. They work within guidelines set by data administration to control the database structure, manage data changes, and maintain DBMS programs.

**Database backup:** A copy of database files that can be used to restore a database to some previous, consistent state.

**Database data:** The portion of a database that contains data that are of interest and use to the application end users.

**Database management system (DBMS):** A set of programs used to define, administer, and process a database and its applications.

**Data Definition Language (DDL):** A language used to describe the structure of a database.

**Data dictionary:** A user-accessible catalog of database and application metadata. An active data dictionary is a dictionary whose contents are updated automatically by the DBMS whenever changes are made to the database or application structure. A passive data dictionary is one whose contents must be updated manually when changes are made.

**Data integrity:** The state of a database in which all constraints are fulfilled; usually refers to interrelation constraints in which the value of a foreign key must be present in the table having that foreign key as its primary key.

**Data item:** (1) A logical group of bytes in a record, usually used with file processing. (2) In the context of the relational model, a synonym for *attribute*.

**Data Manipulation Language (DML):** A language used to describe the processing of a database.

**Data mining:** The application of statistical and mathematical techniques to find patterns in database data.

**Data model:** (1) A model of the users' data requirements, usually expressed in terms of the entity-relationship model. It is sometimes called a users' data model. (2) A language for describing the structure and processing of a database.

**Data structure diagram (DSD):** A graphical display of tables (files) and their relationships. The tables are shown in rectangles, and the relationships are shown by lines. A "many" relationship is shown with a crow's foot on the end of the line, an "optional" relationship is depicted by an oval, and a "mandatory" relationship is shown with hash marks.

**Data sublanguage:** A language for defining and processing a database intended to be embedded in programs written in another language—in most cases, a procedural language such as COBOL, C#, or Visual Basic. A data sublanguage is an incomplete programming language, because it contains only constructs for data definition and processing.

**Deadlock:** A condition that can occur during concurrent processing in which each of two (or more) transactions is waiting to access data that the other transaction has locked. It also is called the *deadly embrace*.

**Deadlock detection:** The process of determining whether two or more transactions are in a state of deadlock.

**Deadlock prevention:** A way of managing transactions so that a deadlock cannot occur.

**Deadly embrace:** See Deadlock.

**Degree:** For relationships in the entity-relationship model, the number of entities participating in the relationship. In almost all cases, such relationships are of degree 2.

**Deletion anomaly:** In a relation, the situation in which the removal of one row of a table deletes facts about two or more themes.

**Denormalization:** The process of intentionally designing a relation that is not normalized. Denormalization is done to improve performance or security.

**Determinant:** One or more attributes that functionally determine another attribute or attributes. In the functional dependency (A, B) D C, the attributes (A, B) are the determinant.

**Dimension:** In an OLAP cube, a characteristic that is associated with a data measure.

**Dirty read:** Reading data that have been changed but not yet committed to a database. Such changes may later be rolled back and removed from the database.

**Distributed database:** A database that is stored and processed on two or more computers.

**Distributed two-phase locking:** A sophisticated form of record locking that must be used when database transactions are processed on two or more machines.

**Domain:** (1) The set of all possible values an attribute can have. (2) A description of the format (data type, length) and the semantics (meaning) of an attribute.

**Domain key/normal form (DK/NF):** A relation in which all constraints are logical consequences of domains and keys. In this text, this definition has been simplified to a relation in which the determinants of all functional dependencies are candidate keys.

**Entity:** Something of importance to a user that needs to be represented in a database. In an entity-relationship model, entities are restricted to things that can be represented by a single table. See **Existence-dependent entity**, **ID-dependent entity**, **Strong entity**, and **Weak entity**.

**Entity class:** A set of entities of the same type; two examples are EMPLOYEE and DEPARTMENT.

**Entity instance:** A particular occurrence of an entity; for example, Employee 100 (an EMPLOYEE) and the Accounting Department (a DEPARTMENT).

**Entity-relationship diagram (E-R diagram):** A graphic used to represent entities and their relationships. Entities normally are shown in squares or rectangles, and relationships are shown in diamonds. The cardinality of the relationship is shown inside the diamond.

**Entity-relationship model (E-R model):** The constructs and conventions used to create a model of the users' data. The things in the users' world are represented by entities, and the associations among those things are represented by relationships. The results usually are documented in an entity-relationship diagram. Also see **Data model**.

**Exclusive lock:** A lock on a data resource that no other transaction can read or update.

**Existence-dependent entity:** The same as a weak entity. An entity that cannot appear in a database unless an instance of one or more other entities also appears in the database. A subclass of existence-dependent entities is ID-dependent entities.

**Explicit lock:** A lock requested by a command from an application program.

**Export:** A function of a DBMS that writes a file of data in bulk. The file is intended to be read by another DBMS or program.

**Extensible Markup Language (XML):** A markup language whose tags can be extended by document designers. See also **XML Schema**.

**Field:** (1) A logical group of bytes in a record used with file processing. (2) In the context of a relational model, a synonym for *attribute*.

**First normal form:** Any table that fits the definition of a relation is said to be in first normal form (1NF).

**Foreign key:** An attribute that is a key of one or more relations other than the one in which it appears.

**Fourth normal form:** A relation in Boyce-Codd normal form in which every multivalue dependency is a functional dependency.

**Functional dependency:** A relationship between attributes in which one attribute or group of attributes determines the value of another. The expressions $X \rightarrow Y$, "X determines Y," and "Y is functionally dependent on X" mean that given a value of X, we can determine the value of Y.

**Granularity:** The size of a database resource that can be locked. Locking the entire database is large granularity; locking a column of a particular row is small granularity.

**Horizontal security:** Limiting access to certain rows of a table or join.

**ID-dependent entity:** An entity that cannot logically exist without the existence of another entity. An APPOINTMENT, for example, cannot exist without a CLIENT to make the appointment. To be an ID-dependent entity, the identifier of the entity must contain the identifier of the entity on which it depends. Such entities are a subset of a weak entity. See also **Strong entity** and **Weak entity**.

**Identifier:** In an entity, a group of one or more attributes that determines entity instances. A unique identifier determines exactly one entity instance. A nonunique identifier determines a group of entity instances.

**Implicit lock:** A lock that is placed automatically by a DBMS.

**Inconsistent backup:** A backup file that contains uncommitted changes.

**Inconsistent read problem:** An anomaly that occurs in concurrent processing in which transactions execute a series of reads that are inconsistent with one another. It can be prevented by two-phase locking and other strategies.

**Index:** Overhead data used to improve access and sorting performance. Indexes can be constructed for a single column or groups of columns. They are especially useful for columns used for control breaks in reports and to specify conditions in joins.

**Inner join:** Synonym for *join*.

**Insertion anomaly:** In a relation, the condition that exists when, to add a complete row to a table, one must add facts about two or more logically different themes.

**Internet Information Server (IIS):** A Windows Web server that processes Active Server Pages (ASPs).

**Intersection relation:** A relation used to represent a many-to-many relationship. It contains the keys of the relations in the relationship. When used to represent entities having a many-to-many relationship, it may have nonkey data if the relationship contains data.

**Isolation level:** See **Transaction isolation level.**

**Java Server Page (JSP):** A combination of HTML and Java that is compiled into a servlet.

**JDBC:** A standard means for accessing DBMS products from Java. Using JDBC, the unique API of a DBMS is hidden and the programmer writes to the standard JDBC interface.

**Join:** A relational algebra operation on two relations, A and B, that produces a third relation, C. A row of A is concatenated with a row of B to form a new row in C if the rows in A and B meet restrictions concerning their values. For example, A1 is an attribute in A, and B1 is an attribute in B. The join of A with B in which A1, B1 will result in a relation C having the concatenation of rows in A and B in which the value of A1 is less than the value of B1. See also **Natural join.**

**Key:** (1) A group of one or more attributes identifying a unique row in a relation. Because relations may not have duplicate rows, every relation must have at least one key that is the composite of all of the attributes in the relation. A key is sometimes called a logical key. A unique key identifies a single row in the relation. A nonunique key identifies a group of rows in the relation. (2) With some relational DBMS products, a key is an index on a column used to improve access and sorting speed. It is sometimes called a physical key.

**Lock:** The process of allocating a database resource to a particular transaction in a concurrent-processing system. The size of the resource locked is known as the lock granularity. With an exclusive lock, no other transaction can read or write the resource. With a shared lock, other transactions can read the resource, but no other transaction can write it.

**Lock granularity:** The size of a lock.

**Log:** A file containing a record of database changes. The log contains before-images and after-images.

**Maximum cardinality:** (1) The maximum number of values that an attribute may have within a semantic object. (2) In a relationship between tables, the maximum number of rows to which a row of one table may relate in the other table.

**Measure:** In OLAP, a data value that is summed, averaged, or processed in some other simple arithmetic manner.

**Metadata:** Data concerning the structure of data in a database stored in the data dictionary. Metadata are used to describe tables, columns, constraints, indexes, and so forth. Compare this with **Application metadata**.

**Minimum cardinality:** In a relationship between tables, the minimum number of rows to which a row of one table may relate in the other table.

**Modification anomaly:** The situation that exists when the storing of one row in a table records facts about two themes, or the deletion of a row removes facts about two themes, or when a data change must be made in multiple rows for consistency.

**Multivalue dependency:** A condition in a relation with three or more attributes in which independent attributes appear to have relationships they do not have. Formally, in a relation R (A, B, C), having key (A, B, C) where A is matched with multiple values of B (or of C or of both), B does not determine C and C does not determine B. An example is the relation EMPLOYEE (EmpNumber, Emp-skill, Dependent-name), where an employee can have multiple values of Emp-skill and Dependent-name. Emp-skill and Dependent-name do not have any relationship, but they do appear to in the relation.

**Natural join:** A join of a relation A having attribute A1 with relation B having attribute B1 where A1 equals B1. The joined relation, C, contains either column A1 or B1 but not both.

**N:M:** An abbreviation for a many-to-many relationship between the rows of two tables.

**Nonrepeatable reads:** The situation that occurs when a transaction reads data it has previously read and finds modifications or deletions caused by a committed transaction.

**Nonunique key:** A key that potentially identifies more than one row.

**Normal form:** A rule or set of rules governing the allowed structure of relations. The rules apply to attributes, functional dependencies, multivalue dependencies, domains, and constraints. The most important normal forms are 1NF, 2NF, 3NF, Boyce-Codd NF, 4NF, 5NF, and domain/key normal form.

**Normalization:** The process of evaluating a relation to determine whether it is in a specified normal form and, if necessary, of converting it to relations in that specified normal form.

**Null value:** An attribute value that has never been supplied. Such values are ambiguous and can mean (a) the value is unknown, (b) the value is not appropriate, or (c) the value is known to be blank.

**Object-oriented DBMS (OODBMS):** A type of DBMS that provides object persistence; has not received commercial acceptance.

**Object-relational DBMS:** A DBMS that provides a relational model interface as well as structures for object persistence. Oracle is the leading object-relational DBMS.

**Object persistence:** The process of storing object data values.

**OLAP cube:** In OLAP, a set of measures and dimensions arranged, normally, in the format of a table.

**1:1:** An abbreviation for a one-to-one relationship between the rows of two tables.

**1:N:** An abbreviation for a one-to-many relationship between the rows of two tables.

**OnLine Analytical Processing (OLAP):** A technique for analyzing data values, called measures, against characteristics associated with those data values, called dimensions.

**Open Database Connectivity (ODBC):** A standard means for accessing DBMS products. Using ODBC, the unique API of a DBMS is hidden, and the programmer writes to the standard ODBC interface.

**Optimistic locking:** A locking strategy that assumes no conflict will occur, processes a transaction, and then checks to determine if conflict did occur. If so, the transaction is aborted. See **Pessimistic locking** and **Deadlock**.

**Outer join:** A join in which all the rows of a table appear in the resulting relation regardless of whether they have a match in the join condition. In a left outer join, all the rows in the left-hand relation appear; in a right outer join, all the rows in the right-hand relation appear.

**Overhead data:** Metadata created by a DBMS to improve performance; for example, indexes and linked lists.

**Owner:** In data administration, the department or other organizational unit in charge of the management of a particular data item. An owner also can be called a data proponent.

**Parent:** A row, record, or node on the "one" side of a one-to-many relationship.

**Partitioned database:** A database in which portions of the database are distributed to two or more computers.

**Pessimistic locking:** A locking strategy that prevents conflict by placing locks before processing database read and write requests. Alos see **Optimistic locking** and **Deadlock**.

**Phantom read:** The situation that occurs when a transaction reads data it has previously read and then finds new rows that were inserted by a committed transaction.

**Physical key:** A column that has an index or other data structure created for it. Such structures are created to improve searching and sorting on the column values. A synonym for *index*.

**Primary key:** A candidate key selected to be the key of a relation.

**Processing rights and responsibilities:** Organizational policies regarding which groups can take which actions on specified data items or other collections of data.

**Program/data independence:** The condition existing when the structure of the data is not defined in application programs. Rather, it is defined in the database, and the application programs obtain it from the DBMS. In this way, changes can be made in the data structures that might not necessarily be made in the application programs.

**Query by Example (QBE):** A style of query interface, first developed by IBM but now used by other vendors, that enables users to express queries by providing examples of the results they seek.

**Query/update language:** A language that can be employed by end users to query a database and make changes to the database data.

**Read committed:** A level of transaction isolation that prohibits dirty reads but allows nonrepeatable reads and phantom reads.

**Read uncommitted:** A level of transaction isolation that allows dirty reads, nonrepeatable reads, and phantom reads to occur.

**Record:** (1) A group of fields pertaining to the same entity; used in file-processing systems. (2) In a relational model, a synonym for row and tuple.

**Recursive relationship:** A relationship among entities, objects, or rows of the same type. For example, if CUSTOMERs refer other CUSTOMERs, the relationship is recursive.

**Referential integrity constraint:** A relationship constraint on foreign key values. A referential integrity constraint specifies that the values of a foreign key must be a proper subset of the values of the primary key to which it refers.

**Relation:** A two-dimensional array containing single-value entries and no duplicate rows. The meaning of the columns is the same in every row. The order of the rows and columns is immaterial.

**Relational database:** A database consisting of relations. In practice, relational databases contain relations with duplicate rows. Most DBMS products include a feature that removes duplicate rows when necessary and appropriate. Such a removal is not done as a matter of course because it can be time-consuming and expensive.

**Relational data model:** A data model in which data are stored in relations, and relationships between rows are represented by data values.

**Relational schema:** A set of relations with referential integrity constraints.

**Relationship:** An association between two entities, objects, or rows of relations.

**Relationship cardinality constraint:** A constraint on the number of rows that can participate in a relationship. Minimum cardinality constraints determine the number of rows that must participate; maximum cardinality constraints specify the largest number of rows that can participate.

**Repeatable read:** A level of transaction isolation that disallows dirty reads and nonrepeatable reads. Phantom reads can occur.

**Replicated database:** A database in which portions of the database are copied to two or more computers.

**Report:** An extraction of data from a database. Reports can be printed, displayed on a computer screen, or stored as a file. A report is part of a database application. Compare this with a form.

**Report band:** See **Band**.

**Resource locking:** See **Lock**.

**Rollback:** The process of recovering a database in which before-images are applied to the database to return to an earlier checkpoint or other point at which the database is logically consistent.

**Rollforward:** The process of recovering a database by applying after-images to a saved copy of the database to bring it to a checkpoint or other point at which the database is logically consistent.

**Row:** A group of columns in a table. All the columns in a row pertain to the same entity. A row is the same as a tuple and a record.

**Schema:** A complete logical view of a database.

**Schema-valid document:** An XML document that conforms to its XML Schema.

**Second normal form:** A relation in first normal form in which all nonkey attributes are dependent on all of the keys.

**Selection:** A relational algebra operation performed on a relation, A, producing a relation, B, with B containing only the rows in A that meet the restrictions specified in the selection.

**Serializable:** A level of transaction isolation that disallows dirty reads, nonrepeatable reads, and phantom reads.

**Servlet:** A module of application logic that runs on a Web server, normally used in conjunction with the Java language.

**Shared lock:** A lock against a data resource in which only one transaction can update the data but many transactions can concurrently read those data.

**Sibling:** A record or node that has the same parent as does another record or node.

**Simple network:** (1) A set of three relations and two relationships in which one of the relations, R, has a many-to-one relationship with the other two relations. The rows in R have two parents, and the parents are of different types. (2) Any set of tables and relationships containing the structure defined in (1).

**Statement level consistency:** All rows impacted by a single SQL statement are protected from changes made by other users during the execution of the statement. Contrast with transaction level consistency.

**Stored procedure:** A collection of SQL statements stored as a file that can be invoked by a single command. Usually, DBMS products provide a language for creating stored procedures that augments SQL with programming language constructs. Oracle provides PL/SQL for this purpose; SQL Server provides TRANSACT-SQL. With some products, stored procedures can be written in a standard language such as Java. Stored procedures are often stored within the database itself.

**Strong entity:** In an entity-relationship model, any entity whose existence in the database does not depend on the existence of any other entity. Also see **ID-dependent entity** and **Weak entity**.

**Structured Query Language (SQL):** A language for defining the structure and processing of a relational database. It can be used as a stand-alone query language, or it can be embedded in application programs. SQL is accepted as a national standard by the American National Standards Institute. It was developed by IBM.

**Subquery:** A SELECT statement that appears in the WHERE clause of a SQL statement. Subqueries can be nested within each other.

**Surrogate key:** A unique, system-supplied identifier used as the primary key of a relation. The values of a surrogate key have no meaning to the users and usually are hidden on forms and reports.

**Third normal form:** A relation in second normal form that has no transitive dependencies.

**Three-tier:** A Web database processing architecture in which the DBMS and the Web server reside on separate computers.

**Transaction:** (1) An atomic transaction. (2) The record of an event in the business world.

**Transaction boundary:** The group of database commands that must be committed or aborted as a unit.

**Transaction isolation level:** The degree to which a database transaction is protected from actions by other transactions. The 1992 SQL standard specified four isolation levels: read uncommitted, read committed, repeatable reads, and serializable.

**Transaction level consistency:** All rows impacted by any of the SQL statements in a transaction are protected from changes during the entire transaction. This level of consistency is expensive to enforce and probably will reduce throughput. It also might mean that a transaction cannot see its own changes. Contrast with **Statement level consistency**.

**Transform-oriented language:** A data sublanguage such as SQL that provides commands and capabilities to transform a set of relations into a new relation.

**Transitive dependency:** In a relation having at least three attributes, such as R (A, B, C), the situation in which A determines B and B determines C, but B does not determine A.

**Tree:** A collection of records, entities, or other data structures in which each element has at most one parent, except for the top element, which has no parent.

**Trigger:** A special type of stored procedure that is invoked by the DBMS when a specified condition occurs. BEFORE triggers are executed before a specified database action, AFTER triggers are executed after a specified database action, and INSTEAD OF triggers are executed in place of a specified database action. INSTEAD OF triggers normally are used to update data in SQL views.

**Tuple:** Same as Row.

**Two-phase locking:** The procedure by which locks are obtained and released in two phases. During the growing phase, the locks are obtained; during the shrinking phase, the locks are released. After a lock is released, no other lock will be granted that transaction. Such a procedure ensures consistency in database updates in a concurrent-processing environment.

**Two-tier:** A Web database processing architecture in which the DBMS and the Web server reside on the same computer.

**Unified Modeling Language (UML):** A set of structures and techniques for modeling and designing object-oriented programs and applications. It is a methodology and a set of tools for such development. UML incorporates the entity-relationship model for data modeling.

**Unique key:** A key that identifies a unique row.

**Vertical security:** Limiting access to certain columns of a table or join.

**Weak entity:** In an entity-relationship model, an entity whose logical existence in the database depends on the existence of another entity. Also see **ID-dependent entity** and **Strong entity**.

**XML Schema Document:** An XML document that describes the structure of a class of XML documents by defining the tags and the valid relationship of those tags.

**XML Web Services:** A set of standards that enables applications to consume each other's services using Internet technology.

# Index

Page numbers followed by f refer to figures.